ECE/TRANS/325 (Vol. II)

ECONOMIC COMMISSION FOR EUROPE

Committee on Inland Transport

European Agreement concerning the International Carriage of Dangerous Goods by Inland Waterways (ADN)

including the Annexed Regulations, applicable as from 1 January 2023

Volume II

UNITED NATIONS
New York and Geneva, 2022

United Nations publication issued by the United Nations Economic Commission for Europe.

ECE/TRANS/325

ISBN: 978-92-1-139225-8
eISBN: 978-92-1-001911-8

ISSN: 2411-8583
eISSN: 2411-8591

Sales number: E.22.VIII.3

Complete set of two volumes
Volumes I and II not to be sold separately

TABLE OF CONTENTS

VOLUME II

Table of contents (cont'd)

ANNEXED REGULATIONS
(continued)

PART 2

Classification

CHAPTER 2.1

GENERAL PROVISIONS

2.1.1   **Introduction**

2.1.1.1   The classes of dangerous goods according to ADN are the following:

Class 1   Explosive substances and articles
Class 2   Gases
Class 3   Flammable liquids
Class 4.1   Flammable solids, self-reactive substances, polymerizing substances and solid desensitized explosives
Class 4.2   Substances liable to spontaneous combustion
Class 4.3   Substances which, in contact with water, emit flammable gases
Class 5.1   Oxidizing substances
Class 5.2   Organic peroxides
Class 6.1   Toxic substances
Class 6.2   Infectious substances
Class 7   Radioactive material
Class 8   Corrosive substances
Class 9   Miscellaneous dangerous substances and articles

2.1.1.2   Each entry in the different classes has been assigned a UN number. The following types of entries are used:

A.   Single entries for well defined substances or articles including entries for substances covering several isomers, e.g.:

UN No. 1090   ACETONE
UN No. 1104   AMYL ACETATES
UN No. 1194   ETHYL NITRITE SOLUTION

B.   Generic entries for a well defined group of substances or articles, which are not n.o.s. entries, e.g.:

UN No. 1133   ADHESIVES
UN No. 1266   PERFUMERY PRODUCTS
UN No. 2757   CARBAMATE PESTICIDE, SOLID, TOXIC
UN No. 3101   ORGANIC PEROXIDE TYPE B, LIQUID

C.   Specific n.o.s. entries covering a group of substances or articles of a particular chemical or technical nature, not otherwise specified, e.g.:

UN No. 1477   NITRATES, INORGANIC, N.O.S.
UN No. 1987   ALCOHOLS, N.O.S.

D.   General n.o.s. entries covering a group of substances or articles having one or more dangerous properties, not otherwise specified, e.g.:

UN No. 1325   FLAMMABLE SOLID, ORGANIC, N.O.S.
UN No. 1993   FLAMMABLE LIQUID, N.O.S.

The entries defined under B, C and D are defined as collective entries.

2.1.1.3   For packing purposes, substances other than those of Classes 1, 2, 5.2, 6.2 and 7, and other than self-reactive substances of Class 4.1 are assigned to packing groups in accordance with the degree of danger they present:

Packing group I: Substances presenting high danger;

Packing group II: Substances presenting medium danger;

Packing group III: Substances presenting low danger.

The packing group(s) to which a substance is assigned is (are) indicated in Table A of Chapter 3.2.

Articles are not assigned to packing groups. For packing purposes any requirement for a specific packaging performance level is set out in the applicable packing instruction.

2.1.1.4   For the purpose of carriage in tank vessels, some substances may be further subdivided.

2.1.2   Principles of classification

2.1.2.1   The dangerous goods covered by the heading of a class are defined on the basis of their properties according to sub-section 2.2.x.1 of the relevant class. Assignment of dangerous goods to a class and a packing group is made according to the criteria mentioned in the same sub-section 2.2.x.1. Assignment of one or several subsidiary hazard(s) to a dangerous substance or article is made according to the criteria of the class or classes corresponding to those hazards, as mentioned in the appropriate sub-section(s) 2.2.x.1.

2.1.2.2   All dangerous goods entries are listed in Table A of Chapter 3.2 in the numerical order of their UN Number. This table contains relevant information on the goods listed, such as name, class, packing group(s), label(s) to be affixed, packing and carriage provisions[1]. The substances listed by name in column (2) of Table A of Chapter 3.2 shall be carried according to their classification in Table A or under the conditions specified in 2.1.2.8.

2.1.2.3   A substance may contain technical impurities (for example those deriving from the production process) or additives for stability or other purposes that do not affect its classification. However, a substance mentioned by name, i.e. listed as a single entry in Table A of Chapter 3.2, containing technical impurities or additives for stability or other purposes affecting its classification shall be considered a solution or mixture (see 2.1.3.3).

2.1.2.4   Dangerous goods which are listed or defined in sub-section 2.2.x.2 of each class are not to be accepted for carriage.

2.1.2.5   Goods not mentioned by name, i.e. goods not listed as single entries in Table A of Chapter 3.2 and not listed or defined in one of the above-mentioned sub-sections 2.2.x.2 shall be assigned to the relevant class in accordance with the procedure of section 2.1.3. In addition, the subsidiary hazard (if any) and the packing group (if any) shall be determined. Once the class, subsidiary hazard (if any) and packing group (if any) have been established the relevant UN number shall be determined. The decision trees in sub-sections 2.2.x.3 (list of collective entries) at the end of each class indicate the relevant parameters for selecting the relevant collective entry (UN number). In all cases the most specific collective entry covering the properties of the substance or article shall be selected, according to the hierarchy indicated in 2.1.1.2 by the letters B, C and D respectively. If the substance or article cannot be classified under entries of type B or C according to 2.1.1.2, then, and only then shall it be classified under an entry of type D.

---

[1]   **Note by the secretariat:** *An alphabetic list of these entries has been prepared by the secretariat and is reproduced in Table B of Chapter 3.2. This table is not an official part of the ADN.*

2.1.2.6	On the basis of the test procedures of Chapter 2.3 and the criteria set out in sub-sections 2.2.x.1 of the various classes when it is so specified, it may be determined that a substance, solution or mixture of a certain class, mentioned by name in Table A of Chapter 3.2, does not meet the criteria of that class. In such a case, the substance, solution or mixture is deemed not to belong to that class.

2.1.2.7	For the purposes of classification, substances with a melting point or initial melting point of 20 °C or lower at a pressure of 101.3 kPa shall be considered to be liquids. A viscous substance for which a specific melting point cannot be determined shall be subjected to the ASTM D 4359-90 test or to the test for determining fluidity (penetrometer test) prescribed in 2.3.4.

2.1.2.8	A consignor who has identified, on the basis of test data, that a substance listed by name in column 2 of Table A of Chapter 3.2 meets classification criteria for a class that is not identified in column 3a or 5 of Table A of Chapter 3.2, may, with the approval of the competent authority, consign the substance:

- Under the most appropriate collective entry listed in sub-sections 2.2.x.3 reflecting all hazards; or

- Under the same UN number and name but with additional hazard communication information as appropriate to reflect the additional subsidiary hazard(s) (documentation, label, placard) provided that the class remains unchanged and that any other carriage conditions (e.g. limited quantity, packaging and tank provisions) that would normally apply to substances possessing such a combination of hazards are the same as those applicable to the substance listed.

NOTE 1: The competent authority granting the approval may be the competent authority of any ADN Contracting Party who may also recognize an approval granted by the competent authority of a country which is not an ADN Contracting Party provided that this approval has been granted in accordance with the procedures applicable according to RID, ADR, ADN, the IMDG Code or the ICAO Technical Instructions.

NOTE 2: When a competent authority grants such approvals, it should inform the United Nations Sub-Committee of Experts on the Transport of Dangerous Goods accordingly and submit a relevant proposal of amendment to the Dangerous Goods List of the UN Model Regulations. Should the proposed amendment be rejected, the competent authority should withdraw its approval.

NOTE 3: For carriage in accordance with 2.1.2.8, see also 5.4.1.1.20.

2.1.3	**Classification of substances, including solutions and mixtures (such as preparations and wastes), not mentioned by name**

2.1.3.1	Substances including solutions and mixtures not mentioned by name shall be classified according to their degree of danger on the basis of the criteria mentioned in sub-section 2.2.x.1 of the various classes. The danger(s) presented by a substance shall be determined on the basis of its physical and chemical characteristics and physiological properties. Such characteristics and properties shall also be taken into account when such experience leads to a more stringent assignment.

2.1.3.2	A substance not mentioned by name in Table A of Chapter 3.2 presenting a single hazard shall be classified in the relevant class under a collective entry listed in sub-section 2.2.x.3 of that class.

2.1.3.3   A solution or mixture meeting the classification criteria of ADN composed of a single predominant substance mentioned by name in Table A of Chapter 3.2 and one or more substances not subject to ADN and/or traces of one or more substances mentioned by name in Table A of Chapter 3.2, shall be assigned the UN number and proper shipping name of the predominant substance mentioned by name in Table A of Chapter 3.2 unless:

(a)   The solution or mixture is mentioned by name in Table A of Chapter 3.2;

(b)   The name and description of the substance mentioned by name in Table A of Chapter 3.2 specifically indicate that they apply only to the pure substance;

(c)   The class, classification code, packing group, or physical state of the solution or mixture is different from that of the substance mentioned by name in Table A of Chapter 3.2; or

(d)   The hazard characteristics and properties of the solution or mixture necessitate emergency response measures that are different from those required for the substance mentioned by name in Table A of Chapter 3.2.

In those other cases, except the one described in (a), the solution or mixture shall be classified as a substance not mentioned by name in the relevant class under a collective entry listed in sub-section 2.2.x.3 of that class taking account of the subsidiary hazards presented by that solution or mixture, if any, unless the solution or mixture does not meet the criteria of any class, in which case it is not subject to ADN.

2.1.3.4   Solutions and mixtures containing a substance belonging to one of the entries mentioned in 2.1.3.4.1 or 2.1.3.4.2 shall be classified in accordance with the provisions of these paragraphs.

2.1.3.4.1   Solutions and mixtures containing one of the following substances mentioned by name shall always be classified under the same entry as the substance they contain, provided they do not have the hazard characteristics as indicated in 2.1.3.5.3:

–   Class 3

UN No. 1921 PROPYLENEIMINE, STABILIZED;

UN No. 3064 NITROGLYCERIN SOLUTION IN ALCOHOL with more than 1% but not more than 5% nitroglycerin;

–   Class 6.1

UN No. 1051 HYDROGEN CYANIDE, STABILIZED, containing less than 3% water;

UN No. 1185 ETHYLENEIMINE, STABILIZED;

UN No. 1259 NICKEL CARBONYL;

UN No. 1613 HYDROCYANIC ACID, AQUEOUS SOLUTION (HYDROGEN CYANIDE, AQUEOUS SOLUTION) with not more than 20% hydrogen cyanide;

UN No. 1614 HYDROGEN CYANIDE, STABILIZED, containing not more than 3% water and absorbed in a porous inert material;

UN No. 1994 IRON PENTACARBONYL;

UN No. 2480 METHYL ISOCYANATE;

UN No. 2481 ETHYL ISOCYANATE;

UN No. 3294 HYDROGEN CYANIDE, SOLUTION IN ALCOHOL, with not more than 45% hydrogen cyanide;

- Class 8

  UN No. 1052 HYDROGEN FLUORIDE, ANHYDROUS;

  UN No. 1744 BROMINE or UN No. 1744 BROMINE SOLUTION;

  UN No. 1790 HYDROFLUORIC ACID with more than 85% hydrogen fluoride;

  UN No. 2576 PHOSPHORUS OXYBROMIDE, MOLTEN.

2.1.3.4.2 Solutions and mixtures containing a substance belonging to one of the following entries of Class 9:

UN No. 2315 POLYCHLORINATED BIPHENYLS, LIQUID;

UN No. 3151 POLYHALOGENATED BIPHENYLS, LIQUID;

UN No. 3151 HALOGENATED MONOMETHYLDIPHENYLMETHANES, LIQUID;

UN No. 3151 POLYHALOGENATED TERPHENYLS, LIQUID;

UN No. 3152 POLYHALOGENATED BIPHENYLS, SOLID;

UN No. 3152 HALOGENATED MONOMETHYLDIPHENYLMETHANES, SOLID;

UN No. 3152 POLYHALOGENATED TERPHENYLS, SOLID; or

UN No. 3432 POLYCHLORINATED BIPHENYLS, SOLID

shall always be classified under the same entry of Class 9 provided that:

- they do not contain any additional dangerous component other than components of packing group III of classes 3, 4.1, 4.2, 4.3, 5.1, 6.1 or 8; and

- they do not have the hazard characteristics as indicated in 2.1.3.5.3.

2.1.3.4.3 Used articles, e.g. transformers and condensers, containing a solution or mixture mentioned in 2.1.3.4.2 shall always be classified under the same entry of Class 9, provided:

(a) they do not contain any additional dangerous components, other than polyhalogenated dibenzodioxins and dibenzofurans of Class 6.1 or components of packing group III of Class 3, 4.1, 4.2, 4.3, 5.1, 6.1 or 8; and

(b) they do not have the hazard characteristics as indicated in 2.1.3.5.3 (a) to (g) and (i).

2.1.3.5 Substances not mentioned by name in Table A of Chapter 3.2, having more than one hazard characteristic and solutions or mixtures meeting the classification criteria of ADN containing several dangerous substances shall be classified under a collective entry (see 2.1.2.5) and packing group of the appropriate class in accordance with their hazard characteristics. Such classification according to the hazard characteristics shall be carried out as follows:

2.1.3.5.1 The physical and chemical characteristics and physiological properties shall be determined by measurement or calculation and the substance, solution or mixture shall be classified according to the criteria mentioned in sub-section 2.2.x.1 of the various classes.

2.1.3.5.2 If this determination is not possible without disproportionate cost or effort (as for some kinds of wastes), the substance, solution or mixture shall be classified in the class of the component presenting the major hazard.

2.1.3.5.3   If the hazard characteristics of the substance, solution or mixture fall within more than one class or group of substances listed below then the substance, solution or mixture shall be classified in the class or group of substances corresponding to the major hazard on the basis of the following order of precedence:

(a)   Material of Class 7 (apart from radioactive material in excepted packages, for which, except for UN 3507 URANIUM HEXAFLUORIDE, RADIOACTIVE MATERIAL, EXCEPTED PACKAGE, special provision 290 of Chapter 3.3 applies, where the other hazardous properties take precedence);

(b)   Substances of Class 1;

(c)   Substances of Class 2;

(d)   Liquid desensitized explosives of Class 3;

(e)   Self-reactive substances and solid desensitized explosives of Class 4.1;

(f)   Pyrophoric substances of Class 4.2;

(g)   Substances of Class 5.2;

(h)   Substances of Class 6.1 meeting the inhalation toxicity criteria of packing group I (Substances meeting the classification criteria of Class 8 and having an inhalation toxicity of dust and mist (LC_{50}) in the range of packing group I and a toxicity through oral ingestion or dermal contact only in the range of packing group III or less, shall be allocated to Class 8);

(i)   Infectious substances of Class 6.2.

2.1.3.5.4   If the hazard characteristics of the substance fall within more than one class or group of substances not listed in 2.1.3.5.3 above, the substance shall be classified in accordance with the same procedure but the relevant class shall be selected according to the precedence of hazards table in 2.1.3.10.

If the hazard characteristics of the substance are such that the substance can be assigned to a UN number or an identification number, then the UN number shall take precedence.

2.1.3.5.5   If the substance to be carried is a waste, with a composition that is not precisely known, its assignment to a UN number and packing group in accordance with 2.1.3.5.2 may be based on the consignor's knowledge of the waste, including all available technical and safety data as requested by safety and environmental legislation in force.[2]

In case of doubt, the highest danger level shall be taken.

If, however, on the basis of the knowledge of the composition of the waste and the physical and chemical properties of the identified components, it is possible to demonstrate that the properties of the waste do not correspond to the properties of the packing group I level, the waste may be classified by default in the most appropriate n.o.s. entry of packing group II.

---

[2]   *Such legislation is for instance the Commission Decision 2000/532/EC of 3 May 2000 replacing Decision 94/3/EC establishing a list of wastes pursuant to Article 1(a) of Council Directive 75/442/EEC on waste and Council Decision 94/904/EC establishing a list of hazardous wastes pursuant to Article 1(4) of Council Directive 91/689/EEC on hazardous wastes (Official Journal of the European Communities No. L 226 of 6 September 2000, page 3), as amended; and Directive 2008/98/EC of the European Parliament and of the Council of 19 November 2008 on waste and repealing certain Directives (Official Journal of the European Union No. L312 of 22 November 2008, pages 3-30), as amended.*

However, if it is known that the waste possesses only environmentally hazardous properties, it may be assigned to packing group III under UN Nos. 3077 or 3082.

This procedure may not be used for wastes containing substances mentioned in 2.1.3.5.3, substances of Class 4.3, substances of the case mentioned in 2.1.3.7 or substances which are not accepted for carriage in accordance with 2.2.x.2.

2.1.3.6   The most specific applicable collective entry (see 2.1.2.5) shall always be used, i.e. a general n.o.s. entry shall only be used if a generic entry or a specific n.o.s. entry cannot be used.

2.1.3.7   Solutions and mixtures of oxidizing substances or substances with an oxidizing subsidiary hazard may have explosive properties. In such a case they are not to be accepted for carriage unless they meet the requirements for Class 1. For solid ammonium nitrate based fertilizers, see also 2.2.51.2.2, thirteenth and fourteenth indent and Manual of Tests and Criteria, Part III, Section 39.

2.1.3.8   Substances of classes 1 to 6.2, 8 and 9, other than those assigned to UN Nos. 3077 and 3082, meeting the criteria of 2.2.9.1.10 are additionally to their hazards of classes 1 to 6.2, 8 and 9 considered to be environmentally hazardous substances. Other substances meeting the criteria of no other class or of no other substance of Class 9, but those of 2.2.9.1.10 are to be assigned to UN Nos. 3077 and 3082 or to identification numbers 9005 and 9006, as appropriate.

Wastes which do not meet the criteria for classification in classes 1 to 9 but are covered by the *Basel Convention on the Control of Transboundary Movements of Hazardous Wastes and their Disposal* may be carried under UN Nos. 3077 or 3082.

2.1.3.10   Table of precedence of hazards

Class and packing group	4.1, II	4.1, III	4.2, II	4.2, III	4.3, I	4.3, II	4.3, III	5.1, I	5.1, II	5.1, III	6.1, I DERMAL	6.1, I ORAL	6.1, II	6.1, III	8, I	8, II	8, III	9
3, I	SOL 4.1 / LIQ 3, I	SOL 4.1 / LIQ 3, I	SOL 4.2 / LIQ 3, I	SOL 4.2 / LIQ 3, I	4.3, I	4.3, I	4.3, I	SOL 5.1, I / LIQ 3, I	SOL 5.1, I / LIQ 3, I	SOL 5.1, I / LIQ 3, I	3, I	3, I	3, I	3, I	3, I	3, I	3, I	3, I
3, II	SOL 4.1 / LIQ 3, II	SOL 4.1 / LIQ 3, II	SOL 4.2 / LIQ 3, II	SOL 4.2 / LIQ 3, II	4.3, I	4.3, II	4.3, II	SOL 5.1, I / LIQ 3, I	SOL 5.1, II / LIQ 3, II	SOL 5.1, II / LIQ 3, II	3, I	3, I	3, II	3, II	8, I	3, II	3, II	3, II
3, III	SOL 4.1 / LIQ 3, III	SOL 4.1 / LIQ 3, III	SOL 4.2 / LIQ 3, III	SOL 4.2 / LIQ 3, III	4.3, I	4.3, II	4.3, III	SOL 5.1, I / LIQ 3, I	SOL 5.1, II / LIQ 3, II	SOL 5.1, III / LIQ 3, III	6.1, I	6.1, I	6.1, II	3, III */	8, I	8, II	3, III	3, III
4.1, II			4.2, II	4.2, II	4.3, I	4.3, II	4.3, II	5.1, I	4.1, II	4.1, II	6.1, I	6.1, I	SOL 4.1, II / LIQ 6.1, II	SOL 4.1, II / LIQ 6.1, II	8, I	SOL 4.1, II / LIQ 8, II	SOL 4.1, II / LIQ 8, II	4.1, II
4.1, III			4.2, II	4.2, III	4.3, I	4.3, II	4.3, III	5.1, I	4.1, II	4.1, III	6.1, I	6.1, I	6.1, II	SOL 4.1, III / LIQ 6.1, III	8, I	8, II	SOL 4.1, III / LIQ 8, III	4.1, III
4.2, II					4.3, I	4.3, II	4.3, II	5.1, I	4.2, II	4.2, II	6.1, I	6.1, I	4.2, II	4.2, II	8, I	4.2, II	4.2, II	4.2, II
4.2, III					4.3, I	4.3, II	4.3, III	5.1, I	5.1, II	4.2, III	6.1, I	6.1, I	6.1, II	4.2, III	8, I	8, II	4.2, III	4.2, III
4.3, I								4.3, I	4.3, I	4.3, I	6.1, I	4.3, I	4.3, I	4.3, I	4.3, I	4.3, I	4.3, I	4.3, I
4.3, II								4.3, I	4.3, II	4.3, II	6.1, I	4.3, I	4.3, II	4.3, II	8, I	4.3, II	4.3, II	4.3, II
4.3, III								4.3, I	4.3, II	4.3, III	6.1, I	6.1, I	6.1, II	4.3, III	8, I	8, II	4.3, III	4.3, III
5.1, I											5.1, I	5.1, I	5.1, I	5.1, I	5.1, I	5.1, I	5.1, I	5.1, I
5.1, II											5.1, I	5.1, I	5.1, II	5.1, II	8, I	5.1, II	5.1, II	5.1, II
5.1, III											5.1, I	5.1, I	6.1, II	5.1, III	8, I	8, II	5.1, III	5.1, III
6.1, I DERMAL															SOL 6.1, I / LIQ 8, I	6.1, I	6.1, I	6.1, I
6.1, I ORAL															SOL 6.1, I / LIQ 8, I	6.1, I	6.1, I	6.1, I
6.1, II INHAL															SOL 6.1, I / LIQ 8, I	6.1, II	6.1, II	6.1, II
6.1, II DERMAL															SOL 6.1, I / LIQ 8, I	SOL 6.1, II / LIQ 8, II	SOL 6.1, II / LIQ 8, II	6.1, II
6.1, II ORAL															8, I	SOL 6.1, II / LIQ 8, II	6.1, II	6.1, II
6.1, III															8, I	8, II	8, III	6.1, III
8, I																		8, I
8, II																		8, II
8, III																		8, III

SOL   =   Solid substances and mixtures
LIQ   =   Liquid substances, mixtures and solutions
DERMAL   =   Dermal toxicity
ORAL   =   Oral toxicity
INHAL   =   Inhalation toxicity
*/   *Class 6.1 for pesticides*

-12-

NOTE 1: *Examples to explain the use of the table*

Classification of a single substance

Description of the substance to be classified:

An amine not mentioned by name meeting the criteria for Class 3, packing group II as well as those for Class 8, packing group I.

Procedure:

The intersection of line 3 II with column 8 I gives 8 I.
This amine has therefore to be classified in Class 8 under:

UN No. 2734 AMINES LIQUID, CORROSIVE, FLAMMABLE, N.O.S. or UN No. 2734 POLYAMINES, LIQUID, CORROSIVE, FLAMMABLE, N.O.S.
packing group I

Classification of a mixture

Description of the mixture to be classified:

Mixture consisting of a flammable liquid classified in Class 3, packing group III, a toxic substance in Class 6.1, packing group II and a corrosive substance in Class 8, packing group I.

Procedure

The intersection of line 3 III with column 6.1 II gives 6.1 II.
The intersection of line 6.1 II with column 8 I gives 8 I LIQ.
This mixture not further defined has therefore to be classified in Class 8 under:

UN No. 2922 CORROSIVE LIQUID, TOXIC, N.O.S.
packing group I.

NOTE 2: *Examples for the classification of mixtures and solutions under a class and a packing group:*

A phenol solution of Class 6.1, (II), in benzene of Class 3, (II) is to be classified in Class 3, (II); this solution is to be classified under UN No. 1992 FLAMMABLE LIQUID, TOXIC, N.O.S., Class 3, (II), by virtue of the toxicity of the phenol.

A solid mixture of sodium arsenate of Class 6.1, (II) and sodium hydroxide of Class 8, (II) is to be classified under UN No. 3290 TOXIC SOLID, CORROSIVE, INORGANIC, N.O.S., in Class 6.1 (II).

A solution of crude or refined naphthalene of Class 4.1, (III) in petrol of Class 3, (II), is to be classified under UN No. 3295 HYDROCARBONS, LIQUID, N.O.S. in Class 3, (II).

A mixture of hydrocarbons of Class 3, (III), and of polychlorinated biphenyls (PCB) of Class 9, (II), is to be classified under UN No. 2315 POLYCHLORINATED BIPHENYLS, LIQUID or UN No. 3432 POLYCHLORINATED BIPHENYLS, SOLID in Class 9, (II).

A mixture of propyleneimine of Class 3, and polychlorinated biphenyls (PCB) of Class 9, (II), is to be classified under UN No. 1921 PROPYLENEIMINE, INHIBITED in Class 3.

2.1.4   **Classification of samples**

2.1.4.1   When the class of a substance is uncertain and it is being carried for further testing, a tentative class, proper shipping name and UN number shall be assigned on the basis of the consignor's knowledge of the substance and application of:

(a)   the classification criteria of Chapter 2.2; and

(b)   the requirements of this Chapter.

The most severe packing group possible for the proper shipping name chosen shall be used.

Where this provision is used the proper shipping name shall be supplemented with the word "SAMPLE" (e.g., "FLAMMABLE LIQUID, N.O.S., SAMPLE"). In certain instances, where a specific proper shipping name is provided for a sample of a substance considered to meet certain classification criteria (e.g., GAS SAMPLE, NON-PRESSURIZED, FLAMMABLE, UN No. 3167) that proper shipping name shall be used. When an N.O.S. entry is used to carry the sample, the proper shipping name need not be supplemented with the technical name as required by special provision 274 of Chapter 3.3.

2.1.4.2   Samples of the substance shall be carried in accordance with the requirements applicable to the tentative assigned proper shipping name provided:

(a)   the substance is not considered to be a substance not accepted for carriage by sub-sections 2.2.x.2 of Chapter 2.2 or by Chapter 3.2;

(b)   the substance is not considered to meet the criteria for Class 1 or considered to be an infectious substance or a radioactive material;

(c)   the substance is in compliance with 2.2.41.1.15 or 2.2.52.1.9 if it is a self-reactive substance or an organic peroxide, respectively;

(d)   the sample is carried in a combination packaging with a net mass per package not exceeding 2.5 kg; and

(e)   the sample is not packed together with other goods.

2.1.4.3   *Samples of energetic materials for testing purposes*

2.1.4.3.1   Samples of organic substances carrying functional groups listed in tables A6.1 and/or A6.3 in Appendix 6 (Screening Procedures) of the Manual of Tests and Criteria may be carried under UN No. 3224 (self-reactive solid type C) or UN No. 3223 (self-reactive liquid type C), as applicable, of Class 4.1 provided that:

(a)   The samples do not contain any:

(i)   Known explosives;

(ii)   Substances showing explosive effects in testing;

(iii)   Compounds designed with the view of producing a practical explosive or pyrotechnic effect; or

(iv)   Components consisting of synthetic precursors of intentional explosives;

(b)   For mixtures, complexes or salts of inorganic oxidizing substances of Class 5.1 with organic material(s), the concentration of the inorganic oxidizing substance is:

    (i)   Less than 15%, by mass, if assigned to packing group I (high hazard) or II (medium hazard); or

    (ii)   Less than 30%, by mass, if assigned to packing group III (low hazard);

(c)   Available data do not allow a more precise classification;

(d)   The sample is not packed together with other goods; and

(e)   The sample is packed in accordance with packing instruction P520 and special packing provisions PP94 or PP95 of 4.1.4.1 of ADR, as applicable.

2.1.5   Classification of articles as articles containing dangerous goods, n.o.s.

NOTE: For articles which do not have a proper shipping name and which contain only dangerous goods within the permitted limited quantity amounts specified in Column (7a) of Table A of Chapter 3.2, UN No. 3363 and special provisions 301 and 672 of Chapter 3.3 may be applied.

2.1.5.1   Articles containing dangerous goods may be classified as otherwise provided by ADN under the proper shipping name for the dangerous goods they contain or in accordance with this section.

For the purposes of this section "article" means machinery, apparatus or other devices containing one or more dangerous goods (or residues thereof) that are an integral element of the article, necessary for its functioning and that cannot be removed for the purpose of carriage.

An inner packaging shall not be an article.

2.1.5.2   Such articles may in addition contain batteries. Lithium batteries that are integral to the article shall be of a type proven to meet the testing requirements of the Manual of Tests and Criteria, part III, sub-section 38.3, except when otherwise specified by ADN (e.g. for pre-production prototype articles containing lithium batteries or for a small production run, consisting of not more than 100 such articles).

2.1.5.3   This section does not apply to articles for which a more specific proper shipping name already exists in Table A of Chapter 3.2.

2.1.5.4   This section does not apply to dangerous goods of Class 1, Class 6.2, Class 7 or radioactive material contained in articles. However, this section applies to articles containing explosives which are excluded from Class 1 in accordance with 2.2.1.1.8.2.

2.1.5.5   Articles containing dangerous goods shall be assigned to the appropriate Class determined by the hazards present using, where applicable, the table of precedence of hazard in 2.1.3.10 for each of the dangerous goods contained in the article. If dangerous goods classified as Class 9 are contained within the article, all other dangerous goods present in the article shall be considered to present a higher hazard.

2.1.5.6   Subsidiary hazards shall be representative of the primary hazards posed by the other dangerous goods contained within the article. When only one item of dangerous goods is present in the article, the subsidiary hazard(s), if any, shall be the subsidiary hazard(s) identified by the subsidiary hazard label(s) in column (5) of Table A of Chapter 3.2. If the article contains more than one item of dangerous goods and these could react dangerously with one another during carriage, each of the dangerous goods shall be enclosed separately (see 4.1.1.6 of ADR).

2.1.6   **Classification of packagings, discarded, empty, uncleaned**

Empty uncleaned packagings, large packagings or IBCs, or parts thereof, carried for disposal, recycling or recovery of their material, other than reconditioning, repair, routine maintenance, remanufacturing or reuse, may be assigned to UN 3509 if they meet the requirements for this entry.

CHAPTER 2.2

CLASS SPECIFIC PROVISIONS

2.2.1   **Class 1**   **Explosive substances and articles**

2.2.1.1   *Criteria*

2.2.1.1.1   The heading of Class 1 covers:

(a)   Explosive substances: solid or liquid substances (or mixtures of substances) capable by chemical reaction of producing gases at such a temperature and pressure and at such a speed as to cause damage to the surroundings.

Pyrotechnic substances: substances or mixtures of substances designed to produce an effect by heat, light, sound, gas or smoke or a combination of these as the result of non-detonating self-sustaining exothermic chemical reactions.

NOTE 1: Substances which are not themselves explosive but which may form an explosive mixture of gas, vapour or dust are not substances of Class 1.

NOTE 2: Also excluded from Class 1 are: water- or alcohol-wetted explosives of which the water or alcohol content exceeds the limits specified and those containing plasticizers - these explosives are assigned to Class 3 or Class 4.1 - and those explosives which, on the basis of their predominant hazard, are assigned to Class 5.2.

(b)   Explosive articles: articles containing one or more explosive or pyrotechnic substances.

NOTE: Devices containing explosive or pyrotechnic substances in such small quantity or of such a character that their inadvertent or accidental ignition or initiation during carriage would not cause any manifestation external to the device by projection, fire, smoke, heat or loud noise are not subject to the requirements of Class 1.

(c)   Substances and articles not mentioned above which are manufactured with a view to producing a practical explosive or pyrotechnic effect.

For the purposes of Class 1, the following definition applies:

Phlegmatized means that a substance (or "phlegmatizer") has been added to an explosive to enhance its safety in handling and carriage. The phlegmatizer renders the explosive insensitive, or less sensitive, to the following actions: heat, shock, impact, percussion or friction. Typical phlegmatizing agents include, but are not limited to: wax, paper, water, polymers (such as chlorofluoropolymers), alcohol and oils (such as petroleum jelly and paraffin).

2.2.1.1.2   Any substance or article having or suspected of having explosive properties shall be considered for assignment to Class 1 in accordance with the tests, procedures and criteria prescribed in Part I, Manual of Tests and Criteria.

A substance or article assigned to Class 1 can only be accepted for carriage when it has been assigned to a name or n.o.s. entry listed in Table A of Chapter 3.2 and meets the criteria of the Manual of Tests and Criteria.

2.2.1.1.3   The substances and articles of Class 1 shall be assigned to a UN Number and a name or n.o.s. entry listed in Table A of Chapter 3.2. Interpretation of the names of substances and articles in Table A of Chapter 3.2 shall be based upon the glossary in 2.2.1.4.

Samples of new or existing explosive substances or articles carried for purposes including: testing, classification, research and development, quality control, or as a commercial sample, other than initiating explosive, may be assigned to UN No. 0190 SAMPLES, EXPLOSIVE.

The assignment of explosive substances and articles not mentioned by name as such in Table A of Chapter 3.2 to an n.o.s entry of Class 1 or UN No. 0190 SAMPLES, EXPLOSIVE as well as the assignment of certain substances the carriage of which is subject to a specific authorization by the competent authority according to the special provisions referred to in Column (6) of Table A of Chapter 3.2 shall be made by the competent authority of the country of origin. This competent authority shall also approve in writing the conditions of carriage of these substances and articles. If the country of origin is not a Contracting Party to ADN, the classification and the conditions of carriage shall be recognized by the competent authority of the first country Contracting Party to ADN reached by the consignment.

2.2.1.1.4   Substances and articles of Class 1 shall have been assigned to a division in accordance with 2.2.1.1.5 and to a compatibility group in accordance with 2.2.1.1.6. The division shall be based on the results of the tests described in section 2.3.1 applying the definitions in 2.2.1.1.5. The compatibility group shall be determined in accordance with the definitions in 2.2.1.1.6. The classification code shall consist of the division number and the compatibility group letter.

2.2.1.1.5   *Definition of divisions*

Division 1.1   Substances and articles which have a mass explosion hazard (a mass explosion is an explosion which affects almost the entire load virtually instantaneously).

Division 1.2   Substances and articles which have a projection hazard but not a mass explosion hazard.

Division 1.3   Substances and articles which have a fire hazard and either a minor blast hazard or a minor projection hazard or both, but not a mass explosion hazard:

(a)   combustion of which gives rise to considerable radiant heat; or

(b)   which burn one after another, producing minor blast or projection effects or both.

Division 1.4   Substances and articles which present only a slight hazard of explosion in the event of ignition or initiation during carriage. The effects are largely confined to the package and no projection of fragments of appreciable size or range is to be expected. An external fire shall not cause virtually instantaneous explosion of almost the entire contents of the package.

Division 1.5   Very insensitive substances having a mass explosion hazard which are so insensitive that there is very little probability of initiation or of transition from burning to detonation under normal conditions of carriage. As a minimum requirement they must not explode in the external fire test.

Division 1.6   Extremely insensitive articles which do not have a mass explosion hazard. The articles predominantly contain extremely insensitive substances and demonstrate a negligible probability of accidental initiation or propagation.

NOTE: *The hazard from articles of Division 1.6 is limited to the explosion of a single article.*

2.2.1.1.6   *Definition of compatibility groups of substances and articles*

A   Primary explosive substance.

B   Article containing a primary explosive substance and not having two or more effective protective features. Some articles, such as detonators for blasting, detonator assemblies for blasting and primers, cap-type, are included, even though they do not contain primary explosives.

C   Propellant explosive substance or other deflagrating explosive substance or article containing such explosive substance.

D   Secondary detonating explosive substance or black powder or article containing a secondary detonating explosive substance, in each case without means of initiation and without a propelling charge, or article containing a primary explosive substance and having two or more effective protective features.

E   Article containing a secondary detonating explosive substance, without means of initiation, with a propelling charge (other than one containing a flammable liquid or gel or hypergolic liquids).

F   Article containing a secondary detonating explosive substance with its own means of initiation, with a propelling charge (other than one containing a flammable liquid or gel or hypergolic liquids) or without a propelling charge.

G   Pyrotechnic substance, or article containing a pyrotechnic substance, or article containing both an explosive substance and an illuminating, incendiary, tear- or smoke-producing substance (other than a water-activated article or one which contains white phosphorus, phosphides, a pyrophoric substance, a flammable liquid or gel or hypergolic liquids).

H   Article containing both an explosive substance and white phosphorus.

J   Article containing both an explosive substance and a flammable liquid or gel.

K   Article containing both an explosive substance and a toxic chemical agent.

L   Explosive substance or article containing an explosive substance and presenting a special hazard (e.g. due to water activation or the presence of hypergolic liquids, phosphides or a pyrophoric substance) necessitating isolation of each type.

N   Articles predominantly containing extremely insensitive substances.

S   Substance or article so packed or designed that any hazardous effects arising from accidental functioning are confined within the package unless the package has been degraded by fire, in which case all blast or projection effects are limited to the extent that they do not significantly hinder or prevent fire-fighting or other emergency response efforts in the immediate vicinity of the package.

NOTE 1: *Each substance or article, packed in a specified packaging, may be assigned to one compatibility group only. Since the criterion of compatibility group S is empirical, assignment to this group is necessarily linked to the tests for assignment of a classification code.*

NOTE 2: *Articles of compatibility groups D and E may be fitted or packed together with their own means of initiation provided that such means have at least two effective protective features designed to prevent an explosion in the event of accidental functioning of the means of initiation. Such articles and packages shall be assigned to compatibility groups D or E.*

NOTE 3: Articles of compatibility groups D and E may be packed together with their own means of initiation, which do not have two effective protective features (i.e. means of initiation assigned to compatibility group B), provided that they comply with mixed packing provision MP 21 of Section 4.1.10 of ADR. Such packages shall be assigned to compatibility groups D or E.

NOTE 4: Articles may be fitted or packed together with their own means of ignition provided that the means of ignition cannot function during normal conditions of carriage.

NOTE 5: Articles of compatibility groups C, D and E may be packed together. Such packages shall be assigned to compatibility group E.

2.2.1.1.7   *Assignment of fireworks to divisions*

2.2.1.1.7.1   Fireworks shall normally be assigned to divisions 1.1, 1.2, 1.3 and 1.4 on the basis of test data derived from Test Series 6 of the Manual of Tests and Criteria. However:

    (a)   waterfalls containing flash composition (see Note 2 of 2.2.1.1.7.5) shall be classified as 1.1G regardless of the results of Test Series 6;

    (b)   since the range of fireworks is very extensive and the availability of test facilities may be limited, assignment to divisions may also be made in accordance with the procedure in 2.2.1.1.7.2.

2.2.1.1.7.2   Assignment of fireworks to UN No. 0333, 0334, 0335 or 0336, and assignment of articles to UN No. 0431 for those used for theatrical effects meeting the definition for article type and the 1.4 G specification in the default fireworks classification table in 2.2.1.1.7.5 may be made on the basis of analogy, without the need for Test Series 6 testing, in accordance with the default fireworks classification table in 2.2.1.1.7.5. Such assignment shall be made with the agreement of the competent authority. Items not specified in the table shall be classified on the basis of test data derived from Test Series 6.

NOTE 1:   The addition of other types of fireworks to column 1 of the table in 2.2.1.1.7.5 shall only be made on the basis of full test data submitted to the UN Sub-Committee of Experts on the Transport of Dangerous Goods for consideration.

NOTE 2:   Test data derived by competent authorities which validates, or contradicts the assignment of fireworks specified in column 4 of the table in 2.2.1.1.7.5 to divisions in column 5 should be submitted to the UN Sub-Committee of Experts on the Transport of Dangerous Goods for information.

2.2.1.1.7.3   Where fireworks of more than one division are packed in the same package they shall be classified on the basis of the highest division unless test data derived from Test Series 6 indicate otherwise.

2.2.1.1.7.4   The classification shown in the table in 2.2.1.1.7.5 applies only for articles packed in fibreboard boxes (4G).

2.2.1.1.7.5   *Default fireworks classification table* [1]

NOTE 1:   References to percentages in the table, unless otherwise stated, are to the mass of all pyrotechnic substances (e.g. rocket motors, lifting charge, bursting charge and effect charge).

---

[1]   This table contains a list of firework classifications which may be used in the absence of Test Series 6 data (see 2.2.1.1.7.2).

NOTE 2: "Flash composition" in this table refers to pyrotechnic substances in powder form or as pyrotechnic units as presented in the fireworks that are used in waterfalls, or to produce an aural effect or used as a bursting charge, or propellant charge unless:

(a) The time taken for the pressure rise in the HSL Flash Composition Test in Appendix 7 of the Manual of Tests and Criteria is demonstrated to be more than 6 ms for 0.5 g of pyrotechnic substance; or

(b) The pyrotechnic substance gives a negative "-" result in the US Flash Composition Test in Appendix 7 of the Manual of Tests and Criteria.

NOTE 3: Dimensions in mm refer to:

(a) for spherical and peanut shells the diameter of the sphere of the shell;

(b) for cylinder shells the length of the shell;

(c) for a shell in mortar, Roman candle, shot tube firework or mine, the inside diameter of the tube comprising or containing the firework;

(d) for a bag mine or cylinder mine, the inside diameter of the mortar intended to contain the mine.

Type	Includes: / Synonym:	Definition	Specification	Classification
Shell, spherical or cylindrical	Spherical display shell: aerial shell, colour shell, dye shell, multi-break shell, multi-effect shell, nautical shell, parachute shell, smoke shell, star shell; report shell: maroon, salute, sound shell, thunderclap, aerial shell kit	Device with or without propellant charge, with delay fuse and bursting charge, pyrotechnic unit(s) or loose pyrotechnic substance and designed to be projected from a mortar	All report shells	1.1G
			Colour shell: ≥ 180 mm	1.1G
			Colour shell: < 180 mm with > 25% flash composition, as loose powder and/or report effects	1.1G
			Colour shell: < 180 mm with ≤ 25% flash composition, as loose powder and/or report effects	1.3G
			Colour shell: ≤ 50 mm, or ≤ 60 g pyrotechnic substance, with ≤ 2% flash composition as loose powder and/or report effects	1.4G
	Peanut shell	Device with two or more spherical aerial shells in a common wrapper propelled by the same propellant charge with separate external delay fuses	The most hazardous spherical aerial shell determines the classification	
	Preloaded mortar, shell in mortar	Assembly comprising a spherical or cylindrical shell inside a mortar from which the shell is designed to be projected	All report shells	1.1G
			Colour shell: ≥ 180 mm	1.1G
			Colour shell: > 25% flash composition as loose powder and/or report effects	1.1G
			Colour shell: > 50 mm and < 180 mm	1.2G
			Colour shell: ≤ 50 mm, or ≤ 60 g pyrotechnic substance, with ≤ 25% flash composition as loose powder and/or report effects	1.3G

Type	Includes: / Synonym:	Definition	Specification	Classification
Shell, spherical or cylindrical (cont'd)	Shell of shells (spherical) *(Reference to percentages for shell of shells are to the gross mass of the fireworks article)*	Device without propellant charge, with delay fuse and bursting charge, containing report shells and inert materials and designed to be projected from a mortar	> 120 mm	1.1G
		Device without propellant charge, with delay fuse and bursting charge, containing report shells ≤ 25g flash composition per report unit, with ≤ 33% flash composition and ≥ 60% inert materials and designed to be projected from a mortar	≤ 120 mm	1.3G
		Device without propellant charge, with delay fuse and bursting charge, containing colour shells and/or pyrotechnic units and designed to be projected from a mortar	> 300 mm	1.1G
		Device without propellant charge, with delay fuse and bursting charge, containing colour shells ≤ 70mm and/or pyrotechnic units, with ≤ 25% flash composition and ≤ 60% pyrotechnic substance and designed to be projected from a mortar	> 200 mm and ≤ 300 mm	1.3G
		Device with propellant charge, with delay fuse and bursting charge, containing colour shells ≤ 70 mm and/or pyrotechnic units, with ≤ 25% flash composition and ≤ 60% pyrotechnic substance and designed to be projected from a mortar	≤ 200 mm	1.3G
Battery/ combination	Barrage, bombardos, cakes, finale box, flowerbed, hybrid, multiple tubes, shell cakes, banger batteries, flash banger batteries	Assembly including several elements either containing the same type or several types each corresponding to one of the types of fireworks listed in this table, with one or two points of ignition	The most hazardous firework type determines the classification	

Type	Includes: / Synonym:	Definition	Specification	Classification
Roman candle	Exhibition candle, candle, bombettes	Tube containing a series of pyrotechnic units consisting of alternate pyrotechnic composition, propellant charge, and transmitting fuse	≥ 50 mm inner diameter, containing flash composition, or < 50 mm with $> 25\%$ flash composition	1.1G
			≥ 50 mm inner diameter, containing no flash composition	1.2G
			< 50 mm inner diameter and $\leq 25\%$ flash composition	1.3G
			≤ 30 mm inner diameter, each pyrotechnic unit ≤ 25 g and $\leq 5\%$ flash composition	1.4G
Shot tube	Single shot Roman candle, small preloaded mortar	Tube containing a pyrotechnic unit consisting of pyrotechnic substance, propellant charge with or without transmitting fuse	≤ 30 mm inner diameter and pyrotechnic unit > 25 g, or $> 5\%$ and $\leq 25\%$ flash composition	1.3G
			≤ 30 mm inner diameter, pyrotechnic unit ≤ 25 g and $\leq 5\%$ flash composition	1.4G
Rocket	Avalanche rocket, signal rocket, whistling rocket, bottle rocket, sky rocket, missile type rocket, table rocket	Tube containing pyrotechnic substance and/or pyrotechnic units, equipped with stick(s) or other means for stabilization of flight, and designed to be propelled into the air	Flash composition effects only	1.1G
			Flash composition $> 25\%$ of the pyrotechnic substance	1.1G
			> 20 g pyrotechnic substance and flash composition $\leq 25\%$	1.3G
			≤ 20 g pyrotechnic substance, black powder bursting charge and ≤ 0.13 g flash composition per report and ≤ 1 g in total	1.4G

Type	Includes: / Synonym:	Definition	Specification	Classification
Mine	Pot-a-feu, ground mine, bag mine, cylinder mine	Tube containing propellant charge and pyrotechnic units and designed to be placed on the ground or to be fixed in the ground. The principal effect is ejection of all the pyrotechnic units in a single burst producing a widely dispersed visual and/or aural effect in the air; or	> 25% flash composition, as loose powder and/ or report effects	1.1G
			≥ 180 mm and ≤ 25% flash composition, as loose powder and/ or report effects	1.1G
		Cloth or paper bag or cloth or paper cylinder containing propellant charge and pyrotechnic units, designed to be placed in a mortar and to function as a mine	< 180 mm and ≤ 25% flash composition, as loose powder and/ or report effects	1.3G
			≤ 150 g pyrotechnic substance, containing ≤ 5% flash composition as loose powder and/ or report effects. Each pyrotechnic unit ≤ 25 g, each report effect < 2g; each whistle, if any, ≤ 3 g	1.4G
Fountain	Volcanos, gerbs, lances, Bengal fire, flitter sparkle, cylindrical fountains, cone fountains, illuminating torch	Non-metallic case containing pressed or consolidated pyrotechnic substance producing sparks and flame NOTE: *Fountains intended to produce a vertical cascade or curtain of sparks are considered to be waterfalls (see row below).*	≥ 1 kg pyrotechnic substance	1.3G
			< 1 kg pyrotechnic substance	1.4G
Waterfall	Cascades, showers	Pyrotechnic fountain intended to produce a vertical cascade or curtain of sparks	Containing flash composition regardless of the results of Test Series 6 (see 2.2.1.1.7.1 (a))	1.1G
			Not containing flash composition	1.3G
Sparkler	Handheld sparklers, non-handheld sparklers, wire sparklers		Perchlorate based sparklers: > 5 g per item or > 10 items per pack	1.3G

Type	Includes: / Synonym:	Definition	Specification	Classification
		Rigid wire partially coated (along one end) with slow burning pyrotechnic substance with or without an ignition tip	Perchlorate based sparklers: ≤ 5 g per item and ≤ 10 items per pack; Nitrate based sparklers: ≤ 30 g per item	1.4G
Bengal stick	Dipped stick	Non-metallic stick partially coated (along one end) with slow-burning pyrotechnic substance and designed to be held in the hand	Perchlorate based items: > 5 g per item or > 10 items per pack	1.3 G
			Perchlorate based items: ≤ 5 g per item and ≤ 10 items per pack; nitrate based items: ≤ 30 g per item	1.4G
Low hazard fireworks and novelties	Table bombs, throwdowns, crackling granules, smokes, fog, snakes, glow worm, serpents, snaps, party poppers	Device designed to produce very limited visible and/ or audible effect which contains small amounts of pyrotechnic and/or explosive composition.	Throwdowns and snaps may contain up to 1.6 mg of silver fulminate; snaps and party poppers may contain up to 16 mg of potassium chlorate/red phosphorous mixture; other articles may contain up to 5 g of pyrotechnic substance, but no flash composition	1.4G
Spinner	Aerial spinner, helicopter, chaser, ground spinner	Non-metallic tube or tubes containing gas- or spark-producing pyrotechnic substance, with or without noise producing composition, with or without aerofoils attached	Pyrotechnic substance per item > 20 g, containing ≤ 3% flash composition as report effects, or whistle composition ≤ 5 g	1.3G
			Pyrotechnic substance per item ≤ 20 g, containing ≤ 3% flash composition as report effects, or whistle composition ≤ 5 g	1.4G

Type	Includes: / Synonym:	Definition	Specification	Classification
Wheels	Catherine wheels, Saxon	Assembly including drivers containing pyrotechnic substance and provided with a means of attaching it to a support so that it can rotate	≥ 1 kg total pyrotechnic substance, no report effect, each whistle (if any) ≤ 25 g and ≤ 50 g whistle composition per wheel	1.3G
			< 1 kg total pyrotechnic substance, no report effect, each whistle (if any) ≤ 5 g and ≤ 10 g whistle composition per wheel	1.4G
Aerial wheel	Flying Saxon, UFO's, rising crown	Tubes containing propellant charges and sparks-flame- and/or noise-producing pyrotechnic substances, the tubes being fixed to a supporting ring	> 200 g total pyrotechnic substance or > 60 g pyrotechnic substance per driver, ≤ 3% flash composition as report effects, each whistle (if any) ≤ 25 g and ≤ 50 g whistle composition per wheel	1.3G
			≤ 200 g total pyrotechnic substance and ≤ 60 g pyrotechnic substance per driver, ≤ 3% flash composition as report effects, each whistle (if any) ≤ 5 g and ≤ 10 g whistle composition per wheel	1.4G
Selection pack	Display selection box, display selection pack, garden selection box, indoor selection box; assortment	A pack of more than one type each corresponding to one of the types of fireworks listed in this table	The most hazardous firework type determines the classification	
Firecracker	Celebration cracker, celebration roll, string cracker	Assembly of tubes (paper or cardboard) linked by a pyrotechnic fuse, each tube intended to produce an aural effect	Each tube ≤ 140 mg of flash composition or ≤ 1 g black powder	1.4G
Banger	Salute, flash banger, lady cracker	Non-metallic tube containing report composition intended to produce an aural effect	> 2 g flash composition per item	1.1G
			≤ 2 g flash composition per item and ≤ 10 g per inner packaging	1.3G
			≤ 1 g flash composition per item and ≤ 10 g per inner packaging or ≤ 10 g black powder per item	1.4G

2.2.1.1.8   *Exclusion from Class 1*

2.2.1.1.8.1   An article or a substance may be excluded from Class 1 by virtue of test results and the Class 1 definition with the approval of the competent authority of any ADN Contracting Party who may also recognize an approval granted by the competent authority of a country which is not an ADN Contracting Party provided that this approval has been granted in accordance with the procedures applicable according to RID, ADR, ADN, the IMDG Code or the ICAO Technical Instructions.

2.2.1.1.8.2   With the approval of the competent authority in accordance with 2.2.1.1.8.1, an article may be excluded from Class 1 when three unpackaged articles, each individually activated by its own means of initiation or ignition or external means to function in the designed mode, meet the following test criteria:

(a)   No external surface shall have a temperature of more than 65 °C. A momentary spike in temperature up to 200 ºC is acceptable;

(b)   No rupture or fragmentation of the external casing or movement of the article or detached parts thereof of more than one metre in any direction;

   NOTE: *Where the integrity of the article may be affected in the event of an external fire these criteria shall be examined by a fire test. One such method is described in ISO 14451-2 using a heating rate of 80 K/min.*

(c)   No audible report exceeding 135 dB(C) peak at a distance of one metre;

(d)   No flash or flame capable of igniting a material such as a sheet of 80 ± 10 g/m² paper in contact with the article; and

(e)   No production of smoke, fumes or dust in such quantities that the visibility in a one cubic metre chamber equipped with appropriately sized blow out panels is reduced more than 50% as measured by a calibrated light (lux) meter or radiometer located one metre from a constant light source located at the midpoint on opposite walls . The general guidance on Optical Density Testing in ISO 5659-1 and the general guidance on the Photometric System described in Section 7.5 in ISO 5659-2 may be used or similar optical density measurement methods designed to accomplish the same purpose may also be employed. A suitable hood cover surrounding the back and sides of the light meter shall be used to minimize effects of scattered or leaking light not emitted directly from the source.

   NOTE 1:   *If during the tests addressing criteria (a), (b), (c) and (d) no or very little smoke is observed the test described in (e) may be waived.*

   NOTE 2:   *The competent authority referred to in 2.2.1.1.8.1 may require testing in packaged form if it is determined that, as packaged for carriage, the article may pose a greater hazard.*

2.2.1.1.9   *Classification documentation*

2.2.1.1.9.1   A competent authority assigning an article or substance into Class 1 shall confirm with the applicant that classification in writing.

2.2.1.1.9.2   A competent authority classification document may be in any form and may consist of more than one page, provided pages are numbered consecutively. The document shall have a unique reference.

2.2.1.1.9.3   The information provided shall be easy to identify, legible and durable.

2.2.1.1.9.4   Examples of the information that may be provided in the classification documents are as follows:

(a)   The name of the competent authority and the provisions in national legislation under which it is granted its authority;

(b)   The modal or national regulations for which the classification document is applicable;

(c)   Confirmation that the classification has been approved, made or agreed in accordance with the UN Model Regulations or the relevant modal regulations;

(d)   The name and address of the person in law to which the classification has been assigned and any company registration which uniquely identifies a company or other body corporate under national legislation;

(e)   The name under which the explosives will be placed onto the market or otherwise supplied for carriage;

(f)   The proper shipping name, UN number, class, division and corresponding compatibility group of the explosives;

(g)   Where appropriate, the maximum net explosive mass of the package or article;

(h)   The name, signature, stamp, seal or other identification of the person authorised by the competent authority to issue the classification document is clearly visible;

(i)   Where safety in carriage or the division is assessed as being dependent upon the packaging, the packaging mark or a description of the permitted:

     –   Inner packagings;

     –   Intermediate packagings;

     –   Outer packagings;

(j)   The classification document states the part number, stock number or other identifying reference under which the explosives will be placed onto the market or otherwise supplied for carriage;

(k)   The name and address of the person in law who manufactured the explosives and any company registration which uniquely identifies a company or other body corporate under national legislation;

(l)   Any additional information regarding the applicable packing instruction and special packing provisions where appropriate;

(m)   The basis for assigning the classification, i.e. whether on the basis of test results, default for fireworks, analogy with classified explosive, by definition from Table A of Chapter 3.2 etc.;

(n)   Any special conditions or limitations that the competent authority has identified as relevant to the safety for carriage of the explosives, the communication of the hazard and international carriage;

(o)   The expiry date of the classification document is given where the competent authority considers one to be appropriate

2.2.1.2   *Substances and articles not accepted for carriage*

2.2.1.2.1   Explosive substances which are unduly sensitive according to the criteria of the Manual of Tests and Criteria, Part I, or are liable to spontaneous reaction, as well as explosive substances and articles which cannot be assigned to a name or n.o.s. entry listed in Table A of Chapter 3.2, shall not be accepted for carriage.

2.2.1.2.2   Articles of compatibility group K shall not be accepted for carriage (1.2K, UN No. 0020 and 1.3K, UN No. 0021).

2.2.1.3   *List of collective entries*

Classification code (see 2.2.1.1.4)	UN No	Name of the substance or article
1.1A	0473	SUBSTANCES, EXPLOSIVE, N.O.S.
1.1B	0461	COMPONENTS, EXPLOSIVE TRAIN, N.O.S.
1.1C	0474	SUBSTANCES, EXPLOSIVE, N.O.S.
	0497	PROPELLANT, LIQUID
	0498	PROPELLANT, SOLID
	0462	ARTICLES, EXPLOSIVE, N.O.S.
1.1D	0475	SUBSTANCES, EXPLOSIVE, N.O.S.
	0463	ARTICLES, EXPLOSIVE, N.O.S.
1.1E	0464	ARTICLES, EXPLOSIVE, N.O.S.
1.1F	0465	ARTICLES, EXPLOSIVE, N.O.S.
1.1G	0476	SUBSTANCES, EXPLOSIVE, N.O.S.
1.1L	0357	SUBSTANCES, EXPLOSIVE, N.O.S.
	0354	ARTICLES, EXPLOSIVE, N.O.S.
1.2B	0382	COMPONENTS, EXPLOSIVE TRAIN, N.O.S.
1.2C	0466	ARTICLES, EXPLOSIVE, N.O.S.
1.2D	0467	ARTICLES, EXPLOSIVE, N.O.S.
1.2E	0468	ARTICLES, EXPLOSIVE, N.O.S.
1.2F	0469	ARTICLES, EXPLOSIVE, N.O.S.
1.2L	0358	SUBSTANCES, EXPLOSIVE, N.O.S.
	0248	CONTRIVANCES, WATER-ACTIVATED with burster, expelling charge or propelling charge
	0355	ARTICLES, EXPLOSIVE, N.O.S.
1.3C	0132	DEFLAGRATING METAL SALTS OF AROMATIC NITRO-DERIVATIVES, N.O.S.
	0477	SUBSTANCES, EXPLOSIVE, N.O.S.
	0495	PROPELLANT, LIQUID
	0499	PROPELLANT, SOLID
	0470	ARTICLES, EXPLOSIVE, N.O.S.
1.3G	0478	SUBSTANCES, EXPLOSIVE, N.O.S.
1.3L	0359	SUBSTANCES, EXPLOSIVE, N.O.S.
	0249	CONTRIVANCES, WATER-ACTIVATED with burster, expelling charge or propelling charge
	0356	ARTICLES, EXPLOSIVE, N.O.S.
1.4B	0350	ARTICLES, EXPLOSIVE, N.O.S.
	0383	COMPONENTS, EXPLOSIVE TRAIN, N.O.S.
1.4C	0479	SUBSTANCES, EXPLOSIVE, N.O.S.
	0351	ARTICLES, EXPLOSIVE, N.O.S.
	0501	PROPELLANT, SOLID
1.4D	0480	SUBSTANCES, EXPLOSIVE, N.O.S.
	0352	ARTICLES, EXPLOSIVE, N.O.S.
1.4E	0471	ARTICLES, EXPLOSIVE, N.O.S.
1.4F	0472	ARTICLES, EXPLOSIVE, N.O.S.

Classification code (see 2.2.1.1.4)	UN No	Name of the substance or article
1.4G	0485	SUBSTANCES, EXPLOSIVE, N.O.S.
	0353	ARTICLES, EXPLOSIVE, N.O.S.
1.4S	0481	SUBSTANCES, EXPLOSIVE, N.O.S.
	0349	ARTICLES, EXPLOSIVE, N.O.S.
	0384	COMPONENTS, EXPLOSIVE TRAIN, N.O.S.
1.5D	0482	SUBSTANCES, EXPLOSIVE, VERY INSENSITIVE (SUBSTANCES, EVI) N.O.S.
1.6N	0486	ARTICLES, EXPLOSIVE, EXTREMELY INSENSITIVE (ARTICLES, EEI)
	0190	SAMPLES, EXPLOSIVE other than initiating explosive *NOTE: Division and Compatibility Group shall be defined as directed by the competent authority and according to the principles in 2.2.1.1.4.*

2.2.1.4   *Glossary of names*

NOTE 1: The descriptions in the glossary are not intended to replace the test procedures, nor to determine the hazard classification of a substance or article of Class 1. Assignment to the correct division and a decision on whether Compatibility Group S is appropriate shall be based on testing of the product in accordance with the Manual of Tests and Criteria, Part I or by analogy with similar products which have already been tested and assigned in accordance with the procedures of the Manual of Tests and Criteria.

NOTE 2: The figures given after the names refer to the relevant UN numbers (Column (1) of Table A of Chapter 3.2). For the classification code, see 2.2.1.1.4.

AMMUNITION, ILLUMINATING, with or without burster, expelling charge or propelling charge: UN Nos. 0171, 0254, 0297

Ammunition designed to produce a single source of intense light for lighting up an area. The term includes illuminating cartridges, grenades and projectiles; and illuminating and target identification bombs.

NOTE: The following articles: CARTRIDGES, SIGNAL; SIGNAL DEVICES HAND; SIGNALS, DISTRESS; FLARES, AERIAL; FLARES, SURFACE are not included in this definition. They are listed separately.

AMMUNITION, INCENDIARY, liquid or gel, with burster, expelling charge or propelling charge: UN No. 0247

Ammunition containing liquid or gelatinous incendiary substance. Except when the incendiary substance is an explosive <u>per se</u>, it also contains one or more of the following: a propelling charge with primer and igniter charge; a fuze with burster or expelling charge.

AMMUNITION, INCENDIARY, WHITE PHOSPHORUS with burster, expelling charge or propelling charge: UN Nos. 0243, 0244

Ammunition containing white phosphorus as incendiary substance. It also contains one or more of the following: a propelling charge with primer and igniter charge; a fuze with burster or expelling charge.

AMMUNITION, INCENDIARY with or without burster, expelling charge or propelling charge: UN Nos. 0009, 0010, 0300

Ammunition containing incendiary composition. Except when the composition is an explosive per se, it also contains one or more of the following: a propelling charge with primer and igniter charge; a fuze with burster or expelling charge.

AMMUNITION, PRACTICE: UN Nos. 0362, 0488

Ammunition without a main bursting charge, containing a burster or expelling charge. Normally it also contains a fuze and a propelling charge.

NOTE: GRENADES, PRACTICE are not included in this definition. They are listed separately.

AMMUNITION, PROOF: UN No. 0363

Ammunition containing pyrotechnic substances, used to test the performance or strength of new ammunition, weapon components or assemblies.

AMMUNITION, SMOKE, WHITE PHOSPHORUS, with burster, expelling charge or propelling charge: UN Nos. 0245, 0246

Ammunition containing white phosphorus as a smoke-producing substance. It also contains one or more of the following: a propelling charge with primer and igniter charge; a fuze with burster or expelling charge. The term includes grenades, smoke.

AMMUNITION, SMOKE with or without burster, expelling charge or propelling charge: UN Nos. 0015, 0016, 0303

Ammunition containing a smoke-producing substance such as chlorosulphonic acid mixture or titanium tetrachloride; or a smoke-producing pyrotechnic composition based on hexachloroethane or red phosphorus. Except when the substance is an explosive per se, the ammunition also contains one or more of the following: a propelling charge with primer and igniter charge; a fuze with burster or expelling charge. The term includes grenades, smoke.

NOTE: SIGNALS, SMOKE are not included in this definition. They are listed separately.

AMMUNITION, TEAR-PRODUCING, with burster, expelling charge or propelling charge: UN Nos. 0018, 0019, 0301

Ammunition containing a tear-producing substance. It also contains one or more of the following: a pyrotechnic substance; a propelling charge with primer and igniter charge; a fuze with burster or expelling charge.

ARTICLES, EXPLOSIVE, EXTREMELY INSENSITIVE (ARTICLES EEI): UN No. 0486

Articles that predominantly contain extremely insensitive substances which demonstrate a negligible probability of accidental initiation or propagation under normal conditions of transport, and which have passed Test Series 7.

ARTICLES, PYROPHORIC: UN No. 0380

Articles which contain a pyrophoric substance (capable of spontaneous ignition when exposed to air) and an explosive substance or component. The term excludes articles containing white phosphorus.

ARTICLES, PYROTECHNIC, for technical purposes: UN Nos. 0428, 0429, 0430, 0431, 0432

Articles which contain pyrotechnic substances and are used for technical purposes such as heat generation, gas generation, theatrical effects, etc.

NOTE: The following articles: all ammunition; CARTRIDGES, SIGNAL; CUTTERS, CABLE, EXPLOSIVE; FIREWORKS; FLARES, AERIAL; FLARES, SURFACE; RELEASE DEVICES, EXPLOSIVE; RIVETS, EXPLOSIVE; SIGNAL DEVICES, HAND; SIGNALS, DISTRESS; SIGNALS, RAILWAY TRACK, EXPLOSIVES; SIGNALS, SMOKE are not included in this definition. They are listed separately.

BLACK POWDER (GUNPOWDER), COMPRESSED or BLACK POWDER (GUNPOWDER), IN PELLETS: UN No. 0028

Substance consisting of a pelletized form of black powder.

BLACK POWDER (GUNPOWDER), granular or as meal: UN No. 0027

Substance consisting of an intimate mixture of charcoal or other carbon and either potassium nitrate or sodium nitrate, with or without sulphur.

BOMBS, WITH FLAMMABLE LIQUID, with bursting charge: UN Nos. 0399, 0400

Articles which are dropped from aircraft, consisting of a tank filled with inflammable liquid and bursting charge.

BOMBS, PHOTO-FLASH: UN No. 0038

Explosive articles which are dropped from aircraft to provide brief, intense illumination for photography. They contain a charge of detonating explosive without means of initiation or with means of initiation containing two or more effective protective features.

BOMBS, PHOTO-FLASH: UN No. 0037

Explosive articles which are dropped from aircraft to provide brief, intense illumination for photography. They contain a charge of detonating explosive with means of initiation not containing two or more effective protective features.

BOMBS, PHOTO-FLASH: UN Nos. 0039, 0299

Explosive articles which are dropped from aircraft to provide brief, intense illumination for photography. They contain a photo-flash composition.

BOMBS with bursting charge: UN Nos. 0034; 0035

Explosive articles which are dropped from aircraft, without means of initiation or with means of initiation containing two or more effective protective features.

BOMBS with bursting charge: UN Nos. 0033, 0291

Explosive articles which are dropped from aircraft, with means of initiation not containing two or more effective protective features.

BOOSTERS WITH DETONATOR: UN Nos. 0225, 0268

Articles consisting of a charge of detonating explosive with means of initiation. They are used to increase the initiating power of detonators or detonating cord.

BOOSTERS without detonator: UN Nos. 0042, 0283

Articles consisting of a charge of detonating explosive without means of initiation. They are used to increase the initiating power of detonators or detonating cord.

BURSTERS, explosive: UN No. 0043

Articles consisting of a small charge of explosive used to open projectiles or other ammunition in order to disperse their contents.

CARTRIDGES, FLASH: UN Nos. 0049, 0050

Articles consisting of a casing, a primer and flash powder, all assembled in one piece ready for firing.

CARTRIDGES FOR TOOLS, BLANK: UN No. 0014

Article, used in tools, consisting of a closed cartridge case with a centre or rim fire primer with or without a charge of smokeless or black powder but with no projectile.

CARTRIDGES FOR WEAPONS, BLANK: UN Nos. 0326, 0413, 0327, 0338, 0014

Ammunition consisting of a closed cartridge case with a centre or rim fire primer and a charge of smokeless or black powder but no projectile. It produces a loud noise and is used for training, saluting, propelling charge, starter pistols, etc. The term includes ammunition, blank.

CARTRIDGES FOR WEAPONS, INERT PROJECTILE: UN Nos. 0328, 0417, 0339, 0012

Ammunition consisting of a projectile without bursting charge but with a propelling charge with or without a primer. The articles may include a tracer, provided that the predominant hazard is that of the propelling charge.

CARTRIDGES FOR WEAPONS with bursting charge: UN Nos. 0006, 0321, 0412

Ammunition consisting of a projectile with a bursting charge without means of initiation or with means of initiation containing two or more effective protective features; and a propelling charge with or without a primer. The term includes fixed (assembled) ammunition, semi-fixed (partially assembled) ammunition and separate loading ammunition when the components are packed together.

CARTRIDGES FOR WEAPONS with bursting charge: UN Nos. 0005, 0007, 0348

Ammunition consisting of a projectile with a bursting charge with means of initiation not containing two or more effective protective features; and a propelling charge with or without a primer. The term includes fixed (assembled) ammunition, semi-fixed (partially assembled) ammunition and separate loading ammunition when the components are packed together.

CARTRIDGES, OIL WELL: UN Nos. 0277, 0278

Articles consisting of a thin casing of fibreboard, metal or other material containing only propellant powder which projects a hardened projectile to perforate an oil well casing.

NOTE: CHARGES, SHAPED are not included in this definition. They are listed separately.

CARTRIDGES, POWER DEVICE: UN Nos. 0275, 0276, 0323, 0381

Articles designed to accomplish mechanical actions. They consist of a casing with a charge of deflagrating explosive and a means of ignition. The gaseous products of the deflagration produce inflation, linear or rotary motion or activate diaphragms, valves or switches or project fastening devices or extinguishing agents.

CARTRIDGES, SIGNAL: UN Nos. 0054, 0312, 0405

Articles designed to fire coloured flares or other signals from signal pistols, etc.

CARTRIDGES, SMALL ARMS: UN Nos. 0417, 0339, 0012

Ammunition consisting of a cartridge case fitted with a centre or rim fire primer and containing both a propelling charge and solid projectile. They are designed to be fired in weapons of calibre not larger than 19.1 mm. Shot-gun cartridges of any calibre are included in this description.

NOTE: CARTRIDGES, SMALL ARMS, BLANK, are not included in this definition. They are listed separately. Some military small arms cartridges are not included in this definition. They are listed under CARTRIDGES FOR WEAPONS, INERT PROJECTILE.

CARTRIDGES, SMALL ARMS, BLANK: UN Nos. 0014, 0327, 0338

Ammunition consisting of a closed cartridge case with a centre or rim fire primer and a charge of smokeless or black powder. The cartridge cases contain no projectiles. The cartridges are designed to be fired from weapons with a calibre of at most 19.1 mm and serve to produce a loud noise and are used for training, saluting, propelling charge, starter pistols, etc.

CASES, CARTRIDGE, EMPTY, WITH PRIMER: UN Nos. 0379; 0055

Articles consisting of a cartridge case made from metal, plastics or other non-inflammable material, in which the only explosive component is the primer.

CASES, COMBUSTIBLE, EMPTY, WITHOUT PRIMER: UN Nos. 0447, 0446

Articles consisting of a cartridge case made partly or entirely from nitrocellulose.

CHARGES, BURSTING, PLASTICS BONDED: UN Nos. 0457, 0458, 0459, 0460

Articles consisting of a charge of detonating explosive, plastics bonded, manufactured in a specific form without a casing and without means of initiation. They are designed as components of ammunition such as warheads.

CHARGES, DEMOLITION: UN No. 0048

Articles containing a charge of a detonating explosive in a casing of fibreboard, plastics, metal or other material. The articles are without means of initiation or with means of initiation containing two or more effective protective features.

NOTE: The following articles: BOMBS; MINES; PROJECTILES are not included in this definition. They are listed separately.

CHARGES, DEPTH: UN No. 0056

Articles consisting of a charge of detonating explosive contained in a drum or projectile without means of initiation or with means of initiation containing two or more effective protective features. They are designed to detonate under water.

CHARGES, EXPLOSIVE, COMMERCIAL without detonator: UN Nos. 0442, 0443, 0444, 0445

Articles consisting of a charge of detonating explosive without means of initiation, used for explosive welding, jointing, forming and other metallurgical processes.

CHARGES, PROPELLING, FOR CANNON: UN Nos. 0242, 0279, 0414

Charges of propellant in any physical form for separate-loading ammunition for cannon.

CHARGES, PROPELLING: UN Nos. 0271, 0272, 0415, 0491

Articles consisting of a charge of a propellant charge in any physical form, with or without a casing, as a component of rocket motors or for reducing the drag of projectiles.

CHARGES, SHAPED, without detonator: UN Nos. 0059, 0439, 0440, 0441

Articles consisting of a casing containing a charge of detonating explosive with a cavity lined with rigid material, without means of initiation. They are designed to produce a powerful, penetrating jet effect.

CHARGES, SHAPED, FLEXIBLE, LINEAR: UN Nos. 0237, 0288

Articles consisting of a V-shaped core of a detonating explosive clad by a flexible sheath.

CHARGES, SUPPLEMENTARY, EXPLOSIVE: UN No. 0060

Articles consisting of a small removable booster placed in the cavity of a projectile between the fuse and the bursting charge.

COMPONENTS, EXPLOSIVE TRAIN, N.O.S.: UN Nos. 0382, 0383, 0384, 0461

Articles containing an explosive designed to transmit detonation or deflagration within an explosive train.

CONTRIVANCES, WATER-ACTIVATED with burster, expelling charge or propelling charge: UN Nos. 0248, 0249

Articles whose functioning depends upon physic-chemical reaction of their contents with water.

CORD, DETONATING, flexible: UN Nos. 0065, 0289

Article consisting of a core of detonating explosive enclosed in spun fabric and a plastics or other covering. The covering is not necessary if the spun fabric is sift-proof.

CORD (FUSE) DETONATING, metal clad: UN Nos. 0102, 0290

Article consisting of a core of detonating explosive clad by a soft metal tube with or without protective covering.

CORD (FUSE) DETONATING, MILD EFFECT, metal clad: UN No. 0104

Article consisting of a core of detonating explosive clad by a soft metal tube with or without a protective covering. The quantity of explosive substance is so small that only a mild effect is manifested outside the cord.

CORD, IGNITER: UN No. 0066

Article consisting of textile yarns covered with black powder or another fast burning pyrotechnic composition and of a flexible protective covering; or it consists of a core of black powder surrounded by a flexible woven fabric. It burns progressively along its length with an external flame and is used to transmit ignition from a device to a charge or primer.

CUTTERS, CABLE, EXPLOSIVE: UN No. 0070

Articles consisting of a knife-edged device which is driven by a small charge of deflagrating explosive into an anvil.

DETONATOR ASSEMBLIES, NON-ELECTRIC for blasting: UN Nos. 0360, 0361, 0500

Non-electric detonators assembled with and activated by such means as safety fuse, shock tube, flash tube or detonating cord. They may be of instantaneous design or incorporate delay elements. Detonating relays incorporating detonating cord are included.

DETONATORS, ELECTRIC for blasting: UN Nos. 0030, 0255, 0456

Articles specially designed for the initiation of blasting explosives. These detonators may be constructed to detonate instantaneously or may contain a delay element. Electric detonators are activated by an electric current.

DETONATORS, ELECTRONIC programmable for blasting: UN Nos. 0511, 0512, 0513

Detonators with enhanced safety and security features, utilizing electronic components to transmit a firing signal with validated commands and secure communications. Detonators of this type cannot be initiated by other means.

DETONATORS FOR AMMUNITION: UN Nos. 0073, 0364, 0365, 0366

Articles consisting of a small metal or plastics tube containing explosives such as lead azide, PETN or combinations of explosives. They are designed to start a detonation train.

DETONATORS, NON-ELECTRIC for blasting: UN Nos. 0029, 0267, 0455

Articles specially designed for the initiation of blasting explosives. These detonators may be constructed to detonate instantaneously or may contain a delay element. Non-electric detonators are activated by such means as shock tube, flash tube, safety fuse, other igniferous device or flexible detonating cord. Detonating relays without detonating cord are included.

EXPLOSIVE, BLASTING, TYPE A: UN No. 0081

Substances consisting of liquid organic nitrates such as nitroglycerine or a mixture of such ingredients with one or more of the following: nitrocellulose; ammonium nitrate or other inorganic nitrates; aromatic nitro-derivatives, or combustible materials, such as wood-meal and aluminium powder. They may contain inert components such as kieselguhr, and additives such as colouring agents and stabilizers. Such explosives shall be in powdery, gelatinous or elastic form. The term includes dynamite; gelatine, blasting and gelatine dynamites.

EXPLOSIVE, BLASTING, TYPE B: UN Nos. 0082, 0331

Substances consisting of

(a)   a mixture of ammonium nitrate or other inorganic nitrates with an explosive such as trinitrotoluene, with or without other substances such as wood-meal and aluminium powder; or

(b)   a mixture of ammonium nitrate or other inorganic nitrates with other combustible substances which are not explosive ingredients. In both cases they may contain inert components such as kieselguhr, and additives such as colouring agents and stabilizers. Such explosives must not contain nitroglycerine, similar liquid organic nitrates or chlorates.

EXPLOSIVE, BLASTING, TYPE C: UN No. 0083

Substances consisting of a mixture of either potassium or sodium chlorate or potassium, sodium or ammonium perchlorate with organic nitro-derivatives or combustible materials such as wood-meal or aluminium powder or a hydrocarbon. They may contain inert components such as kieselguhr and additives such as colouring agents and stabilizers. Such explosives must not contain nitroglycerine or similar liquid organic nitrates.

EXPLOSIVE, BLASTING, TYPE D: UN No. 0084

Substances consisting of a mixture of organic nitrated compounds and combustible materials such as hydrocarbons and aluminium powder. They may contain inert components such as kieselguhr and additives such as colouring agents and stabilizers. Such explosives must not contain nitroglycerine, similar liquid organic nitrates, chlorates and ammonium nitrate. The term generally includes plastic explosives.

EXPLOSIVES, BLASTING, TYPE E: UN Nos. 0241, 0332

Substances consisting of water as an essential ingredient and high proportions of ammonium nitrate or other oxidizers, some or all of which are in solution. The other constituents may include nitro-derivatives such as trinitrotoluene, hydrocarbons or aluminium powder. They may contain inert components such as kieselguhr and additives such as colouring agents and stabilizers. The term includes explosives, emulsion, explosives, slurry and explosives, watergel.

FIREWORKS: UN Nos. 0333, 0334, 0335, 0336, 0337

Pyrotechnic articles designed for entertainment.

FLARES, AERIAL: UN Nos. 0093, 0403, 0404, 0420, 0421;

Articles containing pyrotechnic substances which are designed to be dropped from an aircraft to illuminate, identify, signal or warn.

FLARES, SURFACE: UN Nos. 0092, 0418, 0419

Articles containing pyrotechnic substances which are designed for use on the surface to illuminate, identify, signal or warn.

FLASH POWDER: UN Nos. 0094, 0305

Pyrotechnic substance which, when ignited, produces an intense light.

FRACTURING DEVICES, EXPLOSIVE without detonator, for oil wells: UN No. 0099

Articles consisting of a charge of detonating explosive contained in a casing without means of initiation. They are used to fracture the rock around a drill shaft to assist the flow of crude oil from the rock.

FUSE, IGNITER, tubular, metal clad: UN No. 0103

Article consisting of a metal tube with a core of deflagrating explosive.

FUSE, NON-DETONATING: UN No. 0101

Article consisting of cotton yarns impregnated with fine black powder (quickmatch). It burns with an external flame and is used in ignition trains for fireworks, etc.

FUSE, SAFETY: UN No. 0105

Article consisting of a core of fine grained black powder surrounded by a flexible woven fabric with one or more protective outer coverings. When ignited, it burns at a predetermined rate without any external explosive effect.

FUZES, DETONATING: UN Nos. 0106, 0107, 0257, 0367

Articles with explosive components designed to produce a detonation in ammunition. They incorporate mechanical, electrical, chemical or hydrostatic components to initiate the detonation. They generally incorporate protective features.

FUZES, DETONATING with protective features: UN Nos. 0408, 0409, 0410

Articles with explosive components designed to produce a detonation in ammunition. They incorporate mechanical, electrical, chemical or hydrostatic components to initiate the detonation. The detonating fuze must incorporate two or more effective protective features.

FUZES, IGNITING: UN Nos. 0316, 0317, 0368

Articles with primary explosive components designed to produce a deflagration in ammunition. They incorporate mechanical, electrical, chemical or hydrostatic components to start the deflagration. They generally incorporate protective features.

GRENADES, hand or rifle, with bursting charge: UN Nos. 0284, 0285

Articles which are designed to be thrown by hand or to be projected by a rifle. They are without means of initiation or with means of initiation containing two or more effective protective features.

GRENADES, hand or rifle, with bursting charge: UN Nos. 0292, 0293

Articles which are designed to be thrown by hand or to be projected by a rifle. They are with means of initiation not containing two or more effective protective features.

GRENADES, PRACTICE, hand or rifle: UN Nos. 0110, 0372, 0318, 0452

Articles without a main bursting charge which are designed to be thrown by hand or to be projected by a rifle. They contain the priming device and may contain a spotting charge.

HEXOTONAL: UN No. 0393

Substance consisting of an intimate mixture of cyclotrimethylenetrinitramine (RDX), trinitrotoluene (TNT) and aluminium.

HEXOLITE (HEXOTOL), dry or wetted with less than 15 % water, by mass: UN No. 0118

Substance consisting of an intimate mixture of cyclotrimethylenetrinitramine (RDX) and trinitrotoluene (TNT). The term includes "Composition B".

IGNITERS: UN Nos. 0121, 0314, 0315, 0325, 0454

Articles containing one or more explosive substances designed to produce a deflagration in an explosive train. They may be actuated chemically, electrically or mechanically.

NOTE: The following articles: CORD, IGNITER; FUSE, IGNITER; FUSE, NON-DETONATING; FUZES, IGNITING; LIGHTERS, FUSE; PRIMERS, CAP TYPE; PRIMERS, TUBULAR are not included in this definition. They are listed separately.

JET PERFORATING GUNS, CHARGED, oil well, without detonator: UN Nos. 0124, 0494

Articles consisting of a steel tube or metallic strip, into which are inserted shaped charges connected by detonating cord, without means of initiation.

LIGHTERS, FUSE: UN No. 0131

Articles of various design actuated by friction, percussion or electricity and used to ignite safety fuse.

MINES with bursting charge: UN Nos. 0137, 0138

Articles consisting normally of metal or composition receptacles filled with a detonating explosive, without means of initiation or with means of initiation containing two or more effective protective features. They are designed to be operated by the passage of ships, vehicles or personnel. The term includes "Bangalore torpedoes".

MINES with bursting charge: UN Nos. 0136, 0294

Articles consisting normally of metal or composition receptacles filled with a detonating explosive, with means of initiation not containing two or more effective protective features. They are designed to be operated by the passage of ships, vehicles or personnel. The term includes "Bangalore torpedoes".

OCTOLITE (OCTOL), dry or wetted with less than 15 % water, by mass: UN No. 0266

Substance consisting of an intimate mixture of cyclotetramethylenetetranitramine (HMX) and trinitrotoluene (TNT).

OCTONAL: UN No. 0496

Substance consisting of an intimate mixture of cyclotetramethylenetetranitramine (HMX), trinitrotoluene (TNT) and aluminium.

PENTOLITE, dry or wetted with less than 15 % water, by mass: UN No. 0151

Substance consisting of an intimate mixture of pentaerythrite tetranitrate (PETN) and trinitrotoluene (TNT).

POWDER CAKE (POWDER PASTE), WETTED with not less than 17 % alcohol, by mass; POWDER CAKE (POWDER PASTE), WETTED with not less than 25 % water, by mass: UN Nos. 0433, 0159

Substance consisting of nitrocellulose impregnated with not more than 60 % of nitroglycerine or other liquid organic nitrates or a mixture of these.

POWDER, SMOKELESS: UN Nos. 0160, 0161, 0509

Substance based on nitrocellulose used as propellant. The term includes propellants with a single base (nitrocellulose (NC) alone), those with a double base (such as NC and nitroglycerine (NG)) and those with a triple base (such as NC/NG/nitroguanidine).

NOTE: Cast, pressed or bag-charges of smokeless powder are listed under CHARGES, PROPELLING or CHARGES, PROPELLING, FOR CANNON.

PRIMERS, CAP TYPE: UN Nos. 0044, 0377, 0378

Articles consisting of a metal or plastics cap containing a small amount of primary explosive mixture that is readily ignited by impact. They serve as igniting elements in small arms cartridges and in percussion primers for propelling charges.

PRIMERS, TUBULAR: UN Nos. 0319, 0320, 0376

Articles consisting of a primer for ignition and an auxiliary charge of deflagrating explosive such as black powder used to ignite the propelling charge in a cartridge case for cannon, etc.

PROJECTILES, inert with tracer: UN Nos. 0345, 0424, 0425

Articles such as a shell or bullet, which are projected from a cannon or other gun, rifle or other small arm.

PROJECTILES with burster or expelling charge: UN Nos. 0346, 0347

Articles such as a shell or bullet, which are projected from a cannon or other gun. They are without means of initiation or with means of initiation containing two or more effective protective features. They are used to scatter dyes for spotting or other inert materials.

PROJECTILES with burster or expelling charge: UN Nos. 0426, 0427

Articles such as a shell or bullet, which are projected from a cannon or other gun. They are with means of initiation not containing two or more effective protective features. They are used to scatter dyes for spotting or other inert materials.

PROJECTILES with burster or expelling charge: UN Nos. 0434, 0435

Articles such as a shell or bullet, which are projected from a cannon or other gun, rifle or other small arm. They are used to scatter dyes for spotting or other inert materials.

PROJECTILES with bursting charge: UN Nos. 0168, 0169, 0344

Articles such as a shell or bullet, which are projected from a cannon or other gun. They are without means of initiation or with means of initiation containing two or more effective protective features.

PROJECTILES with bursting charge: UN Nos. 0167, 0324

Articles such as a shell or bullet, which are projected from a cannon or other gun. They are with means of initiation not containing two or more effective protective features.

PROPELLANT, LIQUID: UN Nos. 0495, 0497

Substance consisting of a deflagrating liquid explosive, used for propulsion.

PROPELLANT, SOLID: UN Nos. 0498, 0499, 0501

Substance consisting of a deflagrating solid explosive, used for propulsion.

RELEASE DEVICES, EXPLOSIVE: UN No. 0173

Articles consisting of a small charge of explosive with means of initiation and rods or links. They sever the rods or links to release equipment quickly.

RIVETS, EXPLOSIVE: UN No. 0174

Articles consisting of a small charge of explosive inside a metallic rivet.

ROCKET MOTORS: UN Nos. 0186, 0280, 0281, 0510

Articles consisting of a charge of explosive, generally a solid propellant, contained in a cylinder fitted with one or more nozzles. They are designed to propel a rocket or a guided missile.

ROCKET MOTORS, LIQUID FUELLED: UN Nos. 0395, 0396

Articles consisting of a liquid fuel within a cylinder fitted with one or more nozzles. They are designed to propel a rocket or a guided missile.

ROCKET MOTORS WITH HYPERGOLIC LIQUIDS with or without expelling charge: UN Nos. 0322, 0250

Articles consisting of a hypergolic fuel contained in a cylinder fitted with one or more nozzles. They are designed to propel a rocket or a guided missile.

ROCKETS, LINE THROWING: UN Nos. 0238, 0240, 0453

Articles consisting of a rocket motor which is designed to extend a line.

ROCKETS, LIQUID FUELLED with bursting charge: UN Nos. 0397, 0398

Articles consisting of a liquid fuel within a cylinder fitted with one or more nozzles and fitted with a warhead. The term includes guided missiles.

ROCKETS with bursting charge: UN Nos. 0181, 0182

Articles consisting of a rocket motor and a warhead without means of initiation or with means of initiation containing two or more effective protective features. The term includes guided missiles.

ROCKETS with bursting charge: UN Nos. 0180, 0295

Articles consisting of a rocket motor and a warhead with means of initiation not containing two or more effective protective features. The term includes guided missiles.

ROCKETS with expelling charge: UN Nos. 0436, 0437, 0438

Articles consisting of a rocket motor and a charge to expel the payload from a rocket head. The term includes guided missiles.

ROCKETS with inert head: UN Nos. 0183, 0502

Articles consisting of a rocket motor and an inert head. The term includes guided missiles.

SAFETY DEVICES, PYROTECHNIC: UN No. 0503

Articles which contain pyrotechnic substances or dangerous goods of other classes and are used in vehicles, vessels or aircraft to enhance safety to persons. Examples are: air bag inflators, air bag modules, seat-belt pretensioners and pyromechanical devices. These pyromechanical devices are assembled components for tasks such as but not limited to separation, locking, or occupant restraint.

SAMPLES, EXPLOSIVE, other than initiating explosive UN No. 0190

New or existing explosive substances or articles, not yet assigned to a name in Table A of Chapter 3.2 and carried in conformity with the instructions of the competent authority and generally in small quantities, *inter alia*, for the purposes of testing, classification, research and development, or quality control, or as commercial samples.

NOTE: Explosive substances or articles already assigned to another name in Table A of Chapter 3.2 are not included in this definition.

SIGNAL DEVICES, HAND: UN Nos. 0191, 0373

Portable articles containing pyrotechnic substances which produce visual signals or warnings. The term includes small surface flares such as highway or railway flares and small distress flares.

SIGNALS, DISTRESS, ship: UN Nos. 0194, 0195, 0505, 0506

Articles containing pyrotechnic substances designed to produce signals by means of sound, flame or smoke or any combination thereof.

SIGNALS, RAILWAY TRACK, EXPLOSIVE: UN Nos. 0192, 0193, 0492, 0493

Articles containing a pyrotechnic substance which explodes with a loud report when the article is crushed. They are designed to be placed on a rail.

SIGNALS, SMOKE: UN Nos. 0196, 0197, 0313, 0487, 0507

Articles containing pyrotechnic substances which emit smoke. In addition they may contain devices for emitting audible signals.

SOUNDING DEVICES, EXPLOSIVE: UN Nos. 0374, 0375

Articles consisting of a charge of detonating explosive, without means of initiation or with means of initiation containing two or more effective protective features. They are dropped from ships and function when they reach a predetermined depth or the sea bed.

SOUNDING DEVICES, EXPLOSIVE: UN Nos. 0204, 0296

Articles consisting of a charge of detonating explosive with means of initiation not containing two or more effective protective features. They are dropped from ships and function when they reach a predetermined depth or the sea bed.

SUBSTANCES, EXPLOSIVE, VERY INSENSITIVE (Substances, EVI), N.O.S.: UN No. 0482

Substances presenting a mass explosion hazard but which are so insensitive that there is very little probability of initiation or of transition from burning to detonation under normal conditions of transport, and which have passed Test Series 5.

TORPEDOES, LIQUID FUELLED with inert head: UN No. 0450

Articles consisting of a liquid explosive system to propel the torpedo through the water, with an inert head.

TORPEDOES, LIQUID FUELLED with or without bursting charge: UN No. 0449

Articles consisting of either a liquid explosive system to propel the torpedo through the water, with or without a warhead; or a liquid non-explosive system to propel the torpedo through the water, with a warhead.

TORPEDOES with bursting charge: UN No. 0451

Articles consisting of a non-explosive system to propel the torpedo through the water, and a warhead without means of initiation or with means of initiation containing two or more effective protective features.

TORPEDOES with bursting charge: UN No. 0329

Articles consisting of an explosive system to propel the torpedo through the water, and a warhead without means of initiation or with means of initiation containing two or more effective protective features.

TORPEDOES with bursting charge: UN No. 0330

Articles consisting of an explosive or non-explosive system to propel the torpedo through the water, and a warhead with means of initiation not containing two or more effective protective features.

TRACERS FOR AMMUNITION: UN Nos. 0212, 0306

Sealed articles containing pyrotechnic substances, designed to reveal the trajectory of a projectile.

TRITONAL: UN No. 0390

Substance consisting of trinitrotoluene (TNT) mixed with aluminium.

WARHEADS, ROCKET with burster or expelling charge: UN No. 0370

Articles consisting of an inert payload and a small charge of detonating or deflagrating explosive, without means of initiation or with means of initiation containing two or more effective protective features. They are designed to be fitted to a rocket motor to scatter inert material. The term includes warheads for guided missiles.

WARHEADS, ROCKET with burster or expelling charge: UN No. 0371

Articles consisting of an inert payload and a small charge of detonating or deflagrating explosive, with means of initiation not containing two or more effective protective features. They are designed to be fitted to a rocket motor to scatter inert material. The term includes warheads for guided missiles.

WARHEADS, ROCKET with bursting charge: UN Nos. 0286, 0287

Articles consisting of a detonating explosive, without means of initiation or with means of initiation containing two or more effective protective features. They are designed to be fitted to a rocket. The term includes warheads for guided missiles.

WARHEADS, ROCKET with bursting charge: UN No. 0369

Articles consisting of a detonating explosive, with means of initiation not containing two or more effective protective features. They are designed to be fitted to a rocket. The term includes warheads for guided missiles.

WARHEADS, TORPEDO with bursting charge: UN No. 0221

Articles consisting of a detonating explosive, without means of initiation or with means of initiation containing two or more effective protective features. They are designed to be fitted to a torpedo.

2.2.2   Class 2   Gases

2.2.2.1   *Criteria*

2.2.2.1.1   The heading of Class 2 covers pure gases, mixtures of gases, mixtures of one or more gases with one or more other substances and articles containing such substances.

A gas is a substance which:

(a)   at 50 °C has a vapour pressure greater than 300 kPa (3 bar); or

(b)   is completely gaseous at 20° C at the standard pressure of 101.3 kPa.

NOTE 1: UN No. 1052 HYDROGEN FLUORIDE, ANHYDROUS is nevertheless classified in Class 8.

NOTE 2: A pure gas may contain other components deriving from its production process or added to preserve the stability of the product, provided that the level of these components does not change its classification or its conditions of carriage, such as filling ratio, filling pressure, test pressure.

NOTE 3: N.O.S. entries in 2.2.2.3 may cover pure gases as well as mixtures.

2.2.2.1.2   The substances and articles of Class 2 are subdivided as follows:

1.   *Compressed gas:* a gas which when packaged under pressure for carriage is entirely gaseous at -50 °C; this category includes all gases with a critical temperature less than or equal to -50 °C;

2.   *Liquefied gas:* a gas which when packaged under pressure for carriage is partially liquid at temperatures above -50 °C. A distinction is made between:

High pressure liquefied gas: a gas with a critical temperature above -50 °C and equal to or below +65 °C; and

Low pressure liquefied gas: a gas with a critical temperature above +65 °C;

3.   *Refrigerated liquefied gas*: a gas which when packaged for carriage is made partially liquid because of its low temperature;

4.   *Dissolved gas:* a gas which when packaged under pressure for carriage is dissolved in a liquid phase solvent;

5.   Aerosol dispensers and receptacles, small, containing gas (gas cartridges);

6.   Other articles containing gas under pressure;

7.   Non-pressurized gases subject to special requirements (gas samples);

8.   Chemicals under pressure: liquids, pastes or powders, pressurized with a propellant that meets the definition of a compressed or liquefied gas and mixtures thereof.

9.   *Adsorbed gas:* a gas which when packaged for carriage is adsorbed onto a solid porous material resulting in an internal receptacle pressure of less than 101.3 kPa at 20 °C and less than 300 kPa at 50 °C.

2.2.2.1.3   Substances and articles (except aerosols and chemicals under pressure) of Class 2 are assigned to one of the following groups according to their hazardous properties, as follows:

A   asphyxiant;

O   oxidizing;

F   flammable;

T   toxic;

TF   toxic, flammable;

TC   toxic, corrosive;

TO   toxic, oxidizing;

TFC   toxic, flammable, corrosive;

TOC   toxic, oxidizing, corrosive.

For gases and gas mixtures presenting hazardous properties associated with more than one group according to the criteria, the groups designated by letter T take precedence over all other groups. The groups designated by letter F take precedence over the groups designated by letters A or O.

NOTE 1: *In the UN Model Regulations, the IMDG Code and the ICAO Technical Instructions, gases are assigned to one of the following three divisions, based on the primary hazard:*

Division 2.1:   *flammable gases (corresponding to the groups designated by the capital letter F);*

Division 2.2:   *non-flammable, non-toxic gases (corresponding to the groups designated by the capital letters A or O);*

Division 2.3:   *toxic gases (corresponding to the groups designated by the capital letter T (i.e. T, TF, TC, TO, TFC and TOC).*

NOTE 2: *Receptacles, small containing gas (UN No. 2037) shall be assigned to the groups A to TOC according to the hazard of the contents. For aerosols (UN No. 1950), see 2.2.2.1.6. For chemicals under pressure (UN Nos. 3500 to 3505), see 2.2.2.1.7.*

NOTE 3: *Corrosive gases are considered to be toxic, and are therefore assigned to the group TC, TFC or TOC.*

2.2.2.1.4   If a mixture of Class 2 mentioned by name in Table A of Chapter 3.2 meets different criteria as mentioned in 2.2.2.1.2 and 2.2.2.1.5, this mixture shall be classified according to the criteria and assigned to an appropriate N.O.S. entry.

2.2.2.1.5   Substances and articles (except aerosols and chemicals under pressure) of Class 2 which are not mentioned by name in Table A of Chapter 3.2 shall be classified under a collective entry listed in 2.2.2.3 in accordance with 2.2.2.1.2 and 2.2.2.1.3. The following criteria shall apply:

Asphyxiant gases

Gases which are non-oxidizing, non-flammable and non-toxic and which dilute or replace oxygen normally in the atmosphere.

Flammable gases

Gases which at 20 °C and a standard pressure of 101.3 kPa:

(a)   are ignitable when in a mixture of 13% or less by volume with air; or

(b)   have a flammable range with air of at least 12 percentage points regardless of the lower flammable limit.

Flammability shall be determined by tests or by calculation, in accordance with methods adopted by ISO (see ISO 10156:2017).

Where insufficient data are available to use these methods, tests by a comparable method recognized by the competent authority of the country of origin may be used.

If the country of origin is not a Contracting Party to ADN these methods shall be recognized by the competent authority of the first country Contracting Party to ADN reached by the consignment.

Oxidizing gases

Gases, which may, generally by providing oxygen, cause or contribute to the combustion of other material more than air does. These are pure gases or gas mixtures with an oxidizing power greater than 23.5% as determined by a method specified in ISO 10156:2017.

Toxic gases

NOTE: *Gases meeting the criteria for toxicity in part or completely owing to their corrosivity are to be classified as toxic. See also the criteria under the heading "Corrosive gases" for a possible subsidiary corrosivity hazard.*

Gases which:

(a)   are known to be so toxic or corrosive to humans as to pose a hazard to health; or

(b)   are presumed to be toxic or corrosive to humans because they have a LC_{50} value for acute toxicity equal to or less than 5 000 ml/m³ (ppm) when tested in accordance with 2.2.61.1.

In the case of gas mixtures (including vapours of substances from other classes) the following formula may be used:

$$LC_{50} \text{ Toxic (mixture)} = \frac{1}{\sum_{i=1}^{n} \frac{f_i}{T_i}}$$

where f_i =   mole fraction of the ith component substance of the mixture;

           T_i =   toxicity index of the ith component substance of the mixture.
The T_i equals the LC_{50} value as found in packing instruction P200 of 4.1.4.1 of ADR.
When no LC_{50} value is listed in packing instruction P200 of 4.1.4.1 of ADR, a LC_{50} value available in scientific literature shall be used. When the LC_{50} value is unknown, the toxicity index is determined by using the lowest LC_{50} value of substances of similar physiological and chemical effects, or through testing if this is the only practical possibility.

Corrosive gases

Gases or gas mixtures meeting the criteria for toxicity completely owing to their corrosivity are to be classified as toxic with a subsidiary corrosivity hazard.

A gas mixture that is considered to be toxic due to the combined effects of corrosivity and toxicity has a subsidiary hazard of corrosivity when the mixture is known by human experience to be destructive to the skin, eyes or mucous membranes or when the LC_{50} value of the corrosive components of the mixture is equal to or less than 5 000 ml/m³ (ppm) when the LC_{50} is calculated by the formula:

$$LC_{50} \text{ Corrosive (mixture)} = \frac{1}{\sum_{i=1}^{n} \frac{f_{ci}}{T_{ci}}}$$

where f_{ci} =   mole fraction of the ith corrosive component substance of the mixture;

            T_{ci} =   toxicity index of the ith corrosive component substance of the mixture.
The T_{ci} equals the LC_{50} value as found in packing instruction P200 of 4.1.4.1 of ADR.
When no LC_{50} value is listed in packing instruction P200 of 4.1.4.1 of ADR, a LC_{50} value available in scientific literature shall be used. When the LC_{50} value is unknown the toxicity index is determined by using the lowest LC_{50} value of substances of similar physiological and chemical effects, or through testing if this is the only practical possibility.

2.2.2.1.6   *Aerosols*

Aerosols (UN No. 1950) are assigned to one of the following groups according to their hazardous properties, as follows:

A   asphyxiant;

O   oxidizing;

F   flammable;

T   toxic;

C   corrosive;

CO   corrosive, oxidizing;

FC   flammable, corrosive;

TF   toxic, flammable;

TC   toxic, corrosive;

TO   toxic, oxidizing;

TFC   toxic, flammable, corrosive

TOC   toxic, oxidizing, corrosive.

The classification depends on the nature of the contents of the aerosol dispenser.

NOTE: Gases, which meet the definition of toxic gases according to 2.2.2.1.5 and gases identified as "Considered as pyrophoric" by table note c of Table 2 of packing instruction P200 of ADR, shall not be used as a propellant in an aerosol dispenser. Aerosols with contents meeting the criteria for packing group I for toxicity or corrosivity shall not be accepted for carriage (see also 2.2.2.2.2).

The following criteria shall apply:

(a)   Assignment to group A shall apply when the contents do not meet the criteria for any other group according to sub-paragraphs (b) to (f) below;

(b)   Assignment to group O shall apply when the aerosol contains an oxidizing gas according to 2.2.2.1.5;

(c)   Assignment to group F shall apply if the contents include 85% by mass or more flammable components and the chemical heat of combustion is 30 kJ/g or more.

It shall not apply if the contents contain 1% by mass or less flammable components and the heat of combustion is less than 20 kJ/g.

Otherwise the aerosol shall be tested for flammability in accordance with the tests described in the *Manual of Tests and Criteria*, Part III, section 31. Extremely flammable and flammable aerosols shall be assigned to group F;

NOTE: Flammable components are flammable liquids, flammable solids or flammable gases and gas mixtures as defined in Notes 1 to 3 of sub-section 31.1.3 of Part III of the Manual of Tests and Criteria. This designation does not cover pyrophoric, self-heating or water-reactive substances. The chemical heat of combustion shall be determined by one of the following methods ASTM D 240, ISO/FDIS 13943: 1999 (E/F) 86.1 to 86.3 or NFPA 30B.

(d)   Assignment to group T shall apply when the contents, other than the propellant of aerosol dispensers to be ejected, are classified as Class 6.1, packing groups II or III;

(e)   Assignment to group C shall apply when the contents, other than the propellant of aerosol dispensers to be ejected, meet the criteria for Class 8, packing groups II or III;

(f)   When the criteria for more than one group amongst groups O, F, T, and C are met, assignment to groups CO, FC, TF, TC TO, TFC or TOC shall apply, as relevant.

2.2.2.1.7   *Chemicals under pressure*

Chemicals under pressure (UN Nos. 3500 to 3505) are assigned to one of the following groups according to their hazardous properties, as follows:

A   asphyxiant;

F   flammable;

T   toxic;

C   corrosive;

FC   flammable, corrosive;

TF   toxic, flammable.

The classification depends on the hazard characteristics of the components in the different states:

The propellant;

The liquid; or

The solid.

NOTE 1: Gases, which meet the definition of toxic gases or of oxidizing gases according to 2.2.2.1.5 or gases identified as "Considered as pyrophoric" by table note c of Table 2 of packing instruction P200 in 4.1.4.1 of ADR, shall not be used as a propellant in chemicals under pressure.

NOTE 2: Chemicals under pressure with contents meeting the criteria for packing group I for toxicity or corrosivity or with contents meeting both the criteria for packing group II or III for toxicity and for packing group II or III for corrosivity shall not be accepted for carriage under these UN numbers.

NOTE 3: Chemicals under pressure with components meeting the properties of Class 1; liquid desensitized explosives of Class 3; self-reactive substances and solid desensitized explosives of Class 4.1; Class 4.2; Class 4.3; Class 5.1; Class 5.2; Class 6.2; or Class 7, shall not be used for carriage under these UN numbers.

NOTE 4: A chemical under pressure in an aerosol dispenser shall be carried under UN No. 1950.

The following criteria shall apply:

(a)   Assignment to group A shall apply when the contents do not meet the criteria for any other group according to sub-paragraphs (b) to (e) below;

(b)   Assignment to group F shall apply if one of the components, which can be a pure substance or a mixture, needs to be classified as flammable. Flammable components are flammable liquids and liquid mixtures, flammable solids and solid mixtures or flammable gases and gas mixtures meeting the following criteria:

(i)   A flammable liquid is a liquid having a flashpoint of not more than 93 °C;

(ii)   A flammable solid is a solid which meets the criteria in 2.2.41.1;

(iii)   A flammable gas is a gas which meets the criteria in 2.2.2.1.5;

(c)   Assignment to group T shall apply when the contents, other than the propellant, are classified as dangerous goods of Class 6.1, packing groups II or III;

(d)   Assignment to group C shall apply when the contents, other than the propellant, are classified as dangerous goods of Class 8, packing groups II or III;

(e)   When the criteria for two groups amongst groups F, T, and C are met, assignment to groups FC or TF shall apply, as relevant.

2.2.2.2   *Gases not accepted for carriage*

2.2.2.2.1   Chemically unstable gases of Class 2 shall not be accepted for carriage unless the necessary precautions have been taken to prevent the possibility of a dangerous decomposition or polymerization under normal conditions of carriage or unless carried in accordance with special packing provision (r) of packing instruction P200 (10) of 4.1.4.1 of ADR, as applicable. For the precautions necessary to prevent polymerization, see special provision 386 of Chapter 3.3. To this end particular care shall be taken to ensure that receptacles and tanks do not contain any substances liable to promote these reactions.

2.2.2.2.2   The following substances and mixtures shall not be accepted for carriage:

– UN No. 2186 HYDROGEN CHLORIDE, REFRIGERATED LIQUID;

– UN No. 2421 NITROGEN TRIOXIDE;

– UN No. 2455 METHYL NITRITE;

– Refrigerated liquefied gases which cannot be assigned to classification codes 3A, 3O or 3F, with the exception of substance identification number 9000 AMMONIA ANHYDROUS, DEEPLY REFRIGERATED of classification code 3TC in tank vessels;

– Dissolved gases which cannot be classified under UN Nos. 1001, 1043, 2073 or 3318. For UN No. 1043, see special provision 642;

– Aerosols where gases which are toxic according to 2.2.2.1.5 or pyrophoric according to packing instruction P200 in 4.1.4.1 of ADR are used as propellants;

– Aerosols with contents meeting the criteria for packing group I for toxicity or corrosivity (see 2.2.61 and 2.2.8);

– Receptacles, small, containing gases which are very toxic (LC_{50} lower than 200 ppm) or pyrophoric according to packing instruction P200 in 4.1.4.1 of ADR.

2.2.2.3   *List of collective entries*

Compressed gases		
Classification code	**UN No**	**Name and description**
1A	1956	COMPRESSED GAS, N.O.S.
1O	3156	COMPRESSED GAS, OXIDIZING, N.O.S.
1F	1964	HYDROCARBON GAS MIXTURE, COMPRESSED, N.O.S.
	1954	COMPRESSED GAS, FLAMMABLE, N.O.S.
1T	1955	COMPRESSED GAS, TOXIC, N.O.S.
1TF	1953	COMPRESSED GAS, TOXIC, FLAMMABLE, N.O.S.
1TC	3304	COMPRESSED GAS, TOXIC, CORROSIVE, N.O.S.
1TO	3303	COMPRESSED GAS, TOXIC, OXIDIZING, N.O.S.
1TFC	3305	COMPRESSED GAS, TOXIC, FLAMMABLE, CORROSIVE, N.O.S.
1TOC	3306	COMPRESSED GAS, TOXIC, OXIDIZING, CORROSIVE, N.O.S.

Liquefied gases		
Classification code	**UN No**	**Name and description**
2A	1058	LIQUEFIED GASES, non-flammable, charged with nitrogen, carbon dioxide or air
	1078	REFRIGERANT GAS, N.O.S. such as mixtures of gases, indicated by the letter R, which as: Mixture F1, have a vapour pressure at 70 °C not exceeding 1.3 MPa (13 bar) and a mass density at 50 °C not lower than that of dichlorofluoromethane (1.30 kg/l); Mixture F2, have a vapour pressure at 70 °C not exceeding 1.9 MPa (19 bar) and a mass density at 50 °C not lower than that of dichlorodifluoromethane (1.21 kg/l); Mixture F3, have a vapour pressure at 70 °C not exceeding 3 MPa (30 bar) and a mass density at 50 °C not lower than that of chlorodifluoromethane (1.09 kg/l). ***NOTE:*** *Trichlorofluoromethane (Refrigerant R 11), 1,1,2-trichloro-1,2,2-trifluoroethane (Refrigerant R 113), 1,1,1-trichloro-2,2,2-trifluoroethane (Refrigerant R 113a), 1-chloro-1,2,2-trifluoroethane (Refrigerant R 133) and 1-chloro-1,1,2-trifluoroethane (Refrigerant R 133b) are not substances of Class 2. They may, however, enter into the composition of mixtures F1 to F3.*
	1968	INSECTICIDE GAS, N.O.S.
	3163	LIQUEFIED GAS, N.O.S.
2O	3157	LIQUEFIED GAS, OXIDIZING, N.O.S.
2F	1010	BUTADIENES, STABILIZED or BUTADIENES AND HYDROCARBON MIXTURE, STABILIZED, containing more than 40% butadienes
	1060	METHYLACETYLENE AND PROPADIENE MIXTURE, STABILIZED such as mixtures of methylacetylene and propadiene with hydrocarbons, which as: Mixture P1, contain not more than 63% methylacetylene and propadiene by volume and not more than 24% propane and propylene by volume, the percentage of C_4-saturated hydrocarbons being not less than 14% by volume; and as Mixture P2, contain not more than 48% methylacetylene and propadiene by volume and not more than 50% propane and propylene by volume, the percentage of C_4- saturated hydrocarbons being not less than 5% by volume, as well as mixtures of propadiene with 1 to 4% methylacetylene.

Liquefied gases (cont'd)		
Classification code	UN No	Name and description
	1965	HYDROCARBON GAS MIXTURE, LIQUEFIED, N.O.S such as mixtures, which as: Mixture A, have a vapour pressure at 70 °C not exceeding 1.1 MPa (11 bar) and a mass density at 50 °C not lower than 0.525 kg/l; Mixture A01, have a vapour pressure at 70 °C not exceeding 1.6 MPa (16 bar) and a mass density at 50 °C not lower than 0.516 kg/l; Mixture A02, have a vapour pressure at 70 °C not exceeding 1.6 MPa (16 bar) and a mass density at 50 °C not lower than 0.505 kg/l; Mixture A0, have a vapour pressure at 70 °C not exceeding 1.6 MPa (16 bar) and a mass density at 50 °C not lower than 0.495 kg/l; Mixture A1, have a vapour pressure at 70 °C not exceeding 2.1 MPa (21 bar) and a mass density at 50 °C not lower than 0.485 kg/l; Mixture B1 have a vapour pressure at 70 °C not exceeding 2.6 MPa (26 bar) and a mass density at 50 °C not lower than 0.474 kg/l; Mixture B2 have a vapour pressure at 70 °C not exceeding 2.6 MPa (26 bar) and a mass density at 50 °C not lower than 0.463 kg/l; Mixture B, have a vapour pressure at 70 °C not exceeding 2.6 MPa (26 bar) and a mass density at 50 °C not lower than 0.450 kg/l; Mixture C, have a vapour pressure at 70 °C not exceeding 3.1 MPa (31 bar) and a mass density at 50 °C not lower than 0.440 kg/l; **NOTE 1:** *In the case of the foregoing mixtures, the use of the following names customary in the trade is permitted for describing these substances: for mixture A01, A02 and A0: BUTANE; for mixture C: PROPANE.* **NOTE 2:** *UN No. 1075 PETROLEUM GASES, LIQUEFIED may be used as an alternative entry for UN No. 1965 HYDROCARBON GAS MIXTURE LIQUEFIED, N.O.S. for carriage prior to or following maritime or air carriage.*
	3354	INSECTICIDE GAS, FLAMMABLE, N.O.S.
	3161	LIQUEFIED GAS, FLAMMABLE, N.O.S.
2T	1967	INSECTICIDE GAS, TOXIC, N.O.S.
	3162	LIQUEFIED GAS, TOXIC, N.O.S.
2TF	3355	INSECTICIDE GAS, TOXIC, FLAMMABLE, N.O.S.
	3160	LIQUEFIED GAS, TOXIC, FLAMMABLE, N.O.S.
2TC	3308	LIQUEFIED GAS, TOXIC, CORROSIVE, N.O.S.
2TO	3307	LIQUEFIED GAS, TOXIC, OXIDIZING, N.O.S.
2TFC	3309	LIQUEFIED GAS, TOXIC, FLAMMABLE, CORROSIVE, N.O.S.
2TOC	3310	LIQUEFIED GAS, TOXIC, OXIDIZING, CORROSIVE, N.O.S.

Refrigerated liquefied gases		
Classification code	UN No	Name and description
3A	3158	GAS, REFRIGERATED LIQUID, N.O.S.
3O	3311	GAS, REFRIGERATED LIQUID, OXIDIZING, N.O.S.
3F	3312	GAS, REFRIGERATED LIQUID, FLAMMABLE, N.O.S.

Dissolved gases		
Classification code	UN No	Name and description
4		Only substances listed in Table A of Chapter 3.2 are to be accepted for carriage.

Aerosols and receptacles, small, containing gas		
Classification code	UN No	Name and description
5	1950	AEROSOLS
	2037	RECEPTACLES, SMALL CONTAINING GAS (GAS CARTRIDGES) without a release device, non-refillable

Other articles containing gas under pressure		
Classification code	UN No	Name and description
6A	2857	REFRIGERATING MACHINES containing non-flammable, non-toxic gases or ammonia solutions (UN 2672)
	3164	ARTICLES, PRESSURIZED, PNEUMATIC (containing non-flammable gas) or
	3164	ARTICLES, PRESSURIZED, HYDRAULIC (containing non-flammable gas)
	3538	ARTICLES CONTAINING NON-FLAMMABLE, NON TOXIC GAS, N.O.S.
6F	3150	DEVICES, SMALL, HYDROCARBON GAS POWERED or
	3150	HYDROCARBON GAS REFILLS FOR SMALL DEVICES, with release device
	3358	REFRIGERATING MACHINES containing flammable, non-toxic, liquefied gas
	3478	FUEL CELL CARTRIDGES, containing liquefied flammable gas or
	3478	FUEL CELL CARTRIDGES CONTAINED IN EQUIPMENT, containing liquefied flammable gas or
	3478	FUEL CELL CARTRIDGES PACKED WITH EQUIPMENT, containing liquefied flammable gas
	3479	FUEL CELL CARTRIDGES, containing hydrogen in metal hydride or
	3479	FUEL CELL CARTRIDGES CONTAINED IN EQUIPMENT, containing hydrogen in metal hydride or
	3479	FUEL CELL CARTRIDGES PACKED WITH EQUIPMENT, containing hydrogen in metal hydride
	3529	ENGINE, INTERNAL COMBUSTION, FLAMMABLE GAS POWERED
	3529	ENGINE, FUEL CELL, FLAMMABLE GAS POWERED
	3529	MACHINERY, INTERNAL COMBUSTION, FLAMMABLE GAS POWERED
	3529	MACHINERY, FUEL CELL, FLAMMABLE GAS POWERED
	3537	ARTICLES CONTAINING FLAMMABLE GAS, N.O.S.
6T	3539	ARTICLES CONTAINING TOXIC GAS, N.O.S.

Gas samples		
Classification code	**UN No**	**Name and description**
7F	3167	GAS SAMPLE, NON-PRESSURIZED, FLAMMABLE, N.O.S., not refrigerated liquid
7T	3169	GAS SAMPLE, NON-PRESSURIZED, TOXIC, N.O.S., not refrigerated liquid
7TF	3168	GAS SAMPLE, NON-PRESSURIZED, TOXIC, FLAMMABLE, N.O.S., not refrigerated liquid

Chemicals under pressure		
Classification code	**UN No**	**Name of the substance or article**
8A	3500	CHEMICAL UNDER PRESSURE, N.O.S.
8F	3501	CHEMICAL UNDER PRESSURE, FLAMMABLE, N.O.S.
8T	3502	CHEMICAL UNDER PRESSURE, TOXIC, N.O.S.
8C	3503	CHEMICAL UNDER PRESSURE, CORROSIVE, N.O.S.
8TF	3504	CHEMICAL UNDER PRESSURE, FLAMMABLE, TOXIC, N.O.S.
8FC	3505	CHEMICAL UNDER PRESSURE, FLAMMABLE, CORROSIVE, N.O.S

Adsorbed gases		
Classification code	**UN No.**	**Name of the substance or article**
9A	3511	ADSORBED GAS, N.O.S.
9O	3513	ADSORBED GAS, OXIDIZING, N.O.S.
9F	3510	ADSORBED GAS, FLAMMABLE, N.O.S.
9T	3512	ADSORBED GAS, TOXIC, N.O.S.
9TF	3514	ADSORBED GAS, TOXIC, FLAMMABLE, N.O.S.
9TC	3516	ADSORBED GAS, TOXIC, CORROSIVE, N.O.S.
9TO	3515	ADSORBED GAS, TOXIC, OXIDIZING, N.O.S.
9TFC	3517	ADSORBED GAS, TOXIC, FLAMMABLE, CORROSIVE, N.O.S.
9TOC	3518	ADSORBED GAS, TOXIC, OXIDIZING, CORROSIVE, N.O.S.

2.2.3   **Class 3 Flammable liquids**

2.2.3.1   *Criteria*

2.2.3.1.1   The heading of Class 3 covers substances and articles containing substances of this Class which:

–   are liquids according to subparagraph (a) of the definition for "liquid" in 1.2.1;

–   have at 50 °C a vapour pressure of not more than 300 kPa (3 bar) and are not completely gaseous at 20 °C and at standard pressure of 101.3 kPa; and

–   have a flash-point of not more than 60 °C (see 2.3.3.1 for the relevant test).

The heading of Class 3 also covers liquid substances and molten solid substances with a flash-point of more than 60 °C and which are carried or handed over for carriage whilst heated at temperatures equal to or higher than their flash-point. These substances are assigned to UN No. 3256.

The heading of Class 3 also covers liquid desensitized explosives. Liquid desensitized explosives are explosive substances which arc dissolved or suspended in water or other liquid substances, to form an homogeneous liquid mixture to suppress their explosive properties. Such entries in Table A of Chapter 3.2 are UN Nos. 1204, 2059, 3064, 3343, 3357 and 3379.

For the purpose of carriage in tank vessels, the heading of Class 3 also covers the following substances which:

–   have a flash-point above 60 °C and which are carried or handed over for carriage at a temperature within a range of 15 K below the flash-point;

–   have an auto-ignition temperature of 200 °C or below and which are not mentioned elsewhere.

NOTE 1: Substances having a flash-point above 35 °C, which, do not sustain combustion according to the criteria of 32.2.5 of Part III of the Manual of Tests and Criteria are not substances of Class 3; if, however, these substances are handed over for carriage and carried whilst heated at temperatures equal to or higher than their flash-point, they are substances of Class 3.

NOTE 2: By derogation from paragraph 2.2.3.1.1 above, diesel fuel, gas oil, heating oil (light) including synthetically manufactured products having a flash-point above 60 °C and not more than 100 °C shall be deemed substances of Class 3, UN No. 1202.

NOTE 3: Flammable liquids which are highly toxic by inhalation, as defined in 2.2.61.1.4 to 2.2.61.1.9, and toxic substances having a flash-point of 23 °C or above are substances of Class 6.1 (see 2.2.61.1). Liquids which are highly toxic by inhalation are indicated as "toxic by inhalation" in their proper shipping name in Column (2) or by special provision 354 in Column (6) of Table A of Chapter 3.2.

NOTE 4: Flammable liquid substances and preparations used as pesticides, which are highly toxic, toxic or slightly toxic and have a flash-point of 23 °C or above are substances of Class 6.1 (see 2.2.61.1).

NOTE 5: For the purpose of carriage in tank vessels, substances having a flash-point above 60 °C and not more than 100 °C are substances of Class 9 (identification number 9003).

2.2.3.1.2   The substances and articles of Class 3 are subdivided as follows:

F   Flammable liquids, without subsidiary hazard and articles containing such substances:

F1   Flammable liquids having a flash-point of or below 60 °C;

F2   Flammable liquids having a flash-point above 60 °C which are carried or handed over for carriage at or above their flash-point (elevated temperature substances);

F3   Articles containing inflammable liquids;

F4   Substances having a flash-point above 60 °C which are carried or handed over for carriage at a temperature within a range of 15 K below the flash-point;

F5   Substances having an auto-ignition temperature of 200 °C or below and which are not mentioned elsewhere.

FT   Flammable liquids, toxic:

FT1   Flammable liquids, toxic;

FT2   Pesticides;

FC   Flammable liquids, corrosive;

FTC   Flammable liquids, toxic, corrosive;

D   Liquid desensitized explosives.

2.2.3.1.3   Substances and articles classified in Class 3 are listed in Table A of Chapter 3.2. Substances not mentioned by name in Table A of Chapter 3.2 shall be assigned to the relevant entry of 2.2.3.3 and the relevant packing group in accordance with the provisions of this section. Flammable liquids shall be assigned to one of the following packing groups according to the degree of danger they present for carriage:

Packing Group	Flash-point (closed cup)	Initial boiling point
I	--	≤ 35°C
II [a]	< 23°C	> 35°C
III [a]	≥ 23°C and ≤ 60°C	> 35°C

[a]   See also 2.2.3.1.4

For a liquid with (a) subsidiary hazard(s), the packing group determined in accordance with the table above and the packing group based on the severity of the subsidiary hazard(s) shall be considered; the classification and packing group shall then be determined in accordance with the table of precedence of hazards in 2.1.3.10.

2.2.3.1.4   Viscous flammable liquids such as paints, enamels, lacquers, varnishes, adhesives and polishes having a flash-point of less than 23 °C may be assigned to packing group III in conformity with the procedures prescribed in the *Manual of Tests and Criteria*, Part III, sub-section 32.3, provided that:

(a)   The viscosity[2] and flash-point are in accordance with the following table:

Kinematic viscosity (extrapolated) ν (at near-zero shear rate) mm²/s at 23°C	Flow-time t in seconds	Jet diameter (mm)	Flash-point, closed-cup (°C)
$20 < \nu \le 80$	$20 < t \le 60$	4	above 17
$80 < \nu \le 135$	$60 < t \le 100$	4	above 10
$135 < \nu \le 220$	$20 < t \le 32$	6	above 5
$220 < \nu \le 300$	$32 < t \le 44$	6	above -1
$300 < \nu \le 700$	$44 < t \le 100$	6	above -5
$700 < \nu$	$100 < t$	6	no limit

(b)   Less than 3% of the clear solvent layer separates in the solvent separation test;

(c)   The mixture or any separated solvent does not meet the criteria for Class 6.1 or Class 8;

(d)   The substances are packed in receptacles of not more than 450 litre capacity.

NOTE: *These provisions also apply to mixtures containing no more than 20% nitrocellulose with a nitrogen content not exceeding 12.6% by dry mass. Mixtures containing more than 20% but not more than 55% nitrocellulose with a nitrogen content not exceeding 12.6% by dry mass are substances assigned to UN No. 2059.*

Mixtures having a flash-point below 23 °C and containing:

- *more than 55% nitrocellulose, whatever their nitrogen content; or*

- *not more than 55% nitrocellulose with a nitrogen content above 12.6% by dry mass,*

are substances of Class 1 (UN Nos. 0340 or 0342) or of Class 4.1 (UN Nos. 2555, 2556 or 2557).

2.2.3.1.5   *Viscous liquids*

2.2.3.1.5.1   Except as provided for in 2.2.3.1.5.2, viscous liquids which:

-    have a flash-point of 23 °C or above and less than or equal to 60 °C;

-    are not toxic, corrosive or environmentally hazardous;

---

[2]   *Viscosity determination: Where the substance concerned is non-Newtonian, or where a flow cup method of viscosity determination is otherwise unsuitable, a variable shear-rate viscometer shall be used to determine the dynamic viscosity coefficient of the substance, at 23 °C, at a number of shear rates. The values obtained are plotted against shear rate and then extrapolated to zero shear rate. The dynamic viscosity thus obtained, divided by the density, gives the apparent kinematic viscosity at near-zero shear rate.*

- contain not more than 20% nitrocellulose provided the nitrocellulose contains not more than 12.6% nitrogen by dry mass; and

- are packed in receptacles of not more than 450 litre capacity;

are not subject to ADN, if:

(a) in the solvent separation test (see *Manual of Tests and Criteria*, Part III, sub-section 32.5.1), the height of the separated layer of solvent is less than 3% of the total height; and

(b) the flowtime in the viscosity test (see *Manual of Tests and Criteria*, Part III, sub-section 32.4.3), with a jet diameter of 6 mm is equal to or greater than:

(i) 60 seconds; or

(ii) 40 seconds if the viscous substance contains not more than 60% of Class 3 substances.

2.2.3.1.5.2 Viscous liquids which are also environmentally hazardous, but meet all other criteria in 2.2.3.1.5.1, are not subject to any other provisions of ADN when they are carried in single or combination packagings containing a net quantity per single or inner packaging of 5 litres or less, provided the packagings meet the general provisions of 4.1.1.1, 4.1.1.2 and 4.1.1.4 to 4.1.1.8 of ADR

2.2.3.1.6 If substances of Class 3, as a result of admixtures, come into categories of hazard different from those to which the substances mentioned by name in Table A of Chapter 3.2 belong, these mixtures or solutions shall be assigned to the entries to which they belong on the basis of their actual degree of danger.

NOTE: For the classification of solutions and mixtures (such as preparations and wastes) see also 2.1.3.

2.2.3.1.7 On the basis of the test procedures in accordance with 2.3.3.1 and 2.3.4, and the criteria set out in 2.2.3.1.1, it may also be determined whether the nature of a solution or a mixture mentioned by name or containing a substance mentioned by name is such that the solution or mixture is not subject to the provisions for this Class (see also 2.1.3).

2.2.3.2 *Substances not accepted for carriage*

2.2.3.2.1 Substances of Class 3 which are liable to form peroxides easily (as happens with ethers or with certain heterocyclic oxygenated substances) shall not be accepted for carriage if their peroxide content, calculated as hydrogen peroxide (H_2O_2), exceeds 0.3%. The peroxide content shall be determined as indicated in 2.3.3.3.

2.2.3.2.2 Chemically unstable substances of Class 3 shall not be accepted for carriage unless the necessary precautions have been taken to prevent the possibility of a dangerous decomposition or polymerization under normal conditions of carriage. For the precautions necessary to prevent polymerization, see special provision 386 of Chapter 3.3. To this end particular care shall be taken to ensure that receptacles and tanks do not contain any substances liable to promote these reactions.

2.2.3.2.3 Liquid desensitized explosives other than those listed in Table A of Chapter 3.2 shall not be accepted for carriage as substances of Class 3.

Flammable liquids and articles containing such substances				
Without subsidiary hazard **F**		**F1**	1133	ADHESIVES containing flammable liquid
			1136	COAL TAR DISTILLATES, FLAMMABLE
			1139	COATING SOLUTION (includes surface treatments or coatings used for industrial or other purposes such as vehicle undercoating, drum or barrel lining)
			1197	EXTRACTS, LIQUID, for flavour or aroma
			1210	PRINTING INK, flammable or
			1210	PRINTING INK RELATED MATERIAL (including printing ink thinning or reducing compound), flammable
			1263	PAINT (including paint, lacquer, enamel, stain, shellac, varnish, polish, liquid filler and liquid lacquer base) or
			1263	PAINT RELATED MATERIAL (including paint thinning or reducing compound)
			1266	PERFUMERY PRODUCTS with flammable solvents
			1293	TINCTURES, MEDICINAL
			1306	WOOD PRESERVATIVES, LIQUID
			1866	RESIN SOLUTION, flammable
			1999	TARS, LIQUID, including road oils, and cutback bitumens
			3065	ALCOHOLIC BEVERAGES
			1224	KETONES, LIQUID, N.O.S.
			1268	PETROLEUM DISTILLATES, N.O.S. or
			1268	PETROLEUM PRODUCTS, N.O.S.
			1987	ALCOHOLS, N.O.S.
			1989	ALDEHYDES, N.O.S.
			2319	TERPENE HYDROCARBONS, N.O.S.
			3271	ETHERS, N.O.S.
			3272	ESTERS, N.O.S.
			3295	HYDROCARBONS, LIQUID, N.O.S.
			3336	MERCAPTANS, LIQUID, FLAMMABLE, N.O.S. or
			3336	MERCAPTANS MIXTURE, LIQUID, FLAMMABLE, N.O.S.
			1993	FLAMMABLE LIQUID, N.O.S.
	elevated temperature	**F2**	3256	ELEVATED TEMPERATURE LIQUID, FLAMMABLE, N.O.S., with flash-point above 60 °C, at or above its flash-point
	articles	**F3**	3269	POLYESTER RESIN KIT, liquid base material
			3473	FUEL CELL CARTRIDGES or
			3473	FUEL CELL CARTRIDGES CONTAINED IN EQUIPMENT or
			3473	FUEL CELL CARTRIDGES PACKED WITH EQUIPMENT
			3528	ENGINE, INTERNAL COMBUSTION, FLAMMABLE LIQUID POWERED or
			3528	ENGINE, FUEL CELL, FLAMMABLE LIQUID POWERED or
			3528	MACHINERY, INTERNAL COMBUSTION, FLAMMABLE LIQUID POWERED or
			3528	MACHINERY, FUEL CELL, FLAMMABLE LIQUID POWERED
			3540	ARTICLES CONTAINING FLAMMABLE LIQUID, N.O.S.
		F4	9001	SUBSTANCES HAVING A FLASH-POINT ABOVE 60 °C carried or handed over for carriage at a TEMPERATURE WITHIN A RANGE OF 15 K BELOW THE FLASH-POINT
		F5	9002	SUBSTANCES WITH A SELF-IGNITION TEMPERATURE OF 200 °C AND BELOW, n.o.s.

(cont'd on next page)

	FT1	1228 MERCAPTANS, LIQUID, FLAMMABLE, TOXIC, N.O.S. or 1228 MERCAPTAN MIXTURE, LIQUID, FLAMMABLE, TOXIC, N.O.S. 1986 ALCOHOLS, FLAMMABLE, TOXIC, N.O.S. 1988 ALDEHYDES, FLAMMABLE, TOXIC, N.O.S. 2478 ISOCYANATES, FLAMMABLE, TOXIC, N.O.S. or 2478 ISOCYANATE SOLUTION, FLAMMABLE, TOXIC, N.O.S. 3248 MEDICINE, LIQUID, FLAMMABLE, TOXIC, N.O.S. 3273 NITRILES, FLAMMABLE, TOXIC, N.O.S. 1992 FLAMMABLE LIQUID, TOXIC, N.O.S.

Toxic
FT

Pesticide
(f.p<23 °C)   **FT2**

2758   CARBAMATE PESTICIDE, LIQUID, FLAMMABLE, TOXIC
2760   ARSENICAL PESTICIDE, LIQUID, FLAMMABLE, TOXIC
2762   ORGANOCHLORINE PESTICIDE, LIQUID, FLAMMABLE, TOXIC
2764   TRIAZINE PESTICIDE, LIQUID, FLAMMABLE, TOXIC
2772   THIOCARBAMATE PESTICIDE, LIQUID, FLAMMABLE, TOXIC
2776   COPPER BASED PESTICIDE, LIQUID, FLAMMABLE, TOXIC
2778   MERCURY BASED PESTICIDE, LIQUID, FLAMMABLE, TOXIC
2780   SUBSTITUTED NITROPHENOL PESTICIDE, LIQUID, FLAMMABLE, TOXIC
2782   BIPYRIDILIUM PESTICIDE, LIQUID, FLAMMABLE, TOXIC
2784   ORGANOPHOSPHORUS PESTICIDE, LIQUID, FLAMMABLE, TOXIC
2787   ORGANOTIN PESTICIDE, LIQUID, FLAMMABLE, TOXIC
3024   COUMARIN DERIVATIVE PESTICIDE, LIQUID, FLAMMABLE, TOXIC
3346   PHENOXYACETIC ACID DERIVATIVE PESTICIDE, LIQUID, FLAMMABLE, TOXIC
3350   PYRETHROID PESTICIDE, LIQUID, FLAMMABLE TOXIC
3021   PESTICIDE, LIQUID, FLAMMABLE, TOXIC, N.O.S.
NOTE : The classification of a pesticide under an entry shall be effected on the basis of the active ingredient, of the physical state of the pesticide and any subsidiary hazards it may exhibit.

Corrosive   **FC**

3469   PAINT, FLAMMABLE, CORROSIVE (including paint, lacquer, enamel, stain, shellac, varnish, polish, liquid filler and liquid lacquer base) or
3469   PAINT RELATED MATERIAL, FLAMMABLE, CORROSIVE (including paint thinning or reducing compound)
2733   AMINES, FLAMMABLE, CORROSIVE, N.O.S. or
2733   POLYAMINES, FLAMMABLE, CORROSIVE, N.O.S.
2985   CHLOROSILANES, FLAMMABLE, CORROSIVE, N.O.S.
3274   ALCOHOLATES SOLUTION, N.O.S., in alcohol
2924   FLAMMABLE LIQUID, CORROSIVE, N.O.S.

Toxic,
corrosive   **FTC**

3286   FLAMMABLE LIQUID, TOXIC, CORROSIVE, N.O.S.

Liquid
desensitised   **D**
explosive

3343   NITROGLYCERIN MIXTURE, DESENSITIZED, LIQUID, FLAMMABLE, N.O.S. with not more than 30% nitroglycerin by mass
3357   NITROGLYCERIN MIXTURE, DESENSITIZED, LIQUID, N.O.S. with not more than 30% nitroglycerin by mass
3379   DESENSITIZED EXPLOSIVE, LIQUID, N.O.S.

2.2.41   **Class 4.1   Flammable solids, self-reactive substances, polymerizing substances and solid desensitized explosives**

2.2.41.1   *Criteria*

2.2.41.1.1   The heading of Class 4.1 covers flammable substances and articles, desensitized explosives which are solids according to subparagraph (a) of the definition "solid" in 1.2.1, self-reactive liquids or solids and polymerizing substances.

The following are assigned to Class 4.1:

–   readily flammable solid substances and articles (see paragraphs 2.2.41.1.3 to 2.2.41.1.8);

–   self-reactive solids or liquids (see paragraphs 2.2.41.1.9 to 2.2.41.1.17);

–   solid desensitized explosives (see 2.2.41.1.18);

–   substances related to self-reactive substances (see 2.2.41.1.19);

–   polymerizing substances (see 2.2.41.1.20 and 2.2.41.1.21).

2.2.41.1.2   The substances and articles of Class 4.1 are subdivided as follows:

F   Flammable solids, without subsidiary hazard:

    F1   Organic;

    F2   Organic, molten;

    F3   Inorganic;

    F4   Articles;

FO   Flammable solids, oxidizing;

FT   Flammable solids, toxic:

    FT1   Organic, toxic;

    FT2   Inorganic, toxic;

FC   Flammable solids, corrosive:

    FC1   Organic, corrosive;

    FC2   Inorganic, corrosive;

D   Solid desensitized explosives without subsidiary hazard;

DT   Solid desensitized explosives, toxic;

SR   Self-reactive substances:

    SR1   Not requiring temperature control;

    SR2   Requiring temperature control.

PM   Polymerizing substances

      PM1   Not requiring temperature control;

      PM2   Requiring temperature control.

Flammable solids

Definition and properties

2.2.41.1.3   *Flammable solids* are readily combustible solids and solids which may cause fire through friction.

Readily combustible solids are powdered, granular, or pasty substances which are dangerous if they can be easily ignited by brief contact with an ignition source, such as a burning match, and if the flame spreads rapidly. The danger may come not only from the fire but also from toxic combustion products. Metal powders are especially dangerous because of the difficulty of extinguishing a fire since normal extinguishing agents such as carbon dioxide or water can increase the hazard.

Classification

2.2.41.1.4   Substances and articles classified as flammable solids of Class 4.1 are listed in Table A of Chapter 3.2. The assignment of organic substances and articles not mentioned by name in Table A of Chapter 3.2 to the relevant entry of sub-section 2.2.41.3 in accordance with the provisions of Chapter 2.1 can be based on experience or on the results of the test procedures in accordance with Part III, sub-section 33.2 of the Manual of Tests and Criteria. The assignment of inorganic substances not mentioned by name shall be based on the results of the test procedures in accordance with Part III, sub-section 33.2 of the Manual of Tests and Criteria; experience shall also be taken into account when it leads to a more stringent assignment.

2.2.41.1.5   When substances not mentioned by name are assigned to one of the entries listed in 2.2.41.3 on the basis of the test procedures in accordance with the Manual of Tests and Criteria, Part III, sub-section 33.2, the following criteria apply:

(a)   With the exception of metal powders or powders of metal alloys, powdery, granular or pasty substances shall be classified as readily flammable substances of Class 4.1 if they can be easily ignited by brief contact with an ignition source (e.g. a burning match), or if, in the event of ignition, the flame spreads rapidly, the burning time is less than 45 seconds for a measured distance of 100 mm or the rate of burning is greater than 2.2 mm/s.

(b)   Metal powders or powders of metal alloys shall be assigned to Class 4.1 if they can be ignited by a flame and the reaction spreads over the whole length of the sample in 10 minutes or less.

Solids which may cause fire through friction shall be classified in Class 4.1 by analogy with existing entries (e.g. matches) or in accordance with any appropriate special provision.

2.2.41.1.6   On the basis of the test procedure in accordance with the Manual of Tests and Criteria, Part III, sub-section 33.2 and the criteria set out in 2.2.41.1.4 and 2.2.41.1.5, it may also be determined whether the nature of a substance mentioned by name is such that the substance is not subject to the provisions for this Class.

2.2.41.1.7 If substances of Class 4.1, as a result of admixtures, come into different categories of hazard from those to which the substances mentioned by name in Table A of Chapter 3.2 belong, these mixtures shall be assigned to the entries to which they belong on the basis of their actual degree of danger.

NOTE: For the classification of solutions and mixtures (such as preparations and wastes), see also 2.1.3.

Assignment of packing groups

2.2.41.1.8 Flammable solids classified under the various entries in Table A of Chapter 3.2 shall be assigned to packing groups II or III on the basis of test procedures of the Manual of Tests and Criteria, Part III, sub-section 33.2, in accordance with the following criteria:

(a) Readily flammable solids which, when tested, have a burning time of less than 45 seconds over a measured distance of 100 mm shall be assigned to:

Packing group II: if the flame passes the wetted zone;

Packing group III: if the wetted zone stops the flame for at least four minutes;

(b) Metal powders or powders of metal alloys shall be assigned to:

Packing group II: if, when tested, the reaction spreads over the whole length of the sample in five minutes or less;

Packing group III: if, when tested, the reaction spreads over the whole length of the sample in more than five minutes.

For solids which may cause fire through friction, the packing group shall be assigned by analogy with existing entries or in accordance with any special provision.

Self-reactive substances

Definitions

2.2.41.1.9 For the purposes of ADN, self-reactive substances are thermally unstable substances liable to undergo a strongly exothermic decomposition even without participation of oxygen (air). Substances are not considered to be self-reactive substances of Class 4.1, if:

(a) they are explosives according to the criteria of Class 1;

(b) they are oxidizing substances according to the classification procedure for Class 5.1 (see 2.2.51.1) except that mixtures of oxidizing substances which contain 5.0% or more of combustible organic substances shall be subjected to the classification procedure defined in Note 2;

(c) they are organic peroxides according to the criteria of Class 5.2 (see 2.2.52.1);

(d) their heat of decomposition is less than 300 J/g; or

(e) their self-accelerating decomposition temperature (SADT) (see NOTE 2 below) is greater than 75 °C for a 50 kg package.

NOTE 1: The heat of decomposition can be determined using any internationally recognised method e.g. differential scanning calorimetry and adiabatic calorimetry.

NOTE 2: Mixtures of oxidizing substances meeting the criteria of Class 5.1 which contain 5.0% or more of combustible organic substances, which do not meet the criteria mentioned in (a), (c), (d) or (e) above, shall be subjected to the self-reactive substance classification procedure.

A mixture showing the properties of a self-reactive substance, type B to F, shall be classified as a self-reactive substance of Class 4.1.

A mixture showing the properties of a self-reactive substance, type G, according to the principle given in 20.4.3 (g) of Part II of the Manual of Tests and Criteria shall be considered for classification as a substance of Class 5.1 (see 2.2.51.1).

NOTE 3: The self-accelerating decomposition temperature (SADT) is the lowest temperature at which self-accelerating decomposition may occur with a substance in the packaging as used during carriage. Requirements for the determination of the SADT are given in the Manual of Tests and Criteria, Part II, Chapter 20 and section 28.4.

NOTE 4: Any substance which shows the properties of a self-reactive substance shall be classified as such, even if this substance gives a positive test result according to 2.2.42.1.5 for inclusion in Class 4.2.

Properties

2.2.41.1.10   The decomposition of self-reactive substances can be initiated by heat, contact with catalytic impurities (e.g. acids, heavy-metal compounds, bases), friction or impact. The rate of decomposition increases with temperature and varies with the substance. Decomposition, particularly if no ignition occurs, may result in the evolution of toxic gases or vapours. For certain self-reactive substances, the temperature shall be controlled. Some self-reactive substances may decompose explosively, particularly if confined. This characteristic may be modified by the addition of diluents or by the use of appropriate packagings. Certain self-reactive substances burn vigorously. Self-reactive substances are, for example, some compounds of the types listed below:

aliphatic azo compounds (-C-N=N-C-);
organic azides (-C-N$_3$);
diazonium salts (-CN$_2^+$ Z$^-$);
N-nitroso compounds (-N-N=O); and
aromatic sulphonylhydrazides (-SO$_2$-NH-NH$_2$).

This list is not exhaustive and substances with other reactive groups and some mixtures of substances may have similar properties.

Classification

2.2.41.1.11   Self-reactive substances are classified into seven types according to the degree of danger they present. The types of self-reactive substances range from type A, which is not accepted for carriage in the packaging in which it is tested, to type G, which is not subject to the provisions for self-reactive substances of Class 4.1. The classification of types B to F is directly related to the maximum quantity allowed in one packaging. The principles to be applied for classification as well as the applicable classification procedures, test methods and criteria and an example of a suitable test report are given in Part II of the Manual of Tests and Criteria.

2.2.41.1.12 Self-reactive substances which have already been classified and are already permitted for carriage in packagings are listed in 2.2.41.4, those already permitted for carriage in IBCs are listed in 4.1.4.2 of ADR, packing instruction IBC520 and those already permitted for carriage in portable tanks are listed in 4.2.5.2 of ADR, portable tank instruction T23. Each permitted substance listed is assigned to a generic entry of Table A of Chapter 3.2 (UN Nos. 3221 to 3240), and appropriate subsidiary hazards and remarks providing relevant transport information are given.

The collective entries specify:

–   self-reactive substances types B to F, see 2.2.41.1.11 above;

–   physical state (liquid/solid); and

–   temperature control (when required), see 2.2.41.1.17 below.

The classification of the self-reactive substances listed in 2.2.41.4 is based on the technically pure substance (except where a concentration of less than 100% is specified).

2.2.41.1.13 Classification of self-reactive substances not listed in 2.2.41.4, 4.1.4.2 of ADR, packing instruction IBC520 or 4.2.5.2 of ADR, portable tank instruction T23 and assignment to a collective entry shall be made by the competent authority of the country of origin on the basis of a test report. The statement of approval shall contain the classification and the relevant conditions of carriage. If the country of origin is not a Contracting Party to ADN, the classification and the conditions of carriage shall be recognized by the competent authority of the first country Contracting Party to ADN reached by the consignment.

2.2.41.1.14 Activators, such as zinc compounds, may be added to some self-reactive substances to change their reactivity. Depending on both the type and the concentration of the activator, this may result in a decrease in thermal stability and a change in explosive properties. If either of these properties is altered, the new formulation shall be assessed in accordance with the classification procedure.

2.2.41.1.15 Samples of self-reactive substances or formulations of self-reactive substances not listed in 2.2.41.4, for which a complete set of test results is not available and which are to be carried for further testing or evaluation, shall be assigned to one of the appropriate entries for self-reactive substances type C provided the following conditions are met:

–   the available data indicate that the sample would be no more dangerous than self-reactive substances type B;

–   the sample is packaged in accordance with packing method OP2 of 4.1.4.1 of ADR and the quantity per cargo transport unit and per transport unit is limited to 10 kg;

–   the available data indicate that the control temperature, if any, is sufficiently low to prevent any dangerous decomposition and sufficiently high to prevent any dangerous phase separation.

Desensitization

2.2.41.1.16   In order to ensure safety during carriage, self-reactive substances are in many cases desensitized by use of a diluent. Where a percentage of a substance is stipulated, this refers to the percentage by mass, rounded to the nearest whole number. If a diluent is used, the self-reactive substance shall be tested with the diluent present in the concentration and form used in carriage. Diluents which may allow a self-reactive substance to concentrate to a dangerous extent in the event of leakage from a packaging shall not be used. Any diluent shall be compatible with the self-reactive substance. In this regard, compatible diluents are those solids or liquids which have no detrimental influence on the thermal stability and hazard type of the self-reactive substance. Liquid diluents in formulations requiring temperature control (see 2.2.41.1.14) shall have a boiling point of at least 60 °C and a flash-point not less than 5 °C. The boiling point of the liquid shall be at least 50 °C higher than the control temperature of the self-reactive substance.

Temperature control requirements

2.2.41.1.17   Self-reactive substances with an SADT not greater than 55 °C shall be subject to temperature control during carriage. See 7.1.7.

Solid desensitized explosives

2.2.41.1.18   Solid desensitized explosives are substances which are wetted with water or alcohols or are diluted with other substances to suppress their explosive properties. Such entries in Table A of Chapter 3.2 are: UN Nos. 1310, 1320, 1321, 1322, 1336, 1337, 1344, 1347, 1348, 1349, 1354, 1355, 1356, 1357, 1517, 1571, 2555, 2556, 2557, 2852, 2907, 3317, 3319, 3344, 3364, 3365, 3366, 3367, 3368, 3369, 3370, 3376, 3380 and 3474.

Substances related to self-reactive substances

2.2.41.1.19   Substances that:

(a)   have been provisionally accepted into Class 1 according to Test Series 1 and 2 but exempted from Class 1 by Test Series 6;

(b)   are not self-reactive substances of Class 4.1; and

(c)   are not substances of Classes 5.1 or 5.2;

are also assigned to Class 4.1. UN Nos. 2956, 3241, 3242 and 3251 are such entries.

Polymerizing substances

Definitions and properties

2.2.41.1.20   *Polymerizing substances* are substances which, without stabilization, are liable to undergo a strongly exothermic reaction resulting in the formation of larger molecules or resulting in the formation of polymers under conditions normally encountered in carriage. Such substances are considered to be polymerizing substances of Class 4.1 when:

(a)   Their self-accelerating polymerization temperature (SAPT) is 75 °C or less under the conditions (with or without chemical stabilization as offered for carriage) and in the packaging, IBC or tank in which the substance or mixture is to be carried;

(b)   They exhibit a heat of reaction of more than 300 J/g; and

(c)   They do not meet any other criteria for inclusion in classes 1 to 8.

A mixture meeting the criteria of a polymerizing substance shall be classified as a polymerizing substance of Class 4.1.

Temperature control requirements

2.2.41.1.21   Polymerizing substances are subject to temperature control in carriage if their self-accelerating polymerization temperature (SAPT) is:

(a)   When offered for carriage in a packaging or IBC, 50 °C or less in the packaging or IBC in which the substance is to be carried; or

(b)   When offered for carriage in a tank, 45 °C or less in the tank in which the substance is to be carried.

See 7.1.7.

NOTE: *Substances meeting the criteria of polymerizing substances and also for inclusion in Classes 1 to 8 are subject to the requirements of special provision 386 of Chapter 3.3.*

2.2.41.2   *Substances not accepted for carriage*

2.2.41.2.1   The chemically unstable substances of Class 4.1 shall not be accepted for carriage unless the necessary steps have been taken to prevent their dangerous decomposition or polymerization during carriage. To this end, it shall in particular be ensured that receptacles and tanks do not contain any substance liable to promote these reactions.

2.2.41.2.2   Flammable solids, oxidizing, assigned to UN No. 3097 shall not be accepted for carriage unless they meet the requirements for Class 1 (see also 2.1.3.7).

2.2.41.2.3   The following substances shall not be accepted for carriage:

–   Self-reactive substances of type A (see Manual of Tests and Criteria, Part II, paragraph 20.4.2 (a));

–   Phosphorus sulphides which are not free from yellow and white phosphorus;

–   Solid densitized explosives other than those listed in Table A of Chapter 3.2;

–   Inorganic flammable substances in the molten form other than UN No. 2448 SULPHUR, MOLTEN;

2.2.41.3   *List of collective entries*

Class	Subdivision	Type		Code	UN	Description
Flammable solids F	without subsidiary hazard	organic		F1	3175	SOLIDS CONTAINING FLAMMABLE LIQUID, N.O.S.
					1353	FIBRES IMPREGNATED WITH WEAKLY NITRATED NITROCELLULOSE, N.O.S. or
					1353	FABRICS IMPREGNATED WITH WEAKLY NITRATED NITROCELLULOSE, N.O.S.
					1325	FLAMMABLE SOLID, ORGANIC, N.O.S.
		organic molten		F2	3176	FLAMMABLE SOLID, ORGANIC, MOLTEN, N.O.S.
		inorganic		F3	3089	METAL POWDER, FLAMMABLE, N.O.S. [a] [b]
					3181	METAL SALTS OF ORGANIC COMPOUNDS, FLAMMABLE, N.O.S.
					3182	METAL HYDRIDES, FLAMMABLE, N.O.S. [c]
					3178	FLAMMABLE SOLID, INORGANIC, N.O.S.
		articles		F4	3527	POLYESTER RESIN KIT, solid base material
					3541	ARTICLES CONTAINING FLAMMABLE SOLID, N.O.S.
	oxidizing			FO	3097	FLAMMABLE SOLID, OXIDIZING, N.O.S. (not allowed, see 2.2.41.2.2)
	toxic FT	organic		FT1	2926	FLAMMABLE SOLID, TOXIC, ORGANIC, N.O.S.
		inorganic		FT2	3179	FLAMMABLE SOLID, TOXIC, INORGANIC, N.O.S.
	corrosive FC	organic		FC1	2925	FLAMMABLE SOLID, CORROSIVE, ORGANIC, N.O.S.
		inorganic		FC2	3180	FLAMMABLE SOLID, CORROSIVE, INORGANIC, N.O.S.
Solid desensitized explosives	without subsidiary hazard			D	3319	NITROGLYCERIN MIXTURE, DESENSITIZED, SOLID, N.O.S. with more than 2% but not more than 10% nitroglycerin by mass
					3344	PENTAERYTHRITE TETRANITRATE (PENTAERYTHRITOL TETRANITRATE, PETN) MIXTURE, DESENSITIZED, SOLID, N.O.S. with more than 10% but not more than 20% PETN by mass
					3380	DESENSITIZED EXPLOSIVE, SOLID, N.O.S.
	toxic			DT		Only substances listed in Table A of Chapter 3.2 are to be accepted for carriage as substances of Class 4.1
Self-reactive substances SR	not requiring temperature control			SR1		SELF-REACTIVE LIQUID TYPE A } Not accepted for carriage,
						SELF-REACTIVE SOLID TYPE A } see 2.2.41.2.3
					3221	SELF-REACTIVE LIQUID TYPE B
					3222	SELF-REACTIVE SOLID TYPE B
					3223	SELF-REACTIVE LIQUID TYPE C
					3224	SELF-REACTIVE SOLID TYPE C
					3225	SELF-REACTIVE LIQUID TYPE D
					3226	SELF-REACTIVE SOLID TYPE D
					3227	SELF-REACTIVE LIQUID TYPE E
					3228	SELF-REACTIVE SOLID TYPE E
					3229	SELF-REACTIVE LIQUID TYPE F
					3230	SELF-REACTIVE SOLID TYPE F
						SELF-REACTIVE LIQUID TYPE G } Not subject to the provisions applicable to
						SELF-REACTIVE SOLID TYPE G } Class 4.1, see 2.2.41.1.11
	requiring temperature control			SR2	3231	SELF-REACTIVE LIQUID TYPE B, TEMPERATURE CONTROLLED
					3232	SELF-REACTIVE SOLID TYPE B, TEMPERATURE CONTROLLED
					3233	SELF-REACTIVE LIQUID TYPE C, TEMPERATURE CONTROLLED
					3234	SELF-REACTIVE SOLID TYPE C, TEMPERATURE CONTROLLED
					3235	SELF-REACTIVE LIQUID TYPE D, TEMPERATURE CONTROLLED
					3236	SELF-REACTIVE SOLID TYPE D, TEMPERATURE CONTROLLED
					3237	SELF-REACTIVE LIQUID TYPE E, TEMPERATURE CONTROLLED
					3238	SELF-REACTIVE SOLID TYPE E, TEMPERATURE CONTROLLED
					3239	SELF-REACTIVE LIQUID TYPE F, TEMPERATURE CONTROLLED
					3240	SELF-REACTIVE SOLID TYPE F, TEMPERATURE CONTROLLED

cont'd on next page

---

[a]   *Metals and metal alloys in powdered or other flammable form, liable to spontaneous combustion, are substances of Class 4.2.*

[b]   *Metals and metal alloys in powdered or other flammable form, which in contact with water, emit flammable gases, are substances of Class 4.3.*

[c]   *Metals hydrides which, in contact with water, emit flammable gases, are substances of Class 4.3. Aluminium borohydride or aluminium borohydride in devices are substances of Class 4.2, UN No. 2870.*

2.2.41.3   *List of collective entries (continued)*

| Polymerizing substances PM | not requiring temperature control PM1 | 3531 POLYMERIZING SUBSTANCE, SOLID, STABILIZED, N.O.S.
3532 POLYMERIZING SUBSTANCE, LIQUID, STABILIZED, N.O.S. |
| | requiring temperature control PM2 | 3533 POLYMERIZING SUBSTANCE, SOLID, TEMPERATURE CONTROLLED, N.O.S.
3534 POLYMERIZING SUBSTANCE, LIQUID, TEMPERATURE CONTROLLED, N.O.S. |

2.2.41.4   *List of currently assigned self-reactive substances in packagings*

In the column "Packing Method" codes "OP1" to "OP8" refer to packing methods in 4.1.4.1 of ADR, packing instruction P520 (see also 4.1.7.1 of ADR). Self-reactive substances to be carried shall fulfil the classification and the control and emergency temperatures (derived from the SADT) as listed. For substances permitted in IBCs, see 4.1.4.2 of ADR, packing instruction IBC520 and, for those permitted in tanks according to Chapter 4.2 of ADR, see 4.2.5.2.6 of ADR, portable tank instruction T23. The formulations not listed in this sub-section but listed in packing instruction IBC520 of 4.1.4.2 of ADR and in portable tank instruction T23 of 4.2.5.2.6 of ADR may also be carried packed in accordance with packing method OP8 of packing instruction P520 of 4.1.4.1 of ADR, with the same control and emergency temperatures, if applicable.

NOTE: The classification given in this table is based on the technically pure substance (except where a concentration of less than 100 % is specified). For other concentrations, the substance may be classified differently following the procedures given in Part II of the Manual of Tests and Criteria and in 2.2.41.1.17.

SELF-REACTIVE SUBSTANCE	Concen-tration (%)	Packing method	Control temperature (°C)	Emergency temperature (°C)	UN generic entry	Remarks
ACETONE-PYROGALLOL COPOLYMER 2-DIAZO-1-NAPHTHOL-5-SULPHONATE	100	OP8			3228	
AZODICARBONAMIDE FORMULATION TYPE B, TEMPERATURE CONTROLLED	< 100	OP5			3232	(1) (2)
AZODICARBONAMIDE FORMULATION TYPE C	< 100	OP6			3224	(3)
AZODICARBONAMIDE FORMULATION TYPE C, TEMPERATURE CONTROLLED	< 100	OP6			3234	(4)
AZODICARBONAMIDE FORMULATION TYPE D	< 100	OP7			3226	(5)
AZODICARBONAMIDE FORMULATION TYPE D, TEMPERATURE CONTROLLED	< 100	OP7			3236	(6)
2,2'-AZODI(2,4-DIMETHYL-4-METHOXYVALERONITRILE)	100	OP7	-5	+5	3236	
2,2'-AZODI(2,4-DIMETHYL-VALERONITRILE)	100	OP7	+10	+15	3236	
2,2'-AZODI(ETHYL-2-METHYLPROPIONATE)	100	OP7	+20	+25	3235	
1,1-AZODI(HEXAHYDROBENZONITRILE)	100	OP7			3226	
2,2'-AZODI(ISOBUTYRONITRILE)	100	OP6	+40	+45	3234	
2,2'-AZODI(ISOBUTYRONITRILE) as a water based paste	≤ 50	OP6			3224	
2,2'-AZODI(2-METHYLBUTYRO-NITRILE)	100	OP7	+35	+40	3236	

SELF-REACTIVE SUBSTANCE	Concen-tration (%)	Packing method	Control temperature (°C)	Emergency temperature (°C)	UN generic entry	Remarks
BENZENE-1,3-DISULPHONYL HYDRAZIDE, as a paste	52	OP7			3226	
BENZENE SULPHONYL HYDRAZIDE	100	OP7			3226	
4-(BENZYL(ETHYL)AMINO)-3-ETHOXY-BENZENEDIAZONIUM ZINC CHLORIDE	100	OP7			3226	
4-(BENZYL(METHYL)AMINO)-3-ETHOXYBENZENEDIAZONIUM ZINC CHLORIDE	100	OP7	+40	+45	3236	
3-CHLORO-4-DIETHYLAMINOBENZENE-DIAZONIUM ZINC CHLORIDE	100	OP7			3226	
2-DIAZO-1-NAPHTHOL-4-SULPHONYL CHLORIDE	100	OP5			3222	(2)
2-DIAZO-1-NAPHTHOL-5-SULPHONYL CHLORIDE	100	OP5			3222	(2)
2-DIAZO-1-NAPHTHOL SULPHONIC ACID ESTER MIXTURE, TYPE D	< 100	OP7			3226	(9)
2,5-DIBUTOXY-4-(4-MORPHOLINYL)-BENZENEDIAZONIUM, TETRACHLOROZINCATE (2:1)	100	OP8			3228	
2,5-DIETHOXY-4-MORPHOLINO-BENZENEDIAZONIUM ZINC CHLORIDE	67-100	OP7	+35	+40	3236	
2,5-DIETHOXY-4-MORPHOLINO-BENZENEDIAZONIUM ZINC CHLORIDE	66	OP7	+40	+45	3236	
2,5-DIETHOXY-4-MORPHOLINO-BENZENEDIAZONIUM TETRAFLUOROBORATE	100	OP7	+30	+35	3236	
2,5-DIETHOXY-4-(4-MORPHOLINYL)-BENZENEDIAZONIUM SULPHATE	100	OP7			3226	
2,5-DIETHOXY-4-(PHENYLSULPHONYL)-BENZENEDIAZONIUM ZINC CHLORIDE	67	OP7	+40	+45	3236	
DIETHYLENEGLYCOL BIS (ALLYL CARBONATE) + DI-ISOPROPYLPEROXYDICARBONATE	≥ 88 + ≤ 12	OP8	-10	0	3237	
2,5-DIMETHOXY-4-(4-METHYL-PHENYLSULPHONYL)BENZENE-DIAZONIUM ZINC CHLORIDE	79	OP7	+40	+45	3236	
4-(DIMETHYLAMINO)-BENZENEDIAZONIUM TRICHLOROZINCATE (-1)	100	OP8			3228	
4-DIMETHYLAMINO-6-(2-DIMETHYL-AMINOETHOXY) TOLUENE-2-DIAZONIUM ZINC CHLORIDE	100	OP7	+40	+45	3236	
N,N'-DINITROSO-N,N'- DIMETHYL TEREPHTHALAMIDE, as a paste	72	OP6			3224	
N,N'-DINITROSOPENTAMETHYLENE-TETRAMINE	82	OP6			3224	(7)
DIPHENYLOXIDE-4,4'-DISULPHONYL HYDRAZIDE	100	OP7			3226	
4-DIPROPYLAMINOBENZENE-DIAZONIUM ZINC CHLORIDE	100	OP7			3226	

SELF-REACTIVE SUBSTANCE	Concentration (%)	Packing method	Control temperature (°C)	Emergency temperature (°C)	UN generic entry	Remarks
2-(N,N-ETHOXYCARBONYL-PHENYLAMINO)-3-METHOXY-4-(N-METHYL-N-CYCLOHEXYLAMINO) BENZENEDIAZONIUM ZINC CHLORIDE	63-92	OP7	+ 40	+ 45	3236	
2-(N,N-ETHOXYCARBONYL-PHENYLAMINO)-3-METHOXY-4-(N-METHYL-N-CYCLOHEXYLAMINO) BENZENEDIAZONIUM ZINC CHLORIDE	62	OP7	+ 35	+ 40	3236	
N-FORMYL-2-(NITROMETHYLENE)-1,3-PERHYDROTHIAZINE	100	OP7	+45	+50	3236	
2-(2-HYDROXYETHOXY)-1-(PYRROLIDIN-1-YL)BENZENE-4-DIAZONIUM ZINC CHLORIDE	100	OP7	+ 45	+ 50	3236	
3-(2-HYDROXYETHOXY)-4-(PYRROLIDIN-1-YL)BENZENE DIAZONIUM ZINC CHLORIDE	100	OP7	+40	+45	3236	
(7-METHOXY-5-METHYL-BENZOTHIOPHEN-2-YL) BORONIC ACID	88-100	OP7			3230	(11)
2-(N,N-METHYLAMINOETHYL-CARBONYL)-4-(3,4-DIMETHYL-PHENYLSULPHONYL)BENZENE-DIAZONIUM HYDROGEN SULPHATE	96	OP7	+45	+50	3236	
4-METHYLBENZENESULPHONYL-HYDRAZIDE	100	OP7			3226	
3-METHYL-4-(PYRROLIDIN-1-YL) BENZENEDIAZONIUM TETRAFLUOROBORATE	95	OP6	+45	+50	3234	
4-NITROSOPHENOL	100	OP7	+35	+40	3236	
PHOSPHOROTHIOIC ACID, O-[(CYANOPHENYL METHYLENE) AZANYL] O,O-DIETHYL ESTER	82-91 (Z isomer)	OP8			3227	(10)
SELF-REACTIVE LIQUID, SAMPLE		OP2			3223	(8)
SELF-REACTIVE LIQUID, SAMPLE, TEMPERATURE CONTROLLED		OP2			3233	(8)
SELF-REACTIVE SOLID, SAMPLE		OP2			3224	(8)
SELF-REACTIVE SOLID, SAMPLE, TEMPERATURE CONTROLLED		OP2			3234	(8)
SODIUM 2-DIAZO-1-NAPHTHOL-4-SULPHONATE	100	OP7			3226	
SODIUM 2-DIAZO-1-NAPHTHOL-5-SULPHONATE	100	OP7			3226	
TETRAMINE PALLADIUM (II) NITRATE	100	OP6	+30	+35	3234	

Remarks

(1)   Azodicarbonamide formulations which fulfil the criteria of paragraph 20.4.2 (b) of the *Manual of Tests and Criteria*. The control and emergency temperatures shall be determined by the procedure given in 7.1.7.3.1 to 7.1.7.3.6.

(2)   "EXPLOSIVE" subsidiary hazard label required (Model No. 1, see 5.2.2.2.2).

(3)   Azodicarbonamide formulations which fulfil the criteria of paragraph 20.4.2 (c) of the *Manual of Tests and Criteria*.

(4)   Azodicarbonamide formulations which fulfil the criteria of paragraph 20.4.2 (c) of the *Manual of Tests and Criteria*. The control and emergency temperatures shall be determined by the procedure given in 7.1.7.3.1 to 7.1.7.3.6.

(5)   Azodicarbonamide formulations which fulfil the criteria of paragraph 20.4.2 (d) of the *Manual of Tests and Criteria*.

(6)   Azodicarbonamide formulations which fulfil the criteria of paragraph 20.4.2 (d) of the *Manual of Tests and Criteria*. The control and emergency temperatures shall be determined by the procedure given in 7.1.7.3.1 to 7.1.7.3.6.

(7)   With a compatible diluent having a boiling point of not less than 150 °C.

(8)   See 2.2.41.1.15.

(9)   This entry applies to mixtures of esters of 2-diazo-1-naphthol-4-sulphonic acid and 2-diazo-1-naphthol-5-sulphonic acid which fulfil the criteria of paragraph 20.4.2 (d) of the *Manual of Test and Criteria*.

(10)   This entry applies to the technical mixture in n-butanol within the specified concentration limits of the (Z) isomer.

(11)   The technical compound with the specified concentration limits may contain up to 12% water and up to 1% organic impurities.

2.2.42 **Class 4.2** **Substances liable to spontaneous combustion**

2.2.42.1 *Criteria*

2.2.42.1.1 The heading of Class 4.2 covers:

– *Pyrophoric substances* which are substances, including mixtures and solutions (liquid or solid), which even in small quantities ignite on contact with air within five minutes. These are the Class 4.2 substances, the most liable to spontaneous combustion; and

– *Self-heating substances and articles* which are substances and articles, including mixtures and solutions, which, on contact with air, without energy supply, are liable to self-heating. These substances will ignite only in large amounts (kilogrammes) and after long periods of time (hours or days).

2.2.42.1.2 The substances and articles of Class 4.2 are subdivided as follows:

S Substances liable to spontaneous combustion, without subsidiary hazard:

S1 Organic, liquid;

S2 Organic, solid;

S3 Inorganic, liquid;

S4 Inorganic, solid;

S5 Organometallic;

S6 Articles;

SW Substances liable to spontaneous combustion, which, in contact with water, emit flammable gases;

SO Substances liable to spontaneous combustion, oxidizing;

ST Substances liable to spontaneous combustion, toxic:

ST1 Organic, toxic, liquid;

ST2 Organic, toxic, solid;

ST3 Inorganic, toxic, liquid;

ST4 Inorganic, toxic, solid;

SC Substances liable to spontaneous combustion, corrosive:

SC1 Organic, corrosive, liquid;

SC2 Organic, corrosive, solid;

SC3 Inorganic, corrosive, liquid;

SC4 Inorganic, corrosive, solid.

Properties

2.2.42.1.3   Self-heating of a substance is a process where the gradual reaction of that substance with oxygen (in air) generates heat. If the rate of heat production exceeds the rate of heat loss, then the temperature of the substance will rise which, after an induction time, may lead to self-ignition and combustion.

Classification

2.2.42.1.4   Substances and articles classified in Class 4.2 are listed in Table A of Chapter 3.2. The assignment of substances and articles not mentioned by name in Table A of Chapter 3.2 to the relevant specific N.O.S. entry of 2.2.42.3 in accordance with the provisions of Chapter 2.1 can be based on experience or the results of the test procedures in accordance with the Manual of Tests and Criteria, Part III, sub-section 33.4. Assignment to general N.O.S. entries of Class 4.2 shall be based on the results of the test procedures in accordance with the Manual of Tests and Criteria, Part III, sub-section 33.4; experience shall also be taken into account when it leads to a more stringent assignment.

2.2.42.1.5   When substances or articles not mentioned by name are assigned to one of the entries listed in 2.2.42.3 on the basis of the test procedures in accordance with the Manual of Tests and Criteria, Part III, sub-section 33.4, the following criteria shall apply:

(a)   Solids liable to spontaneous combustion (pyrophoric) shall be assigned to Class 4.2 when they ignite on falling from a height of 1 m or within five minutes;

(b)   Liquids liable to spontaneous combustion (pyrophoric) shall be assigned to Class 4.2 when:

(i)   on being poured on an inert carrier, they ignite within five minutes, or

(ii)   in the event of a negative result of the test according to (i), when poured on a dry, indented filter paper (Whatman No. 3 filter), they ignite or carbonize it within five minutes;

(c)   Substances in which, in a 10 cm sample cube, at 140 °C test temperature, spontaneous combustion or a rise in temperature to over 200 °C is observed within 24 hours shall be assigned to Class 4.2. This criterion is based on the temperature of the spontaneous combustion of charcoal, which is at 50 °C for a sample cube of 27 m³. Substances with a temperature of spontaneous combustion higher than 50 °C for a volume of 27 m³ are not to be assigned to Class 4.2.

NOTE 1: *Substances carried in packages with a volume of not more than 3 m³ are exempted from Class 4.2 if, tested with a 10 cm sample cube at 120 °C, no spontaneous combustion nor a rise in temperature to over 180 °C is observed within 24 hours.*

NOTE 2: *Substances carried in packages with a volume of not more than 450 litres are exempted from Class 4.2 if, tested with a 10 cm sample cube at 100 °C, no spontaneous combustion nor a rise in temperature to over 160 °C is observed within 24 hours.*

NOTE 3:   *Since organometallic substances can be classified in Class 4.2 or 4.3 with additional subsidiary hazards, depending on their properties, a specific classification flow chart for these substances is given in 2.3.5.*

2.2.42.1.6   If substances of Class 4.2, as a result of admixtures, come into different categories of hazard from those to which the substances mentioned by name in Table A of Chapter 3.2 belong, these mixtures shall be assigned to the entries to which they belong on the basis of their actual degree of danger.

NOTE: *For the classification of solutions and mixtures (such as preparations and wastes), see also 2.1.3.*

2.2.42.1.7   On the basis of the test procedure in the Manual of Tests and Criteria, Part III, sub-section 33.4 and the criteria set out in 2.2.42.1.5, it may also be determined whether the nature of a substance mentioned by name is such that the substance is not subject to the provisions for this Class.

Assignment of packing groups

2.2.42.1.8   Substances and articles classified under the various entries in Table A of Chapter 3.2 shall be assigned to packing groups I, II or III on the basis of test procedures of the Manual of Tests and Criteria, Part III, sub-section 33.4, in accordance with the following criteria:

(a)   Substances liable to spontaneous combustion (pyrophoric) shall be assigned to packing group I;

(b)   Self-heating substances and articles in which, in a 2.5 cm sample cube, at 140 °C test temperature, spontaneous combustion or a rise in temperature to over 200 °C is observed within 24 hours, shall be assigned to packing group II;

Substances with a temperature of spontaneous combustion higher than 50 °C for a volume of 450 litres are not to be assigned to packing group II;

(c)   Slightly self-heating substances in which, in a 2.5 cm sample cube, the phenomena referred to under (b) are not observed, in the given conditions, but in which in a 10 cm sample cube at 140 °C test temperature spontaneous combustion or a rise in temperature to over 200 °C is observed within 24 hours, shall be assigned to packing group III.

2.2.42.2   **Substances not accepted for carriage**

The following substances shall not be accepted for carriage:

–   UN No. 3255 tert-BUTYL HYPOCHLORITE; and

–   Self-heating solids, oxidizing, assigned to UN No. 3127 unless they meet the requirements for Class 1 (see 2.1.3.7).

2.2.42.3   *List of collective entries*

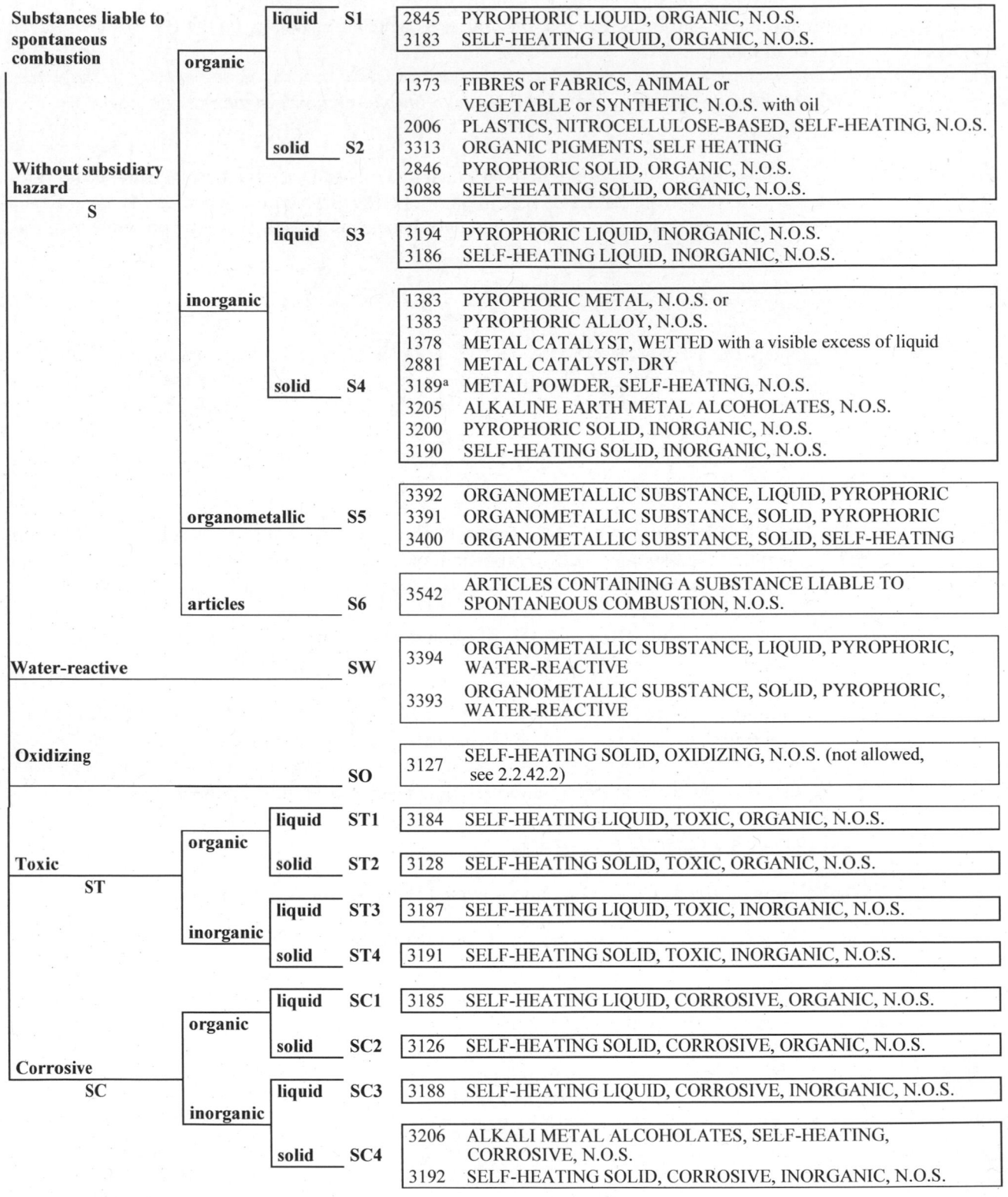

Substances liable to spontaneous combustion		liquid	**S1**	2845	PYROPHORIC LIQUID, ORGANIC, N.O.S.
				3183	SELF-HEATING LIQUID, ORGANIC, N.O.S.
	organic				
		solid	**S2**	1373	FIBRES or FABRICS, ANIMAL or VEGETABLE or SYNTHETIC, N.O.S. with oil
				2006	PLASTICS, NITROCELLULOSE-BASED, SELF-HEATING, N.O.S.
				3313	ORGANIC PIGMENTS, SELF HEATING
Without subsidiary hazard				2846	PYROPHORIC SOLID, ORGANIC, N.O.S.
S				3088	SELF-HEATING SOLID, ORGANIC, N.O.S.
		liquid	**S3**	3194	PYROPHORIC LIQUID, INORGANIC, N.O.S.
				3186	SELF-HEATING LIQUID, INORGANIC, N.O.S.
	inorganic				
		solid	**S4**	1383	PYROPHORIC METAL, N.O.S. or
				1383	PYROPHORIC ALLOY, N.O.S.
				1378	METAL CATALYST, WETTED with a visible excess of liquid
				2881	METAL CATALYST, DRY
				3189[a]	METAL POWDER, SELF-HEATING, N.O.S.
				3205	ALKALINE EARTH METAL ALCOHOLATES, N.O.S.
				3200	PYROPHORIC SOLID, INORGANIC, N.O.S.
				3190	SELF-HEATING SOLID, INORGANIC, N.O.S.
	organometallic		**S5**	3392	ORGANOMETALLIC SUBSTANCE, LIQUID, PYROPHORIC
				3391	ORGANOMETALLIC SUBSTANCE, SOLID, PYROPHORIC
				3400	ORGANOMETALLIC SUBSTANCE, SOLID, SELF-HEATING
	articles		**S6**	3542	ARTICLES CONTAINING A SUBSTANCE LIABLE TO SPONTANEOUS COMBUSTION, N.O.S.
Water-reactive			**SW**	3394	ORGANOMETALLIC SUBSTANCE, LIQUID, PYROPHORIC, WATER-REACTIVE
				3393	ORGANOMETALLIC SUBSTANCE, SOLID, PYROPHORIC, WATER-REACTIVE
Oxidizing			**SO**	3127	SELF-HEATING SOLID, OXIDIZING, N.O.S. (not allowed, see 2.2.42.2)
Toxic	**organic**	liquid	**ST1**	3184	SELF-HEATING LIQUID, TOXIC, ORGANIC, N.O.S.
ST		solid	**ST2**	3128	SELF-HEATING SOLID, TOXIC, ORGANIC, N.O.S.
	inorganic	liquid	**ST3**	3187	SELF-HEATING LIQUID, TOXIC, INORGANIC, N.O.S.
		solid	**ST4**	3191	SELF-HEATING SOLID, TOXIC, INORGANIC, N.O.S.
Corrosive	**organic**	liquid	**SC1**	3185	SELF-HEATING LIQUID, CORROSIVE, ORGANIC, N.O.S.
SC		solid	**SC2**	3126	SELF-HEATING SOLID, CORROSIVE, ORGANIC, N.O.S.
	inorganic	liquid	**SC3**	3188	SELF-HEATING LIQUID, CORROSIVE, INORGANIC, N.O.S.
		solid	**SC4**	3206	ALKALI METAL ALCOHOLATES, SELF-HEATING, CORROSIVE, N.O.S.
				3192	SELF-HEATING SOLID, CORROSIVE, INORGANIC, N.O.S.

---

[a]   *Dust and powder of metals, non toxic in a non-spontaneous combustible form which nevertheless, in contact with water, emit flammable gases, are substances of Class 4.3.*

2.2.43   **Class 4.3   Substances which, in contact with water, emit flammable gases**

2.2.43.1   *Criteria*

2.2.43.1.1   The heading of Class 4.3 covers substances which react with water to emit flammable gases liable to form explosive mixtures with air, and articles containing such substances.

2.2.43.1.2   Substances and articles of Class 4.3 are subdivided as follows:

W   Substances which, in contact with water, emit flammable gases, without subsidiary hazard, and articles containing such substances:

W1   Liquid;

W2   Solid;

W3   Articles;

WF1   Substances which, in contact with water, emit flammable gases, liquid, flammable;

WF2   Substances which, in contact with water, emit flammable gases, solid, flammable;

WS   Substances which, in contact with water, emit flammable gases, solid, self-heating;

WO   Substances which, in contact with water, emit flammable gases, oxidizing, solid;

WT   Substances which, in contact with water, emit flammable gases, toxic:

WT1   Liquid;

WT2   Solid;

WC   Substances which, in contact with water, emit flammable gases, corrosive:

WC1   Liquid;

WC2   Solid;

WFC   Substances which, in contact with water, emit flammable gases, flammable, corrosive.

Properties

2.2.43.1.3   Certain substances in contact with water may emit flammable gases that can form explosive mixtures with air. Such mixtures are easily ignited by all ordinary sources of ignition, for example naked lights, sparking handtools or unprotected lamps. The resulting blast wave and flames may endanger people and the environment. The test method referred to in 2.2.43.1.4 below is used to determine whether the reaction of a substance with water leads to the development of a dangerous amount of gases which may be flammable. This test method shall not be applied to pyrophoric substances.

Classification

2.2.43.1.4   Substances and articles classified in Class 4.3 are listed in Table A of Chapter 3.2. The assignment of substances and articles not mentioned by name in Table A of Chapter 3.2 to the relevant entry of 2.2.43.3 in accordance with the provisions of Chapter 2.1 shall be based on the results of the test procedure in accordance with the Manual of Tests and Criteria, Part III, sub-section 33.5; experience shall also be taken into account when it leads to a more stringent assignment.

2.2.43.1.5   When substances not mentioned by name are assigned to one of the entries listed in 2.2.43.3 on the basis of the test procedure in accordance with the Manual of Tests and Criteria, Part III, sub-section 33.5, the following criteria shall apply:

A substance shall be assigned to Class 4.3 if:

(a)   spontaneous ignition of the gas emitted takes place in any step of the test procedure; or

(b)   there is an evolution of flammable gas at a rate greater than 1 litre per kilogram of the substance to be tested per hour.

NOTE: Since organometallic substances can be classified in Classes 4.2 or 4.3 with additional subsidiary hazards, depending on their properties, a specific classification flow chart for these substances is given in 2.3.5.

2.2.43.1.6   If substances of Class 4.3, as a result of admixtures, come into different categories of hazard from those to which the substances mentioned by name in Table A of Chapter 3.2 belong, these mixtures shall be assigned to the entries to which they belong on the basis of their actual degree of danger.

NOTE: For the classification of solutions and mixtures (such as preparations and wastes) see also 2.1.3.

2.2.43.1.7   On the basis of the test procedures in accordance with the Manual of Tests and Criteria, Part III, sub-section 33.5, and the criteria set out in paragraph 2.2.43.1.5, it may also be determined whether the nature of a substance mentioned by name is such that the substance is not subject to the provisions for this Class.

Assignment of packing groups

2.2.43.1.8   Substances and articles classified under the various entries in Table A of Chapter 3.2 shall be assigned to packing groups I, II or III on the basis of test procedures of the Manual of Tests and Criteria, Part III, sub-section 33.5, in accordance with the following criteria:

(a)   Packing group I shall be assigned to any substance which reacts vigorously with water at ambient temperature and generally demonstrates a tendency for the gas produced to ignite spontaneously, or one which reacts readily with water at ambient temperatures such that the rate of evolution of flammable gas is equal to or greater than 10 litres per kilogram of substance over any one minute period;

(b)   Packing group II shall be assigned to any substance which reacts readily with water at ambient temperature such that the maximum rate of evolution of flammable gas is equal to or greater than 20 litres per kilogram of substance per hour, and which does not meet the criteria of packing group I;

(c)   Packing group III shall be assigned to any substance which reacts slowly with water at ambient temperature such that the maximum rate of evolution of flammable gas is greater than 1 litre per kilogram of substance per hour, and which does not meet the criteria of packing groups I or II.

2.2.43.2   **Substances not accepted for carriage**

Water-reactive solids, oxidizing, assigned to UN No. 3133, shall not be accepted for carriage unless they meet the requirements for Class 1 (see also 2.1.3.7).

2.2.43.3 *List of collective entries*

Substances which, in contact with water, emit flammable gases		liquid	W1	1389 ALKALI METAL AMALGAM, LIQUID 1391 ALKALI METAL DISPERSION or 1391 ALKALINE EARTH METAL DISPERSION 1392 ALKALINE EARTH METAL AMALGAM, LIQUID 1420 POTASSIUM METAL ALLOYS, LIQUID 1421 ALKALI METAL ALLOY, LIQUID, N.O.S. 1422 POTASSIUM SODIUM ALLOYS, LIQUID 3398 ORGANOMETALLIC SUBSTANCE, LIQUID, WATER-REACTIVE 3148 WATER-REACTIVE LIQUID, N.O.S.
Without subsidiary hazard W		solid	W2 [a]	1390 ALKALI METAL AMIDES 3401 ALKALI METAL AMALGAM, SOLID 3402 ALKALINE EARTH METAL AMALGAM, SOLID 3170 ALUMINIUM SMELTING BY-PRODUCTS or 3170 ALUMINIUM REMELTING BY-PRODUCTS 3403 POTASSIUM METAL ALLOYS, SOLID 3404 POTASSIUM SODIUM ALLOYS, SOLID 1393 ALKALINE EARTH METAL ALLOY, N.O.S. 1409 METAL HYDRIDES, WATER-REACTIVE, N.O.S. 3208 METALLIC SUBSTANCE, WATER-REACTIVE, N.O.S. 3395 ORGANOMETALLIC SUBSTANCE, SOLID, WATER-REACTIVE 2813 WATER-REACTIVE SOLID, N.O.S.
		articles	W3	3292 BATTERIES, CONTAINING SODIUM or 3292 CELLS, CONTAINING SODIUM 3543 ARTICLES CONTAINING A SUBSTANCE WHICH IN CONTACT WITH WATER EMITS FLAMMABLE GASES, N.O.S.
Liquid, flammable			WF1	3482 ALKALI METAL DISPERSION, FLAMMABLE or 3482 ALKALINE EARTH METAL DISPERSION, FLAMMABLE 3399 ORGANOMETALLIC SUBSTANCE, LIQUID, WATER-REACTIVE, FLAMMABLE
Solid, flammable			WF2	3396 ORGANOMETALLIC SUBSTANCE, SOLID, WATER-REACTIVE, FLAMMABLE 3132 WATER-REACTIVE SOLID, FLAMMABLE, N.O.S.
Solid, self-heating			WS [b]	3397 ORGANOMETALLIC SUBSTANCE, SOLID, WATER-REACTIVE, SELF-HEATING 3209 METALLIC SUBSTANCE, WATER-REACTIVE, SELF-HEATING, N.O.S. 3135 WATER-REACTIVE SOLID, SELF-HEATING, N.O.S.
Solid, oxidizing			WO	3133 WATER-REACTIVE SOLID, OXIDIZING, N.O.S. (not allowed, see 2.2.43.2)
Toxic WT		liquid	WT1	3130 WATER-REACTIVE LIQUID, TOXIC, N.O.S.
		solid	WT2	3134 WATER-REACTIVE SOLID, TOXIC, N.O.S.
Corrosive WC		liquid	WC1	3129 WATER-REACTIVE LIQUID, CORROSIVE, N.O.S.
		solid	WC2	3131 WATER-REACTIVE SOLID, CORROSIVE, N.O.S.
Flammable, corrosive			WFC [c]	2988 CHLOROSILANES, WATER-REACTIVE, FLAMMABLE, CORROSIVE, NO.S. (No other collective entry with this classification code available; if need be, classification under a collective entry with a classification code to be determined according to the table of precedence of hazards in 2.1.3.10.)

---

[a]   *Metals and metal alloys which, in contact with water, do not emit flammable gases and are not pyrophoric or self-heating, but which are readily flammable, are substances of Class 4.1. Alkaline-earth metals and alkaline-earth metal alloys in pyrophoric form are substances of Class 4.2. Dust and powders of metals in pyrophoric form are substances of Class 4.2. Metals and metal alloys in pyrophoric form are substances of Class 4.2. Compounds of phosphorus with heavy metals such as iron, copper, etc. are not subject to the provisions of ADN.*

[b]   *Metals and metal alloys in pyrophoric form are substances of Class 4.2.*

[c]   *Chlorosilanes, having a flash-point of less than 23 °C and which, in contact with water, do not emit flammable gases, are substances of Class 3. Chlorosilanes, having a flash-point equal to or greater than 23 °C and which, in contact with water, do not emit flammable gases, are substances of Class 8.*

2.2.51 **Class 5.1** **Oxidizing substances**

2.2.51.1 *Criteria*

2.2.51.1.1 The heading of Class 5.1 covers substances which, while in themselves not necessarily combustible, may, generally by yielding oxygen, cause or contribute to the combustion of other materials and articles containing such substances.

2.2.51.1.2 The substances of Class 5.1 and articles containing such substances are subdivided as follows:

O   Oxidizing substances without subsidiary hazard or articles containing such substances:

    O1   Liquid;

    O2   Solid;

    O3   Articles;

OF   Oxidizing substances, solid, flammable;

OS   Oxidizing substances, solid, self-heating;

OW   Oxidizing substances, solid which, in contact with water, emit flammable gases;

OT   Oxidizing substances, toxic:

    OT1   Liquid;

    OT2   Solid;

OC   Oxidizing substances, corrosive:

    OC1   Liquid;

    OC2   Solid;

OTC   Oxidizing substances, toxic, corrosive.

2.2.51.1.3 Substances and articles classified in Class 5.1 are listed in Table A of Chapter 3.2. The assignment of substances and articles not mentioned by name in Table A of Chapter 3.2 to the relevant entry of 2.2.51.3 in accordance with the provisions of Chapter 2.1 can be based on the tests, methods and criteria in paragraphs 2.2.51.1.6 to 2.2.51.1.10 below and the Manual of Tests and Criteria, Part III, Section 34.4 or, for solid ammonium nitrate based fertilizers, Section 39 subject to the restrictions of 2.2.51.2.2, thirteenth and fourteenth indents. In the event of divergence between test results and known experience, judgement based on known experience shall take precedence over test results.

2.2.51.1.4 If substances of Class 5.1, as a result of admixtures, come into different categories of hazard from those to which the substances mentioned by name in Table A of Chapter 3.2 belong, these mixtures or solutions shall be assigned to the entries to which they belong on the basis of their actual degree of danger.

NOTE: For the classification of solutions and mixtures (such as preparations and wastes), see also Section 2.1.3.

2.2.51.1.5   On the basis of the test procedures in the Manual of Tests and Criteria, Part III, Section 34.4 or, for solid ammonium nitrate based fertilizers, Section 39, and the criteria set out in 2.2.51.1.6 to 2.2.51.1.10 it may also be determined whether the nature of a substance mentioned by name in Table A of Chapter 3.2 is such that the substance is not subject to the provisions for this class.

Oxidizing solids

Classification

2.2.51.1.6   When oxidizing solid substances not mentioned by name in Table A of Chapter 3.2 are assigned to one of the entries listed in 2.2.51.3 on the basis of the test procedure in accordance with the Manual of Tests and Criteria, Part III, sub-section 34.4.1 (test O.1) or alternatively, sub section 34.4.3 (test O.3), the following criteria shall apply:

(a)   In the test O.1, a solid substance shall be assigned to Class 5.1 if, in the 4:1 or the 1:1 sample-to-cellulose ratio (by mass) tested, it ignites or burns or exhibits mean burning times equal to or less than that of a 3:7 mixture (by mass) of potassium bromate and cellulose; or

(b)   In the test O.3, a solid substance shall be assigned to Class 5.1 if, in the 4:1 or the 1:1 sample-to-cellulose ratio (by mass) tested, it exhibits a mean burning rate equal to or greater than the mean burning rate of a 1:2 mixture (by mass) of calcium peroxide and cellulose.

2.2.51.1.7   By exception, solid ammonium nitrate based fertilizers shall be classified in accordance with the procedure as set out in the Manual of Tests and Criteria, Part III, Section 39.

Assignment of packing groups

2.2.51.1.8   Oxidizing solids classified under the various entries in Table A of Chapter 3.2 shall be assigned to packing groups I, II or III on the basis of test procedures of the Manual of Tests and Criteria, Part III, sub-section 34.4.1 (test O.1) or sub-section 34.4.3 (test O.3), in accordance with the following criteria:

(a)   Test O.1:

     (i)   Packing group I: any substance which, in the 4:1 or 1:1 sample-to-cellulose ratio (by mass) tested, exhibits a mean burning time less than the mean burning time of a 3:2 mixture, by mass, of potassium bromate and cellulose;

     (ii)   Packing group II: any substance which, in the 4:1 or 1:1 sample-to-cellulose ratio (by mass) tested, exhibits a mean burning time equal to or less than the mean burning time of a 2:3 mixture (by mass) of potassium bromate and cellulose and the criteria for packing group I are not met;

     (iii)   Packing group III: any substance which, in the 4:1 or 1:1 sample-to-cellulose ratio (by mass) tested, exhibits a mean burning time equal to or less than the mean burning time of a 3:7 mixture (by mass) of potassium bromate and cellulose and the criteria for packing groups I and II are not met;

(b)   Test O.3:

     (i)   Packing group I: any substance which, in the 4:1 or 1:1 sample-to-cellulose ratio (by mass) tested, exhibits a mean burning rate greater than the mean burning rate of a 3:1 mixture (by mass) of calcium peroxide and cellulose;

(ii)   Packing group II: any substance which, in the 4:1 or 1:1 sample-to-cellulose ratio (by mass) tested, exhibits a mean burning rate equal to or greater than the mean burning rate of a 1:1 mixture (by mass) of calcium peroxide and cellulose, and the criteria for packing group I are not met;

(iii)   Packing group III: any substance which, in the 4:1 or 1:1 sample-to-cellulose ratio (by mass) tested, exhibits a mean burning rate equal to or greater than the mean burning rate of a 1:2 mixture (by mass) of calcium peroxide and cellulose, and the criteria for packing groups I and II are not met.

Oxidizing liquids

Classification

2.2.51.1.9   When oxidizing liquid substances not mentioned by name in Table A of Chapter 3.2 are assigned to one of the entries listed in sub-section 2.2.51.3 on the basis of the test procedure in accordance with the Manual of Tests and Criteria, Part III, sub-section 34.4.2, the following criteria shall apply:

A liquid substance shall be assigned to Class 5.1 if, in the 1:1 mixture, by mass, of substance and cellulose tested, it exhibits a pressure rise of 2070 kPa gauge or more and a mean pressure rise time equal to or less than the mean pressure rise time of a 1:1 mixture, by mass, of 65% aqueous nitric acid and cellulose.

Assignment of packing groups

2.2.51.1.10   Oxidizing liquids classified under the various entries in Table A of Chapter 3.2 shall be assigned to packing groups I, II or III on the basis of test procedures of the Manual of Tests and Criteria, Part III, section 34.4.2, in accordance with the following criteria:

(a)   Packing group I: any substance which, in the 1:1 mixture, by mass, of substance and cellulose tested, spontaneously ignites; or the mean pressure rise time of a 1:1 mixture, by mass, of substance and cellulose is less than that of a 1:1 mixture, by mass, of 50% perchloric acid and cellulose;

(b)   Packing group II: any substance which, in the 1:1 mixture, by mass, of substance and cellulose tested, exhibits a mean pressure rise time less than or equal to the mean pressure rise time of a 1:1 mixture, by mass, of 40% aqueous sodium chlorate solution and cellulose; and the criteria for packing group I are not met;

(c)   Packing group III: any substance which, in the 1:1 mixture, by mass, of substance and cellulose tested, exhibits a mean pressure rise time less than or equal to the mean pressure rise time of a 1:1 mixture, by mass, of 65% aqueous nitric acid and cellulose; and the criteria for packing groups I and II are not met.

2.2.51.2   *Substances not accepted for carriage*

2.2.51.2.1   The chemically unstable substances of Class 5.1 shall not be accepted for carriage unless the necessary steps have been taken to prevent their dangerous decomposition or polymerization during carriage. To this end it shall in particular be ensured that receptacles and tanks do not contain any material liable to promote these reactions.

2.2.51.2.2   The following substances and mixtures shall not be accepted for carriage:

–   oxidizing solids, self-heating, assigned to UN No. 3100, oxidizing solids, water-reactive, assigned to UN No. 3121 and oxidizing solids, flammable, assigned to UN No. 3137, unless they meet the requirements for Class 1 (see also 2.1.3.7);

–   hydrogen peroxide, not stabilized or hydrogen peroxide, aqueous solutions, not stabilized containing more than 60 % hydrogen peroxide;

–   tetranitromethane not free from combustible impurities;

–   perchloric acid solutions containing more than 72 % (mass) acid, or mixtures of perchloric acid with any liquid other than water;

–   chloric acid solution containing more than 10 % chloric acid or mixtures of chloric acid with any liquid other than water;

–   halogenated fluor compounds other than UN Nos. 1745 BROMINE PENTAFLUORIDE; 1746 BROMINE TRIFLUORIDE and 2495 IODINE PENTAFLUORIDE of Class 5.1 as well as UN Nos. 1749 CHLORINE TRIFLUORIDE and 2548 CHLORINE PENTAFLUORIDE of Class 2;

–   ammonium chlorate and its aqueous solutions and mixtures of a chlorate with an ammonium salt;

–   ammonium chlorite and its aqueous solutions and mixtures of a chlorite with an ammonium salt;

–   mixtures of a hypochlorite with an ammonium salt;

–   ammonium bromate and its aqueous solutions and mixtures of a bromate with an ammonium salt;

–   ammonium permanganate and its aqueous solutions and mixtures of a permanganate with an ammonium salt;

–   ammonium nitrate containing more than 0.2 % combustible substances (including any organic substance calculated as carbon) unless it is a constituent of a substance or article of Class 1;

–   ammonium nitrate based fertilizers with compositions that lead to exit boxes 4, 6, 8, 15, 31, or 33 of the flowchart of paragraph 39.5.1 of the Manual of Tests and Criteria, Part III, Section 39, unless they have been assigned a suitable UN number in Class 1;

–   ammonium nitrate based fertilizers with compositions that lead to exit boxes 20, 23 or 39 of the flowchart of paragraph 39.5.1 of the Manual of Tests and Criteria, Part III, Section 39, unless they have been assigned a suitable UN number in Class 1 or, provided that the suitability for carriage has been demonstrated and that this has been approved by the competent authority, in Class 5.1 other than UN No. 2067;

NOTE: The term "competent authority" means the competent authority of the country of origin. If the country of origin is not a Contracting Party to ADR, the classification and conditions of carriage shall be recognized by the competent authority of the first country Contracting Party to ADR reached by the consignment.

–   ammonium nitrite and its aqueous solutions and mixtures of an inorganic nitrite with an ammonium salt;

–   mixtures of potassium nitrate, sodium nitrite and an ammonium salt.

2.2.51.3   *List of collective entries*

Oxidizing substances and articles containing such substances	Liquid	O1	3210	CHLORATES, INORGANIC, AQUEOUS SOLUTION, N.O.S.
			3211	PERCHLORATES, INORGANIC, AQUEOUS SOLUTION, N.O.S.
			3213	BROMATES, INORGANIC, AQUEOUS SOLUTION, N.O.S.
			3214	PERMANGANATES, INORGANIC, AQUEOUS SOLUTION, N.O.S.
			3216	PERSULPHATES, INORGANIC, AQUEOUS SOLUTION, N.O.S.
			3218	NITRATES, INORGANIC, AQUEOUS SOLUTION, N.O.S.
			3219	NITRITES, INORGANIC, AQUEOUS SOLUTION, N.O.S.
			3139	OXIDIZING LIQUID, N.O.S.
			1450	BROMATES, INORGANIC, N.O.S
			1461	CHLORATES, INORGANIC, N.O.S.
			1462	CHLORITES, INORGANIC, N.O.S.
Without subsidiary hazard			1477	NITRATES, INORGANIC, N.O.S
	Solid	O2	1481	PERCHLORATES, INORGANIC, N.O.S.
O			1482	PERMANGANATES, INORGANIC, N.O.S.
			1483	PEROXIDES, INORGANIC, N.O.S
			2627	NITRITES, INORGANIC, N.O.S.
			3212	HYPOCHLORITES, INORGANIC, N.O.S.
			3215	PERSULPHATES, INORGANIC, N.O.S.
			1479	OXIDIZING SOLID, N.O.S.
	Articles	O3	3356	OXYGEN GENERATOR, CHEMICAL
			3544	ARTICLES CONTAINING OXIDIZING SUBSTANCE, N.O.S.
Solid, flammable		OF	3137	OXIDIZING SOLID, FLAMMABLE, N.O.S. (not allowed, see 2.2.51.2)
Solid, self-heating		OS	3100	OXIDIZING SOLID, SELF-HEATING, N.O.S. (not allowed, see 2.2.51.2)
Solid, water reactive		OW	3121	OXIDIZING SOLID, WATER REACTIVE, N.O.S. (not allowed, see 2.2.51.2)
Toxic	Liquid	OT1	3099	OXIDIZING LIQUID, TOXIC, N.O.S.
OT	Solid	OT2	3087	OXIDIZING SOLID, TOXIC, N.O.S.
Corrosive	Liquid	OC1	3098	OXIDIZING LIQUID, CORROSIVE, N.O.S.
OC	Solid	OC2	3085	OXIDIZING SOLID, CORROSIVE, N.O.S.
Toxic, corrosive		OTC	(No collective entry with this classification code available; if need be, classification under a collective entry with a classification code to be determined according to the table of precedence of hazards in 2.1.3.10.)	

2.2.52   **Class 5.2**   **Organic peroxides**

2.2.52.1   *Criteria*

2.2.52.1.1   The heading of Class 5.2 covers organic peroxides and formulations of organic peroxides.

2.2.52.1.2   The substances of Class 5.2 are subdivided as follows:

     P1   Organic peroxides, not requiring temperature control;

     P2   Organic peroxides, requiring temperature control.

Definition

2.2.52.1.3   *Organic peroxides* are organic substances which contain the bivalent -O-O- structure and may be considered derivatives of hydrogen peroxide, where one or both of the hydrogen atoms have been replaced by organic radicals.

Properties

2.2.52.1.4   Organic peroxides are liable to exothermic decomposition at normal or elevated temperatures. The decomposition can be initiated by heat, contact with impurities (e.g. acids, heavy-metal compounds, amines), friction or impact. The rate of decomposition increases with temperature and varies with the organic peroxide formulation. Decomposition may result in the evolution of harmful, or flammable, gases or vapours. For certain organic peroxides the temperature shall be controlled during carriage. Some organic peroxides may decompose explosively, particularly if confined. This characteristic may be modified by the addition of diluents or by the use of appropriate packagings. Many organic peroxides burn vigorously. Contact of organic peroxides with the eyes is to be avoided. Some organic peroxides will cause serious injury to the cornea, even after brief contact, or will be corrosive to the skin.

NOTE: Test methods for determining the flammability of organic peroxides are set out in the Manual of Tests and Criteria, Part III, sub-section 32.4. Because organic peroxides may react vigorously when heated, it is recommended to determine their flash-point using small sample sizes such as described in ISO 3679:1983.

Classification

2.2.52.1.5   Any organic peroxide shall be considered for classification in Class 5.2 unless the organic peroxide formulation contains:

     (a)   not more than 1.0 % available oxygen from the organic peroxides when containing not more than 1.0 % hydrogen peroxide;

     (b)   not more than 0.5 % available oxygen from the organic peroxides when containing more than 1.0 % but not more than 7.0 % hydrogen peroxide.

NOTE: The available oxygen content (%) of an organic peroxide formulation is given by the formula

$$16 \times 3 \, (n_i \times c_i / m_i)$$

where:

n_i =   *number of peroxygen groups per molecule of organic peroxide i;*
c_i =   *concentration (mass %) of organic peroxide i; and*
m_i =   *molecular mass of organic peroxide i.*

2.2.52.1.6   Organic peroxides are classified into seven types according to the degree of danger they present. The types of organic peroxide range from type A, which is not accepted for carriage in the packaging in which it is tested, to type G, which is not subject to the provisions of Class 5.2. The classification of types B to F is directly related to the maximum quantity allowed in one package. The principles to be applied to the classification of substances not listed in 2.2.52.4 are set out in the Manual of Tests and Criteria, Part II.

2.2.52.1.7   Organic peroxides which have already been classified and are already permitted for carriage in packagings are listed in 2.2.52.4, those already permitted for carriage in IBCs are listed in 4.1.4.2 of ADR, packing instruction IBC520 and those already permitted for carriage in tanks in accordance with Chapters 4.2 and 4.3 of ADR are listed in 4.2.5.2 of ADR, portable tank instruction T23. Each permitted substance listed is assigned to a generic entry of Table A of Chapter 3.2 (UN Nos. 3101 to 3120) and appropriate subsidiary hazards and remarks providing relevant transport information are given.

These generic entries specify:

–   the type (B to F) of organic peroxide (see 2.2.52.1.6 above);

–   physical state (liquid/solid); and

–   temperature control (when required), see 2.2.52.1.15 and 2.2.52.1.16.

Mixtures of these formulations may be classified as the same type of organic peroxide as that of the most dangerous component and be carried under the conditions of carriage given for this type. However, as two stable components can form a thermally less stable mixture, the self-accelerating decomposition temperature (SADT) of the mixture shall be determined and, if necessary, the control and emergency temperatures derived from the SADT in accordance with paragraph 7.1.7.3.6.

2.2.52.1.8   Classification of organic peroxides not listed in 2.2.52.4, 4.1.4.2 of ADR, packing instruction IBC520 or 4.2.5.2 of ADR, portable tank instruction T23, and assignment to a collective entry shall be made by the competent authority of the country of origin. The statement of approval shall contain the classification and the relevant conditions of carriage. If the country of origin is not a Contracting Party to ADN, the classification and conditions of carriage shall be recognized by the competent authority of the first country Contracting Party to ADN reached by the consignment.

2.2.52.1.9   Samples of organic peroxides or formulations of organic peroxides not listed in 2.2.52.4, for which a complete set of test results is not available and which are to be carried for further testing or evaluation, shall be assigned to one of the appropriate entries for organic peroxides of type C provided the following conditions are met:

–   the available data indicate that the sample would be no more dangerous than organic peroxides of type B;

–   the sample is packaged in accordance with packing method OP2 of 4.1.4.1 of ADR and the quantity per cargo transport unit is limited to 10 kg;

–   the available data indicate that the control temperature, if any, is sufficiently low to prevent any dangerous decomposition and sufficiently high to prevent any dangerous phase separation.

Desensitization of organic peroxides

2.2.52.1.10   In order to ensure safety during carriage, organic peroxides are in many cases desensitized by organic liquids or solids, inorganic solids or water. Where a percentage of a substance is stipulated, this refers to the percentage by mass, rounded to the nearest whole number. In general, desensitization shall be such that, in case of spillage, the organic peroxide will not concentrate to a dangerous extent.

2.2.52.1.11   Unless otherwise stated for the individual organic peroxide formulation, the following definition(s) shall apply to diluents used for desensitization:

–   diluents of type A are organic liquids which are compatible with the organic peroxide and which have a boiling point of not less than 150 °C. Type A diluents may be used for desensitizing all organic peroxides.

–   diluents of type B are organic liquids which are compatible with the organic peroxide and which have a boiling point of less than 150 °C but not less than 60 °C and a flash-point of not less than 5 °C.

Type B diluents may be used for desensitization of all organic peroxides provided that the boiling point of the liquid is at least 60 °C higher than the SADT in a 50 kg package.

2.1.52.1.12   Diluents, other than type A or type B, may be added to organic peroxide formulations as listed in 2.2.52.4 provided that they are compatible. However, replacement of all or part of a type A or type B diluent by another diluent with differing properties requires that the organic peroxide formulation be re-assessed in accordance with the normal acceptance procedure for Class 5.2.

2.2.52.1.13   Water may only be used for the desensitization of organic peroxides which are listed in 2.2.52.4 or in the competent authority decision according to 2.2.52.1.8 as being "with water" or "as a stable dispersion in water". Samples of organic peroxides or formulations of organic peroxides not listed in 2.2.52.4 may also be desensitized with water provided the requirements of 2.2.52.1.9 are met.

2.2.52.1.14   Organic and inorganic solids may be used for desensitization of organic peroxides provided that they are compatible. Compatible liquids and solids are those which have no detrimental influence on the thermal stability and hazard type of the organic peroxide formulation.

Temperature control requirements

2.2.52.1.15   The following organic peroxides shall be subject to temperature control during carriage:

–   organic peroxides of types B and C with an SADT ≤ 50 °C;

–   organic peroxides of type D showing a medium effect when heated under confinement with an SADT ≤ 50 °C or showing a low or no effect when heated under confinement with an SADT ≤ 45 °C; and

–   organic peroxides of types E and F with an SADT ≤ 45 °C.

NOTE: *Provisions for the determination of the effects of heating under confinement are given in the Manual of Tests and Criteria, Part II, Section 20 and test series E in Section 25.*

See 7.1.7.

2.2.52.1.16   Where applicable, control and emergency temperatures are listed in 2.2.52.4. The actual temperature during carriage may be lower than the control temperature but shall be selected so as to avoid dangerous separation of phases.

2.2.52.2   *Substances not accepted for carriage*

Organic peroxides of type A shall not be accepted for carriage under the provisions of Class 5.2 (see Manual of Tests and Criteria, Part II, paragraph 20.4.3 (a)).

2.2.52.3   *List of collective entries*

Organic peroxides				
			ORGANIC PEROXIDE TYPE A, LIQUID	} Not accepted for carriage,
			ORGANIC PEROXIDE TYPE A, SOLID	} see 2.2.52.2
		3101	ORGANIC PEROXIDE TYPE B, LIQUID	
		3102	ORGANIC PEROXIDE TYPE B, SOLID	
		3103	ORGANIC PEROXIDE TYPE C, LIQUID	
		3104	ORGANIC PEROXIDE TYPE C, SOLID	
Not requiring temperature control	**P1**	3105	ORGANIC PEROXIDE TYPE D, LIQUID	
		3106	ORGANIC PEROXIDE TYPE D, SOLID	
		3107	ORGANIC PEROXIDE TYPE E, LIQUID	
		3108	ORGANIC PEROXIDE TYPE E, SOLID	
		3109	ORGANIC PEROXIDE TYPE F, LIQUID	
		3110	ORGANIC PEROXIDE TYPE F, SOLID	
			ORGANIC PEROXIDE TYPE G, LIQUID	} Not subject to the provisions
			ORGANIC PEROXIDE TYPE G, SOLID	} applicable to Class 5.2, see 2.2.52.1.6
		3545	ARTICLES CONTAINING ORGANIC PEROXIDE, N.O.S.	

		3111	ORGANIC PEROXIDE TYPE B, LIQUID, TEMPERATURE CONTROLLED
		3112	ORGANIC PEROXIDE TYPE B, SOLID, TEMPERATURE CONTROLLED
		3113	ORGANIC PEROXIDE TYPE C, LIQUID, TEMPERATURE CONTROLLED
		3114	ORGANIC PEROXIDE TYPE C, SOLID, TEMPERATURE CONTROLLED
Requiring temperature control	**P2**	3115	ORGANIC PEROXIDE TYPE D, LIQUID, TEMPERATURE CONTROLLED
		3116	ORGANIC PEROXIDE TYPE D, SOLID, TEMPERATURE CONTROLLED
		3117	ORGANIC PEROXIDE TYPE E, LIQUID, TEMPERATURE CONTROLLED
		3118	ORGANIC PEROXIDE TYPE E, SOLID, TEMPERATURE CONTROLLED
		3119	ORGANIC PEROXIDE TYPE F, LIQUID, TEMPERATURE CONTROLLED
		3120	ORGANIC PEROXIDE TYPE F, SOLID, TEMPERATURE CONTROLLED
		3545	ARTICLES CONTAINING ORGANIC PEROXIDE, N.O.S.

2.2.52.4   *List of currently assigned organic peroxides in packagings*

In the column "Packing Method", codes "OP1" to "OP8" refer to packing methods in 4.1.4.1 of ADR, packing instruction P520 (see also 4.1.7.1 of ADR). Organic peroxides to be carried shall fulfil the classification and the control and emergency temperatures (derived from the SADT) as listed. For substances permitted in IBCs, see 4.1.4.2 of ADR, packing instruction IBC520 and, for those permitted in tanks according to Chapters 4.2 and 4.3 of ADR, see 4.2.5.2.6 of ADR, portable tank instruction T23. The formulations not listed in this sub-section but listed in packing instruction IBC520 of 4.1.4.2 of ADR and in portable tank instruction T23 of 4.2.5.2.6 of ADR may also be carried packed in accordance with packing method OP8 of packing instruction P520 of 4.1.4.1 of ADR, with the same control and emergency temperatures, if applicable.

ORGANIC PEROXIDE	Concentration (%)	Diluent type A (%)	Diluent type B (%) 1)	Inert solid (%)	Water	Packing Method	Control temperature (°C)	Emergency temperature (°C)	Number (Generic entry)	Subsidiary hazards and remarks
ACETYL ACETONE PEROXIDE	≤42	≥48			≥8	OP7			3105	2)
"	≤32 as a paste					OP7			3106	20)
"	≤35	≥57			≥8	OP8			3107	32)
ACETYL CYCLOHEXANESULPHONYL PEROXIDE	≤82				≥12	OP4	-10	0	3112	3)
"	≤32		≥68			OP7	-10	0	3115	
tert-AMYL HYDROPEROXIDE	≤88	≥6			≥6	OP8			3107	
tert-AMYL PEROXYACETATE	≤62	≥38				OP7			3105	
tert-AMYL PEROXYBENZOATE	≤100					OP5			3103	
tert-AMYL PEROXY-2-ETHYLHEXANOATE	≤100					OP7	+20	+25	3115	
tert-AMYL PEROXY-2-ETHYLHEXYL CARBONATE	≤100					OP7			3105	
tert-AMYL PEROXY ISOPROPYL CARBONATE	≤77	≥23				OP5			3103	
tert-AMYL PEROXYNEODECANOATE	≤77		≥23			OP7	0	+10	3115	
"	≤47					OP8	0	+10	3119	
tert-AMYL PEROXYPIVALATE	≤77	≥53	≥23			OP5	+10	+15	3113	
tert-AMYLPEROXY-3,5,5-TRIMETHYLHEXANOATE	≤100					OP7			3105	
tert-BUTYL CUMYL PEROXIDE	>42 – 100					OP8			3109	
"	≤52			≥48		OP8			3108	
n-BUTYL-4,4-DI-(tert-BUTYLPEROXY)VALERATE	>52 – 100					OP5			3103	
"	≤52			≥48		OP8			3108	
tert-BUTYL HYDROPEROXIDE	>79 – 90				≥10	OP5			3103	13)
"	≤80	≥20				OP7			3105	4) 13)
"	≤79				>14	OP8			3107	13) 23)
"	≤72				≥28	OP8			3109	13)
tert-BUTYL HYDROPEROXIDE + DI-tert-BUTYLPEROXIDE	<82 + >9				≥7	OP5			3103	13)
tert-BUTYL MONOPEROXYMALEATE	>52 – 100					OP5			3102	3)
"	≤52	≥48				OP6			3103	
"	≤52			≥48		OP8			3108	
"	≤52 as a paste					OP8			3108	
tert-BUTYL PEROXYACETATE	>52 – 77	≥23				OP5			3101	3)
"	>32 – 52	≥48				OP6			3103	3)
"	≤32		≥68			OP8			3109	

ORGANIC PEROXIDE	Concentration (%)	Diluent type A (%)	Diluent type B (%) 1)	Inert solid (%)	Water	Packing Method	Control temperature (°C)	Emergency temperature (°C)	Number (Generic entry)	Subsidiary hazards and remarks
tert-BUTYL PEROXYBENZOATE	>77 – 100					OP5			3103	
"	>52 – 77	≥23				OP7			3105	
"	≤52			≥48		OP7			3106	
tert-BUTYL PEROXYBUTYL FUMARATE	≤52	≥48				OP7			3105	
tert-BUTYL PEROXYCROTONATE	≤77	≥23				OP7			3105	
tert-BUTYL PEROXYDIETHYLACETATE	≤100					OP5	+20	+25	3113	
tert-BUTYL PEROXY-2-ETHYLHEXANOATE	>52 – 100					OP6	+20	+25	3113	
"	>32 – 52		≥48			OP8	+30	+35	3117	
"	≤52			≥48		OP8	+20	+25	3118	
"	≤32		≥68			OP8	+40	+45	3119	
tert-BUTYL PEROXY-2-ETHYLHEXANOATE + 2,2-DI-(tert-BUTYLPEROXY)BUTANE	≤12 + ≤14	≥14		≥60		OP7			3106	
"	≤31 + ≤36		≥33			OP7	+35	+40	3115	
tert-BUTYL PEROXY-2-ETHYLHEXYLCARBONATE	≤100					OP7			3105	
tert-BUTYL PEROXYISOBUTYRATE	>52 – 77		≥23			OP5	+15	+20	3111	3)
"	≤52		≥48			OP7	+15	+20	3115	
tert-BUTYLPEROXY ISOPROPYLCARBONATE	≤77	≥23				OP5			3103	
"	≤62		≥38			OP7			3105	
1-(2-tert-BUTYLPEROXY ISOPROPYL)-3-ISOPROPENYLBENZENE	≤77	≥23				OP7			3105	
"	≤42			≥58		OP8			3108	
tert-BUTYL PEROXY-2-METHYLBENZOATE	≤100					OP5			3103	
tert-BUTYL PEROXYNEODECANOATE	>77 – 100		≥23			OP7	-5	+5	3115	
"	≤77					OP7	0	+10	3115	
"	≤52 as a stable dispersion in water					OP8	0	+10	3119	
"	≤42 as a stable dispersion in water (frozen)					OP8	0	+10	3118	
"	≤32	≥68				OP8	0	+10	3119	
tert-BUTYL PEROXYNEOHEPTANOATE	≤77	≥23				OP7	0	+10	3115	
"	≤42 as a stable dispersion in water					OP8	0	+10	3117	
tert-BUTYL PEROXYPIVALATE	>67 – 77	≥23				OP5	0	+10	3113	
"	>27 – 67		≥33			OP7	0	+10	3115	

ORGANIC PEROXIDE	Concentration (%)	Diluent type A (%)	Diluent type B (%) 1)	Inert solid (%)	Water	Packing Method	Control temperature (°C)	Emergency temperature (°C)	Number (Generic entry)	Subsidiary hazards and remarks
"	≤27		≥73			OP8	+30	+35	3119	
tert-BUTYLPEROXY STEARYLCARBONATE	≤100					OP7			3106	
tert-BUTYL PEROXY-3,5,5-TRIMETHYLHEXANOATE	>37 – 100					OP7			3105	
"	≤42			≥58		OP7			3106	
"	≤37		≥63			OP8			3109	
3-CHLOROPEROXYBENZOIC ACID	>57 – 86			≥14		OP1			3102	3)
"	≤57			≥3	≥40	OP7			3106	
"	≤77			≥6	≥17	OP7			3106	
CUMYL HYDROPEROXIDE	>90 – 98	≤10				OP8			3107	13)
"	≤90	≥10				OP8			3109	13) 18)
CUMYL PEROXYNEODECANOATE	≤87	≥13				OP7	-10	0	3115	
"	≤77		≥23			OP7	-10	0	3115	
"	≤52 as a stable dispersion in water					OP8	-10	0	3119	
CUMYL PEROXYNEOHEPTANOATE	≤77	≥23				OP7	-10	0	3115	
CUMYL PEROXYPIVALATE	≤77		≥23			OP7	-5	+5	3115	
CYCLOHEXANONE PEROXIDE(S)	≤91					OP6			3104	13)
"	≤72	≥28				OP7			3105	5)
"	≤72 as a paste				≥9	OP7			3106	5) 20)
"	≤32			≥68					Exempt	29)
([3R-(3R,5aS,6S,8aS,9R,10R,12S,12aR**)]-DECAHYDRO-10-METHOXY-3,6,9-TRIMETHYL-3,12-EPOXY-12H-PYRANO[4,3-j]-1,2-BENZODIOXEPIN	≤100					OP7			3106	
DIACETONE ALCOHOL PEROXIDES	≤57		≥26		≥8	OP7	+40	+45	3115	6)
DIACETYL PEROXIDE	≤27		≥73			OP7	+20	+25	3115	7) 13)
DI-tert-AMYL PEROXIDE	≤100					OP8			3107	
2,2-DI-(tert-AMYLPEROXY)BUTANE	≤57	≥43				OP7			3105	
1,1-DI-(tert-AMYLPEROXY)CYCLOHEXANE	≤82	≥18				OP6			3103	
DIBENZOYL PEROXIDE	>52 - 100			≤48		OP2			3102	3)
"	>77 - 94				≥6	OP4			3102	3)
"	≤77				≥23	OP6			3104	
"	≤62			≥28	≥10	OP7			3106	
"	>52 – 62 as a paste					OP7			3106	20)
"	>35 – 52			≥48		OP7			3106	
"	>36 – 42	≥18			≤40	OP8			3107	

ORGANIC PEROXIDE	Concentration (%)	Diluent type A (%)	Diluent type B (%) 1)	Inert solid (%)	Water	Packing Method	Control temperature (°C)	Emergency temperature (°C)	Number (Generic entry)	Subsidiary hazards and remarks
"	≤ 56.5 as a paste				≥ 15	OP8			3108	
"	≤ 52 as a paste					OP8			3108	20)
"	≤ 42 as a stable dispersion in water					OP8			3109	
"	≤ 35			≥ 65					Exempt	29)
DI-(4-tert-BUTYLCYCLOHEXYL) PEROXYDICARBONATE	≤ 100					OP6	+30	+35	3114	
"	≤ 42 as a stable dispersion in water					OP8	+30	+35	3119	
"	≤ 42 (as a paste)					OP8	+35	+40	3118	
DI-tert-BUTYL PEROXIDE	> 52 – 100					OP8			3107	
"	≤ 52		≥ 48			OP8			3109	25)
DI-tert-BUTYL PEROXYAZELATE	≤ 52	≥ 48				OP7			3105	
2,2-DI-(tert-BUTYLPEROXY)BUTANE	≤ 52	≥ 48				OP6			3103	
1,6-Di-((tert-BUTYLPEROXYCARBONYLOXY) HEXANE	≤ 72	≥ 28				OP5			3103	
1,1-DI-(tert-BUTYLPEROXY) CYCLOHEXANE	> 80 - 100					OP5			3101	3)
"	≤ 72		≥ 28			OP5			3103	30)
"	> 52 - 80	≥ 20				OP5			3103	
"	> 42 – 52	≥ 48				OP7			3105	
"	≤ 42	≥ 13		≥ 45		OP7			3106	
"	≤ 42	≥ 58				OP8			3109	
"	≤ 27	≥ 25				OP8			3107	21)
"	≤ 13	≥ 13	≥ 74			OP8			3109	
1,1-DI-(tert-BUTYLPEROXY) CYCLOHEXANE + tert-BUTYL PEROXY-2-ETHYLHEXANOATE	≤ 43 + ≤ 16	≥ 41				OP 7			3105	
DI-n-BUTYL PEROXYDICARBONATE	> 27 - 52		≥ 48			OP7	-15	-5	3115	
"	≤ 27		≥ 73			OP8	-10	0	3117	
"	≤ 42 as a stable dispersion in water (frozen)					OP8	-15	-5	3118	
DI-sec-BUTYL PEROXYDICARBONATE	> 52 - 100					OP4	-20	-10	3113	
"	≤ 52		≥ 48			OP7	-15	-5	3115	
DI-(tert-BUTYLPEROXYISOPROPYL) BENZENE(S)	> 42 -100			≤ 57		OP7			3106	
"	≤ 42			≥ 58					Exempt	29)
DI-(tert-BUTYLPEROXY) PHTHALATE	> 42 - 52	≥ 48				OP7			3105	

ORGANIC PEROXIDE	Concentration (%)	Diluent type A (%)	Diluent type B (%) 1)	Inert solid (%)	Water	Packing Method	Control temperature (°C)	Emergency temperature (°C)	Number (Generic entry)	Subsidiary hazards and remarks
"	≤ 52 as a paste					OP7			3106	20)
"	≤ 42	≥ 58				OP8			3107	
2,2-DI-(tert-BUTYLPEROXY)PROPANE	≤ 52	≥ 48				OP7			3105	
"	≤ 42	≥ 13		≥ 45		OP7			3106	
1,1-DI-(tert-BUTYLPEROXY)-3,3,5-TRIMETHYLCYCLOHEXANE	> 90 - 100					OP5			3101	3)
"	≤ 90		≥ 10			OP5			3103	30)
"	> 57 – 90	≥ 10				OP5			3103	
"	≤ 77		≥ 23			OP5			3103	
"	≤ 57			≥ 43		OP8			3110	
"	≤ 57	≥ 43				OP8			3107	
"	≤ 32	≥ 26	≥ 42			OP8			3107	
DICETYL PEROXYDICARBONATE	≤ 100					OP8	+30	+35	3120	
"	≤ 42 as a stable dispersion in water					OP8	+30	+35	3119	
DI-4-CHLOROBENZOYL PEROXIDE	≤ 77				≥ 23	OP5			3102	3)
"	≤ 52 as a paste					OP7			3106	20)
"	≤ 32			≥ 68					Exempt	29)
DICUMYL PEROXIDE	> 52 - 100					OP8			3110	12)
"	≤ 52			≥ 48					Exempt	29)
DICYCLOHEXYL PEROXYDICARBONATE	> 91 - 100					OP3	+10	+15	3112	3)
"	≤ 91				≥ 9	OP5	+10	+15	3114	
"	≤ 42 as a stable dispersion in water					OP8	+15	+20	3119	
DIDECANOYL PEROXIDE	≤ 100					OP6	+30	+35	3114	
2,2-DI-(4,4-DI (tert-BUTYLPEROXY) CYCLOHEXYL) PROPANE	≤ 42			≥ 58		OP7			3106	
"	≤ 22		≥ 78			OP8			3107	
DI-2,4-DICHLOROBENZOYL PEROXIDE	≤ 77				≥ 23	OP5			3102	3)
"	≤ 52 as a paste					OP8	+ 20	+ 25	3118	
"	≤ 52 as a paste with silicon oil					OP7			3106	
DI-(2-ETHOXYETHYL) PEROXYDICARBONATE	≤ 52		≥ 48			OP7	-10	0	3115	

ORGANIC PEROXIDE	Concentration (%)	Diluent type A (%)	Diluent type B (%) 1)	Inert solid (%)	Water	Packing Method	Control temperature (°C)	Emergency temperature (°C)	Number (Generic entry)	Subsidiary hazards and remarks
DI-(2-ETHYLHEXYL) PEROXYDICARBONATE	> 77 – 100					OP5	-20	-10	3113	
"	≤ 77		≥ 23			OP7	-15	-5	3115	
"	≤ 62 as a stable dispersion in water					OP8	-15	-5	3119	
"	≤ 52 as a stable dispersion in water (frozen)					OP8	-15	-5	3120	
2,2-DIHYDROPEROXYPROPANE	≤ 27			≥ 73		OP5			3102	3)
DI-(1-HYDROXYCYCLOHEXYL) PEROXIDE	≤ 100					OP7			3106	
DIISOBUTYRYL PEROXIDE	> 32 – 52		≥ 48			OP5	-20	-10	3111	3)
"	≤ 32		≥ 68			OP7	-20	-10	3115	
"	≤ 42 (as a stable dispersion in water)					OP8	-20	-10	3119	
DIISOPROPYLBENZENE DIHYDROPEROXIDE	≤ 82	≥ 5			≥ 5	OP7			3106	24)
DIISOPROPYL PEROXYDICARBONATE	> 52-100					OP2	-15	-5	3112	3)
"	≤ 52		≥ 48			OP7	-20	-10	3115	
"	≤ 32	≥ 68				OP7	-15	-5	3115	
DILAUROYL PEROXIDE	≤ 100					OP7			3106	
"	≤ 42 as a stable dispersion in water					OP8			3109	
DI-(3-METHOXYBUTYL) PEROXYDICARBONATE	≤ 52		≥ 48			OP7	-5	+5	3115	3)
DI-(2-METHYLBENZOYL) PEROXIDE	≤ 87				≥ 13	OP5	+30	+35	3112	3)
DI-(3-METHYLBENZOYL) PEROXIDE + BENZOYL (3-METHYLBENZOYL) PEROXIDE + DIBENZOYL PEROXIDE	≤ 20 + ≤ 18 + ≤ 4		≥ 58			OP7	+35	+40	3115	
DI-(4-METHYLBENZOYL) PEROXIDE□	≤ 52 as a paste with silicon oil					OP7			3106	
2,5-DIMETHYL-2,5-DI-(BENZOYLPEROXY)HEXANE	> 82-100					OP5			3102	3)
"	≤ 82					OP7			3106	
"	≤ 82			≥ 18		OP5			3104	
2,5-DIMETHYL-2,5-DI-(tert-BUTYLPEROXY)HEXANE	> 90 – 100					OP5			3103	
"	> 52-90	≥ 10				OP7			3105	
"	≤ 77			≥ 23		OP8			3108	
"	≤ 52	≥ 48				OP8			3109	
"	≤ 47 as a paste				≥ 18	OP8			3108	

ORGANIC PEROXIDE	Concentration (%)	Diluent type A (%)	Diluent type B (%) 1)	Inert solid (%)	Water	Packing Method	Control temperature (°C)	Emergency temperature (°C)	Number (Generic entry)	Subsidiary hazards and remarks
2,5-DIMETHYL-2,5-DI-(tert-BUTYLPEROXY)HEXYNE-3	>86-100					OP5			3101	3)
"	>52-86	≥14				OP5			3103	26)
"	≤52			≥48		OP7			3106	
2,5-DIMETHYL-2,5-DI-(2-ETHYLHEXANOYLPEROXY)HEXANE□	≤100					OP5	+20	+25	3113	
2,5-DIMETHYL-2,5-DIHYDROPEROXYHEXANE□	≤82	≥23			≥18	OP6			3104	
2,5-DIMETHYL-2,5-DI-(3,5,5-TRIMETHYLHEXANOYLPEROXY)HEXANE	≤77					OP7			3105	
1,1-DIMETHYL-3-HYDROXYBUTYL PEROXYNEOHEPTANOATE	≤52	≥48				OP8	0	+10	3117	
DIMYRISTYL PEROXYDICARBONATE	≤100					OP7	+20	+25	3116	
"	≤42 as a stable dispersion in water					OP8	+20	+25	3119	
DI-(2-NEODECANOYLPEROXYISOPROPYL)BENZENE	≤52	≥48				OP7	-10	0	3115	
DI-n-NONANOYL PEROXIDE	≤100					OP7	0	+10	3116	
DI-n-OCTANOYL PEROXIDE	≤100					OP5	+10	+15	3114	
DI-(2-PHENOXYETHYL) PEROXYDICARBONATE	>85 – 100					OP5			3102	3)
"	≤85				≥15	OP7			3106	
DIPROPIONYL PEROXIDE	≤27		≥73			OP8	+15	+20	3117	
DI-n-PROPYL PEROXYDICARBONATE	≤100					OP3	-25	-15	3113	
"	≤77		≥23			OP5	-20	-10	3113	
DISUCCINIC ACID PEROXIDE	>72 – 100					OP4			3102	3) 17)
"	≤72				≥28	OP7			3116	
DI-(3,5,5-TRIMETHYLHEXANOYL) PEROXIDE	>38-52	≥48				OP8	+10	+15	3119	
"	>52-82	≥18				OP7	0	+10	3115	
"	≤52 as a stable dispersion in water					OP8	+10	+15	3119	
"	≤38	≥62				OP8	+20	+25	3119	
ETHYL 3,3-DI-(tert-AMYLPEROXY)BUTYRATE	≤67	≥33				OP7			3105	
ETHYL 3,3-DI-(tert-BUTYLPEROXY)BUTYRATE	>77 – 100					OP5			3103	
"	≤77	≥23				OP7			3105	
"	≤52			≥48		OP7			3106	
1-(2-ETHYLHEXANOYLPEROXY)-1,3-DIMETHYLBUTYL PEROXYPIVALATE	≤52	≥45	≥10			OP7	-20	-10	3115	

ORGANIC PEROXIDE	Concentration (%)	Diluent type A (%)	Diluent type B (%) 1)	Inert solid (%)	Water	Packing Method	Control temperature (°C)	Emergency temperature (°C)	Number (Generic entry)	Subsidiary hazards and remarks
tert-HEXYL PEROXYNEODECANOATE	≤71	≥29				OP7	0	+10	3115	
tert-HEXYL PEROXYPIVALATE	≤72		≥28			OP7	+10	+15	3115	
"	≤52 as a stable dispersion in water					OP8	+15	+20	3117	
3-HYDROXY-1,1-DIMETHYLBUTYL PEROXYNEODECANOATE	≤77	≥23				OP 7	-5	+5	3115	
"	≤52	≥48				OP 8	-5	+5	3117	
"	≤52 as a stable dispersion in water					OP 8	-5	+5	3119	
ISOPROPYL sec-BUTYL PEROXYDICARBONATE +DI-sec-BUTYL PEROXYDICARBONATE +DI-ISOPROPYL PEROXYDICARBONATE	≤32 + ≤15 – 18 + ≤12 – 15	≥38				OP7	-20	-10	3115	
"	≤52 + ≤28 + ≤22					OP5	-20	-10	3111	3)
ISOPROPYLCUMYL HYDROPEROXIDE	≤72	≥28				OP8			3109	13)
p-MENTHYL HYDROPEROXIDE	>72 - 100					OP7			3105	13)
"	≤72	≥28				OP8			3109	27)
METHYLCYCLOHEXANONE PEROXIDE(S)	≤67		≥33			OP7	+35	+40	3115	
METHYL ETHYL KETONE PEROXIDE(S)	see remark 8)	≥48				OP5			3101	3) 8) 13)
"	see remark 9)	≥55				OP7			3105	9)
"	see remark 10)	≥60				OP8			3107	10)
METHYL ISOBUTYL KETONE PEROXIDE(S)	≤62	≥19				OP7			3105	22)
METHYL ISOPROPYL KETONE PEROXIDE(S)	See remark 31)	≥70				OP8			3109	31)
ORGANIC PEROXIDE, LIQUID, SAMPLE						OP2			3103	11)
ORGANIC PEROXIDE, LIQUID, SAMPLE, TEMPERATURE CONTROLLED						OP2			3113	11)
ORGANIC PEROXIDE, SOLID, SAMPLE						OP2			3104	11)
ORGANIC PEROXIDE, SOLID, SAMPLE, TEMPERATURE CONTROLLED						OP2			3114	11)
3,3,5,7,7-PENTAMETHYL-1,2,4-TRIOXEPANE	≤100					OP8			3107	
PEROXYACETIC ACID, TYPE D, stabilized	≤43					OP7			3105	13) 14) 19)
PEROXYACETIC ACID, TYPE E, stabilized	≤43					OP8			3107	13) 15) 19)
PEROXYACETIC ACID, TYPE F, stabilized	≤43					OP8			3109	13) 16) 19)
PEROXYLAURIC ACID	≤100					OP8	+35	+40	3118	
1-PHENYLETHYL HYDROPEROXIDE	≤38		≥62			OP8			3109	

ORGANIC PEROXIDE	Concentration (%)	Diluent type A (%)	Diluent type B (%) 1)	Inert solid (%)	Water	Packing Method	Control temperature (°C)	Emergency temperature (°C)	Number (Generic entry)	Subsidiary hazards and remarks
PINANYL HYDROPEROXIDE	> 56 – 100					OP7			3105	13)
"	≤ 56	≥ 44				OP8			3109	
POLYETHER POLY-tert-BUTYLPEROXY-CARBONATE	≤ 52		≥ 48			OP8			3107	
1,1,3,3-TETRAMETHYLBUTYL HYDROPEROXIDE	≤ 100					OP7			3105	
1,1,3,3-TETRAMETHYLBUTYL PEROXY-2-ETHYLHEXANOATE	≤ 100					OP7	+15	+20	3115	
1,1,3,3- TETRAMETHYLBUTYL PEROXYNEODECANOATE	≤ 72		≥ 28			OP7	-5	+5	3115	
"	≤ 52 as a stable dispersion in water					OP8	-5	+5	3119	
1,1,3,3-TETRAMETHYLBUTYL PEROXYPIVALATE	≤ 77	≥ 23				OP7	0	+10	3115	
3,6,9-TRIETHYL-3,6,9-TRIMETHYL-1,4,7 TRIPEROXONANE	≤ 17	≥ 18		≥ 65		OP8			3110	
"	≤ 42	≥ 58				OP7			3105	28)

Remarks (refer to the last column of the Table in 2.2.52.4):

1)   Diluent type B may always be replaced by diluent type A. The boiling point of diluent type B shall be at least 60°C higher than the SADT of the organic peroxide.

2)   Available oxygen ≤ 4.7%.

3)   "EXPLOSIVE" subsidiary hazard label required (Model No.1, see 5.2.2.2.2).

4)   Diluent may be replaced by di-tert-butyl peroxide.

5)   Available oxygen ≤ 9%.

6)   With ≤ 9% hydrogen peroxide; available oxygen ≤ 10%.

7)   Only non-metallic packagings allowed.

8)   Available oxygen > 10% and ≤ 10.7%, with or without water.

9)   Available oxygen ≤ 10%, with or without water.

10) Available oxygen ≤ 8.2%, with or without water.

11) See 2.2.52.1.9.

12) Up to 2000 kg per receptacle assigned to ORGANIC PEROXIDE TYPE F on the basis of largescale trials.

13) "CORROSIVE" subsidiary hazard label required (Model No.8, see 5.2.2.2.2).

14) Peroxyacetic acid formulations which fulfil the criteria of the Manual of Tests and Criteria, paragraph 20.4.3 (d).

15) Peroxyacetic acid formulations which fulfil the criteria of the Manual of Tests and Criteria, paragraph 20.4.3 (e).

16) Peroxyacetic acid formulations which fulfil the criteria of the Manual of Tests and Criteria, paragraph 20.4.3 (f).

17) Addition of water to this organic peroxide will decrease its thermal stability.

18) No "CORROSIVE" subsidiary hazard label (Model No.8, see 5.2.2.2.2) required for concentrations below 80%.

19) Mixtures with hydrogen peroxide, water and acid(s).

20) With diluent type A, with or without water.

21) With ≥ 25% diluent type A by mass, and in addition ethylbenzene.

22) With ≥ 19% diluent type A by mass, and in addition methyl isobutyl ketone.

23) With < 6% di-tert-butyl peroxide.

24) With ≤ 8% 1-isopropylhydroperoxy-4-isopropylhydroxybenzene.

25) Diluent type B with boiling point > 110 °C.

26) With < 0.5% hydroperoxides content.

27) For concentrations more than 56%, "CORROSIVE" subsidiary hazard label required (Model No.8, see 5.2.2.2.2).

28) Available active oxygen ≤ 7.6% in diluent type A having a 95% boil-off point in the range of 200 - 260 °C.

29) Not subject to the requirements of ADN for Class 5.2.

30) Diluent type B with boiling point > 130 °C.

31) Active oxygen ≤ 6.7%.

32) Active oxygen ≤ 4.15%.

2.2.61   **Class 6.1**   **Toxic substances**

2.2.61.1   *Criteria*

2.2.61.1.1   The heading of Class 6.1 covers substances of which it is known by experience or regarding which it is presumed from experiments on animals that in relatively small quantities they are able by a single action or by action of short duration to cause damage to human health, or death, by inhalation, by cutaneous absorption or by ingestion.

NOTE: *Genetically modified microorganisms and organisms shall be assigned to this Class if they meet the conditions for this Class.*

2.2.61.1.2   Substances of Class 6.1 are subdivided as follows:

T   Toxic substances without subsidiary hazard:

　　　　T1   Organic, liquid;

　　　　T2   Organic, solid;

　　　　T3   Organometallic substances;

　　　　T4   Inorganic, liquid;

　　　　T5   Inorganic, solid;

　　　　T6   Liquid, used as pesticides;

　　　　T7   Solid, used as pesticides;

　　　　T8   Samples;

　　　　T9   Other toxic substances;

　　　　T10   Articles;

　TF   Toxic substances, flammable:

　　　　TF1   Liquid;

　　　　TF2   Liquid, used as pesticides;

　　　　TF3   Solid;

　TS   Toxic substances, self-heating, solid;

　TW   Toxic substances, which, in contact with water, emit flammable gases:

　　　　TW1   Liquid;

　　　　TW2   Solid;

　TO   Toxic substances, oxidizing:

　　　　TO1   Liquid;

　　　　TO2   Solid;

TC   Toxic substances, corrosive:

　　TC1   Organic, liquid;

　　TC2   Organic, solid;

　　TC3   Inorganic, liquid;

　　TC4   Inorganic, solid;

TFC   Toxic substances, flammable, corrosive.

TFW   Toxic flammable substances, which, in contact with water, emit flammable gases.

Definitions

2.2.61.1.3   For the purposes of ADN:

LD$_{50}$ (median lethal dose) for acute oral toxicity is the statistically derived single dose of a substance that can be expected to cause death within 14 days in 50 per cent of young adult albino rats when administered by the oral route. The LD$_{50}$ value is expressed in terms of mass of test substance per mass of test animal (mg/kg);

LD$_{50}$ for acute dermal toxicity is that dose of the substance which, administered by continuous contact for 24 hours with the bare skin of albino rabbits, is most likely to cause death within 14 days in one half of the animals tested. The number of animals tested shall be sufficient to give a statistically significant result and be in conformity with good pharmacological practice. The result is expressed in milligrams per kg body mass;

LC$_{50}$ for acute toxicity on inhalation is that concentration of vapour, mist or dust which, administered by continuous inhalation to both male and female young adult albino rats for one hour, is most likely to cause death within 14 days in one half of the animals tested. A solid substance shall be tested if at least 10% (by mass) of its total mass is likely to be dust in a respirable range, e.g. the aerodynamic diameter of that particle-fraction is 10 µm or less. A liquid substance shall be tested if a mist is likely to be generated in a leakage of the transport containment. Both for solid and liquid substances more than 90% (by mass) of a specimen prepared for inhalation toxicity shall be in the respirable range as defined above. The result is expressed in milligrams per litre of air for dusts and mists or in millilitres per cubic metre of air (parts per million) for vapours.

Classification and assignment of packing groups

2.2.61.1.4   Substances of Class 6.1 shall be classified in three packing groups according to the degree of danger they present for carriage, as follows:

Packing group I:	highly toxic substances
Packing group II:	toxic substances
Packing group III:	slightly toxic substances.

2.2.61.1.5   Substances, mixtures, solutions and articles classified in Class 6.1 are listed in Table A of Chapter 3.2. The assignment of substances, mixtures and solutions not mentioned by name in Table A of Chapter 3.2 to the relevant entry of sub-section 2.2.61.3 and to the relevant packing group in accordance with the provisions of Chapter 2.1, shall be made according to the following criteria in 2.2.61.1.6 to 2.2.61.1.11.

2.2.61.1.6   To assess the degree of toxicity, account shall be taken of human experience of instances of accidental poisoning, as well as special properties possessed by any individual substances: liquid state, high volatility, any special likelihood of cutaneous absorption, and special biological effects.

2.2.61.1.7   In the absence of observations on humans, the degree of toxicity shall be assessed using the available data from animal experiments in accordance with the table below:

	Packing group	Oral toxicity LD_{50} (mg/kg)	Dermal toxicity LD_{50} (mg/kg)	Inhalation toxicity by dusts and mists LC_{50} (mg/l)
Highly toxic	I	≤ 5.0	≤ 50	≤ 0.2
Toxic	II	> 5.0 and ≤ 50	> 50 and ≤ 200	> 0.2 and ≤ 2.0
Slightly toxic	III [a]	> 50 and ≤ 300	> 200 and $\leq 1\ 000$	> 2.0 and ≤ 4.0

[a]   *Tear gas substances shall be included in packing group II even if data concerning their toxicity correspond to packing group III criteria.*

2.2.61.1.7.1   Where a substance exhibits different degrees of toxicity for two or more kinds of exposure, it shall be classified under the highest such degree of toxicity.

2.2.61.1.7.2   Substances meeting the criteria of Class 8 and with an inhalation toxicity of dusts and mists (LC_{50}) leading to packing group I shall only be accepted for an allocation to Class 6.1 if the toxicity through oral ingestion or dermal contact is at least in the range of packing groups I or II. Otherwise an assignment to Class 8 shall be made if appropriate (see 2.2.8.1.4.5).

2.2.61.1.7.3   The criteria for inhalation toxicity of dusts and mists are based on LC_{50} data relating to 1-hour exposure, and where such information is available it shall be used. However, where only LC_{50} data relating to 4-hour exposure are available, such figures can be multiplied by four and the product substituted in the above criteria, i.e. LC_{50} value multiplied by four (4 hour) is considered the equivalent of LC_{50} (1 hour).

Inhalation toxicity of vapours

2.2.61.1.8   Liquids giving off toxic vapours shall be classified into the following groups where "V" is the saturated vapour concentration (in ml/m³ of air) (volatility) at 20 °C and standard atmospheric pressure:

	Packing group	
Highly toxic	I	Where $V \geq 10\ LC_{50}$ and $LC_{50} \leq 1\ 000$ ml/m³
Toxic	II	Where $V \geq LC_{50}$ and $LC_{50} \leq 3\ 000$ ml/m³ and the criteria for packing group I are not met
Slightly toxic	III[a]	Where $V \geq 1/5\ LC_{50}$ and $LC_{50} \leq 5\ 000$ ml/m³ and the criteria for packing groups I and II are not met

[a]   *Tear gas substances shall be included in packing group II even if data concerning their toxicity correspond to packing group III criteria.*

These criteria for inhalation toxicity of vapours are based on LC_{50} data relating to 1-hour exposure, and where such information is available, it shall be used.

However, where only LC_{50} data relating to 4-hour exposure to the vapours are available, such figures can be multiplied by two and the product substituted in the above criteria, i.e. LC_{50} (4 hour) $\times$ 2 is considered the equivalent of LC_{50} (1 hour).

GROUP BORDERLINES INHALATION TOXICITY OF VAPOURS

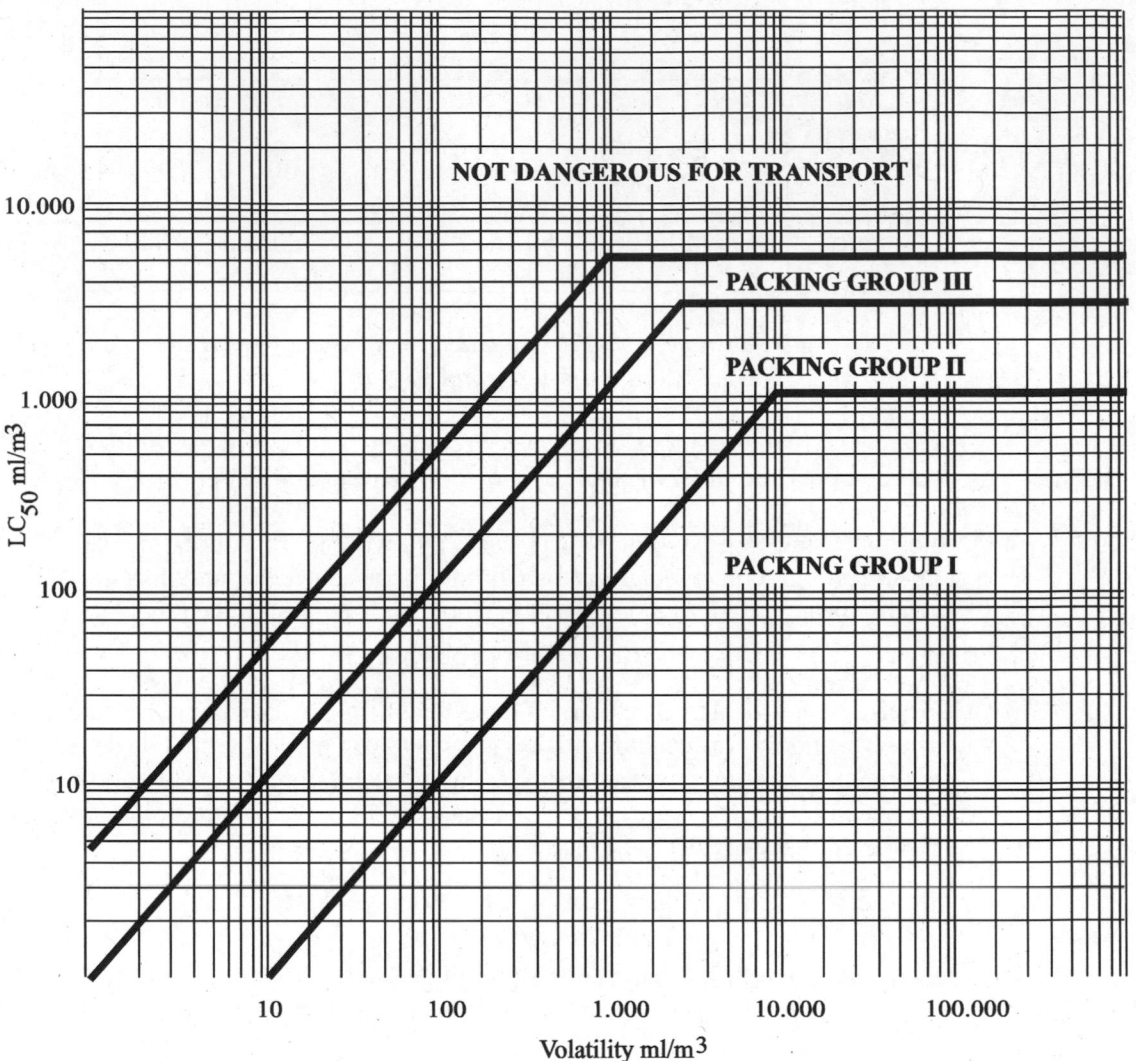

In this figure, the criteria are expressed in graphical form, as an aid to easy classification. However, due to approximations inherent in the use of graphs, substances falling on or near group borderlines shall be checked using numerical criteria.

Mixtures of liquids

2.2.61.1.9   Mixtures of liquids which are toxic on inhalation shall be assigned to packing groups according to the following criteria:

2.2.61.1.9.1   If LC_{50} is known for each of the toxic substances constituting the mixture, the packing group may be determined as follows:

(a)   calculation of the LC_{50} of the mixture:

$$LC_{50} \text{ (mixture)} = \dfrac{1}{\displaystyle\sum_{i=1}^{1} \dfrac{f_i}{LC_{50i}}}$$

where f_i =   molar fraction of constituent i of the mixture;

LC_{50i} =   average lethal concentration of constituent i in ml/m^3.

(b)   calculation of volatility of each mixture constituent:

$$V_i = P_i \times \dfrac{10^6}{101.3} \text{ (ml/m}^3)$$

where P_i =   partial pressure of constituent i in kPa at 20 °C and at standard atmospheric pressure.

(c)   calculation of the ratio of volatility to LC_{50}:

$$R = \sum_{i=1}^{n} \dfrac{V_i}{LC_{50i}}$$

(d)   the values calculated for LC_{50} (mixture) and R are then used to determine the packing group of the mixture:

Packing group I $R \geq 10$ and LC_{50} (mixture) $\leq 1\ 000$ ml/m^3;

Packing group II $R \geq 1$ and LC_{50} (mixture) $\leq 3\ 000$ ml/m^3, if the mixture does not meet the criteria for packing group I;

Packing group III $R \geq 1/5$ and LC_{50} (mixture) $\leq 5\ 000$ ml/m^3, if the mixture does not meet the criteria of packing groups I or II.

2.2.61.1.9.2   In the absence of LC_{50} data on the toxic constituent substances, the mixture may be assigned to a group based on the following simplified threshold toxicity tests. When these threshold tests are used, the most restrictive group shall be determined and used for carrying the mixture.

2.2.61.1.9.3   A mixture is assigned to packing group I only if it meets both of the following criteria:

(a)   A sample of the liquid mixture is vaporized and diluted with air to create a test atmosphere of 1000 ml/m^3 vaporized mixture in air. Ten albino rats (5 male and 5 female) are exposed to the test atmosphere for 1 hour and observed for 14 days. If five or more of the animals die within the 14-day observation period, the mixture is presumed to have an LC_{50} equal to or less than 1000 ml/m^3;

(b)   A sample of vapour in equilibrium with the liquid mixture is diluted with 9 equal volumes of air to form a test atmosphere. Ten albino rats (5 male and 5 female) are exposed to the test atmosphere for 1 hour and observed for 14 days. If five or more of the animals die within the 14-day observation period, the mixture is presumed to have a volatility equal to or greater than 10 times the mixture LC_{50}.

2.2.61.1.9.4   A mixture is assigned to packing group II only if it meets both of the following criteria, and does not meet the criteria for packing group I:

(a)   A sample of the liquid mixture is vaporized and diluted with air to create a test atmosphere of 3000 ml/m^3 vaporized mixture in air. Ten albino rats (5 male and 5 female) are exposed to the test atmosphere for 1 hour and observed for 14 days. If five or more of the animals die within the 14-day observation period, the mixture is presumed to have an LC_{50} equal to or less than 3000 ml/m^3;

(b)   A sample of the vapour in equilibrium with the liquid mixture is used to form a test atmosphere. Ten albino rats (5 male and 5 female) are exposed to the test atmosphere for 1 hour and observed for 14 days. If five or more of the animals die within the 14-day observation period, the mixture is presumed to have a volatility equal to or greater than the mixture LC_{50}.

2.2.61.1.9.5   A mixture is assigned to packing group III only if it meets both of the following criteria, and does not meet the criteria for packing groups I or II:

(a)   A sample of the liquid mixture is vaporized and diluted with air to create a test atmosphere of 5000 ml/m^3 vaporized mixture in air. Ten albino rats (5 male and 5 female) are exposed to the test atmosphere for 1 hour and observed for 14 days. If five or more of the animals die within the 14-day observation period, the mixture is presumed to have an LC_{50} equal to or less than 5000 ml/m^3;

(b)   The vapour concentration (volatility) of the liquid mixture is measured and if the vapour concentration is equal to or greater than 1000 ml/m^3, the mixture is presumed to have a volatility equal to or greater than 1/5 the mixture LC_{50}.

Methods for determining oral and dermal toxicity of mixtures

2.2.61.1.10   When classifying and assigning the appropriate packing group to mixtures in Class 6.1 in accordance with the oral and dermal toxicity criteria (see 2.2.61.1.3), it is necessary to determine the acute LD_{50} of the mixture.

If a mixture contains only one active substance, and the LD_{50} of that constituent is known, in the absence of reliable acute oral and dermal toxicity data on the actual mixture to be carried, the oral or dermal LD_{50} may be obtained by the following method:

$$LD_{50} \text{ value of preparation} = \frac{LD_{50} \text{ value of active substance} \times 100}{\text{percentage of active substance by mass}}$$

2.2.61.1.10.2   If a mixture contains more than one active constituent, there are three possible approaches that may be used to determine the oral or dermal LD_{50} of the mixture. The preferred method is to obtain reliable acute oral and dermal toxicity data on the actual mixture to be carried. If reliable, accurate data are not available, then either of the following methods may be performed:

(a)   Classify the formulation according to the most hazardous constituent of the mixture as if that constituent were present in the same concentration as the total concentration of all active constituents; or

(b)   Apply the formula:

$$\frac{C_A}{T_A} + \frac{C_B}{T_B} + \ldots + \frac{C_Z}{T_Z} = \frac{100}{T_M}$$

where:

C   =   the percentage concentration of constituent A, B, ... Z in the mixture;

T   =   the oral LD_{50} values of constituent A, B, ... Z;

T_M =   the oral LD_{50} value of the mixture.

NOTE: This formula can also be used for dermal toxicities provided that this information is available on the same species for all constituents. The use of this formula does not take into account any potentiation or protective phenomena.

Classification of pesticides

2.2.61.1.11   All active pesticide substances and their preparations for which the LC_{50} and/or LD_{50} values are known and which are classified in Class 6.1 shall be classified under appropriate packing groups in accordance with the criteria given in 2.2.61.1.6 to 2.2.61.1.9. Substances and preparations which are characterized by subsidiary hazards shall be classified according to the precedence of hazards Table in 2.1.3.10 with the assignment of appropriate packing groups.

2.2.61.1.11.1   If the oral or dermal LD_{50} value for a pesticide preparation is not known, but the LD_{50} value of its active substance(s) is known, the LD_{50} value for the preparation may be obtained by applying the procedures in 2.2.61.1.10.

NOTE: LD_{50} toxicity data for a number of common pesticides may be obtained from the most current edition of the document "The WHO Recommended Classification of Pesticides by Hazard and Guidelines to Classification" available from the International Programme on Chemical Safety, World Health Organization (WHO), 1211 Geneva 27, Switzerland. While that document may be used as a source of LD50 data for pesticides, its classification system shall not be used for purposes of transport classification of, or assignment of packing groups to, pesticides, which shall be in accordance with the requirements of ADN.

2.2.61.1.11.2   The proper shipping name used in the carriage of the pesticide shall be selected on the basis of the active ingredient, of the physical state of the pesticide and any subsidiary hazards it may exhibit (see 3.1.2).

2.2.61.1.12   If substances of Class 6.1, as a result of admixtures, come into categories of hazard different from those to which the substances mentioned by name in Table A of Chapter 3.2 belong, these mixtures or solutions shall be assigned to the entries to which they belong on the basis of their actual degree of danger.

NOTE: For the classification of solutions and mixtures (such as preparations and wastes), see also 2.1.3.

2.2.61.1.13   On the basis of the criteria of 2.2.61.1.6 to 2.2.61.1.11, it may also be determined whether the nature of a solution or mixture mentioned by name or containing a substance mentioned by name is such that the solution or mixture is not subject to the requirements for this Class.

2.2.61.1.14　　Substances, solutions and mixtures, with the exception of substances and preparations used as pesticides, which are not classified as acute toxic category 1, 2 or 3 according to Regulation (EC) No 1272/2008[3], may be considered as substances not belonging to class 6.1.

2.2.61.2　　*Substances not accepted for carriage*

2.2.61.2.1　　Chemically unstable substances of Class 6.1 shall not be accepted for carriage unless the necessary precautions have been taken to prevent the possibility of a dangerous decomposition or polymerization under normal conditions of carriage. For the precautions necessary to prevent polymerization, see special provision 386 of Chapter 3.3. To this end particular care shall be taken to ensure that receptacles and tanks do not contain any substances liable to promote these reactions.

2.2.61.2.2　　The following substances and mixtures shall not be accepted for carriage:

–　　Hydrogen cyanide, anhydrous or in solution, which do not meet the descriptions of UN Nos. 1051, 1613, 1614 and 3294;

–　　Metal carbonyls, having a flash-point below 23 °C, other than UN Nos. 1259 NICKEL CARBONYL and 1994 IRON PENTACARBONYL;

–　　2,3,7,8-TETRACHLORODIBENZO-p-DIOXINE (TCDD) in concentrations considered highly toxic in accordance with the criteria in 2.2.61.1.7;

–　　UN No. 2249 DICHLORODIMETHYL ETHER, SYMMETRICAL;

–　　Preparations of phosphides without additives inhibiting the emission of toxic flammable gases.

---

[3]　　*Regulation (EC) No 1272/2008 of the European Parliament and of the Council of 16 December 2008 on classification, labelling and packaging of substances and mixtures, amending and repealing Directive 67/548/EEC and 1999/45/EC; and amending Regulation (EC) No 1907/2006, published in the Official Journal of the European Union, L 353, 31 December 2008, p 1-1355.*

Toxic substances <u>without</u> subsidiary hazard(s)

Organic	**liquid** [a]	**T1**	1583 CHLOROPICRIN MIXTURE, N.O.S. 1602 DYE, LIQUID, TOXIC, N.O.S., or 1602 DYE INTERMEDIATE, LIQUID, TOXIC, N.O.S. 1693 TEAR GAS SUBSTANCE, LIQUID, N.O.S. 1851 MEDICINE, LIQUID, TOXIC, N.O.S. 2206 ISOCYANATES, TOXIC, N.O.S. or 2206 ISOCYANATE SOLUTION, TOXIC, N.O.S. 3140 ALKALOIDS, LIQUID, N.O.S. or 3140 ALKALOID SALTS, LIQUID, N.O.S. 3142 DISINFECTANT, LIQUID, TOXIC, N.O.S. 3144 NICOTINE COMPOUND, LIQUID, N.O.S. or 3144 NICOTINE PREPARATION, LIQUID, N.O.S. 3172 TOXINS, EXTRACTED FROM LIVING SOURCES, LIQUID, N.O.S. 3276 NITRILES, LIQUID, TOXIC, N.O.S 3278 ORGANOPHOSPHORUS COMPOUND, LIQUID, TOXIC, N.O.S. 3381 TOXIC BY INHALATION LIQUID, N.O.S. with an LC_{50} lower than or equal to 200 ml/m^3 and saturated vapour concentration greater than or equal to 500 LC_{50} 3382 TOXIC BY INHALATION LIQUID, N.O.S. with an LC_{50} lower than or equal to 1000 ml/m^3 and saturated vapour concentration greater than or equal to 10 LC_{50} 2810 TOXIC LIQUID, ORGANIC, N.O.S.
	solid [a, b]	**T2**	1544 ALKALOIDS, SOLID, N.O.S. or 1544 ALKALOID SALTS, SOLID, N.O.S. 1601 DISINFECTANT, SOLID, TOXIC, N.O.S. 1655 NICOTINE COMPOUND, SOLID, N.O.S., or 1655 NICOTINE PREPARATION, SOLID, N.O.S. 3448 TEAR GAS SUBSTANCE, SOLID, N.O.S. 3143 DYE, SOLID, TOXIC, N.O.S. or 3143 DYE INTERMEDIATE, SOLID, TOXIC, N.O.S. 3462 TOXINS, EXTRACTED FROM LIVING SOURCES, SOLID, N.O.S. 3249 MEDICINE, SOLID, TOXIC, N.O.S. 3464 ORGANOPHOSPHORUS COMPOUND, SOLID, TOXIC, N.O.S. 3439 NITRILES, SOLID, TOXIC, N.O.S. 2811 TOXIC SOLID, ORGANIC, N.O.S.
Organometallic [c, d]		**T3**	2026 PHENYLMERCURIC COMPOUND, N.O.S. 2788 ORGANOTIN COMPOUND, LIQUID, N.O.S. 3146 ORGANOTIN COMPOUND, SOLID, N.O.S. 3280 ORGANOARSENIC COMPOUND, LIQUID, N.O.S. 3465 ORGANOARSENIC COMPOUND, SOLID, N.O.S. 3281 METAL CARBONYLS, LIQUID, N.O.S. 3466 METAL CARBONYLS, SOLID, N.O.S. 3282 ORGANOMETALLIC COMPOUND, LIQUID, TOXIC, N.O.S. 3467 ORGANOMETALLIC COMPOUND, SOLID, TOXIC, N.O.S.

(cont'd on next page)

---

[a]   *Substances and preparations containing alkaloids or nicotine used as pesticides shall be classified under UN No. 2588 PESTICIDES, SOLID, TOXIC, N.O.S., UN No. 2902 PESTICIDES, LIQUID, TOXIC, N.O.S. or UN No. 2903 PESTICIDES, LIQUID, TOXIC, FLAMMABLE, N.O.S.*

[b]   *Active substances and triturations or mixtures of substances intended for laboratories and experiments and for the manufacture of pharmaceutical products with other substances shall be classified according to their toxicity (see 2.2.61.1.7 to 2.2.61.1.11).*

[c]   *Self-heating substances, slightly toxic and spontaneously combustible organometallic compounds, are substances of Class 4.2.*

[d]   *Water-reactive substances, slightly toxic, and water-reactive organometallic compounds, are substances of Class 4.3.*

Toxic substances <u>without</u> subsidiary hazard(s) *(cont'd)*

	liquid [e] **T4**	1556 ARSENIC COMPOUND, LIQUID, N.O.S., inorganic including: Arsenates, n.o.s., Arsenites, n.o.s.; and Arsenic sulphides, n.o.s.
		1935 CYANIDE SOLUTION, N.O.S.
		2024 MERCURY COMPOUND, LIQUID, N.O.S.
		3141 ANTIMONY COMPOUND, INORGANIC, LIQUID, N.O.S.
		3440 SELENIUM COMPOUND, LIQUID, N.O.S.
		3381 TOXIC BY INHALATION LIQUID, N.O.S. with an LC_{50} lower than or equal to 200 ml/m^3 and saturated vapour concentration greater than or equal to 500 LC_{50}
		3382 TOXIC BY INHALATION LIQUID, N.O.S. with an LC_{50} lower than or equal to 1000 ml/m^3 and saturated vapour concentration greater than or equal to 10 LC_{50}
		3287 TOXIC LIQUID, INORGANIC, N.O.S.

Inorganic

	solids [f, g] **T5**	1549 ANTIMONY COMPOUND, INORGANIC, SOLID, N.O.S
		1557 ARSENIC COMPOUND, SOLID, N.O.S., including: Arsenates, n.o.s.; Arsenites, n.o.s.; and Arsenic sulphides, n.o.s.
		1564 BARIUM COMPOUND, N.O.S.
		1566 BERYLLIUM COMPOUND, N.O.S.
		1588 CYANIDES, INORGANIC, SOLID, N.O.S.
		1707 THALLIUM COMPOUND, N.O.S.
		2025 MERCURY COMPOUND, SOLID, N.O.S.
		2291 LEAD COMPOUND, SOLUBLE, N.O.S.
		2570 CADMIUM COMPOUND
		2630 SELENATES or
		2630 SELENITES
		2856 FLUOROSILICATES, N.O.S.
		3283 SELENIUM COMPOUND, SOLID, N.O.S.
		3284 TELLURIUM COMPOUND, N.O.S.
		3285 VANADIUM COMPOUND, N.O.S.
		3288 TOXIC SOLID, INORGANIC, N.O.S.

	liquid [h] **T6**	2992 CARBAMATE PESTICIDE, LIQUID, TOXIC
		2994 ARSENICAL PESTICIDE, LIQUID, TOXIC
		2996 ORGANOCHLORINE PESTICIDE, LIQUID, TOXIC
		2998 TRIAZINE PESTICIDE, LIQUID, TOXIC
		3006 THIOCARBAMATE PESTICIDE, LIQUID, TOXIC
		3010 COPPER BASED PESTICIDE, LIQUID, TOXIC
		3012 MERCURY BASED PESTICIDE, LIQUID, TOXIC
		3014 SUBSTITUTED NITROPHENOL PESTICIDE, LIQUID, TOXIC
		3016 BIPYRIDILIUM PESTICIDE, LIQUID, TOXIC
		3018 ORGANOPHOSPHORUS PESTICIDE, LIQUID, TOXIC
		3020 ORGANOTIN PESTICIDE, LIQUID, TOXIC
		3026 COUMARIN DERIVATIVE PESTICIDE, LIQUID, TOXIC
		3348 PHENOXYACETIC ACID DERIVATIVE PESTICIDE, LIQUID, TOXIC
		3352 PYRETHROID PESTICIDE, LIQUID, TOXIC
		2902 PESTICIDE, LIQUID, TOXIC, N.O.S

Pesticides
(cont'd on next page)

---

[e] *Mercury fulminate, wetted with not less than 20% water, or mixture of alcohol and water by mass is a substance of Class 1, UN No. 0135.*

[f] *Ferricyanides, ferrocyanides, alkaline thiocyanates and ammonium thiocyanates are not subject to the provisions of ADN.*

[g] *Lead salts and lead pigments which, when mixed in a ratio of 1:1,000 with 0.07M hydrochloric acid and stirred for one hour at a temperature of 23 °C ± 2 °C, exhibit a solubility of 5% or less, are not subject to the provisions of ADN.*

[h] *Articles impregnated with this pesticide, such as fibreboard plates, paper strips, cotton-wool balls, sheets of plastics material, in hermetically closed wrappings, are not subject to the provisions of ADN.*

List of collective entries (cont'd)

Toxic substances <u>without</u> subsidiary hazard(s) *(cont'd)*

Pesticides *(cont'd)*		
Solid[h]	T7	2757 CARBAMATE PESTICIDE, SOLID, TOXIC 2759 ARSENICAL PESTICIDE, SOLID, TOXIC 2761 ORGANOCHLORINE PESTICIDE, SOLID, TOXIC 2763 TRIAZINE PESTICIDE, SOLID, TOXIC 2771 THIOCARBAMATE PESTICIDE, SOLID, TOXIC 2775 COPPER BASED PESTICIDE, SOLID, TOXIC 2777 MERCURY BASED PESTICIDE, SOLID, TOXIC 2779 SUBSTITUTED NITROPHENOL PESTICIDE, SOLID, TOXIC 2781 BIPYRIDILIUM PESTICIDE, SOLID, TOXIC 2783 ORGANOPHOSPHORUS PESTICIDE, SOLID, TOXIC 2786 ORGANOTIN PESTICIDE, SOLID, TOXIC 3027 COUMARIN DERIVATIVE PESTICIDE, SOLID, TOXIC 3048 ALUMINIUM PHOSPHIDE PESTICIDE 3345 PHENOXYACETIC ACID DERIVATIVE PESTICIDE, SOLID, TOXIC 3349 PYRETHROID PESTICIDE, SOLID, TOXIC 2588 PESTICIDE, SOLID, TOXIC, N.O.S.
Samples	T8	3315 CHEMICAL SAMPLE, TOXIC
Other toxic substances [i]	T9	3243 SOLIDS CONTAINING TOXIC LIQUID, N.O.S.
Articles	T10	3546 ARTICLES CONTAINING TOXIC SUBSTANCE, N.O.S.

Toxic substances <u>with</u> subsidiary hazard(s)

| Flammable TF | Liquid [j, k] | TF1 | 3071 MERCAPTANS, LIQUID, TOXIC, FLAMMABLE, N.O.S. or
3071 MERCAPTAN MIXTURE, LIQUID, TOXIC, FLAMMABLE, N.O.S.
3080 ISOCYANATES, TOXIC, FLAMMABLE, N.O.S. or
3080 ISOCYANATE SOLUTION, TOXIC, FLAMMABLE, N.O.S.
3275 NITRILES, TOXIC, FLAMMABLE, N.O.S.
3279 ORGANOPHOSPHORUS COMPOUND, TOXIC, FLAMMABLE, N.O.S.
3383 TOXIC BY INHALATION LIQUID, FLAMMABLE, N.O.S. with an LC_{50} lower than or equal to 200 ml/m^3 and saturated vapour concentration greater than or equal to 500 LC_{50}
3384 TOXIC BY INHALATION LIQUID, FLAMMABLE, N.O.S. with an LC_{50} lower than or equal to 1000 ml/m^3 and saturated vapour concentration greater than or equal to 10 LC_{50}
2929 TOXIC LIQUID, FLAMMABLE, ORGANIC, N.O.S. |

(cont'd on next page)

---

[h]   *Articles impregnated with this pesticide, such as fibreboard plates, paper strips, cotton-wool balls, sheets of plastics material, in hermetically closed wrappings, are not subject to the provisions of ADN.*

[i]   *Mixtures of solids which are not subject to the provisions of ADN and of toxic liquids may be carried under UN No. 3243 without first applying the classification criteria of Class 6.1, provided there is no free liquid visible at the time the substance is loaded or at the time the packaging or cargo transport unit is closed. Each packaging shall correspond to a design type that has passed a leakproofness test at the packing group II level. This entry shall not be used for solids containing a packing group I liquid.*

[j]   *Highly toxic and toxic flammable liquids having a flash-point below 23 °C are substances of Class 3 except those which are highly toxic by inhalation, as defined in 2.2.61.1.4 to 2.2.61.1.9. Liquids which are highly toxic by inhalation are indicated as "toxic by inhalation" in their proper shipping name in Column (2) or by special provision 354 in Column (6) of Table A of Chapter 3.2.*

[k]   *Flammable liquids, slightly toxic, with the exception of substances and preparations used as pesticides, having a flash-point between 23 °C and 60 °C inclusive, are substances of Class 3.*

Flammable TF (cont'd)				
	pesticides, liquid (flash-point not less than 23 °C)	TF2	2991	CARBAMATE PESTICIDE, LIQUID, TOXIC, FLAMMABLE
			2993	ARSENICAL PESTICIDE, LIQUID, TOXIC, FLAMMABLE
			2995	ORGANOCHLORINE PESTICIDE, LIQUID, TOXIC, FLAMMABLE
			2997	TRIAZINE PESTICIDE, LIQUID, TOXIC, FLAMMABLE
			3005	THIOCARBAMATE PESTICIDE, LIQUID, TOXIC, FLAMMABLE
			3009	COPPER BASED PESTICIDE, LIQUID, TOXIC, FLAMMABLE
			3011	MERCURY BASED PESTICIDE, LIQUID, TOXIC, FLAMMABLE
			3013	SUBSTITUTED NITROPHENOL PESTICIDE, LIQUID, TOXIC, FLAMMABLE
			3015	BIPYRIDILIUM PESTICIDE, LIQUID, TOXIC, FLAMMABLE
			3017	ORGANOPHOSPHORUS PESTICIDE, LIQUID, TOXIC, FLAMMABLE
			3019	ORGANOTIN PESTICIDE, LIQUID, TOXIC, FLAMMABLE
			3025	COUMARIN DERIVATIVE PESTICIDE, LIQUID, TOXIC, FLAMMABLE
			3347	PHENOXYACETIC ACID DERIVATIVE PESTICIDE, LIQUID, TOXIC, FLAMMABLE
			3351	PYRETHROID PESTICIDE, LIQUID, TOXIC, FLAMMABLE
			2903	PESTICIDE, LIQUID, TOXIC, FLAMMABLE, N.O.S.
	solid	TF3	1700	TEAR GAS CANDLES
			2930	TOXIC SOLID, FLAMMABLE, ORGANIC, N.O.S.
			3535	TOXIC SOLID, FLAMMABLE, INORGANIC, N.O.S.
Solid, self-heating [c] TS			3124	TOXIC SOLID, SELF-HEATING, N.O.S.
Water-reactive [d] TW	liquid	TW1	3385	TOXIC BY INHALATION LIQUID, WATER-REACTIVE, N.O.S. with an LC_{50} lower than or equal to 200 ml/m^3 and saturated vapour concentration greater than or equal to 500 LC_{50}
			3386	TOXIC BY INHALATION LIQUID, WATER-REACTIVE, N.O.S. with an LC_{50} lower than or equal to 1000 ml/m^3 and saturated vapour concentration greater than or equal to 10 LC_{50}
			3123	TOXIC LIQUID, WATER-REACTIVE, N.O.S.
	solid [n]	TW2	3125	TOXIC SOLID, WATER-REACTIVE, N.O.S.
Oxidizing [l] TO	liquid	TO1	3387	TOXIC BY INHALATION LIQUID, OXIDIZING, N.O.S. with an LC_{50} lower than or equal to 200 ml/m^3 and saturated vapour concentration greater than or equal to 500 LC_{50}
			3388	TOXIC BY INHALATION LIQUID, OXIDIZING, N.O.S. with an LC_{50} lower than or equal to 1000 ml/m^3 and saturated vapour concentration greater than or equal to 10 LC_{50}
			3122	TOXIC LIQUID, OXIDIZING, N.O.S.
	solid	TO2	3086	TOXIC SOLID, OXIDIZING, N.O.S.
Corrosive [m] TC	organic liquid	TC1	3277	CHLOROFORMATES, TOXIC, CORROSIVE, N.O.S.
			3361	CHLOROSILANES, TOXIC, CORROSIVE, N.O.S.
			3389	TOXIC BY INHALATION LIQUID, CORROSIVE, N.O.S. with an LC_{50} lower than or equal to 200 ml/m^3 and saturated vapour concentration greater than or equal to 500 LC_{50}
			3390	TOXIC BY INHALATION LIQUID, CORROSIVE, N.O.S. with an LC_{50} lower than or equal to 1000 ml/m^3 and saturated vapour concentration greater than or equal to 10 LC_{50}
			2927	TOXIC LIQUID, CORROSIVE, ORGANIC, N.O.S.
	organic solid	TC2	2928	TOXIC SOLID, CORROSIVE, ORGANIC, N.O.S.

(cont'd on next page)

---

[c]   *Self-heating substances, slightly toxic and spontaneously combustible organometallic compounds, are substances of Class 4.2.*

[d]   *Water-reactive substances, slightly toxic, and water-reactive organometallic compounds, are substances of Class 4.3.*

[l]   *Oxidizing substances, slightly toxic, are substances of Class 5.1.*

[m]   *Substances slightly toxic and slightly corrosive, are substances of Class 8.*

[n]   *Metal phosphides assigned to UN Nos. 1360, 1397, 1432, 1714, 2011 and 2013 are substances of Class 4.3.*

Toxic substances <u>with</u> subsidiary hazard(s) (cont'd)

Corrosive [m] **TC** *(cont'd)*	**inorganic**	**liquid**	**TC3**	3389 TOXIC BY INHALATION LIQUID, CORROSIVE, N.O.S. with an LC_{50} lower than or equal to 200 ml/m³ and saturated vapour concentration greater than or equal to 500 LC_{50}
				3390 TOXIC BY INHALATION LIQUID, CORROSIVE, N.O.S. with an LC_{50} lower than or equal to 1000 ml/m³ and saturated vapour concentration greater than or equal to 10 LC_{50}
				3289 TOXIC LIQUID, CORROSIVE, INORGANIC, N.O.S.
		solid	**TC4**	3290 TOXIC SOLID, CORROSIVE, INORGANIC, N.O.S.
Flammable, corrosive **TFC**				2742 CHLOROFORMATES, TOXIC, CORROSIVE, FLAMMABLE, N.O.S.
				3362 CHLOROSILANES, TOXIC, CORROSIVE, FLAMMABLE, N.O.S.
				3488 TOXIC BY INHALATION LIQUID, FLAMMABLE, CORROSIVE, N.O.S. with an LC_{50} lower than or equal to 200 ml/m³ and saturated vapour concentration greater than or equal to 500 LC_{50}
				3489 TOXIC BY INHALATION LIQUID, FLAMMABLE, CORROSIVE, N.O.S. with an LC_{50} lower than or equal to 1000 ml/m³ and saturated vapour concentration greater than or equal to 10 LC_{50}
Flammable, water-reactive **TFW**				3490 TOXIC BY INHALATION LIQUID, WATER-REACTIVE, FLAMMABLE, N.O.S. with an LC_{50} lower than or equal to 200 ml/m³ and saturated vapour concentration greater than or equal to 500 LC_{50}
				3491 TOXIC BY INHALATION LIQUID, WATER-REACTIVE, FLAMMABLE, N.O.S. with an LC_{50} lower than or equal to 1000 ml/m³ and saturated vapour concentration greater than or equal to 10 LC_{50}

---

[m]   *Substances slightly toxic and slightly corrosive, are substances of Class 8.*

2.2.62   **Class 6.2   Infectious substances**

2.2.62.1   *Criteria*

2.2.62.1.1   The heading of Class 6.2 covers infectious substances. For the purposes of ADN, infectious substances are substances which are known or are reasonably expected to contain pathogens. Pathogens are defined as micro-organisms (including bacteria, viruses, parasites, fungi) and other agents such as prions, which can cause disease in humans or animals.

NOTE 1: Genetically modified microorganisms and organisms, biological products, diagnostic specimens and intentionally infected live animals shall be assigned to this Class if they meet the conditions for this Class.

The carriage of unintentionally or naturally infected live animals is subject only to the relevant rules and regulations of the respective countries of origin, transit and destination.

NOTE 2: Toxins from plant, animal or bacterial sources which do not contain any infectious substances or organisms or which are not contained in them are substances of Class 6.1, UN No. 3172 or 3462.

2.2.62.1.2   Substances of Class 6.2 are subdivided as follows:

I1   Infectious substances affecting humans;

I2   Infectious substances affecting animals only;

I3   Clinical waste;

I4   Biological substances, category B.

Definitions

2.2.62.1.3   For the purposes of ADN:

"Biological products" are those products derived from living organisms which are manufactured and distributed in accordance with the requirements of appropriate national authorities, which may have special licensing requirements, and are used either for prevention, treatment, or diagnosis of disease in humans or animals, or for development, experimental or investigational purposes related thereto. They include, but are not limited to, finished or unfinished products such as vaccines;

"Cultures" are the result of a process by which pathogens are intentionally propagated. This definition does not include human or animal patient specimens as defined in this paragraph;

"Medical or clinical wastes" are wastes derived from the veterinary treatment of animals, the medical treatment of humans or from bio-research;

"Patient specimens" are those, collected directly from humans or animals, including, but not limited to, excreta, secreta, blood and its components, tissue and tissue fluid swabs, and body parts being carried for purposes such as research, diagnosis, investigational activities, disease treatment and prevention.

Classification

2.2.62.1.4   Infectious substances shall be classified in Class 6.2 and assigned to UN Nos 2814, 2900, 3291, 3373 or 3549, as appropriate.

Infectious substances are divided into the following categories:

2.2.62.1.4.1   Category A: An infectious substance which is carried in a form that, when exposure to it occurs, is capable of causing permanent disability, life-threatening or fatal disease in otherwise healthy humans or animals. Indicative examples of substances that meet these criteria are given in the table in this paragraph.

NOTE: *An exposure occurs when an infectious substance is released outside of the protective packaging, resulting in physical contact with humans or animals.*

(a)   Infectious substances meeting these criteria which cause disease in humans or both in humans and animals shall be assigned to UN No. 2814. Infectious substances which cause disease only in animals shall be assigned to UN No. 2900;

(b)   Assignment to UN No. 2814 or UN No. 2900 shall be based on the known medical history and symptoms of the source human or animal, endemic local conditions, or professional judgement concerning individual circumstances of the source human or animal.

NOTE 1: *The proper shipping name for UN No. 2814 is "INFECTIOUS SUBSTANCE, AFFECTING HUMANS". The proper shipping name for UN No. 2900 is "INFECTIOUS SUBSTANCE, AFFECTING ANIMALS only".*

NOTE 2: *The following table is not exhaustive. Infectious substances, including new or emerging pathogens, which do not appear in the table but which meet the same criteria shall be assigned to Category A. In addition, if there is doubt as to whether or not a substance meets the criteria it shall be included in Category A.*

NOTE 3: *In the following table, the micro-organisms written in italics are bacteria or fungi.*

INDICATIVE EXAMPLES OF INFECTIOUS SUBSTANCES INCLUDED IN CATEGORY A IN ANY FORM UNLESS OTHERWISE INDICATED (2.2.62.1.4.1)	
UN Number and name	**Microorganism**
UN No. 2814 Infectious substances affecting humans	*Bacillus anthracis (cultures only)*
	Brucella abortus (cultures only)
	Brucella melitensis (cultures only)
	Brucella suis (cultures only)
	Burkholderia mallei - Pseudomonas mallei – Glanders *(cultures only)*
	Burkholderia pseudomallei – Pseudomonas pseudomallei (cultures only)
	Chlamydia psittaci - avian strains (cultures only)
	Clostridium botulinum (cultures only)
	Coccidioides immitis (cultures only)
	Coxiella burnetii (cultures only)
	Crimean-Congo haemorrhagic fever virus
	Dengue virus (cultures only)
	Eastern equine encephalitis virus (cultures only)
	Escherichia coli, verotoxigenic (cultures only) [a]
	Ebola virus
	Flexal virus
	Francisella tularensis (cultures only)
	Guanarito virus
	Hantaan virus
	Hantavirus causing haemorrhagic fever with renal syndrome
	Hendra virus
	Hepatitis B virus (cultures only)
	Herpes B virus (cultures only)
	Human immunodeficiency virus (cultures only)
	Highly pathogenic avian influenza virus (cultures only)
	Japanese Encephalitis virus (cultures only)
	Junin virus
	Kyasanur Forest disease virus
	Lassa virus
	Machupo virus
	Marburg virus
	Monkeypox virus
	Mycobacterium tuberculosis (cultures only) [a]
	Nipah virus
	Omsk haemorrhagic fever virus
	Poliovirus (cultures only)
	Rabies virus (cultures only)
	Rickettsia prowazekii (cultures only)
	Rickettsia rickettsii (cultures only)
	Rift Valley fever virus (cultures only)
	Russian spring-summer encephalitis virus (cultures only)
	Sabia virus
	Shigella dysenteriae type 1 (cultures only) [a]
	Tick-borne encephalitis virus (cultures only)
	Variola virus
	Venezuelan equine encephalitis virus (cultures only)
	West Nile virus (cultures only)
	Yellow fever virus (cultures only)
	Yersinia pestis (cultures only)

---

[a]   *Nevertheless, when the cultures are intended for diagnostic or clinical purposes, they may be classified as infectious substances of Category B.*

INDICATIVE EXAMPLES OF INFECTIOUS SUBSTANCES INCLUDED IN CATEGORY A IN ANY FORM UNLESS OTHERWISE INDICATED (2.2.62.1.4.1)	
UN Number and name	**Microorganism**
UN No. 2900 Infectious substances affecting animals only	African swine fever virus (cultures only) Avian paramyxovirus Type 1 - Velogenic Newcastle disease virus (cultures only) Classical swine fever virus (cultures only) Foot and mouth disease virus (cultures only) Lumpy skin disease virus (cultures only) *Mycoplasma mycoides* - Contagious bovine pleuropneumonia (cultures only) Peste des petits ruminants virus (cultures only) Rinderpest virus (cultures only) Sheep-pox virus (cultures only) Goatpox virus (cultures only) Swine vesicular disease virus (cultures only) Vesicular stomatitis virus (cultures only)

2.2.62.1.4.2   Category B: An infectious substance which does not meet the criteria for inclusion in Category A. Infectious substances in Category B shall be assigned to UN No. 3373.

NOTE: *The proper shipping name of UN No. 3373 is "BIOLOGICAL SUBSTANCE, CATEGORY B".*

2.2.62.1.5   *Exemptions*

2.2.62.1.5.1   Substances which do not contain infectious substances or substances which are unlikely to cause disease in humans or animals are not subject to the provisions of ADN unless they meet the criteria for inclusion in another class.

2.2.62.1.5.2   Substances containing microorganisms which are non-pathogenic to humans or animals are not subject to ADN unless they meet the criteria for inclusion in another class.

2.2.62.1.5.3   Substances in a form that any present pathogens have been neutralized or inactivated such that they no longer pose a health risk are not subject to ADN unless they meet the criteria for inclusion in another class.

NOTE: *Medical equipment which has been drained of free liquid is deemed to meet the requirements of this paragraph and is not subject to the provisions of ADN.*

2.2.62.1.5.4   Substances where the concentration of pathogens is at a level naturally encountered (including foodstuff and water samples) and which are not considered to pose a significant risk of infection are not subject to ADN unless they meet the criteria for inclusion in another class.

2.2.62.1.5.5   Dried blood spots, collected by applying a drop of blood onto absorbent material, are not subject to ADN.

2.2.62.1.5.6   Faecal occult blood screening samples are not subject to ADN.

2.2.62.1.5.7   Blood or blood components which have been collected for the purposes of transfusion or for the preparation of blood products to be used for transfusion or transplantation and any tissues or organs intended for use in transplantation as well as samples drawn in connection with such purposes are not subject to ADN.

2.2.62.1.5.8   Human or animal specimens for which there is minimal likelihood that pathogens are present are not subject to ADN if the specimen is carried in a packaging which will prevent any leakage and which is marked with the words "Exempt human specimen" or "Exempt animal specimen", as appropriate.

The packaging is deemed to comply with the above requirements if it meets the following conditions:

(a)   The packaging consists of three components:

(i)   a leak-proof primary receptacle(s);

(ii)   a leak-proof secondary packaging; and

(iii)   an outer packaging of adequate strength for its capacity, mass and intended use, and with at least one surface having minimum dimensions of 100 mm × 100 mm;

(b)   For liquids, absorbent material in sufficient quantity to absorb the entire contents is placed between the primary receptacle(s) and the secondary packaging so that, during carriage, any release or leak of a liquid substance will not reach the outer packaging and will not compromise the integrity of the cushioning material;

(c)   When multiple fragile primary receptacles are placed in a single secondary packaging, they are either individually wrapped or separated to prevent contact between them.

NOTE 1: An element of professional judgement is required to determine if a substance is exempt under this paragraph. That judgement should be based on the known medical history, symptoms and individual circumstances of the source, human or animal, and endemic local conditions. Examples of specimens which may be carried under this paragraph include blood or urine tests to monitor cholesterol levels, blood glucose levels, hormone levels, or prostate specific antibodies (PSA); those required to monitor organ function such as heart, liver or kidney function for humans or animals with non-infectious diseases, or for therapeutic drug monitoring; those conducted for insurance or employment purposes and intended to determine the presence of drugs or alcohol; pregnancy tests; biopsies to detect cancer; and antibody detection in humans or animals in the absence of any concern for infection (e.g. evaluation of vaccine induced immunity, diagnosis of autoimmune disease, etc.).

NOTE 2: For air transport, packagings for specimens exempted under this paragraph shall meet the conditions in (a) to (c).

2.2.62.1.5.9   Except for:

(a)   Medical waste (UN Nos. 3291 and 3549);

(b)   Medical devices or equipment contaminated with or containing infectious substances in Category A (UN No. 2814 or UN No. 2900); and

(c)   Medical devices or equipment contaminated with or containing other dangerous goods that meet the definition of another class, medical devices or equipment potentially contaminated with or containing infectious substances which are being carried for disinfection, cleaning, sterilization, repair, or equipment evaluation are not subject to provisions of ADN other than those of this paragraph if packed in packagings designed and constructed in such a way that, under normal conditions of carriage, they cannot break, be punctured or leak their contents. Packagings shall be designed to meet the construction requirements listed in 6.1.4 or 6.6.4 of ADR.

These packagings shall meet the general packing requirements of 4.1.1.1 and 4.1.1.2 of ADR and be capable of retaining the medical devices and equipment when dropped from a height of 1.2 m.

The packagings shall be marked "USED MEDICAL DEVICE" or "USED MEDICAL EQUIPMENT". When using overpacks, these shall be marked in the same way, except when the inscription remains visible.

2.2.62.1.6 to 2.2.62.1.8   *(Reserved)*

2.2.62.1.9   *Biological products*

For the purposes of ADN, biological products are divided into the following groups:

(a)   those which are manufactured and packaged in accordance with the requirements of appropriate national authorities and carried for the purposes of final packaging or distribution, and use for personal health care by medical professionals or individuals. Substances in this group are not subject to the provisions of ADN;

(b)   those which do not fall under paragraph (a) and are known or reasonably believed to contain infectious substances and which meet the criteria for inclusion in Category A or Category B. Substances in this group shall be assigned to UN No. 2814, UN No. 2900 or UN No. 3373, as appropriate.

NOTE: *Some licensed biological products may present a biohazard only in certain parts of the world. In that case, competent authorities may require these biological products to be in compliance with local requirements for infectious substances or may impose other restrictions.*

2.2.62.1.10   *Genetically modified micro-organisms and organisms*

Genetically modified micro-organisms not meeting the definition of infectious substance shall be classified according to section 2.2.9.

2.2.62.1.11   *Medical or clinical wastes*

2.2.62.1.11.1   Medical or clinical waste containing:

(a)   Category A infectious substances shall be assigned to UN No. 2814, UN No. 2900 or UN No. 3549, as appropriate. Solid medical waste containing Category A infectious substances generated from the medical treatment of humans or veterinary treatment of animals may be assigned to UN No. 3549. The UN No. 3549 entry shall not be used for waste from bio-research or liquid waste;

(b)   Category B infectious substances shall be assigned to UN No. 3291.

NOTE 1: *The proper shipping name for UN No. 3549 is "MEDICAL WASTE, CATEGORY A, AFFECTING HUMANS, solid" or "MEDICAL WASTE, CATEGORY A, AFFECTING ANIMALS only, solid".*

NOTE 2: Medical or clinical wastes assigned to number 18 01 03 (Wastes from human or animal health care and/or related research – wastes from natal care, diagnosis, treatment or prevention of disease in humans – wastes whose collection and disposal is subject to special requirement in order to prevent infection) or 18 02 02 (Wastes from human or animal health care and/or related research – wastes from research, diagnosis, treatment or prevention of disease involving animals – wastes whose collection and disposal is subject to special requirements in order to prevent infection) according to the list of wastes annexed to the Commission Decision 2000/532/EC[4] as amended, shall be classified according to the provisions set out in this paragraph, based on the medical or veterinary diagnosis concerning the patient or the animal.

2.2.62.1.11.2 Medical or clinical wastes which are reasonably believed to have a low probability of containing infectious substances shall be assigned to UN No. 3291. For the assignment, international, regional or national waste catalogues may be taken into account.

NOTE 1: The proper shipping name for UN No. 3291 is "CLINICAL WASTE, UNSPECIFIED, N.O.S." or "(BIO) MEDICAL WASTE, N.O.S". or "REGULATED MEDICAL WASTE, N.O.S.".

NOTE 2: Notwithstanding the classification criteria set out above, medical or clinical wastes assigned to number 18 01 04 (Wastes from human or animal health care and/or related research – wastes from natal care, diagnosis, treatment or prevention of disease in humans – wastes whose collection and disposal is not subject to special requirements in order to prevent infection) or 18 02 03 (Wastes from human or animal health care and/or related research – wastes from research, diagnosis, treatment or prevention of disease involving animals – wastes whose collection and disposal is not subject to special requirements in order to prevent infection) according to the list of wastes annexed to the Commission Decision 2000/532/EC[4] as amended, are not subject to the provisions of ADN.

2.2.62.1.11.3 Decontaminated medical or clinical wastes which previously contained infectious substances are not subject to the provisions of ADN unless they meet the criteria for inclusion in another class.

2.2.62.1.11.4 *(Deleted)*

2.2.62.1.12 *Infected animals*

2.2.62.1.12.1 Unless an infectious substance cannot be consigned by any other means, live animals shall not be used to consign such a substance. A live animal which has been intentionally infected and is known or suspected to contain an infectious substance shall only be carried under terms and conditions approved by the competent authority.

---

[4] *Commission Decision 2000/532/EC of 3 May 2000 replacing Decision 94/3/EC establishing a list of wastes pursuant to Article 1(a) of Council Directive 75/442/EEC on waste (replaced by Directive 2006/12/EC of the European Parliament and of the Council (Official Journal of the European Communities No. L 114 of 27 April 2006, page 9)) and Council Decision 94/904/EC establishing a list of hazardous waste pursuant to Article 1(4) of Council Directive 91/689/EEC on hazardous waste (Official Journal of the European Communities No. L 226 of 6 September 2000, page 3).*

NOTE: *The approval of the competent authorities shall be issued on the basis of the relevant rules for the carriage of live animals, taking into consideration dangerous goods aspects. The authorities that are competent to lay down these conditions and rules for approval shall be regulated at national level.*

If there is no approval by a competent authority of a Contracting Party to ADN, the competent authority of a Contracting Party to ADN may recognize an approval issued by the competent authority of a country that is not a Contracting Party to ADN.

Rules for the carriage of livestock are, for example, contained in Council Regulation (EC) No 1/2005 of 22 December 2004 on the protection of animals during transport (Official Journal of the European Community No L 3 of 5 January 2005) as amended.

2.2.62.1.12.2   *(Deleted)*

2.2.62.2   Substances not accepted for carriage

Live vertebrate or invertebrate animals shall not be used to carry an infectious agent unless the agent cannot be carried by other means or unless this carriage has been approved by the competent authority (see 2.2.62.1.12.1).

2.2.62.3   List of collective entries

Effects on humans	I1	2814	INFECTIOUS SUBSTANCE, AFFECTING HUMANS
Effects on animals only	I2	2900	INFECTIOUS SUBSTANCE, AFFECTING ANIMALS only
Clinical waste	I3	3291 3291 3291 3549 3549	CLINICAL WASTE, UNSPECIFIED, N.O.S. or (BIO)MEDICAL WASTE, N.O.S. or REGULATED MEDICAL WASTE, N.O.S. MEDICAL WASTE, CATEGORY A, AFFECTING HUMANS, solid or MEDICAL WASTE, CATEGORY A, AFFECTING ANIMALS only, solid
Biological substances	I4	3373	BIOLOGICAL SUBSTANCE, CATEGORY B

2.2.7   **Class 7   Radioactive material**

2.2.7.1   *Definitions*

2.2.7.1.1   *Radioactive material* means any material containing radionuclides where both the activity concentration and the total activity in the consignment exceed the values specified in 2.2.7.2.2.1 to 2.2.7.2.2.6.

2.2.7.1.2   *Contamination*

Contamination means the presence of a radioactive substance on a surface in quantities in excess of 0.4 Bq/cm^2 for beta and gamma emitters and low toxicity alpha emitters, or 0.04 Bq/cm^2 for all other alpha emitters.

Non-fixed contamination means contamination that can be removed from a surface during routine conditions of carriage.

Fixed contamination means contamination other than non-fixed contamination.

2.2.7.1.3   *Definitions of specific terms*

A_1 and A_2

A_1 means the activity value of special form radioactive material which is listed in the Table in 2.2.7.2.2.1 or derived in 2.2.7.2.2.2 and is used to determine the activity limits for the requirements of ADN.

A_2 means the activity value of radioactive material, other than special form radioactive material, which is listed in the Table in 2.2.7.2.2.1 or derived in 2.2.7.2.2.2 and is used to determine the activity limits for the requirements of ADN.

Fissile nuclides means uranium-233, uranium-235, plutonium-239 and plutonium-241. Fissile material means a material containing any of the fissile nuclides. Excluded from the definition of fissile material are the following:

(a)   Natural uranium or depleted uranium which is unirradiated;

(b)   Natural uranium or depleted uranium which has been irradiated in thermal reactors only;

(c)   Material with fissile nuclides less than a total of 0.25 g;

(d)   Any combination of (a), (b) and/or (c).

These exclusions are only valid if there is no other material with fissile nuclides in the package or in the consignment if shipped unpackaged.

Low dispersible radioactive material means either a solid radioactive material or a solid radioactive material in a sealed capsule, that has limited dispersibility and is not in powder form.

Low specific activity (LSA) material means radioactive material which by its nature has a limited specific activity, or radioactive material for which limits of estimated average specific activity apply. External shielding materials surrounding the LSA material shall not be considered in determining the estimated average specific activity.

Low toxicity alpha emitters are: natural uranium; depleted uranium; natural thorium; uranium-235 or uranium-238; thorium-232; thorium-228 and thorium-230 when contained in ores or physical and chemical concentrates; or alpha emitters with a half-life of less than 10 days.

Specific activity of a radionuclide means the activity per unit mass of that nuclide. The specific activity of a material shall mean the activity per unit mass of the material in which the radionuclides are essentially uniformly distributed.

Special form radioactive material means either:

(a)   An indispersible solid radioactive material; or

(b)   A sealed capsule containing radioactive material.

Surface contaminated object (SCO) means a solid object which is not itself radioactive but which has radioactive material distributed on its surface.

Unirradiated thorium means thorium containing not more than 10^{-7} g of uranium-233 per gram of thorium-232.

Unirradiated uranium means uranium containing not more than 2×10^3 Bq of plutonium per gram of uranium-235, not more than 9×10^6 Bq of fission products per gram of uranium-235 and not more than 5×10^{-3} g of uranium-236 per gram of uranium-235.

Uranium - natural, depleted, enriched means the following:

Natural uranium means uranium (which may be chemically separated) containing the naturally occurring distribution of uranium isotopes (approximately 99.28% uranium-238, and 0.72% uranium-235 by mass).

Depleted uranium means uranium containing a lesser mass percentage of uranium-235 than in natural uranium.

Enriched uranium means uranium containing a greater mass percentage of uranium-235 than 0.72%.

In all cases, a very small mass percentage of uranium-234 is present.

2.2.7.2   ***Classification***

2.2.7.2.1   *General provisions*

2.2.7.2.1.1   Radioactive material shall be assigned to one of the UN numbers specified in Table 2.2.7.2.1.1, in accordance with 2.2.7.2.4 and 2.2.7.2.5, taking into account the material characteristics determined in 2.2.7.2.3.

UN Nos.	Proper shipping name and description [a]
Excepted packages (1.7.1.5)	
UN 2908	RADIOACTIVE MATERIAL, EXCEPTED PACKAGE - EMPTY PACKAGING
UN 2909	RADIOACTIVE MATERIAL, EXCEPTED PACKAGE – ARTICLES MANUFACTURED FROM NATURAL URANIUM or DEPLETED URANIUM or NATURAL THORIUM
UN 2910	RADIOACTIVE MATERIAL, EXCEPTED PACKAGE - LIMITED QUANTITY OF MATERIAL
UN 2911	RADIOACTIVE MATERIAL, EXCEPTED PACKAGE - INSTRUMENTS or ARTICLES
UN 3507	URANIUM HEXAFLUORIDE, RADIOACTIVE MATERIAL, EXCEPTED PACKAGE less than 0.1 kg per package, non-fissile or fissile-excepted [b, c]
Low specific activity radioactive material (2.2.7.2.3.1)	
UN 2912	RADIOACTIVE MATERIAL, LOW SPECIFIC ACTIVITY (LSA-I), non-fissile or fissile-excepted [b]
UN 3321	RADIOACTIVE MATERIAL, LOW SPECIFIC ACTIVITY (LSA-II), non fissile or fissile-excepted [b]
UN 3322	RADIOACTIVE MATERIAL, LOW SPECIFIC ACTIVITY (LSA-III), non fissile or fissile-excepted [b]
UN 3324	RADIOACTIVE MATERIAL, LOW SPECIFIC ACTIVITY (LSA-II), FISSILE
UN 3325	RADIOACTIVE MATERIAL, LOW SPECIFIC ACTIVITY (LSA-III), FISSILE
Surface contaminated objects (2.2.7.2.3.2)	
UN 2913	RADIOACTIVE MATERIAL, SURFACE CONTAMINATED OBJECTS (SCO-I, SCO-II or SCO-III), non-fissile or fissile-excepted [b]
UN 3326	RADIOACTIVE MATERIAL, SURFACE CONTAMINATED OBJECTS (SCO-I or SCO-II), FISSILE
Type A packages (2.2.7.2.4.4)	
UN 2915	RADIOACTIVE MATERIAL, TYPE A PACKAGE, non-special form, non-fissile or fissile-excepted [b]
UN 3327	RADIOACTIVE MATERIAL, TYPE A PACKAGE, FISSILE, non-special form
UN 3332	RADIOACTIVE MATERIAL, TYPE A PACKAGE, SPECIAL FORM, non fissile or fissile-excepted [b]
UN 3333	RADIOACTIVE MATERIAL, TYPE A PACKAGE, SPECIAL FORM, FISSILE
Type B(U) packages (2.2.7.2.4.6)	
UN 2916	RADIOACTIVE MATERIAL, TYPE B(U) PACKAGE, non-fissile or fissile-excepted [b]
UN 3328	RADIOACTIVE MATERIAL, TYPE B(U) PACKAGE, FISSILE
Type B(M) packages (2.2.7.2.4.6)	
UN 2917	RADIOACTIVE MATERIAL, TYPE B(M) PACKAGE, non-fissile or fissile-excepted [b]
UN 3329	RADIOACTIVE MATERIAL, TYPE B(M) PACKAGE, FISSILE
Type C packages (2.2.7.2.4.6)	
UN 3323	RADIOACTIVE MATERIAL, TYPE C PACKAGE, non fissile or fissile-excepted [b]
UN 3330	RADIOACTIVE MATERIAL, TYPE C PACKAGE, FISSILE

Special arrangement	
(2.2.7.2.5)	
UN 2919	RADIOACTIVE MATERIAL, TRANSPORTED UNDER SPECIAL ARRANGEMENT, non-fissile or fissile-excepted [b]
UN 3331	RADIOACTIVE MATERIAL, TRANSPORTED UNDER SPECIAL ARRANGEMENT, FISSILE
Uranium hexafluoride	
(2.2.7.2.4.5)	
UN 2977	RADIOACTIVE MATERIAL, URANIUM HEXAFLUORIDE, FISSILE
UN 2978	RADIOACTIVE MATERIAL, URANIUM HEXAFLUORIDE, non-fissile or fissile-excepted [b]
UN 3507	URANIUM HEXAFLUORIDE, RADIOACTIVE MATERIAL, EXCEPTED PACKAGE less than 0.1 kg per package, non-fissile or fissile-excepted [b, c]

[a] *The proper shipping name is found in the column "proper shipping name and description" and is restricted to that part shown in capital letters. In the cases of UN Nos. 2909, 2911, 2913 and 3326, where alternative proper shipping names are separated by the word "or" only the relevant proper shipping name shall be used.*

[b] *The term "fissile-excepted" refers only to material excepted under 2.2.7.2.3.5.*

[c] *For UN No. 3507, see also special provision 369 in Chapter 3.3.*

2.2.7.2.2   *Determination of radionuclide values*

2.2.7.2.2.1   The following basic values for individual radionuclides are given in Table 2.2.7.2.2.1:

(a) A_1 and A_2 in TBq;

(b)   Activity concentration limits for exempt material in Bq/g; and

(c)   Activity limits for exempt consignments in Bq.

Table 2.2.7.2.2.1: Basic radionuclides values for individual radionuclides

Radionuclide (atomic number)	A_1 (TBq)	A_2 (TBq)	Activity concentration limit for exempt material (Bq/g)	Activity limit for an exempt consignment (Bq)
Actinium (89)				
Ac-225 (a)	8×10^{-1}	6×10^{-3}	1×10^1	1×10^4
Ac-227 (a)	9×10^{-1}	9×10^{-5}	1×10^{-1}	1×10^3
Ac-228	6×10^{-1}	5×10^{-1}	1×10^1	1×10^6
Silver (47)				
Ag-105	2×10^0	2×10^0	1×10^2	1×10^6
Ag-108m (a)	7×10^{-1}	7×10^{-1}	1×10^1 (b)	1×10^6 (b)
Ag-110m (a)	4×10^{-1}	4×10^{-1}	1×10^1	1×10^6
Ag-111	2×10^0	6×10^{-1}	1×10^3	1×10^6
Aluminium (13)				
Al-26	1×10^{-1}	1×10^{-1}	1×10^1	1×10^5
Americium (95)				
Am-241	1×10^1	1×10^{-3}	1×10^0	1×10^4
Am-242m (a)	1×10^1	1×10^{-3}	1×10^0 (b)	1×10^4 (b)
Am-243 (a)	5×10^0	1×10^{-3}	1×10^0 (b)	1×10^3 (b)
Argon (18)				
Ar-37	4×10^1	4×10^1	1×10^6	1×10^8
Ar-39	4×10^1	2×10^1	1×10^7	1×10^4
Ar-41	3×10^{-1}	3×10^{-1}	1×10^2	1×10^9
Arsenic (33)				
As-72	3×10^{-1}	3×10^{-1}	1×10^1	1×10^5
As-73	4×10^1	4×10^1	1×10^3	1×10^7
As-74	1×10^0	9×10^{-1}	1×10^1	1×10^6
As-76	3×10^{-1}	3×10^{-1}	1×10^2	1×10^5
As-77	2×10^1	7×10^{-1}	1×10^3	1×10^6
Astatine (85)				
At-211 (a)	2×10^1	5×10^{-1}	1×10^3	1×10^7
Gold (79)				
Au-193	7×10^0	2×10^0	1×10^2	1×10^7
Au-194	1×10^0	1×10^0	1×10^1	1×10^6

Radionuclide (atomic number)	A_1 (TBq)	A_2 (TBq)	Activity concentration limit for exempt material (Bq/g)	Activity limit for an exempt consignment (Bq)
Au-195	1×10^1	6×10^0	1×10^2	1×10^7
Au-198	1×10^0	6×10^{-1}	1×10^2	1×10^6
Au-199	1×10^1	6×10^{-1}	1×10^2	1×10^6
Barium (56)				
Ba-131 (a)	2×10^0	2×10^0	1×10^2	1×10^6
Ba-133	3×10^0	3×10^0	1×10^2	1×10^6
Ba-133m	2×10^1	6×10^{-1}	1×10^2	1×10^6
Ba-135m	2×10^1	6×10^{-1}	1×10^2	1×10^6
Ba-140 (a)	5×10^{-1}	3×10^{-1}	1×10^1 (b)	1×10^5 (b)
Beryllium (4)				
Be-7	2×10^1	2×10^1	1×10^3	1×10^7
Be-10	4×10^1	6×10^{-1}	1×10^4	1×10^6
Bismuth (83)				
Bi-205	7×10^{-1}	7×10^{-1}	1×10^1	1×10^6
Bi-206	3×10^{-1}	3×10^{-1}	1×10^1	1×10^5
Bi-207	7×10^{-1}	7×10^{-1}	1×10^1	1×10^6
Bi-210	1×10^0	6×10^{-1}	1×10^3	1×10^6
Bi-210m (a)	6×10^{-1}	2×10^{-2}	1×10^1	1×10^5
Bi-212 (a)	7×10^{-1}	6×10^{-1}	1×10^1 (b)	1×10^5 (b)
Berkelium (97)				
Bk-247	8×10^0	8×10^{-4}	1×10^0	1×10^4
Bk-249 (a)	4×10^1	3×10^{-1}	1×10^3	1×10^6
Bromine (35)				
Br-76	4×10^{-1}	4×10^{-1}	1×10^1	1×10^5
Br-77	3×10^0	3×10^0	1×10^2	1×10^6
Br-82	4×10^{-1}	4×10^{-1}	1×10^1	1×10^6
Carbon (6)				
C-11	1×10^0	6×10^{-1}	1×10^1	1×10^6
C-14	4×10^1	3×10^0	1×10^4	1×10^7
Calcium (20)				
Ca-41	Unlimited	Unlimited	1×10^5	1×10^7

Radionuclide (atomic number)	A_1 (TBq)	A_2 (TBq)	Activity concentration limit for exempt material (Bq/g)	Activity limit for an exempt consignment (Bq)
Ca-45	4×10^1	1×10^0	1×10^4	1×10^7
Ca-47 (a)	3×10^0	3×10^{-1}	1×10^1	1×10^6
Cadmium (48)				
Cd-109	3×10^1	2×10^0	1×10^4	1×10^6
Cd-113m	4×10^1	5×10^{-1}	1×10^3	1×10^6
Cd-115 (a)	3×10^0	4×10^{-1}	1×10^2	1×10^6
Cd-115m	5×10^{-1}	5×10^{-1}	1×10^3	1×10^6
Cerium (58)				
Ce-139	7×10^0	2×10^0	1×10^2	1×10^6
Ce-141	2×10^1	6×10^{-1}	1×10^2	1×10^7
Ce-143	9×10^{-1}	6×10^{-1}	1×10^2	1×10^6
Ce-144 (a)	2×10^{-1}	2×10^{-1}	1×10^2 (b)	1×10^5 (b)
Californium (98)				
Cf-248	4×10^1	6×10^{-3}	1×10^1	1×10^4
Cf-249	3×10^0	8×10^{-4}	1×10^0	1×10^3
Cf-250	2×10^1	2×10^{-3}	1×10^1	1×10^4
Cf-251	7×10^0	7×10^{-4}	1×10^0	1×10^3
Cf-252	1×10^{-1}	3×10^{-3}	1×10^1	1×10^4
Cf-253 (a)	4×10^1	4×10^{-2}	1×10^2	1×10^5
Cf-254	1×10^{-3}	1×10^{-3}	1×10^0	1×10^3
Chlorine (17)				
Cl-36	1×10^1	6×10^{-1}	1×10^4	1×10^6
Cl-38	2×10^{-1}	2×10^{-1}	1×10^1	1×10^5
Curium (96)				
Cm-240	4×10^1	2×10^{-2}	1×10^2	1×10^5
Cm-241	2×10^0	1×10^0	1×10^2	1×10^6
Cm-242	4×10^1	1×10^{-2}	1×10^2	1×10^5
Cm-243	9×10^0	1×10^{-3}	1×10^0	1×10^4
Cm-244	2×10^1	2×10^{-3}	1×10^1	1×10^4
Cm-245	9×10^0	9×10^{-4}	1×10^0	1×10^3
Cm-246	9×10^0	9×10^{-4}	1×10^0	1×10^3

Radionuclide (atomic number)	A_1 (TBq)	A_2 (TBq)	Activity concentration limit for exempt material (Bq/g)	Activity limit for an exempt consignment (Bq)
Cm-247 (a)	3×10^0	1×10^{-3}	1×10^0	1×10^4
Cm-248	2×10^{-2}	3×10^{-4}	1×10^0	1×10^3
Cobalt (27)				
Co-55	5×10^{-1}	5×10^{-1}	1×10^1	1×10^6
Co-56	3×10^{-1}	3×10^{-1}	1×10^1	1×10^5
Co-57	1×10^1	1×10^1	1×10^2	1×10^6
Co-58	1×10^0	1×10^0	1×10^1	1×10^6
Co-58m	4×10^1	4×10^1	1×10^4	1×10^7
Co-60	4×10^{-1}	4×10^{-1}	1×10^1	1×10^5
Chromium (24)				
Cr-51	3×10^1	3×10^1	1×10^3	1×10^7
Caesium (55)				
Cs-129	4×10^0	4×10^0	1×10^2	1×10^5
Cs-131	3×10^1	3×10^1	1×10^3	1×10^6
Cs-132	1×10^0	1×10^0	1×10^1	1×10^5
Cs-134	7×10^{-1}	7×10^{-1}	1×10^1	1×10^4
Cs-134m	4×10^1	6×10^{-1}	1×10^3	1×10^5
Cs-135	4×10^1	1×10^0	1×10^4	1×10^7
Cs-136	5×10^{-1}	5×10^{-1}	1×10^1	1×10^5
Cs-137 (a)	2×10^0	6×10^{-1}	1×10^1 (b)	1×10^4 (b)
Copper (29)				
Cu-64	6×10^0	1×10^0	1×10^2	1×10^6
Cu-67	1×10^1	7×10^{-1}	1×10^2	1×10^6
Dysprosium (66)				
Dy-159	2×10^1	2×10^1	1×10^3	1×10^7
Dy-165	9×10^{-1}	6×10^{-1}	1×10^3	1×10^6
Dy-166 (a)	9×10^{-1}	3×10^{-1}	1×10^3	1×10^6
Erbium (68)				
Er-169	4×10^1	1×10^0	1×10^4	1×10^7
Er-171	8×10^{-1}	5×10^{-1}	1×10^2	1×10^6
Europium (63)				

Radionuclide (atomic number)	A_1 (TBq)	A_2 (TBq)	Activity concentration limit for exempt material (Bq/g)	Activity limit for an exempt consignment (Bq)
Eu-147	2×10^0	2×10^0	1×10^2	1×10^6
Eu-148	5×10^{-1}	5×10^{-1}	1×10^1	1×10^6
Eu-149	2×10^1	2×10^1	1×10^2	1×10^7
Eu-150 (short lived)	2×10^0	7×10^{-1}	1×10^3	1×10^6
Eu-150 (long lived)	7×10^{-1}	7×10^{-1}	1×10^1	1×10^6
Eu-152	1×10^0	1×10^0	1×10^1	1×10^6
Eu-152m	8×10^{-1}	8×10^{-1}	1×10^2	1×10^6
Eu-154	9×10^{-1}	6×10^{-1}	1×10^1	1×10^6
Eu-155	2×10^1	3×10^0	1×10^2	1×10^7
Eu-156	7×10^{-1}	7×10^{-1}	1×10^1	1×10^6
Fluorine (9)				
F-18	1×10^0	6×10^{-1}	1×10^1	1×10^6
Iron (26)				
Fe-52 (a)	3×10^{-1}	3×10^{-1}	1×10^1	1×10^6
Fe-55	4×10^1	4×10^1	1×10^4	1×10^6
Fe-59	9×10^{-1}	9×10^{-1}	1×10^1	1×10^6
Fe-60 (a)	4×10^1	2×10^{-1}	1×10^2	1×10^5
Gallium (31)				
Ga-67	7×10^0	3×10^0	1×10^2	1×10^6
Ga-68	5×10^{-1}	5×10^{-1}	1×10^1	1×10^5
Ga-72	4×10^{-1}	4×10^{-1}	1×10^1	1×10^5
Gadolinium (64)				
Gd-146 (a)	5×10^{-1}	5×10^{-1}	1×10^1	1×10^6
Gd-148	2×10^1	2×10^{-3}	1×10^1	1×10^4
Gd-153	1×10^1	9×10^0	1×10^2	1×10^7
Gd-159	3×10^0	6×10^{-1}	1×10^3	1×10^6
Germanium (32)				
Ge-68 (a)	5×10^{-1}	5×10^{-1}	1×10^1	1×10^5
Ge-69	1×10^0	1×10^0	1×10^1	1×10^6
Ge-71	4×10^1	4×10^1	1×10^4	1×10^8
Ge-77	3×10^{-1}	3×10^{-1}	1×10^1	1×10^5

Radionuclide (atomic number)	A_1 (TBq)	A_2 (TBq)	Activity concentration limit for exempt material (Bq/g)	Activity limit for an exempt consignment (Bq)
Hafnium (72)				
Hf-172 (a)	6×10^{-1}	6×10^{-1}	1×10^1	1×10^6
Hf-175	3×10^0	3×10^0	1×10^2	1×10^6
Hf-181	2×10^0	5×10^{-1}	1×10^1	1×10^6
Hf-182	Unlimited	Unlimited	1×10^2	1×10^6
Mercury (80)				
Hg-194 (a)	1×10^0	1×10^0	1×10^1	1×10^6
Hg-195m (a)	3×10^0	7×10^{-1}	1×10^2	1×10^6
Hg-197	2×10^1	1×10^1	1×10^2	1×10^7
Hg-197m	1×10^1	4×10^{-1}	1×10^2	1×10^6
Hg-203	5×10^0	1×10^0	1×10^2	1×10^5
Holmium (67)				
Ho-166	4×10^{-1}	4×10^{-1}	1×10^3	1×10^5
Ho-166m	6×10^{-1}	5×10^{-1}	1×10^1	1×10^6
Iodine (53)				
I-123	6×10^0	3×10^0	1×10^2	1×10^7
I-124	1×10^0	1×10^0	1×10^1	1×10^6
I-125	2×10^1	3×10^0	1×10^3	1×10^6
I-126	2×10^0	1×10^0	1×10^2	1×10^6
I-129	Unlimited	Unlimited	1×10^2	1×10^5
I-131	3×10^0	7×10^{-1}	1×10^2	1×10^6
I-132	4×10^{-1}	4×10^{-1}	1×10^1	1×10^5
I-133	7×10^{-1}	6×10^{-1}	1×10^1	1×10^6
I-134	3×10^{-1}	3×10^{-1}	1×10^1	1×10^5
I-135 (a)	6×10^{-1}	6×10^{-1}	1×10^1	1×10^6
Indium (49)				
In-111	3×10^0	3×10^0	1×10^2	1×10^6
In-113m	4×10^0	2×10^0	1×10^2	1×10^6
In-114m (a)	1×10^1	5×10^{-1}	1×10^2	1×10^6
In-115m	7×10^0	1×10^0	1×10^2	1×10^6
Iridium (77)				

Radionuclide (atomic number)	A_1 (TBq)	A_2 (TBq)	Activity concentration limit for exempt material (Bq/g)	Activity limit for an exempt consignment (Bq)
Ir-189 (a)	1×10^1	1×10^1	1×10^2	1×10^7
Ir-190	7×10^{-1}	7×10^{-1}	1×10^1	1×10^6
Ir-192	1×10^0(c)	6×10^{-1}	1×10^1	1×10^4
Ir-193m	4×10^1	4×10^0	1×10^4	1×10^7
Ir-194	3×10^{-1}	3×10^{-1}	1×10^2	1×10^5
Potassium (19)				
K-40	9×10^{-1}	9×10^{-1}	1×10^2	1×10^6
K-42	2×10^{-1}	2×10^{-1}	1×10^2	1×10^6
K-43	7×10^{-1}	6×10^{-1}	1×10^1	1×10^6
Krypton (36)				
Kr-79	4×10^0	2×10^0	1×10^3	1×10^5
Kr-81	4×10^1	4×10^1	1×10^4	1×10^7
Kr-85	1×10^1	1×10^1	1×10^5	1×10^4
Kr-85m	8×10^0	3×10^0	1×10^3	1×10^{10}
Kr-87	2×10^{-1}	2×10^{-1}	1×10^2	1×10^9
Lanthanum (57)				
La-137	3×10^1	6×10^0	1×10^3	1×10^7
La-140	4×10^{-1}	4×10^{-1}	1×10^1	1×10^5
Lutetium (71)				
Lu-172	6×10^{-1}	6×10^{-1}	1×10^1	1×10^6
Lu-173	8×10^0	8×10^0	1×10^2	1×10^7
Lu-174	9×10^0	9×10^0	1×10^2	1×10^7
Lu-174m	2×10^1	1×10^1	1×10^2	1×10^7
Lu-177	3×10^1	7×10^{-1}	1×10^3	1×10^7
Magnesium (12)				
Mg-28 (a)	3×10^{-1}	3×10^{-1}	1×10^1	1×10^5
Manganese (25)				
Mn-52	3×10^{-1}	3×10^{-1}	1×10^1	1×10^5
Mn-53	Unlimited	Unlimited	1×10^4	1×10^9
Mn-54	1×10^0	1×10^0	1×10^1	1×10^6
Mn-56	3×10^{-1}	3×10^{-1}	1×10^1	1×10^5

Radionuclide (atomic number)	A_1 (TBq)	A_2 (TBq)	Activity concentration limit for exempt material (Bq/g)	Activity limit for an exempt consignment (Bq)
Molybdenum (42)				
Mo-93	4×10^1	2×10^1	1×10^3	1×10^8
Mo-99 (a)	1×10^0	6×10^{-1}	1×10^2	1×10^6
Nitrogen (7)				
N-13	9×10^{-1}	6×10^{-1}	1×10^2	1×10^9
Sodium (11)				
Na-22	5×10^{-1}	5×10^{-1}	1×10^1	1×10^6
Na-24	2×10^{-1}	2×10^{-1}	1×10^1	1×10^5
Niobium (41)				
Nb-93m	4×10^1	3×10^1	1×10^4	1×10^7
Nb-94	7×10^{-1}	7×10^{-1}	1×10^1	1×10^6
Nb-95	1×10^0	1×10^0	1×10^1	1×10^6
Nb-97	9×10^{-1}	6×10^{-1}	1×10^1	1×10^6
Neodymium (60)				
Nd-147	6×10^0	6×10^{-1}	1×10^2	1×10^6
Nd-149	6×10^{-1}	5×10^{-1}	1×10^2	1×10^6
Nickel (28)				
Ni-57	6×10^{-1}	6×10^{-1}	1×10^1	1×10^6
Ni-59	Unlimited	Unlimited	1×10^4	1×10^8
Ni-63	4×10^1	3×10^1	1×10^5	1×10^8
Ni-65	4×10^{-1}	4×10^{-1}	1×10^1	1×10^6
Neptunium (93)				
Np-235	4×10^1	4×10^1	1×10^3	1×10^7
Np-236 (short-lived)	2×10^1	2×10^0	1×10^3	1×10^7
Np-236 (long-lived)	9×10^0	2×10^{-2}	1×10^2	1×10^5
Np-237	2×10^1	2×10^{-3}	1×10^0 (b)	1×10^3 (b)
Np-239	7×10^0	4×10^{-1}	1×10^2	1×10^7
Osmium (76)				
Os-185	1×10^0	1×10^0	1×10^1	1×10^6
Os-191	1×10^1	2×10^0	1×10^2	1×10^7
Os-191m	4×10^1	3×10^1	1×10^3	1×10^7

Radionuclide (atomic number)	A_1 (TBq)	A_2 (TBq)	Activity concentration limit for exempt material (Bq/g)	Activity limit for an exempt consignment (Bq)
Os-193	2×10^0	6×10^{-1}	1×10^2	1×10^6
Os-194 (a)	3×10^{-1}	3×10^{-1}	1×10^2	1×10^5
Phosphorus (15)				
P-32	5×10^{-1}	5×10^{-1}	1×10^3	1×10^5
P-33	4×10^1	1×10^0	1×10^5	1×10^8
Protactinium (91)				
Pa-230 (a)	2×10^0	7×10^{-2}	1×10^1	1×10^6
Pa-231	4×10^0	4×10^{-4}	1×10^0	1×10^3
Pa-233	5×10^0	7×10^{-1}	1×10^2	1×10^7
Lead (82)				
Pb-201	1×10^0	1×10^0	1×10^1	1×10^6
Pb-202	4×10^1	2×10^1	1×10^3	1×10^6
Pb-203	4×10^0	3×10^0	1×10^2	1×10^6
Pb-205	Unlimited	Unlimited	1×10^4	1×10^7
Pb-210 (a)	1×10^0	5×10^{-2}	1×10^1 (b)	1×10^4 (b)
Pb-212 (a)	7×10^{-1}	2×10^{-1}	1×10^1 (b)	1×10^5 (b)
Palladium (46)				
Pd-103 (a)	4×10^1	4×10^1	1×10^3	1×10^8
Pd-107	Unlimited	Unlimited	1×10^5	1×10^8
Pd-109	2×10^0	5×10^{-1}	1×10^3	1×10^6
Promethium (61)				
Pm-143	3×10^0	3×10^0	1×10^2	1×10^6
Pm-144	7×10^{-1}	7×10^{-1}	1×10^1	1×10^6
Pm-145	3×10^1	1×10^1	1×10^3	1×10^7
Pm-147	4×10^1	2×10^0	1×10^4	1×10^7
Pm-148m (a)	8×10^{-1}	7×10^{-1}	1×10^1	1×10^6
Pm-149	2×10^0	6×10^{-1}	1×10^3	1×10^6
Pm-151	2×10^0	6×10^{-1}	1×10^2	1×10^6
Polonium (84)				
Po-210	4×10^1	2×10^{-2}	1×10^1	1×10^4
Praseodymium (59)				

Radionuclide (atomic number)	A_1 (TBq)	A_2 (TBq)	Activity concentration limit for exempt material (Bq/g)	Activity limit for an exempt consignment (Bq)
Pr-142	4×10^{-1}	4×10^{-1}	1×10^2	1×10^5
Pr-143	3×10^0	6×10^{-1}	1×10^4	1×10^6
Platinum (78)				
Pt-188 (a)	1×10^0	8×10^{-1}	1×10^1	1×10^6
Pt-191	4×10^0	3×10^0	1×10^2	1×10^6
Pt-193	4×10^1	4×10^1	1×10^4	1×10^7
Pt-193m	4×10^1	5×10^{-1}	1×10^3	1×10^7
Pt-195m	1×10^1	5×10^{-1}	1×10^2	1×10^6
Pt-197	2×10^1	6×10^{-1}	1×10^3	1×10^6
Pt-197m	1×10^1	6×10^{-1}	1×10^2	1×10^6
Plutonium (94)				
Pu-236	3×10^1	3×10^{-3}	1×10^1	1×10^4
Pu-237	2×10^1	2×10^1	1×10^3	1×10^7
Pu-238	1×10^1	1×10^{-3}	1×10^0	1×10^4
Pu-239	1×10^1	1×10^{-3}	1×10^0	1×10^4
Pu-240	1×10^1	1×10^{-3}	1×10^0	1×10^3
Pu-241 (a)	4×10^1	6×10^{-2}	1×10^2	1×10^5
Pu-242	1×10^1	1×10^{-3}	1×10^0	1×10^4
Pu-244 (a)	4×10^{-1}	1×10^{-3}	1×10^0	1×10^4
Radium (88)				
Ra-223 (a)	4×10^{-1}	7×10^{-3}	1×10^2 (b)	1×10^5 (b)
Ra-224 (a)	4×10^{-1}	2×10^{-2}	1×10^1 (b)	1×10^5 (b)
Ra-225 (a)	2×10^{-1}	4×10^{-3}	1×10^2	1×10^5
Ra-226 (a)	2×10^{-1}	3×10^{-3}	1×10^1 (b)	1×10^4 (b)
Ra-228 (a)	6×10^{-1}	2×10^{-2}	1×10^1 (b)	1×10^5 (b)
Rubidium (37)				
Rb-81	2×10^0	8×10^{-1}	1×10^1	1×10^6
Rb-83 (a)	2×10^0	2×10^0	1×10^2	1×10^6
Rb-84	1×10^0	1×10^0	1×10^1	1×10^6
Rb-86	5×10^{-1}	5×10^{-1}	1×10^2	1×10^5
Rb-87	Unlimited	Unlimited	1×10^4	1×10^7

Radionuclide (atomic number)	A_1 (TBq)	A_2 (TBq)	Activity concentration limit for exempt material (Bq/g)	Activity limit for an exempt consignment (Bq)
Rb(nat)	Unlimited	Unlimited	1×10^4	1×10^7
Rhenium (75)				
Re-184	1×10^0	1×10^0	1×10^1	1×10^6
Re-184m	3×10^0	1×10^0	1×10^2	1×10^6
Re-186	2×10^0	6×10^{-1}	1×10^3	1×10^6
Re-187	Unlimited	Unlimited	1×10^6	1×10^9
Re-188	4×10^{-1}	4×10^{-1}	1×10^2	1×10^5
Re-189 (a)	3×10^0	6×10^{-1}	1×10^2	1×10^6
Re(nat)	Unlimited	Unlimited	1×10^6	1×10^9
Rhodium (45)				
Rh-99	2×10^0	2×10^0	1×10^1	1×10^6
Rh-101	4×10^0	3×10^0	1×10^2	1×10^7
Rh-102	5×10^{-1}	5×10^{-1}	1×10^1	1×10^6
Rh-102m	2×10^0	2×10^0	1×10^2	1×10^6
Rh-103m	4×10^1	4×10^1	1×10^4	1×10^8
Rh-105	1×10^1	8×10^{-1}	1×10^2	1×10^7
Radon (86)				
Rn-222 (a)	3×10^{-1}	4×10^{-3}	1×10^1 (b)	1×10^8 (b)
Ruthenium (44)				
Ru-97	5×10^0	5×10^0	1×10^2	1×10^7
Ru-103 (a)	2×10^0	2×10^0	1×10^2	1×10^6
Ru-105	1×10^0	6×10^{-1}	1×10^1	1×10^6
Ru-106 (a)	2×10^{-1}	2×10^{-1}	1×10^2 (b)	1×10^5 (b)
Sulphur (16)				
S-35	4×10^1	3×10^0	1×10^5	1×10^8
Antimony (51)				
Sb-122	4×10^{-1}	4×10^{-1}	1×10^2	1×10^4
Sb-124	6×10^{-1}	6×10^{-1}	1×10^1	1×10^6
Sb-125	2×10^0	1×10^0	1×10^2	1×10^6
Sb-126	4×10^{-1}	4×10^{-1}	1×10^1	1×10^5
Scandium (21)				

Radionuclide (atomic number)	A_1 (TBq)	A_2 (TBq)	Activity concentration limit for exempt material (Bq/g)	Activity limit for an exempt consignment (Bq)
Sc-44	5×10^{-1}	5×10^{-1}	1×10^1	1×10^5
Sc-46	5×10^{-1}	5×10^{-1}	1×10^1	1×10^6
Sc-47	1×10^1	7×10^{-1}	1×10^2	1×10^6
Sc-48	3×10^{-1}	3×10^{-1}	1×10^1	1×10^5
Selenium (34)				
Se-75	3×10^0	3×10^0	1×10^2	1×10^6
Se-79	4×10^1	2×10^0	1×10^4	1×10^7
Silicon (14)				
Si-31	6×10^{-1}	6×10^{-1}	1×10^3	1×10^6
Si-32	4×10^1	5×10^{-1}	1×10^3	1×10^6
Samarium (62)				
Sm-145	1×10^1	1×10^1	1×10^2	1×10^7
Sm-147	Unlimited	Unlimited	1×10^1	1×10^4
Sm-151	4×10^1	1×10^1	1×10^4	1×10^8
Sm-153	9×10^0	6×10^{-1}	1×10^2	1×10^6
Tin (50)				
Sn-113 (a)	4×10^0	2×10^0	1×10^3	1×10^7
Sn-117m	7×10^0	4×10^{-1}	1×10^2	1×10^6
Sn-119m	4×10^1	3×10^1	1×10^3	1×10^7
Sn-121m (a)	4×10^1	9×10^{-1}	1×10^3	1×10^7
Sn-123	8×10^{-1}	6×10^{-1}	1×10^3	1×10^6
Sn-125	4×10^{-1}	4×10^{-1}	1×10^2	1×10^5
Sn-126 (a)	6×10^{-1}	4×10^{-1}	1×10^1	1×10^5

Radionuclide (atomic number)	A_1 (TBq)	A_2 (TBq)	Activity concentration limit for exempt material (Bq/g)	Activity limit for an exempt consignment (Bq)
Strontium (38)				
Sr-82 (a)	2×10^{-1}	2×10^{-1}	1×10^1	1×10^5
Sr-83	1×10^0	1×10^0	1×10^1	1×10^6
Sr-85	2×10^0	2×10^0	1×10^2	1×10^6
Sr-85m	5×10^0	5×10^0	1×10^2	1×10^7
Sr-87m	3×10^0	3×10^0	1×10^2	1×10^6
Sr-89	6×10^{-1}	6×10^{-1}	1×10^3	1×10^6
Sr-90 (a)	3×10^{-1}	3×10^{-1}	1×10^2 (b)	1×10^4 (b)
Sr-91 (a)	3×10^{-1}	3×10^{-1}	1×10^1	1×10^5
Sr-92 (a)	1×10^0	3×10^{-1}	1×10^1	1×10^6
Tritium (1)				
T(H-3)	4×10^1	4×10^1	1×10^6	1×10^9
Tantalum (73)				
Ta-178 (long-lived)	1×10^0	8×10^{-1}	1×10^1	1×10^6
Ta-179	3×10^1	3×10^1	1×10^3	1×10^7
Ta-182	9×10^{-1}	5×10^{-1}	1×10^1	1×10^4
Terbium (65)				
Tb-149	8×10^{-1}	8×10^{-1}	1×10^1	1×10^6
Tb-157	4×10^1	4×10^1	1×10^4	1×10^7
Tb-158	1×10^0	1×10^0	1×10^1	1×10^6
Tb-160	1×10^0	6×10^{-1}	1×10^1	1×10^6
Tb-161	3×10^1	7×10^{-1}	1×10^3	1×10^6
Technetium (43)				
Tc-95m (a)	2×10^0	2×10^0	1×10^1	1×10^6
Tc-96	4×10^{-1}	4×10^{-1}	1×10^1	1×10^6
Tc-96m (a)	4×10^{-1}	4×10^{-1}	1×10^3	1×10^7
Tc-97	Unlimited	Unlimited	1×10^3	1×10^8
Tc-97m	4×10^1	1×10^0	1×10^3	1×10^7
Tc-98	8×10^{-1}	7×10^{-1}	1×10^1	1×10^6
Tc-99	4×10^1	9×10^{-1}	1×10^4	1×10^7
Tc-99m	1×10^1	4×10^0	1×10^2	1×10^7

Radionuclide (atomic number)	A_1 (TBq)	A_2 (TBq)	Activity concentration limit for exempt material (Bq/g)	Activity limit for an exempt consignment (Bq)
Tellurium (52)				
Te-121	2×10^0	2×10^0	1×10^1	1×10^6
Te-121m	5×10^0	3×10^0	1×10^2	1×10^6
Te-123m	8×10^0	1×10^0	1×10^2	1×10^7
Te-125m	2×10^1	9×10^{-1}	1×10^3	1×10^7
Te-127	2×10^1	7×10^{-1}	1×10^3	1×10^6
Te-127m (a)	2×10^1	5×10^{-1}	1×10^3	1×10^7
Te-129	7×10^{-1}	6×10^{-1}	1×10^2	1×10^6
Te-129m (a)	8×10^{-1}	4×10^{-1}	1×10^3	1×10^6
Te-131m (a)	7×10^{-1}	5×10^{-1}	1×10^1	1×10^6
Te-132 (a)	5×10^{-1}	4×10^{-1}	1×10^2	1×10^7
Thorium (90)				
Th-227	1×10^1	5×10^{-3}	1×10^1	1×10^4
Th-228 (a)	5×10^{-1}	1×10^{-3}	1×10^0 (b)	1×10^4 (b)
Th-229	5×10^0	5×10^{-4}	1×10^0 (b)	1×10^3 (b)
Th-230	1×10^1	1×10^{-3}	1×10^0	1×10^4
Th-231	4×10^1	2×10^{-2}	1×10^3	1×10^7
Th-232	Unlimited	Unlimited	1×10^1	1×10^4
Th-234 (a)	3×10^{-1}	3×10^{-1}	1×10^3 (b)	1×10^5 (b)
Th(nat)	Unlimited	Unlimited	1×10^0 (b)	1×10^3 (b)
Titanium (22)				
Ti-44 (a)	5×10^{-1}	4×10^{-1}	1×10^1	1×10^5
Thallium (81)				
Tl-200	9×10^{-1}	9×10^{-1}	1×10^1	1×10^6
Tl-201	1×10^1	4×10^0	1×10^2	1×10^6
Tl-202	2×10^0	2×10^0	1×10^2	1×10^6
Tl-204	1×10^1	7×10^{-1}	1×10^4	1×10^4
Thulium (69)				
Tm-167	7×10^0	8×10^{-1}	1×10^2	1×10^6
Tm-170	3×10^0	6×10^{-1}	1×10^3	1×10^6
Tm-171	4×10^1	4×10^1	1×10^4	1×10^8

Radionuclide (atomic number)	A_1 (TBq)	A_2 (TBq)	Activity concentration limit for exempt material (Bq/g)	Activity limit for an exempt consignment (Bq)
Uranium (92)				
U-230 (fast lung absorption) (a)(d)	4×10^1	1×10^{-1}	1×10^1 (b)	1×10^5 (b)
U-230 (medium lung absorption) (a)(e)	4×10^1	4×10^{-3}	1×10^1	1×10^4
U-230 (slow lung absorption) (a)(f)	3×10^1	3×10^{-3}	1×10^1	1×10^4
U-232 (fast lung absorption) (d)	4×10^1	1×10^{-2}	1×10^0 (b)	1×10^3 (b)
U-232 (medium lung absorption) (e)	4×10^1	7×10^{-3}	1×10^1	1×10^4
U-232 (slow lung absorption) (f)	1×10^1	1×10^{-3}	1×10^1	1×10^4
U-233 (fast lung absorption) (d)	4×10^1	9×10^{-2}	1×10^1	1×10^4
U-233 (medium lung absorption) (e)	4×10^1	2×10^{-2}	1×10^2	1×10^5
U-233 (slow lung absorption) (f)	4×10^1	6×10^{-3}	1×10^1	1×10^5
U-234 (fast lung absorption) (d)	4×10^1	9×10^{-2}	1×10^1	1×10^4
U-234 (medium lung absorption) (e)	4×10^1	2×10^{-2}	1×10^2	1×10^5
U-234 (slow lung absorption) (f)	4×10^1	6×10^{-3}	1×10^1	1×10^5
U-235 (all lung absorption types) (a)(d)(e)(f)	Unlimited	Unlimited	1×10^1 (b)	1×10^4 (b)
U-236 (fast lung absorption) (d)	Unlimited	Unlimited	1×10^1	1×10^4
U-236 (medium lung absorption) (e)	4×10^1	2×10^{-2}	1×10^2	1×10^5
U-236 (slow lung absorption) (f)	4×10^1	6×10^{-3}	1×10^1	1×10^4
U-238 (all lung absorption types) (d)(e)(f)	Unlimited	Unlimited	1×10^1 (b)	1×10^4 (b)
U (nat)	Unlimited	Unlimited	1×10^0 (b)	1×10^3 (b)
U (enriched to 20% or less) (g)	Unlimited	Unlimited	1×10^0	1×10^3
U (dep)	Unlimited	Unlimited	1×10^0	1×10^3
Vanadium (23)				
V-48	4×10^{-1}	4×10^{-1}	1×10^1	1×10^5
V-49	4×10^1	4×10^1	1×10^4	1×10^7
Tungsten (74)				
W-178 (a)	9×10^0	5×10^0	1×10^1	1×10^6
W-181	3×10^1	3×10^1	1×10^3	1×10^7
W-185	4×10^1	8×10^{-1}	1×10^4	1×10^7
W-187	2×10^0	6×10^{-1}	1×10^2	1×10^6
W-188 (a)	4×10^{-1}	3×10^{-1}	1×10^2	1×10^5

Radionuclide (atomic number)	A_1 (TBq)	A_2 (TBq)	Activity concentration limit for exempt material (Bq/g)	Activity limit for an exempt consignment (Bq)
Xenon (54)				
Xe-122 (a)	4×10^{-1}	4×10^{-1}	1×10^2	1×10^9
Xe-123	2×10^0	7×10^{-1}	1×10^2	1×10^9
Xe-127	4×10^0	2×10^0	1×10^3	1×10^5
Xe-131m	4×10^1	4×10^1	1×10^4	1×10^4
Xe-133	2×10^1	1×10^1	1×10^3	1×10^4
Xe-135	3×10^0	2×10^0	1×10^3	1×10^{10}
Yttrium (39)				
Y-87 (a)	1×10^0	1×10^0	1×10^1	1×10^6
Y-88	4×10^{-1}	4×10^{-1}	1×10^1	1×10^6
Y-90	3×10^{-1}	3×10^{-1}	1×10^3	1×10^5
Y-91	6×10^{-1}	6×10^{-1}	1×10^3	1×10^6
Y-91m	2×10^0	2×10^0	1×10^2	1×10^6
Y-92	2×10^{-1}	2×10^{-1}	1×10^2	1×10^5
Y-93	3×10^{-1}	3×10^{-1}	1×10^2	1×10^5
Ytterbium (70)				
Yb-169	4×10^0	1×10^0	1×10^2	1×10^7
Yb-175	3×10^1	9×10^{-1}	1×10^3	1×10^7
Zinc (30)				
Zn-65	2×10^0	2×10^0	1×10^1	1×10^6
Zn-69	3×10^0	6×10^{-1}	1×10^4	1×10^6
Zn-69m (a)	3×10^0	6×10^{-1}	1×10^2	1×10^6
Zirconium (40)				
Zr-88	3×10^0	3×10^0	1×10^2	1×10^6
Zr-93	Unlimited	Unlimited	1×10^3 (b)	1×10^7 (b)
Zr-95 (a)	2×10^0	8×10^{-1}	1×10^1	1×10^6
Zr-97 (a)	4×10^{-1}	4×10^{-1}	1×10^1 (b)	1×10^5 (b)

(a) A_1 and/or A_2 values for these parent radionuclides include contributions from their progeny with half-lives less than 10 days, as listed in the following:

Mg-28	Al-28
Ar-42	K-42
Ca-47	Sc-47
Ti-44	Sc-44
Fe-52	Mn-52m
Fe-60	Co-60m
Zn-69m	Zn-69
Ge-68	Ga-68
Rb-83	Kr-83m
Sr-82	Rb-82
Sr-90	Y-90
Sr-91	Y-91m
Sr-92	Y-92
Y-87	Sr-87m
Zr-95	Nb-95m
Zr-97	Nb-97m, Nb-97
Mo-99	Tc-99m
Tc-95m	Tc-95
Tc-96m	Tc-96
Ru-103	Rh-103m
Ru-106	Rh-106
Pd-103	Rh-103m
Ag-108m	Ag-108
Ag-110m	Ag-110
Cd-115	In-115m
In-114m	In-114
Sn-113	In-113m
Sn-121m	Sn-121
Sn-126	Sb-126m
Te-118	Sb-118
Te-127m	Te-127
Te-129m	Te-129
Te-131m	Te-131
Te-132	I-132
I-135	Xe-135m
Xe-122	I-122
Cs-137	Ba-137m
Ba-131	Cs-131
Ba-140	La-140
Ce-144	Pr-144m, Pr-144
Pm-148m	Pm-148
Gd-146	Eu-146
Dy-166	Ho-166
Hf-172	Lu-172
W-178	Ta-178
W-188	Re-188
Re-189	Os-189m
Os-194	Ir-194
Ir-189	Os-189m
Pt-188	Ir-188
Hg-194	Au-194
Hg-195m	Hg-195
Pb-210	Bi-210
Pb-212	Bi-212, Tl-208, Po-212

Bi-210m	Tl-206
Bi-212	Tl-208, Po-212
At-211	Po-211
Rn-222	Po-218, Pb-214, At-218, Bi-214, Po-214
Ra-223	Rn-219, Po-215, Pb-211, Bi-211, Po-211, Tl-207
Ra-224	Rn-220, Po-216, Pb-212, Bi-212, Tl-208, Po-212
Ra-225	Ac-225, Fr-221, At-217, Bi-213, Tl-209, Po-213, Pb-209
Ra-226	Rn-222, Po-218, Pb-214, At-218, Bi-214, Po-214
Ra-228	Ac-228
Ac-225	Fr-221, At-217, Bi-213, Tl-209, Po-213, Pb-209
Ac-227	Fr-223
Th-228	Ra-224, Rn-220, Po-216, Pb-212, Bi-212, Tl-208, Po-212
Th-234	Pa-234m, Pa-234
Pa-230	Ac-226, Th-226, Fr-222, Ra-222, Rn-218, Po-214
U-230	Th-226, Ra-222, Rn-218, Po-214
U-235	Th-231
Pu-241	U-237
Pu-244	U-240, Np-240m
Am-242m	Am-242, Np-238
Am-243	Np-239
Cm-247	Pu-243
Bk-249	Am-245
Cf-253	Cm-249

(b) Parent nuclides and their progeny included in secular equilibrium are listed in the following (the activity to be taken into account is that of the parent nuclide only):

Sr-90	Y-90
Zr-93	Nb-93m
Zr-97	Nb-97
Ru-106	Rh-106
Ag-108m	Ag-108
Cs-137	Ba-137m
Ce-144	Pr-144
Ba-140	La-140
Bi-212	Tl-208 (0.36), Po-212 (0.64)
Pb-210	Bi-210, Po-210
Pb-212	Bi-212, Tl-208 (0.36), Po-212 (0.64)
Rn-222	Po-218, Pb-214, Bi-214, Po-214
Ra-223	Rn-219, Po-215, Pb-211, Bi-211, Tl-207
Ra-224	Rn-220, Po-216, Pb-212, Bi-212, Tl-208 (0.36), Po-212 (0.64)
Ra-226	Rn-222, Po-218, Pb-214, Bi-214, Po-214, Pb-210, Bi-210, Po-210
Ra-228	Ac-228
Th-228	Ra-224, Rn-220, Po-216, Pb212, Bi-212, Tl208 (0.36), Po-212 (0.64)
Th-229	Ra-225, Ac-225, Fr-221, At-217, Bi-213, Po-213, Pb-209
Th-nat[5]	Ra-228, Ac-228, Th-228, Ra-224, Rn-220, Po-216, Pb-212, Bi-212, l208(0.36), Po-212 (0.64)
Th-234	Pa-234m
U-230	Th-226, Ra-222, Rn-218, Po-214
U-232	Th-228, Ra-224, Rn-220, Po-216, Pb-212, Bi-212, Tl-208 (0.36), Po-212 (0.64)
U-235	Th-231
U-238	Th-234, Pa-234m

---

[5] *In the case of Th-natural, the parent nuclide is Th-232, in the case of U-natural the parent nuclide is U-238.*

U-nat[5]	Th-234, Pa-234m, U-234, Th-230, Ra-226, Rn-222, Po-218, Pb-214, Bi-214, Po-214, Pb-210, Bi-210, Po-210
Np-237	Pa-233
Am-242m	Am-242
Am-243	Np-239

(c)   The quantity may be determined from a measurement of the rate of decay or a measurement of the dose rate at a prescribed distance from the source.

(d)   These values apply only to compounds of uranium that take the chemical form of UF_6, UO_2F_2 and $UO_2(NO_3)_2$ in both normal and accident conditions of carriage.

(e)   These values apply only to compounds of uranium that take the chemical form of UO_3, UF_4, UCl_4 and hexavalent compounds in both normal and accident conditions of carriage.

(f)   These values apply to all compounds of uranium other than those specified in (d) and (e) above.

(g)   These values apply to unirradiated uranium only.

2.2.7.2.2.2   For individual radionuclides:

(a)   Which are not listed in Table 2.2.7.2.2.1 the determination of the basic radionuclide values referred to in 2.2.7.2.2.1 shall require multilateral approval. For these radionuclides, activity concentration limits for exempt material and activity limits for exempt consignments shall be calculated in accordance with the principles established in "Radiation Protection and Safety of Radiation Sources: International Basic Safety Standards", IAEA Safety Standards Series No. GSR Part 3, IAEA, Vienna (2014). It is permissible to use an A_2 value calculated using a dose coefficient for the appropriate lung absorption type as recommended by the International Commission on Radiological Protection, if the chemical forms of each radionuclide under both normal and accident conditions of carriage are taken into consideration. Alternatively, the radionuclide values in Table 2.2.7.2.2.2 may be used without obtaining competent authority approval;

(b)   In instruments or articles in which the radioactive material is enclosed or is included as a component part of the instrument or other manufactured article and which meet 2.2.7.2.4.1.3 (c), alternative basic radionuclide values to those in Table 2.2.7.2.2.1 for the activity limit for an exempt consignment are permitted and shall require multilateral approval. Such alternative activity limits for an exempt consignment shall be calculated in accordance with the principles set out in GSR Part 3.

---

[5]   *In the case of Th-natural, the parent nuclide is Th-232, in the case of U-natural the parent nuclide is U-238.*

Table 2.2.7.2.2.2: Basic radionuclide values for unknown radionuclides or mixtures

Radioactive contents	A_1 (TBq)	A_2 (TBq)	Activity concentration limit for exempt material (Bq/g)	Activity limit for exempt consignments (Bq)
Only beta or gamma emitting nuclides are known to be present	0.1	0.02	1×10^1	1×10^4
Alpha emitting nuclides but no neutron emitters are known to be present	0.2	9×10^{-5}	1×10^{-1}	1×10^3
Neutron emitting nuclides are known to be present or no relevant data are available	0.001	9×10^{-5}	1×10^{-1}	1×10^3

2.2.7.2.2.3   In the calculations of A_1 and A_2 for a radionuclide not in Table 2.2.7.2.2.1, a single radioactive decay chain in which the radionuclides are present in their naturally occurring proportions, and in which no progeny nuclide has a half-life either longer than 10 days or longer than that of the parent nuclide, shall be considered as a single radionuclide; and the activity to be taken into account and the A_1 or A_2 value to be applied shall be those corresponding to the parent nuclide of that chain. In the case of radioactive decay chains in which any progeny nuclide has a half-life either longer than 10 days or greater than that of the parent nuclide, the parent and such progeny nuclides shall be considered as mixtures of different nuclides.

2.2.7.2.2.4   For mixtures of radionuclides, the basic radionuclide values referred to in 2.2.7.2.2.1 may be determined as follows:

$$X_m = \frac{1}{\sum_i \dfrac{f(i)}{X(i)}}$$

where,

f(i)   is the fraction of activity or activity concentration of radionuclide i in the mixture;

X(i)   is the appropriate value of A_1 or A_2, or the activity concentration limit for exempt material or the activity limit for an exempt consignment as appropriate for the radionuclide i; and

X_m is the derived value of A_1 or A_2, or the activity concentration limit for exempt material or the activity limit for an exempt consignment in the case of a mixture.

2.2.7.2.2.5   When the identity of each radionuclide is known but the individual activities of some of the radionuclides are not known, the radionuclides may be grouped and the lowest radionuclide value, as appropriate, for the radionuclides in each group may be used in applying the formulas in 2.2.7.2.2.4 and 2.2.7.2.4.4. Groups may be based on the total alpha activity and the total beta/gamma activity when these are known, using the lowest radionuclide values for the alpha emitters or beta/gamma emitters, respectively.

2.2.7.2.2.6   For individual radionuclides or for mixtures of radionuclides for which relevant data are not available, the values shown in Table 2.2.7.2.2.2 shall be used.

2.2.7.2.3   *Determination of other material characteristics*

2.2.7.2.3.1   Low specific activity (LSA) material

2.2.7.2.3.1.1   *(Reserved)*

2.2.7.2.3.1.2   LSA material shall be in one of three groups:

       (a)   LSA-I

           (i)   uranium and thorium ores and concentrates of such ores, and other ores containing naturally occurring radionuclides;

           (ii)   natural uranium, depleted uranium, natural thorium or their compounds or mixtures, that are unirradiated and in solid or liquid form;

           (iii)   radioactive material for which the A_2 value is unlimited. Fissile material may be included only if excepted under 2.2.7.2.3.5;

           (iv)   other radioactive material in which the activity is distributed throughout and the estimated average specific activity does not exceed 30 times the values for activity concentration specified in 2.2.7.2.2.1 to 2.2.7.2.2.6. Fissile material may be included only if excepted under 2.2.7.2.3.5;

       (b)   LSA-II

           (i)   water with tritium concentration up to 0.8 TBq/l;

           (ii)   other material in which the activity is distributed throughout and the estimated average specific activity does not exceed 10^{-4} A_2/g for solids and gases, and 10^{-5} A_2/g for liquids;

       (c)   LSA-III - Solids (e.g. consolidated wastes, activated materials), excluding powders in which:

           (i)   the radioactive material is distributed throughout a solid or a collection of solid objects, or is essentially uniformly distributed in a solid compact binding agent (such as concrete, bitumen and ceramic);

           (ii)   the estimated average specific activity of the solid, excluding any shielding material, does not exceed 2×10^{-3} A_2/g.

2.2.7.2.3.1.3 to 2.2.7.2.3.1.5   *(Deleted)*

2.2.7.2.3.2   Surface contaminated object (SCO)

SCO is classified in one of three groups:

       (a)   SCO-I: A solid object on which:

           (i)   the non-fixed contamination on the accessible surface averaged over 300 cm^2 (or the area of the surface if less than 300 cm^2) does not exceed 4 Bq/cm^2 for beta and gamma emitters and low toxicity alpha emitters, or 0.4 Bq/cm^2 for all other alpha emitters; and

(ii)   the fixed contamination on the accessible surface averaged over 300 cm^2 (or the area of the surface if less than 300 cm^2) does not exceed 4×10^4 Bq/cm^2 for beta and gamma emitters and low toxicity alpha emitters, or 4×10^3 Bq/cm^2 for all other alpha emitters; and

(iii)   the non-fixed contamination plus the fixed contamination on the inaccessible surface averaged over 300 cm^2 (or the area of the surface if less than 300 cm^2) does not exceed 4×10^4 Bq/cm^2 for beta and gamma emitters and low toxicity alpha emitters, or 4×10^3 Bq/cm^2 for all other alpha emitters;

(b)   SCO-II: A solid object on which either the fixed or non-fixed contamination on the surface exceeds the applicable limits specified for SCO-I in (a) above and on which:

(i)   the non-fixed contamination on the accessible surface averaged over 300 cm^2 (or the area of the surface if less than 300 cm^2) does not exceed 400 Bq/cm^2 for beta and gamma emitters and low toxicity alpha emitters, or 40 Bq/cm^2 for all other alpha emitters; and

(ii)   the fixed contamination on the accessible surface, averaged over 300 cm^2 (or the area of the surface if less than 300 cm^2) does not exceed 8×10^5 Bq/cm^2 for beta and gamma emitters and low toxicity alpha emitters, or 8×10^4 Bq/cm^2 for all other alpha emitters; and

(iii)   the non-fixed contamination plus the fixed contamination on the inaccessible surface averaged over 300 cm^2 (or the area of the surface if less than 300 cm^2) does not exceed 8×10^5 Bq/cm^2 for beta and gamma emitters and low toxicity alpha emitters, or 8×10^4 Bq/cm^2 for all other alpha emitters.

(c)   SCO-III: A large solid object which, because of its size, cannot be carried in a type of package described in ADN and for which:

(i)   all openings are sealed to prevent release of radioactive material during conditions defined in 4.1.9.2.4 (e) of ADR;

(ii)   the inside of the object is as dry as practicable;

(iii)   the non-fixed contamination on the external surfaces does not exceed the limits specified in 4.1.9.1.2 of ADR; and

(iv)   the non-fixed contamination plus the fixed contamination on the inaccessible surface averaged over 300 cm^2 does not exceed 8×10^5 Bq/cm^2 for beta and gamma emitters and low toxicity alpha emitters, or 8×10^4 Bq/cm^2 for all other alpha emitters.

2.2.7.2.3.3   Special form radioactive material

2.2.7.2.3.3.1   Special form radioactive material shall have at least one dimension not less than 5 mm. When a sealed capsule constitutes part of the special form radioactive material, the capsule shall be so manufactured that it can be opened only by destroying it. The design for special form radioactive material requires unilateral approval.

2.2.7.2.3.3.2   Special form radioactive material shall be of such a nature or shall be so designed that if it is subjected to the tests specified in 2.2.7.2.3.3.4 to 2.2.7.2.3.3.8, it shall meet the following requirements:

(a)   It would not break or shatter under the impact, percussion and bending tests 2.2.7.2.3.3.5 (a), (b), (c), 2.2.7.2.3.3.6 (a) as applicable;

(b)   It would not melt or disperse in the applicable heat test 2.2.7.2.3.3.5 (d) or 2.2.7.2.3.3.6 (b) as applicable; and

(c)   The activity in the water from the leaching tests specified in 2.2.7.2.3.3.7 and 2.2.7.2.3.3.8 would not exceed 2 kBq; or alternatively for sealed sources, the leakage rate for the volumetric leakage assessment test specified in ISO 9978:1992 "Radiation Protection - Sealed Radioactive Sources - Leakage Test Methods", would not exceed the applicable acceptance threshold acceptable to the competent authority.

2.2.7.2.3.3.3   Demonstration of compliance with the performance standards in 2.2.7.2.3.3.2 shall be in accordance with 6.4.12.1 and 6.4.12.2 of ADR.

2.2.7.2.3.3.4   Specimens that comprise or simulate special form radioactive material shall be subjected to the impact test, the percussion test, the bending test, and the heat test specified in 2.2.7.2.3.3.5 or alternative tests as authorized in 2.2.7.2.3.3.6. A different specimen may be used for each of the tests. Following each test, a leaching assessment or volumetric leakage test shall be performed on the specimen by a method no less sensitive than the methods given in 2.2.7.2.3.3.7 for indispersible solid material or 2.2.7.2.3.3.8 for encapsulated material.

2.2.7.2.3.3.5   The relevant test methods are:

(a)   Impact test: The specimen shall drop onto the target from a height of 9 m. The target shall be as defined in 6.4.14 of ADR;

(b)   Percussion test: The specimen shall be placed on a sheet of lead which is supported by a smooth solid surface and struck by the flat face of a mild steel bar so as to cause an impact equivalent to that resulting from a free drop of 1.4 kg from a height of 1 m. The lower part of the bar shall be 25 mm in diameter with the edges rounded off to a radius of (3.0 ± 0.3) mm. The lead, of hardness number 3.5 to 4.5 on the Vickers scale and not more than 25 mm thick, shall cover an area greater than that covered by the specimen. A fresh surface of lead shall be used for each impact. The bar shall strike the specimen so as to cause maximum damage;

(c)   Bending test: The test shall apply only to long, slender sources with both a minimum length of 10 cm and a length to minimum width ratio of not less than 10. The specimen shall be rigidly clamped in a horizontal position so that one half of its length protrudes from the face of the clamp. The orientation of the specimen shall be such that the specimen will suffer maximum damage when its free end is struck by the flat face of a steel bar. The bar shall strike the specimen so as to cause an impact equivalent to that resulting from a free vertical drop of 1.4 kg from a height of 1 m. The lower part of the bar shall be 25 mm in diameter with the edges rounded off to a radius of (3.0 ± 0.3) mm;

(d)   Heat test: The specimen shall be heated in air to a temperature of 800 °C and held at that temperature for a period of 10 minutes and shall then be allowed to cool.

2.2.7.2.3.3.6   Specimens that comprise or simulate radioactive material enclosed in a sealed capsule may be excepted from:

(a)   The tests prescribed in 2.2.7.2.3.3.5 (a) and (b) provided that the specimens are alternatively subjected to the impact test prescribed in ISO 2919:2012: "Radiation Protection - Sealed Radioactive Sources - General requirements and classification":

(i)   The Class 4 impact test if the mass of the special form radioactive material is equal to or less than 200 g;

(ii)   The Class 5 impact test if the mass of the special form radioactive material is more than 200 g but less than 500 g;

(b)   The test prescribed in 2.2.7.2.3.3.5 (d) provided they are alternatively subjected to the Class 6 temperature test specified in ISO 2919:2012 "Radiation protection - Sealed radioactive sources - General requirements and classification".

2.2.7.2.3.3.7   For specimens which comprise or simulate indispersible solid material, a leaching assessment shall be performed as follows:

(a)   The specimen shall be immersed for 7 days in water at ambient temperature. The volume of water to be used in the test shall be sufficient to ensure that at the end of the 7 day test period the free volume of the unabsorbed and unreacted water remaining shall be at least 10% of the volume of the solid test sample itself. The water shall have an initial pH of 6-8 and a maximum conductivity of 1 mS/m at 20 °C;

(b)   The water and the specimen shall then be heated to a temperature of (50 ± 5) °C and maintained at this temperature for 4 hours;

(c)   The activity of the water shall then be determined;

(d)   The specimen shall then be kept for at least 7 days in still air at not less than 30 °C and relative humidity not less than 90%;

(e)   The specimen shall then be immersed in water of the same specification as in (a) above and the water and the specimen heated to (50 ± 5) °C and maintained at this temperature for 4 hours;

(f)   The activity of the water shall then be determined.

2.2.7.2.3.3.8   For specimens which comprise or simulate radioactive material enclosed in a sealed capsule, either a leaching assessment or a volumetric leakage assessment shall be performed as follows:

(a)   The leaching assessment shall consist of the following steps:

(i)   the specimen shall be immersed in water at ambient temperature. The water shall have an initial pH of 6-8 with a maximum conductivity of 1 mS/m at 20 °C;

(ii)   the water and specimen shall then be heated to a temperature of (50 ± 5) °C and maintained at this temperature for 4 hours;

(iii)   the activity of the water shall then be determined;

(iv)   the specimen shall then be kept for at least 7 days in still air at not less than 30°C and relative humidity of not less than 90%;

(v)   the process in (i), (ii) and (iii) shall be repeated;

(b) The alternative volumetric leakage assessment shall comprise any of the tests prescribed in ISO 9978:1992 "Radiation Protection - Sealed radioactive sources - Leakage test methods", provided that they are acceptable to the competent authority.

2.2.7.2.3.4   Low dispersible radioactive material

2.2.7.2.3.4.1   The design for low dispersible radioactive material shall require multilateral approval. Low dispersible radioactive material shall be such that the total amount of this radioactive material in a package, taking into account the provisions of 6.4.8.14 of ADR, shall meet the following requirements:

(a) The dose rate at 3 m from the unshielded radioactive material does not exceed 10 mSv/h;

(b) If subjected to the tests specified in 6.4.20.3 and 6.4.20.4 of ADR, the airborne release in gaseous and particulate forms of up to 100 μm aerodynamic equivalent diameter would not exceed 100 A_2. A separate specimen may be used for each test; and

(c) If subjected to the test specified in 2.2.7.2.3.4.3 the activity in the water would not exceed 100 A_2. In the application of this test, the damaging effects of the tests specified in (b) above shall be taken into account.

2.2.7.2.3.4.2   Low dispersible radioactive material shall be tested as follows:

A specimen that comprises or simulates low dispersible radioactive material shall be subjected to the enhanced thermal test specified in 6.4.20.3 of ADR and the impact test specified in 6.4.20.4 of ADR. A different specimen may be used for each of the tests. Following each test, the specimen shall be subjected to the leach test specified in 2.2.7.2.3.4.3. After each test it shall be determined if the applicable requirements of 2.2.7.2.3.4.1 have been met.

2.2.7.2.3.4.3   A solid material sample representing the entire contents of the package shall be immersed for 7 days in water at ambient temperature. The volume of water to be used in the test shall be sufficient to ensure that at the end of the 7-day test period the free volume of the unabsorbed and unreacted water remaining shall be at least 10 % of the volume of the solid test sample itself. The water shall have an initial pH of 6-8 and a maximum conductivity of 1 mS/m at 20 °C. The total activity of the free volume of water shall be measured following the 7-day immersion of the test sample.

2.2.7.2.3.4.4   Demonstration of compliance with the performance standards in 2.2.7.2.3.4.1, 2.2.7.2.3.4.2 and 2.2.7.2.3.4.3 shall be in accordance with 6.4.12.1 and 6.4.12.2 of ADR.

2.2.7.2.3.5   Fissile material

Fissile material and packages containing fissile material shall be classified under the relevant entry as "FISSILE" in accordance with Table 2.2.7.2.1.1 unless excepted by one of the provisions of sub-paragraphs (a) to (f) below and carried subject to the requirements of 7.1.4.14.7.4.3. All provisions apply only to material in packages that meets the requirements of 6.4.7.2 of ADR unless unpackaged material is specifically allowed in the provision.

(a) Uranium enriched in uranium-235 to a maximum of 1% by mass, and with a total plutonium and uranium-233 content not exceeding 1% of the mass of uranium-235, provided that the fissile nuclides are distributed essentially homogeneously throughout the material. In addition, if uranium-235 is present in metallic, oxide or carbide forms, it shall not form a lattice arrangement;

(b) Liquid solutions of uranyl nitrate enriched in uranium-235 to a maximum of 2% by mass, with a total plutonium and uranium-233 content not exceeding 0.002% of the mass of uranium, and with a minimum nitrogen to uranium atomic ratio (N/U) of 2;

(c)   Uranium with a maximum uranium enrichment of 5% by mass uranium-235 provided:

   (i)   There is no more than 3.5 g of uranium-235 per package;

   (ii)   The total plutonium and uranium-233 content does not exceed 1% of the mass of uranium-235 per package;

   (iii)   Carriage of the package is subject to the consignment limit provided in 7.1.4.14.7.4.3 (c);

(d)   Fissile nuclides with a total mass not greater than 2.0 g per package provided the package is carried subject to the consignment limit provided in 7.1.4.14.7.4.3 (d);

(e)   Fissile nuclides with a total mass not greater than 45 g either packaged or unpackaged subject to the requirements of 7.1.4.14.7.4.3 (e);

(f)   A fissile material that meets the requirements of 7.1.4.14.7.4.3 (b), 2.2.7.2.3.6 and 5.1.5.2.1.

2.2.7.2.3.6   Fissile material excepted from classification as "FISSILE" under 2.2.7.2.3.5 (f) shall be subcritical without the need for accumulation control under the following conditions:

(a)   The conditions of 6.4.11.1 (a) of ADR;

(b)   The conditions consistent with the assessment provisions stated in 6.4.11.12 (b) and 6.4.11.13 (b) of ADR for packages.

2.2.7.2.4   *Classification of packages or unpacked material*

The quantity of radioactive material in a package shall not exceed the relevant limits for the package type as specified below.

2.2.7.2.4.1   Classification as excepted package

2.2.7.2.4.1.1   A package may be classified as an excepted package if it meets one of the following conditions:

(a)   It is an empty package having contained radioactive material;

(b)   It contains instruments or articles not exceeding the activity limits specified in columns (2) and (3) of Table 2.2.7.2.4.1.2;

(c)   It contains articles manufactured of natural uranium, depleted uranium or natural thorium;

(d)   It contains radioactive material not exceeding the activity limits specified in column (4) of Table 2.2.7.2.4.1.2; or

(e)   It contains less than 0.1 kg of uranium hexafluoride not exceeding the activity limits specified in column (4) of Table 2.2.7.2.4.1.2.

2.2.7.2.4.1.2   A package containing radioactive material may be classified as an excepted package provided that the dose rate at any point on its external surface does not exceed 5 µSv/h.

Table 2.2.7.2.4.1.2: Activity limits for excepted packages

Physical state of contents	Instruments or article		Materials
	Item limits [a]	Package limits [a]	Package limits [a]
(1)	(2)	(3)	(4)
Solids			
special form	$10^{-2}\,A_1$	A_1	$10^{-3}\,A_1$
other form	$10^{-2}\,A_2$	A_2	$10^{-3}\,A_2$
Liquids	$10^{-3}\,A_2$	$10^{-1}\,A_2$	$10^{-4}\,A_2$
Gases			
Tritium	$2 \times 10^{-2}\,A_2$	$2 \times 10^{-1}\,A_2$	$2 \times 10^{-2}\,A_2$
special form	$10^{-3}\,A_1$	$10^{-2}\,A_1$	$10^{-3}\,A_1$
other forms	$10^{-3}\,A_2$	$10^{-2}\,A_2$	$10^{-3}\,A_2$

[a] *For mixtures of radionuclides, see 2.2.7.2.2.4 to 2.2.7.2.2.6.*

2.2.7.2.4.1.3   Radioactive material which is enclosed in or is included as a component part of an instrument or other manufactured article may be classified under UN No. 2911 RADIOACTIVE MATERIAL, EXCEPTED PACKAGE - INSTRUMENTS or ARTICLES provided that:

(a)   The dose rate at 10 cm from any point on the external surface of any unpackaged instrument or article is not greater than 0.1 mSv/h;

(b)   Each instrument or manufactured article bears the mark "RADIOACTIVE" on its external surface except for the following:

(i)   radioluminescent time-pieces or devices;

(ii)   consumer products that have either received regulatory approval in accordance with 1.7.1.4 (e) or do not individually exceed the activity limit for an exempt consignment in Table 2.2.7.2.2.1 (column 5), provided such products are transported in a package that bears the mark "RADIOACTIVE" on its internal surface in such a manner that a warning of the presence of radioactive material is visible on opening the package; and

(iii)   other instruments or articles too small to bear the mark "RADIOACTIVE", provided that they are transported in a package that bears the mark "RADIOACTIVE" on its internal surface in such a manner that a warning of the presence of radioactive material is visible on opening the package;

(c)   The active material is completely enclosed by non-active components (a device performing the sole function of containing radioactive material shall not be considered to be an instrument or manufactured article);

(d)   The limits specified in columns 2 and 3 of Table 2.2.7.2.4.1.2 are met for each individual item and each package, respectively;

(e)   *(Reserved)*;

(f)   If the package contains fissile material, one of the provisions of 2.2.7.2.3.5 (a) to (f) applies.

2.2.7.2.4.1.4   Radioactive material in forms other than as specified in 2.2.7.2.4.1.3 and with an activity not exceeding the limits specified in column 4 of Table 2.2.7.2.4.1.2, may be classified under UN No. 2910 RADIOACTIVE MATERIAL, EXCEPTED PACKAGE - LIMITED QUANTITY OF MATERIAL provided that:

(a)   The package retains its radioactive contents under routine conditions of carriage;

(b)   The package bears the mark "RADIOACTIVE" on either:

     (i)   An internal surface in such a manner that a warning of the presence of radioactive material is visible on opening the package; or

     (ii)   The outside of the package, where it is impractical to mark an internal surface; and

(c)   If the package contains fissile material, one of the provisions of 2.2.7.2.3.5 (a) to (f) applies.

2.2.7.2.4.1.5   Uranium hexafluoride not exceeding the limits specified in Column 4 of Table 2.2.7.2.4.1.2 may be classified under UN 3507 URANIUM HEXAFLUORIDE, RADIOACTIVE MATERIAL, EXCEPTED PACKAGE, less than 0.1 kg per package, non-fissile or fissile-excepted provided that:

(a)   The mass of uranium hexafluoride in the package is less than 0.1 kg;

(b)   The conditions of 2.2.7.2.4.5.2 and 2.2.7.2.4.1.4 (a) and (b) are met.

2.2.7.2.4.1.6   Articles manufactured of natural uranium, depleted uranium or natural thorium and articles in which the sole radioactive material is unirradiated natural uranium, unirradiated depleted uranium or unirradiated natural thorium may be classified under UN No. 2909 RADIOACTIVE MATERIAL, EXCEPTED PACKAGE - ARTICLES MANUFACTURED FROM NATURAL URANIUM or DEPLETED URANIUM or NATURAL THORIUM, provided that the outer surface of the uranium or thorium is enclosed in an inactive sheath made of metal or some other substantial material.

2.2.7.2.4.1.7   An empty packaging which had previously contained radioactive material may be classified under UN No. 2908 RADIOACTIVE MATERIAL, EXCEPTED PACKAGE - EMPTY PACKAGING, provided that:

(a)   It is in a well-maintained condition and securely closed;

(b)   The outer surface of any uranium or thorium in its structure is covered with an inactive sheath made of metal or some other substantial material;

(c)   The level of internal non-fixed contamination, when averaged over any 300 cm^2, does not exceed:

     (i)   400 Bq/cm^2 for beta and gamma emitters and low toxicity alpha emitters; and

     (ii)   40 Bq/cm^2 for all other alpha emitters;

(d)   Any labels which may have been displayed on it in conformity with 5.2.2.1.11.1 are no longer visible; and

(e)   If the packaging has contained fissile material, one of the provisions of 2.2.7.2.3.5 (a) to (f) or one of the provisions for exclusion in 2.2.7.1.3 applies.

2.2.7.2.4.2   Classification as Low specific activity (LSA) material

Radioactive material may only be classified as LSA material if the definition of LSA in 2.2.7.1.3 and the conditions of 2.2.7.2.3.1, 4.1.9.2 and 7.5.11 CV33 (2) of ADR are met.

2.2.7.2.4.3   Classification as Surface contaminated object (SCO)

Radioactive material may be classified as SCO if the definition of SCO in 2.2.7.1.3 and the conditions of 2.2.7.2.3.2, 4.1.9.2 and 7.5.11 CV33 (2) of ADR are met.

2.2.7.2.4.4   Classification as Type A package

Packages containing radioactive material may be classified as Type A packages provided that the following conditions are met:

Type A packages shall not contain activities greater than either of the following:

(a)   For special form radioactive material - A_1;

(b)   For all other radioactive material - A_2.

For mixtures of radionuclides whose identities and respective activities are known, the following condition shall apply to the radioactive contents of a Type A package:

$$\Sigma_i \frac{B(i)}{A_1(i)} + \Sigma_j \frac{C(j)}{A_2(j)} \leq 1$$

where   B(i)   is the activity of radionuclide i as special form radioactive material;

          $A_1(i)$ is the A_1 value for radionuclide i;

          C (j)   is the activity of radionuclide j as other than special form radioactive material;

          A_2 (j)   is the A_2 value for radionuclide j.

2.2.7.2.4.5   *Classification of uranium hexafluoride*

2.2.7.2.4.5.1   Uranium hexafluoride shall only be assigned to:

(a)   UN No. 2977, RADIOACTIVE MATERIAL, URANIUM HEXAFLUORIDE, FISSILE;

(b)   UN No. 2978, RADIOACTIVE MATERIAL, URANIUM HEXAFLUORIDE, non-fissile or fissile-excepted; or

(c)   UN No. 3507, URANIUM HEXAFLUORIDE, RADIOACTIVE MATERIAL, EXCEPTED PACKAGE less than 0.1 kg per package, non-fissile or fissile-excepted.

2.2.7.2.4.5.2   The contents of a package containing uranium hexafluoride shall comply with the following requirements:

(a)   For UN Nos. 2977 and 2978, the mass of uranium hexafluoride shall not be different from that allowed for the package design, and for UN No. 3507, the mass of uranium hexafluoride shall be less than 0.1 kg;

(b)   The mass of uranium hexafluoride shall not be greater than a value that would lead to an ullage smaller than 5% at the maximum temperature of the package as specified for the plant systems where the package shall be used; and

(c)   The uranium hexafluoride shall be in solid form and the internal pressure shall not be above atmospheric pressure when presented for carriage.

2.2.7.2.4.6   Classification as Type B(U), Type B(M) or Type C packages

2.2.7.2.4.6.1   Packages not otherwise classified in 2.2.7.2.4 (2.2.7.2.4.1 to 2.2.7.2.4.5) shall be classified in accordance with the competent authority certificate of approval for the package issued by the country of origin of design.

2.2.7.2.4.6.2   The contents of a Type B(U), Type B(M) or Type C package shall be as specified in the certificate of approval.

2.2.7.2.5   *Special arrangements*

Radioactive material shall be classified as transported under special arrangement when it is intended to be carried in accordance with 1.7.4.

2.2.8   **Class 8**   **Corrosive substances**

2.2.8.1   *Definition, general provisions and criteria*

2.2.8.1.1   Corrosive substances are substances which, by chemical action, will cause irreversible damage to the skin, or, in the case of leakage, will materially damage, or even destroy, other goods or the means of transport. The heading of this class also covers other substances which form a corrosive liquid only in the presence of water, or which produce corrosive vapour or mist in the presence of natural moisture of the air.

2.2.8.1.2   For substances and mixtures that are corrosive to skin, general classification provisions are provided in 2.2.8.1.4. Skin corrosion refers to the production of irreversible damage to the skin, namely, visible necrosis through the epidermis and into the dermis occurring after exposure to a substance or mixture.

2.2.8.1.3   Liquids and solids which may become liquid during carriage, which are judged not to be skin corrosive shall still be considered for their potential to cause corrosion to certain metal surfaces in accordance with the criteria in 2.2.8.1.5.3 (c) (ii).

2.2.8.1.4   *General classification provisions*

2.2.8.1.4.1   Substances and articles of Class 8 are subdivided as follows:

C1-C11   Corrosive substances without subsidiary hazard and articles containing such substances:

     C1-C4   Acid substances:

          C1   Inorganic, liquid;

          C2   Inorganic, solid;

          C3   Organic, liquid;

          C4   Organic, solid;

     C5-C8   Basic substances:

          C5   Inorganic, liquid;

          C6   Inorganic, solid;

          C7   Organic, liquid;

          C8   Organic, solid;

     C9-C10   Other corrosive substances:

          C9   Liquid;

          C10   Solid;

     C11   Articles.

CF   Corrosive substances, flammable:

     CF1   Liquid;

     CF2   Solid;

CS   Corrosive substances, self-heating:

     CS1   Liquid;

     CS2   Solid;

CW	Corrosive substances which, in contact with water, emit flammable gases:	
	CW1	Liquid;
	CW2	Solid;
CO	Corrosive substances, oxidizing:	
	CO1	Liquid;
	CO2	Solid;
CT	Corrosive substances, toxic and articles containing such substances:	
	CT1	Liquid;
	CT2	Solid;
	CT3	Articles;

CFT   Corrosive substances, flammable, liquid, toxic;

COT   Corrosive substances, oxidizing, toxic.

Classification and assignment of packing groups

2.2.8.1.4.2   Substances and mixtures of Class 8 are divided among the three packing groups according to their degree of danger in carriage:

(a)   Packing group I: very dangerous substances and mixtures;

(b)   Packing group II: substances and mixtures presenting medium danger;

(c)   Packing group III: substances and mixtures that present minor danger.

2.2.8.1.4.3   Allocation of substances listed in Table A of Chapter 3.2 to the packing groups in Class 8 has been made on the basis of experience taking into account such additional factors as inhalation risk (see 2.2.8.1.4.5) and reactivity with water (including the formation of dangerous decomposition products).

2.2.8.1.4.4   New substances and mixtures can be assigned to packing groups on the basis of the length of time of contact necessary to produce irreversible damage of intact skin tissue in accordance with the criteria in 2.2.8.1.5. Alternatively, for mixtures, the criteria in 2.2.8.1.6 can be used.

2.2.8.1.4.5   A substance or mixture meeting the criteria of Class 8 having an inhalation toxicity of dusts and mists (LC_{50}) in the range of packing group I, but toxicity through oral ingestion or dermal contact only in the range of packing group III or less, shall be allocated to Class 8 (see 2.2.61.1.7.2).

2.2.8.1.5   *Packing group assignment for substances and mixtures*

2.2.8.1.5.1   Existing human and animal data including information from single or repeated exposure shall be the first line of evaluation, as they give information directly relevant to effects on the skin.

2.2.8.1.5.2   In assigning the packing group in accordance with 2.2.8.1.4.4, account shall be taken of human experience in instances of accidental exposure. In the absence of human experience the assignment shall be based on data obtained from experiments in accordance with OECD Test Guidelines Nos. 404[6], 435[7], 431[8] or 430[9]. A substance or mixture which is determined not to be corrosive in accordance with one of these or non-classified in accordance with OECD Test Guideline No. 439[10] may be considered not to be corrosive to skin for the purposes of ADN without further testing. If the test results indicate that the substance or mixture is corrosive and not assigned to packing group I, but the test method does not allow discrimination between packing groups II and III, it shall be considered to be packing group II. If the test results indicate that the substance or mixture is corrosive, but the test method does not allow discrimination between packing groups, it shall be assigned to packing group I if no other test results indicate a different packing group.

2.2.8.1.5.3   Packing groups are assigned to corrosive substances in accordance with the following criteria (see table 2.2.8.1.5.3):

(a)   Packing group I is assigned to substances that cause irreversible damage of intact skin tissue within an observation period up to 60 minutes starting after the exposure time of three minutes or less;

(b)   Packing group II is assigned to substances that cause irreversible damage of intact skin tissue within an observation period up to 14 days starting after the exposure time of more than three minutes but not more than 60 minutes;

(c)   Packing group III is assigned to substances that:

(i)   Cause irreversible damage of intact skin tissue within an observation period up to 14 days starting after the exposure time of more than 60 minutes but not more than 4 hours; or

(ii)   Are judged not to cause irreversible damage of intact skin tissue but which exhibit a corrosion rate on either steel or aluminium surfaces exceeding 6.25 mm a year at a test temperature of 55 °C when tested on both materials. For the purposes of testing steel, type S235JR+CR (1.0037 resp. St 37-2), S275J2G3+ CR (1.0144 resp. St 44-3), ISO 3574, Unified Numbering System (UNS) G10200 or SAE 1020, and for testing aluminium, non-clad, types 7075–T6 or AZ5GU-T6 shall be used. An acceptable test is prescribed in the Manual of Tests and Criteria, Part III, Section 37.

NOTE: *Where an initial test on either steel or aluminium indicates the substance being tested is corrosive the follow up test on the other metal is not required.*

---

[6]   OECD Guideline for the testing of chemicals No. 404 "Acute Dermal Irritation/Corrosion" 2015.
[7]   OECD Guideline for the testing of chemicals No. 435 "In Vitro Membrane Barrier Test Method for Skin Corrosion" 2015.
[8]   OECD Guideline for the testing of chemicals No. 431 "In vitro skin corrosion: reconstructed human epidermis (RHE) test method" 2016.
[9]   OECD Guideline for the testing of chemicals No. 430 "In Vitro Skin Corrosion: Transcutaneous Electrical Resistance Test Method (TER)" 2015.
[10]   OECD Guideline for the testing of chemicals No. 439 "In Vitro Skin Irritation: Reconstructed Human Epidermis Test Method" 2015.

Table 2.2.8.1.5.3: Table summarizing the criteria in 2.2.8.1.5.3

Packing Group	Exposure Time	Observation Period	Effect
I	≤ 3 min	≤ 60 min	Irreversible damage of intact skin
II	> 3 min ≤ 1 h	≤ 14 d	Irreversible damage of intact skin
III	> 1 h ≤ 4 h	≤ 14 d	Irreversible damage of intact skin
III	-	-	Corrosion rate on either steel or aluminium surfaces exceeding 6.25 mm a year at a test temperature of 55 °C when tested on both materials

2.2.8.1.6   *Alternative packing group assignment methods for mixtures: Step-wise approach*

2.2.8.1.6.1   General provisions

For mixtures it is necessary to obtain or derive information that allows the criteria to be applied to the mixture for the purpose of classification and assignment of packing groups. The approach to classification and assignment of packing groups is tiered, and is dependent upon the amount of information available for the mixture itself, for similar mixtures and/or for its ingredients. The flow chart of Figure 2.2.8.1.6.1 below outlines the process to be followed:

Figure 2.2.8.1.6.1: Step-wise approach to classify and assign packing group of corrosive mixtures

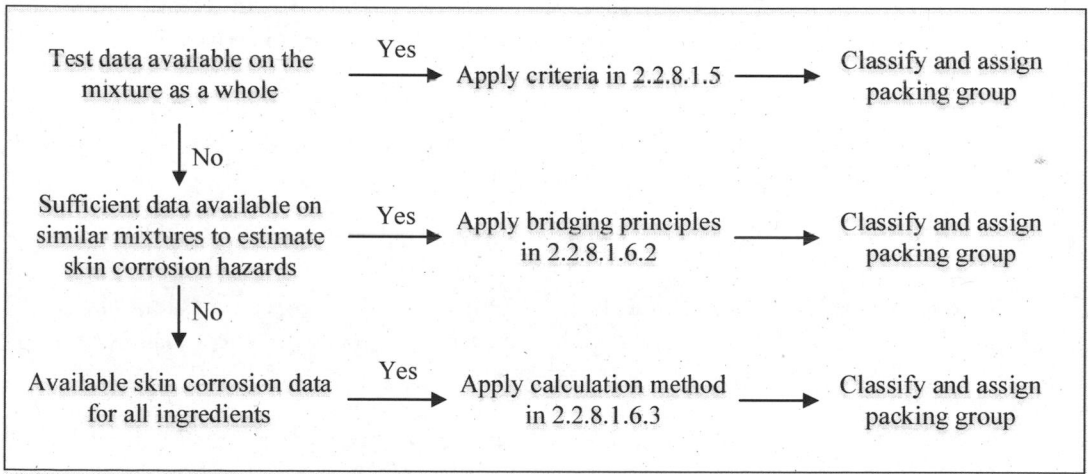

2.2.8.1.6.2   Bridging principles

Where a mixture has not been tested to determine its skin corrosion potential, but there are sufficient data on both the individual ingredients and similar tested mixtures to adequately classify and assign a packing group for the mixture, these data will be used in accordance with the following bridging principles. This ensures that the classification process uses the available data to the greatest extent possible in characterizing the hazards of the mixture.

(a)   Dilution: If a tested mixture is diluted with a diluent which does not meet the criteria for Class 8 and does not affect the packing group of other ingredients, then the new diluted mixture may be assigned to the same packing group as the original tested mixture.

   NOTE: *In certain cases, diluting a mixture or substance may lead to an increase in the corrosive properties. If this is the case, this bridging principle cannot be used.*

(b)   Batching: The skin corrosion potential of a tested production batch of a mixture can be assumed to be substantially equivalent to that of another untested production batch of the same commercial product when produced by or under the control of the same manufacturer, unless there is reason to believe there is significant variation such that the skin corrosion potential of the untested batch has changed. If the latter occurs, a new classification is necessary.

(c)   Concentration of mixtures of packing group I: If a tested mixture meeting the criteria for inclusion in packing group I is concentrated, the more concentrated untested mixture may be assigned to packing group I without additional testing.

(d)   Interpolation within one packing group: For three mixtures (A, B and C) with identical ingredients, where mixtures A and B have been tested and are in the same skin corrosion packing group, and where untested mixture C has the same Class 8 ingredients as mixtures A and B but has concentrations of Class 8 ingredients intermediate to the concentrations in mixtures A and B, then mixture C is assumed to be in the same skin corrosion packing group as A and B.

(e)   Substantially similar mixtures: Given the following:

    (i)   Two mixtures: (A+B) and (C+B);

    (ii)   The concentration of ingredient B is the same in both mixtures;

    (iii)   The concentration of ingredient A in mixture (A+B) equals the concentration of ingredient C in mixture (C+B);

    (iv)   Data on skin corrosion for ingredients A and C are available and substantially equivalent, i.e. they are the same skin corrosion packing group and do not affect the skin corrosion potential of B.

    If mixture (A+B) or (C+B) is already classified based on test data, then the other mixture may be assigned to the same packing group.

2.2.8.1.6.3   Calculation method based on the classification of the substances

2.2.8.1.6.3.1   Where a mixture has not been tested to determine its skin corrosion potential, nor is sufficient data available on similar mixtures, the corrosive properties of the substances in the mixture shall be considered to classify and assign a packing group.

Applying the calculation method is only allowed if there are no synergistic effects that make the mixture more corrosive than the sum of its substances. This restriction applies only if packing group II or III would be assigned to the mixture.

2.2.8.1.6.3.2   When using the calculation method, all Class 8 ingredients present at a concentration of $\geq 1\%$ shall be taken into account, or $< 1\%$ if these ingredients are still relevant for classifying the mixture to be corrosive to skin.

2.2.8.1.6.3.3   To determine whether a mixture containing corrosive substances shall be considered a corrosive mixture and to assign a packing group, the calculation method in the flow chart in Figure 2.2.8.1.6.3 shall be applied. For this calculation method, generic concentration limits apply where 1% is used in the first step for the assessment of the packing group I substances, and where 5% is used for the other steps respectively.

2.2.8.1.6.3.4   When a specific concentration limit (SCL) is assigned to a substance following its entry in Table A of Chapter 3.2 or in a special provision, this limit shall be used instead of the generic concentration limits (GCL).

2.2.8.1.6.3.5 For this purpose, the summation formula for each step of the calculation method shall be adapted. This means that, where applicable, the generic concentration limit shall be substituted by the specific concentration limit assigned to the substance(s) (SCL$_i$), and the adapted formula is a weighted average of the different concentration limits assigned to the different substances in the mixture:

$$\frac{PGx_1}{GCL} + \frac{PGx_2}{SCL_2} + \cdots + \frac{PGx_i}{SCL_i} \geq 1$$

Where:

PG x_i = concentration of substance 1, 2 …i in the mixture, assigned to packing group x (I, II or III)

GCL = generic concentration limit

SCL$_i$ = specific concentration limit assigned to substance i

The criterion for a packing group is fulfilled when the result of the calculation is ≥ 1. The generic concentration limits to be used for the evaluation in each step of the calculation method are those found in Figure 2.2.8.1.6.3.

Examples for the application of the above formula can be found in the note below.

NOTE: *Examples for the application of the above formula*

Example 1: A mixture contains one corrosive substance in a concentration of 5% assigned to packing group I without a specific concentration limit:

Calculation for packing group I: $\dfrac{5}{5\,(GCL)} = 1$ ➜ *assign to Class 8, packing group I.*

Example 2: A mixture contains three substances corrosive to skin; two of them (A and B) have specific concentration limits; for the third one (C) the generic concentration limit applies. The rest of the mixture needs not to be taken into consideration:

Substance X in the mixture and its packing group assignment within Class 8	Concentration (conc) in the mixture in %	Specific concentration limit (SCL) for packing group I	Specific concentration limit (SCL) for packing group II	Specific concentration limit (SCL) for packing group III
A, assigned to packing group I	3	30%	none	none
B, assigned to packing group I	2	20%	10%	none
C, assigned to packing group III	10	none	none	none

Calculation for packing group I: $\dfrac{3\,(conc\ A)}{30\,(SCL\ PGI)} + \dfrac{2\,(conc\ B)}{20\,(SCL\ PGI)} = 0,2 < 1$

The criterion for packing group I is not fulfilled.

Calculation for packing group II: $\dfrac{3\,(conc\ A)}{5\,(GCL\ PG\ II)} + \dfrac{2\,(conc\ B)}{10\,(SCL\ PG\ II)} = 0,8 < 1$

The criterion for packing group II is not fulfilled.

Calculation for packing group III: $\quad \dfrac{3\,(conc\ A)}{5\,(GCL\ PGIII)} + \dfrac{2\,(conc\ B)}{5\,(GCL\ PG\ III)} + \dfrac{10\,(conc\ C)}{5\ GCL\ PG\ III)} = 3 \geq 1$

The criterion for packing group III is fulfilled, the mixture shall be assigned to Class 8, packing group III.

Figure 2.2.8.1.6.3: Calculation method

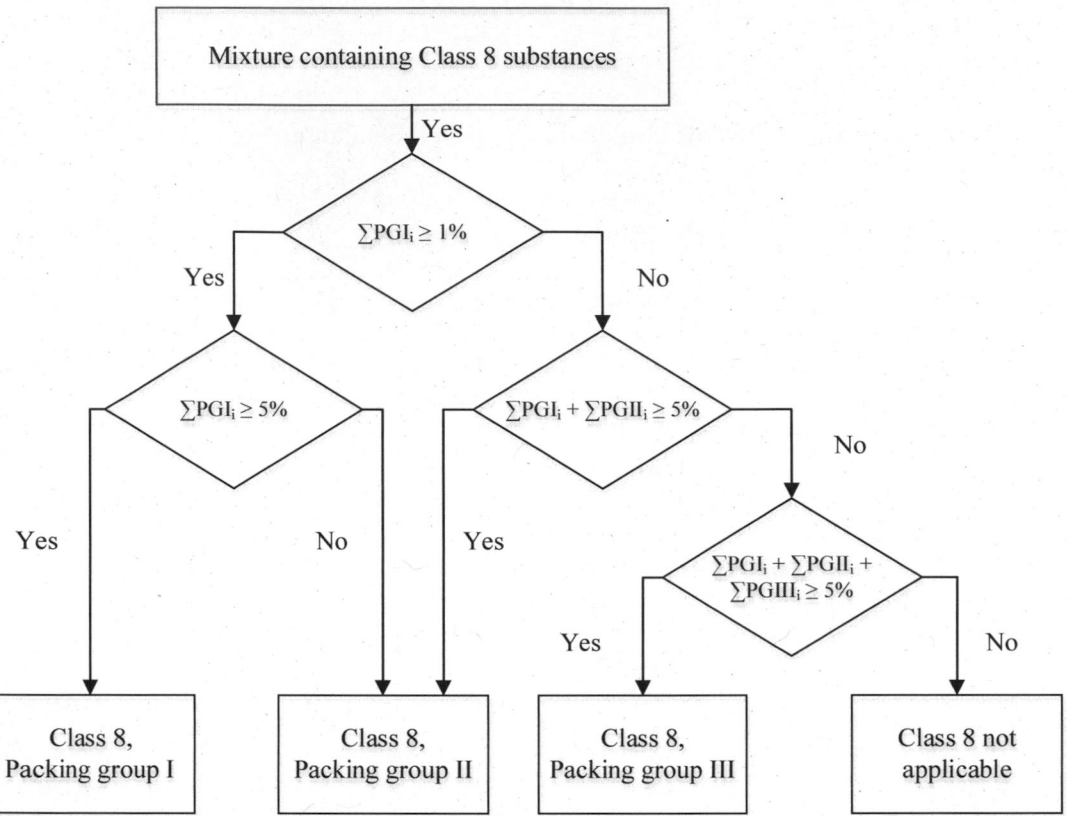

2.2.8.1.7   If substances of Class 8, as a result of admixtures, come into categories of risk different from those to which the substances mentioned by name in Table A of Chapter 3.2 belong, these mixtures or solutions shall be assigned to the entries to which they belong, on the basis of their actual degree of danger.

NOTE: *For the classification of solutions and mixtures (such as preparations and wastes), see also 2.1.3.*

2.2.8.1.8   On the basis of the criteria set out in paragraph 2.2.8.1.6, it may also be determined whether the nature of a solution or mixture mentioned by name or containing a substance mentioned by name is such that the solution or mixture is not subject to the provisions for this class.

2.2.8.1.9   *(Deleted)*

NOTE: *UN No. 1910 calcium oxide and UN No. 2812 sodium aluminate, listed in the UN Model Regulations, are not subject to the provisions of ADN.*

2.2.8.2   *Substances not accepted for carriage*

2.2.8.2.1   Chemically unstable substances of Class 8 shall not be accepted for carriage unless the necessary precautions have been taken to prevent the possibility of a dangerous decomposition or polymerization under normal conditions of carriage. For the precautions necessary to prevent polymerization, see special provision 386 of Chapter 3.3. To this end particular care shall be taken to ensure that receptacles and tanks do not contain any substances liable to promote these reactions.

2.2.8.2.2   The following substances shall not be accepted for carriage:

– UN No. 1798 NITROHYDROCHLORIC ACID;

– chemically unstable mixtures of spent sulphuric acid;

– chemically unstable mixtures of nitrating acid or mixtures of residual sulphuric and nitric acids, not denitrated;

– perchloric acid aqueous solution with more than 72% pure acid, by mass, or mixtures of perchloric acid with any liquid other than water.

2.2.8.3　　*List of collective entries*

Corrosive substances <u>without</u> subsidiary hazard and articles containing such substances

Acid **C1-C4**	inorganic	liquid	C1	2584 2584 2693 2837 3264	ALKYLSULPHONIC ACIDS, LIQUID with more than 5% free sulphuric acid or ARYLSULPHONIC ACIDS, LIQUID with more than 5% free sulphuric acid BISULPHITES, AQUEOUS SOLUTION, N.O.S. BISULPHATES, AQUEOUS SOLUTION CORROSIVE LIQUID, ACIDIC, INORGANIC, N.O.S.
		solid	C2	1740 2583 2583 3260	HYDROGENDIFLUORIDES, SOLID, N.O.S. ALKYLSULPHONIC ACIDS, SOLID with more than 5% free sulphuric acid or ARYLSULPHONIC ACIDS, SOLID with more than 5% free sulphuric acid CORROSIVE SOLID, ACIDIC, INORGANIC, N.O.S.
	organic	liquid	C3	2586 2586 2987 3145 3265	ALKYLSULPHONIC ACIDS, LIQUID with not more than 5% free sulphuric acid or ARYLSULPHONIC ACIDS, LIQUID with not more than 5% free sulphuric acid CHLOROSILANES, CORROSIVE, N.O.S. ALKYLPHENOLS, LIQUID, N.O.S. (including C_2-C_{12} homologues) CORROSIVE LIQUID, ACIDIC, ORGANIC, N.O.S
		solid	C4	2430 2585 2585 3261	ALKYLPHENOLS, SOLID, N.O.S. (including C_2-C_{12} homologues) ALKYLSULPHONIC ACIDS, SOLID with not more than 5% free sulphuric acid or ARYLSULPHONIC ACIDS, SOLID with not more than 5% free sulphuric acid CORROSIVE SOLID, ACIDIC, ORGANIC, N.O.S.
Basic **C5-C8**	inorganic	liquid	C5	1719 2797 3266	CAUSTIC ALKALI LIQUID, N.O.S. BATTERY FLUID, ALKALI CORROSIVE LIQUID, BASIC, INORGANIC, N.O.S.
		solid	C6	3262	CORROSIVE SOLID, BASIC, INORGANIC, N.O.S.
	organic	liquid	C7	2735 2735 3267	AMINES, LIQUID, CORROSIVE, N.O.S. or POLYAMINES, LIQUID, CORROSIVE, N.O.S. CORROSIVE LIQUID, BASIC, ORGANIC, N.O.S.
		solid	C8	3259 3259 3263	AMINES, SOLID, CORROSIVE, N.O.S., or POLYAMINES, SOLID, CORROSIVE, N.O.S. CORROSIVE SOLID, BASIC, ORGANIC, N.O.S.
Other corrosive substances **C9-C10**		liquid	C9	1903 2801 2801 3066 3066 1760	DISINFECTANT, LIQUID, CORROSIVE, N.O.S DYE, LIQUID, CORROSIVE, N.O.S. or DYE INTERMEDIATE, LIQUID, CORROSIVE, N.O.S. PAINT (including paint, enamel, stain, shellac, varnish, polish, liquid filler and lacquer base) or PAINT RELATED MATERIAL (including paint thinning or reducing compound) CORROSIVE LIQUID, N.O.S.
		solid [a]	C10	3147 3147 3244 1759	DYE, SOLID, CORROSIVE, N.O.S. or DYE INTERMEDIATE, SOLID, CORROSIVE, N.O.S. SOLIDS CONTAINING CORROSIVE LIQUID, N.O.S. CORROSIVE SOLID, N.O.S.
Articles			C11	1774 2028 2794 2795 2800 3028 3477 3477 3477 3547	FIRE EXTINGUISHER CHARGES, corrosive liquid BOMBS, SMOKE, NON-EXPLOSIVE with corrosive liquid, without initiating device BATTERIES, WET, FILLED WITH ACID, electric storage BATTERIES, WET, FILLED WITH ALKALI, electric storage BATTERIES, WET, NON-SPILLABLE, electric storage BATTERIES, DRY, CONTAINING POTASSIUM HYDROXIDE SOLID, electric storage FUEL CELL CARTRIDGES containing corrosive substances, or FUEL CELL CARTRIDGES CONTAINED IN EQUIPMENT, containing corrosive substances, or FUEL CELL CARTRIDGES PACKED WITH EQUIPMENT, containing corrosive substances ARTICLES CONTAINING CORROSIVE SUBSTANCE, N.O.S.

(cont'd on next page)

---

[a]　　Mixtures of solids which are not subject to the provisions of ADN and of corrosive liquids may be carried under UN No. 3244 without being subject to the classification criteria of Class 8, provided there is no free liquid visible at the time the substance is loaded or at the time the packaging or cargo transport unit is closed. Each packaging shall correspond to a design type which has passed the leakproofness test for Packing group II level.

Corrosive substances <u>with</u> subsidiary hazard(s) and articles containing such substances

(cont'd)	liquid	CF1	3470	PAINT, CORROSIVE, FLAMMABLE (including paint, enamel, stain, shellac, varnish, polish, liquid filler and lacquer base) or
			3470	PAINT RELATED MATERIAL, CORROSIVE, FLAMMABLE (including paint thinning or reducing compound)
			2734	AMINES, LIQUID, CORROSIVE, FLAMMABLE, N.O.S. or
			2734	POLYAMINES, LIQUID, CORROSIVE, FLAMMABLE, N.O.S.
			2986	CHLOROSILANES, CORROSIVE, FLAMMABLE, N.O.S.
Flammable [b]			2920	CORROSIVE LIQUID, FLAMMABLE, N.O.S.
CF	solid	CF2	2921	CORROSIVE SOLID, FLAMMABLE, N.O.S.
Self-heating	liquid	CS1	3301	CORROSIVE LIQUID, SELF-HEATING, N.O.S.
CS	solid	CS2	3095	CORROSIVE SOLID, SELF-HEATING, N.O.S.
Water-reactive	liquid [b]	CW1	3094	CORROSIVE LIQUID, WATER-REACTIVE, N.O.S.
CW	solid	CW2	3096	CORROSIVE SOLID, WATER-REACTIVE, N.O.S.
Oxidizing	liquid	CO1	3093	CORROSIVE LIQUID, OXIDIZING, N.O.S.
CO	solid	CO2	3084	CORROSIVE SOLID, OXIDIZING, N.O.S.
Toxic [d]	liquid [c]	CT1	3471	HYDROGENDIFLUORIDES SOLUTION, N.O.S.
			2922	CORROSIVE LIQUID, TOXIC, N.O.S.
CT	solid [e]	CT2	2923	CORROSIVE SOLID, TOXIC, N.O.S.
	articles	CT3	3506	MERCURY CONTAINED IN MANUFACTURED ARTICLES
Flammable, liquid, toxic [d]		CFT		No collective entry with this classification code available; if need be, classification under a collective entry with a classification code to be determined according to table of precedence of hazards in 2.1.3.10.
Oxidizing, toxic [d, e]		COT		No collective entry with this classification code available; if need be, classification under a collective entry with a classification code to be determined according to table of precedence of hazards in 2.1.3.10.

---

[b] *Chlorosilanes which, in contact with water or moist air, emit flammable gases, are substances of Class 4.3.*

[c] *Chloroformates having predominantly toxic properties are substances of Class 6.1.*

[d] *Corrosive substances which are highly toxic by inhalation, as defined in 2.2.61.1.4 to 2.2.61.1.9 are substances of Class 6.1.*

[e] *UN No. 2505 AMMONIUM FLUORIDE, UN No. 1812 POTASSIUM FLUORIDE, UN No. 1690 SODIUM FLUORIDE, SOLD, UN No. 2674 SODIUM FLUOROSILICATE, UN No. 2856 FLUOROSILICATES, N.O.S., UN No. 3415 SODIUM FLUORIDE SOLUTION and UN No. 3422 POTASSIUM FLUORIDE SOLUTION are substances of Class 6.1.*

2.2.9 **Class 9** **Miscellaneous dangerous substances and articles**

2.2.9.1 *Criteria*

2.2.9.1.1 The heading of Class 9 covers substances and articles which, during carriage, present a danger not covered by the heading of other classes.

2.2.9.1.2 The substances and articles of Class 9 are subdivided as follows:

M1 Substances which, on inhalation as fine dust, may endanger health;

M2 Substances and articles which, in the event of fire, may form dioxins;

M3 Substances evolving flammable vapour;

M4 Lithium batteries;

M5 Life-saving appliances;

M6-M8 Environmentally hazardous substances:

M6 Pollutant to the aquatic environment, liquid;

M7 Pollutant to the aquatic environment, solid;

M8 Genetically modified micro-organisms and organisms;

M9-M10 Elevated temperature substances:

M9 Liquid;

M10 Solid;

M11 Other substances and articles presenting a danger during carriage, but not meeting the definitions of another class.

M12 Other substances and articles presenting a danger during carriage in tank vessels, but not meeting the definitions of another class.

Definitions and classification

2.2.9.1.3 Substances and articles classified in Class 9 are listed in Table A of Chapter 3.2. The assignment of substances and articles not mentioned by name in Table A of Chapter 3.2 to the relevant entry of that Table or of sub-section 2.2.9.3 shall be done in accordance with 2.2.9.1.4 to 2.2.9.1.8, 2.2.9.1.10, 2.2.9.1.11, 2.2.9.1.13 and 2.2.9.1.14 below.

Substances which, on inhalation as fine dust, may endanger health

2.2.9.1.4 Substances which, on inhalation as fine dust, may endanger health include asbestos and mixtures containing asbestos.

Substances and articles which, in the event of fire, may form dioxins

2.2.9.1.5 Substances and articles which, in the event of fire, may form dioxins include polychlorinated biphenyls (PCBs) and terphenyls (PCTs) and polyhalogenated biphenyls and terphenyls and mixtures containing these substances, as well as articles such as transformers, condensers and articles containing those substances or mixtures.

NOTE: Mixtures with a PCB or PCT content of not more than 50 mg/kg are not subject to the provisions of ADN.

Substances evolving flammable vapour

2.2.9.1.6   Substances evolving flammable vapour include polymers containing flammable liquids with a flash-point not exceeding 55 °C.

Lithium batteries

2.2.9.1.7   Lithium batteries shall meet the following requirements, except when otherwise provided for in ADN (e.g. for prototype batteries and small production runs under special provision 310 or damaged batteries under special provision 376).

NOTE: For UN 3536 LITHIUM BATTERIES INSTALLED IN CARGO TRANSPORT UNIT, see special provision 389 in Chapter 3.3.

Cells and batteries, cells and batteries contained in equipment, or cells and batteries packed with equipment, containing lithium in any form shall be assigned to UN Nos. 3090, 3091, 3480 or 3481 as appropriate. They may be carried under these entries if they meet the following provisions:

(a)   Each cell or battery is of the type proved to meet the requirements of each test of the *Manual of Tests and Criteria*, Part III, sub-section 38.3;

NOTE: Batteries shall be of a design type proved to meet the testing requirements of the Manual of Tests and Criteria, part III, sub-section 38.3, irrespective of whether the cells of which they are composed are of a tested type.

(b)   Each cell and battery incorporates a safety venting device or is designed to preclude a violent rupture under normal conditions of carriage;

(c)   Each cell and battery is equipped with an effective means of preventing external short circuits;

(d)   Each battery containing cells or series of cells connected in parallel is equipped with effective means as necessary to prevent dangerous reverse current flow (e.g., diodes, fuses, etc.);

(e)   Cells and batteries shall be manufactured under a quality management programme that includes:

(i)   description of the organizational structure and responsibilities of personnel with regard to design and product quality;

(ii)   The relevant inspection and test, quality control, quality assurance, and process operation instructions that will be used;

(iii)   Process controls that should include relevant activities to prevent and detect internal short circuit failure during manufacture of cells;

(iv)   Quality records, such as inspection reports, test data, calibration data and certificates. Test data shall be kept and made available to the competent authority upon request;

(v)   Management reviews to ensure the effective operation of the quality management programme;

(vi)   A process for control of documents and their revision;

(vii)   A means for control of cells or batteries that are not conforming to the type tested as mentioned in (a) above;

(viii) Training programmes and qualification procedures for relevant personnel; and

(ix)   Procedures to ensure that there is no damage to the final product.

> **NOTE:**   *In-house quality management programmes may be accepted. Third party certification is not required, but the procedures listed in (i) to (ix) above shall be properly recorded and traceable. A copy of the quality management programme shall be made available to the competent authority upon request.*

(f)   Lithium batteries, containing both primary lithium metal cells and rechargeable lithium ion cells, that are not designed to be externally charged (see special provision 387 of Chapter 3.3) shall meet the following conditions:

(i)   The rechargeable lithium ion cells can only be charged from the primary lithium metal cells;

(ii)   Overcharge of the rechargeable lithium ion cells is precluded by design;

(iii)   The battery has been tested as a lithium primary battery;

(iv)   Component cells of the battery shall be of a type proved to meet the respective testing requirements of the Manual of Tests and Criteria, part III, sub-section 38.3;

(g)   Except for button cells installed in equipment (including circuit boards), manufacturers and subsequent distributors of cells or batteries manufactured after 30 June 2003 shall make available the test summary as specified in the Manual of Tests and Criteria, Part III, sub-section 38.3, paragraph 38.3.5.

Lithium batteries are not subject to the provisions of ADN if they meet the requirements of special provision 188 of Chapter 3.3.

Life-saving appliances

2.2.9.1.8   Life-saving appliances include life-saving appliances and motor vehicle components which meet the descriptions of special provisions 235 or 296 of Chapter 3.3.

Environmentally hazardous substances

2.2.9.1.9   *(Deleted)*

Pollutants to the aquatic environment

2.2.9.1.10   *Environmentally hazardous substances (aquatic environment)*

2.2.9.1.10.1   For carriage in packages or in bulk, substances, solutions and mixtures meeting the criteria for Acute 1, Chronic 1 or Chronic 2 in Chapter 2.4 (see also 2.1.3.8) shall be considered to be environmentally hazardous (aquatic environment). Substances which cannot be assigned to other classes in ADN or to other Class 9 entries and which meet these criteria shall be assigned to UN Nos. 3077, ENVIRONMENTALLY HAZARDOUS SUBSTANCE, SOLID, N.O.S., or 3082, ENVIRONMENTALLY HAZARDOUS SUBSTANCE, LIQUID, N.O.S, and to packing group III.

2.2.9.1.10.2   For carriage in tank vessels, the substances, solutions and mixtures referred to in 2.2.9.1.10.1 and those meeting the criteria for Acute 2, Acute 3 or Chronic 3 in Chapter 2.4 shall be considered to be environmentally hazardous.

Substances classified as environmentally hazardous which meet the criteria for Acute or Chronic Category 1 shall be assigned to group 'N1'.

Substances classified as environmentally hazardous which meet the criteria for Chronic Categories 2 or 3 shall be assigned to group 'N2'.

Substances classified as environmentally hazardous which meet the criteria for Acute Categories 2 or 3 shall be assigned to group 'N3'.

Substances which meet the criteria of 2.2.9.1.10.1 shall be assigned to UN Nos. 3082, ENVIRONMENTALLY HAZARDOUS SUBSTANCE, LIQUID, N.O.S, or 3077, ENVIRONMENTALLY HAZARDOUS SUBSTANCE, SOLID, N.O.S., MOLTEN. Those that meet the additional criteria in this paragraph shall be assigned to identification Nos. 9005, ENVIRONMENTALLY HAZARDOUS SUBSTANCE, SOLID, N.O.S, MOLTEN, or 9006, ENVIRONMENTALLY HAZARDOUS SUBSTANCE, LIQUID, N.O.S.

2.2.9.1.10.3   Substances or mixtures classified as environmentally hazardous substances (aquatic environment) on the basis of Regulation 1272/2008/EC[3]

Notwithstanding the provisions of 2.2.9.1.10.1, if data for classification according to the criteria of 2.4.3 and 2.4.4 are not available, a substance or mixture:

(a)   Shall be classified as an environmentally hazardous substance (aquatic environment) if it has to be assigned category(ies) Aquatic Acute 1, Aquatic Chronic 1 or Aquatic Chronic 2 according to Regulation 1272/2008/EC[3];

(b)   May be regarded as not being an environmentally hazardous substance (aquatic environment) for carriage in packages or in bulk in the sense of 2.2.9.10.1 if it does not have to be assigned such a category according to the said Regulation.

2.2.9.1.10.4   (*Reserved*)

2.2.9.1.10.5   For carriage in tank vessels, substances, solutions and mixtures are considered as floating substances, solutions and mixtures (floaters) if they meet the following criteria: [11]

Water solubility	< 0.1%
Vapour pressure	< 0.3 kPa
Relative density	≤ 1,000.

For carriage in tank vessels, substances, solutions and mixtures are considered as substances, solutions and mixtures that sink (sinkers) if they meet the following criteria: [11]

Water solubility	< 0.1%
Relative density	> 1,000.

---

[3]   *Regulation (EC) No 1272/2008 of the European Parliament and of the Council of 16 December 2008 on classification, labelling and packaging of substances and mixtures, amending and repealing Directive 67/548/EEC and 1999/45/EC; and amending Regulation (EC) No 1907/2006, published in the Official Journal of the European Union, L 353, 31 December 2008, p 1-1355.*

[11]   *The values of relative density, vapour pressure and water solubility to be used according to the GESAMP model are the values at 20°C.*

Genetically modified micro-organisms or organisms

2.2.9.1.11   Genetically modified micro-organisms (GMMOs) and genetically modified organisms (GMOs) are micro-organisms and organisms in which genetic material has been purposely altered through genetic engineering in a way that does not occur naturally. They are assigned to Class 9 (UN No. 3245) if they do not meet the definition of toxic substances or infectious substances, but are capable of altering animals, plants or microbiological substances in a way not normally the result of natural reproduction.

NOTE 1:   GMMOs and GMOs which are infectious are substances of Class 6.2, UN Nos. 2814, 2900 or 3373).

NOTE 2:   GMMOs or GMOs are not subject to the provisions of ADN when authorized for use by the competent authorities of the countries of origin, transit and destination. [12]

NOTE 3:   Genetically modified live animals which, in accordance with the current state of scientific knowledge, have no known pathogenic effect on humans, animals and plants and are carried in receptacles that are suitable for safely preventing both the escape of the animals and unauthorized access to them, are not subject to the provisions of ADN. The provisions specified by the International Air Transport Association (IATA) for air transport "Live Animals Regulations, LAR" can be drawn on as guidelines for suitable receptacles for the transport of live animals.

NOTE 4:   Live animals shall not be used to carry genetically modified micro-organisms classified in Class 9 unless the substance can be carried no other way. Genetically modified live animals shall be carried under terms and conditions of the competent authorities of the countries of origin and destination.

2.2.9.1.12   *(Deleted)*

Elevated temperature substances

2.2.9.1.13   Elevated temperature substances include substances which are carried or handed over for carriage in the liquid state at or above 100 °C and, in the case of those with a flash-point, below their flash-point. They also include solids which are carried or handed over for carriage at or above 240 °C.

NOTE 1: Elevated temperature substances may be assigned to Class 9 only if they do not meet the criteria of any other class.

NOTE 2: Substances having a flash-point above 60 °C which are carried or handed over for carriage within a range of 15 K below the flash-point are substances of Class 3, identification number 9001.

Other substances and articles presenting a danger during carriage but not meeting the definitions of another class

---

[12]   *See Part C of Directive 2001/18/EC of the European Parliament and of the Council on the deliberate release into the environment of genetically modified organisms and repealing Council Directive 90/220/EEC (Official Journal of the European Communities, No. L 106, of 17 April 2001, pp 8-14) and Regulation (EC) No. 1829/2003 of the European Parliament and of the Council on genetically modified food and feed (Official Journal of the European Union, No. L 268, of 18 October 2003, pp 1-23), which set out the authorization procedures for the European Union.*

2.2.9.1.14   The following other miscellaneous substances not meeting the definitions of another class are assigned to Class 9:

Solid ammonia compounds having a flash-point below 60 °C

Low hazard dithionites

Highly volatile liquids

Substances emitting noxious fumes

Substances containing allergens

Chemical kits and first aid kits

Electric double layer capacitors (with an energy storage capacity greater than 0.3 Wh).

Vehicles, engines and machinery, internal combustion.

Articles containing miscellaneous dangerous goods

The following miscellaneous substances not meeting the definition of another class are assigned to Class 9 when they are carried in bulk or in tank vessels:

–   UN 2071 AMMONIUM NITRATE BASED FERTILIZERS;

   NOTE: Solid ammonium nitrate based fertilizers shall be classified in accordance with the procedures as set out in the Manual of Tests and Criteria, Part III, Section 39.

–   UN 2216 FISH MEAL, STABILIZED (humidity between 5% by mass and 12% by mass with not more than 15% fat by mass); or

–   UN 2216 FISH SCRAP, STABILIZED (humidity between 5% by mass and 12% by mass with not more than 15% fat by mass);

–   Identification No. 9003 SUBSTANCES HAVING A FLASH-POINT ABOVE 60 °C AND NOT MORE THAN 100 °C which cannot be assigned to another class or another entry of Class 9. If these substances can also be assigned to Identification No. 9005 or Identification No. 9006, then Identification No. 9003 shall take precedence.

–   Identification No. 9004, 4,4'-DIPHENYLMETHANE DIISOCYANATE;

–   Identification No. 9005, ENVIRONMENTALLY HAZARDOUS SUBSTANCE, SOLID, N.O.S, MOLTEN, which cannot be assigned to UN No. 3077;

–   Identification No. 9006, ENVIRONMENTALLY HAZARDOUS SUBSTANCE, LIQUID, N.O.S., which cannot be assigned to UN No. 3082.

NOTE: UN No. 1845 carbon dioxide, solid (dry ice),[13] *UN No. 2807 magnetized material, UN No. 3334 aviation regulated liquid, n.o.s. and UN No. 3335 aviation regulated solid, n.o.s., listed in the UN Model Regulations, are not subject to the provisions of ADN.*

Assignment of the packing groups

2.2.9.1.15   When indicated in column 4 of Table A of Chapter 3.2, substances and articles of Class 9 are assigned to one of the following packing groups according to their degree of danger:

Packing group II: substances presenting medium danger;

Packing group III: substances presenting low danger.

---

[13]   *For UN No. 1845 carbon dioxide, solid (dry ice), see 5.5.3.*

2.2.9.2   *Substances and articles not accepted for carriage*

The following substances and articles shall not be accepted for carriage:

–   Lithium batteries which do not meet the relevant conditions of special provisions 188, 230, 310, 636 or 670 of Chapter 3.3;

–   Uncleaned empty containment vessels for apparatus such as transformers, condensers and hydraulic apparatus containing substances assigned to UN Nos. 2315, 3151, 3152 or 3432.

2.2.9.3 *List of entries*

Substances which, on inhalation as fine dust, may endanger health	M1	2212 ASBESTOS, AMPHIBOLE (amosite, tremolite, actinolite, anthophyllite, crocidolite) 2590 ASBESTOS, CHRYSOTILE
Substances and articles which, in the event of fire, may form dioxins	M2	2315 POLYCHLORINATED BIPHENYLS, LIQUID 3432 POLYCHLORINATED BIPHENYLS, SOLID 3151 POLYHALOGENATED BIPHENYLS, LIQUID or 3151 HALOGENATED MONOMETHYLDIPHENYLMETHANES, LIQUID or 3151 POLYHALOGENATED TERPHENYLS, LIQUID 3152 POLYHALOGENATED BIPHENYLS, SOLID or 3152 HALOGENATED MONOMETHYLDIPHENYLMETHANES, SOLID or 3152 POLYHALOGENATED TERPHENYLS, SOLID
Substances evolving flammable vapour	M3	2211 POLYMERIC BEADS, EXPANDABLE, evolving flammable vapour 3314 PLASTICS MOULDING COMPOUND in dough, sheet or extruded rope form evolving flammable vapour
Lithium batteries	M4	3090 LITHIUM METAL BATTERIES (including lithium alloy battcrics) 3091 LITHIUM METAL BATTERIES CONTAINED IN EQUIPMENT (including lithium alloy batteries) or 3091 LITHIUM METAL BATTERIES PACKED WITH EQUIPMENT (including lithium alloy batteries) 3480 LITHIUM ION BATTERIES (including lithium ion polymer batteries) 3481 LITHIUM ION BATTERIES CONTAINED IN EQUIPMENT (including lithium ion polymer batteries) or 3481 LITHIUM ION BATTERIES PACKED WITH EQUIPMENT (including lithium ion polymer batteries) 3536 LITHIUM BATTERIES INSTALLED IN CARGO TRANSPORT UNIT lithium ion batteries or lithium metal batteries
Life-saving appliances	M5	2990 LIFE SAVING APPLIANCES, SELF INFLATING 3072 LIFE-SAVING APPLIANCES NOT SELF-INFLATING containing dangerous goods as equipment 3268 SAFETY DEVICES, electrically initiated
Environmentally hazardous substances — **pollutant to the aquatic environment, liquid**	M6	3082 ENVIRONMENTALLY HAZARDOUS SUBSTANCE, LIQUID, N.O.S.
pollutant to the aquatic environment, solid	M7	3077 ENVIRONMENTALLY HAZARDOUS SUBSTANCE, SOLID, N.O.S.
genetically modified micro-organisms and organisms	M8	3245 GENETICALLY MODIFIED MICROORGANISMS or 3245 GENETICALLY MODIFIED ORGANISMS

(cont'd on next page)

Elevated temperature substances	liquid	M9	3257 ELEVATED TEMPERATURE LIQUID, N.O.S., at or above 100 °C and below its flash-point (including molten metal, molten salts, etc.)
	solid	M10	3258 ELEVATED TEMPERATURE SOLID, N.O.S., at or above 240 °C
Other substances and articles presenting a danger during carriage, but not meeting the definitions of another class		M11	Only substances and articles listed in Table A of Chapter 3.2 are subject to the provisions for Class 9 under this classification code, as follows: 1841 ACETALDEHYDE AMMONIA 1931 ZINC DITHIONITE (ZINC HYDROSULPHITE) 1941 DIBROMODIFLUOROMETHANE 1990 BENZALDEHYDE 2071 AMMONIUM NITRATE BASED FERTILIZER (only in bulk) 2216 FISH MEAL, STABILISED 2216 FISH SCRAP, STABILISED 2969 CASTOR BEANS, or 2969 CASTOR MEAL, or 2969 CASTOR POMACE, or 2969 CASTOR FLAKE 3166 VEHICLE, FLAMMABLE GAS POWERED or 3166 VEHICLE, FLAMMABLE LIQUID POWERED or 3166 VEHICLE, FUEL CELL, FLAMMABLE GAS POWERED or 3166 VEHICLE, FUEL CELL, FLAMMABLE LIQUID POWERED 3171 BATTERY POWERED VEHICLE or 3171 BATTERY POWERED EQUIPMENT 3316 CHEMICAL KIT, or 3316 FIRST AID KIT 3359 FUMIGATED CARGO TRANSPORT UNIT 3363 DANGEROUS GOODS IN ARTICLES or 3363 DANGEROUS GOODS IN MACHINERY or 3363 DANGEROUS GOODS IN APPARATUS 3499 CAPACITOR, ELECTRIC DOUBLE LAYER (with an energy storage capacity greater than 0.3Wh) 3508 CAPACITOR, ASYMMETRIC (with an energy storage capacity greater than 0.3Wh) 3509 PACKAGINGS, DISCARDED, EMPTY, UNCLEANED 3530 ENGINE, INTERNAL COMBUSTION or 3530 MACHINERY, INTERNAL COMBUSTION 3548 ARTICLES CONTAINING MISCELLANEOUS DANGEROUS GOODS N.O.S.
Other substances and articles presenting a danger during carriage in tank vessels, but not meeting the definitions of another class		M12	Only substances and articles listed in Table A of Chapter 3.2 are subject to the provisions for Class 9 under this classification code, as follows: 9003 SUBSTANCES WITH A FLASH-POINT ABOVE 60 °C AND NOT MORE THAN 100 °C, which do not belong to another class 9004 DIPHENYLMETHANE-4, 4'-DIISOCYANATE 9005 ENVIRONMENTALLY HAZARDOUS SUBSTANCE, SOLID, N.O.S., MOLTEN 9006 ENVIRONMENTALLY HAZARDOUS SUBSTANCE, LIQUID, N.O.S.

CHAPTER 2.3

TEST METHODS

2.3.0   **General**

Unless otherwise provided for in Chapter 2.2 or in this Chapter, the test methods to be used for the classification of dangerous goods are those described in the Manual of Tests and Criteria.

2.3.1   **Exudation test for blasting explosives of Type A**

2.3.1.1   Blasting explosives of type A (UN No. 0081) shall, if they contain more than 40% liquid nitric ester, in addition to the testing specified in the Manual of Tests and Criteria, satisfy the following exudation test.

2.3.1.2   The apparatus for testing blasting explosive for exudation (figs. 1 to 3) consists of a hollow bronze cylinder. This cylinder, which is closed at one end by a plate of the same metal, has an internal diameter of 15.7 mm and a depth of 40 mm.

It is pierced by 20 holes 0.5 mm in diameter (four sets of five holes) on the circumference. A bronze piston, cylindrically fashioned over a length of 48 mm and having a total length of 52 mm, slides into the vertically placed cylinder.

The piston, whose diameter is 15.6 mm, is loaded with a mass of 2 220 g so that a pressure of 120 kPa (1.20 bar) is exerted on the base of the cylinder.

2.3.1.3   A small plug of blasting explosive weighing 5 to 8 g, 30 mm long and 15 mm in diameter, is wrapped in very fine gauze and placed in the cylinder; the piston and its loading mass are then placed on it so that the blasting explosive is subjected to a pressure of 120 kPa (1.20 bar). The time taken for the appearance of the first signs of oily droplets (nitroglycerine) at the outer orifices of the cylinder holes is noted.

2.3.1.4   The blasting explosive is considered satisfactory if the time elapsing before the appearance of the liquid exudations is more than five minutes, the test having been carried out at a temperature of 15 °C to 25 °C.

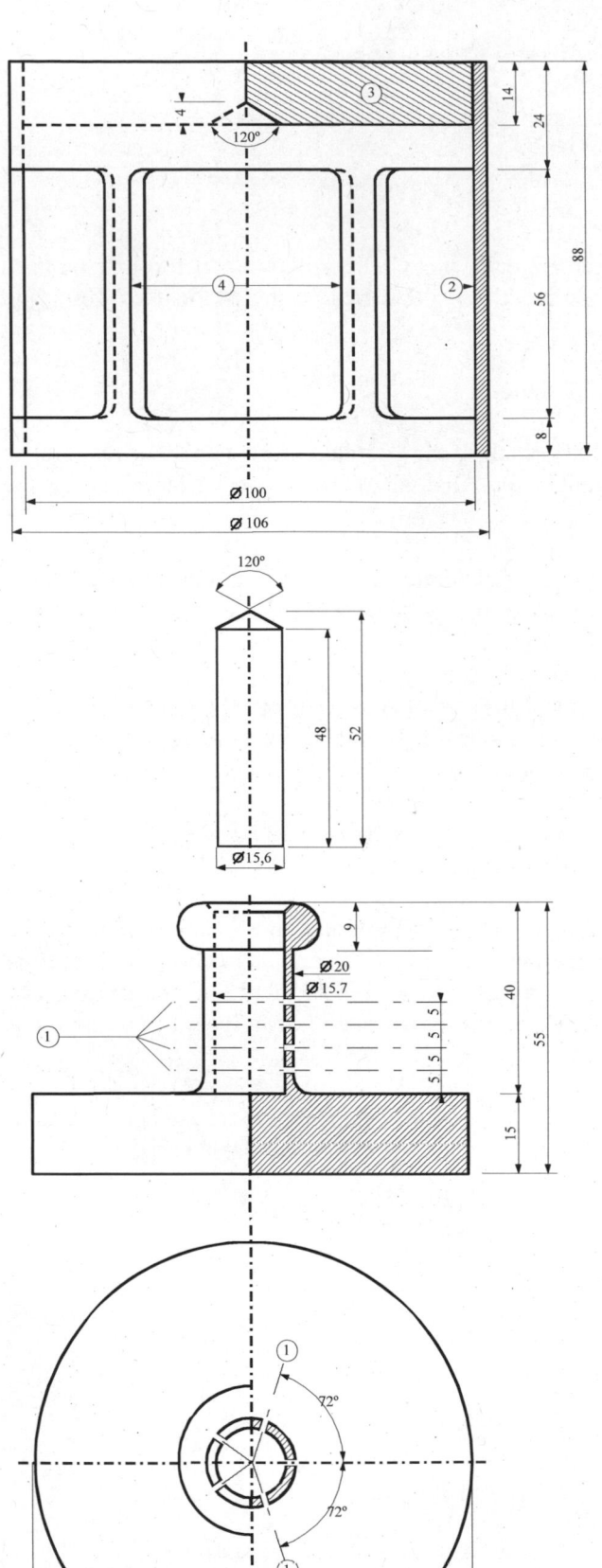

Test of blasting explosive for exudation

Fig.1: Bell-form charge, mass 2220 g, capable of being suspended from a bronze piston

Fig.2: Cylindrical bronze piston, dimensions in mm

Fig.3: Hollow bronze cylinder, closed at one end; Plan and cut dimensions in mm

Fig. 1 to 3

(1) 4 series of 5 holes at 0.5 Ø
(2) copper
(3) lead plate with centre cone at the inferior face
(4) 4 openings, approximately 46x56, set at even intervals on the periphery

2.3.2   **Tests relating to nitrated cellulose mixtures of Class 1 and Class 4.1**

2.3.2.1   In order to determine the criteria of the nitrocellulose, the Bergmann-Junk test or the methyl violet paper test in the Manual of Tests and Criteria Appendix 10 shall be performed (see Chapter 3.3, special provisions 393 and 394). If there is doubt that the ignition temperature of the nitrocellulose is considerably higher than 132 °C in the case of the Bergmann-Junk test or higher than 134.5 °C in the case of the methyl violet paper test, the ignition temperature test described in 2.3.2.5 should be carried out before these tests are performed. If the ignition temperature of nitrocellulose mixtures is higher than 180 °C or the ignition temperature of plasticized nitrocellulose is higher than 170 °C, the Bergmann-Junk test or the methyl violet paper test can be carried out safely.

2.3.2.2   Before undergoing the tests in 2.3.2.5, the samples shall be dried for not less than 15 hours at the ambient temperature in a vacuum desiccator containing fused and granulated calcium chloride, the sample substance being spread in a thin layer; for this purpose, substances which are neither in powder form nor fibrous shall be ground, or grated, or cut into small pieces. The pressure in the desiccator shall be brought below 6.5 kPa (0.065 bar).

2.3.2.3   Before being dried as prescribed in 2.3.2.2 above, plasticized nitrocellulose shall undergo preliminary drying in a well-ventilated oven, with its temperature set at 70 °C, until the loss of mass per quarter-hour is less than 0.3 % of the original mass.

2.3.2.4   Weakly nitrated nitrocellulose shall first undergo preliminary drying as prescribed in 2.3.2.3 above; drying shall then be completed by keeping the nitrocellulose for at least 15 hours over concentrated sulphuric acid in a desiccator.

2.3.2.5   *Ignition temperature (see 2.3.2.1)*

(a)   The ignition temperature is determined by heating 0.2 g of substance enclosed in a glass test tube immersed in a Wood's alloy bath. The test tube is placed in the bath when the latter has reached 100 °C. The temperature of the bath is then progressively increased by 5 °C per minute;

(b)   The test tubes must have the following dimensions:

        length   125 mm
        internal diameter   15 mm
        thickness of wall   0.5 mm

and shall be immersed to a depth of 20 mm;

(c)   The test shall be repeated three times, the temperature at which ignition of the substance occurs, i.e., slow or rapid combustion, deflagration or detonation, being noted each time;

(d)   The lowest temperature recorded in the three tests is the ignition temperature.

2.3.3   **Tests relating to flammable liquids of Classes 3, 6.1 and 8**

2.3.3.1   *Determination of flash-point*

2.3.3.1.1   The following methods for determining the flash-point of flammable liquids may be used:

International standards:

ISO 1516 (Determination of flash/no flash – Closed cup equilibrium method)

ISO 1523 (Determination of flash point – Closed cup equilibrium method)

ISO 2719 (Determination of flash point – Pensky-Martens closed cup method)

ISO 13736 (Determination of flash point – Abel closed-cup method)

ISO 3679 (Determination of flash point – Rapid equilibrium closed cup method)

ISO 3680 (Determination of flash/no flash – Rapid equilibrium closed cup method)

National standards:

American Society for Testing Materials International, 100 Barr Harbor Drive, PO Box C700, West Conshohocken, Pennsylvania, USA 19428-2959:

ASTM D3828-07a, Standard Test Methods for Flash Point by Small Scale Closed-Cup Tester

ASTM D56-05, Standard Test Method for Flash Point by Tag Closed-Cup Tester

ASTM D3278-96(2004)e1, Standard Test Methods for Flash Point of Liquids by Small Scale Closed-Cup Apparatus

ASTM D93-08, Standard Test Methods for Flash Point by Pensky-Martens Closed-Cup Tester

Association française de normalisation, AFNOR, 11, rue de Pressensé, F-93571 La Plaine Saint-Denis Cedex:

French Standard NF M 07 - 019

French Standards NF M 07 - 011 / NF T 30 - 050 / NF T 66 - 009

French Standard NF M 07 - 036

Deutsches Institut für Normung, Burggrafenstr. 6, D-10787 Berlin:

Standard DIN 51755 (flash-points below 65 °C)

State Committee of the Council of Ministers for Standardization, RUS-113813, GSP, Moscow, M-49 Leninsky Prospect, 9:

GOST 12.1.044-84

2.3.3.1.2   To determine the flash-point of paints, gums and similar viscous products containing solvents, only apparatus and test methods suitable for determining the flash-point for viscous liquids shall be used, in accordance with the following standards:

(a)   International Standard ISO 3679:1983;

(b)   International Standard ISO 3680:1983;

(c)   International Standard ISO 1523:1983;

(d)   International Standards EN ISO 13736 and EN ISO 2719, Method B.

2.3.3.1.3   The standards listed in 2.3.3.1.1 shall only be used for flash-point ranges which are specified therein. The possibility of chemical reactions between the substance and the sample holder shall be considered when selecting the standard to be used. The apparatus shall, as far as is consistent with safety, be placed in a draught-free position. For safety, a method utilizing a small sample size, around 2 ml, shall be used for organic peroxides and self-reactive substances (also known as "energetic" substances), or for toxic substances.

2.3.3.1.4   When the flash-point, determined by a non-equilibrium method is found to be 23 ± 2 °C or 60 ± 2 °C, it shall be confirmed for each temperature range by an equilibrium method.

2.3.3.1.5   In the event of a dispute as to the classification of a flammable liquid, the classification proposed by the consignor shall be accepted if a check-test of the flash-point yields a result not differing by more than 2 °C from the limits (23 °C and 60 °C respectively) stated in 2.2.3.1. If the difference is more than 2 °C, a second check-test shall be carried out, and the lowest figure of the flash-points obtained in either check-test shall be adopted.

2.3.3.2   *Determination of initial boiling point*

The following methods for determining the initial boiling point of flammable liquids may be used:

International standards:

ISO 3924 (Petroleum products – Determination of boiling range distribution – Gas chromatography method)

ISO 4626 (Volatile organic liquids – Determination of boiling range of organic solvents used as raw materials)

ISO 3405 (Petroleum products – Determination of distillation characteristics at atmospheric pressure)

National standards:

American Society for Testing Materials International, 100 Barr Harbor Drive, PO Box C700, West Conshohocken, Pennsylvania, USA 19428-2959:

ASTM D86-07a, Standard Test Method for Distillation of Petroleum Products at Atmospheric Pressure

ASTM D1078-05, Standard Test Method for Distillation Range of Volatile Organic Liquids

Further acceptable methods:

Method A.2 as described in Part A of the Annex to Commission Regulation (EC) No 440/2008[1].

---

[1]   *Commission Regulation (EC) No 440/2008 of 30 May 2008 laying down test methods pursuant to Regulation (EC) No 1907/2006 of the European Parliament and of the Council on the Registration, Evaluation, Authorisation and Restriction of Chemicals (REACH) (Official Journal of the European Union, No. L 142 of 31.05.2008, p.1-739 and No. L 143 of 03.06.2008, p.55).*

2.3.3.3   *Test for determining peroxide content*

To determine the peroxide content of a liquid, the procedure is as follows:

A quantity p (about 5 g, weighed to the nearest 0.01 g) of the liquid to be titrated is placed in an Erlenmeyer flask; 20 cm^3 of acetic anhydride and about 1 g of powdered solid potassium iodide are added; the flask is shaken and, after 10 minutes, heated for 3 minutes to about 60 °C. When it has been left to cool for 5 minutes, 25 cm^3 of water are added. After this, it is left standing for half an hour, then the liberated iodine is titrated with a decinormal solution of sodium thiosulphate, no indicator being added; complete discoloration indicates the end of the reaction. If n is the number of cm^3 of thiosulphate solution required, the percentage of peroxide (calculated as H_2O_2) present in the sample is obtained by the formula:

$$\frac{17n}{100p}$$

2.3.4   **Test for determining fluidity**

To determine the fluidity of liquid, viscous or pasty substances and mixtures, the following test method shall be used.

2.3.4.1   *Test apparatus*

Commercial penetrometer conforming to ISO 2137:1985, with a guide rod of 47.5 g ± 0.05 g; sieve disc of duralumin with conical bores and a mass of 102.5 g ± 0.05 g (see Figure 1); penetration vessel with an inside diameter of 72 mm to 80 mm for reception of the sample.

2.3.4.2   *Test procedure*

The sample is poured into the penetration vessel not less than half an hour before the measurement. The vessel is then hermetically closed and left standing until the measurement. The sample in the hermetically closed penetration vessel is heated to 35 °C ± 0.5 °C and is placed on the penetrometer table immediately prior to measurement (not more than two minutes). The point S of the sieve disc is then brought into contact with the surface of the liquid and the rate of penetration is measured.

2.3.4.3   *Evaluation of test results*

A substance is pasty if, after the centre S has been brought into contact with the surface of the sample, the penetration indicated by the dial gauge:

(a)   after a loading time of 5 s ± 0.1 s, is less than 15.0 mm ± 0.3 mm; or

(b)   after a loading time of 5 s ± 0.1 s, is greater than 15.0 mm ± 0.3 mm, but the additional penetration after another 55 s ± 0.5 s is less than 5.0 mm ± 0.5 mm.

NOTE: In the case of samples having a flow point, it is often impossible to produce a steady level surface in the penetration vessel and, hence, to establish satisfactory initial measuring conditions for the contact of the point S. Furthermore, with some samples, the impact of the sieve disc can cause an elastic deformation of the surface and, in the first few seconds, simulate a deeper penetration. In all these cases, it may be appropriate to make the evaluation in paragraph (b) above.

Figure 1 – Penetrometer

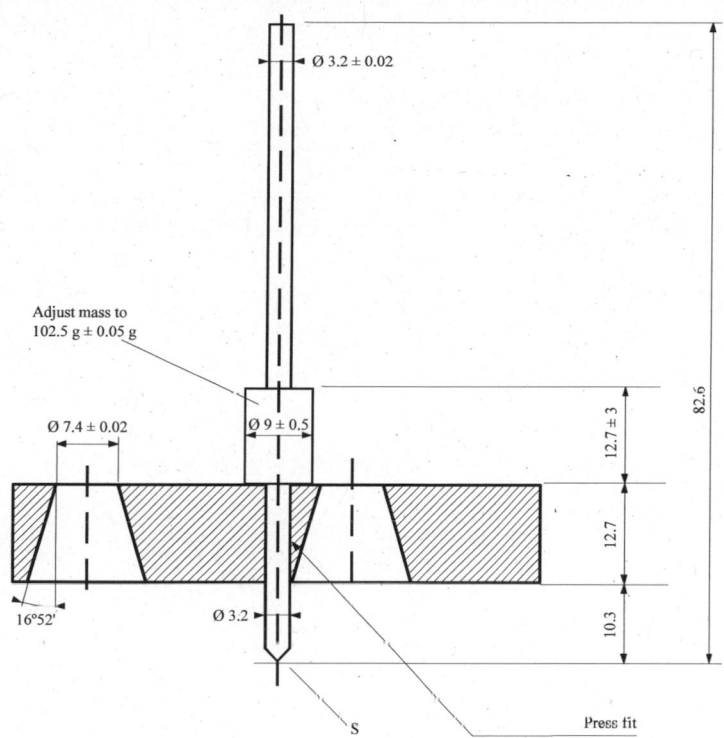

Ø 3.2 ± 0.02

Adjust mass to
102.5 g ± 0.05 g

Ø 7.4 ± 0.02

Ø 9 ± 0.5

82.6

12.7 ± 3

12.7

10.3

16°52'

Ø 3.2

S

Press fit

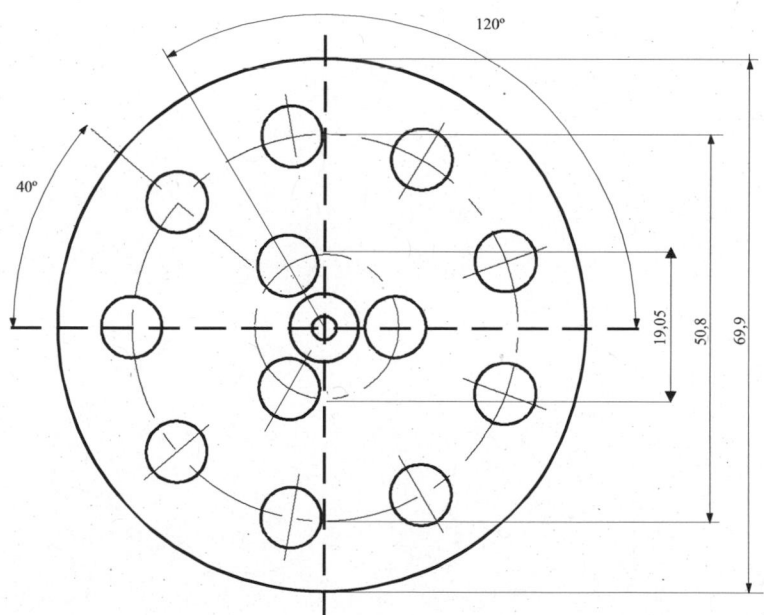

120°

40°

19,05

50,8

69,9

Tolerances not specified are ± 0.1 mm.

2.3.5   **Classification of organometallic substances in Classes 4.2 and 4.3**

Depending on their properties as determined in accordance with tests N.1 to N.5 of the *Manual of Tests and Criteria*, Part III, section 33, organometallic substances may be classified in Classes 4.2 or 4.3, as appropriate, in accordance with the flowchart scheme given in Figure 2.3.5.

NOTE 1: *Depending on their other properties and on the precedence of hazard table (see 2.1.3.10), organometallic substances may have to be classified in other classes as appropriate.*

NOTE 2*: Flammable solutions with organometallic compounds in concentrations which are not liable to spontaneous combustion or, in contact with water, do not emit flammable gases in dangerous quantities, are substances of Class 3.*

Figure 2.3.5   Flowchart scheme for the classification of organometallic substances in Classes 4.2 and 4.3 [b]

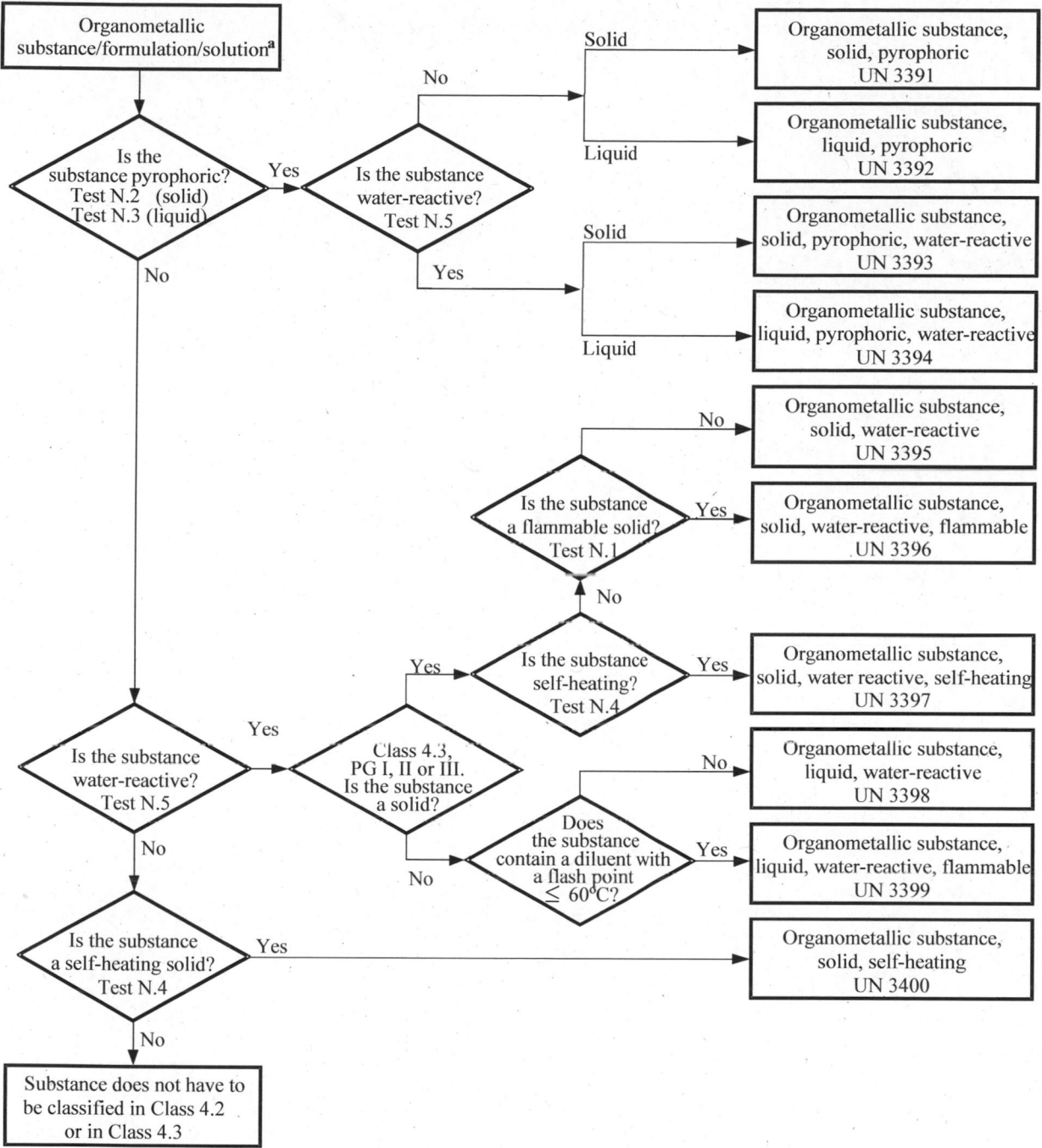

---

[a]   *If applicable (and testing is relevant, taking into account reactivity properties, class 6.1 and 8 properties should be considered according to the precedence of hazard table of 2.1.3.10.*

[b]   *Test methods N.1 to N.5 can be found in the Manual of Tests and Criteria, Part III, Section 33.*

CHAPTER 2.4

CRITERIA FOR SUBSTANCES HAZARDOUS TO THE AQUATIC ENVIRONMENT

2.4.1   General definitions

2.4.1.1   Environmentally hazardous substances include, inter alia, liquid or solid substances pollutant to the aquatic environment and solutions and mixtures of such substances (such as preparations and wastes). For the purposes of this Chapter, 'substance' means chemical elements and their compounds in the natural state or obtained by any production process, including any additive necessary to preserve the stability of the product and any impurities deriving from the process used, but excluding any solvent which may be separated without affecting the stability of the substance or changing its composition.

2.4.1.2   The aquatic environment may be considered in terms of the aquatic organisms that live in the water, and the aquatic ecosystem of which they are part.[1] The basis, therefore, of the identification of hazard is the aquatic toxicity of the substance or mixture, although this may be modified by further information on the degradation and bioaccumulation behaviour.

2.4.1.3   While the following classification procedure is intended to apply to all substances and mixtures, it is recognized that in some cases, e.g. metals or poorly soluble inorganic compounds, special guidance will be necessary.[2]

2.4.1.4   The following definitions apply for acronyms or terms used in this section:

- BCF: Bioconcentration Factor;

- BOD: Biochemical Oxygen Demand;

- COD: Chemical Oxygen Demand;

- GLP: Good Laboratory Practices;

- EC_x: the concentration associated with x% response;

- EC_{50}: the effective concentration of substance that causes 50% of the maximum response;

- ErC_{50}: EC_{50} in terms of reduction of growth;

- K_{ow}: octanol/water partition coefficient;

- LC_{50} (50% lethal concentration): the concentration of a substance in water which causes the death of 50% (one half) in a group of test animals;

- $L(E)C_{50}$: LC_{50} or EC_{50};

- NOEC (No Observed Effect Concentration): the test concentration immediately below the lowest tested concentration with statistically significant adverse effect. The NOEC has no statistically significant adverse effect compared to the control;

- OECD Test Guidelines: test guidelines published by the Organisation for Economic Co-operation and Development (OECD).

---

[1]   *This does not address aquatic pollutants for which there may be a need to consider effects beyond the aquatic environment such as the impacts on human health, etc.*

[2]   *See annex 10 of GHS.*

2.4.2   Definitions and data requirements

2.4.2.1   The basic elements for classification of environmentally hazardous substances (aquatic environment) are as follows:

(a)   Acute aquatic toxicity;

(b)   Chronic aquatic toxicity;

(c)   Potential for or actual bioaccumulation; and

(d)   Degradation (biotic or abiotic) for organic chemicals.

2.4.2.2   While data from internationally harmonized test methods are preferred, in practice, data from national methods may also be used where they are considered as equivalent. In general, it has been agreed that freshwater and marine species toxicity data can be considered as equivalent data and are preferably to be derived using OECD Test Guidelines or equivalent according to the principles of Good Laboratory Practices (GLP). Where such data are not available, classification should be based on the best available data.

2.4.2.3   **Acute aquatic toxicity** means the intrinsic property of a substance to be injurious to an organism in a short-term aquatic exposure to that substance.

Acute (short-term) hazard, for classification purposes, means the hazard of a chemical caused by its acute toxicity to an organism during short-term aquatic exposure to that chemical.

Acute aquatic toxicity shall normally be determined using a fish 96-hour LC_{50} (OECD Test Guideline 203 or equivalent), a crustacea species 48-hour EC_{50} (OECD Test Guideline 202 or equivalent) and/or an algal species 72- or 96-hour EC_{50} (OECD Test Guideline 201 or equivalent). These species are considered as surrogate for all aquatic organisms, and data on other species such as Lemna may also be considered if the test methodology is suitable.

2.4.2.4   **Chronic aquatic toxicity** means the intrinsic property of a substance to cause adverse effects to aquatic organisms during aquatic exposures which are determined in relation to the life-cycle of the organism.

Long-term hazard, for classification purposes, means the hazard of a chemical caused by its chronic toxicity following long-term exposure in the aquatic environment.

Chronic toxicity data are less available than acute data and the range of testing procedures less standardized. Data generated according to OECD Test Guidelines 210 (Fish Early Life Stage) or 211 (Daphnia Reproduction) and 201 (Algal Growth Inhibition) can be accepted. Other validated and internationally accepted tests could also be used. The NOECs or other equivalent ECx shall be used.

2.4.2.5   **Bioaccumulation** means net result of uptake, transformation and elimination of a substance in an organism due to all routes of exposure (i.e. air, water, sediment/soil and food).

The **potential for bioaccumulation** shall normally be determined by using the octanol/water partition coefficient, usually reported as a log K_{ow} determined by OECD Test Guidelines 107, 117 or 123. While this represents a potential to bioaccumulate, an experimentally determined Bioconcentration Factor (BCF) provides a better measure and should be used in preference when available. A BCF should be determined according to OECD Test Guideline 305.

2.4.2.6   **Degradation** means the decomposition of organic molecules to smaller molecules and eventually to carbon dioxide, water and salts.

Environmental degradation may be biotic or abiotic (e.g. hydrolysis) and the criteria reflect this fact. Ready biodegradation can most easily be defined using the biodegradability tests (A-F) of OECD Test Guideline 301. A pass level in these tests can be considered as indicative of rapid degradation in most environments. These are freshwater tests and thus the use of the results from OECD Test Guideline 306, which is more suitable for marine environments, has also been included. Where such data are not available, a BOD_5 (5 days)/COD ratio ≥ 0.5 is considered as indicative of rapid degradation. Abiotic degradation such as hydrolysis, primary degradation, both abiotic and biotic, degradation in non-aquatic media and proven rapid degradation in the environment may all be considered in defining rapid degradability.[3]

Substances shall be considered rapidly degradable in the environment if the following criteria are met:

(a)   In 28-day ready biodegradation studies, the following levels of degradation are achieved:

(i)   Tests based on dissolved organic carbon: 70%;

(ii)   Tests based on oxygen depletion or carbon dioxide generation: 60% of theoretical maxima;

These levels of biodegradation shall be achieved within 10 days of the start of degradation, which point is taken as the time when 10% of the substance has been degraded, unless the substance is identified as a complex, multi-component substance with structurally similar constituents. In this case, and where there is sufficient justification, the 10-day window condition may be waived and the pass level applied at 28 days[4]; or

(b)   In those cases where only BOD and COD data are available, when the ratio of BOD_5/COD is > 0.5; or

(c)   If other convincing scientific evidence is available to demonstrate that the substance or mixture can be degraded (biotically and/or abiotically) in the aquatic environment to a level above 70% within a 28-day period.

2.4.3   **Substance classification categories and criteria**

NOTE: Chronic Category 4 of Chapter 4.1 of GHS is reproduced in this section for information, although it is not relevant in the context of ADN.

2.4.3.1   The following substances shall be considered to be environmentally hazardous (aquatic environment):

(a)   For carriage in packages, substances which meet the criteria for Acute 1, Chronic 1 or Chronic 2, according to table 2.4.3.1 below; and

(b)   For carriage in tank vessels, substances which meet the criteria for Acute 1, Acute 2 or Acute 3, or Chronic 1, Chronic 2 or Chronic 3, according to table 2.4.3.1 below.

---

[3]   *Special guidance on data interpretation is provided in Chapter 4.1 and Annex 9 to GHS.*
[4]   *See Chapter 4.1 and Annex 9, paragraph A9.4.2.2.3 of the GHS.*

Table 2.4.3.1: Categories for substances hazardous to the aquatic environment *(see Note 1)*

(a) Acute (short-term) aquatic hazard

<u>**Category Acute 1:**</u> *(Note 2)*

96 h LC_{50} (for fish)	≤ 1 mg/l and/or
48 h EC_{50} (for crustacea)	≤ 1 mg/l and/or
72 or 96 h ErC_{50} (for algae or other aquatic plants)	≤ 1 mg/l *(see Note 3)*

<u>**Category Acute 2:**</u>

96 h LC_{50} (for fish)	> 1 but ≤ 10 mg/l and/or
48 h EC_{50} (for crustacea)	>1 but ≤ 10 mg/l and/or
72 or 96 h ErC_{50} (for algae or other aquatic plants)	>1 but ≤ 10 mg/l *(see Note 3)*

<u>**Category Acute 3:**</u>

96 h LC_{50} (for fish)	>10 but ≤ 100 mg/l and/or
48 h EC_{50} (for crustacea)	>10 but ≤ 100 mg/l and/or
72 or 96 h ErC_{50} (for algae or other aquatic plants)	>10 but ≤ 100 mg/l *(see Note 3)*

(b) Long-term aquatic hazard *(see also figure 2.4.3.1)*

(i) Non-rapidly degradable substances *(see Note 4)* for which there are adequate chronic toxicity data available

<u>**Category Chronic 1:**</u> (see *Note 2*)

Chronic NOEC or EC_x (for fish)	≤ 0.1 mg/l and/or
Chronic NOEC or EC_x (for crustacea)	≤ 0.1 mg/l and/or
Chronic NOEC or EC_x (for algae or other aquatic plants)	≤ 0.1 mg/l

<u>**Category Chronic 2:**</u>

Chronic NOEC or EC_x (for fish)	≤ 1 mg/l and/or
Chronic NOEC or EC_x (for crustacea)	≤ 1 mg/l and/or
Chronic NOEC or EC_x (for algae or other aquatic plants)	≤ 1 mg/l

(ii) Rapidly degradable substances for which there are adequate chronic toxicity data available

<u>**Category Chronic 1:**</u> *(see Note 2)*

Chronic NOEC or EC_x (for fish)	≤ 0.01 mg/l and/or
Chronic NOEC or EC_x (for crustacea)	≤ 0.01 mg/l and/or
Chronic NOEC or EC_x (for algae or other aquatic plants)	≤ 0.01 mg/l

<u>**Category Chronic 2:**</u>

Chronic NOEC or EC_x (for fish)	≤ 0.1 mg/l and/or
Chronic NOEC or EC_x (for crustacea)	≤ 0.1 mg/l and/or
Chronic NOEC or EC_x (for algae or other aquatic plants)	≤ 0.1 mg/l

<u>**Category Chronic 3:**</u>

Chronic NOEC or EC_x (for fish)	≤ 1 mg/l and/or
Chronic NOEC or EC_x (for crustacea)	≤ 1 mg/l and/or
Chronic NOEC or EC_x (for algae or other aquatic plants)	≤ 1 mg/l

      (iii)   Substances for which adequate chronic toxicity data are not available

Category Chronic 1: *(see Note 2)*

96 h LC_{50} (for fish)	≤ 1 mg/l and/or
48 h EC_{50} (for crustacea)	≤ 1 mg/l and/or
72 or 96 h ErC_{50} (for algae or other aquatic plants)	≤ 1 mg/l *(see Note 3)*

and the substance is not rapidly degradable and/or the experimentally determined BCF is ≥ 500 (or, if absent, the log $K_{ow} \geq 4$) *(see Notes 4 and 5).*

Category Chronic 2:

96 h LC_{50} (for fish)	> 1 but ≤ 10 mg/l and/or
48 h EC_{50} (for crustacea)	> 1 but ≤ 10 mg/l and/or
72 or 96 h ErC_{50} (for algae or other aquatic plants)	> 1 but ≤ 10 mg/l *(see Note 3)*

and the substance is not rapidly degradable and/or the experimentally determined BCF is ≥ 500 (or, if absent, the log $K_{ow} \geq 4$) *(see Notes 4 and 5).*

Category Chronic 3:

96 h LC_{50} (for fish)	> 10 but ≤ 100 mg/l and/or
48 h EC_{50} (for crustacea)	> 10 but ≤ 100 mg/l and/or
72 or 96 h ErC_{50} (for algae or other aquatic plants)	> 10 but ≤ 100 mg/l *(see Note 3)*

and the substance is not rapidly degradable and/or the experimentally determined BCF is ≥ 500 (or, if absent, the log $K_{ow} \geq 4$) *(see Notes 4 and 5).*

(c)   **"Safety net" classification**

Category Chronic 4:

Poorly soluble substances for which no acute toxicity is recorded at levels up to the water solubility, and which are not rapidly degradable and have a log $K_{ow} \geq 4$, indicating a potential to bioaccumulate, will be classified in this category unless other scientific evidence exists showing classification to be unnecessary. Such evidence would include an experimentally determined BCF < 500, or a chronic toxicity NOECs > 1 mg/l, or evidence of rapid degradation in the environment.

Substances which come under Category Chronic 4 alone are not considered to be environmentally hazardous in the sense of ADN.

NOTE 1: The organisms, fish, crustacea and algae are tested as surrogate species covering a range of trophic levels and taxa, and the test methods are highly standardized. Data on other organisms may also be considered, however, provided they represent equivalent species and test endpoints.

NOTE 2: When classifying substances as Acute 1 and/or Chronic 1 it is necessary at the same time to indicate an appropriate M factor (see 2.4.4.6.4) to apply the summation method.

NOTE 3: Where the algal toxicity ErC_{50} (= EC_{50} (growth rate)) falls more than 100 times below the next most sensitive species and results in a classification based solely on this effect, consideration shall be given to whether this toxicity is representative of the toxicity to aquatic plants. Where it can be shown that this is not the case, professional judgement shall be used in deciding if classification shall be applied. Classification shall be based on the ErC_{50}. In circumstances where the basis of the EC_{50} is not specified and no ErC_{50} is recorded, classification shall be based on the lowest EC_{50} available.

NOTE 4: Lack of rapid degradability is based on either a lack of ready biodegradability or other evidence of lack of rapid degradation. When no useful data on degradability are available, either experimentally determined or estimated data, the substance shall be regarded as not rapidly degradable.

NOTE 5: Potential to bioaccumulate, based on an experimentally derived BCF ≥ 500 or, if absent, a log $K_{ow} \geq 4$ provided log K_{ow} is an appropriate descriptor for the bioaccumulation potential of the substance. Measured log K_{ow} values take precedence over estimated values and measured BCF values take precedence over log K_{ow} values.

Figure 2.4.3.1: Categories for substances long-term hazardous to the aquatic environment

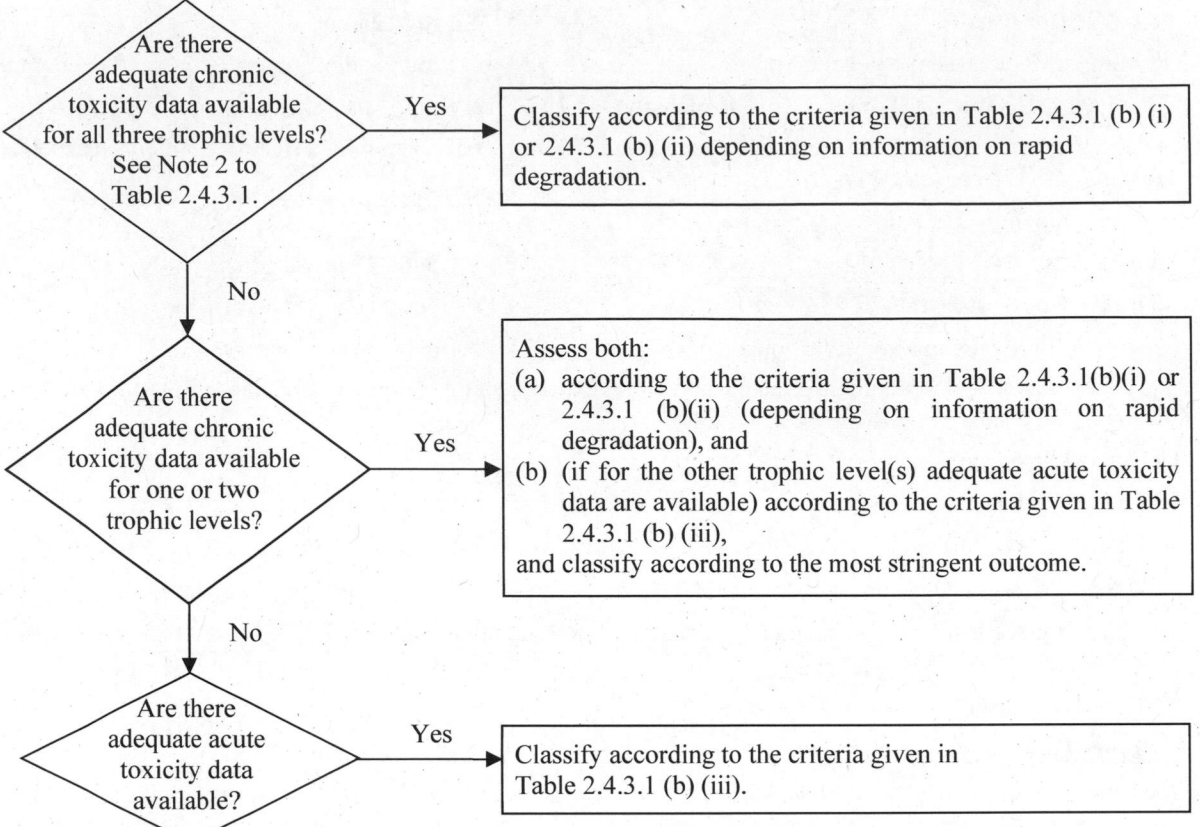

2.4.3.2　　　The classification scheme in Table 2.4.3.2 below summarizes the classification criteria for substances.

Table 2.4.3.2: Classification scheme for substances hazardous to the aquatic environment

	Classification categories		
Acute hazard (*Note 1*)	**Long-term hazard** (*Note 2*)		
	Adequate chronic toxicity data available		**Adequate chronic toxicity data not available** (*Note 1*)
	Non-rapidly degradable substances (*Note 3*)	**Rapidly degradable substances** (*Note 3*)	
Category: Acute 1	**Category: Chronic 1**	**Category: Chronic 1**	**Category: Chronic 1**
$L(E)C_{50} \leq 1.00$	NOEC or $EC_x \leq 0.1$	NOEC or $EC_x \leq 0.01$	$L(E)C_{50} \leq 1.00$ and lack of rapid degradability and/or $BCF \geq 500$ or, if absent log $K_{ow} \geq 4$
Category: Acute 2	**Category: Chronic 2**	**Category: Chronic 2**	**Category: Chronic 2**
$1.00 < L(E)C_{50} \leq 10.0$	$0.1 < $ NOEC or $EC_x \leq 1$	$0.01 < $ NOEC or $EC_x \leq 0.1$	$1.00 < L(E)C_{50} \leq 10.0$ and lack of rapid degradability and/or $BCF \geq 500$ or, if absent log $K_{ow} \geq 4$
Category: Acute 3		**Category: Chronic 3**	**Category: Chronic 3**
$10.0 < L(E)C_{50} \leq 100$		$0.1 < $ NOEC or $EC_x \leq 1$	$10.0 < L(E)C_{50} \leq 100$ and lack of rapid degradability and/or $BCF \geq 500$ or, if absent log $K_{ow} \geq 4$
	Category: Chronic 4 (*Note 4*) Example: (*Note 5*) No acute toxicity and lack of rapid degradability and $BCF \geq 500$ or, if absent log $K_{ow} \geq 4$, unless NOECs > 1 mg/l		

NOTE 1: *Acute toxicity band based on L(E)C$_{50}$ values in mg/l for fish, crustacea and/or algae or other aquatic plants (or Quantitative Structure Activity Relationships (QSAR) estimation if no experimental data[5]).*

NOTE 2: *Substances are classified in the various chronic categories unless there are adequate chronic toxicity data available for all three trophic levels above the water solubility or above 1 mg/l. ("Adequate" means that the data sufficiently cover the endpoint of concern. Generally this would mean measured test data, but in order to avoid unnecessary testing it can on a case by case basis also be estimated data, e.g. (Q)SAR, or for obvious cases expert judgement).*

NOTE 3: *Chronic toxicity band based on NOEC or equivalent EC$_x$ values in mg/l for fish or crustacea or other recognized measures for chronic toxicity.*

NOTE 4: *The system also introduces a "safety net" classification (referred to as category Chronic 4) for use when the data available do not allow classification under the formal criteria but there are nevertheless some grounds for concern.*

NOTE 5: *For poorly soluble substances for which no acute toxicity has been demonstrated at the solubility limit, and are both not rapidly degraded and have a potential to bioaccumulate, this category should apply unless it can be demonstrated that the substance does not require classification for aquatic long-term hazards.*

---

[5]　*Special guidance is provided in Chapter 4.1, paragraph 4.1.2.13 and Annex 9, Section A9.6 of the GHS.*

2.4.4   **Classification categories and criteria for mixtures**

NOTE: Chronic Category 4 of Chapter 4.1 of GHS is reproduced in this section for information, although it is not relevant in the context of ADN.

2.4.4.1   The classification system for mixtures covers all classification categories which are used for substances, meaning categories Acute 1 to 3 and Chronic 1 to 4. In order to make use of all available data for purposes of classifying the aquatic environmental hazards of the mixture, the following assumption has been made and is applied where appropriate.

The "relevant ingredients" of a mixture are those which are present in a concentration equal to or greater than 0.1% (by mass) for ingredients classified as Acute and/or Chronic 1 and equal to or greater than 1% for other ingredients, unless there is a presumption (e.g. in the case of highly toxic ingredients) that an ingredient present at less than 0.1% can still be relevant for classifying the mixture for aquatic environmental hazards.

2.4.4.2   The approach for classification of aquatic environmental hazards is tiered and is dependent upon the type of information available for the mixture itself and for its ingredients. Elements of the tiered approach include:

(a)   Classification based on tested mixtures;

(b)   Classification based on bridging principles;

(c)   Use of 'summation of classified ingredients' and/or an 'additivity formula'.

Figure 2.4.4.2 outlines the process to be followed.

Figure 2.4.4.2: Tiered approach to classification of mixtures for acute and long-term environmental hazards

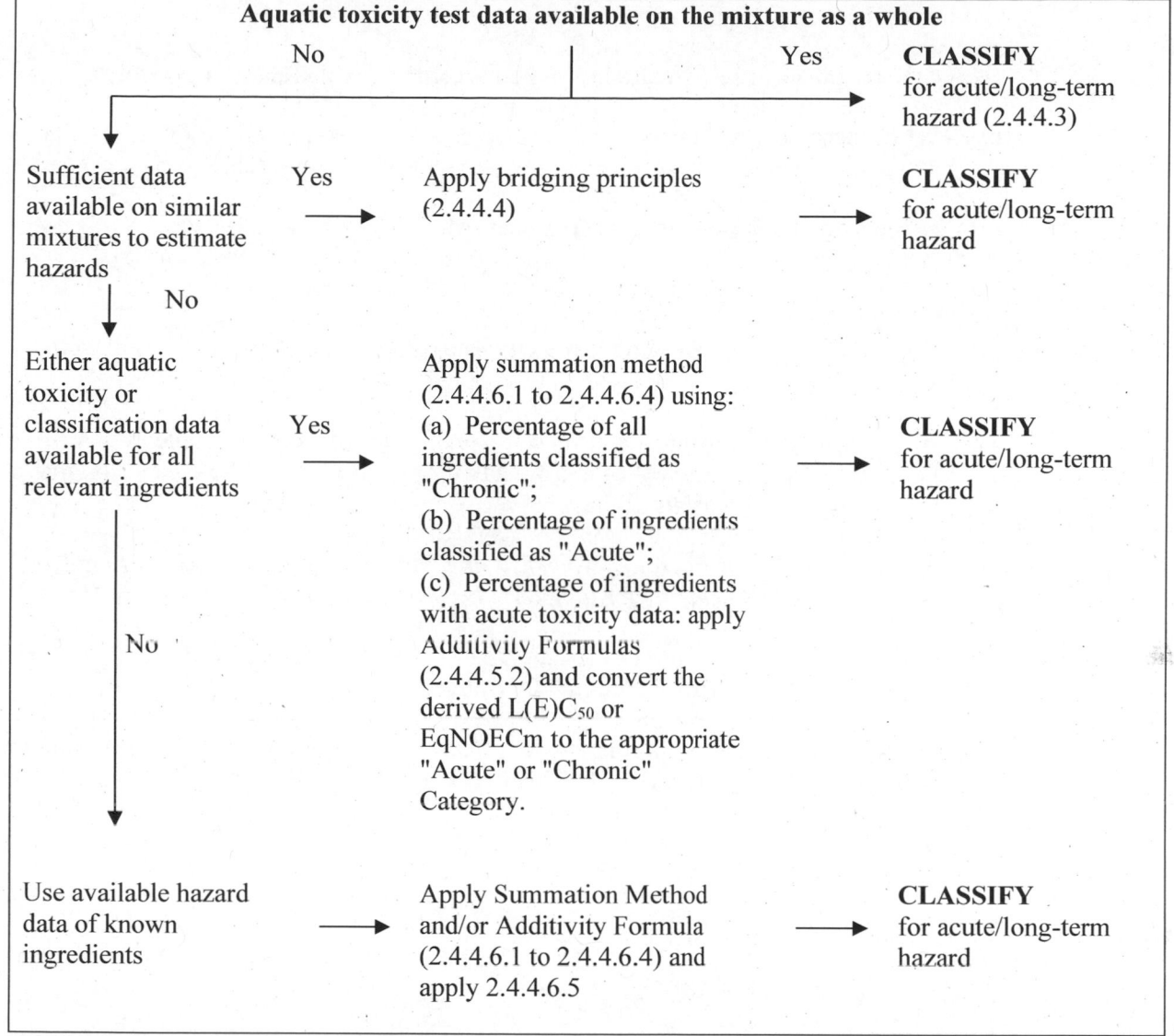

2.4.4.3 *Classification of mixtures when toxicity data are available for the complete mixture*

2.4.4.3.1 When the mixture as a whole has been tested to determine its aquatic toxicity, this information shall be used for classifying the mixture according to the criteria that have been agreed for substances. The classification is normally based on the data for fish, crustacea and algae/plants (2.4.2.3 and 2.4.2.4). When adequate acute or chronic data for the mixture as a whole are lacking, "bridging principles" or "summation method" shall be applied (see 2.4.4.4 and 2.4.4.5).

2.4.4.3.2 The long-term hazard classification of mixtures requires additional information on degradability and in certain cases bioaccumulation. There are no degradability and bioaccumulation data for mixtures as a whole. Degradability and bioaccumulation tests for mixtures are not used as they are usually difficult to interpret, and such tests may be meaningful only for single substances.

2.4.4.3.3　*Classification for categories Acute 1, 2 and 3*

(a)　When there are adequate acute toxicity test data (LC_{50} or EC_{50}) available for the mixture as a whole showing $L(E)C_{50} \leq 100$ mg/l:

Classify the mixture as Acute 1, 2 or 3 in accordance with Table 2.4.3.1 (a);

(b)　When there are acute toxicity test data (LC_{50}(s) or EC_{50}(s) available for the mixture as a whole showing $L(E)C_{50}$(s) > 100 mg/l, or above the water solubility:

No need to classify for acute hazard under ADN.

2.4.4.3.4　*Classification for categories Chronic 1, 2 and 3*

(a)　When there are adequate chronic toxicity data (EC_x or NOEC) available for the mixture as a whole showing EC_x or NOEC of the tested mixture ≤ 1mg/l:

(i)　classify the mixture as Chronic 1, 2 or 3 in accordance with Table 2.4.3.1 (b) (ii) (rapidly degradable) if the available information allows the conclusion that all relevant ingredients of the mixture are rapidly degradable;

NOTE: *In this situation, when EC_x or NOEC of the tested mixture > 1 mg/l, there is no need to classify for long-term hazard under ADN.*

(ii)　classify the mixture as Chronic 1, 2 or 3 in all other cases in accordance with Table 2.4.3.1 (b) (i) (non-rapidly degradable);

(b)　When there are adequate chronic toxicity data (EC_x or NOEC) available for the mixture as a whole showing EC_x(s) or NOEC(s) of the tested mixture > 1mg/l or above the water solubility:

No need to classify for long-term hazard under ADN.

2.4.4.3.5　*Classification for category Chronic 4*

If there are nevertheless reasons for concern:

Classify the mixture as Chronic 4 (safety net classification) in accordance with Table 2.4.3.1 (c).

2.4.4.4　*Classification of mixtures when toxicity data are not available for the complete mixture: bridging principles*

2.4.4.4.1　Where the mixture itself has not been tested to determine its aquatic environmental hazard, but there are sufficient data on the individual ingredients and similar tested mixtures to adequately characterize the hazards of the mixture, these data shall be used in accordance with the following agreed bridging rules. This ensures that the classification process uses the available data to the greatest extent possible in characterizing the hazards of the mixture without the necessity for additional testing in animals.

2.4.4.4.2　*Dilution*

Where a new mixture is formed by diluting a tested mixture or a substance with a diluent which has an equivalent or lower aquatic hazard classification than the least toxic original ingredient and which is not expected to affect the aquatic hazards of other ingredients, then the resulting mixture shall be classified as equivalent to the original tested mixture or substance. Alternatively, the method explained in 2.4.4.5 may be applied.

2.4.4.4.3　　　　*Batching*

The aquatic hazard classification of a tested production batch of a mixture can be assumed to be substantially equivalent to that of another untested production batch of the same commercial product when produced by or under the control of the same manufacturer, unless there is reason to believe there is significant variation such that the aquatic hazard classification of the untested batch has changed. If the latter occurs, new classification is necessary.

2.4.4.4.4　　　　*Concentration of mixtures which are classified with the most severe classification categories (Chronic 1 and Acute 1)*

If a tested mixture is classified as Chronic 1 and/or Acute 1, and the ingredients of the mixture which are classified as Chronic 1 and/or Acute 1 are further concentrated, the more concentrated untested mixture shall be classified with the same classification category as the original tested mixture without additional testing.

2.4.4.4.5　　　　*Interpolation within one toxicity category*

For three mixtures (A, B and C) with identical ingredients, where mixtures A and B have been tested and are in the same toxicity category, and where untested mixture C has the same toxicologically active ingredients as mixtures A and B but has concentrations of toxicologically active ingredients intermediate to the concentrations in mixtures A and B, then mixture C is assumed to be in the same category as A and B.

2.4.4.4.6　　　　*Substantially similar mixtures*

Given the following:

(a)　　Two mixtures:

　　　(i)　　A + B;

　　　(ii)　　C + B;

(b)　　The concentration of ingredient B is essentially the same in both mixtures;

(c)　　The concentration of ingredient A in mixture (i) equals that of ingredient C in mixture (ii);

(d)　　Data on aquatic hazards for A and C are available and are substantially equivalent, i.e. they are in the same hazard category and are not expected to affect the aquatic toxicity of B.

If mixture (i) or (ii) is already classified based on test data, then the other mixture can be assigned the same hazard category.

2.4.4.5　　　*Classification of mixtures when toxicity data are available for all ingredients or only for some ingredients of the mixture*

2.4.4.5.1　　　　The classification of a mixture is based on summation of the concentrations of its classified ingredients. The percentage of ingredients classified as 'Acute' or 'Chronic' will feed straight into the summation method. Details of the summation method are described in 2.4.4.6.1 to 2.4.4.6.4.

2.4.4.5.2   Mixtures may be made of a combination of both ingredients that are classified (as Acute 1 to 3 and/or Chronic 1 to 4) and those for which adequate toxicity test data are available. When adequate toxicity data are available for more than one ingredient in the mixture, the combined toxicity of those ingredients shall be calculated using the following additivity formulas (a) or (b), depending on the nature of the toxicity data:

(a)   Based on acute aquatic toxicity:

$$\frac{\sum C_i}{L(E)C_{50m}} = \sum_n \frac{C_i}{L(E)C_{50i}}$$

where:

C_i =   concentration of ingredient i (mass percentage);

$L(E)C_{50i}$ = LC_{50} or EC_{50} for ingredient i (mg/l);

n   =   number of ingredients, and i is running from 1 to n;

$L(E)C_{50m}$ = $L(E)C_{50}$ of the part of the mixture with test data;

The calculated toxicity shall be used to assign that portion of the mixture an acute hazard category which is then subsequently used in applying the summation method;

(b)   Based on chronic aquatic toxicity:

$$\frac{\sum C_i + \sum C_j}{EqNOEC_m} = \sum_n \frac{C_i}{NOEC_i} + \sum_n \frac{C_j}{0.1 \times NOEC_j}$$

where:

C_i =   concentration of ingredient i (mass percentage) covering the rapidly degradable ingredients;

C_j =   concentration of ingredient j (mass percentage) covering the non-rapidly degradable ingredients;

$NOEC_i$ =   NOEC (or other recognized measures for chronic toxicity) for ingredient i covering the rapidly degradable ingredients, in mg/l;

$NOEC_j$ =   NOEC (or other recognized measures for chronic toxicity) for ingredient j covering the non-rapidly degradable ingredients, in mg/l;

n   =   number of ingredients, and i and j are running from 1 to n;

$EqNOEC_m$=   equivalent NOEC of the part of the mixture with test data;

The equivalent toxicity thus reflects the fact that non-rapidly degrading substances are classified one hazard category level more "severe" than rapidly degrading substances.

The calculated equivalent toxicity shall be used to assign that portion of the mixture a long-term hazard category, in accordance with the criteria for rapidly degradable substances (Table 2.4.3.1 (b) (ii)), which is then subsequently used in applying the summation method.

2.4.4.5.3   When applying the additivity formula for part of the mixture, it is preferable to calculate the toxicity of this part of the mixture using for each ingredient toxicity values that relate to the same taxonomic group (i.e. fish, crustacea or algae) and then to use the highest toxicity (lowest value) obtained (i.e. use the most sensitive of the three groups). However, when toxicity data for each ingredient are not available in the same taxonomic group, the toxicity value of each ingredient shall be selected in the same manner that toxicity values are selected for the classification of substances, i.e. the highest toxicity (from the most sensitive test organism) is used. The calculated acute and chronic toxicity may then be used to classify this part of the mixture as Acute 1, 2 or 3 and/or Chronic 1, 2, or 3 using the same criteria described for substances.

2.4.4.5.4   If a mixture is classified in more than one way, the method yielding the more conservative result shall be used.

2.4.4.6   *Summation method*

2.4.4.6.1   *Classification procedures*

In general, a more severe classification for mixtures overrides a less severe classification, e.g. a classification with Chronic 1 overrides a classification with Chronic 2. As a consequence, the classification procedure is already completed if the result of the classification is Chronic 1. A more severe classification than Chronic 1 is not possible; therefore, it is not necessary to pursue the classification procedure further.

2.4.4.6.2   *Classification for categories Acute 1, 2 and 3*

2.4.4.6.2.1   First, all ingredients classified as Acute 1 are considered. If the sum of the concentrations (in %) of these ingredients is $\geq 25\%$, the whole mixture is classified as Acute 1. If the result of the calculation is a classification of the mixture as Acute 1, the classification process is completed.

2.4.4.6.2.2   In cases where the mixture is not classified as Acute 1, classification of the mixture as Acute 2 shall be considered. A mixture is classified as Acute 2 if 10 times the sum of all ingredients classified as Acute 1 plus the sum of all ingredients classified as Acute 2 is $\geq 25\%$. If the result of the calculation is classification of the mixture as Acute 2, the classification process is completed.

2.4.4.6.2.3   In cases where the mixture is not classified either as Acute 1 or Acute 2, classification of the mixture as Acute 3 shall be considered. A mixture is classified as Acute 3 if 100 times the sum of all ingredients classified as Acute 1 plus 10 times the sum of all ingredients classified as Acute 2 plus the sum of all ingredients classified as Acute 3 is $\geq 25\%$.

2.4.4.6.2.4   The classification of mixtures for acute hazards based on this summation of the concentrations of classified ingredients is summarized in Table 2.4.4.6.2.4.

Table 2.4.4.6.2.4:   Classification of a mixture for acute hazards based on summation of the concentrations of classified ingredients

Sum of the concentrations (in %) of ingredients classified as:	Mixture classified as:
Acute 1 × M[a] $\geq 25\%$	Acute 1
(M × 10 x Acute 1) + Acute 2 $\geq 25\%$	Acute 2
(M × 100 × Acute 1) + (10 × Acute 2) + Acute 3 $\geq 25\%$	Acute 3

[a] *For explanation of the M factor, see 2.4.4.6.4.*

2.4.4.6.3   *Classification for categories Chronic 1, 2, 3 and 4*

2.4.4.6.3.1   First, all ingredients classified as Chronic 1 are considered. If the sum of the concentrations (in %) of these ingredients is ≥ 25%, the mixture shall be classified as Chronic 1. If the result of the calculation is a classification of the mixture as Chronic 1, the classification procedure is completed.

2.4.4.6.3.2   In cases where the mixture is not classified as Chronic 1, classification of the mixture as Chronic 2 shall be considered. A mixture is classified as Chronic 2 if 10 times the sum of the concentrations (in %) of all ingredients classified as Chronic 1 plus the sum of the concentrations (in %) of all ingredients classified as Chronic 2 is ≥ 25%. If the result of the calculation is classification of the mixture as Chronic 2, the classification process is completed.

2.4.4.6.3.3   In cases where the mixture is not classified either as Chronic 1 or Chronic 2, classification of the mixture as Chronic 3 shall be considered. A mixture is classified as Chronic 3 if 100 times the sum of all ingredients classified as Chronic 1 plus 10 times the sum of all ingredients classified as Chronic 2 plus the sum of all ingredients classified as Chronic 3 is ≥ 25%.

2.4.4.6.3.4   If the mixture is still not classified in Category Chronic 1, 2 or 3, classification of the mixture as Chronic 4 need not be considered for the purposes of ADN. A mixture is classified as Chronic 4 if the sum of the percentages of ingredients classified as Chronic 1, 2, 3 and 4 is ≥ 25%.

2.4.4.6.3.5   The classification of mixtures for long-term hazards based on this summation of the concentrations of classified ingredients is summarized in Table 2.4.4.6.3.5 below.

Table 2.4.4.6.3.5: Classification of a mixture for long-term hazards based on summation of the concentrations of classified ingredients

Sum of the concentrations (in %) of ingredients classified as:	Mixture classified as:
Chronic 1 × M [a] ≥ 25%	Chronic 1
(M × 10 × Chronic 1) + Chronic 2 ≥ 25%	Chronic 2
(M × 100 × Chronic 1) + (10 × Chronic 2) + Chronic 3 ≥ 25%	Chronic 3
Chronic 1 + Chronic 2 + Chronic 3 + Chronic 4 ≥ 25 %	Chronic 4

[a]   *For explanation of the M factor, see 2.4.4.6.4.*

2.4.4.6.4   *Mixtures with highly toxic ingredients*

Acute 1 or Chronic 1 ingredients with acute toxicities well below 1 mg/l and/or chronic toxicities well below 0.1 mg/l (if non-rapidly degradable) and 0.01 mg/l (if rapidly degradable) may influence the toxicity of the mixture and shall be given increased weight in applying the summation method. When a mixture contains ingredients classified as Acute or Chronic 1, the tiered approach described in 2.4.4.6.2 and 2.4.4.6.3 shall be applied using a weighted sum by multiplying the concentrations of Acute 1 and Chronic 1 ingredients by a factor, instead of merely adding up the percentages. This means that the concentration of "Acute 1" in the left column of Table 2.4.4.6.2.4 and the concentration of "Chronic 1" in the left column of Table 2.4.4.6.3.4 are multiplied by the appropriate multiplying factor. The multiplying factors to be applied to these ingredients are defined using the toxicity value, as summarized in Table 2.4.4.6.4 below. Therefore, in order to classify a mixture containing Acute/Chronic 1 ingredients, the classifier needs to be informed of the value of the M factor in order to apply the summation method. Alternatively, the additivity formula (see 2.4.4.5.2) may be used when toxicity data are available for all highly toxic ingredients in the mixture and there is convincing evidence that all other ingredients, including those for which specific acute and/or chronic toxicity data are not available, are of low or no toxicity and do not significantly contribute to the environmental hazard of the mixture.

Table 2.4.4.6.4 Multiplying factors for highly toxic ingredients of mixtures

Acute toxicity	M factor	Chronic toxicity	M factor	
L(E)C$_{50}$ value		NOEC value	NRD [a] ingredients	RD [b] ingredients
$0.1 < L(E)C_{50} \leq 1$	1	$0.01 < NOEC \leq 0.1$	1	–
$0.01 < L(E)C_{50} \leq 0.1$	10	$0.001 < NOEC \leq 0.01$	10	1
$0.001 < L(E)C_{50} \leq 0.01$	100	$0.0001 < NOEC \leq 0.001$	100	10
$0.0001 < L(E)C_{50} \leq 0.001$	1 000	$0.00001 < NOEC \leq 0.0001$	1 000	100
$0.00001 < L(E)C_{50} \leq 0.0001$	10 000	$0.000001 < NOEC \leq 0.00001$	10 000	1 000
(continue in factor 10 intervals)		(continue in factor 10 intervals)		

[a] *Non-rapidly degradable.*
[b] *Rapidly degradable.*

2.4.4.6.5 *Classification of mixtures with ingredients without any useable information*

In the event that no useable information on acute and/or chronic aquatic toxicity is available for one or more relevant ingredients, it is concluded that the mixture cannot be attributed (a) definitive hazard category(ies). In this situation, the mixture shall be classified based on the known ingredients only.

PART 3

Dangerous goods list, special provisions and exemptions related to limited and excepted quantities

CHAPTER 3.1

GENERAL

3.1.1 **Introduction**

In addition to the provisions referred to or given in the tables of this Part, the general requirements of each Part, Chapter and/or Section are to be observed. These general requirements are not given in the tables. When a general requirement is contradictory to a special provision, the special provision prevails.

3.1.2 **Proper shipping name**

NOTE: For proper shipping names used for the carriage of samples, see 2.1.4.1.

3.1.2.1   The proper shipping name is that portion of the entry most accurately describing the goods in Table A or Table C in Chapter 3.2, which is shown in upper case characters (plus any numbers, Greek letters, "sec", "tert", and the letters "m", "n", "o", "p", which form an integral part of the name). Particulars concerning the vapour pressure (vp) and the boiling point (bp) in column (2) of Table C in chapter 3.2 are part of the proper shipping name. An alternative proper shipping name may be shown in brackets following the main proper shipping name. In Table A, it is shown in upper case characters (e.g., ETHANOL (ETHYL ALCOHOL)). In Table C, it is shown in lower case characters (e.g. ACETONITRILE (methyl cyanide)). Portions of an entry appearing in lower case need not be considered as part of the proper shipping name unless otherwise stated above.

3.1.2.2   When a combination of several distinct proper shipping names are listed under a single UN number, and these are separated by "and" or "or" in lower case or are punctuated by commas, only the most appropriate shall be shown in the transport document and package marks. Examples illustrating the selection of the proper shipping name for such entries are:

(a)   UN 1057 LIGHTERS or LIGHTER REFILLS - The proper shipping name is the most appropriate of the following possible combinations:

LIGHTERS

LIGHTER REFILLS;

(b)   UN 2793 FERROUS METAL BORINGS, SHAVINGS, TURNINGS or CUTTINGS in a form liable to self-heating. The proper shipping name is the most appropriate of the following combinations:

FERROUS METAL BORINGS

FERROUS METAL SHAVINGS

FERROUS METAL TURNINGS

FERROUS METAL CUTTINGS.

3.1.2.3   Proper shipping names may be used in the singular or plural as appropriate. In addition, when qualifying words are used as part of the proper shipping name, their sequence on documentation or package marks is optional. For instance, "DIMETHYLAMINE AQUEOUS SOLUTION" may alternatively be shown "AQUEOUS SOLUTION OF DIMETHYLAMINE". Commercial or military names for goods of Class 1 which contain the proper shipping name supplemented by additional descriptive text may be used.

3.1.2.4   Many substances have an entry for both the liquid and solid state (see definitions for liquid and solid in 1.2.1), or for the solid and solution. These are allocated separate UN numbers which are not necessarily adjacent to each other[1].

3.1.2.5   Unless it is already included in capital letters in the name indicated in Table A or Table C in Chapter 3.2, the qualifying word "MOLTEN" shall be added as part of the proper shipping name when a substance, which is a solid in accordance with the definition in 1.2.1, is offered for carriage in the molten state (e.g. ALKYLPHENOL, SOLID, N.O.S., MOLTEN).

3.1.2.6   Except for self-reactive substances and organic peroxides and unless it is already included in capital letters in the name indicated in Column (2) of Table A of Chapter 3.2, the word "STABILIZED" shall be added as part of the proper shipping name of a substance which without stabilization would be forbidden from carriage in accordance with paragraphs 2.2.X.2 due to it being liable to dangerously react under conditions normally encountered in carriage (e.g.: "TOXIC LIQUID, ORGANIC, N.O.S., STABILIZED").

When temperature control is used to stabilize such substances to prevent the development of any dangerous excess pressure, or the evolution of excessive heat, or when chemical stabilization is used in combination with temperature control, then:

(a)   For liquids and solids where the SAPT[2] (measured without or with inhibitor, when chemical stabilization is applied) is less than or equal to that prescribed in 2.2.41.1.21, the provisions of 2.2.41.1.17, special provision 386 of Chapter 3.3, 7.1.7, special provision V8 of Chapter 7.2 of ADR, special provision S4 of Chapter 8.5 of ADR and the requirements of Chapter 9.6 of ADR apply except that the term "SADT" as used in these paragraphs is understood to include also "SAPT" when the substance concerned reacts by polymerization;

(b)   Unless it is already included in capital letters in the name indicated in Column (2) of Table A in Chapter 3.2, the words "TEMPERATURE CONTROLLED" shall be added as part of the proper shipping name;

(c)   For gases: the conditions of carriage shall be approved by the competent authority.

3.1.2.7   Hydrates may be carried under the proper shipping name for the anhydrous substance.

3.1.2.8   ***Generic or "not otherwise specified" (N.O.S.) names***

3.1.2.8.1   Generic and "not otherwise specified" proper shipping names that are assigned to special provision 274 or 318 in Column (6) of Table A in Chapter 3.2 or remark 27 in column (20) of Table C in Chapter 3.2 shall be supplemented with the technical name of the goods unless a national law or international convention prohibits its disclosure if it is a controlled substance. For explosive substances and articles of Class 1, the dangerous goods description may be supplemented by additional descriptive text to indicate commercial or military names. Technical names shall be entered in brackets immediately following the proper shipping name. An appropriate modifier, such as "contains" or "containing" or other qualifying words such as "mixture", "solution", etc. and the percentage of the technical constituent may also be used. For example: "UN 1993 FLAMMABLE LIQUID, N.O.S. (CONTAINS XYLENE AND BENZENE), 3, II".

---

[1]   *Details are provided in the alphabetical index (Table B of Chapter 3.2), e.g.:*
       NITROXYLENES, LIQUID   6.1   1665
       NITROXYLENES, SOLID   6.1   3447
[2]   *For the definition of self-accelerating polymerization temperature (SAPT), see 1.2.1.*

3.1.2.8.1.1   The technical name shall be a recognized chemical name or biological name, or other name currently used in scientific and technical handbooks, journals and texts. Trade names shall not be used for this purpose. In the case of pesticides, only ISO common name(s), other name(s) in the World Health Organization (WHO) Recommended Classification of Pesticides by Hazard and Guidelines to Classification, or the name(s) of the active substance(s) may be used.

3.1.2.8.1.2   When a mixture of dangerous goods or articles containing dangerous goods are described by one of the "N.O.S." or "generic" entries to which special provision 274 has been allocated in Column (6) of Table A in Chapter 3.2, not more than the two constituents which most predominantly contribute to the hazard or hazards of the mixture or of the articles need to be shown, excluding controlled substances when their disclosure is prohibited by national law or international convention. If a package containing a mixture is labelled with any subsidiary hazard label, one of the two technical names shown in parentheses shall be the name of the constituent which compels the use of the subsidiary hazard label.

   NOTE: see 5.4.1.2.2.

3.1.2.8.1.3   Examples illustrating the selection of the proper shipping name supplemented with the technical name of goods for such N.O.S. entries are:

   UN 2902 PESTICIDE, LIQUID, TOXIC, N.O.S. (drazoxolon);

   UN 3394 ORGANOMETALLIC SUBSTANCE, LIQUID, PYROPHORIC, WATER-REACTIVE (trimethylgallium).

   UN 3540 ARTICLES CONTAINING FLAMMABLE LIQUID, N.O.S. (pyrrolidine)

3.1.2.8.1.4   For UN Nos. 3077 and 3082 only, the technical name may be a name shown in capital letters in column 2 of Table A of Chapter 3.2, provided that this name does not include "N.O.S." and that special provision 274 is not assigned. The name which most appropriately describes the substance or mixture shall be used, e.g.:

   UN 3082, ENVIRONMENTALLY HAZARDOUS SUBSTANCE, LIQUID, N.O.S. (PAINT)

   UN 3082, ENVIRONMENTALLY HAZARDOUS SUBSTANCE, LIQUID, N.O.S. (PERFUMERY PRODUCTS).

3.1.2.8.1.5   *(Deleted)*

3.1.3   Solutions or mixtures

   NOTE: Where a substance is specifically mentioned by name in Table A of Chapter 3.2, it shall be identified in carriage by the proper shipping name in Column (2) of Table A of Chapter 3.2. Such substances may contain technical impurities (for example those deriving from the production process) or additives for stability or other purposes that do not affect its classification. However, a substance mentioned by name containing technical impurities or additives for stability or other purposes affecting its classification shall be considered a solution or mixture (see 2.1.3.3).

3.1.3.1   A solution or mixture is not subject to ADN if the characteristics, properties, form or physical state of the solution or mixture are such that it does not meet the criteria, including human experience criteria, for inclusion in any class.

3.1.3.2   A solution or mixture meeting the classification criteria of ADN composed of a single predominant substance mentioned by name in Table A of Chapter 3.2 and one or more substances not subject to ADN and/or traces of one or more substances mentioned by name in Table A of Chapter 3.2, shall be assigned the UN number and proper shipping name of the predominant substance mentioned by name in Table A of Chapter 3.2 unless:

(a)   The solution or mixture is mentioned by name in Table A of Chapter 3.2;

(b)   The name and description of the substance mentioned by name in Table A of Chapter 3.2 specifically indicate that they apply only to the pure substance;

(c)   The class, classification code, packing group, or physical state of the solution or mixture is different from that of the substance mentioned by name in Table A of Chapter 3.2; or

(d)   The hazard characteristics and properties of the solution or mixture necessitate emergency response measures that are different from those required for the substance mentioned by name in Table A of Chapter 3.2.

Qualifying words such as "SOLUTION" or "MIXTURE", as appropriate, shall be added as part of the proper shipping name, for example, "ACETONE SOLUTION". In addition, the concentration of the mixture or solution may also be indicated after the basic description of the mixture or solution, for example, "ACETONE 75% SOLUTION".

3.1.3.3   A solution or mixture meeting the classification criteria of ADN that is not mentioned by name in Table A of Chapter 3.2 and that is composed of two or more dangerous goods shall be assigned to an entry that has the proper shipping name, description, class, classification code and packing group that most precisely describe the solution or mixture.

DANGEROUS GOODS LIST

3.2.1   **Table A:**   **List of dangerous goods in numerical order**

Explanations concerning Table A:

As a rule, each row of Table A deals with the substance(s) or article(s) covered by a specific UN number or an identification number. However, when substances or articles belonging to the same UN number have different chemical properties, physical properties and/or carriage conditions, several consecutive rows may be used for that UN number or identification number.

Each column of Table A is dedicated to a specific subject as indicated in the explanatory notes below. The intersection of columns and rows (cell) contains information concerning the subject treated in that column, for the substance(s) or article(s) of that row:

–   The first four cells identify the substance(s) or article(s) belonging to that row (additional information in that respect may be given by the special provisions referred to in Column (6));

–   The following cells give the applicable special provisions, either in the form of complete information or in coded form. The codes cross-refer to detailed information that is to be found in the numbers indicated in the explanatory notes below. An empty cell means either that there is no special provision and that only the general requirements apply, or that the carriage restriction indicated in the explanatory notes is in force. When used in this table, an alphanumeric code starting with the letters "SP" designates a special provision of Chapter 3.3.

The applicable general requirements are not referred to in the corresponding cells.

Explanatory notes for each column:

Column (1)   "UN number/identification number".

                Contains the UN number or the identification number:

–   of the dangerous substance or article if the substance or article has been assigned its own specific UN number or identification number, or

–   of the generic or n.o.s. entry to which the dangerous substances or articles not mentioned by name shall be assigned in accordance with the criteria ("decision trees") of Part 2.

Column (2)   "Name and description"

                Contains, in upper case characters, the name of the substance or article, if the substance or article has been assigned its own specific UN number or identification number, or of the generic or n.o.s. entry to which it has been assigned in accordance with the criteria ("decision trees") of Part 2. This name shall be used as the proper shipping name or, when applicable, as part of the proper shipping name (see 3.1.2 for further details on the proper shipping name).

A descriptive text in lower case characters is added after the proper shipping name to clarify the scope of the entry if the classification and/or carriage conditions of the substance or article may be different under certain conditions.

Column (3a)   "Class"

Contains the number of the Class, whose heading covers the dangerous substance or article. This Class number is assigned in accordance with the procedures and criteria of Part 2.

Column (3b)   "Classification code"

Contains the classification code of the dangerous substance or article.

– For dangerous substances or articles of Class 1, the code consists of a division number and compatibility group letter, which are assigned in accordance with the procedures and criteria of 2.2.1.1.4.

– For dangerous substances or articles of Class 2, the code consists of a number and one or more letters representing the hazardous property group, which are explained in 2.2.2.1.2 and 2.2.2.1.3.

– For dangerous substances or articles of Classes 3, 4.1, 4.2, 4.3, 5.1, 5.2, 6.1, 6.2 and 9, the codes are explained in 2.2.x.1.2. [1]

– For dangerous substances or articles of Class 8, the codes are explained in 2.2.8.1.4.1;

– Dangerous substances or articles of Class 7 do not have a classification code.

Column (4)   "Packing group"

Contains the packing group number(s) (I, II or III) assigned to the dangerous substance. These packing group numbers are assigned on the basis of the procedures and criteria of Part 2. Certain articles and substances are not assigned to packing groups.

Column (5)   "Labels"

Contains the model number of the labels/placards (see 5.2.2.2 and 5.3.1.1.7) that have to be affixed to packages, containers, tank-containers, portable tanks, MEGCs, vehicles and wagons. However:

– For substances or articles of Class 7, 7X means label model No. 7A, 7B or 7C as appropriate according to the category (see 5.1.5.3.4 and 5.2.2.1.11.1) or placard No. 7D (see 5.3.1.1.3 and 5.3.1.1.7.2).

The general provisions on labelling/placarding (e.g. number of labels, their location) are to be found in 5.2.2.1 for packages, and in 5.3.1, for containers, tank-containers, MEGCs, portable tanks, vehicles and wagons.

NOTE: Special provisions, indicated in Column (6), may change the above labelling provisions.

---

[1] *x = the Class number of the dangerous substance or article, without dividing point if applicable.*

Column (6)	"Special provisions"

Contains the numeric codes of special provisions that have to be met. These provisions concern a wide array of subjects, mainly connected with the contents of Columns (1) to (5) (e.g. carriage prohibitions, exemptions from certain requirements, explanations concerning the classification of certain forms of the dangerous goods concerned and additional labelling or marking provisions), and are listed in Chapter 3.3 in numerical order. If Column (6) is empty, no special provisions apply to the contents of Columns (1) to (5) for the dangerous goods concerned. Special provisions specific to inland navigation begin at 800.

Column (7a)	"Limited Quantities"

Provides the maximum quantity per inner packaging or article for carrying dangerous goods as limited quantities in accordance with Chapter 3.4.

Column (7b)	"Excepted Quantities"

Contains an alphanumeric code with the following meaning:

- "E0" signifies that no exemption from the provisions of ADN exists for the dangerous goods packed in excepted quantities;

- All the other alphanumerical codes starting with the letter "E" signify that the provisions of ADN are not applicable if the conditions indicated in Chapter 3.5 are fulfilled.

Column (8)	"Carriage permitted"

This column contains the alphabetic codes concerning the permitted form of carriage in inland navigation vessels.

If column (8) is empty, the substance or article may only be carried in packages.

If column (8) contains code "B", carriage is permitted in packages or in bulk (see 7.1.1.11).

If column (8) contains code "T", carriage is permitted in packages and in tank vessels. In the event of carriage in tank vessels, the requirements of Table C are applicable (see 7.2.1.21).

Column (9)	"Equipment required"

This column contains the alphanumeric codes for the equipment required for the carriage of the dangerous substance or article (see 8.1.5).

Column (10)	"Ventilation"

This column contains the alphanumeric codes of the special requirements concerning ventilation applicable to carriage with the following meaning:

- alphanumeric codes starting with the letters "VE" mean that special additional conditions are applicable to carriage. These can be found in 7.1.6.12 and establish special requirements.

Column (11)   "Provisions concerning loading, unloading and carriage"

This column contains the alphanumeric codes of the special requirements applicable to carriage with the following meaning:

– alphanumeric codes starting with the letters "CO", "ST" and "RA" mean that special additional conditions are applicable to carriage in bulk. These can be found in 7.1.6.11 and establish special requirements.

– alphanumeric codes starting with the letters "LO" mean that special additional conditions are applicable prior to loading. These can be found in 7.1.6.13 and establish special requirements.

– alphanumeric codes starting with the letters "HA" mean that special additional conditions are applicable to the handling and stowage of the cargo. These can be found in 7.1.6.14 and establish special requirements.

– alphanumeric codes starting with the letters "IN" mean that special additional conditions are applicable to the inspection of holds during carriage. These can be found in 7.1.6.16 and establish special requirements.

Column (12)   "Number of blue cones/lights"

This column contains the number of cones/lights which should constitute the marking of the vessel during the carriage of this dangerous substance or article (see 7.1.5).

Column (13)   "Additional requirements/Remarks"

This column contains additional requirements or observations concerning the carriage of this dangerous substance or article.

UN No. or ID No.	Name and description	Class	Classification Code	Packing group	Labels	Special provisions	Limited quantities	Excepted quantities	Carriage permitted	Equipment required	Ventilation	Provisions concerning loading, unloading and carriage	Number of blue cones/ lights	Remarks
		2.2	2.2	2.1.1.3	5.2.2	3.3	3.4	3.5.1.2	3.2.1	8.1.5	7.1.6	7.1.6	7.1.5	3.2.1
(1)	(2)	(3a)	(3b)	(4)	(5)	(6)	(7a)	(7b)	(8)	(9)	(10)	(11)	(12)	(13)
0004	AMMONIUM PICRATE dry or wetted with less than 10% water, by mass	1	1.1D		1		0	E0		PP		LO01	HA01, HA02, HA03	3	
0005	CARTRIDGES FOR WEAPONS with bursting charge	1	1.1F		1		0	E0		PP		LO01	HA01, HA02, HA03	3	
0006	CARTRIDGES FOR WEAPONS with bursting charge	1	1.1E		1		0	E0		PP		LO01	HA01, HA02, HA03	3	
0007	CARTRIDGES FOR WEAPONS with bursting charge	1	1.2F		1		0	E0		PP		LO01	HA01, HA02, HA03	3	
0009	AMMUNITION, INCENDIARY with or without burster, expelling charge or propelling charge	1	1.2G		1		0	E0		PP		LO01	HA01, HA03	3	
0010	AMMUNITION, INCENDIARY with or without burster, expelling charge or propelling charge	1	1.3G		1		0	E0		PP		LO01	HA01, HA03	3	
0012	CARTRIDGES FOR WEAPONS, INERT PROJECTILE or CARTRIDGES, SMALL ARMS	1	1.4S		1.4	364	5 kg	E0		PP		LO01	HA01, HA03	0	
0014	CARTRIDGES FOR WEAPONS, BLANK or CARTRIDGES, SMALL ARMS, BLANK or CARTRIDGES FOR TOOLS, BLANK	1	1.4S		1.4	364	5 kg	E0		PP		LO01	HA01, HA03	0	
0015	AMMUNITION, SMOKE with or without burster, expelling charge or propelling charge	1	1.2G		1		0	E0		PP		LO01	HA01, HA03	3	
0015	AMMUNITION, SMOKE with or without burster, expelling charge or propelling charge, containing corrosive substances	1	1.2G		1+8		0	E0		PP		LO01	HA01, HA03	3	
0015	AMMUNITION, SMOKE with or without burster, expelling charge or propelling charge, containing toxic by inhalation substances	1	1.2G		1+6.1		0	E0		PP		LO01	HA01, HA03	3	
0016	AMMUNITION, SMOKE with or without burster, expelling charge or propelling charge	1	1.3G		1		0	E0		PP		LO01	HA01, HA03	3	
0016	AMMUNITION, SMOKE with or without burster, expelling charge or propelling charge, containing corrosive substances	1	1.3G		1+8		0	E0		PP		LO01	HA01, HA03	3	
0016	AMMUNITION, SMOKE with or without burster, expelling charge or propelling charge, containing toxic by inhalation substances	1	1.3G		1+6.1		0	E0		PP		LO01	HA01, HA03	3	
0018	AMMUNITION, TEAR-PRODUCING with burster, expelling charge or propelling charge	1	1.2G		1+6.1+8	802	0	E0		PP		LO01	HA01, HA03	3	
0019	AMMUNITION, TEAR-PRODUCING with burster, expelling charge or propelling charge	1	1.3G		1+6.1+8	802	0	E0		PP		LO01	HA01, HA03	3	
0020	AMMUNITION, TOXIC with burster, expelling charge or propelling charge	1	1.2K						CARRIAGE PROHIBITED					
0021	AMMUNITION, TOXIC with burster, expelling charge or propelling charge	1	1.3K						CARRIAGE PROHIBITED					
0027	BLACK POWDER (GUNPOWDER), granular or as a meal	1	1.1D		1		0	E0		PP		LO01	HA01, HA02, HA03	3	

-211-

UN No. or ID No.	Name and description	Class	Classification Code	Packing group	Labels	Special provisions	Limited and excepted quantities		Carriage permitted	Equipment required	Ventilation	Provisions concerning loading, unloading and carriage	Number of blue cones/ lights	Remarks
	3.1.2	2.2	2.2	2.1.1.3	5.2.2	3.3	3.4	3.5.1.2	3.2.1	8.1.5	7.1.6	7.1.6	7.1.5	3.2.1
(1)	(2)	(3a)	(3b)	(4)	(5)	(6)	(7a)	(7b)	(8)	(9)	(10)	(11)	(12)	(13)
0028	BLACK POWDER (GUNPOWDER), COMPRESSED or BLACK POWDER (GUNPOWDER), IN PELLETS	1	1.1D		1		0	E0		PP		LO01 HA01, HA02, HA03	3	
0029	DETONATORS, NON-ELECTRIC for blasting	1	1.1B		1		0	E0		PP		LO01 HA01, HA02, HA03	3	
0030	DETONATORS, ELECTRIC for blasting	1	1.1B		1		0	E0		PP		LO01 HA01, HA02, HA03	3	
0033	BOMBS with bursting charge	1	1.1F		1		0	E0		PP		LO01 HA01, HA02, HA03	3	
0034	BOMBS with bursting charge	1	1.1D		1		0	E0		PP		LO01 HA01, HA02, HA03	3	
0035	BOMBS with bursting charge	1	1.2D		1		0	E0		PP		LO01 HA01, HA03	3	
0037	BOMBS, PHOTO-FLASH	1	1.1F		1		0	E0		PP		LO01 HA01, HA02, HA03	3	
0038	BOMBS, PHOTO-FLASH	1	1.1D		1		0	E0		PP		LO01 HA01, HA02, HA03	3	
0039	BOMBS, PHOTO-FLASH	1	1.2G		1		0	E0		PP		LO01 HA01, HA03	3	
0042	BOOSTERS without detonator	1	1.1D		1		0	E0		PP		LO01 HA01, HA02, HA03	3	
0043	BURSTERS, explosive	1	1.1D		1		0	E0		PP		LO01 HA01, HA02, HA03	3	
0044	PRIMERS, CAP TYPE	1	1.4S		1.4		0	E0		PP		LO01 HA01, HA03	0	
0048	CHARGES, DEMOLITION	1	1.1D		1		0	E0		PP		LO01 HA01, HA02, HA03	3	
0049	CARTRIDGES, FLASH	1	1.1G		1		0	E0		PP		LO01 HA01, HA02, HA03	3	
0050	CARTRIDGES, FLASH	1	1.3G		1		0	E0		PP		LO01 HA01, HA03	3	
0054	CARTRIDGES, SIGNAL	1	1.3G		1		0	E0		PP		LO01 HA01, HA03	3	
0055	CASES, CARTRIDGE, EMPTY, WITH PRIMER	1	1.4S		1.4	364	5 kg	E0		PP		LO01 HA01, HA03	0	
0056	CHARGES, DEPTH	1	1.1D		1		0	E0		PP		LO01 HA01, HA02, HA03	3	

UN No. or ID No.	Name and description	Class	Classification Code	Packing group	Labels	Special provisions	Limited quantities	Excepted quantities	Carriage permitted	Equipment required	Ventilation	Provisions concerning loading, unloading and carriage	Number of blue cones/lights	Remarks
(1)	(2)	2.2 (3a)	2.2 (3b)	2.1.1.3 (4)	5.2.2 (5)	3.3 (6)	3.4 (7a)	3.5.1.2 (7b)	3.2.1 (8)	8.1.5 (9)	7.1.6 (10)	7.1.6 (11)	7.1.5 (12)	3.2.1 (13)
0059	CHARGES, SHAPED without detonator	1	1.1D		1		0	E0		PP		LO01	HA01, HA02, HA03	3	
0060	CHARGES, SUPPLEMENTARY, EXPLOSIVE	1	1.1D		1		0	E0		PP		LO01	HA01, HA02, HA03	3	
0065	CORD, DETONATING, flexible	1	1.1D		1		0	E0		PP		LO01	HA01, HA02, HA03	3	
0066	CORD, IGNITER	1	1.4G		1.4		0	E0		PP		LO01	HA01, HA03	1	
0070	CUTTERS, CABLE, EXPLOSIVE	1	1.4S		1.4		0	E0		PP		LO01	HA01, HA03	0	
0072	CYCLOTRIMETHYLENETRINITRAMINE (CYCLONITE; HEXOGEN; RDX), WETTED with not less than 15% water, by mass	1	1.1D		1	266	0	E0		PP		LO01	HA01, HA02, HA03	3	
0073	DETONATORS FOR AMMUNITION	1	1.1B		1		0	E0		PP		LO01	HA01, HA02, HA03	3	
0074	DIAZODINITROPHENOL, WETTED with not less than 40% water, or mixture of alcohol and water, by mass	1	1.1A		1	266	0	E0		PP		LO01	HA01, HA02, HA03	3	
0075	DIETHYLENEGLYCOL DINITRATE, DESENSITIZED with not less than 25% non-volatile, water-insoluble phlegmatizer, by mass	1	1.1D		1	266	0	E0		PP		LO01	HA01, HA02, HA03	3	
0076	DINITROPHENOL, dry or wetted with less than 15% water, by mass	1	1.1D		1+6.1	802	0	E0		PP		LO01	HA01, HA02, HA03	3	
0077	DINITROPHENOLATES, alkali metals, dry or wetted with less than 15% water, by mass	1	1.3C		1+6.1	802	0	E0		PP		LO01	HA01, HA02, HA03	3	
0078	DINITRORESORCINOL, dry or wetted with less than 15% water, by mass	1	1.1D		1		0	E0		PP		LO01	HA01, HA02, HA03	3	
0079	HEXANITRODIPHENYLAMINE (DIPICRYLAMINE; HEXYL)	1	1.1D		1		0	E0		PP		LO01	HA01, HA02, HA03	3	
0081	EXPLOSIVE, BLASTING, TYPE A	1	1.1D		1	616 617	0	E0		PP		LO01	HA01, HA02, HA03	3	
0082	EXPLOSIVE, BLASTING, TYPE B	1	1.1D		1	617	0	E0		PP		LO01	HA01, HA02, HA03	3	
0083	EXPLOSIVE, BLASTING, TYPE C	1	1.1D		1	267 617	0	E0		PP		LO01	HA01, HA02, HA03	3	
0084	EXPLOSIVE, BLASTING, TYPE D	1	1.1D		1	617	0	E0		PP		LO01	HA01, HA02, HA03	3	

UN No. or ID No.	Name and description	Class	Classification Code	Packing group	Labels	Special provisions	Limited and excepted quantities		Carriage permitted	Equipment required	Venti-lation	Provisions concerning loading, unloading and carriage	Number of blue cones/ lights	Remarks
							3.4	3.5.1.2	3.2.1	8.1.5	7.1.6	7.1.6	7.1.5	3.2.1
	3.1.2	2.2	2.2	2.1.1.3	5.2.2	3.3								
(1)	(2)	(3a)	(3b)	(4)	(5)	(6)	(7a)	(7b)	(8)	(9)	(10)	(11)	(12)	(13)
0092	FLARES, SURFACE	1	1.3G		1		0	E0		PP		LO01 HA01, HA03	3	
0093	FLARES, AERIAL	1	1.3G		1		0	E0		PP		LO01 HA01, HA03	3	
0094	FLASH POWDER	1	1.1G		1		0	E0		PP		LO01 HA01, HA02, HA03	3	
0099	FRACTURING DEVICES, EXPLOSIVE without detonator, for oil wells	1	1.1D		1		0	E0		PP		LO01 HA01, HA02, HA03	3	
0101	FUSE, NON-DETONATING	1	1.3G		1		0	E0		PP		LO01 HA01, HA03	3	
0102	CORD (FUSE), DETONATING, metal clad	1	1.2D		1		0	E0		PP		LO01 HA01, HA03	3	
0103	FUSE, IGNITER, tubular, metal clad	1	1.4G		1.4		0	E0		PP		LO01 HA01, HA03	1	
0104	CORD (FUSE), DETONATING, MILD EFFECT, metal clad	1	1.4D		1.4		0	E0		PP		LO01 HA01, HA03	1	
0105	FUSE, SAFETY	1	1.4S		1.4		0	E0		PP		LO01 HA01, HA03	0	
0106	FUZES, DETONATING	1	1.1B		1		0	E0		PP		LO01 HA01, HA02, HA03	3	
0107	FUZES, DETONATING	1	1.2B		1		0	E0		PP		LO01 HA01, HA02, HA03	3	
0110	GRENADES, PRACTICE, hand or rifle	1	1.4S		1.4		0	E0		PP		LO01 HA01, HA03	0	
0113	GUANYLNITROSAMINOGUANYLIDENE HYDRAZINE, WETTED with not less than 30% water, by mass	1	1.1A		1	266	0	E0		PP		LO01 HA01, HA02, HA03	3	
0114	GUANYLNITROSAMINOGUANYLTETRAZENE (TETRAZENE), WETTED with not less than 30% water, or mixture of alcohol and water, by mass	1	1.1A		1	266	0	E0		PP		LO01 HA01, HA02, HA03	3	
0118	HEXOLITE (HEXOTOL), dry or wetted with less than 15% water, by mass	1	1.1D		1		0	E0		PP		LO01 HA01, HA02, HA03	3	
0121	IGNITERS	1	1.1G		1		0	E0		PP		LO01 HA01, HA02, HA03	3	
0124	JET PERFORATING GUNS, CHARGED, oil well, without detonator	1	1.1D		1		0	E0		PP		LO01 HA01, HA02, HA03	3	
0129	LEAD AZIDE, WETTED with not less than 20% water, or mixture of alcohol and water, by mass	1	1.1A		1	266	0	E0		PP		LO01 HA01, HA02, HA03	3	

UN No. or ID No. (1)	Name and description (2)	Class (3a)	Classification Code (3b)	Packing group (4)	Labels (5)	Special provisions (6)	Limited quantities (7a)	Excepted quantities (7b)	Carriage permitted (8)	Equipment required (9)	Ventilation (10)	Provisions concerning loading, unloading and carriage (11)	Number of blue cones/lights (12)	Remarks (13)
0130	LEAD STYPHNATE (LEAD TRINITRORESORCINATE), WETTED with not less than 20% water, or mixture of alcohol and water, by mass	1	1.1A		1	266	0	E0		PP		LO01 HA01, HA02, HA03	3	
0131	LIGHTERS, FUSE	1	1.4S		1.4		0	E0				LO01 HA01, HA03	0	
0132	DEFLAGRATING METAL SALTS OF AROMATIC NITRODERIVATIVES, N.O.S.	1	1.3C		1	274	0	E0		PP		LO01 HA01, HA03	3	
0133	MANNITOL HEXANITRATE (NITROMANNITE), WETTED with not less than 40% water, or mixture of alcohol and water, by mass	1	1.1D		1	266	0	E0		PP		LO01 HA01, HA02, HA03	3	
0135	MERCURY FULMINATE, WETTED with not less than 20% water, or mixture of alcohol and water, by mass	1	1.1A		1	266	0	E0		PP		LO01 HA01, HA02, HA03	3	
0136	MINES with bursting charge	1	1.1F		1		0	E0		PP		LO01 HA01, HA02, HA03	3	
0137	MINES with bursting charge	1	1.1D		1		0	E0		PP		LO01 HA01, HA02, HA03	3	
0138	MINES with bursting charge	1	1.2D		1		0	E0		PP		LO01 HA01, HA02, HA03	3	
0143	NITROGLYCERIN, DESENSITIZED with not less than 40% non-volatile water-insoluble phlegmatizer, by mass	1	1.1D		1+6.1	266 271 802	0	E0		PP		LO01 HA01, HA02, HA03	3	
0144	NITROGLYCERIN SOLUTION IN ALCOHOL with more than 1% but not more than 10% nitroglycerin	1	1.1D		1	358	0	E0		PP		LO01 HA01, HA02, HA03	3	
0146	NITROSTARCH, dry or wetted with less than 20% water, by mass	1	1.1D		1		0	E0		PP		LO01 HA01, HA02, HA03	3	
0147	NITRO UREA	1	1.1D		1		0	E0		PP		LO01 HA01, HA02, HA03	3	
0150	PENTAERYTHRITE TETRANITRATE (PENTAERYTHRITOL TETRANITRATE; PETN), WETTED with not less than 25% water, by mass, or DESENSITIZED with not less than 15% phlegmatizer, by mass	1	1.1D		1	266	0	E0		PP		LO01 HA01, HA02, HA03	3	
0151	PENTOLITE, dry or wetted with less than 15% water, by mass	1	1.1D		1		0	E0		PP		LO01 HA01, HA02, HA03	3	
0153	TRINITROANILINE (PICRAMIDE)	1	1.1D		1		0	E0		PP		LO01 HA01, HA02, HA03	3	
0154	TRINITROPHENOL (PICRIC ACID), dry or wetted with less than 30% water, by mass	1	1.1D		1		0	E0		PP		LO01 HA01, HA02, HA03	3	

UN No. or ID No. (1)	Name and description 3.1.2 (2)	Class 2.2 (3a)	Classification Code 2.2 (3b)	Packing group 2.1.1.3 (4)	Labels 5.2.2 (5)	Special provisions 3.3 (6)	Limited and excepted quantities 3.4 (7a)	3.5.1.2 (7b)	Carriage permitted 3.2.1 (8)	Equipment required 8.1.5 (9)	Ventilation 7.1.6 (10)	Provisions concerning loading, unloading and carriage 7.1.6 (11)	Number of blue cones/lights 7.1.5 (12)	Remarks 3.2.1 (13)
0155	TRINITROCHLOROBENZENE (PICRYL CHLORIDE)	1	1.1D		1		0	E0		PP		LO01 HA01, HA02, HA03	3	
0159	POWDER CAKE (POWDER PASTE), WETTED with not less than 25% water, by mass	1	1.3C		1	266	0	E0		PP		LO01 HA01, HA03	3	
0160	POWDER, SMOKELESS	1	1.1C		1		0	E0		PP		LO01 HA01, HA02, HA03	3	
0161	POWDER, SMOKELESS	1	1.3C		1		0	E0		PP		LO01 HA01, HA03	3	
0167	PROJECTILES with bursting charge	1	1.1F		1		0	E0		PP		LO01 HA01, HA02, HA03	3	
0168	PROJECTILES with bursting charge	1	1.1D		1		0	E0		PP		LO01 HA01, HA02, HA03	3	
0169	PROJECTILES with bursting charge	1	1.2D		1		0	E0		PP		LO01 HA01, HA03	3	
0171	AMMUNITION, ILLUMINATING with or without burster, expelling charge or propelling charge	1	1.2G		1		0	E0		PP		LO01 HA01, HA03	3	
0173	RELEASE DEVICES, EXPLOSIVE	1	1.4S		1.4		0	E0		PP		LO01 HA01, HA03	0	
0174	RIVETS, EXPLOSIVE	1	1.4S		1.4		0	E0		PP		LO01 HA01, HA03	0	
0180	ROCKETS with bursting charge	1	1.1F		1		0	E0		PP		LO01 HA01, HA02, HA03	3	
0181	ROCKETS with bursting charge	1	1.1E		1		0	E0		PP		LO01 HA01, HA02, HA03	3	
0182	ROCKETS with bursting charge	1	1.2E		1		0	E0		PP		LO01 HA01, HA03	3	
0183	ROCKETS with inert head	1	1.3C		1		0	E0		PP		LO01 HA01, HA03	3	
0186	ROCKET MOTORS	1	1.3C		1		0	E0		PP		LO01 HA01, HA03	3	
0190	SAMPLES, EXPLOSIVE, other than initiating explosive	1				16 274	0	E0		PP		LO01 HA01, HA02, HA03	3	
0191	SIGNAL DEVICES, HAND	1	1.4G		1.4		0	E0		PP		LO01 HA01, HA03	1	
0192	SIGNALS, RAILWAY TRACK, EXPLOSIVE	1	1.1G		1		0	E0		PP		LO01 HA01, HA02, HA03	3	
0193	SIGNALS, RAILWAY TRACK, EXPLOSIVE	1	1.4S		1.4		0	E0		PP		LO01 HA01, HA03	0	

UN No. or ID No.	Name and description	Class	Classification Code	Packing group	Labels	Special provisions	Limited and excepted quantities		Carriage permitted	Equipment required	Ventilation	Provisions concerning loading, unloading and carriage	Number of blue cones/ lights	Remarks
		2.2	2.2	2.1.1.3	5.2.2	3.3	3.4	3.5.1.2	3.2.1	8.1.5	7.1.6	7.1.6	7.1.5	3.2.1
(1)	(2)	(3a)	(3b)	(4)	(5)	(6)	(7a)	(7b)	(8)	(9)	(10)	(11)	(12)	(13)
0194	SIGNALS, DISTRESS, ship	1	1.1G		1		0	E0		PP		L001	HA01, HA02, HA03	3	
0195	SIGNALS, DISTRESS, ship	1	1.3G		1		0	E0		PP		L001	HA01, HA03	3	
0196	SIGNALS, SMOKE	1	1.1G		1		0	E0		PP		L001	HA01, HA02, HA03	3	
0197	SIGNALS, SMOKE	1	1.4G		1.4		0	E0		PP		L001	HA01, HA03	1	
0204	SOUNDING DEVICES, EXPLOSIVE	1	1.2F		1		0	E0		PP		L001	HA01, HA02, HA03	3	
0207	TETRANITROANILINE	1	1.1D		1		0	E0		PP		L001	HA01, HA02, HA03	3	
0208	TRINITROPHENYLMETHYLNITRAMINE (TETRYL)	1	1.1D		1		0	E0		PP		L001	HA01, HA02, HA03	3	
0209	TRINITROTOLUENE (TNT), dry or wetted with less than 30% water, by mass	1	1.1D		1		0	E0		PP		L001	HA01, HA02, HA03	3	
0212	TRACERS FOR AMMUNITION	1	1.3G		1		0	E0		PP		L001	HA01, HA02, HA03	3	
0213	TRINITROANISOLE	1	1.1D		1		0	E0		PP		L001	HA01, HA02, HA03	3	
0214	TRINITROBENZENE, dry or wetted with less than 30% water, by mass	1	1.1D		1		0	E0		PP		L001	HA01, HA02, HA03	3	
0215	TRINITROBENZOIC ACID, dry or wetted with less than 30% water, by mass	1	1.1D		1		0	E0		PP		L001	HA01, HA02, HA03	3	
0216	TRINITRO-m-CRESOL	1	1.1D		1		0	E0		PP		L001	HA01, HA02, HA03	3	
0217	TRINITRONAPHTHALENE	1	1.1D		1		0	E0		PP		L001	HA01, HA02, HA03	3	
0218	TRINITROPHENETOLE	1	1.1D		1		0	E0		PP		L001	HA01, HA02, HA03	3	
0219	TRINITRORESORCINOL (STYPHNIC ACID), dry or wetted with less than 20% water, or mixture of alcohol and water, by mass	1	1.1D		1		0	E0		PP		L001	HA01, HA02, HA03	3	
0220	UREA NITRATE, dry or wetted with less than 20% water, by mass	1	1.1D		1		0	E0		PP		L001	HA01, HA02, HA03	3	

UN No. or ID No.	Name and description	Class	Classi-fication Code	Packing group	Labels	Special provis-ions	Limited and excepted quantities		Carriage permitted	Equipment required	Venti-lation	Provisions concerning loading, unloading and carriage	Number of blue cones/ lights	Remarks
							3.4	3.5.1.2	3.2.1	8.1.5	7.1.6	7.1.6	7.1.5	3.2.1
(1)	3.1.2 (2)	2.2 (3a)	2.2 (3b)	2.1.1.3 (4)	5.2.2 (5)	3.3 (6)	(7a)	(7b)	(8)	(9)	(10)	(11)	(12)	(13)
0221	WARHEADS, TORPEDO with bursting charge	1	1.1D		1		0	E0		PP		LO01 HA01, HA02, HA03	3	
0222	AMMONIUM NITRATE	1	1.1D		1	370	0	E0		PP		LO01 HA01, HA02, HA03	3	
0224	BARIUM AZIDE, dry or wetted with less than 50% water, by mass	1	1.1A		1+6.1	802	0	E0		PP		LO01 HA01, HA02, HA03	3	
0225	BOOSTERS WITH DETONATOR	1	1.1B		1		0	E0		PP		LO01 HA01, HA02, HA03	3	
0226	CYCLOTETRAMETHYLENETETRANITRAMINE (HMX; OCTOGEN), WETTED with not less than 15% water, by mass	1	1.1D		1	266	0	E0		PP		LO01 HA01, HA02, HA03	3	
0234	SODIUM DINITRO-o-CRESOLATE, dry or wetted with less than 15% water, by mass	1	1.3C		1		0	E0		PP		LO01 HA01, HA03	3	
0235	SODIUM PICRAMATE, dry or wetted with less than 20% water, by mass	1	1.3C		1		0	E0		PP		LO01 HA01, HA03	3	
0236	ZIRCONIUM PICRAMATE, dry or wetted with less than 20% water, by mass	1	1.3C		1		0	E0		PP		LO01 HA01, HA03	3	
0237	CHARGES, SHAPED, FLEXIBLE, LINEAR	1	1.4D		1.4		0	E0		PP		LO01 HA01, HA03	1	
0238	ROCKETS, LINE-THROWING	1	1.2G		1		0	E0		PP		LO01 HA01, HA03	3	
0240	ROCKETS, LINE-THROWING	1	1.3G		1		0	E0		PP		LO01 HA01, HA03	3	
0241	EXPLOSIVE, BLASTING, TYPE E	1	1.1D		1	617	0	E0		PP		LO01 HA01, HA02, HA03	3	
0242	CHARGES, PROPELLING, FOR CANNON	1	1.3C		1		0	E0		PP		LO01 HA01, HA03	3	
0243	AMMUNITION, INCENDIARY, WHITE PHOSPHORUS with burster, expelling charge or propelling charge	1	1.2H		1		0	E0		PP		LO01 HA01, HA03	3	
0244	AMMUNITION, INCENDIARY, WHITE PHOSPHORUS with burster, expelling charge or propelling charge	1	1.3H		1		0	E0		PP		LO01 HA01, HA03	3	
0245	AMMUNITION, SMOKE, WHITE PHOSPHORUS with burster, expelling charge or propelling charge	1	1.2H		1		0	E0		PP		LO01 HA01, HA03	3	
0246	AMMUNITION, SMOKE, WHITE PHOSPHORUS with burster, expelling charge or propelling charge	1	1.3H		1		0	E0		PP		LO01 HA01, HA03	3	
0247	AMMUNITION, INCENDIARY, liquid or gel, with burster, expelling charge or propelling charge	1	1.3J		1		0	E0		PP		LO01 HA01, HA03	3	
0248	CONTRIVANCES, WATER-ACTIVATED with burster, expelling charge or propelling charge	1	1.2L		1	274	0	E0		PP		LO01 HA01, HA03	3	
0249	CONTRIVANCES, WATER-ACTIVATED with burster, expelling charge or propelling charge	1	1.3L		1	274	0	E0		PP		LO01 HA01, HA03	3	

UN No. or ID No. (1) 3.1.2	Name and description (2) 3.1.2	Class (3a) 2.2	Classification Code (3b) 2.2	Packing group (4) 2.1.1.3	Labels (5) 5.2.2	Special provisions (6) 3.3	Limited and excepted quantities 3.4 (7a)	Limited and excepted quantities 3.5.1.2 (7b)	Carriage permitted (8) 3.2.1	Equipment required (9) 8.1.5	Ventilation (10) 7.1.6	Provisions concerning loading, unloading and carriage (11) 7.1.6	Number of blue cones/lights (12) 7.1.5	Remarks (13) 3.2.1
0250	ROCKET MOTORS WITH HYPERGOLIC LIQUIDS with or without expelling charge	1	1.3L		1		0	E0		PP		LO01 HA01, HA03	3	
0254	AMMUNITION, ILLUMINATING with or without burster, expelling charge or propelling charge	1	1.3G		1		0	E0		PP		LO01 HA01, HA03	3	
0255	DETONATORS, ELECTRIC for blasting	1	1.4B		1.4		0	E0		PP		LO01 HA01, HA02, HA03	1	
0257	FUZES, DETONATING	1	1.4B		1.4		0	E0		PP		LO01 HA01, HA02, HA03	1	
0266	OCTOLITE (OCTOL), dry or wetted with less than 15% water, by mass	1	1.1D		1		0	E0		PP		LO01 HA01, HA02, HA03	3	
0267	DETONATORS, NON-ELECTRIC for blasting	1	1.4B		1.4		0	E0		PP		LO01 HA01, HA02, HA03	1	
0268	BOOSTERS WITH DETONATOR	1	1.2B		1		0	E0		PP		LO01 HA01, HA02, HA03	3	
0271	CHARGES, PROPELLING	1	1.1C		1		0	E0		PP		LO01 HA01, HA02, HA03	3	
0272	CHARGES, PROPELLING	1	1.3C		1		0	E0		PP		LO01 HA01, HA03	3	
0275	CARTRIDGES, POWER DEVICE	1	1.3C		1		0	E0		PP		LO01 HA01, HA03	3	
0276	CARTRIDGES, POWER DEVICE	1	1.4C		1.4		0	E0		PP		LO01 HA01, HA03	3	
0277	CARTRIDGES, OIL WELL	1	1.3C		1		0	E0		PP		LO01 HA01, HA03	3	
0278	CARTRIDGES, OIL WELL	1	1.4C		1.4		0	E0		PP		LO01 HA01, HA03	1	
0279	CHARGES, PROPELLING, FOR CANNON	1	1.1C		1		0	E0		PP		LO01 HA01, HA02, HA03	3	
0280	ROCKET MOTORS	1	1.1C		1		0	E0		PP		LO01 HA01, HA02, HA03	3	
0281	ROCKET MOTORS	1	1.2C		1		0	E0		PP		LO01 HA01, HA03	3	
0282	NITROGUANIDINE (PICRITE), dry or wetted with less than 20% water, by mass	1	1.1D		1		0	E0		PP		LO01 HA01, HA02, HA03	3	
0283	BOOSTERS without detonator	1	1.2D		1		0	E0		PP		LO01 HA01, HA03	3	
0284	GRENADES, hand or rifle, with bursting charge	1	1.1D		1		0	E0		PP		LO01 HA01, HA02, HA03	3	

UN No. or ID No. (1)	Name and description 3.1.2 (2)	Class 2.2 (3a)	Classification Code 2.2 (3b)	Packing group 2.1.1.3 (4)	Labels 5.2.2 (5)	Special provisions 3.3 (6)	Limited quantities 3.4 (7a)	Excepted quantities 3.5.1.2 (7b)	Carriage permitted 3.2.1 (8)	Equipment required 8.1.5 (9)	Ventilation 7.1.6 (10)	Provisions concerning loading, unloading and carriage 7.1.6 (11)	Number of blue cones/lights 7.1.5 (12)	Remarks 3.2.1 (13)
0285	GRENADES, hand or rifle, with bursting charge	1	1.2D		1		0	E0		PP		LO01	HA01, HA03	3	
0286	WARHEADS, ROCKET with bursting charge	1	1.1D		1		0	E0		PP		LO01	HA01, HA02, HA03	3	
0287	WARHEADS, ROCKET with bursting charge	1	1.2D		1		0	E0		PP		LO01	HA01, HA03	3	
0288	CHARGES, SHAPED, FLEXIBLE, LINEAR	1	1.1D		1		0	E0		PP		LO01	HA01, HA02, HA03	3	
0289	CORD, DETONATING, flexible	1	1.4D		1.4		0	E0		PP		LO01	HA01, HA03	1	
0290	CORD (FUSE), DETONATING, metal clad	1	1.1D		1		0	E0		PP		LO01	HA01, HA02, HA03	3	
0291	BOMBS with bursting charge	1	1.2F		1		0	E0		PP		LO01	HA01, HA02, HA03	3	
0292	GRENADES, hand or rifle, with bursting charge	1	1.1F		1		0	E0		PP		LO01	HA01, HA02, HA03	3	
0293	GRENADES, hand or rifle, with bursting charge	1	1.2F		1		0	E0		PP		LO01	HA01, HA02, HA03	3	
0294	MINES with bursting charge	1	1.2F		1		0	E0		PP		LO01	HA01, HA02, HA03	3	
0295	ROCKETS with bursting charge	1	1.2F		1		0	E0		PP		LO01	HA01, HA02, HA03	3	
0296	SOUNDING DEVICES, EXPLOSIVE	1	1.1F		1		0	E0		PP		LO01	HA01, HA02, HA03	3	
0297	AMMUNITION, ILLUMINATING with or without burster, expelling charge or propelling charge	1	1.4G		1.4		0	E0		PP		LO01	HA01, HA03	1	
0299	BOMBS, PHOTO-FLASH	1	1.3G		1		0	E0		PP		LO01	HA01, HA03	3	
0300	AMMUNITION, INCENDIARY with or without burster, expelling charge or propelling charge	1	1.4G		1.4		0	E0		PP		LO01	HA01, HA03	1	
0301	AMMUNITION, TEAR-PRODUCING with burster, expelling charge or propelling charge	1	1.4G	802	1.4+6.1+8		0	E0		PP		LO01	HA01, HA03	1	
0303	AMMUNITION, SMOKE with or without burster, expelling charge or propelling charge	1	1.4G		1.4		0	E0		PP		LO01	HA01, HA03	1	
0303	AMMUNITION, SMOKE with or without burster, expelling charge or propelling charge, containing corrosive substances	1	1.4G		1.4+8		0	E0		PP		LO01	HA01, HA03	1	

UN No. or ID No.	Name and description	Class	Classification Code	Packing group	Labels	Special provisions	Limited and excepted quantities		Carriage permitted	Equipment required	Ventilation	Provisions concerning loading, unloading and carriage	Number of blue cones/lights	Remarks
		2.2	2.2	2.1.1.3	5.2.2	3.3	3.4	3.5.1.2	3.2.1	8.1.5	7.1.6	7.1.6	7.1.5	3.2.1
(1)	(2)	(3a)	(3b)	(4)	(5)	(6)	(7a)	(7b)	(8)	(9)	(10)	(11)	(12)	(13)
0303	AMMUNITION, SMOKE with or without burster, expelling charge or propelling charge, containing toxic by inhalation substances	1	1.4G		1.4+6.1		0	E0		PP		LO01 HA01, HA03	1	
0305	FLASH POWDER	1	1.3G		1		0	E0		PP		LO01 HA01, HA03	3	
0306	TRACERS FOR AMMUNITION	1	1.4G		1.4		0	E0		PP		LO01 HA01, HA03	1	
0312	CARTRIDGES, SIGNAL	1	1.4G		1.4		0	E0		PP		LO01 HA01, HA03	1	
0313	SIGNALS, SMOKE	1	1.2G		1		0	E0		PP		LO01 HA01, HA03	3	
0314	IGNITERS	1	1.2G		1		0	E0		PP		LO01 HA01, HA03	3	
0315	IGNITERS	1	1.3G		1		0	E0		PP		LO01 HA01, HA03	3	
0316	FUZES, IGNITING	1	1.3G		1		0	E0		PP		LO01 HA01, HA03	3	
0317	FUZES, IGNITING	1	1.4G		1.4		0	E0		PP		LO01 HA01, HA03	1	
0318	GRENADES, PRACTICE, hand or rifle	1	1.3G		1		0	E0		PP		LO01 HA01, HA03	3	
0319	PRIMERS, TUBULAR	1	1.3G		1		0	E0		PP		LO01 HA01, HA03	3	
0320	PRIMERS, TUBULAR	1	1.4G		1.4		0	E0		PP		LO01 HA01, HA03	1	
0321	CARTRIDGES FOR WEAPONS with bursting charge	1	1.2E		1		0	E0		PP		LO01 HA01, HA03	3	
0322	ROCKET MOTORS WITH HYPERGOLIC LIQUIDS with or without expelling charge	1	1.2L		1		0	E0		PP		LO01 HA01, HA03	3	
0323	CARTRIDGES, POWER DEVICE	1	1.4S		1.4	347	0	E0		PP		LO01 HA01, HA03	0	
0324	PROJECTILES with bursting charge	1	1.2F		1		0	E0		PP		LO01 HA01, HA02, HA03	3	
0325	IGNITERS	1	1.4G		1.4		0	E0		PP		LO01 HA01, HA03	1	
0326	CARTRIDGES FOR WEAPONS, BLANK	1	1.1C		1		0	E0		PP		LO01 HA01, HA02, HA03	3	
0327	CARTRIDGES FOR WEAPONS, BLANK or CARTRIDGES, SMALL ARMS, BLANK	1	1.3C		1		0	E0		PP		LO01 HA01, HA03	3	
0328	CARTRIDGES FOR WEAPONS, INERT PROJECTILE	1	1.2C		1		0	E0		PP		LO01 HA01, HA03	3	
0329	TORPEDOES with bursting charge	1	1.1E		1		0	E0		PP		LO01 HA01, HA02, HA03	3	

UN No. or ID No.	Name and description	Class	Classi-fication Code	Packing group	Labels	Special provis-ions	Limited and excepted quantities		Carriage permitted	Equipment required	Venti-lation	Provisions concerning loading, unloading and carriage	Number of blue cones/ lights	Remarks
	3.1.2	2.2	2.2	2.1.1.3	5.2.2	3.3	3.4	3.5.1.2	3.2.1	8.1.5	7.1.6	7.1.6	7.1.5	3.2.1
(1)	(2)	(3a)	(3b)	(4)	(5)	(6)	(7a)	(7b)	(8)	(9)	(10)	(11)	(12)	(13)
0330	TORPEDOES with bursting charge	1	1.1F		1		0	E0		PP		LO01 HA01, HA02, HA03	3	
0331	EXPLOSIVE, BLASTING, TYPE B (AGENT, BLASTING, TYPE B)	1	1.5D		1.5	617	0	E0		PP		LO01 HA01, HA03	3	
0332	EXPLOSIVE, BLASTING, TYPE E (AGENT, BLASTING, TYPE E)	1	1.5D		1.5	617	0	E0		PP		LO01 HA01, HA03	3	
0333	FIREWORKS	1	1.1G		1	645	0	E0		PP		LO01 HA01, HA02, HA03	3	
0334	FIREWORKS	1	1.2G		1	645	0	E0		PP		LO01 HA01, HA03	3	
0335	FIREWORKS	1	1.3G		1	645	0	E0		PP		LO01 HA01, HA03	3	
0336	FIREWORKS	1	1.4G		1.4	645 651	0	E0		PP		LO01 HA01, HA03	1	
0337	FIREWORKS	1	1.4S		1.4	645	0	E0		PP		LO01 HA01, HA03	0	
0338	CARTRIDGES FOR WEAPONS, BLANK or CARTRIDGES, SMALL ARMS, BLANK	1	1.4C		1.4		0	E0		PP		LO01 HA01, HA03	1	
0339	CARTRIDGES FOR WEAPONS, INERT PROJECTILE or CARTRIDGES, SMALL ARMS	1	1.4C		1.4		0	E0		PP		LO01 HA01, HA03	1	
0340	NITROCELLULOSE, dry or wetted with less than 25% water (or alcohol), by mass	1	1.1D		1	393	0	E0		PP		LO01 HA01, HA02, HA03	3	
0341	NITROCELLULOSE, unmodified or plasticized with less than 18% plasticizing substance, by mass	1	1.1D		1	393	0	E0		PP		LO01 HA01, HA02, HA03	3	
0342	NITROCELLULOSE, WETTED with not less than 25% alcohol, by mass	1	1.3C		1	105 393	0	E0		PP		LO01 HA01, HA03	3	
0343	NITROCELLULOSE, PLASTICIZED with not less than 18% plasticizing substance, by mass	1	1.3C		1	105 393	0	E0		PP		LO01 HA01, HA03	3	
0344	PROJECTILES with bursting charge	1	1.4D		1.4		0	E0		PP		LO01 HA01, HA03	1	
0345	PROJECTILES, inert with tracer	1	1.4S		1.4		0	E0		PP		LO01 HA01, HA03	0	
0346	PROJECTILES with burster or expelling charge	1	1.2D		1		0	E0		PP		LO01 HA01, HA03	3	
0347	PROJECTILES with burster or expelling charge	1	1.4D		1.4		0	E0		PP		LO01 HA01, HA03	1	
0348	CARTRIDGES FOR WEAPONS with bursting charge	1	1.4F		1.4		0	E0		PP		LO01 HA01, HA02, HA03	1	
0349	ARTICLES, EXPLOSIVE, N.O.S.	1	1.4S		1.4	178 274 347	0	E0		PP		LO01 HA01, HA03	0	

UN No. or ID No. (1) 3.1.2	Name and description (2) 3.1.2	Class (3a) 2.2	Classification Code (3b) 2.2	Packing group (4) 2.1.1.3	Labels (5) 5.2.2	Special provisions (6) 3.3	Limited (7a) 3.4	excepted quantities (7b) 3.5.1.2	Carriage permitted (8) 3.2.1	Equipment required (9) 8.1.5	Ventilation (10) 7.1.6	Provisions concerning loading, unloading and carriage (11) 7.1.6	Number of blue cones/ lights (12) 7.1.5	Remarks (13) 3.2.1
0350	ARTICLES, EXPLOSIVE, N.O.S.	1	1.4B		1.4	178 274	0	E0		PP		LO01 HA01, HA02, HA03	1	
0351	ARTICLES, EXPLOSIVE, N.O.S.	1	1.4C		1.4	178 274	0	E0		PP		LO01 HA01, HA03	1	
0352	ARTICLES, EXPLOSIVE, N.O.S.	1	1.4D		1.4	178 274	0	E0		PP		LO01 HA01, HA03	1	
0353	ARTICLES, EXPLOSIVE, N.O.S.	1	1.4G		1.4	178 274	0	E0		PP		LO01 HA01, HA03	1	
0354	ARTICLES, EXPLOSIVE, N.O.S.	1	1.1L		1	178 274	0	E0		PP		LO01 HA01, HA02, HA03	3	
0355	ARTICLES, EXPLOSIVE, N.O.S.	1	1.2L		1	178 274	0	E0		PP		LO01 HA01, HA03	3	
0356	ARTICLES, EXPLOSIVE, N.O.S.	1	1.3L		1	178 274	0	E0		PP		LO01 HA01, HA03	3	
0357	SUBSTANCES, EXPLOSIVE, N.O.S.	1	1.1L		1	178 274	0	E0		PP		LO01 HA01, HA02, HA03	3	
0358	SUBSTANCES, EXPLOSIVE, N.O.S.	1	1.2L		1	178 274	0	E0		PP		LO01 HA01, HA03	3	
0359	SUBSTANCES, EXPLOSIVE, N.O.S.	1	1.3L		1	178 274	0	E0		PP		LO01 HA01, HA03	3	
0360	DETONATOR ASSEMBLIES, NON-ELECTRIC for blasting	1	1.1B		1		0	E0		PP		LO01 HA01, HA02, HA03	3	
0361	DETONATOR ASSEMBLIES, NON-ELECTRIC for blasting	1	1.4B		1.4		0	E0		PP		LO01 HA01, HA02, HA03	1	
0362	AMMUNITION, PRACTICE	1	1.4G		1.4		0	E0		PP		LO01 HA01, HA03	1	
0363	AMMUNITION, PROOF	1	1.4G		1.4		0	E0		PP		LO01 HA01, HA03	1	
0364	DETONATORS FOR AMMUNITION	1	1.2B		1		0	E0		PP		LO01 HA01, HA02, HA03	3	
0365	DETONATORS FOR AMMUNITION	1	1.4B		1.4		0	E0		PP		LO01 HA01, HA02, HA03	1	
0366	DETONATORS FOR AMMUNITION	1	1.4S		1.4	347	0	E0		PP		LO01 HA01, HA03	0	
0367	FUZES, DETONATING	1	1.4S		1.4	347	0	E0		PP		LO01 HA01, HA03	0	
0368	FUZES, IGNITING	1	1.4S		1.4		0	E0		PP		LO01 HA01, HA03	0	
0369	WARHEADS, ROCKET with bursting charge	1	1.1F		1		0	E0		PP		LO01 HA01, HA02, HA03	3	

UN No. or ID No.	Name and description	Class	Classification Code	Packing group	Labels	Special provisions	Limited and excepted quantities		Carriage permitted	Equipment required	Venti-lation	Provisions concerning loading, unloading and carriage	Number of blue cones/ lights	Remarks
		2.2	2.2	2.1.1.3	5.2.2	3.3	3.4	3.5.1.2	3.2.1	8.1.5	7.1.6	7.1.6	7.1.5	3.2.1
(1)	(2)	(3a)	(3b)	(4)	(5)	(6)	(7a)	(7b)	(8)	(9)	(10)	(11)	(12)	(13)
0370	WARHEADS, ROCKET with burster or expelling charge	1	1.4D		1.4		0	E0		PP		LO01 HA01, HA03	1	
0371	WARHEADS, ROCKET with burster or expelling charge	1	1.4F		1.4		0	E0		PP		LO01 HA01, HA02, HA03	1	
0372	GRENADES, PRACTICE, hand or rifle	1	1.2G		1		0	E0		PP		LO01 HA01, HA03	3	
0373	SIGNAL DEVICES, HAND	1	1.4S		1.4		0	E0		PP		LO01 HA01, HA03	0	
0374	SOUNDING DEVICES, EXPLOSIVE	1	1.1D		1		0	E0		PP		LO01 HA01, HA02, HA03	3	
0375	SOUNDING DEVICES, EXPLOSIVE	1	1.2D		1		0	E0		PP		LO01 HA01, HA03	3	
0376	PRIMERS, TUBULAR	1	1.4S		1.4		0	E0		PP		LO01 HA01, HA03	0	
0377	PRIMERS, CAP TYPE	1	1.1B		1		0	E0		PP		LO01 HA01, HA02, HA03	3	
0378	PRIMERS, CAP TYPE	1	1.4B		1.4		0	E0		PP		LO01 HA01, HA02, HA03	1	
0379	CASES, CARTRIDGE, EMPTY, WITH PRIMER	1	1.4C		1.4		0	E0		PP		LO01 HA01, HA03	1	
0380	ARTICLES, PYROPHORIC	1	1.2L		1		0	E0		PP		LO01 HA01, HA03	3	
0381	CARTRIDGES, POWER DEVICE	1	1.2C		1		0	E0		PP		LO01 HA01, HA03	3	
0382	COMPONENTS, EXPLOSIVE TRAIN, N.O.S.	1	1.2B		1	178 274	0	E0		PP		LO01 HA01, HA02, HA03	3	
0383	COMPONENTS, EXPLOSIVE TRAIN, N.O.S.	1	1.4B		1.4	178 274	0	E0		PP		LO01 HA01, HA02, HA03	1	
0384	COMPONENTS, EXPLOSIVE TRAIN, N.O.S.	1	1.4S		1.4	178 274 347	0	E0		PP		LO01 HA01, HA03	0	
0385	5-NITROBENZOTRIAZOL	1	1.1D		1		0	E0		PP		LO01 HA01, HA02, HA03	3	
0386	TRINITROBENZENESULPHONIC ACID	1	1.1D		1		0	E0		PP		LO01 HA01, HA02, HA03	3	
0387	TRINITROFLUORENONE	1	1.1D		1		0	E0		PP		LO01 HA01, HA02, HA03	3	

UN No. or ID No.	Name and description	Class	Classi-fication Code	Packing group	Labels	Special provis-ions	Limited and excepted quantities		Carriage permitted	Equipment required	Venti-lation	Provisions concerning loading, unloading and carriage	Number of blue cones/ lights	Remarks
(1)	3.1.2 (2)	2.2 (3a)	2.2 (3b)	2.1.1.3 (4)	5.2.2 (5)	3.3 (6)	3.4 (7a)	3.5.1.2 (7b)	3.2.1 (8)	8.1.5 (9)	7.1.6 (10)	7.1.6 (11)	7.1.5 (12)	3.2.1 (13)
0388	TRINITROTOLUENE (TNT) AND TRINITROBENZENE MIXTURE or TRINITROTOLUENE (TNT) AND TRINITROBENZENE AND HEXANITROSTILBENE	1	1.1D		1		0	E0		PP		LO01 HA01, HA02, HA03	3	
0389	TRINITROTOLUENE (TNT) MIXTURE CONTAINING TRINITROBENZENE AND HEXANITROSTILBENE	1	1.1D		1		0	E0		PP		LO01 HA01, HA02, HA03	3	
0390	TRITONAL	1	1.1D		1		0	E0		PP		LO01 HA01, HA02, HA03	3	
0391	CYCLOTRIMETHYLENETRINITRAMINE (CYCLONITE; HEXOGEN; RDX) AND CYCLOTETRAMETHYLENETETRANITRAMINE (HMX; OCTOGEN) MIXTURE, WETTED with not less than 15% water, by mass or DESENSITIZED with not less than 10% phlegmatiser by mass	1	1.1D		1	266	0	E0		PP		LO01 HA01, HA02, HA03	3	
0392	HEXANITROSTILBENE	1	1.1D		1		0	E0		PP		LO01 HA01, HA02, HA03	3	
0393	HEXOTONAL	1	1.1D		1		0	E0		PP		LO01 HA01, HA02, HA03	3	
0394	TRINITRORESORCINOL (STYPHNIC ACID), WETTED with not less than 20% water, or mixture of alcohol and water, by mass	1	1.1D		1		0	E0		PP		LO01 HA01, HA02, HA03	3	
0395	ROCKET MOTORS, LIQUID FUELLED	1	1.2J		1		0	E0		PP		LO01 HA01, HA03	3	
0396	ROCKET MOTORS, LIQUID FUELLED	1	1.3J		1		0	E0		PP		LO01 HA01, HA03	3	
0397	ROCKETS, LIQUID FUELLED with bursting charge	1	1.1J		1		0	E0		PP		LO01 HA01, HA02, HA03	3	
0398	ROCKETS, LIQUID FUELLED with bursting charge	1	1.2J		1		0	E0		PP		LO01 HA01, HA03	3	
0399	BOMBS WITH FLAMMABLE LIQUID with bursting charge	1	1.1J		1		0	E0		PP		LO01 HA01, HA02, HA03	3	
0400	BOMBS WITH FLAMMABLE LIQUID with bursting charge	1	1.2J		1		0	E0		PP		LO01 HA01, HA03	3	
0401	DIPICRYL SULPHIDE, dry or wetted with less than 10% water, by mass	1	1.1D		1		0	E0		PP		LO01 HA01, HA02, HA03	3	
0402	AMMONIUM PERCHLORATE	1	1.1D		1	152	0	E0		PP		LO01 HA01, HA02, HA03	3	
0403	FLARES, AERIAL	1	1.4G		1.4		0	E0		PP		LO01 HA01, HA03	1	
0404	FLARES, AERIAL	1	1.4S		1.4		0	E0		PP		LO01 HA01, HA03	0	

UN No. or ID No. (1)	Name and description 3.1.2 (2)	Class 2.2 (3a)	Classification Code 2.2 (3b)	Packing group 2.1.1.3 (4)	Labels 5.2.2 (5)	Special provisions 3.3 (6)	Limited and excepted quantities 3.4 (7a)	3.5.1.2 (7b)	Carriage permitted 3.2.1 (8)	Equipment required 8.1.5 (9)	Ventilation 7.1.6 (10)	Provisions concerning loading, unloading and carriage 7.1.6 (11)	Number of blue cones/lights 7.1.5 (12)	Remarks 3.2.1 (13)
0405	CARTRIDGES, SIGNAL	1	1.4S		1.4		0	E0		PP		LO01 HA01, HA03	0	
0406	DINITROSOBENZENE	1	1.3C		1		0	E0		PP		LO01 HA01, HA03	3	
0407	TETRAZOL-1-ACETIC ACID	1	1.4C		1.4		0	E0		PP		LO01 HA01, HA03	1	
0408	FUZES, DETONATING with protective features	1	1.1D		1		0	E0		PP		LO01 HA01, HA02, HA03	3	
0409	FUZES, DETONATING with protective features	1	1.2D		1		0	E0		PP		LO01 HA01, HA03	3	
0410	FUZES, DETONATING with protective features	1	1.4D		1.4		0	E0		PP		LO01 HA01, HA03	1	
0411	PENTAERYTHRITE TETRANITRATE (PENTAERYTHRITOL TETRANITRATE; PETN) with not less than 7% wax, by mass	1	1.1D		1	131	0	E0		PP		LO01 HA01, HA02, HA03	3	
0412	CARTRIDGES FOR WEAPONS with bursting charge	1	1.4E		1.4		0	E0		PP		LO01 HA01, HA03	1	
0413	CARTRIDGES FOR WEAPONS, BLANK	1	1.2C		1		0	E0		PP		LO01 HA01, HA03	3	
0414	CHARGES, PROPELLING, FOR CANNON	1	1.2C		1		0	E0		PP		LO01 HA01, HA03	3	
0415	CHARGES, PROPELLING	1	1.2C		1		0	E0		PP		LO01 HA01, HA03	3	
0417	CARTRIDGES FOR WEAPONS, INERT PROJECTILE or CARTRIDGES, SMALL ARMS	1	1.3C		1		0	E0		PP		LO01 HA01, HA03	3	
0418	FLARES, SURFACE	1	1.1G		1		0	E0		PP		LO01 HA01, HA02, HA03	3	
0419	FLARES, SURFACE	1	1.2G		1		0	E0		PP		LO01 HA01, HA03	3	
0420	FLARES, AERIAL	1	1.1G		1		0	E0		PP		LO01 HA01, HA02, HA03	3	
0421	FLARES, AERIAL	1	1.2G		1		0	E0		PP		LO01 HA01, HA03	3	
0424	PROJECTILES, inert with tracer	1	1.3G		1		0	E0		PP		LO01 HA01, HA03	3	
0425	PROJECTILES, inert with tracer	1	1.4G		1.4		0	E0		PP		LO01 HA01, HA03	1	
0426	PROJECTILES with burster or expelling charge	1	1.2F		1		0	E0		PP		LO01 HA01, HA02, HA03	3	
0427	PROJECTILES with burster or expelling charge	1	1.4F		1.4		0	E0		PP		LO01 HA01, HA02, HA03	1	

UN No. or ID No. (1) 3.1.2	Name and description (2) 3.1.2	Class (3a) 2.2	Classification Code (3b) 2.2	Packing group (4) 2.1.1.3	Labels (5) 5.2.2	Special provisions (6) 3.3	Limited quantities (7a) 3.4	excepted quantities (7b) 3.5.1.2	Carriage permitted (8) 3.2.1	Equipment required (9) 8.1.5	Ventilation (10) 7.1.6	Provisions concerning loading, unloading and carriage (11) 7.1.6	Number of blue cones/lights (12) 7.1.5	Remarks (13) 3.2.1
0428	ARTICLES, PYROTECHNIC for technical purposes	1	1.1G		1		0	E0		PP		LO01 HA01, HA02, HA03	3	
0429	ARTICLES, PYROTECHNIC for technical purposes	1	1.2G		1		0	E0		PP		LO01 HA01, HA03	3	
0430	ARTICLES, PYROTECHNIC for technical purposes	1	1.3G		1		0	E0		PP		LO01 HA01, HA03	3	
0431	ARTICLES, PYROTECHNIC for technical purposes	1	1.4G		1.4		0	E0		PP		LO01 HA01, HA03	1	
0432	ARTICLES, PYROTECHNIC for technical purposes	1	1.4S		1.4		0	E0		PP		LO01 HA01, HA03	0	
0433	POWDER CAKE (POWDER PASTE), WETTED with not less than 17% alcohol, by mass	1	1.1C		1	266	0	E0		PP		LO01 HA01, HA02, HA03	3	
0434	PROJECTILES with burster or expelling charge	1	1.2G		1		0	E0		PP		LO01 HA01, HA03	3	
0435	PROJECTILES with burster or expelling charge	1	1.4G		1.4		0	E0		PP		LO01 HA01, HA03	1	
0436	ROCKETS with expelling charge	1	1.2C		1		0	E0		PP		LO01 HA01, HA03	3	
0437	ROCKETS with expelling charge	1	1.3C		1		0	E0		PP		LO01 HA01, HA03	3	
0438	ROCKETS with expelling charge	1	1.4C		1.4		0	E0		PP		LO01 HA01, HA03	1	
0439	CHARGES, SHAPED, without detonator	1	1.2D		1		0	E0		PP		LO01 HA01, HA03	3	
0440	CHARGES, SHAPED, without detonator	1	1.4D		1.4		0	E0		PP		LO01 HA01, HA03	1	
0441	CHARGES, SHAPED, without detonator	1	1.4S		1.4	347	0	E0		PP		LO01 HA01, HA03	0	
0442	CHARGES, EXPLOSIVE, COMMERCIAL without detonator	1	1.1D		1		0	E0		PP		LO01 HA01, HA02, HA03	3	
0443	CHARGES, EXPLOSIVE, COMMERCIAL without detonator	1	1.2D		1		0	E0		PP		LO01 HA01, HA03	3	
0444	CHARGES, EXPLOSIVE, COMMERCIAL without detonator	1	1.4D		1.4		0	E0		PP		LO01 HA01, HA03	1	
0445	CHARGES, EXPLOSIVE, COMMERCIAL without detonator	1	1.4S		1.4	347	0	E0		PP		LO01 HA01, HA03	0	
0446	CASES, COMBUSTIBLE, EMPTY, WITHOUT PRIMER	1	1.4C		1.4		0	E0		PP		LO01 HA01, HA03	1	
0447	CASES, COMBUSTIBLE, EMPTY, WITHOUT PRIMER	1	1.3C		1		0	E0		PP		LO01 HA01, HA03	3	
0448	5-MERCAPTOTETRAZOL-1-ACETIC ACID	1	1.4C		1.4		0	E0		PP		LO01 HA01, HA03	1	
0449	TORPEDOES, LIQUID FUELLED with or without bursting charge	1	1.1J		1		0	E0		PP		LO01 HA01, HA02, HA03	3	

UN No. or ID No. (1)	Name and description (2)	Class (3a)	Classification Code (3b)	Packing group (4)	Labels (5)	Special provisions (6)	Limited and excepted quantities 3.4 (7a)	Limited and excepted quantities 3.5.1.2 (7b)	Carriage permitted (8)	Equipment required (9)	Ventilation (10)	Provisions concerning loading, unloading and carriage (11)	Number of blue cones/lights (12)	Remarks (13)
0450	TORPEDOES, LIQUID FUELLED with inert head	1	1.3J		1		0	E0		PP		LO01 HA01, HA03	3	
0451	TORPEDOES with bursting charge	1	1.1D		1		0	E0		PP		LO01 HA01, HA02, HA03	3	
0452	GRENADES, PRACTICE, hand or rifle	1	1.4G		1.4		0	E0		PP		LO01 HA01, HA03	1	
0453	ROCKETS, LINE-THROWING	1	1.4G		1.4		0	E0		PP		LO01 HA01, HA03	1	
0454	IGNITERS	1	1.4S		1.4		0	E0		PP		LO01 HA01, HA03	0	
0455	DETONATORS, NON-ELECTRIC for blasting	1	1.4S		1.4	347	0	E0		PP		LO01 HA01, HA03	0	
0456	DETONATORS, ELECTRIC for blasting	1	1.4S		1.4	347	0	E0		PP		LO01 HA01, HA03	0	
0457	CHARGES, BURSTING, PLASTICS BONDED	1	1.1D		1		0	E0		PP		LO01 HA01, HA02, HA03	3	
0458	CHARGES, BURSTING, PLASTICS BONDED	1	1.2D		1		0	E0		PP		LO01 HA01, HA03	3	
0459	CHARGES, BURSTING, PLASTICS BONDED	1	1.4D		1.4		0	E0		PP		LO01 HA01, HA03	1	
0460	CHARGES, BURSTING, PLASTICS BONDED	1	1.4S		1.4	347	0	E0		PP		LO01 HA01, HA03	0	
0461	COMPONENTS, EXPLOSIVE TRAIN, N.O.S.	1	1.1B		1	178 274	0	E0		PP		LO01 HA01, HA02, HA03	3	
0462	ARTICLES, EXPLOSIVE, N.O.S.	1	1.1C		1	178 274	0	E0		PP		LO01 HA01, HA02, HA03	3	
0463	ARTICLES, EXPLOSIVE, N.O.S.	1	1.1D		1	178 274	0	E0		PP		LO01 HA01, HA02, HA03	3	
0464	ARTICLES, EXPLOSIVE, N.O.S.	1	1.1E		1	178 274	0	E0		PP		LO01 HA01, HA02, HA03	3	
0465	ARTICLES, EXPLOSIVE, N.O.S.	1	1.1F		1	178 274	0	E0		PP		LO01 HA01, HA02, HA03	3	
0466	ARTICLES, EXPLOSIVE, N.O.S.	1	1.2C		1	178 274	0	E0		PP		LO01 HA01, HA03	3	
0467	ARTICLES, EXPLOSIVE, N.O.S.	1	1.2D		1	178 274	0	E0		PP		LO01 HA01, HA03	3	
0468	ARTICLES, EXPLOSIVE, N.O.S.	1	1.2E		1	178 274	0	E0		PP		LO01 HA01, HA03	3	
0469	ARTICLES, EXPLOSIVE, N.O.S.	1	1.2F		1	178 274	0	E0		PP		LO01 HA01, HA02, HA03	3	

UN No. or ID No.	Name and description	Class	Classification Code	Packing group	Labels	Special provisions	Limited and excepted quantities		Carriage permitted	Equipment required	Venti-lation	Provisions concerning loading, unloading and carriage	Number of blue cones/lights	Remarks
		2.2	2.2	2.1.1.3	5.2.2	3.3	3.4	3.5.1.2	3.2.1	8.1.5	7.1.6	7.1.6	7.1.5	3.2.1
(1)	(2)	(3a)	(3b)	(4)	(5)	(6)	(7a)	(7b)	(8)	(9)	(10)	(11)	(12)	(13)
0470	ARTICLES, EXPLOSIVE, N.O.S.	1	1.3C		1	178 274	0	E0		PP		LO01 HA01, HA03	3	
0471	ARTICLES, EXPLOSIVE, N.O.S.	1	1.4E		1.4	178 274	0	E0		PP		LO01 HA01, HA03	1	
0472	ARTICLES, EXPLOSIVE, N.O.S.	1	1.4F		1.4	178 274	0	E0		PP		LO01 HA01, HA02, HA03	1	
0473	SUBSTANCES, EXPLOSIVE, N.O.S.	1	1.1A		1	178 274	0	E0		PP		LO01 HA01, HA02, HA03	3	
0474	SUBSTANCES, EXPLOSIVE, N.O.S.	1	1.1C		1	178 274	0	E0		PP		LO01 HA01, HA02, HA03	3	
0475	SUBSTANCES, EXPLOSIVE, N.O.S.	1	1.1D		1	178 274	0	E0		PP		LO01 HA01, HA02, HA03	3	
0476	SUBSTANCES, EXPLOSIVE, N.O.S.	1	1.1G		1	178 274	0	E0		PP		LO01 HA01, HA02, HA03	3	
0477	SUBSTANCES, EXPLOSIVE, N.O.S.	1	1.3C		1	178 274	0	E0		PP		LO01 HA01, HA03	3	
0478	SUBSTANCES, EXPLOSIVE, N.O.S.	1	1.3G		1	178 274	0	E0		PP		LO01 HA01, HA03	3	
0479	SUBSTANCES, EXPLOSIVE, N.O.S.	1	1.4C		1.4	178 274	0	E0		PP		LO01 HA01, HA03	1	
0480	SUBSTANCES, EXPLOSIVE, N.O.S.	1	1.4D		1.4	178 274	0	E0		PP		LO01 HA01, HA03	1	
0481	SUBSTANCES, EXPLOSIVE, N.O.S.	1	1.4S		1.4	178 274 347	0	E0		PP		LO01 HA01, HA03	0	
0482	SUBSTANCES, EXPLOSIVE, VERY INSENSITIVE (SUBSTANCES, EVI), N.O.S.	1	1.5D		1.5	178 274	0	E0		PP		LO01 HA01, HA03	3	
0483	CYCLOTRIMETHYLENETRINITRAMINE (CYCLONITE; HEXOGEN; RDX), DESENSITIZED	1	1.1D		1		0	E0		PP		LO01 HA01, HA02, HA03	3	
0484	CYCLOTETRAMETHYLENETETRANITRAMINE (HMX; OCTOGEN), DESENSITIZED	1	1.1D		1		0	E0		PP		LO01 HA01, HA02, HA03	3	
0485	SUBSTANCES, EXPLOSIVE, N.O.S.	1	1.4G		1.4	178 274	0	E0		PP		LO01 HA01, HA03	1	
0486	ARTICLES, EXPLOSIVE, EXTREMELY INSENSITIVE (ARTICLES, EEI)	1	1.6N		1.6		0	E0		PP		LO01 HA01, HA03	3	
0487	SIGNALS, SMOKE	1	1.3G		1		0	E0		PP		LO01 HA01, HA03	3	
0488	AMMUNITION, PRACTICE	1	1.3G		1		0	E0		PP		LO01 HA01, HA03	3	

(1) UN No. or ID No.	(2) Name and description 3.1.2	(3a) Class 2.2	(3b) Classification Code 2.2	(4) Packing group 2.1.1.3	(5) Labels 5.2.2	(6) Special provisions 3.3	(7a) 3.4	(7b) 3.5.1.2	(8) Carriage permitted 3.2.1	(9) Equipment required 8.1.5	(10) Ventilation 7.1.6	(11) Provisions concerning loading, unloading and carriage 7.1.6	(12) Number of blue cones/lights 7.1.5	(13) Remarks 3.2.1
0489	DINITROGLYCOLURIL (DINGU)	1	1.1D		1		0	E0		PP		LO01	HA01, HA02, HA03	3	
0490	NITROTRIAZOLONE (NTO)	1	1.1D		1		0	E0		PP		LO01	HA01, HA02, HA03	3	
0491	CHARGES, PROPELLING	1	1.4C		1.4		0	E0		PP		LO01	HA01, HA03	1	
0492	SIGNALS, RAILWAY TRACK, EXPLOSIVE	1	1.3G		1		0	E0		PP		LO01	HA01, HA03	3	
0493	SIGNALS, RAILWAY TRACK, EXPLOSIVE	1	1.4G		1.4		0	E0		PP		LO01	HA01, HA03	1	
0494	JET PERFORATING GUNS, CHARGED, oil well, without detonator	1	1.4D		1.4		0	E0		PP		LO01	HA01, HA03	1	
0495	PROPELLANT, LIQUID	1	1.3C		1	224	0	E0		PP		LO01	HA01, HA03	3	
0496	OCTONAL	1	1.1D		1		0	E0		PP		LO01	HA01, HA02, HA03	3	
0497	PROPELLANT, LIQUID	1	1.1C		1	224	0	E0		PP		LO01	HA01, HA02, HA03	3	
0498	PROPELLANT, SOLID	1	1.1C		1		0	E0		PP		LO01	HA01, HA02, HA03	3	
0499	PROPELLANT, SOLID	1	1.3C		1		0	E0		PP		LO01	HA01, HA03	3	
0500	DETONATOR ASSEMBLIES, NON-ELECTRIC for blasting	1	1.4S		1.4	347	0	E0		PP		LO01	HA01, HA03	0	
0501	PROPELLANT, SOLID	1	1.4C		1.4		0	E0		PP		LO01	HA01, HA03	1	
0502	ROCKETS with inert head	1	1.2C		1		0	E0		PP		LO01	HA01, HA03	3	
0503	SAFETY DEVICES, PYROTECHNIC	1	1.4G		1.4	235 289	0	E0		PP		LO01	HA01, HA03	1	
0504	1H-TETRAZOLE	1	1.1D		1		0	E0		PP		LO01	HA01, HA02, HA03	3	
0505	SIGNALS, DISTRESS, ship	1	1.4G		1.4		0	E0		PP		LO01	HA01, HA03	1	
0506	SIGNALS, DISTRESS, ship	1	1.4S		1.4		0	E0		PP		LO01	HA01, HA03	0	
0507	SIGNALS, SMOKE	1	1.4S		1.4		0	E0		PP		LO01	HA01, HA03	0	
0508	1-HYDROXY-BENZOTRIAZOLE, ANHYDROUS, dry or wetted with less than 20% water, by mass	1	1.3C		1		0	E0		PP		LO01	HA01, HA03	3	
0509	POWDER, SMOKELESS	1	1.4C		1.4		0	E0		PP		LO01	HA01, HA03	1	

UN No. or ID No.	Name and description	Class	Classification Code	Packing group	Labels	Special provisions	Limited and excepted quantities		Carriage permitted	Equipment required	Venti-lation	Provisions concerning loading, unloading and carriage	Number of blue cones/ lights	Remarks
		2.2	2.2	2.1.1.3	5.2.2	3.3	3.4	3.5.1.2	3.2.1	8.1.5	7.1.6	7.1.6	7.1.5	3.2.1
(1)	(2)	(3a)	(3b)	(4)	(5)	(6)	(7a)	(7b)	(8)	(9)	(10)	(11)	(12)	(13)
0510	ROCKET MOTORS	1	1.4C		1.4		0	E0		PP		LO01	HA01, HA03	1	
511	DETONATORS, ELECTRONIC programmable for blasting	1	1.1B		1		0	E0		PP		LO01	HA01, HA02, HA03	3	
512	DETONATORS, ELECTRONIC programmable for blasting	1	1.4B		1.4		0	E0		PP		LO01	HA01, HA02, HA03	1	
513	DETONATORS, ELECTRONIC programmable for blasting	1	1.4S		1.4	347	0	E0		PP		LO01	HA01, HA03	0	
1001	ACETYLENE, DISSOLVED	2	4F		2.1	662	0	E0		PP, EX, A	VE01			1	
1002	AIR, COMPRESSED	2	1A		2.2	392 397 655 662	120 ml	E1		PP				0	
1003	AIR, REFRIGERATED LIQUID	2	3O		2.2+5.1		0	E0		PP				0	
1005	AMMONIA, ANHYDROUS	2	2TC		2.3+8	23 379	0	E0	T	PP, EP, TOX, A	VE02			2	
1006	ARGON, COMPRESSED	2	1A		2.2	378 392 653 662	120 ml	E1		PP				0	
1008	BORON TRIFLUORIDE	2	2TC		2.3+8	373	0	E0		PP, EP, TOX, A	VE02			2	
1009	BROMOTRIFLUOROMETHANE (REFRIGERANT GAS R 13B1)	2	2A		2.2	662	120 ml	E1		PP				0	
1010	BUTADIENES, STABILIZED or BUTADIENES AND HYDROCARBON MIXTURE, STABILIZED, containing more than 40% butadienes	2	2F		2.1	386 618 662 676	0	E0	T	PP, EX, A	VE01			1	
1011	BUTANE	2	2F		2.1	392 657 662 674	0	E0	T	PP, EX, A	VE01			1	
1012	BUTYLENE	2	2F		2.1	398 662	0	E0	T	PP, EX, A	VE01			1	
1013	CARBON DIOXIDE	2	2A		2.2	663	120 ml	E1		PP				0	
1016	CARBON MONOXIDE, COMPRESSED	2	1TF		2.3+2.1		0	E0		PP, EP, EX, TOX, A	VE01, VE02			2	
1017	CHLORINE	2	2TOC		2.3+5.1+8		0	E0		PP, EP, TOX, A	VE02			2	
1018	CHLORODIFLUOROMETHANE (REFRIGERANT GAS R 22)	2	2A		2.2	662	120 ml	E1		PP				0	
1020	CHLOROPENTAFLUORO-ETHANE (REFRIGERANT GAS R 115)	2	2A		2.2	662	120 ml	E1	T	PP				0	
1021	1-CHLORO-1,2,2,2-TETRAFLUOROETHANE (REFRIGERANT GAS R 124)	2	2A		2.2	662	120 ml	E1		PP				0	
1022	CHLOROTRIFLUOROMETHANE (REFRIGERANT GAS R 13)	2	2A		2.2	662	120 ml	E1		PP				0	

UN No. or ID No.	Name and description	Class	Classification Code	Packing group	Labels	Special provisions	Limited and excepted quantities		Carriage permitted	Equipment required	Ventilation	Provisions concerning loading, unloading and carriage	Number of blue cones/lights	Remarks
							3.4	3.5.1.2	3.2.1	8.1.5	7.1.6	7.1.6	7.1.5	3.2.1
3.1.2	3.1.2	2.2	2.2	2.1.1.3	5.2.2	3.3								
(1)	(2)	(3a)	(3b)	(4)	(5)	(6)	(7a)	(7b)	(8)	(9)	(10)	(11)	(12)	(13)
1023	COAL GAS, COMPRESSED	2	1TF		2.3+2.1		0	E0		PP, EP, EX, TOX, A	VE01, VE02		2	
1026	CYANOGEN	2	2TF		2.3+2.1		0	E0		PP, EP, EX, TOX, A	VE01, VE02		2	
1027	CYCLOPROPANE	2	2F		2.1	662	0	E0		PP, EX, A	VE01		1	
1028	DICHLORODIFLUORO-METHANE (REFRIGERANT GAS R 12)	2	2A		2.2	662	120 ml	E1		PP			0	
1029	DICHLOROFLUORO-METHANE (REFRIGERANT GAS R 21)	2	2A		2.2	662	120 ml	E1		PP			0	
1030	1,1-DIFLUOROETHANE (REFRIGERANT GAS R 152a)	2	2F		2.1	662	0	E0	T	PP, EX, A	VE01		1	
1032	DIMETHYLAMINE, ANHYDROUS	2	2F		2.1	662	0	E0		PP, EX, A	VE01		1	
1033	DIMETHYL ETHER	2	2F		2.1	662	0	E0	T	PP, EX, A	VE01		1	
1035	ETHANE	2	2F		2.1	662	0	E0		PP, EX, A	VE01		1	
1036	ETHYLAMINE	2	2F		2.1	662	0	E0		PP, EX, A	VE01		1	
1037	ETHYL CHLORIDE	2	2F		2.1	662	0	E0	T	PP, EX, A	VE01		1	
1038	ETHYLENE, REFRIGERATED LIQUID	2	3F		2.1		0	E0		PP, EX, A	VE01		1	
1039	ETHYL METHYL ETHER	2	2F		2.1	662	0	E0		PP, EX, A	VE01		1	
1040	ETHYLENE OXIDE	2	2TF		2.3+2.1	342	0	E0		PP, EP, EX, TOX, A	VE01, VE02		2	
1040	ETHYLENE OXIDE WITH NITROGEN up to a total pressure of 1 MPa (10 bar) at 50 °C	2	2TF		2.3+2.1	342	0	E0	T	PP, EP, EX, TOX, A	VE01, VE02		2	
1041	ETHYLENE OXIDE AND CARBON DIOXIDE MIXTURE with more than 9% but not more than 87% ethylene oxide	2	2F		2.1	662	0	E0		PP, EX, A	VE01		1	
1043	FERTILIZER AMMONIATING SOLUTION with free ammonia	2	4A		2.2	642	120 ml	E0		PP			0	
1044	FIRE EXTINGUISHERS with compressed or liquefied gas	2	6A		2.2	225 594	0	E0		PP			0	
1045	FLUORINE, COMPRESSED	2	1TOC		2.3+5.1+8	662	0	E0		PP, EP, TOX, A	VE02		2	
1046	HELIUM, COMPRESSED.	2	1A		2.2	378 392 653 662	120 ml	E1		PP			0	
1048	HYDROGEN BROMIDE, ANHYDROUS	2	2TC		2.3+8	802	0	E0		PP, EP, TOX, A	VE02		2	
1049	HYDROGEN, COMPRESSED	2	1F		2.1	392 662	0	E0		PP, EX, A	VE01		1	
1050	HYDROGEN CHLORIDE, ANHYDROUS	2	2TC		2.3+8	662	0	E0		PP, EP, TOX, A	VE02		2	
1051	HYDROGEN CYANIDE, STABILIZED containing less than 3% water	6.1	TF1	I	6.1+3	386 603 676 802	0	E1		PP, EP, EX, TOX, A	VE01, VE02		2	
1052	HYDROGEN FLUORIDE, ANHYDROUS	8	CT1	I	8+6.1	802	0	E0		PP, EP, TOX, A	VE02		2	
1053	HYDROGEN SULPHIDE	2	2TF		2.3+2.1		0	E0		PP, EP, EX, TOX, A	VE01, VE02		2	
1055	ISOBUTYLENE	2	2F		2.1	662	0	E0	T	PP, EX, A	VE01		1	

UN No. or ID No.	Name and description	Class	Classification Code	Packing group	Labels	Special provisions	Limited and excepted quantities		Carriage permitted	Equipment required	Ventilation	Provisions concerning loading, unloading and carriage	Number of blue cones/lights	Remarks
3.1.2	3.1.2	2.2	2.2	2.1.1.3	5.2.2	3.3	3.4	3.5.1.2	3.2.1	8.1.5	7.1.6	7.1.6	7.1.5	3.2.1
(1)	(2)	(3a)	(3b)	(4)	(5)	(6)	(7a)	(7b)	(8)	(9)	(10)	(11)	(12)	(13)
1056	KRYPTON, COMPRESSED	2	1A		2.2	378 392 662	120 ml	E1		PP			0	
1057	LIGHTERS or LIGHTER REFILLS containing flammable gas	2	6F		2.1	201 654 658	0	E0		PP, EX, A	VE01		1	
1058	LIQUEFIED GASES, non-flammable, charged with nitrogen, carbon dioxide or air	2	2A		2.2	392 662	120 ml	E1		PP			0	
1060	METHYLACETYLENE AND PROPADIENE MIXTURE, STABILIZED such as mixture P1 or mixture P2	2	2F		2.1	386 581 662 676	0	E0		PP, EX, A	VE01		1	
1061	METHYLAMINE, ANHYDROUS	2	2F		2.1	662	0	E0		PP, EX, A	VE01		1	
1062	METHYL BROMIDE with not more than 2% chloropicrin	2	2T		2.3	23	0	E0		PP, EP, TOX, A	VE02		2	
1063	METHYL CHLORIDE (REFRIGERANT GAS R 40)	2	2F		2.1	662	0	E0	T	PP, EX, A	VE01		1	
1064	METHYL MERCAPTAN	2	2TF		2.3+2.1		0	E0		PP, EP, EX, TOX, A	VE01, VE02		2	
1065	NEON, COMPRESSED	2	1A		2.2	378 392 662	120 ml	E1		PP			0	
1066	NITROGEN, COMPRESSED	2	1A		2.2	378 392 653 662	120 ml	E1		PP			0	
1067	DINITROGEN TETROXIDE (NITROGEN DIOXIDE)	2	2TOC		2.3+5.1+8		0	E0		PP, EP, TOX, A	VE02		2	
1069	NITROSYL CHLORIDE	2	2TC		2.3+8		0	E0		PP, EP, TOX, A	VE02		2	
1070	NITROUS OXIDE	2	2O		2.2+5.1	584 662	0	E0		PP			0	
1071	OIL GAS, COMPRESSED	2	1TF		2.3+2.1		0	E0		PP, EP, EX, TOX, A	VE01, VE02		2	
1072	OXYGEN, COMPRESSED	2	1O		2.2+5.1	355 655 662	0	E0		PP			0	
1073	OXYGEN, REFRIGERATED LIQUID	2	3O		2.2+5.1		0	E0		PP			0	
1075	PETROLEUM GASES, LIQUEFIED	2	2F		2.1	274 392 583 639 662 674	0	E0	T	PP, EX, A	VE01		1	
1076	PHOSGENE	2	2TC		2.3+8		0	E0		PP, EP, TOX, A	VE02		2	
1077	PROPYLENE	2	2F		2.1	662	0	E0		PP, EX, A	VE01		1	
1078	REFRIGERANT GAS, N.O.S., such as mixture F1, mixture F2 or mixture F3	2	2A		2.2	274 582 662	120 ml	E1		PP			0	
1079	SULPHUR DIOXIDE	2	2TC		2.3+8		0	E0		PP, EP, TOX, A	VE02		2	

UN No. or ID No.	Name and description	Class	Classification Code	Packing group	Labels	Special provisions	Limited quantities	Excepted quantities	Carriage permitted	Equipment required	Ventilation	Provisions concerning loading, unloading and carriage	Number of blue cones/lights	Remarks
	3.1.2	2.2	2.2	2.1.1.3	5.2.2	3.3	3.4	3.5.1.2	3.2.1	8.1.5	7.1.6	7.1.6	7.1.5	3.2.1
(1)	(2)	(3a)	(3b)	(4)	(5)	(6)	(7a)	(7b)	(8)	(9)	(10)	(11)	(12)	(13)
1080	SULPHUR HEXAFLUORIDE	2	2A		2.2	392 662	120 ml	E1		PP			0	
1081	TETRAFLUOROETHYLENE, STABILIZED	2	2F		2.1	386 662 676	0	E0		PP, EX, A	VE01		1	
1082	TRIFLUOROCHLOROETHYLENE, STABILIZED (REFRIGERANT GAS R 1113)	2	2TF		2.3+2.1	386 676	0	E0		PP, EP, EX, TOX, A	VE01, VE02		2	
1083	TRIMETHYLAMINE, ANHYDROUS	2	2F		2.1	662	0	E0	T	PP, EX, A	VE01		1	
1085	VINYL BROMIDE, STABILIZED	2	2F		2.1	386 662 676	0	E0		PP, EX, A	VE01		1	
1086	VINYL CHLORIDE, STABILIZED	2	2F		2.1	386 662 676	0	E0	T	PP, EX, A	VE01		1	
1087	VINYL METHYL ETHER, STABILIZED	2	2F		2.1	386 662 676	0	E0		PP, EX, A	VE01		1	
1088	ACETAL	3	F1	II	3		1 L	E2	T	PP, EX, A	VE01		1	
1089	ACETALDEHYDE	3	F1	I	3		0	E0	T	PP, EX, A	VE01		1	
1090	ACETONE	3	F1	II	3		1 L	E2	T	PP, EX, A	VE01		1	
1091	ACETONE OILS	3	F1	II	3		1 L	E2	T	PP, EX, A	VE01		1	
1092	ACROLEIN, STABILIZED	6.1	TF1	I	6.1+3	354 386 676 802	0	E0	T	PP, EP, EX, TOX, A	VE01, VE02		2	
1093	ACRYLONITRILE, STABILIZED	3	FT1	I	3+6.1	386 676 802	0	E0	T	PP, EP, EX, TOX, A	VE01, VE02		2	
1098	ALLYL ALCOHOL	6.1	TF1	I	6.1+3	354 802	0	E0	T	PP, EP, EX, TOX, A	VE01, VE02		2	
1099	ALLYL BROMIDE	3	FT1	I	3+6.1	802	0	E0	T	PP, EP, EX, TOX, A	VE01, VE02		2	
1100	ALLYL CHLORIDE	3	FT1	I	3+6.1	802	0	E0	T	PP, EP, EX, TOX, A	VE01, VE02		2	
1104	AMYL ACETATES	3	F1	III	3		5 L	E1		PP, EX, A	VE01		0	
1105	PENTANOLS	3	F1	II	3		1 L	E2		PP, EX, A	VE01		1	
1105	PENTANOLS	3	F1	III	3		5 L	E1		PP, EX, A	VE01		0	
1106	AMYLAMINE	3	FC	II	3+8		1 L	E2	T	PP, EP, EX, A	VE01		1	
1106	AMYLAMINE	3	FC	III	3+8		5 L	E1		PP, EP, EX, A	VE01		0	
1107	AMYL CHLORIDE	3	F1	II	3		1 L	E2	T	PP, EX, A	VE01		1	
1108	1-PENTENE (n-AMYLENE)	3	F1	I	3		0	E3	T	PP, EX, A	VE01		1	
1109	AMYL FORMATES	3	F1	III	3		5 L	E1		PP, EX, A	VE01		0	
1110	n-AMYL METHYL KETONE	3	F1	III	3		5 L	E1		PP, EX, A	VE01		0	
1111	AMYL MERCAPTAN	3	F1	II	3		1 L	E2		PP, EX, A	VE01		1	
1112	AMYL NITRATE	3	F1	III	3		5 L	E1		PP, EX, A	VE01		0	
1113	AMYL NITRITE	3	F1	II	3		1 L	E2		PP, EX, A	VE01		1	
1114	BENZENE	3	F1	II	3		1 L	E2	T	PP, EX, A	VE01		1	
1120	BUTANOLS	3	F1	II	3		1 L	E2	T	PP, EX, A	VE01		1	

UN No. or ID No.	Name and description	Class	Classification Code	Packing group	Labels	Special provisions	Limited and excepted quantities		Carriage permitted	Equipment required	Venti-lation	Provisions concerning loading, unloading and carriage	Number of blue cones/ lights	Remarks
		2.2	2.2	2.1.1.3	5.2.2	3.3	3.4	3.5.1.2	3.2.1	8.1.5	7.1.6	7.1.6	7.1.5	3.2.1
(1)	(2)	(3a)	(3b)	(4)	(5)	(6)	(7a)	(7b)	(8)	(9)	(10)	(11)	(12)	(13)
1120	BUTANOLS	3	F1	III	3		5 L	E1	T	PP, EX, A	VE01		0	
1123	BUTYL ACETATES	3	F1	II	3		1 L	E2	T	PP, EX, A	VE01		1	
1123	BUTYL ACETATES	3	F1	III	3		5 L	E1	T	PP, EX, A	VE01		0	
1125	n-BUTYLAMINE	3	FC	II	3+8		1 L	E2	T	PP, EP, EX, A	VE01		1	
1126	1-BROMOBUTANE	3	F1	II	3		1 L	E2		PP, EX, A	VE01		1	
1127	CHLOROBUTANES	3	F1	II	3		1 L	E2	T	PP, EX, A	VE01		1	
1128	n-BUTYL FORMATE	3	F1	II	3		1 L	E2	T	PP, EX, A	VE01		1	
1129	BUTYRALDEHYDE	3	F1	II	3		1 L	E2	T	PP, EX, A	VE01		1	
1130	CAMPHOR OIL	3	F1	III	3		5 L	E1	T	PP, EX, A	VE01		0	
1131	CARBON DISULPHIDE	3	FT1	I	3+6.1	802	0	E0	T	PP, EX, TOX, A	VE01, VE02		2	
1133	ADHESIVES containing flammable liquid	3	F1	I	3		500 ml	E3		PP, EX, A	VE01		1	
1133	ADHESIVES containing flammable liquid (vapour pressure at 50 °C more than 110 kPa)	3	F1	II	3	640C	5 L	E2		PP, EX, A	VE01		1	
1133	ADHESIVES containing flammable liquid (vapour pressure at 50 °C not more than 110 kPa)	3	F1	II	3	640D	5 L	E2		PP, EX, A	VE01		1	
1133	ADHESIVES containing flammable liquid	3	F1	III	3		5 L	E1		PP, EX, A	VE01		0	
1133	ADHESIVES containing flammable liquid (having a flash-point below 23 °C and viscous according to 2.2.3.1.4) (vapour pressure at 50 °C more than 110 kPa)	3	F1	III	3		5 L	E1		PP, EX, A	VE01		0	
1133	ADHESIVES containing flammable liquid (having a flash-point below 23 °C and viscous according to 2.2.3.1.4) (vapour pressure at 50 °C not more than 110 kPa)	3	F1	III	3		5 L	E1		PP, EX, A	VE01		0	
1134	CHLOROBENZENE	3	F1	III	3		5 L	E1	T	PP, EX, A	VE01		0	
1135	ETHYLENE CHLOROHYDRIN	6.1	TF1	I	6.1+3	354 802	0	E0	T	PP, EP, EX, TOX, A	VE01, VE02		2	
1136	COAL TAR DISTILLATES, FLAMMABLE	3	F1	II	3		1 L	E2		PP, EX, A	VE01		1	
1136	COAL TAR DISTILLATES, FLAMMABLE	3	F1	III	3		5 L	E1		PP, EX, A	VE01		0	
1139	COATING SOLUTION (includes surface treatments or coatings used for industrial or other purposes such as vehicle under coating, drum or barrel lining)	3	F1	I	3		500 ml	E3		PP, EX, A	VE01		1	
1139	COATING SOLUTION (includes surface treatments or coatings used for industrial or other purposes such as vehicle under coating, drum or barrel lining) (vapour pressure at 50°C more than 110 kPa)	3	F1	II	3	640C	5 L	E2		PP, EX, A	VE01		1	
1139	COATING SOLUTION (includes surface treatments or coatings used for industrial or other purposes such as vehicle under coating, drum or barrel lining) (vapour pressure at 50°C not more than 110 kPa)	3	F1	II	3	640D	5 L	E2		PP, EX, A	VE01		1	
1139	COATING SOLUTION (includes surface treatments or coatings used for industrial or other purposes such as vehicle under coating, drum or barrel lining)	3	F1	III	3		5 L	E1		PP, EX, A	VE01		0	
1139	COATING SOLUTION (includes surface treatments or coatings used for industrial or other purposes such as vehicle under coating, drum or barrel lining) (having a flash-point below 23°C and viscous according to 2.2.3.1.4) (vapour pressure at 50°C)	3	F1	III	3		5 L	E1		PP, EX, A	VE01		0	

UN No. or ID No. (1)	Name and description 3.1.2 (2)	Class 2.2 (3a)	Classification Code 2.2 (3b)	Packing group 2.1.1.3 (4)	Labels 5.2.2 (5)	Special provisions 3.3 (6)	Limited quantities 3.4 (7a)	Excepted quantities 3.5.1.2 (7b)	Carriage permitted 3.2.1 (8)	Equipment required 8.1.5 (9)	Ventilation 7.1.6 (10)	Provisions concerning loading, unloading and carriage 7.1.6 (11)	Number of blue cones/lights 7.1.5 (12)	Remarks 3.2.1 (13)
1139	COATING SOLUTION (includes surface treatments or coatings used for industrial or other purposes such as vehicle under coating, drum or barrel lining) (having a flash-point below 23°C and viscous according to 2.2.3.1.4) (vapour pressure at 50°C not more than 110 kPa)	3	F1	III	3		5 L	E1		PP, EX, A	VE01		0	
1143	CROTONALDEHYDE or CROTONALDEHYDE, STABILIZED	6.1	TF1	I	6.1+3	324 354 386 676 802	0	E0	T	PP, EP, EX, TOX, A	VE01, VE02		2	
1144	CROTONYLENE	3	F1	I	3		0	E3		PP, EX, A	VE01		1	
1145	CYCLOHEXANE	3	F1	II	3		1 L	E2	T	PP, EX, A	VE01		1	
1146	CYCLOPENTANE	3	F1	II	3		1 L	E2	T	PP, EX, A	VE01		1	
1147	DECAHYDRONAPHTHALENE	3	F1	III	3		5 L	E1		PP, EX, A	VE01		0	
1148	DIACETONE ALCOHOL	3	F1	II	3		1 L	E2		PP, EX, A	VE01		1	
1148	DIACETONE ALCOHOL	3	F1	III	3		5 L	E1	T	PP, EX, A	VE01		0	
1149	DIBUTYL ETHERS	3	F1	III	3		5 L	E1	T	PP, EX, A	VE01		0	
1150	1,2-DICHLOROETHYLENE	3	F1	II	3		1 L	E2	T	PP, EX, A	VE01		1	
1152	DICHLOROPENTANES	3	F1	III	3		5 L	E1		PP, EX, A	VE01		0	
1153	ETHYLENE GLYCOL DIETHYL ETHER	3	F1	II	3		1 L	E2	T	PP, EX, A	VE01		1	
1153	ETHYLENE GLYCOL DIETHYL ETHER	3	F1	III	3		5 L	E1	T	PP, EX, A	VE01		0	
1154	DIETHYLAMINE	3	FC	II	3+8		1 L	E2	T	PP, EP, EX, A	VE01		1	
1155	DIETHYL ETHER (ETHYL ETHER)	3	F1	I	3		0	E3	T	PP, EX, A	VE01		1	
1156	DIETHYL KETONE	3	F1	II	3		1 L	E2	T	PP, EX, A	VE01		1	
1157	DIISOBUTYL KETONE	3	F1	III	3		5 L	E1	T	PP, EX, A	VE01		0	
1158	DIISOPROPYLAMINE	3	FC	II	3+8		1 L	E2	T	PP, EP, EX, A	VE01		1	
1159	DIISOPROPYL ETHER	3	F1	II	3		1 L	E2	T	PP, EX, A	VE01		1	
1160	DIMETHYLAMINE AQUEOUS SOLUTION	3	FC	II	3+8		1 L	E2	T	PP, EP, EX, A	VE01		1	
1161	DIMETHYL CARBONATE	3	F1	II	3		1 L	E2	T	PP, EX, A	VE01		1	
1162	DIMETHYLDICHLOROSILANE	3	FC	II	3+8		0	E0	T	PP, EP, EX, A	VE01		1	
1163	DIMETHYLHYDRAZINE, UNSYMMETRICAL	6.1	TFC	I	6.1+3+8	354 802	0	E0	T	PP, EP, EX, TOX, A	VE01, VE02		2	
1164	DIMETHYL SULPHIDE	3	F1	II	3		1 L	E2		PP, EX, A	VE01		1	
1165	DIOXANE	3	F1	II	3		1 L	E2	T	PP, EX, A	VE01		1	
1166	DIOXOLANE	3	F1	II	3		1 L	E2		PP, EX, A	VE01		1	
1167	DIVINYL ETHER, STABILIZED	3	F1	I	3	386 676	0	E3	T	PP, EX, A	VE01		1	
1170	ETHANOL (ETHYL ALCOHOL) or ETHANOL SOLUTION (ETHYL ALCOHOL SOLUTION)	3	F1	II	3	144 601	1 L	E2	T	PP, EX, A	VE01		1	
1170	ETHANOL SOLUTION (ETHYL ALCOHOL SOLUTION)	3	F1	III	3	144 601	5 L	E1	T	PP, EX, A	VE01		0	
1171	ETHYLENE GLYCOL MONOETHYL ETHER	3	F1	III	3		5 L	E1	T	PP, EX, A	VE01		0	
1172	ETHYLENE GLYCOL MONOETHYL ETHER ACETATE	3	F1	III	3		5 L	E1	T	PP, EX, A	VE01		0	
1173	ETHYL ACETATE	3	F1	II	3		1 L	E2	T	PP, EX, A	VE01		1	
1175	ETHYLBENZENE	3	F1	II	3		1 L	E2	T	PP, EX, A	VE01		1	
1176	ETHYL BORATE	3	F1	II	3		1 L	E2		PP, EX, A	VE01		1	

UN No. or ID No.	Name and description	Class	Classification Code	Packing group	Labels	Special provisions	Limited and excepted quantities		Carriage permitted	Equipment required	Venti-lation	Provisions concerning loading, unloading and carriage	Number of blue cones/ lights	Remarks
3.1.2	3.1.2	2.2	2.2	2.1.1.3	5.2.2	3.3	3.4	3.5.1.2	3.2.1	8.1.5	7.1.6	7.1.6	7.1.5	3.2.1
(1)	(2)	(3a)	(3b)	(4)	(5)	(6)	(7a)	(7b)	(8)	(9)	(10)	(11)	(12)	(13)
1177	2-ETHYLBUTYL ACETATE	3	F1	III	3		5 L	E1	T	PP, EX, A	VE01		0	
1178	2-ETHYLBUTYRALDEHYDE	3	F1	II	3		1 L	E2		PP, EX, A	VE01		1	
1179	ETHYL BUTYL ETHER	3	F1	II	3		1 L	E2	T	PP, EX, A	VE01		1	
1180	ETHYL BUTYRATE	3	F1	III	3		5 L	E1		PP, EX, A	VE01		0	
1181	ETHYL CHLOROACETATE	6.1	TF1	II	6.1+3	802	100 ml	E4		PP, EP, EX, TOX, A	VE01, VE02		2	
1182	ETHYL CHLOROFORMATE	6.1	TFC	I	6.1+3+8	354 802	0	E0		PP, EP, EX, TOX, A	VE01, VE02		2	
1183	ETHYLDICHLOROSILANE	4.3	WFC	I	4.3+3+8		0	E0		PP, EP, EX, A	VE01	HA08	1	
1184	ETHYLENE DICHLORIDE	3	FT1	II	3+6.1	802	1 L	E2	T	PP, EP, EX, TOX, A	VE01, VE02		2	
1185	ETHYLENEIMINE, STABILIZED	6.1	TF1	I	6.1+3	354 386 676 802	0	E0		PP, EP, EX, TOX, A	VE01, VE02		2	
1188	ETHYLENE GLYCOL MONOMETHYL ETHER	3	F1	III	3		5 L	E1	T	PP, EX, A	VE01		0	
1189	ETHYLENE GLYCOL MONOMETHYL ETHER ACETATE	3	F1	III	3		5 L	E1		PP, EX, A	VE01		0	
1190	ETHYL FORMATE	3	F1	II	3		1 L	E2		PP, EX, A	VE01		1	
1191	OCTYL ALDEHYDES	3	F1	III	3		5 L	E1	T	PP, EX, A	VE01		0	
1192	ETHYL LACTATE	3	F1	III	3		5 L	E1		PP, EX, A	VE01		0	
1193	ETHYL METHYL KETONE (METHYL ETHYL KETONE)	3	F1	II	3		1 L	E2	T	PP, EX, A	VE01		1	
1194	ETHYL NITRITE SOLUTION	3	FT1	I	3+6.1	802	0	E0		PP, EP, EX, TOX, A	VE01, VE02		2	
1195	ETHYL PROPIONATE	3	F1	II	3		1 L	E2		PP, EX, A	VE01		1	
1196	ETHYLTRICHLOROSILANE	3	FC	II	3+8		0	E0		PP, EP, EX, A	VE01		1	
1197	EXTRACTS, LIQUID, for flavour or aroma (vapour pressure at 50 °C more than 110 kPa)	3	F1	II	3	601 640C	5 L	E2		PP, EP, EX, A	VE01		1	
1197	EXTRACTS, LIQUID, for flavour or aroma (vapour pressure at 50 °C not more than 110 kPa)	3	F1	II	3	601 640D	5 L	E2		PP, EX, A	VE01		1	
1197	EXTRACTS, LIQUID, for flavour or aroma	3	F1	III	3	601	5 L	E1		PP, EX, A	VE01		0	
1197	EXTRACTS, LIQUID, for flavour or aroma (having a flash-point below 23 °C and viscous according to 2.2.3.1.4) (vapour pressure at 50 °C more than 110 kPa)	3	F1	III	3	601	5 L	E1		PP, EX, A	VE01		0	
1197	EXTRACTS, LIQUID, for flavour or aroma (having a flash-point below 23 °C and viscous according to 2.2.3.1.4) (vapour pressure at 50 °C not more than 110 kPa)	3	F1	III	3	601	5 L	E1		PP, EX, A	VE01		0	
1198	FORMALDEHYDE SOLUTION, FLAMMABLE	3	FC	III	3+8		5 L	E1	T	PP, EP, EX, A	VE01		0	
1199	FURALDEHYDES	6.1	TF1	II	6.1+3	802	100 ml	E4	T	PP, EP, EX, TOX, A	VE01, VE02		2	
1201	FUSEL OIL	3	F1	II	3		1 L	E2		PP, EX, A	VE01		1	
1201	FUSEL OIL	3	F1	III	3		5 L	E1		PP, EX, A	VE01		0	
1202	GAS OIL or DIESEL FUEL or HEATING OIL, LIGHT (flash-point not more than 60 °C)	3	F1	III	3	640K	5 L	E1	T	PP, EX, A	VE01		0	

UN No. or ID No. (1)	Name and description 3.1.2 (2)	Class 2.2 (3a)	Classification Code 2.2 (3b)	Packing group 2.1.1.3 (4)	Labels 5.2.2 (5)	Special provisions 3.3 (6)	Limited and excepted quantities 3.4 (7a)	3.5.1.2 (7b)	Carriage permitted 3.2.1 (8)	Equipment required 8.1.5 (9)	Ventilation 7.1.6 (10)	Provisions concerning loading, unloading and carriage 7.1.6 (11)	Number of blue cones/lights 7.1.5 (12)	Remarks 3.2.1 (13)
1202	DIESEL FUEL complying with standard EN 590:2013 + A1:2017 or GAS OIL or HEATING OIL, LIGHT with a flash-point as specified in EN 590:2013 + A1:2017	3	F1	III	3	640L	5 L	E1	T	PP, EX, A	VE01		0	
1202	GAS OIL or DIESEL FUEL or HEATING OIL, LIGHT (flash-point more than 60 °C and not more than 100 °C)	3	F1	III	3	640M	5 L	E1	T	PP, EX, A	VE01		0	
1203	MOTOR SPIRIT or GASOLINE or PETROL	3	F1	II	3	243 534	1 L	E2	T	PP, EX, A	VE01		1	
1204	NITROGLYCERIN SOLUTION IN ALCOHOL with not more than 1% nitroglycerin	3	D	II	3	601	1 L	E0	T	PP, EX, A	VE01		1	
1206	HEPTANES	3	F1	II	3		1 L	E2	T	PP, EX, A	VE01		1	
1207	HEXALDEHYDE	3	F1	III	3		5 L	E1		PP, EX, A	VE01		0	
1208	HEXANES	3	F1	II	3		1 L	E2	T	PP, EX, A	VE01		1	
1210	PRINTING INK, flammable or PRINTING INK RELATED MATERIAL (including printing ink thinning or reducing compound), flammable	3	F1	I	3	163 367	500 ml	E3		PP, EX, A	VE01		1	
1210	PRINTING INK, flammable or PRINTING INK RELATED MATERIAL (including printing ink thinning or reducing compound), flammable (vapour pressure at 50 °C more than 110 kPa)	3	F1	II	3	163 367 640C	5 L	E2		PP, EX, A			1	
1210	PRINTING INK, flammable or PRINTING INK RELATED MATERIAL (including printing ink thinning or reducing compound), flammable (vapour pressure at 50 °C not more than 110 kPa)	3	F1	II	3	163 367 640D	5 L	E2		PP, EX, A	VE01		1	
1210	PRINTING INK, flammable or PRINTING INK RELATED MATERIAL (including printing ink thinning or reducing compound), flammable	3	F1	III	3	163 367	5 L	E1		PP, EX, A	VE01		0	
1210	PRINTING INK, flammable or PRINTING INK RELATED MATERIAL (including printing ink thinning or reducing compound), flammable (having a flash-point below 23 °C and viscous according to 2.2.3.1.4) (vapour pressure at 50 °C more than 110 kPa)	3	F1	III	3	163 367	5 L	E1		PP, EX, A	VE01		0	
1210	PRINTING INK, flammable or PRINTING INK RELATED MATERIAL (including printing ink thinning or reducing compound), flammable (having a flash-point below 23 °C and viscous according to 2.2.3.1.4) (vapour pressure at 50 °C not more than 110 kPa)	3	F1	III	3	163 367	5 L	E1		PP, EX, A	VE01		0	
1212	ISOBUTANOL (ISOBUTYL ALCOHOL)	3	F1	III	3		5 L	E1	T	PP, EX, A	VE01		0	
1213	ISOBUTYL ACETATE	3	F1	II	3		1 L	E2	T	PP, EX, A	VE01		1	
1214	ISOBUTYLAMINE	3	FC	II	3+8		1 L	E2	T	PP, EP, EX, A	VE01		1	
1216	ISOOCTENES	3	F1	II	3		1 L	E2	T	PP, EX, A	VE01		1	
1218	ISOPRENE, STABILIZED	3	F1	I	3	386 676	0	E3	T	PP, EX, A	VE01		1	
1219	ISOPROPANOL (ISOPROPYL ALCOHOL)	3	F1	II	3	601	1 L	E2	T	PP, EX, A	VE01		1	
1220	ISOPROPYL ACETATE	3	F1	II	3		1 L	E2	T	PP, EX, A	VE01		1	
1221	ISOPROPYLAMINE	3	FC	I	3+8		0	E0	T	PP, EP, EX, A	VE01		1	
1222	ISOPROPYL NITRATE	3	F1	II	3		1 L	E2		PP, EX, A	VE01		1	
1223	KEROSENE	3	F1	III	3		5 L	E1	T	PP, EX, A	VE01		0	

UN No. or ID No. (1)	Name and description (2) 3.1.2	Class (3a) 2.2	Classification Code (3b) 2.2	Packing group (4) 2.1.1.3	Labels (5) 5.2.2	Special provisions (6) 3.3	Limited and excepted quantities 3.4 (7a)	3.5.1.2 (7b)	Carriage permitted (8) 3.2.1	Equipment required (9) 8.1.5	Ventilation (10) 7.1.6	Provisions concerning loading, unloading and carriage (11) 7.1.6	Number of blue cones/lights (12) 7.1.5	Remarks (13) 3.2.1
1224	KETONES, LIQUID, N.O.S. (vapour pressure at 50 °C more than 110 kPa)	3	F1	II	3	274 640C	1 L	E2	T	PP, EX, A	VE01		1	
1224	KETONES, LIQUID, N.O.S. (vapour pressure at 50 °C not more than 110 kPa)	3	F1	II	3	274 640D	1 L	E2	T	PP, EX, A	VE01		1	
1224	KETONES, LIQUID, N.O.S.	3	F1	III	3	274	5 L	E1	T	PP, EX, A	VE01		0	
1228	MERCAPTANS, LIQUID, FLAMMABLE, TOXIC, N.O.S. or MERCAPTAN MIXTURE, LIQUID, FLAMMABLE, TOXIC, N.O.S.	3	FT1	II	3+6.1	274 802	1 L	E0		PP, EP, EX, TOX, A	VE01, VE02		2	
1228	MERCAPTANS, LIQUID, FLAMMABLE, TOXIC, N.O.S. or MERCAPTAN MIXTURE, LIQUID, FLAMMABLE, TOXIC, N.O.S.	3	FT1	III	3+6.1	274 802	5 L	E1		PP, EP, EX, TOX, A	VE01, VE02		0	
1229	MESITYL OXIDE	3	F1	III	3		5 L	E1	T	PP, EX, A	VE01		0	
1230	METHANOL	3	FT1	II	3+6.1	279 802	1 L	E2	T	PP, EP, EX, TOX, A	VE01, VE02		2	
1231	METHYL ACETATE	3	F1	II	3		1 L	E2	T	PP, EX, A	VE01		1	
1233	METHYLAMYL ACETATE	3	F1	III	3		5 L	E1	T	PP, EX, A	VE01		0	
1234	METHYLAL	3	F1	II	3		1 L	E2	T	PP, EX, A	VE01		1	
1235	METHYLAMINE, AQUEOUS SOLUTION	3	FC	II	3+8		1 L	E2	T	PP, EP, EX, A	VE01		1	
1237	METHYL BUTYRATE	3	F1	II	3		1 L	E2	T	PP, EX, A	VE01		1	
1238	METHYL CHLOROFORMATE	6.1	TFC	I	6.1+3+8	354 802	0	E0		PP, EP, EX, TOX, A	VE01, VE02		2	
1239	METHYL CHLOROMETHYL ETHER	6.1	TF1	I	6.1+3	354 802	0	E0		PP, EP, EX, TOX, A	VE01, VE02		2	
1242	METHYLDICHLOROSILANE	4.3	WFC	I	4.3+3+8		0	E0		PP, EP, EX, A	VE01	HA08	1	
1243	METHYL FORMATE	3	F1	I	3		0	E3	T	PP, EX, A	VE01		1	
1244	METHYLHYDRAZINE	6.1	TFC	I	6.1+3+8	354 802	0	E0	T	PP, EP, EX, TOX, A	VE01, VE02		2	
1245	METHYL ISOBUTYL KETONE	3	F1	II	3		1 L	E2	T	PP, EX, A	VE01		1	
1246	METHYL ISOPROPENYL KETONE, STABILIZED	3	F1	II	3	386 676	1 L	E2		PP, EX, A	VE01		1	
1247	METHYL METHACRYLATE MONOMER, STABILIZED	3	F1	II	3	386 676	1 L	E2	T	PP, EX, A	VE01		1	
1248	METHYL PROPIONATE	3	F1	II	3		1 L	E2		PP, EX, A	VE01		1	
1249	METHYL PROPYL KETONE	3	F1	II	3		1 L	E2		PP, EX, A	VE01		1	
1250	METHYLTRICHLOROSILANE	3	FC	III	3+8		0	E0		PP, EP, EX, A	VE01		1	
1251	METHYL VINYL KETONE, STABILIZED	6.1	TFC	I	6.1+3+8	354 386 676 802	0	E0		PP, EP, EX, TOX, A	VE01, VE02		2	
1259	NICKEL CARBONYL	6.1	TF1	I	6.1+3	802	0	E0		PP, EP, EX, TOX, A	VE01, VE02		2	
1261	NITROMETHANE	3	F1	II	3		1 L	E0		PP, EX, A	VE01		1	
1262	OCTANES	3	F1	II	3		1 L	E2	T	PP, EX, A	VE01		1	
1263	PAINT (including paint, lacquer, enamel, stain, shellac, varnish, polish, liquid filler and liquid lacquer base) or PAINT RELATED MATERIAL (including paint thinning and reducing compound)	3	F1	I	3	163 367 650	500 ml	E3		PP, EX, A	VE01		1	

(1) UN No. or ID No.	(2) Name and description 3.1.2	(3a) Class 2.2	(3b) Classification Code 2.2	(4) Packing group 2.1.1.3	(5) Labels 5.2.2	(6) Special provisions 3.3	(7a) Limited quantities 3.4	(7b) excepted quantities 3.5.1.2	(8) Carriage permitted 3.2.1	(9) Equipment required 8.1.5	(10) Ventilation 7.1.6	(11) Provisions concerning loading, unloading and carriage 7.1.6	(12) Number of blue cones/lights 7.1.5	(13) Remarks 3.2.1
1263	PAINT (including paint, lacquer, enamel, stain, shellac, varnish, polish, liquid filler and liquid lacquer base) or PAINT RELATED MATERIAL (including paint thinning and reducing compound) (vapour pressure at 50 °C more than 110 kPa)	3	F1	II	3	163 367 640C 650	5 L	E2		PP, EX, A	VE01		1	
1263	PAINT (including paint, lacquer, enamel, stain, shellac, varnish, polish, liquid filler and liquid lacquer base) or PAINT RELATED MATERIAL (including paint thinning and reducing compound) (vapour pressure at 50 °C not more than 110 kPa)	3	F1	II	3	163 367 640D 650	5 L	E2		PP, EX, A	VE01		1	
1263	PAINT (including paint, lacquer, enamel, stain, shellac, varnish, polish, liquid filler and liquid lacquer base) or PAINT RELATED MATERIAL (including paint thinning and reducing compound)	3	F1	III	3	163 367 650	5 L	E1		PP, EX, A	VE01		0	
1263	PAINT (including paint, lacquer, enamel, stain, shellac, varnish, polish, liquid filler and liquid lacquer base) or PAINT RELATED MATERIAL (including paint thinning and reducing compound) (having a flash-point below 23 °C and viscous according to 2.2.3.1.4) (vapour pressure at 50 °C more than 110 kPa)	3	F1	III	3	163 367 650	5 L	E1		PP, EX, A	VE01		0	
1263	PAINT (including paint, lacquer, enamel, stain, shellac, varnish, polish, liquid filler and liquid lacquer base) or PAINT RELATED MATERIAL (including paint thinning and reducing compound) (having a flash-point below 23 °C and viscous according to 2.2.3.1.4) (vapour pressure at 50 °C not more than 110 kPa)	3	F1	III	3	163 367 650	5 L	E1		PP, EX, A	VE01		0	
1264	PARALDEHYDE	3	F1	III	3		5 L	E1	T	PP, EX, A	VE01		0	
1265	PENTANES, liquid	3	F1	I	3		0	E3	T	PP, EX, A	VE01		1	
1265	PENTANES, liquid	3	F1	II	3		1 L	E2	T	PP, EX, A	VE01		1	
1266	PERFUMERY PRODUCTS with flammable solvents (vapour pressure at 50 °C more than 110 kPa)	3	F1	II	3	163 640C	5 L	E2		PP, EX, A	VE01		1	
1266	PERFUMERY PRODUCTS with flammable solvents (vapour pressure at 50 °C not more than 110 kPa)	3	F1	II	3	163 640D	5 L	E2		PP, EX, A	VE01		1	
1266	PERFUMERY PRODUCTS with flammable solvents	3	F1	III	3	163	5 L	E1		PP, EX, A	VE01		0	
1266	PERFUMERY PRODUCTS with flammable solvents (having a flash-point below 23 °C and viscous according to 2.2.3.1.4) (vapour pressure at 50 °C more than 110 kPa)	3	F1	III	3	163	5 L	E1		PP, EX, A	VE01		0	
1266	PERFUMERY PRODUCTS with flammable solvents (having a flash-point below 23 °C and viscous according to 2.2.3.1.4) (vapour pressure at 50 °C not more than 110 kPa)	3	F1	III	3	163	5 L	E1		PP, EX, A	VE01		0	
1267	PETROLEUM CRUDE OIL	3	F1	I	3	357	500 ml	E3	T	PP, EX, A	VE01		1	
1267	PETROLEUM CRUDE OIL (vapour pressure at 50 °C more than 110 kPa)	3	F1	II	3	357 640C	1 L	E2	T	PP, EX, A	VE01		1	

UN No. or ID No.	Name and description	Class	Classification Code	Packing group	Labels	Special provisions	Limited and excepted quantities		Carriage permitted	Equipment required	Ventilation	Provisions concerning loading, unloading and carriage	Number of blue cones/ lights	Remarks
		2.2	2.2	2.1.1.3	5.2.2	3.3	3.4	3.5.1.2	3.2.1	8.1.5	7.1.6	7.1.6	7.1.5	3.2.1
(1)	(2)	(3a)	(3b)	(4)	(5)	(6)	(7a)	(7b)	(8)	(9)	(10)	(11)	(12)	(13)
1267	PETROLEUM CRUDE OIL (vapour pressure at 50 °C not more than 110 kPa)	3	F1	II	3	357 640D	1 L	E2	T	PP, EX, A	VE01		1	
1267	PETROLEUM CRUDE OIL	3	F1	III	3	357	5 L	E1	T	PP, EX, A	VE01		0	
1268	PETROLEUM DISTILLATES, N.O.S. or PETROLEUM PRODUCTS, N.O.S.	3	F1	I	3		500 ml	E3	T	PP, EX, A	VE01		1	
1268	PETROLEUM DISTILLATES, N.O.S. or PETROLEUM PRODUCTS, N.O.S. (vapour pressure at 50 °C more than 110 kPa)	3	F1	II	3	640C	1 L	E2	T	PP, EX, A	VE01		1	
1268	PETROLEUM DISTILLATES, N.O.S. or PETROLEUM PRODUCTS, N.O.S. (vapour pressure at 50 °C not more than 110 kPa)	3	F1	II	3	640D	1 L	E2	T	PP, EX, A	VE01		1	
1268	PETROLEUM DISTILLATES, N.O.S. or PETROLEUM PRODUCTS, N.O.S.	3	F1	III	3		5 L	E1	T	PP, EX, A	VE01		0	
1272	PINE OIL	3	F1	III	3		5 L	E1	T	PP, EX, A	VE01		0	
1274	n-PROPANOL (PROPYL ALCOHOL, NORMAL)	3	F1	II	3		1 L	E2	T	PP, EX, A	VE01		1	
1274	n-PROPANOL (PROPYL ALCOHOL, NORMAL)	3	F1	III	3		5 L	E1	T	PP, EX, A	VE01		0	
1275	PROPIONALDEHYDE	3	F1	II	3		1 L	E2	T	PP, EX, A	VE01		1	
1276	n-PROPYL ACETATE	3	F1	II	3		1 L	E2	T	PP, EX, A	VE01		1	
1277	PROPYLAMINE	3	FC	II	3+8		1 L	E2	T	PP, EP, EX, A	VE01		1	
1278	1-CHLOROPROPANE	3	F1	II	3		1 L	E0	T	PP, EX, A	VE01		1	
1279	1,2-DICHLOROPROPANE	3	F1	II	3		1 L	E2	T	PP, EX, A	VE01		1	
1280	PROPYLENE OXIDE	3	F1	I	3		0	E3	T	PP, EX, A	VE01		1	
1281	PROPYL FORMATES	3	F1	II	3		1 L	E2	T	PP, EX, A	VE01		1	
1282	PYRIDINE	3	F1	II	3		1 L	E2	T	PP, EX, A	VE01		1	
1286	ROSIN OIL (vapour pressure at 50 °C more than 110 kPa)	3	F1	II	3	640C	5 L	E2		PP, EX, A	VE01		1	
1286	ROSIN OIL (vapour pressure at 50 °C not more than 110 kPa)	3	F1	II	3	640D	5 L	E2		PP, EX, A	VE01		1	
1286	ROSIN OIL	3	F1	III	3		5 L	E1		PP, EX, A	VE01		0	
1286	ROSIN OIL (having a flash-point below 23 °C and viscous according to 2.2.3.1.4) (vapour pressure at 50 °C more than 110 kPa)	3	F1	III	3		5 L	E1		PP, EX, A	VE01		0	
1286	ROSIN OIL (having a flash-point below 23 °C and viscous according to 2.2.3.1.4) (vapour pressure at 50 °C not more than 110 kPa)	3	F1	III	3		5 L	E1		PP, EX, A	VE01		0	
1287	RUBBER SOLUTION (vapour pressure at 50 °C more than 110 kPa)	3	F1	II	3	640C	5 L	E2		PP, EX, A	VE01		1	
1287	RUBBER SOLUTION (vapour pressure at 50 °C not more than 110 kPa)	3	F1	II	3	640D	5 L	E2		PP, EX, A	VE01		1	
1287	RUBBER SOLUTION	3	F1	III	3		5 L	E1		PP, EX, A	VE01		0	
1287	RUBBER SOLUTION (having a flash-point below 23 °C and viscous according to 2.2.3.1.4) (vapour pressure at 50 °C more than 110 kPa)	3	F1	III	3		5 L	E1		PP, EX, A	VE01		0	
1287	RUBBER SOLUTION (having a flash-point below 23 °C and viscous according to 2.2.3.1.4) (vapour pressure at 50 °C not more than 110 kPa)	3	F1	III	3		5 L	E1	T	PP, EX, A	VE01		0	
1288	SHALE OIL	3	F1	II	3		1 L	E2	T	PP, EX, A	VE01		1	

UN No. or ID No. (1)	Name and description 3.1.2 (2)	Class 2.2 (3a)	Classification Code 2.2 (3b)	Packing group 2.1.1.3 (4)	Labels 5.2.2 (5)	Special provisions 3.3 (6)	Limited and excepted quantities 3.4 (7a)	Limited and excepted quantities 3.5.1.2 (7b)	Carriage permitted 3.2.1 (8)	Equipment required 8.1.5 (9)	Ventilation 7.1.6 (10)	Provisions concerning loading, unloading and carriage 7.1.6 (11)	Number of blue cones/lights 7.1.5 (12)	Remarks 3.2.1 (13)
1288	SHALE OIL	3	F1	III	3		5 L	E1		PP, EX, A	VE01		0	
1289	SODIUM METHYLATE SOLUTION in alcohol	3	FC	II	3+8		1 L	E2		PP, EP, EX, A	VE01		1	
1289	SODIUM METHYLATE SOLUTION in alcohol	3	FC	III	3+8		5 L	E1	T	PP, EP, EX, A	VE01		0	
1292	TETRAETHYL SILICATE	3	F1	III	3		5 L	E1		PP, EX, A	VE01		0	
1293	TINCTURES, MEDICINAL	3	F1	II	3	601	1 L	E2		PP, EX, A	VE01		1	
1293	TINCTURES, MEDICINAL	3	F1	III	3	601	5 L	E1		PP, EX, A	VE01		0	
1294	TOLUENE	3	F1	II	3		1 L	E2	T	PP, EX, A	VE01		1	
1295	TRICHLOROSILANE	4.3	WFC	I	4.3+3+8		0	E0		PP, EP, EX, A	VE01	HA08	1	
1296	TRIETHYLAMINE	3	FC	II	3+8		1 L	E2	T	PP, EP, EX, A	VE01		1	
1297	TRIMETHYLAMINE, AQUEOUS SOLUTION, not more than 50% trimethylamine, by mass	3	FC	I	3+8		0	E0		PP, EP, EX, A	VE01		1	
1297	TRIMETHYLAMINE, AQUEOUS SOLUTION, not more than 50% trimethylamine, by mass	3	FC	II	3+8		1 L	E2		PP, EP, EX, A	VE01		1	
1297	TRIMETHYLAMINE, AQUEOUS SOLUTION, not more than 50% trimethylamine, by mass	3	FC	III	3+8		5 L	E1		PP, EP, EX, A	VE01		0	
1298	TRIMETHYLCHLOROSILANE	3	FC	II	3+8		0	E0		PP, EP, EX, A	VE01		1	
1299	TURPENTINE	3	F1	III	3		5 L	E1		PP, EX, A	VE01		0	
1300	TURPENTINE SUBSTITUTE	3	F1	II	3		1 L	E2		PP, EX, A	VE01		1	
1300	TURPENTINE SUBSTITUTE	3	F1	III	3		5 L	E1	T	PP, EX, A	VE01		0	
1301	VINYL ACETATE, STABILIZED	3	F1	II	3	386 676	1 L	E2	T	PP, EX, A	VE01		1	
1302	VINYL ETHYL ETHER, STABILIZED	3	F1	I	3	386 676	0	E3		PP, EX, A	VE01		1	
1303	VINYLIDENE CHLORIDE, STABILIZED	3	F1	I	3	386 676	0	E3		PP, EX, A	VE01		1	
1304	VINYL ISOBUTYL ETHER, STABILIZED	3	F1	II	3	386 676	1 L	E2		PP, EX, A	VE01		1	
1305	VINYLTRICHLOROSILANE, STABILIZED	3	FC	II	3+8		0	E0		PP, EP, EX, A	VE01		1	
1306	WOOD PRESERVATIVES, LIQUID (vapour pressure at 50 °C more than 110 kPa)	3	F1	II	3	640C	5 L	E2		PP, EX, A	VE01		1	
1306	WOOD PRESERVATIVES, LIQUID (vapour pressure at 50 °C not more than 110 kPa)	3	F1	II	3	640D	5 L	E2		PP, EX, A	VE01		1	
1306	WOOD PRESERVATIVES, LIQUID	3	F1	III	3		5 L	E1		PP, EX, A	VE01		0	
1306	WOOD PRESERVATIVES, LIQUID (having a flash-point below 23 °C and viscous according to 2.2.3.1.4) (vapour pressure at 50 °C more than 110 kPa)	3	F1	III	3		5 L	E1		PP, EX, A	VE01		0	
1306	WOOD PRESERVATIVES, LIQUID (having a flash-point below 23 °C and viscous according to 2.2.3.1.4) (vapour pressure at 50 °C not more than 110 kPa)	3	F1	III	3		5 L	E1		PP, EX, A	VE01		0	
1307	XYLENES	3	F1	II	3		1 L	E2	T	PP, EX, A	VE01		1	
1307	XYLENES	3	F1	III	3		5 L	E1	T	PP, EX, A	VE01		0	
1308	ZIRCONIUM SUSPENDED IN A FLAMMABLE LIQUID	3	F1	I	3		0	E0		PP, EX, A	VE01		1	
1308	ZIRCONIUM SUSPENDED IN A FLAMMABLE LIQUID (vapour pressure at 50 °C more than 110 kPa)	3	F1	II	3	640C	1 L	E2		PP, EX, A	VE01		1	
1308	ZIRCONIUM SUSPENDED IN A FLAMMABLE LIQUID (vapour pressure at 50 °C not more than 110 kPa)	3	F1	II	3	640D	1 L	E2		PP, EX, A	VE01		1	

UN No. or ID No. (1) 3.1.2	Name and description (2) 3.1.2	Class (3a) 2.2	Classification Code (3b) 2.2	Packing group (4) 2.1.1.3	Labels (5) 5.2.2	Special provisions (6) 3.3	Limited and excepted quantities (7a) 3.4	(7b) 3.5.1.2	Carriage permitted (8) 3.2.1	Equipment required (9) 8.1.5	Ventilation (10) 7.1.6	Provisions concerning loading, unloading and carriage (11) 7.1.6	Number of blue cones/lights (12) 7.1.5	Remarks (13) 3.2.1
1308	ZIRCONIUM SUSPENDED IN A FLAMMABLE LIQUID	3	F1	III	3		5 L	E1		PP, EX, A	VE01		0	
1309	ALUMINIUM POWDER, COATED	4.1	F3	II	4.1		1 kg	E2		PP			1	
1309	ALUMINIUM POWDER, COATED	4.1	F3	III	4.1		5 kg	E1		PP			0	
1310	AMMONIUM PICRATE, WETTED with not less than 10% water, by mass	4.1	D	I	4.1		0	E0		PP			1	
1312	BORNEOL	4.1	F1	III	4.1		5 kg	E1		PP			0	
1313	CALCIUM RESINATE	4.1	F3	III	4.1		5 kg	E1		PP			0	
1314	CALCIUM RESINATE, FUSED	4.1	F3	III	4.1		5 kg	E1		PP			0	
1318	COBALT RESINATE, PRECIPITATED	4.1	F3	III	4.1		5 kg	E1		PP			0	
1320	DINITROPHENOL, WETTED with not less than 15% water, by mass	4.1	DT	I	4.1+6.1	802	0	E0		PP, EP			2	
1321	DINITROPHENOLATES, WETTED with not less than 15% water, by mass	4.1	DT	I	4.1+6.1	802	0	E0		PP, EP			2	
1322	DINITRORESORCINOL, WETTED with not less than 15% water, by mass	4.1	D	I	4.1		0	E0		PP			1	
1323	FERROCERIUM	4.1	F3	II	4.1	249	1 kg	E2		PP			1	
1324	FILMS, NITROCELLULOSE BASE, gelatin coated, except scrap	4.1	F1	III	4.1		5 kg	E1		PP			0	
1325	FLAMMABLE SOLID, ORGANIC, N.O.S.	4.1	F1	II	4.1	274	1 kg	E2		PP			1	
1325	FLAMMABLE SOLID, ORGANIC, N.O.S.	4.1	F1	III	4.1	274	5 kg	E1		PP			0	
1326	HAFNIUM POWDER, WETTED with not less than 25% water	4.1	F3	II	4.1	586	1 kg	E2		PP			1	
1327	Hay, Straw or Bhusa	4.1	F1		4.1				NOT SUBJECT TO ADN					
1328	HEXAMETHYLENETETRAMINE	4.1	F1	III	4.1		5 kg	E1		PP			0	
1330	MANGANESE RESINATE	4.1	F3	III	4.1		5 kg	E0		PP			0	
1331	MATCHES, 'STRIKE ANYWHERE'	4.1	F1	III	4.1	293	5 kg	E1		PP			0	
1332	METALDEHYDE	4.1	F1	III	4.1		5 kg	E1		PP			0	
1333	CERIUM, slabs, ingots or rods	4.1	F3	II	4.1		1 kg	E2		PP			1	
1334	NAPHTHALENE, CRUDE or NAPHTHALENE, REFINED	4.1	F1	III	4.1	501	5 kg	E1	B	PP		CO01	0	
1336	NITROGUANIDINE (PICRITE), WETTED with not less than 20% water, by mass	4.1	D	I	4.1		0	E0		PP			1	
1337	NITROSTARCH, WETTED with not less than 20% water, by mass	4.1	D	I	4.1		0	E0		PP			1	
1338	PHOSPHORUS, AMORPHOUS	4.1	F3	III	4.1		5 kg	E1		PP			0	
1339	PHOSPHORUS HEPTASULPHIDE, free from yellow and white phosphorus	4.1	F3	II	4.1	602	1 kg	E2		PP			1	
1340	PHOSPHORUS PENTASULPHIDE, free from yellow and white phosphorus	4.3	WF2	II	4.3+4.1	602	500 g	E2		PP, EX, A	VE01	HA08	1	
1341	PHOSPHORUS SESQUISULPHIDE, free from yellow and white phosphorus	4.1	F3	II	4.1	602	1 kg	E2		PP			1	
1343	PHOSPHORUS TRISULPHIDE, free from yellow and white phosphorus	4.1	F3	II	4.1	602	1 kg	E2		PP			1	
1344	TRINITROPHENOL (PICRIC ACID), WETTED with not less than 30% water, by mass	4.1	D	I	4.1	602	0	E0		PP			1	

UN No. or ID No.	Name and description	Class	Classi-fication Code	Packing group	Labels	Special provisions	Limited quantities	Excepted quantities	Carriage permitted	Equipment required	Venti-lation	Provisions concerning loading, unloading and carriage	Number of blue cones/ lights	Remarks
		2.2	2.2	2.1.1.3	5.2.2	3.3	3.4	3.5.1.2	3.2.1	8.1.5	7.1.6	7.1.6	7.1.5	3.2.1
(1)	(2)	(3a)	(3b)	(4)	(5)	(6)	(7a)	(7b)	(8)	(9)	(10)	(11)	(12)	(13)
1345	RUBBER SCRAP or RUBBER SHODDY, powdered or granulated, not exceeding 840 microns and rubber content exceeding 45 %	4.1	F1	II	4.1		1 kg	E2		PP			1	
1346	SILICON POWDER, AMORPHOUS	4.1	F3	III	4.1	32	5 kg	E1		PP			0	
1347	SILVER PICRATE, WETTED with not less than 30% water, by mass	4.1	D	I	4.1		0	E0		PP			1	
1348	SODIUM DINITRO-o-CRESOLATE, WETTED with not less than 15% water, by mass	4.1	DT	I	4.1+6.1	802	0	E0		PP, EP			2	
1349	SODIUM PICRAMATE, WETTED with not less than 20% water, by mass	4.1	D	I	4.1		0	E0		PP			1	
1350	SULPHUR	4.1	F3	III	4.1	242	5 kg	E1	B	PP			0	
1352	TITANIUM POWDER, WETTED with not less than 25% water	4.1	F3	II	4.1	586	1 kg	E2		PP			1	
1353	FIBRES or FABRICS IMPREGNATED WITH WEAKLY NITRATED NITROCELLULOSE, N.O.S.	4.1	F1	III	4.1	502	5 kg	E1		PP			0	
1354	TRINITROBENZENE, WETTED with not less than 30% water, by mass	4.1	D	I	4.1		0	E0		PP			1	
1355	TRINITROBENZOIC ACID, WETTED with not less than 30% water, by mass	4.1	D	I	4.1		0	E0		PP			1	
1356	TRINITROTOLUENE (TNT), WETTED with not less than 30% water, by mass	4.1	D	I	4.1		0	E0		PP			1	
1357	UREA NITRATE, WETTED with not less than 20% water, by mass	4.1	D	I	4.1	227	0	E0		PP			1	
1358	ZIRCONIUM POWDER, WETTED with not less than 25% water	4.1	F3	II	4.1	586	1 kg	E2		PP			1	
1360	CALCIUM PHOSPHIDE	4.3	WT2	I	4.3+6.1	802	0	E0		PP, EP, EX, TOX, A	VE01, VE02	HA08	2	
1361	CARBON, animal or vegetable origin	4.2	S2	II	4.2	665 803	0	E0		PP			0	
1361	CARBON, animal or vegetable origin	4.2	S2	III	4.2		0	E0		PP			0	
1362	CARBON, ACTIVATED	4.2	S2	III	4.2	646	0	E1	B	PP			0	
1363	COPRA	4.2	S2	III	4.2		0	E0	B	PP		IN01, IN02	0	IN01 and IN02 apply only when this substance is carried in bulk or without packaging
1364	COTTON WASTE, OILY	4.2	S2	III	4.2		0	E0	B	PP			0	
1365	COTTON, WET	4.2	S2	III	4.2		0	E0	B	PP			0	
1369	p-NITROSODIMETHYLANILINE	4.2	S2	II	4.2		0	E2		PP			0	
1372	Fibres, animal or fibres, vegetable burnt, wet or damp	4.2	S2	III	4.2				NOT SUBJECT TO ADN					
1373	FIBRES or FABRICS, ANIMAL or VEGETABLE or SYNTHETIC, N.O.S. with oil	4.2	S2	III	4.2		0	E0	B	PP			0	
1374	FISH MEAL (FISH SCRAP), UNSTABILIZED	4.2	S2	II	4.2	300	0	E2		PP			0	
1376	IRON OXIDE, SPENT or IRON SPONGE, SPENT obtained from coal gas purification	4.2	S4	III	4.2	592	0	E0		PP			0	
1378	METAL CATALYST, WETTED with a visible excess of liquid	4.2	S4	II	4.2	274	0	E0	B	PP			0	
1379	PAPER, UNSATURATED OIL TREATED, incompletely dried (including carbon paper)	4.2	S2	III	4.2		0	E0		PP			0	

UN No. or ID No. (1)	Name and description (2)	Class (3a)	Classification Code (3b)	Packing group (4)	Labels (5)	Special provisions (6)	Limited quantities (7a)	Excepted quantities (7b)	Carriage permitted (8)	Equipment required (9)	Ventilation (10)	Provisions concerning loading, unloading and carriage (11)	Number of blue cones/lights (12)	Remarks (13)
1380	PENTABORANE	4.2	ST3	I	4.2+6.1	802	0	E0		PP, EP, TOX, A	VE02		2	
1381	PHOSPHORUS, WHITE or YELLOW, UNDER WATER or IN SOLUTION	4.2	ST3	I	4.2+6.1	503 802	0	E0		PP, EP, TOX, A	VE02		2	
1381	PHOSPHORUS, WHITE or YELLOW, DRY	4.2	ST4	I	4.2+6.1	503 802	0	E0		PP, EP			2	
1382	POTASSIUM SULPHIDE, ANHYDROUS or POTASSIUM SULPHIDE with less than 30% water of crystallization	4.2	S4	II	4.2	504	0	E2		PP			0	
1383	PYROPHORIC METAL, N.O.S. or PYROPHORIC ALLOY, N.O.S.	4.2	S4	I	4.2	274	0	E0		PP			0	
1384	SODIUM DITHIONITE (SODIUM HYDROSULPHITE)	4.2	S4	II	4.2		0	E2		PP			0	
1385	SODIUM SULPHIDE, ANHYDROUS or SODIUM SULPHIDE with less than 30% water of crystallization	4.2	S4	II	4.2	504	0	E2		PP			0	
1386	SEED CAKE with more than 1.5% oil and not more than 11% moisture	4.2	S2	III	4.2	800	0	E0	B	PP		IN01, IN02	0	IN01 and IN02 apply only when this substance is carried in bulk or without packaging
1387	Wool waste, wet	4.2	S2						NOT SUBJECT TO ADN					
1389	ALKALI METAL AMALGAM, LIQUID	4.3	W1	I	4.3	182	0	E0		PP, EX, A	VE01	HA08	0	
1390	ALKALI METAL AMIDES	4.3	W2	II	4.3	182 505	500 g	E2		PP, EX, A	VE01	HA08	0	
1391	ALKALI METAL DISPERSION or ALKALINE EARTH METAL DISPERSION	4.3	W1	I	4.3	182 183 506	0	E0		PP, EX, A	VE01	HA08	1	
1392	ALKALINE EARTH METAL AMALGAM, LIQUID	4.3	W1	I	4.3	183 506	0	E0		PP, EX, A	VE01	HA08	0	
1393	ALKALINE EARTH METAL ALLOY, N.O.S.	4.3	W2	II	4.3	183 506	500 g	E2		PP, EX, A	VE01	HA08	0	
1394	ALUMINIUM CARBIDE	4.3	W2	II	4.3		500 g	E2		PP, EP, EX, A	VE01	HA08	0	
1395	ALUMINIUM FERROSILICON POWDER	4.3	WT2	II	4.3+6.1	802	500 g	E2		PP, EP, EX, TOX, A	VE01, VE02	HA08	2	
1396	ALUMINIUM POWDER, UNCOATED	4.3	W2	II	4.3		500 g	E2		PP, EX, A	VE01	HA08	0	
1396	ALUMINIUM POWDER, UNCOATED	4.3	W2	III	4.3		1 kg	E1		PP, EX, A	VE01	HA08	0	
1397	ALUMINIUM PHOSPHIDE	4.3	WT2	I	4.3+6.1	507 802	0	E0		PP, EP, EX, TOX, A	VE01, VE02	HA08	2	
1398	ALUMINIUM SILICON POWDER, UNCOATED	4.3	W2	III	4.3	37	1 kg	E1	B	PP, EX, A	VE01, VE03	LO03 HA07, HA08 IN01, IN03	0	VE03, LO03, HA07, IN01 and IN03 apply only when this substance is carried in bulk or without packaging
1400	BARIUM	4.3	W2	II	4.3		500 g	E2		PP, EX, A	VE01	HA08	0	
1401	CALCIUM	4.3	W2	II	4.3		500 g	E2		PP, EX, A	VE01	HA08	0	
1402	CALCIUM CARBIDE	4.3	W2	I	4.3		0	E0		PP, EX, A	VE01	HA08	0	
1402	CALCIUM CARBIDE	4.3	W2	II	4.3		500 g	E2		PP, EX, A	VE01	HA08	0	
1403	CALCIUM CYANAMIDE with more than 0.1% calcium carbide	4.3	W2	III	4.3	38	1 kg	E1		PP, EX, A	VE01	HA08	0	
1404	CALCIUM HYDRIDE	4.3	W2	I	4.3		0	E0		PP, EX, A	VE01	HA08	0	
1405	CALCIUM SILICIDE	4.3	W2	II	4.3		500 g	E2		PP, EX, A	VE01	HA08	0	
1405	CALCIUM SILICIDE	4.3	W2	III	4.3		1 kg	E1		PP, EX, A	VE01	HA08	0	

UN No. or ID No. (1)	Name and description (2)	Class (3a)	Classification Code (3b)	Packing group (4)	Labels (5)	Special provisions (6)	Limited quantities (7a)	Excepted quantities (7b)	Carriage permitted (8)	Equipment required (9)	Ventilation (10)	Provisions concerning loading, unloading and carriage (11)	Number of blue cones/lights (12)	Remarks (13)
1407	CAESIUM	4.3	W2	I	4.3		0	E0		PP, EX, A	VE01	HA08	0	
1408	FERROSILICON with 30% or more but less than 90% silicon	4.3	WT2	III	4.3+6.1	39 801 802	1 kg	E1	B	PP, EP, EX, TOX, A	VE01, VE02, VE03	HA07, HA08 LO03 IN01, IN02, IN03	0	VE03, LO03, HA07, IN01, IN02 and IN03 apply only when this substance is carried in bulk or without packaging
1409	METAL HYDRIDES, WATER-REACTIVE, N.O.S.	4.3	W2	I	4.3	274 508	0	E0		PP, EX, A	VE01	HA08	0	
1409	METAL HYDRIDES, WATER-REACTIVE, N.O.S.	4.3	W2	II	4.3	274 508	500 g	E2		PP, EX, A	VE01	HA08	0	
1410	LITHIUM ALUMINIUM HYDRIDE	4.3	W2	I	4.3		0	E0		PP, EX, A	VE01	HA08	1	
1411	LITHIUM ALUMINIUM HYDRIDE, ETHEREAL	4.3	WF1	I	4.3+3		0	E0		PP, EX, A	VE01	HA08	0	
1413	LITHIUM BOROHYDRIDE	4.3	W2	I	4.3		0	E0		PP, EX, A	VE01	HA08	0	
1414	LITHIUM HYDRIDE	4.3	W2	I	4.3		0	E0		PP, EX, A	VE01	HA08	0	
1415	LITHIUM	4.3	W2	I	4.3		0	E0		PP, EX, A	VE01	HA08	0	
1417	LITHIUM SILICON	4.3	W2	II	4.3		500 g	E2		PP, EX, A	VE01	HA08	0	
1418	MAGNESIUM POWDER or MAGNESIUM ALLOYS POWDER	4.3	WS	I	4.3+4.2		0	E0		PP, EX, A	VE01	HA08	0	
1418	MAGNESIUM POWDER or MAGNESIUM ALLOYS POWDER	4.3	WS	II	4.3+4.2		0	E2		PP, EX, A	VE01	HA08	0	
1418	MAGNESIUM POWDER or MAGNESIUM ALLOYS POWDER	4.3	WS	III	4.3+4.2		0	E1		PP, EX, A	VE01	HA08	0	
1419	MAGNESIUM ALUMINIUM PHOSPHIDE	4.3	WT2	I	4.3+6.1	802	0	E0		PP, EP, EX, TOX, A	VE01, VE02	HA08	2	
1420	POTASSIUM METAL ALLOYS, LIQUID	4.3	W1	I	4.3		0	E0		PP, EX, A	VE01	HA08	0	
1421	ALKALI METAL ALLOY, LIQUID, N.O.S.	4.3	W1	I	4.3	182	0	E0		PP, EX, A	VE01	HA08	0	
1422	POTASSIUM SODIUM ALLOYS, LIQUID	4.3	W1	I	4.3		0	E0		PP, EX, A	VE01	HA08	0	
1423	RUBIDIUM	4.3	W2	I	4.3		0	E0		PP, EX, A	VE01	HA08	0	
1426	SODIUM BOROHYDRIDE	4.3	W2	I	4.3		0	E0		PP, EX, A	VE01	HA08	0	
1427	SODIUM HYDRIDE	4.3	W2	I	4.3		0	E0		PP, EX, A	VE01	HA08	0	
1428	SODIUM	4.3	W2	I	4.3		0	E0		PP, EX, A	VE01	HA08	0	
1431	SODIUM METHYLATE	4.2	SC4	II	4.2+8		0	E2		PP, EP	VE01	HA08	2	
1432	SODIUM PHOSPHIDE	4.3	WT2	I	4.3+6.1	802	0	E0		PP, EP, EX, TOX, A	VE01, VE02	HA08	2	
1433	STANNIC PHOSPHIDES	4.3	WT2	I	4.3+6.1	802	0	E0		PP, EP, EX, TOX, A	VE01, VE02	HA08	2	
1435	ZINC ASHES	4.3	W2	III	4.3		1 kg	E1	B	PP, EX, A	VE01, VE03	HA07, HA08 LO03 IN01, IN03	0	VE03, LO03, HA07, IN01 and IN03 apply only when this substance is carried in bulk or without packaging
1436	ZINC POWDER or ZINC DUST	4.3	WS	I	4.3+4.2		0	E0		PP, EX, A	VE01	HA08	0	
1436	ZINC POWDER or ZINC DUST	4.3	WS	II	4.3+4.2		0	E2		PP, EX, A	VE01	HA08	0	
1436	ZINC POWDER or ZINC DUST	4.3	WS	III	4.3+4.2		0	E1		PP, EX, A	VE01	HA08	0	
1437	ZIRCONIUM HYDRIDE	4.1	F3	II	4.1		1 kg	E2		PP			1	
1438	ALUMINIUM NITRATE	5.1	O2	III	5.1		5 kg	E1	B	PP		CO02, LO04	0	CO02 and LO04 apply only when this substance is carried in bulk or without packaging

UN No. or ID No. (1)	Name and description 3.1.2 (2)	Class 2.2 (3a)	Classification Code 2.2 (3b)	Packing group 2.1.1.3 (4)	Labels 5.2.2 (5)	Special provisions 3.3 (6)	Limited and excepted quantities 3.4 (7a)	Limited and excepted quantities 3.5.1.2 (7b)	Carriage permitted 3.2.1 (8)	Equipment required 8.1.5 (9)	Ventilation 7.1.6 (10)	Provisions concerning loading, unloading and carriage 7.1.6 (11)	Number of blue cones/lights 7.1.5 (12)	Remarks 3.2.1 (13)
1439	AMMONIUM DICHROMATE	5.1	O2	II	5.1		1 kg	E2		PP			0	
1442	AMMONIUM PERCHLORATE	5.1	O2	II	5.1	152	1 kg	E2		PP			0	
1444	AMMONIUM PERSULPHATE	5.1	O2	III	5.1		5 kg	E1		PP			0	
1445	BARIUM CHLORATE, SOLID	5.1	OT2	II	5.1+6.1	802	1 kg	E2		PP, EP			2	
1446	BARIUM NITRATE	5.1	OT2	II	5.1+6.1	802	1 kg	E2		PP, EP			2	
1447	BARIUM PERCHLORATE, SOLID	5.1	OT2	II	5.1+6.1	802	1 kg	E2		PP, EP			2	
1448	BARIUM PERMANGANATE	5.1	OT2	II	5.1+6.1	802	1 kg	E2		PP, EP			2	
1449	BARIUM PEROXIDE	5.1	OT2	II	5.1+6.1	802	1 kg	E2		PP, EP			2	
1450	BROMATES, INORGANIC, N.O.S.	5.1	O2	II	5.1	274 350	1 kg	E2		PP			0	
1451	CAESIUM NITRATE	5.1	O2	III	5.1		5 kg	E1	B	PP	CO02, LO04	CO02, LO04	0	CO02 and LO04 apply only when this substance is carried in bulk or without packaging
1452	CALCIUM CHLORATE	5.1	O2	II	5.1		1 kg	E2		PP			0	
1453	CALCIUM CHLORITE	5.1	O2	II	5.1		1 kg	E2		PP			0	
1454	CALCIUM NITRATE	5.1	O2	III	5.1	208	5 kg	E1	B	PP	CO02, LO04	CO02, LO04	0	CO02 and LO04 apply only when this substance is carried in bulk or without packaging
1455	CALCIUM PERCHLORATE	5.1	O2	II	5.1		1 kg	E2		PP			0	
1456	CALCIUM PERMANGANATE	5.1	O2	II	5.1		1 kg	E2		PP			0	
1457	CALCIUM PEROXIDE	5.1	O2	II	5.1		1 kg	E2		PP			0	
1458	CHLORATE AND BORATE MIXTURE	5.1	O2	II	5.1		1 kg	E2		PP			0	
1458	CHLORATE AND BORATE MIXTURE	5.1	O2	III	5.1		5 kg	E1		PP			0	
1459	CHLORATE AND MAGNESIUM CHLORIDE MIXTURE, SOLID	5.1	O2	II	5.1		1 kg	E2		PP			0	
1459	CHLORATE AND MAGNESIUM CHLORIDE MIXTURE, SOLID	5.1	O2	III	5.1		5 kg	E1		PP			0	
1461	CHLORATES, INORGANIC, N.O.S.	5.1	O2	II	5.1	274 351	1 kg	E2		PP			0	
1462	CHLORITES, INORGANIC, N.O.S.	5.1	O2	II	5.1	274 352 509	1 kg	E2		PP			0	
1463	CHROMIUM TRIOXIDE, ANHYDROUS	5.1	OTC	II	5.1+6.1+8	510	1 kg	E2		PP, EP			2	
1465	DIDYMIUM NITRATE	5.1	O2	III	5.1		5 kg	E1	B	PP	CO02, LO04	CO02, LO04	0	CO02 and LO04 apply only when this substance is carried in bulk or without packaging
1466	FERRIC NITRATE	5.1	O2	III	5.1		5 kg	E1	B	PP	CO02, LO04	CO02, LO04	0	CO02 and LO04 apply only when this substance is carried in bulk or without packaging
1467	GUANIDINE NITRATE	5.1	O2	III	5.1		5 kg	E1	B	PP	CO02, LO04	CO02, LO04	0	CO02 and LO04 apply only when this substance is carried in bulk or without packaging

UN No. or ID No. (1)	Name and description 3.1.2 (2)	Class 2.2 (3a)	Classification Code 2.2 (3b)	Packing group 2.1.1.3 (4)	Labels 5.2.2 (5)	Special provisions 3.3 (6)	Limited and excepted quantities 3.4 (7a)	Limited and excepted quantities 3.5.1.2 (7b)	Carriage permitted 3.2.1 (8)	Equipment required 8.1.5 (9)	Venti-lation 7.1.6 (10)	Provisions concerning loading, unloading and carriage 7.1.6 (11)	Number of blue cones/lights 7.1.5 (12)	Remarks 3.2.1 (13)
1469	LEAD NITRATE	5.1	OT2	II	5.1+6.1	802	1 kg	E2		PP, EP			2	
1470	LEAD PERCHLORATE, SOLID	5.1	OT2	II	5.1+6.1	802	1 kg	E2		PP, EP			2	
1471	LITHIUM HYPOCHLORITE, DRY or LITHIUM HYPOCHLORITE MIXTURE	5.1	O2	II	5.1		1 kg	E2		PP			0	
1471	LITHIUM HYPOCHLORITE, DRY or LITHIUM HYPOCHLORITE MIXTURE	5.1	O2	III	5.1		5 kg	E1		PP			0	
1472	LITHIUM PEROXIDE	5.1	O2	II	5.1		1 kg	E2		PP			0	
1473	MAGNESIUM BROMATE	5.1	O2	II	5.1		1 kg	E2		PP			0	
1474	MAGNESIUM NITRATE	5.1	O2	III	5.1	332	5 kg	E1	B	PP		CO02, LO04	0	CO02 and LO04 apply only when this substance is carried in bulk or without packaging
1475	MAGNESIUM PERCHLORATE	5.1	O2	II	5.1		1 kg	E2		PP			0	
1476	MAGNESIUM PEROXIDE	5.1	O2	II	5.1		1 kg	E2		PP			0	
1477	NITRATES, INORGANIC, N.O.S.	5.1	O2	II	5.1	511	1 kg	E2		PP			0	
1477	NITRATES, INORGANIC, N.O.S.	5.1	O2	III	5.1	511	5 kg	E1	B	PP		CO02, LO04	0	CO02 and LO04 apply only when this substance is carried in bulk or without packaging
1479	OXIDIZING SOLID, N.O.S.	5.1	O2	I	5.1	274	0	E0		PP			0	
1479	OXIDIZING SOLID, N.O.S.	5.1	O2	II	5.1	274	1 kg	E2		PP			0	
1479	OXIDIZING SOLID, N.O.S.	5.1	O2	III	5.1	274	5 kg	E1		PP			0	
1481	PERCHLORATES, INORGANIC, N.O.S.	5.1	O2	II	5.1		1 kg	E2		PP			0	
1481	PERCHLORATES, INORGANIC, N.O.S.	5.1	O2	III	5.1		5 kg	E1		PP			0	
1482	PERMANGANATES, INORGANIC, N.O.S.	5.1	O2	II	5.1	274 353	1 kg	E2		PP			0	
1482	PERMANGANATES, INORGANIC, N.O.S.	5.1	O2	III	5.1	274 353	5 kg	E1		PP			0	
1483	PEROXIDES, INORGANIC, N.O.S.	5.1	O2	II	5.1		1 kg	E2		PP			0	
1483	PEROXIDES, INORGANIC, N.O.S.	5.1	O2	III	5.1		5 kg	E1		PP			0	
1484	POTASSIUM BROMATE	5.1	O2	II	5.1		1 kg	E2		PP			0	
1485	POTASSIUM CHLORATE	5.1	O2	II	5.1		1 kg	E2		PP			0	
1486	POTASSIUM NITRATE	5.1	O2	III	5.1		5 kg	E1	B	PP		CO02, LO04	0	CO02 and LO04 apply only when this substance is carried in bulk or without packaging
1487	POTASSIUM NITRATE AND SODIUM NITRITE MIXTURE	5.1	O2	II	5.1	607	1 kg	E2		PP			0	
1488	POTASSIUM NITRITE	5.1	O2	II	5.1		1 kg	E2		PP			0	
1489	POTASSIUM PERCHLORATE	5.1	O2	II	5.1		1 kg	E2		PP			0	
1490	POTASSIUM PERMANGANATE	5.1	O2	II	5.1		1 kg	E2		PP			0	
1491	POTASSIUM PEROXIDE	5.1	O2	I	5.1		0	E0		PP			0	
1492	POTASSIUM PERSULPHATE	5.1	O2	III	5.1		5 kg	E1		PP			0	
1493	SILVER NITRATE	5.1	O2	II	5.1		1 kg	E2		PP			0	
1494	SODIUM BROMATE	5.1	O2	II	5.1		1 kg	E2		PP			0	
1495	SODIUM CHLORATE	5.1	O2	II	5.1		1 kg	E2		PP			0	
1496	SODIUM CHLORITE	5.1	O2	II	5.1		1 kg	E2		PP			0	

UN No. or ID No.	Name and description	Class	Classi-fication Code	Packing group	Labels	Special provis-ions	Limited and excepted quantities		Carriage permitted	Equipment required	Venti-lation	Provisions concerning loading, unloading and carriage	Number of blue cones/ lights	Remarks
							3.4	3.5.1.2	3.2.1	8.1.5	7.1.6	7.1.6	7.1.5	3.2.1
	3.1.2	2.2	2.2	2.1.1.3	5.2.2	3.3								
(1)	(2)	(3a)	(3b)	(4)	(5)	(6)	(7a)	(7b)	(8)	(9)	(10)	(11)	(12)	(13)
1498	SODIUM NITRATE	5.1	O2	III	5.1		5 kg	E1	B	PP		CO02, LO04	0	CO02 and LO04 apply only when this substance is carried in bulk or without packaging
1499	SODIUM NITRATE AND POTASSIUM NITRATE MIXTURE	5.1	O2	III	5.1		5 kg	E1	B	PP		CO02, LO04	0	CO02 and LO04 apply only when this substance is carried in bulk or without packaging
1500	SODIUM NITRITE	5.1	OT2	III	5.1+6.1	802	5 kg	E1		PP, EP			0	
1502	SODIUM PERCHLORATE	5.1	O2	II	5.1		1 kg	E2		PP			0	
1503	SODIUM PERMANGANATE	5.1	O2	II	5.1		1 kg	E2		PP			0	
1504	SODIUM PEROXIDE	5.1	O2	I	5.1		0	E0		PP			0	
1505	SODIUM PERSULPHATE	5.1	O2	III	5.1		5 kg	E1		PP			0	
1506	STRONTIUM CHLORATE	5.1	O2	II	5.1		1 kg	E2		PP			0	
1507	STRONTIUM NITRATE	5.1	O2	III	5.1		5 kg	E1	B	PP		CO02, LO04	0	CO02 and LO04 apply only when this substance is carried in bulk or without packaging
1508	STRONTIUM PERCHLORATE	5.1	O2	II	5.1		1 kg	E2		PP			0	
1509	STRONTIUM PEROXIDE	5.1	O2	II	5.1		1 kg	E2		PP			0	
1510	TETRANITROMETHANE	6.1	TO1	I	6.1+5.1	354 609 802	0	E0		PP, EP, TOX, A	VE02		2	
1511	UREA HYDROGEN PEROXIDE	5.1	OC2	III	5.1+8	802	5 kg	E1		PP, EP			0	
1512	ZINC AMMONIUM NITRITE	5.1	O2	II	5.1		1 kg	E2		PP			0	
1513	ZINC CHLORATE	5.1	O2	II	5.1		1 kg	E2		PP			0	
1514	ZINC NITRATE	5.1	O2	II	5.1		1 kg	E2		PP			0	
1515	ZINC PERMANGANATE	5.1	O2	II	5.1		1 kg	E2		PP			0	
1516	ZINC PEROXIDE	5.1	O2	II	5.1		1 kg	E2		PP			0	
1517	ZIRCONIUM PICRAMATE, WETTED with not less than 20% water, by mass	4.1	D	I	4.1		0	E0		PP			1	
1541	ACETONE CYANOHYDRIN, STABILIZED	6.1	T1	I	6.1	354 802	0	E0	T	PP, EP, TOX, A	VE02		2	
1544	ALKALOIDS, SOLID, N.O.S. or ALKALOID SALTS, SOLID, N.O.S.	6.1	T2	I	6.1	43 274 802	0	E5		PP, EP			2	
1544	ALKALOIDS, SOLID, N.O.S. or ALKALOID SALTS, SOLID, N.O.S.	6.1	T2	II	6.1	43 274 802	500 g	E4		PP, EP			2	
1544	ALKALOIDS, SOLID, N.O.S. or ALKALOID SALTS, SOLID, N.O.S.	6.1	T2	III	6.1	43 274 802	5 kg	E1		PP, EP			0	
1545	ALLYL ISOTHIOCYANATE, STABILIZED	6.1	TF1	II	6.1+3	386 676 802	100 ml	E0	T	PP, EP, EX, TOX, A	VE01, VE02		2	
1546	AMMONIUM ARSENATE	6.1	T5	II	6.1	802	500 g	E4		PP, EP			2	
1547	ANILINE	6.1	T1	II	6.1	279 802	100 ml	E4	T	PP, EP, TOX, A	VE02		2	

UN No. or ID No.	Name and description	Class	Classi-fication Code	Packing group	Labels	Special provis-ions	Limited and excepted quantities		Carriage permitted	Equipment required	Venti-lation	Provisions concerning loading, unloading and carriage	Number of blue cones/lights	Remarks
	3.1.2	2.2	2.2	2.1.1.3	5.2.2	3.3	3.4	3.5.1.2	3.2.1	8.1.5	7.1.6	7.1.6	7.1.5	3.2.1
(1)	(2)	(3a)	(3b)	(4)	(5)	(6)	(7a)	(7b)	(8)	(9)	(10)	(11)	(12)	(13)
1548	ANILINE HYDROCHLORIDE	6.1	T2	III	6.1	802	5 kg	E1		PP, EP			0	
1549	ANTIMONY COMPOUND, INORGANIC, SOLID, N.O.S.	6.1	T5	III	6.1	45 274 512 802	5 kg	E1		PP, EP			0	
1550	ANTIMONY LACTATE	6.1	T5	III	6.1	802	5 kg	E1		PP, EP			0	
1551	ANTIMONY POTASSIUM TARTRATE	6.1	T5	III	6.1	802	5 kg	E1		PP, EP			0	
1553	ARSENIC ACID, LIQUID	6.1	T4	I	6.1	802	0	E5		PP, EP, TOX, A	VE02		2	
1554	ARSENIC ACID, SOLID	6.1	T5	II	6.1	802	500 g	E4		PP, EP			2	
1555	ARSENIC BROMIDE	6.1	T5	II	6.1	802	500 g	E4		PP, EP			2	
1556	ARSENIC COMPOUND, LIQUID, N.O.S., inorganic, including: Arsenates, n.o.s., Arsenites, n.o.s.; and Arsenic sulphides, n.o.s.	6.1	T4	I	6.1	43 274 802	0	E5		PP, EP, TOX, A	VE02		2	
1556	ARSENIC COMPOUND, LIQUID, N.O.S., inorganic, including: Arsenates, n.o.s., Arsenites, n.o.s.; and Arsenic sulphides, n.o.s.	6.1	T4	II	6.1	43 274 802	100 ml	E4		PP, EP, TOX, A	VE02		2	
1556	ARSENIC COMPOUND, LIQUID, N.O.S., inorganic, including: Arsenates, n.o.s., Arsenites, n.o.s.; and Arsenic sulphides, n.o.s.	6.1	T4	III	6.1	43 274 802	5 L	E1		PP, EP, TOX, A	VE02		0	
1557	ARSENIC COMPOUND, SOLID, N.O.S., inorganic, including: Arsenates, n.o.s., Arsenites, n.o.s.; and Arsenic sulphides, n.o.s.	6.1	T5	I	6.1	43 274 802	0	E5		PP, EP			2	
1557	ARSENIC COMPOUND, SOLID, N.O.S., inorganic, including: Arsenates, n.o.s., Arsenites, n.o.s.; and Arsenic sulphides, n.o.s.	6.1	T5	II	6.1	43 274 802	500 g	E4		PP, EP			2	
1557	ARSENIC COMPOUND, SOLID, N.O.S., inorganic, including: Arsenates, n.o.s., Arsenites, n.o.s.; and Arsenic sulphides, n.o.s.	6.1	T5	III	6.1	43 274 802	5 kg	E1		PP, EP			0	
1558	ARSENIC	6.1	T5	II	6.1	802	500 g	E4		PP, EP			2	
1559	ARSENIC PENTOXIDE	6.1	T5	II	6.1	802	500 g	E4		PP, EP			2	
1560	ARSENIC TRICHLORIDE	6.1	T4	I	6.1	802	0	E0		PP, EP, TOX, A	VE02		2	
1561	ARSENIC TRIOXIDE	6.1	T5	II	6.1	802	500 g	E4		PP, EP			2	
1562	ARSENICAL DUST	6.1	T5	II	6.1	802	500 g	E4		PP, EP			2	
1564	BARIUM COMPOUND, N.O.S.	6.1	T5	II	6.1	177 274 513 587 802	500 g	E4		PP, EP			2	
1564	BARIUM COMPOUND, N.O.S.	6.1	T5	III	6.1	177 274 513 587 802	5 kg	E1		PP, EP			0	
1565	BARIUM CYANIDE	6.1	T5	I	6.1	802	0	E5		PP, EP			2	
1566	BERYLLIUM COMPOUND, N.O.S.	6.1	T5	II	6.1	274 514 802	500 g	E4		PP, EP			2	

UN No. or ID No. (3.1.2)	Name and description (3.1.2)	Class (2.2)	Classification Code (2.2)	Packing group (2.1.1.3)	Labels (5.2.2)	Special provisions (3.3)	Limited and excepted quantities		Carriage permitted (3.2.1)	Equipment required (8.1.5)	Ventilation (7.1.6)	Provisions concerning loading, unloading and carriage (7.1.6)	Number of blue cones/lights (7.1.5)	Remarks (3.2.1)
							3.4 (7a)	3.5.1.2 (7b)						
(1)	(2)	(3a)	(3b)	(4)	(5)	(6)	(7a)	(7b)	(8)	(9)	(10)	(11)	(12)	(13)
1566	BERYLLIUM COMPOUND, N.O.S.	6.1	T5	III	6.1	274 514 802	5 kg	E1		PP, EP			0	
1567	BERYLLIUM POWDER	6.1	TF3	II	6.1+4.1	802	500 g	E4		PP, EP			2	
1569	BROMOACETONE	6.1	TF1	II	6.1+3	802	0	E0		PP, EP, EX, TOX, A	VE01, VE02		2	
1570	BRUCINE	6.1	T2	I	6.1	43 802	0	E5		PP, EP			2	
1571	BARIUM AZIDE, WETTED with not less than 50% water, by mass	4.1	DT	I	4.1+6.1	568 802	0	E0		PP, EP			2	
1572	CACODYLIC ACID	6.1	T5	II	6.1	802	500 g	E4		PP, EP			2	
1573	CALCIUM ARSENATE	6.1	T5	II	6.1	802	500 g	E4		PP, EP			2	
1574	CALCIUM ARSENATE AND CALCIUM ARSENITE MIXTURE, SOLID	6.1	T5	II	6.1	802	500 g	E4		PP, EP			2	
1575	CALCIUM CYANIDE	6.1	T5	I	6.1	802	0	E5		PP, EP			2	
1577	CHLORODINITROBENZENES, LIQUID	6.1	T1	II	6.1	279 802	100 ml	E4		PP, EP, TOX, A	VE02		2	
1578	CHLORONITROBENZENES, SOLID	6.1	T2	II	6.1	279 802	500 g	E4	T	PP, EP, TOX, A	VE02		2	
1579	4-CHLORO-o-TOLUIDINE HYDROCHLORIDE, SOLID	6.1	T2	III	6.1	802	5 kg	E1		PP, EP			0	
1580	CHLOROPICRIN	6.1	T1	I	6.1	354 802	0	E0		PP, EP, TOX, A	VE02		2	
1581	CHLOROPICRIN AND METHYL BROMIDE MIXTURE with more than 2% chloropicrin	2	2T		2.3		0	E0		PP, EP, TOX, A	VE02		2	
1582	CHLOROPICRIN AND METHYL CHLORIDE MIXTURE	2	2T		2.3		0	E0		PP, EP, TOX, A	VE02		2	
1583	CHLOROPICRIN MIXTURE, N.O.S.	6.1	T1	I	6.1	274 315 515 802	0	E0		PP, EP, TOX, A	VE02		2	
1583	CHLOROPICRIN MIXTURE, N.O.S.	6.1	T1	II	6.1	274 515 802	100 ml	E0		PP, EP, TOX, A	VE02		2	
1583	CHLOROPICRIN MIXTURE, N.O.S.	6.1	T1	III	6.1	274 515 802	5 L	E0		PP, EP, TOX, A	VE02		0	
1585	COPPER ACETOARSENITE	6.1	T5	II	6.1	802	500 g	E4		PP, EP			2	
1586	COPPER ARSENITE	6.1	T5	II	6.1	802	500 g	E4		PP, EP			2	
1587	COPPER CYANIDE	6.1	T5	II	6.1	802	500 g	E4		PP, EP			2	
1588	CYANIDES, INORGANIC, SOLID, N.O.S.	6.1	T5	I	6.1	47 274 802	0	E5		PP, EP			2	
1588	CYANIDES, INORGANIC, SOLID, N.O.S.	6.1	T5	II	6.1	47 274 802	500 g	E4		PP, EP			2	

UN No. or ID No. (1)	Name and description 3.1.2 (2)	Class 2.2 (3a)	Classification Code 2.2 (3b)	Packing group 2.1.1.3 (4)	Labels 5.2.2 (5)	Special provisions 3.3 (6)	Limited and excepted quantities 3.4 (7a)	3.5.1.2 (7b)	Carriage permitted 3.2.1 (8)	Equipment required 8.1.5 (9)	Ventilation 7.1.6 (10)	Provisions concerning loading, unloading and carriage 7.1.6 (11)	Number of blue cones/lights 7.1.5 (12)	Remarks 3.2.1 (13)
1588	CYANIDES, INORGANIC, SOLID, N.O.S.	6.1	T5	III	6.1	47 274 802	5 kg	E1		PP, EP			0	
1589	CYANOGEN CHLORIDE, STABILIZED	2	2TC		2.3+8	386 676	0	E0		PP, EP, TOX, A	VE02		2	
1590	DICHLOROANILINES, LIQUID	6.1	T1	II	6.1	279 802	100 ml	E4		PP, EP, TOX, A	VE02		2	
1591	o-DICHLOROBENZENE	6.1	T1	III	6.1	279 802	5 L	E1	T	PP, EP, TOX, A	VE02		0	
1593	DICHLOROMETHANE	6.1	T1	III	6.1	516 802	5 L	E1	T	PP, EP, TOX, A	VE02		0	
1594	DIETHYL SULPHATE	6.1	T1	II	6.1	802	100 ml	E4	T	PP, EP, TOX, A	VE02		2	
1595	DIMETHYL SULPHATE	6.1	TC1	I	6.1+8	354 802	0	E0	T	PP, EP, TOX, A	VE02		2	
1596	DINITROANILINES	6.1	T2	II	6.1	802	500 g	E4		PP, EP			2	
1597	DINITROBENZENES, LIQUID	6.1	T1	II	6.1	802	100 ml	E4		PP, EP, TOX, A	VE02		2	
1597	DINITROBENZENES, LIQUID	6.1	T1	III	6.1	802	5 L	E1		PP, EP, TOX, A	VE02		0	
1598	DINITRO-o-CRESOL	6.1	T2	II	6.1	43 802	500 g	E4		PP, EP			2	
1599	DINITROPHENOL SOLUTION	6.1	T1	II	6.1	802	100 ml	E4		PP, EP, A			2	
1599	DINITROPHENOL SOLUTION	6.1	T1	III	6.1	802	5 L	E1		PP, EP, A			0	
1600	DINITROTOLUENES, MOLTEN	6.1	T1	II	6.1	802	0	E0		PP, EP, TOX, A	VE02		2	
1601	DISINFECTANT, SOLID, TOXIC, N.O.S.	6.1	T2	I	6.1	274 802	0	E5		PP, EP			2	
1601	DISINFECTANT, SOLID, TOXIC, N.O.S.	6.1	T2	II	6.1	274 802	500 g	E4		PP, EP			2	
1601	DISINFECTANT, SOLID, TOXIC, N.O.S.	6.1	T2	III	6.1	274 802	5 kg	E1		PP, EP			0	
1602	DYE, LIQUID, TOXIC, N.O.S. or DYE INTERMEDIATE, LIQUID, TOXIC, N.O.S.	6.1	T1	I	6.1	274 802	0	E5		PP, EP, TOX, A	VE02		2	
1602	DYE, LIQUID, TOXIC, N.O.S. or DYE INTERMEDIATE, LIQUID, TOXIC, N.O.S.	6.1	T1	II	6.1	274 802	100 ml	E4		PP, EP, TOX, A	VE02		2	
1602	DYE, LIQUID, TOXIC, N.O.S. or DYE INTERMEDIATE, LIQUID, TOXIC, N.O.S.	6.1	T1	III	6.1	274 802	5 L	E1		PP, EP, TOX, A	VE02		0	
1603	ETHYL BROMOACETATE	6.1	TF1	II	6.1+3	802	100 ml	E0		PP, EP, EX, TOX, A	VE01, VE02		2	
1604	ETHYLENEDIAMINE	8	CF1	II	8+3		1 L	E2	T	PP, EP, EX, A	VE01		1	
1605	ETHYLENE DIBROMIDE	6.1	T1	I	6.1	354 802	0	E0	T	PP, EP, TOX, A	VE02		2	
1606	FERRIC ARSENATE	6.1	T5	II	6.1	802	500 g	E4		PP, EP			2	
1607	FERRIC ARSENITE	6.1	T5	II	6.1	802	500 g	E4		PP, EP			2	
1608	FERROUS ARSENATE	6.1	T5	II	6.1	802	500 g	E4		PP, EP			2	
1611	HEXAETHYL TETRAPHOSPHATE	6.1	T1	II	6.1	802	100 ml	E4		PP, EP, TOX, A	VE02		2	
1612	HEXAETHYL TETRAPHOSPHATE AND COMPRESSED GAS MIXTURE	2	1T		2.3		0	E0		PP, EP, TOX, A	VE02		2	
1613	HYDROCYANIC ACID, AQUEOUS SOLUTION (HYDROGEN CYANIDE, AQUEOUS SOLUTION) with not more than 20% hydrogen cyanide	6.1	TF1	I	6.1+3	48 802	0	E0		PP, EP, EX, TOX, A	VE01, VE02		2	

UN No. or ID No.	Name and description	Class	Classification Code	Packing group	Labels	Special provisions	Limited and excepted quantities		Carriage permitted	Equipment required	Ventilation	Provisions concerning loading, unloading and carriage	Number of blue cones/ lights	Remarks
							3.4	3.5.1.2	3.2.1	8.1.5	7.1.6	7.1.6	7.1.5	3.2.1
3.1.2	3.1.2	2.2	2.2	2.1.1.3	5.2.2	3.3	(7a)	(7b)	(8)	(9)	(10)	(11)	7.1.5	3.2.1
(1)	(2)	(3a)	(3b)	(4)	(5)	(6)	(7a)	(7b)	(8)	(9)	(10)	(11)	(12)	(13)
1614	HYDROGEN CYANIDE, STABILIZED, containing less than 3% water and absorbed in a porous inert material	6.1	TF1	I	6.1+3	386 603 676 802	0	E0		PP, EP, EX, TOX, A	VE01, VE02		2	
1616	LEAD ACETATE	6.1	T5	III	6.1	802	5 kg	E1		PP, EP			0	
1617	LEAD ARSENATES	6.1	T5	II	6.1	802	500 g	E4		PP, EP			2	
1618	LEAD ARSENITES	6.1	T5	II	6.1	802	500 g	E4		PP, EP			2	
1620	LEAD CYANIDE	6.1	T5	II	6.1	802	500 g	E4		PP, EP			2	
1621	LONDON PURPLE	6.1	T5	II	6.1	43 802	500 g	E4		PP, EP			2	
1622	MAGNESIUM ARSENATE	6.1	T5	II	6.1	802	500 g	E4		PP, EP			2	
1623	MERCURIC ARSENATE	6.1	T5	II	6.1	802	500 g	E4		PP, EP			2	
1624	MERCURIC CHLORIDE	6.1	T5	II	6.1	802	500 g	E4		PP, EP			2	
1625	MERCURIC NITRATE	6.1	T5	II	6.1	802	500 g	E4		PP, EP			2	
1626	MERCURIC POTASSIUM CYANIDE	6.1	T5	I	6.1	802	0	E5		PP, EP			2	
1627	MERCUROUS NITRATE	6.1	T5	II	6.1	802	500 g	E4		PP, EP			2	
1629	MERCURY ACETATE	6.1	T5	II	6.1	802	500 g	E4		PP, EP			2	
1630	MERCURY AMMONIUM CHLORIDE	6.1	T5	II	6.1	802	500 g	E4		PP, EP			2	
1631	MERCURY BENZOATE	6.1	T5	II	6.1	802	500 g	E4		PP, EP			2	
1634	MERCURY BROMIDES	6.1	T5	II	6.1	802	500 g	E4		PP, EP			2	
1636	MERCURY CYANIDE	6.1	T5	II	6.1	802	500 g	E4		PP, EP			2	
1637	MERCURY GLUCONATE	6.1	T5	II	6.1	802	500 g	E4		PP, EP			2	
1638	MERCURY IODIDE	6.1	T5	II	6.1	802	500 g	E4		PP, EP			2	
1639	MERCURY NUCLEATE	6.1	T5	II	6.1	802	500 g	E4		PP, EP			2	
1640	MERCURY OLEATE	6.1	T5	II	6.1	802	500 g	E4		PP, EP			2	
1641	MERCURY OXIDE	6.1	T5	II	6.1	802	500 g	E4		PP, EP			2	
1642	MERCURY OXYCYANIDE, DESENSITIZED	6.1	T5	II	6.1	802	500 g	E4		PP, EP			2	
1643	MERCURY POTASSIUM IODIDE	6.1	T5	II	6.1	802	500 g	E4		PP, EP			2	
1644	MERCURY SALICYLATE	6.1	T5	II	6.1	802	500 g	E4		PP, EP			2	
1645	MERCURY SULPHATE	6.1	T5	II	6.1	802	500 g	E4		PP, EP			2	
1646	MERCURY THIOCYANATE	6.1	T5	II	6.1	802	500 g	E4		PP, EP			2	
1647	METHYL BROMIDE AND ETHYLENE DIBROMIDE MIXTURE, LIQUID	6.1	T1	I	6.1	354 802	0	E0		PP, EP, TOX, A	VE02		2	
1648	ACETONITRILE	3	F1	II	3		1 L	E2	T	PP, EX, A	VE01		1	
1649	MOTOR FUEL ANTI-KNOCK MIXTURE	6.1	T3	I	6.1	802	0	E0		PP, EP, TOX, A	VE02		2	
1650	beta-NAPHTHYLAMINE, SOLID	6.1	T2	II	6.1	802	500 g	E4		PP, EP			2	
1651	NAPHTHYLTHIOUREA	6.1	T2	II	6.1	43 802	500 g	E4		PP, EP			2	
1652	NAPHTHYLUREA	6.1	T2	II	6.1	802	500 g	E4		PP, EP			2	
1653	NICKEL CYANIDE	6.1	T5	II	6.1	802	500 g	E4		PP, EP			2	
1654	NICOTINE	6.1	T1	II	6.1	802	100 ml	E4		PP, EP, TOX, A	VE02		2	
1655	NICOTINE COMPOUND, SOLID, N.O.S. or NICOTINE PREPARATION, SOLID, N.O.S.	6.1	T2	I	6.1	43 274 802	0	E5		PP, EP				
1655	NICOTINE COMPOUND, SOLID, N.O.S. or NICOTINE PREPARATION, SOLID, N.O.S.	6.1	T2	II	6.1	43 274 802	500 g	E4		PP, EP			2	

UN No. or ID No. (1)	Name and description 3.1.2 (2)	Class 2.2 (3a)	Classification Code 2.2 (3b)	Packing group 2.1.1.3 (4)	Labels 5.2.2 (5)	Special provisions 3.3 (6)	Limited and excepted quantities 3.4 (7a)	3.5.1.2 (7b)	Carriage permitted 3.2.1 (8)	Equipment required 8.1.5 (9)	Ventilation 7.1.6 (10)	Provisions concerning loading, unloading and carriage 7.1.6 (11)	Number of blue cones/ lights 7.1.5 (12)	Remarks 3.2.1 (13)
1655	NICOTINE COMPOUND, SOLID, N.O.S. or NICOTINE PREPARATION, SOLID, N.O.S.	6.1	T2	III	6.1	43 274 802	5 kg	E1		PP, EP			0	
1656	NICOTINE HYDROCHLORIDE, LIQUID or SOLUTION	6.1	T1	II	6.1	43 802	100 ml	E4		PP, EP, TOX, A	VE02		2	
1656	NICOTINE HYDROCHLORIDE, LIQUID or SOLUTION	6.1	T1	III	6.1	43 802	5 L	E1		PP, EP, TOX, A	VE02		0	
1657	NICOTINE SALICYLATE	6.1	T2	II	6.1	802	500 g	E4		PP, EP			2	
1658	NICOTINE SULPHATE, SOLUTION	6.1	T1	II	6.1	802	100 ml	E4		PP, EP, TOX, A	VE02		2	
1658	NICOTINE SULPHATE, SOLUTION	6.1	T1	III	6.1	802	5 L	E1		PP, EP, TOX, A	VE02		0	
1659	NICOTINE TARTRATE	6.1	T2	II	6.1	802	500 g	E4		PP, EP			2	
1660	NITRIC OXIDE, COMPRESSED	2	1TOC		2.3+5.1+8		0	E0		PP, EP, TOX, A	VE02		2	
1661	NITROANILINES (o-, m-, p-)	6.1	T2	II	6.1	279 802	500 g	E4		PP, EP			2	
1662	NITROBENZENE	6.1	T1	II	6.1	279 802	100 ml	E4	T	PP, EP, TOX, A	VE02		2	
1663	NITROPHENOLS (o-, m-, p-)	6.1	T2	III	6.1	279 802	5 kg	E1	T	PP, EP			0	
1664	NITROTOLUENES, LIQUID	6.1	T1	II	6.1	802	100 ml	E4	T	PP, EP, TOX, A	VE02		2	
1665	NITROXYLENES, LIQUID	6.1	T1	II	6.1	802	100 ml	E4		PP, EP, TOX, A	VE02		2	
1669	PENTACHLOROETHANE	6.1	T1	II	6.1	802	100 ml	E4		PP, EP, TOX, A	VE02		2	
1670	PERCHLOROMETHYL MERCAPTAN	6.1	T1	I	6.1	354 802	0	E0		PP, EP, TOX, A	VE02		2	
1671	PHENOL, SOLID	6.1	T2	II	6.1	279 802	500 g	E4		PP, EP			2	
1672	PHENYLCARBYLAMINE CHLORIDE	6.1	T1	I	6.1	802	0	E0		PP, EP, TOX, A	VE02		2	
1673	PHENYLENEDIAMINES (o-, m-, p-)	6.1	T2	III	6.1	279 802	5 kg	E1		PP, EP			0	
1674	PHENYLMERCURIC ACETATE	6.1	T3	II	6.1	43 802	500 g	E4		PP, EP, TOX, A	VE02		2	
1677	POTASSIUM ARSENATE	6.1	T5	II	6.1	802	500 g	E4		PP, EP			2	
1678	POTASSIUM ARSENITE	6.1	T5	II	6.1	802	500 g	E4		PP, EP			2	
1679	POTASSIUM CUPROCYANIDE	6.1	T5	II	6.1	802	500 g	E4		PP, EP			2	
1680	POTASSIUM CYANIDE, SOLID	6.1	T5	I	6.1	802	0	E5		PP, EP			2	
1683	SILVER ARSENITE	6.1	T5	II	6.1	802	500 g	E4		PP, EP			2	
1684	SILVER CYANIDE	6.1	T5	II	6.1	802	500 g	E4		PP, EP			2	
1685	SODIUM ARSENATE	6.1	T5	II	6.1	802	500 g	E4		PP, EP			2	
1686	SODIUM ARSENITE, AQUEOUS SOLUTION	6.1	T4	II	6.1	43 802	100 ml	E4		PP, EP			2	
1686	SODIUM ARSENITE, AQUEOUS SOLUTION	6.1	T4	III	6.1	43 802	5 L	E1		PP, EP			0	
1687	SODIUM AZIDE	6.1	T5	II	6.1	802	500 g	E4		PP, EP			2	
1688	SODIUM CACODYLATE	6.1	T5	II	6.1	802	500 g	E4		PP, EP			2	
1689	SODIUM CYANIDE, SOLID	6.1	T5	I	6.1	802	0	E5		PP, EP			2	
1690	SODIUM FLUORIDE, SOLID	6.1	T5	III	6.1	802	5 kg	E1	B	PP, EP			0	
1691	STRONTIUM ARSENITE	6.1	T5	II	6.1	802	500 g	E4		PP, EP			2	
1692	STRYCHNINE or STRYCHNINE SALTS	6.1	T2	I	6.1	802	0	E5		PP, EP			2	

UN No. or ID No. (1) 3.1.2	Name and description (2) 3.1.2	Class (3a) 2.2	Classification Code (3b) 2.2	Packing group (4) 2.1.1.3	Labels (5) 5.2.2	Special provisions (6) 3.3	Limited quantities (7a) 3.4	Limited and excepted quantities (7b) 3.5.1.2	Carriage permitted (8) 3.2.1	Equipment required (9) 8.1.5	Ventilation (10) 7.1.6	Provisions concerning loading, unloading and carriage (11) 7.1.6	Number of blue cones/ lights (12) 7.1.5	Remarks (13) 3.2.1
1693	TEAR GAS SUBSTANCE, LIQUID, N.O.S.	6.1	T1	I	6.1	274 802	0	E0		PP, EP, TOX, A	VE02		2	
1693	TEAR GAS SUBSTANCE, LIQUID, N.O.S.	6.1	T1	II	6.1	274 802	0	E0		PP, EP, TOX, A	VE02		2	
1694	BROMOBENZYL CYANIDES, LIQUID	6.1	T1	I	6.1	138 802	0	E0		PP, EP, TOX, A	VE02		2	
1695	CHLOROACETONE, STABILIZED	6.1	TFC	I	6.1+3+8	354 802	0	E0		PP, EP, EX, TOX, A	VE01, VE02		2	
1697	CHLOROACETOPHENONE, SOLID	6.1	T2	II	6.1	802	0	E0		PP, EP, TOX, A	VE02		2	
1698	DIPHENYLAMINECHLOROARSINE	6.1	T3	I	6.1	802	0	E0		PP, EP, TOX, A	VE02		2	
1699	DIPHENYLCHLOROARSINE, LIQUID	6.1	T3	I	6.1	802	0	E0		PP, EP, TOX, A	VE02		2	
1700	TEAR GAS CANDLES	6.1	TF3	II	6.1+4.1	802	0	E0		PP, EP			2	
1701	XYLYL BROMIDE, LIQUID	6.1	T1	II	6.1	802	0	E0		PP, EP, TOX, A	VE02		2	
1702	1,1,2,2-TETRACHLOROETHANE	6.1	T1	II	6.1	802	100 ml	E4		PP, EP, TOX, A	VE02		2	
1704	TETRAETHYL DITHIOPYROPHOSPHATE	6.1	T1	II	6.1	43 802	100 ml	E4		PP, EP			2	
1707	THALLIUM COMPOUND, N.O.S.	6.1	T5	II	6.1	43 274 802	500 g	E4		PP, EP			2	
1708	TOLUIDINES, LIQUID	6.1	T1	II	6.1	279 802	100 ml	E4	T	PP, EP, TOX, A	VE02		2	
1709	2,4-TOLUYLENEDIAMINE, SOLID	6.1	T2	III	6.1	802	5 kg	E1		PP, EP			0	
1710	TRICHLOROETHYLENE	6.1	T1	III	6.1	802	5 L	E1	T	PP, EP, TOX, A	VE02		0	
1711	XYLIDINES, LIQUID	6.1	T1	II	6.1	802	100 ml	E4		PP, EP, TOX, A	VE02		2	
1712	ZINC ARSENATE, ZINC ARSENITE or ZINC ARSENATE AND ZINC ARSENITE MIXTURE	6.1	T5	II	6.1	802	500 g	E4		PP, EP			2	
1713	ZINC CYANIDE	6.1	T5	I	6.1	802	0	E5		PP, EP			2	
1714	ZINC PHOSPHIDE	4.3	WT2	I	4.3+6.1	802	0	E0		PP, EP	VE01, VE02	HA08	2	
1715	ACETIC ANHYDRIDE	8	CF1	II	8+3		1 L	E2	T	PP, EP, EX, A	VE01		1	
1716	ACETYL BROMIDE	8	C3	II	8		1 L	E2		PP, EP			0	
1717	ACETYL CHLORIDE	3	FC	II	3+8		1 L	E2	T	PP, EP, EX, A	VE01		1	
1718	BUTYL ACID PHOSPHATE	8	C3	III	8		5 L	E1	T	PP, EP			0	
1719	CAUSTIC ALKALI LIQUID, N.O.S.	8	C5	II	8	274	1 L	E2	T	PP, EP			0	
1719	CAUSTIC ALKALI LIQUID, N.O.S.	8	C5	III	8	274	5 L	E1	T	PP, EP			0	
1722	ALLYL CHLOROFORMATE	6.1	TFC	I	6.1+3+8	802	0	E0		PP, EP, EX, TOX, A	VE01, VE02		2	
1723	ALLYL IODIDE	3	FC	II	3+8		1 L	E2		PP, EP, EX, A	VE01		1	
1724	ALLYLTRICHLOROSILANE, STABILIZED	8	CF1	II	8+3	386 676	0	E0		PP, EP, EX, A	VE01		1	
1725	ALUMINIUM BROMIDE, ANHYDROUS	8	C2	II	8	588	1 kg	E2		PP, EP			0	
1726	ALUMINIUM CHLORIDE, ANHYDROUS	8	C2	II	8	588	1 kg	E2		PP, EP			0	
1727	AMMONIUM HYDROGENDIFLUORIDE, SOLID	8	C2	II	8		1 kg	E2		PP, EP			0	
1728	AMYLTRICHLOROSILANE	8	C3	II	8		0	E0		PP, EP			0	
1729	ANISOYL CHLORIDE	8	C4	II	8		1 kg	E2		PP, EP			0	
1730	ANTIMONY PENTACHLORIDE, LIQUID	8	C1	II	8		1 L	E2		PP, EP			0	
1731	ANTIMONY PENTACHLORIDE SOLUTION	8	C1	II	8		1 L	E2		PP, EP			0	
1731	ANTIMONY PENTACHLORIDE SOLUTION	8	C1	III	8		5 L	E1		PP, EP			0	

UN No. or ID No.	Name and description	Class	Classification Code	Packing group	Labels	Special provisions	Limited quantities	Excepted quantities	Carriage permitted	Equipment required	Ventilation	Provisions concerning loading, unloading and carriage	Number of blue cones/lights	Remarks
		2.2	2.2	2.1.1.3	5.2.2	3.3	3.4	3.5.1.2	3.2.1	8.1.5	7.1.6	7.1.6	7.1.5	3.2.1
(1)	(2)	(3a)	(3b)	(4)	(5)	(6)	(7a)	(7b)	(8)	(9)	(10)	(11)	(12)	(13)
1732	ANTIMONY PENTAFLUORIDE	8	CT1	II	8+6.1	802	1 L	E0		PP, EP, TOX, A	VE02		2	
1733	ANTIMONY TRICHLORIDE	8	C2	II	8		1 kg	E2		PP, EP			0	
1736	BENZOYL CHLORIDE	8	C3	II	8		1 L	E2		PP, EP			0	
1737	BENZYL BROMIDE	6.1	TC1	II	6.1+8	802	0	E4		PP, EP, TOX, A	VE02		2	
1738	BENZYL CHLORIDE	6.1	TC1	II	6.1+8	802	0	E4	T	PP, EP, TOX, A	VE02		2	
1739	BENZYL CHLOROFORMATE	8	C9	I	8		0	E0		PP, EP			0	
1740	HYDROGENDIFLUORIDES, SOLID, N.O.S.	8	C2	II	8	517	1 kg	E2		PP, EP			0	
1740	HYDROGENDIFLUORIDES, SOLID, N.O.S.	8	C2	III	8	517	5 kg	E1		PP, EP			0	
1741	BORON TRICHLORIDE	2	2TC		2.3+8		0	E0		PP, EP, TOX, A	VE02		2	
1742	BORON TRIFLUORIDE ACETIC ACID COMPLEX, LIQUID	8	C3	II	8		1 L	E2	T	PP, EP			0	
1743	BORON TRIFLUORIDE PROPIONIC ACID COMPLEX, LIQUID	8	C3	II	8		1 L	E2		PP, EP			0	
1744	BROMINE or BROMINE SOLUTION	8	CT1	I	8+6.1	802	0	E0		PP, EP, TOX, A	VE02		2	
1745	BROMINE PENTAFLUORIDE	5.1	OTC	I	5.1+6.1+8	802	0	E0		PP, EP, TOX, A	VE02		2	
1746	BROMINE TRIFLUORIDE	5.1	OTC	I	5.1+6.1+8	802	0	E0		PP, EP, TOX, A	VE02		2	
1747	BUTYLTRICHLOROSILANE	8	CF1	II	8+3		0	E2		PP, EP, EX, A	VE01		1	
1748	CALCIUM HYPOCHLORITE, DRY or CALCIUM HYPOCHLORITE MIXTURE, DRY with more than 39% available chlorine (8.8% available oxygen)	5.1	O2	II	5.1	314	1 kg	E2		PP			0	
1748	CALCIUM HYPOCHLORITE, DRY or CALCIUM HYPOCHLORITE MIXTURE, DRY with more than 39% available chlorine (8.8% available oxygen)	5.1	O2	III	5.1	316	5 kg	E1		PP			0	
1749	CHLORINE TRIFLUORIDE	2	2TOC		2.3+5.1+8		0	E0		PP, EP, TOX, A	VE02		2	
1750	CHLOROACETIC ACID SOLUTION	6.1	TC1	II	6.1+8	802	100 ml	E4	T	PP, EP, TOX, A	VE02		2	
1751	CHLOROACETIC ACID, SOLID	6.1	TC2	II	6.1+8	802	500 g	E4		PP, EP			2	
1752	CHLOROACETYL CHLORIDE	6.1	TC1	I	6.1+8	354 802	0	E0		PP, EP, TOX, A	VE02		2	
1753	CHLOROPHENYLTRICHLOROSILANE	8	C3	II	8		0	E0		PP, EP			0	
1754	CHLOROSULPHONIC ACID (with or without sulphur trioxide)	8	C1	I	8		0	E0		PP, EP			0	
1755	CHROMIC ACID SOLUTION	8	C1	II	8	518	1 L	E2		PP, EP			0	
1755	CHROMIC ACID SOLUTION	8	C1	III	8	518	5 L	E1		PP, EP			0	
1756	CHROMIC FLUORIDE, SOLID	8	C2	II	8		1 kg	E2		PP, EP			0	
1757	CHROMIC FLUORIDE SOLUTION	8	C1	II	8		1 L	E2		PP, EP			0	
1757	CHROMIC FLUORIDE SOLUTION	8	C1	III	8		5 L	E1		PP, EP			0	
1758	CHROMIUM OXYCHLORIDE	8	C1	I	8		0	E0		PP, EP			0	
1759	CORROSIVE SOLID, N.O.S.	8	C10	I	8	274	0	E0		PP, EP			0	
1759	CORROSIVE SOLID, N.O.S.	8	C10	II	8	274	1 kg	E2		PP, EP			0	
1759	CORROSIVE SOLID, N.O.S.	8	C10	III	8	274	5 kg	E1		PP, EP			0	
1760	CORROSIVE LIQUID, N.O.S.	8	C9	I	8	274	0	E0	T	PP, EP			0	
1760	CORROSIVE LIQUID, N.O.S.	8	C9	II	8	274	1 L	E2	T	PP, EP			0	
1760	CORROSIVE LIQUID, N.O.S.	8	C9	III	8	274	5 L	E1	T	PP, EP			0	
1761	CUPRIETHYLENEDIAMINE SOLUTION	8	CT1	II	8+6.1	802	1 L	E2		PP, EP, A	VE02		2	
1761	CUPRIETHYLENEDIAMINE SOLUTION	8	CT1	III	8+6.1	802	5 L	E1		PP, EP, A	VE02		0	
1762	CYCLOHEXENYLTRICHLOROSILANE	8	C3	II	8		0	E0		PP, EP			0	
1763	CYCLOHEXYLTRICHLOROSILANE	8	C3	II	8		0	E0		PP, EP			0	
1764	DICHLOROACETIC ACID	8	C3	II	8		1 L	E2	T	PP, EP			0	

UN No. or ID No.	Name and description	Class	Classification Code	Packing group	Labels	Special provisions	Limited and exempted quantities		Carriage permitted	Equipment required	Ventilation	Provisions concerning loading, unloading and carriage	Number of blue cones/ lights	Remarks
							3.4	3.5.1.2						
3.1.2	3.1.2	2.2	2.2	2.1.1.3	5.2.2	3.3	3.4	3.5.1.2	3.2.1	8.1.5	7.1.6	7.1.6	7.1.5	3.2.1
(1)	(2)	(3a)	(3b)	(4)	(5)	(6)	(7a)	(7b)	(8)	(9)	(10)	(11)	(12)	(13)
1765	DICHLOROACETYL CHLORIDE	8	C3	II	8		1 L	E2		PP, EP			0	
1766	DICHLOROPHENYLTRICHLOROSILANE	8	C3	II	8		0	E0		PP, EP			0	
1767	DIETHYLDICHLOROSILANE	8	CF1	II	8+3		0	E0		PP, EP, EX, A	VE01		1	
1768	DIFLUOROPHOSPHORIC ACID, ANHYDROUS	8	C1	II	8		1 L	E2		PP, EP			0	
1769	DIPHENYLDICHLOROSILANE	8	C3	II	8		0	E0		PP, EP			0	
1770	DIPHENYLMETHYL BROMIDE	8	C10	II	8		1 kg	E2		PP, EP			0	
1771	DODECYLTRICHLOROSILANE	8	C3	II	8		0	E0		PP, EP			0	
1773	FERRIC CHLORIDE, ANHYDROUS	8	C2	III	8	590	5 kg	E1		PP, EP			0	
1774	FIRE EXTINGUISHER CHARGES, corrosive liquid	8	C11	II	8		1 L	E0		PP, EP			0	
1775	FLUOROBORIC ACID	8	C1	II	8		1 L	E2		PP, EP			0	
1776	FLUOROPHOSPHORIC ACID, ANHYDROUS	8	C1	II	8		1 L	E2		PP, EP			0	
1777	FLUOROSULPHONIC ACID	8	C1	I	8		0	E0		PP, EP			0	
1778	FLUOROSILICIC ACID	8	C1	II	8		1 L	E2	T	PP, EP			0	
1779	FORMIC ACID with more than 85% acid by mass	8	CF1	II	8+3		1 L	E2	T	PP, EP, EX, A	VE01		1	
1780	FUMARYL CHLORIDE	8	C3	II	8		1 L	E2	T	PP, EP			0	
1781	HEXADECYLTRICHLOROSILANE	8	C3	II	8		0	E0		PP, EP			0	
1782	HEXAFLUOROPHOSPHORIC ACID	8	C1	II	8		1 L	E2		PP, EP			0	
1783	HEXAMETHYLENEDIAMINE SOLUTION	8	C7	II	8		1 L	E2	T	PP, EP			0	
1783	HEXAMETHYLENEDIAMINE SOLUTION	8	C7	III	8		5 L	E1	T	PP, EP			0	
1784	HEXYLTRICHLOROSILANE	8	C3	II	8		0	E0		PP, EP			0	
1786	HYDROFLUORIC ACID AND SULPHURIC ACID MIXTURE	8	CT1	I	8+6.1	802	0	E0		PP, EP, TOX, A	VE02		2	
1787	HYDRIODIC ACID	8	C1	II	8		1 L	E2		PP, EP			0	
1787	HYDRIODIC ACID	8	C1	III	8		5 L	E1		PP, EP			0	
1788	HYDROBROMIC ACID	8	C1	II	8	519	1 L	E2		PP, EP			0	
1788	HYDROBROMIC ACID	8	C1	III	8	519	5 L	E1		PP, EP			0	
1789	HYDROCHLORIC ACID	8	C1	II	8	520	1 L	E2	T	PP, EP			0	
1789	HYDROCHLORIC ACID	8	C1	III	8	520	5 L	E1		PP, EP			0	
1790	HYDROFLUORIC ACID with more than 85% hydrofluoric acid	8	CT1	I	8+6.1	640I 802	0	E0		PP, EP, TOX, A	VE02		2	
1790	HYDROFLUORIC ACID with more than 60% but not more than 85% hydrofluoric acid	8	CT1	I	8+6.1	640J 802	0	E0		PP, EP, TOX, A	VE02		2	
1790	HYDROFLUORIC ACID with not more than 60% hydrofluoric acid	8	CT1	II	8+6.1	802	1 L	E2		PP, EP, TOX, A	VE02		2	
1791	HYPOCHLORITE SOLUTION	8	C9	II	8	521	1 L	E2		PP, EP			0	
1791	HYPOCHLORITE SOLUTION	8	C9	III	8	521	5 L	E1		PP, EP			0	
1792	IODINE MONOCHLORIDE, SOLID	8	C2	II	8		1 kg	E0		PP, EP			0	
1793	ISOPROPYL ACID PHOSPHATE	8	C3	III	8		5 L	E1		PP, EP			0	
1794	LEAD SULPHATE with more than 3% free acid	8	C2	II	8	591	1 kg	E2		PP, EP			0	
1796	NITRATING ACID MIXTURE with more than 50% nitric acid	8	CO1	I	8+5.1		0	E0		PP, EP			2	
1796	NITRATING ACID MIXTURE with not more than 50% nitric acid	8	C1	II	8		1 L	E0		PP, EP			0	
1798	NITROHYDROCHLORIC ACID	8	COT						CARRIAGE PROHIBITED					
1799	NONYLTRICHLOROSILANE	8	C3	II	8		0	E0		PP, EP			0	
1800	OCTADECYLTRICHLOROSILANE	8	C3	II	8		0	E0		PP, EP			0	
1801	OCTYLTRICHLOROSILANE	8	C3	II	8		0	E0		PP, EP			0	

UN No. or ID No. (1)	Name and description (2)	Class (3a)	Classification Code (3b)	Packing group (4)	Labels (5)	Special provisions (6)	Limited quantities 3.4 (7a)	Excepted quantities 3.5.1.2 (7b)	Carriage permitted (8)	Equipment required (9)	Ventilation (10)	Provisions concerning loading, unloading and carriage (11)	Number of blue cones/lights (12)	Remarks (13)
		2.2	2.2	2.1.1.3	5.2.2	3.3	3.4	3.5.1.2	3.2.1	8.1.5	7.1.6	7.1.6	7.1.5	3.2.1
1802	PERCHLORIC ACID with not more than 50% acid, by mass	8	CO1	II	8+5.1	522	1 L	E0		PP, EP			0	
1803	PHENOLSULPHONIC ACID, LIQUID	8	C3	II	8		1 L	E2		PP, EP			0	
1804	PHENYLTRICHLOROSILANE	8	C3	II	8		0	E0		PP, EP			0	
1805	PHOSPHORIC ACID, SOLUTION	8	C1	III	8		5 L	E1	T	PP, EP			0	
1806	PHOSPHORUS PENTACHLORIDE	8	C2	II	8		1 kg	E0		PP, EP			0	
1807	PHOSPHORUS PENTOXIDE	8	C2	II	8		1 kg	E2		PP, EP			0	
1808	PHOSPHORUS TRIBROMIDE	8	C1	II	8		1 L	E0		PP, EP			0	
1809	PHOSPHORUS TRICHLORIDE	6.1	TC3	I	6.1+8	354 802	0	E0		PP, EP, TOX, A	VE02		2	
1810	PHOSPHORUS OXYCHLORIDE	6.1	TC3	I	6.1+8	354	0	E0		PP, EP, TOX, A	VE02		2	
1811	POTASSIUM HYDROGENDIFLUORIDE, SOLID	8	CT2	II	8+6.1	802	1 kg	E2		PP, EP			2	
1812	POTASSIUM FLUORIDE, SOLID	6.1	T5	III	6.1	802	5 kg	E1	B	PP, EP			0	
1813	POTASSIUM HYDROXIDE, SOLID	8	C6	II	8		1 kg	E2		PP, EP			0	
1814	POTASSIUM HYDROXIDE SOLUTION	8	C5	II	8		1 L	E2	T	PP, EP			0	
1814	POTASSIUM HYDROXIDE SOLUTION	8	C5	III	8		5 L	E1	T	PP, EP			0	
1815	PROPIONYL CHLORIDE	3	FC	II	3+8		1 L	E2		PP, EP, EX, A	VE01		1	
1816	PROPYLTRICHLOROSILANE	8	CF1	II	8+3		0	E0		PP, EP, EX, A	VE01		1	
1817	PYROSULPHURYL CHLORIDE	8	C1	II	8		1 L	E2		PP, EP			0	
1818	SILICON TETRACHLORIDE	8	C1	II	8		0	E0		PP, EP			0	
1819	SODIUM ALUMINATE SOLUTION	8	C5	II	8		1 L	E2		PP, EP			0	
1819	SODIUM ALUMINATE SOLUTION	8	C5	III	8		5 L	E1		PP, EP			0	
1823	SODIUM HYDROXIDE, SOLID	8	C6	II	8		1 kg	E2	T	PP, EP			0	
1824	SODIUM HYDROXIDE SOLUTION	8	C5	II	8		1 L	E2	T	PP, EP			0	
1824	SODIUM HYDROXIDE SOLUTION	8	C5	III	8		5 L	E1	T	PP, EP			0	
1825	SODIUM MONOXIDE	8	C6	II	8		1 kg	E2		PP, EP			0	
1826	NITRATING ACID MIXTURE, SPENT, with more than 50% nitric acid	8	CO1	I	8+5.1	113	0	E0		PP, EP			0	
1826	NITRATING ACID MIXTURE, SPENT, with not more than 50% nitric acid	8	C1	II	8	113	1 L	E0		PP, EP			0	
1827	STANNIC CHLORIDE, ANHYDROUS	8	C1	II	8		1 L	E2		PP, EP			0	
1828	SULPHUR CHLORIDES	8	C1	I	8		0	E0		PP, EP			0	
1829	SULPHUR TRIOXIDE, STABILIZED	8	C1	I	8	386 623 676	0	E0		PP, EP			0	
1830	SULPHURIC ACID with more than 51% acid	8	C1	II	8		1 L	E2	T	PP, EP			0	
1831	SULPHURIC ACID, FUMING	8	CT1	I	8+6.1	802	0	E0	T	PP, EP, TOX, A	VE02		2	
1832	SULPHURIC ACID, SPENT	8	C1	II	8	113	1 L	E0	T	PP, EP			0	
1833	SULPHUROUS ACID	8	C1	II	8		1 L	E2		PP, EP			0	
1834	SULPHURYL CHLORIDE	6.1	TC3	I	6.1+8	354	0	E0		PP, EP, TOX, A	VE02		2	
1835	TETRAMETHYL AMMONIUM HYDROXIDE, SOLUTION	8	C7	II	8		1 L	E2		PP, EP			0	
1835	TETRAMETHYL AMMONIUM HYDROXIDE SOLUTION	8	C7	III	8		5 L	E1		PP, EP			0	
1836	THIONYL CHLORIDE	8	C1	I	8		0	E0		PP, EP			0	
1837	THIOPHOSPHORYL CHLORIDE	8	C1	II	8		1 L	E0		PP, EP			0	
1838	TITANIUM TETRACHLORIDE	6.1	TC3	I	6.1+8	354	0	E0		PP, EP, TOX, A	VE02		2	
1839	TRICHLOROACETIC ACID	8	C4	II	8		1 kg	E2		PP, EP			0	

UN No. or ID No. (1)	Name and description (2)	Class (3a)	Classification Code (3b)	Packing group (4)	Labels (5)	Special provisions (6)	Limited and excepted quantities (7a)	Limited and excepted quantities (7b)	Carriage permitted (8)	Equipment required (9)	Venti-lation (10)	Provisions concerning loading, unloading and carriage (11)	Number of blue cones/lights (12)	Remarks (13)
		2.2	2.2	2.1.1.3	5.2.2	3.3	3.4	3.5.1.2	3.2.1	8.1.5	7.1.6	7.1.6	7.1.5	3.2.1
1840	ZINC CHLORIDE SOLUTION	8	C1	III	8		5 L	E1		PP, EP			0	
1841	ACETALDEHYDE AMMONIA	9	M11	III	9		5 kg	E1		PP			0	
1843	AMMONIUM DINITRO-o-CRESOLATE, SOLID	6.1	T2	II	6.1	802	500 g	E4		PP, EP			2	
1845	Carbon dioxide, solid (Dry ice)	9	M11				NOT SUBJECT TO ADN except for 5.5.3								
1846	CARBON TETRACHLORIDE	6.1	T1	II	6.1	802	100 ml	E4	T	PP, EP, TOX, A	VE02		2	
1847	POTASSIUM SULPHIDE, HYDRATED with not less than 30% water of crystallization	8	C6	II	8	523	1 kg	E2		PP, EP			0	
1848	PROPIONIC ACID with not less than 10% and less than 90% acid by mass	8	C3	III	8		5 L	E1	T	PP, EP			0	
1849	SODIUM SULPHIDE, HYDRATED with not less than 30% water	8	C6	II	8	523	1 kg	E2		PP, EP			0	
1851	MEDICINE, LIQUID, TOXIC, N.O.S.	6.1	T1	II	6.1	221 601 802	100 ml	E4		PP, EP, TOX, A	VE02		2	
1851	MEDICINE, LIQUID, TOXIC, N.O.S.	6.1	T1	III	6.1	221 601 802	5 L	E1		PP, EP, TOX, A	VE02		0	
1854	BARIUM ALLOYS, PYROPHORIC	4.2	S4	I	4.2		0	E0		PP			0	
1855	CALCIUM, PYROPHORIC or CALCIUM ALLOYS, PYROPHORIC	4.2	S4	I	4.2		0	E0		PP			0	
1856	Rags, oily	4.2	S2				NOT SUBJECT TO ADN								
1857	Textile waste, wet	4.2	S2				NOT SUBJECT TO ADN								
1858	HEXAFLUOROPROPYLENE (REFRIGERANT GAS R 1216)	2	2A		2:2	662	120 ml	E1		PP			0	
1859	SILICON TETRAFLUORIDE	2	2TC		2.3+8		0	E0		PP, EP, TOX, A	VE02		2	
1860	VINYL FLUORIDE, STABILIZED	2	2F		2.1	386 662 676	0	E0		PP, EX, A	VE01		1	
1862	ETHYL CROTONATE	3	F1	II	3		1 L	E2		PP, EX, A	VE01		1	
1863	FUEL, AVIATION, TURBINE ENGINE	3	F1	I	3		500 ml	E3		PP, EX, A	VE01		1	
1863	FUEL, AVIATION, TURBINE ENGINE (vapour pressure at 50 °C more than 110 kPa)	3	F1	II	3	640C	1 L	E2	T	PP, EX, A	VE01		1	
1863	FUEL, AVIATION, TURBINE ENGINE (vapour pressure at 50 °C not more than 110 kPa)	3	F1	II	3	640D	1 L	E2	T	PP, EX, A	VE01		1	
1863	FUEL, AVIATION, TURBINE ENGINE	3	F1	III	3		5 L	E1	T	PP, EX, A	VE01		0	
1865	n-PROPYL NITRATE	3	F1	II	3		1 L	E2		PP, EX, A	VE01		1	
1866	RESIN SOLUTION, flammable	3	F1	I	3		500 ml	E3		PP, EX, A	VE01		1	
1866	RESIN SOLUTION, flammable (vapour pressure at 50 °C more than 110 kPa)	3	F1	II	3	640C	5 L	E2		PP, EX, A	VE01		1	
1866	RESIN SOLUTION, flammable (vapour pressure at 50 °C not more than 110 kPa)	3	F1	II	3	640D	5 L	E2		PP, EX, A	VE01		1	
1866	RESIN SOLUTION, flammable	3	F1	III	3		5 L	E1		PP, EX, A	VE01		0	
1866	RESIN SOLUTION, flammable (having a flash-point below 23 °C and viscous according to 2.2.3.1.4) (vapour pressure at 50 °C more than 110 kPa)	3	F1	III	3		5 L	E1		PP, EX, A	VE01		0	
1866	RESIN SOLUTION, flammable (having a flash-point below 23 °C and viscous according to 2.2.3.1.4) (vapour pressure at 50 °C not more than 110 kPa)	3	F1	III	3		5 L	E1		PP, EX, A	VE01		0	

(1)	(2)	(3a)	(3b)	(4)	(5)	(6)	(7a)	(7b)	(8)	(9)	(10)	(11)	(12)	(13)
UN No. or ID No.	Name and description	Class	Classification Code	Packing group	Labels	Special provisions	Limited and excepted quantities		Carriage permitted	Equipment required	Venti-lation	Provisions concerning loading, unloading and carriage	Number of blue cones/lights	Remarks
	3.1.2	2.2	2.2	2.1.1.3	5.2.2	3.3	3.4	3.5.1.2	3.2.1	8.1.5	7.1.6	7.1.6	7.1.5	3.2.1
							(7a)	(7b)						(13)
1868	DECABORANE	4.1	FT2	II	4.1+6.1	802	1 kg	E0		PP, EP			2	
1869	MAGNESIUM or MAGNESIUM ALLOYS with more than 50% magnesium in pellets, turnings or ribbons	4.1	F3	III	4.1	59	5 kg	E1		PP			0	
1870	POTASSIUM BOROHYDRIDE	4.3	W2	I	4.3		0	E0		PP, EX, A	VE01	HA08	0	
1871	TITANIUM HYDRIDE	4.1	F3	II	4.1		1 kg	E2		PP			1	
1872	LEAD DIOXIDE	5.1	O2	III	5.1		5 kg	E1		PP			0	
1873	PERCHLORIC ACID with more than 50% but not more than 72% acid, by mass	5.1	OC1	I	5.1+8	60	0	E0		PP, EP			0	
1884	BARIUM OXIDE	6.1	T5	III	6.1	802	5 kg	E1		PP, EP			0	
1885	BENZIDINE	6.1	T2	II	6.1	802	500 g	E4		PP, EP			2	
1886	BENZYLIDENE CHLORIDE	6.1	T1	II	6.1	802	100 ml	E4		PP, EP, TOX, A	VE02		2	
1887	BROMOCHLOROMETHANE	6.1	T1	III	6.1	802	5 L	E1		PP, EP, TOX, A	VE02		0	
1888	CHLOROFORM	6.1	T1	III	6.1	802	5 L	E1	T	PP, EP, TOX, A	VE02		0	
1889	CYANOGEN BROMIDE	6.1	TC2	I	6.1+8	802	0	E0		PP, EP	VE02		2	
1891	ETHYL BROMIDE	3	FT1	II	3+6.1	802	1 L	E2		PP, EP, TOX, A	VE02		2	
1892	ETHYLDICHLOROARSINE	6.1	T3	I	6.1	354 802	0	E0		PP, EP, TOX, A	VE02		2	
1894	PHENYLMERCURIC HYDROXIDE	6.1	T3	II	6.1	802	500 g	E4		PP, EP, TOX, A	VE02		2	
1895	PHENYLMERCURIC NITRATE	6.1	T3	II	6.1	802	500 g	E4		PP, EP, TOX, A	VE02		2	
1897	TETRACHLOROETHYLENE	6.1	T1	III	6.1	802	5 L	E1	T	PP, EP, TOX, A	VE02		0	
1898	ACETYL IODIDE	8	C3	II	8		1 L	E2		PP, EP			0	
1902	DIISOOCTYL ACID PHOSPHATE	8	C3	III	8		5 L	E1		PP, EP			0	
1903	DISINFECTANT, LIQUID, CORROSIVE, N.O.S.	8	C9	I	8	274	0	E0		PP, EP			0	
1903	DISINFECTANT, LIQUID, CORROSIVE, N.O.S.	8	C9	II	8	274	1 L	E2		PP, EP			0	
1903	DISINFECTANT, LIQUID, CORROSIVE, N.O.S.	8	C9	III	8	274	5 L	E1		PP, EP			0	
1905	SELENIC ACID	8	C2	I	8		0	E0		PP, EP			0	
1906	SLUDGE ACID	8	C1	II	8		1 L	E2		PP, EP			0	
1907	SODA LIME with more than 4% sodium hydroxide	8	C6	III	8	62	5 kg	E1		PP, EP			0	
1908	CHLORITE SOLUTION	8	C9	II	8	521	1 L	E2		PP, EP			0	
1908	CHLORITE SOLUTION	8	C9	III	8	521	5 L	E1		PP, EP			0	
1910	Calcium oxide	8	C6						NOT SUBJECT TO ADN					
1911	DIBORANE	2	2TF		2.3+2.1	228 662	0	E0	T	PP, EP, EX, TOX, A	VE01, VE02		2	
1912	METHYL CHLORIDE AND METHYLENE CHLORIDE MIXTURE	2	2F		2.1		0	E0	T	PP, EX, A	VE01		1	
1913	NEON, REFRIGERATED LIQUID	2	3A		2.2	593	120 ml	E1		PP			0	
1914	BUTYL PROPIONATES	3	F1	III	3		5 L	E1		PP, EX, A	VE01		0	
1915	CYCLOHEXANONE	3	F1	III	3		5 L	E1	T	PP, EX, A	VE01		0	
1916	2,2'-DICHLORODIETHYL ETHER	6.1	TF1	II	6.1+3	802	100 ml	E4		PP, EP, EX, TOX, A	VE01, VE02		2	
1917	ETHYL ACRYLATE, STABILIZED	3	F1	II	3	386 676	1 L	E2	T	PP, EX, A	VE01		1	
1918	ISOPROPYLBENZENE	3	F1	III	3		5 L	E1	T	PP, EX, A	VE01		0	
1919	METHYL ACRYLATE, STABILIZED	3	F1	II	3	386 676	1 L	E2	T	PP, EX, A	VE01		1	
1920	NONANES	3	F1	III	3		5 L	E1	T	PP, EX, A	VE01		0	

UN No. or ID No.	Name and description	Class	Classification Code	Packing group	Labels	Special provisions	Limited and excepted quantities		Carriage permitted	Equipment required	Ventilation	Provisions concerning loading, unloading and carriage	Number of blue cones/lights	Remarks
		2.2	2.2	2.1.1.3	5.2.2	3.3	3.4	3.5.1.2	3.2.1	8.1.5	7.1.6	7.1.6	7.1.5	3.2.1
(1)	(2)	(3a)	(3b)	(4)	(5)	(6)	(7a)	(7b)	(8)	(9)	(10)	(11)	(12)	(13)
1921	PROPYLENEIMINE, STABILIZED	3	FT1	I	3+6.1	386 676 802	0	E0		PP, EP, EX, TOX, A	VE01, VE02		2	
1922	PYRROLIDINE	3	FC	II	3+8		1 L	E2	T	PP, EP, EX, A	VE01		1	
1923	CALCIUM DITHIONITE (CALCIUM HYDROSULPHITE)	4.2	S4	II	4.2		0	E2		PP			0	
1928	METHYL MAGNESIUM BROMIDE IN ETHYL	4.3	WF1	I	4.3+3		0	E0		PP, EX, A	VE01	HA08	1	
1929	POTASSIUM DITHIONITE (POTASSIUM HYDROSULPHITE)	4.2	S4	II	4.2		0	E2		PP			0	
1931	ZINC DITHIONITE (ZINC HYDROSULPHITE)	9	M11	III	9		5 kg	E1		PP			0	
1932	ZIRCONIUM SCRAP	4.2	S4	III	4.2	524 592	0	E0		PP			0	
1935	CYANIDE SOLUTION, N.O.S.	6.1	T4	I	6.1	274 525 802	0	E5		PP, EP, TOX, A	VE02		2	
1935	CYANIDE SOLUTION, N.O.S.	6.1	T4	II	6.1	274 525 802	100 ml	E4		PP, EP, TOX, A	VE02		2	
1935	CYANIDE SOLUTION, N.O.S.	6.1	T4	III	6.1	274 525 802	5 L	E1		PP, EP, TOX, A	VE02		0	
1938	BROMOACETIC ACID, SOLUTION	8	C3	II	8		1 L	E2		PP, EP			0	
1938	BROMOACETIC ACID SOLUTION	8	C3	III	8		5 L	E1		PP, EP			0	
1939	PHOSPHORUS OXYBROMIDE	8	C2	II	8		1 kg	E0		PP, EP			0	
1940	THIOGLYCOLIC ACID	8	C3	II	8		1 L	E2		PP, EP			0	
1941	DIBROMODIFLUOROMETHANE	9	M11	III	9		5 L	E1		PP			0	
1942	AMMONIUM NITRATE with not more than 0.2% combustible substances, including any organic substance calculated as carbon, to the exclusion of any other added substance	5.1	O2	III	5.1	306 611	5 kg	E1	B	PP		ST01, CO02, LO04 / HA09	0	CO02 and HA09 apply only when this substance is carried in bulk or without packaging
1944	MATCHES, SAFETY (book, card or strike on box)	4.1	F1	III	4.1	293	5 kg	E1		PP			0	
1945	MATCHES, WAX 'VESTA'	4.1	F1	III	4.1	293	5 kg	E1		PP			0	
1950	AEROSOLS, asphyxiant	2	5A		2.2	190 327 344 625	1 L	E0		PP	VE04		0	
1950	AEROSOLS, corrosive	2	5C		2.2+8	190 327 344 625	1 L	E0		PP, EP	VE04		0	
1950	AEROSOLS, corrosive, oxidizing	2	5CO		2.2+5.1+8	190 327 344 625	1 L	E0		PP, EP	VE04		0	
1950	AEROSOLS, flammable	2	5F		2.1	190 327 344 625	1 L	E0		PP, EX, A	VE01, VE04		1	

UN No. or ID No. (1)	Name and description 3.1.2 (2)	Class 2.2 (3a)	Classification Code 2.2 (3b)	Packing group 2.1.1.3 (4)	Labels 5.2.2 (5)	Special provisions 3.3 (6)	Limited quantities 3.4 (7a)	Excepted quantities 3.5.1.2 (7b)	Carriage permitted 3.2.1 (8)	Equipment required 8.1.5 (9)	Ventilation 7.1.6 (10)	Provisions concerning loading, unloading and carriage 7.1.6 (11)	Number of blue cones/ lights 7.1.5 (12)	Remarks 3.2.1 (13)
1950	AEROSOLS, flammable, corrosive	2	5FC		2.1+8	190 327 344 625	1 L	E0		PP, EP, EX, A	VE01, VE04		1	
1950	AEROSOLS, oxidizing	2	5O		2.2+5.1	190 327 344 625	1 L	E0		PP	VE04		0	
1950	AEROSOLS, toxic	2	5T		2.2+6.1	190 327 344 625 802	120 ml	E0		PP, EP, TOX, A	VE02, VE04		2	
1950	AEROSOLS, toxic, corrosive	2	5TC		2.2+6.1+8	190 327 344 625 802	120 ml	E0		PP, EP, TOX, A	VE02, VE04		2	
1950	AEROSOLS, toxic, flammable	2	5TF		2.1+6.1	190 327 344 625 802	120 ml	E0		PP, EP, EX, TOX, A	VE01, VE02, VE04		2	
1950	AEROSOLS, toxic, flammable, corrosive	2	5TFC		2.1+6.1+8	190 327 344 625 802	120 ml	E0		PP, EP, EX, TOX, A	VE01, VE02, VE04		2	
1950	AEROSOLS, toxic, oxidizing	2	5TO		2.2+5.1+6.1	190 327 344 625 802	120 ml	E0		PP, EP, TOX, A	VE02, VE04		2	
1950	AEROSOLS, toxic, oxidizing, corrosive	2	5TOC		2.2+5.1+6.1 +8	190 327 344 625 802	120 ml	E0		PP, EP, TOX, A	VE02, VE04		2	
1951	ARGON, REFRIGERATED LIQUID	2	3A		2.2	593	120 ml	E1		PP			0	
1952	ETHYLENE OXIDE AND CARBON DIOXIDE MIXTURE with not more than 9% ethylene oxide	2	2A		2.2	392 662	120 ml	E1		PP			0	
1953	COMPRESSED GAS, TOXIC, FLAMMABLE, N.O.S.	2	1TF		2.3+2.1	274	0	E0		PP, EP, EX, TOX, A	VE01, VE02		2	
1954	COMPRESSED GAS, FLAMMABLE, N.O.S.	2	1F		2.1	274 392 662	0	E0		PP, EX, A	VE01		1	
1955	COMPRESSED GAS, TOXIC, N.O.S.	2	1T		2.3	274	0	E0		PP, EP, TOX, A	VE02		2	

UN No. or ID No. (1) 3.1.2	Name and description (2) 3.1.2	Class (3a) 2.2	Classification Code (3b) 2.2	Packing group (4) 2.1.1.3	Labels (5) 5.2.2	Special provisions (6) 3.3	Limited and excepted quantities (7a) 3.4	(7b) 3.5.1.2	Carriage permitted (8) 3.2.1	Equipment required (9) 8.1.5	Ventilation (10) 7.1.6	Provisions concerning loading, unloading and carriage (11) 7.1.6	Number of blue cones/lights (12) 7.1.5	Remarks (13) 3.2.1
1956	COMPRESSED GAS, N.O.S.	2	1A		2.2	274 378 392 655 662	120 ml	E1		PP			0	
1957	DEUTERIUM, COMPRESSED	2	1F		2.1	662	0	E0		PP, EX, A	VE01		1	
1958	1,2-DICHLORO-1,1,2,2-TETRAFLUOROETHANE (REFRIGERANT GAS R 114)	2	2A		2.2	662	120 ml	E1		PP			0	
1959	1,1-DIFLUOROETHYLENE (REFRIGERANT GAS R 1132a)	2	2F		2.1	662	0	E0		PP, EX, A	VE01		1	
1961	ETHANE, REFRIGERATED LIQUID	2	3F		2.1		0	E0		PP, EX, A	VE01		1	
1962	ETHYLENE	2	2F		2.1	662	0	E0		PP, EX, A	VE01		1	
1963	HELIUM, REFRIGERATED LIQUID	2	3A		2.2	593	120 ml	E1		PP	VE01		0	
1964	HYDROCARBON GAS MIXTURE, COMPRESSED, N.O.S.	2	1F		2.1	274 662	0	E0		PP, EX, A	VE01		1	
1965	HYDROCARBON GAS MIXTURE, LIQUEFIED, N.O.S. such as mixtures A, A01, A02, A0, A1, B1, B2, B or C	2	2F		2.1	274 392 583 662 674	0	E0	T	PP, EX, A	VE01		1	
1966	HYDROGEN, REFRIGERATED LIQUID	2	3F		2.1		0	E0		PP, EX, A	VE01		1	
1967	INSECTICIDE GAS, TOXIC, N.O.S.	2	2T		2.3	274	0	E0		PP, EP, TOX, A	VE02		2	
1968	INSECTICIDE GAS, N.O.S.	2	2A		2.2	274 662	120 ml	E1		PP			0	
1969	ISOBUTANE	2	2F		2.1	392 657 662 674	0	E0	T	PP, EX, A	VE01		1	
1970	KRYPTON, REFRIGERATED LIQUID	2	3A		2.2	593	120 ml	E1		PP			0	
1971	METHANE, COMPRESSED or NATURAL GAS, COMPRESSED with high methane content	2	1F		2.1	392 662	0	E0		PP, EX, A	VE01		1	
1972	METHANE, REFRIGERATED LIQUID or NATURAL GAS, REFRIGERATED LIQUID with high methane content	2	3F		2.1	392	0	E0	T	PP, EX, A	VE01		1	
1973	CHLORODIFLUOROMETHANE AND CHLOROPENTAFLUOROETHANE MIXTURE with fixed boiling point, with approximately 49% chlorodifluoromethane (REFRIGERANT GAS R 502)	2	2A		2.2	662	120 ml	E1		PP			0	
1974	CHLORODIFLUOROBROMOMETHANE (REFRIGERANT GAS R 12B1)	2	2A		2.2	662	0	E0		PP	VE01		1	
1975	NITRIC OXIDE AND DINITROGEN TETROXIDE MIXTURE (NITRIC OXIDE AND NITROGEN DIOXIDE MIXTURE)	2	2TOC		2.3+5.1+8		0	E0		PP, EP, TOX, A	VE02		2	
1976	OCTAFLUOROCYCLOBUTANE (REFRIGERANT GAS RC 318)	2	2A		2.2	662	120 ml	E1		PP			0	
1977	NITROGEN, REFRIGERATED LIQUID	2	3A		2.2	345 346 593	120 ml	E1		PP			0	

UN No. or ID No. (1)	Name and description 3.1.2 (2)	Class 2.2 (3a)	Classification Code 2.2 (3b)	Packing group 2.1.1.3 (4)	Labels 5.2.2 (5)	Special provisions 3.3 (6)	Limited and excepted quantities 3.4 (7a)	3.5.1.2 (7b)	Carriage permitted 3.2.1 (8)	Equipment required 8.1.5 (9)	Ventilation 7.1.6 (10)	Provisions concerning loading, unloading and carriage 7.1.6 (11)	Number of blue cones/lights 7.1.5 (12)	Remarks 3.2.1 (13)
1978	PROPANE	2	2F		2.1	392 657 662 674	0	E0	T	PP, EX, A	VE01		1	
1982	TETRAFLUOROMETHANE (REFRIGERANT GAS R 14)	2	2A		2.2	662	120 ml	E1		PP			0	
1983	1-CHLORO-2,2,2-TRIFLUOROETHANE (REFRIGERANT GAS R 133a)	2	2A		2.2	662	120 ml	E1		PP			0	
1984	TRIFLUOROMETHANE (REFRIGERANT GAS R 23)	2	2A		2.2	662	120 ml	E1		PP			0	
1986	ALCOHOLS, FLAMMABLE, TOXIC, N.O.S.	3	FT1	I	3+6.1	274 802	0	E0	T	PP, EP, EX, TOX, A	VE01, VE02		2	
1986	ALCOHOLS, FLAMMABLE, TOXIC, N.O.S.	3	FT1	II	3+6.1	274 802	1 L	E2	T	PP, EP, EX, TOX, A	VE01, VE02		2	
1986	ALCOHOLS, FLAMMABLE, TOXIC, N.O.S.	3	FT1	III	3+6.1	274 802	5 L	E1	T	PP, EP, EX, TOX, A	VE01, VE02		0	
1987	ALCOHOLS, N.O.S. (vapour pressure at 50 °C more than 110 kPa)	3	F1	II	3	274 601 640C	1 L	E2	T	PP, EX, A	VE01		1	
1987	ALCOHOLS, N.O.S. (vapour pressure at 50 °C not more than 110 kPa)	3	F1	II	3	274 601 640D	1 L	E2	T	PP, EX, A	VE01		1	
1987	ALCOHOLS, N.O.S.	3	F1	III	3	274 601	5 L	E1	T	PP, EX, A	VE01		0	
1988	ALDEHYDES, FLAMMABLE, TOXIC, N.O.S.	3	FT1	I	3+6.1	274 802	0	E0		PP, EP, EX, TOX, A	VE01, VE02		2	
1988	ALDEHYDES, FLAMMABLE, TOXIC, N.O.S.	3	FT1	II	3+6.1	274 802	1 L	E2		PP, EP, EX, TOX, A	VE01, VE02		2	
1988	ALDEHYDES, FLAMMABLE, TOXIC, N.O.S.	3	FT1	III	3+6.1	274 802	5 L	E1		PP, EP, EX, TOX, A	VE01, VE02		0	
1989	ALDEHYDES, N.O.S.	3	F1	I	3	274	0	E3		PP, EX, A	VE01		1	
1989	ALDEHYDES, N.O.S. (vapour pressure at 50 °C more than 110 kPa)	3	F1	II	3	274 640C	1 L	E2	T	PP, EX, A	VE01		1	
1989	ALDEHYDES, N.O.S. (vapour pressure at 50 °C not more than 110 kPa)	3	F1	II	3	274 640D	1 L	E2	T	PP, EX, A	VE01		1	
1989	ALDEHYDES, N.O.S.	3	F1	III	3	274	5 L	E1	T	PP, EX, A	VE01		0	
1990	BENZALDEHYDE	9	M11	III	9		5 L	E1	T	PP			0	
1991	CHLOROPRENE, STABILIZED	3	FT1	I	3+6.1	386 676 802	0	E0	T	PP, EP, EX, TOX, A	VE01, VE02		2	
1992	FLAMMABLE LIQUID, TOXIC, N.O.S.	3	FT1	I	3+6.1	274 802	0	E0	T	PP, EP, EX, TOX, A	VE01, VE02		2	
1992	FLAMMABLE LIQUID, TOXIC, N.O.S.	3	FT1	II	3+6.1	274 802	1 L	E2	T	PP, EP, EX, TOX, A	VE01, VE02		2	
1992	FLAMMABLE LIQUID, TOXIC, N.O.S.	3	FT1	III	3+6.1	274 802	5 L	E1	T	PP, EP, EX, TOX, A	VE01, VE02		0	
1993	FLAMMABLE LIQUID, N.O.S.	3	F1	I	3	274	0	E3	T	PP, EX, A	VE01		1	

UN No. or ID No. (1)	Name and description (2)	Class (3a)	Classification Code (3b)	Packing group (4)	Labels (5)	Special provisions (6)	Limited and excepted quantities 3.4 (7a)	Limited and excepted quantities 3.5.1.2 (7b)	Carriage permitted (8)	Equipment required (9)	Ventilation (10)	Provisions concerning loading, unloading and carriage (11)	Number of blue cones/lights (12)	Remarks (13)
1993	FLAMMABLE LIQUID, N.O.S. (vapour pressure at 50 °C more than 110 kPa)	3	F1	II	3	274 601 640C	1 L	E2	T	PP, EX, A	VE01		1	
1993	FLAMMABLE LIQUID, N.O.S. (vapour pressure at 50 °C not more than 110 kPa)	3	F1	II	3	274 601 640D	1 L	E2	T	PP, EX, A	VE01		1	
1993	FLAMMABLE LIQUID, N.O.S.	3	F1	III	3	274 601	5 L	E1	T	PP, EX, A	VE01		0	
1993	FLAMMABLE LIQUID, N.O.S. (having a flash-point below 23 °C and viscous according to 2.2.3.1.4) (vapour pressure at 50 °C more than 110 kPa)	3	F1	III	3	274 601	5 L	E1	T	PP, EX, A	VE01		0	
1993	FLAMMABLE LIQUID, N.O.S. (having a flash-point below 23 °C and viscous according to 2.2.3.1.4) (vapour pressure at 50 °C not more than 110 kPa)	3	F1	III	3	274 601	5 L	E1	T	PP, EX, A	VE01		0	
1994	IRON PENTACARBONYL	6.1	TF1	I	6.1+3	354 802	0	E0		PP, EP, EX, TOX, A	VE01, VE02		2	
1999	TARS, LIQUID, including road oils, and cutback bitumens (vapour pressure at 50°C more than 110 kPa)	3	F1	II	3	640C	5 L	E2		PP, EX, A	VE01		1	
1999	TARS, LIQUID, including road oils, and cutback bitumens (vapour pressure at 50°C not more than 110 kPa)	3	F1	II	3	640D	5 L	E2		PP, EX, A	VE01		1	
1999	TARS, LIQUID, including road asphalt and oils, bitumen and cut backs	3	F1	III	3		5 L	E1	T	PP, EX, A	VE01		0	
1999	TARS, LIQUID, including road oils, and cutback bitumens (having a flash-point below 23°C and viscous according to 2.2.3.1.4) (vapour pressure at 50°C more than 110 kPa)	3	F1	III	3		5 L	E1		PP, EX, A	VE01		0	
1999	TARS, LIQUID, including road oils, and cutback bitumens (having a flash-point below 23°C and viscous according to 2.2.3.1.4) (vapour pressure at 50°C not more than 110 kPa)	3	F1	III	3		5 L	E1	T	PP, EX, A	VE01		0	
2000	CELLULOID in block, rods, rolls, sheets, tubes, etc., except scrap	4.1	F1	III	4.1	383 502	5 kg	E1		PP			0	
2001	COBALT NAPHTHENATES, POWDER	4.1	F3	III	4.1		5 kg	E1		PP			0	
2002	CELLULOID, SCRAP	4.2	S2	III	4.2	526 592	0	E0		PP			0	
2004	MAGNESIUM DIAMIDE	4.2	S4	II	4.2		0	E2		PP			0	
2006	PLASTICS, NITROCELLULOSE-BASED, SELF-HEATING, N.O.S.	4.2	S2	III	4.2	274 528	0	E0		PP			0	
2008	ZIRCONIUM POWDER, DRY	4.2	S4	I	4.2	524 540	0	E0		PP			0	
2008	ZIRCONIUM POWDER, DRY	4.2	S4	II	4.2	524 540	0	E2		PP			0	
2008	ZIRCONIUM POWDER, DRY	4.2	S4	III	4.2	524 540	0	E1		PP			0	
2009	ZIRCONIUM, DRY, finished sheets, strip or coiled wire	4.2	S4	III	4.2	524 592	0	E1		PP			0	

UN No. or ID No. (1)	Name and description 3.1.2 (2)	Class 2.2 (3a)	Classi-fication Code 2.2 (3b)	Packing group 2.1.1.3 (4)	Labels 5.2.2 (5)	Special provisions 3.3 (6)	Limited and excepted quantities 3.4 (7a)	3.5.1.2 (7b)	Carriage permitted 3.2.1 (8)	Equipment required 8.1.5 (9)	Venti-lation 7.1.6 (10)	Provisions concerning loading, unloading and carriage 7.1.6 (11)	Number of blue cones/lights 7.1.5 (12)	Remarks 3.2.1 (13)
2010	MAGNESIUM HYDRIDE	4.3	W2	I	4.3		0	E0		PP, EX, A	VE01	HA08	0	
2011	MAGNESIUM PHOSPHIDE	4.3	WT2	I	4.3+6.1	802	0	E0		PP, EP, EX, TOX, A	VE01, VE02	HA08	2	
2012	POTASSIUM PHOSPHIDE	4.3	WT2	I	4.3+6.1	802	0	E0		PP, EP, EX, TOX, A	VE01, VE02	HA08	2	
2013	STRONTIUM PHOSPHIDE	4.3	WT2	I	4.3+6.1	802	0	E0		PP, EP, EX, TOX, A	VE01, VE02	HA08	2	
2014	HYDROGEN PEROXIDE, AQUEOUS SOLUTION with not less than 20% but not more than 60% hydrogen peroxide (stabilized as necessary)	5.1	OC1	II	5.1+8		1 L	E2	T	PP, EP			0	
2015	HYDROGEN PEROXIDE, STABILIZED or HYDROGEN PEROXIDE, AQUEOUS SOLUTION, STABILIZED with more than 70% hydrogen peroxide	5.1	OC1	I	5.1+8	640N	0	E0		PP, EP			0	
2015	HYDROGEN PEROXIDE, AQUEOUS SOLUTION, STABILIZED with more than 60% hydrogen peroxide and not more than 70% hydrogen peroxide	5.1	OC1	I	5.1+8	640O	0	E0		PP, EP			0	
2016	AMMUNITION, TOXIC, NON-EXPLOSIVE without burster or expelling charge, non-fuzed	6.1	T2		6.1	802	0	E0		PP, EP			2	
2017	AMMUNITION, TEAR-PRODUCING, NON-EXPLOSIVE without burster or expelling charge, non-fuzed	6.1	TC2		6.1+8	802	0	E0		PP, EP			2	
2018	CHLOROANILINES, SOLID	6.1	T2	II	6.1	802	500 g	E4		PP, EP			2	
2019	CHLOROANILINES, LIQUID	6.1	T1	II	6.1	802	100 ml	E4		PP, EP, TOX, A	VE02		2	
2020	CHLOROPHENOLS, SOLID	6.1	T2	III	6.1	205 802	5 kg	E1		PP, EP			0	
2021	CHLOROPHENOLS, LIQUID	6.1	T1	III	6.1	802	5 L	E1	T	PP, EP, TOX, A	VE02		0	
2022	CRESYLIC ACID	6.1	TC1	II	6.1+8	802	100 ml	E4	T	PP, EP, TOX, A	VE01, VE02		2	
2023	EPICHLOROHYDRIN	6.1	TF1	II	6.1+3	279 802	100 ml	E4	T	PP, EP, EX, TOX, A	VE01, VE02		2	
2024	MERCURY COMPOUND, LIQUID, N.O.S.	6.1	T4	I	6.1	43 274 802	0	E5		PP, EP, TOX, A	VE02		2	
2024	MERCURY COMPOUND, LIQUID, N.O.S.	6.1	T4	II	6.1	43 274 802	100 ml	E4		PP, EP, TOX, A	VE02		2	
2024	MERCURY COMPOUND, LIQUID, N.O.S.	6.1	T4	III	6.1	43 274 802	5 L	E1		PP, EP, TOX, A	VE02		0	
2025	MERCURY COMPOUND, SOLID, N.O.S.	6.1	T5	I	6.1	43 66 274 529 802	0	E5		PP, EP			2	
2025	MERCURY COMPOUND, SOLID, N.O.S.	6.1	T5	II	6.1	43 66 274 529 802	500 g	E4		PP, EP			2	

UN No. or ID No.	Name and description	Class	Classification Code	Packing group	Labels	Special provisions	Limited quantities	Excepted quantities	Carriage permitted	Equipment required	Venti-lation	Provisions concerning loading, unloading and carriage	Number of blue cones/lights	Remarks
		3.1.2	2.2	2.2	2.1.1.3	5.2.2	3.3	3.4	3.5.1.2	3.2.1	8.1.5	7.1.6	7.1.6	7.1.5	3.2.1
(1)	(2)	(3a)	(3b)	(4)	(5)	(6)	(7a)	(7b)	(8)	(9)	(10)	(11)	(12)	(13)
2025	MERCURY COMPOUND, SOLID, N.O.S.	6.1	T5	III	6.1	43 66 274 529 802	5 kg	E1		PP, EP			0	
2026	PHENYLMERCURIC COMPOUND, N.O.S.	6.1	T3	I	6.1	43 274 802	0	E5		PP, EP, TOX, A	VE02		2	
2026	PHENYLMERCURIC COMPOUND, N.O.S.	6.1	T3	II	6.1	43 274 802	500 g	E4		PP, EP, TOX, A	VE02		2	
2026	PHENYLMERCURIC COMPOUND, N.O.S.	6.1	T3	III	6.1	43 274 802	5 kg	E1		PP, EP, TOX, A	VE02		0	
2027	SODIUM ARSENITE, SOLID	6.1	T5	II	6.1	43 802	500 g	E4		PP, EP			2	
2028	BOMBS, SMOKE, NON-EXPLOSIVE with corrosive liquid, without initiating device	8	C11	II	8		0	E0		PP, EP			0	
2029	HYDRAZINE, ANHYDROUS	8	CFT	I	8+3+6.1	802	0	E0		PP, EP, EX, TOX, A	VE01, VE02		2	
2030	HYDRAZINE AQUEOUS SOLUTION, with more than 37% hydrazine by mass	8	CT1	I	8+6.1	530 802	0	E0		PP, EP, TOX, A	VE02		2	
2030	HYDRAZINE AQUEOUS SOLUTION, with more than 37% hydrazine by mass	8	CT1	II	8+6.1	530 802	1 L	E0		PP, EP, TOX, A	VE02		2	
2030	HYDRAZINE AQUEOUS SOLUTION, with more than 37% hydrazine by mass	8	CT1	III	8+6.1	530 802	5 L	E1		PP, EP, TOX, A	VE02		0	
2031	NITRIC ACID, other than red fuming, with more than 70% nitric acid	8	CO1	I	8+5.1		0	E0	T	PP, EP			0	
2031	NITRIC ACID, other than red fuming, with at least 65%, but not more than 70% nitric acid	8	CO1	II	8+5.1		1 L	E2	T	PP, EP			0	
2031	NITRIC ACID, other than red fuming, with less than 65% nitric acid	8	C1	II	8		1 L	E2	T	PP,EP			0	
2032	NITRIC ACID, RED FUMING	8	COT	I	8+5.1+6.1	802	0	E0	T	PP, EP, TOX, A	VE02		2	
2033	POTASSIUM MONOXIDE	8	C6	II	8		1 kg	E2		PP, EP			0	
2034	HYDROGEN AND METHANE MIXTURE, COMPRESSED	2	1F		2.1	662	0	E0		PP, EX, A	VE01		1	
2035	1,1,1-TRIFLUOROETHANE (REFRIGERANT GAS R 143a)	2	2F		2.1	662	0	E0		PP, EX, A	VE01		1	
2036	XENON	2	2A		2.2	378 392 662	120 ml	E1		PP			0	
2037	RECEPTACLES, SMALL, CONTAINING GAS (GAS CARTRIDGES) without a release device, non-refillable	2	5A		2.2	191 303 327 344	1 L	E0		PP			0	

UN No. or ID No. (1)	Name and description 3.1.2 (2)	Class 2.2 (3a)	Classification Code 2.2 (3b)	Packing group 2.1.1.3 (4)	Labels 5.2.2 (5)	Special provisions 3.3 (6)	Limited and excepted quantities 3.4 (7a)	3.5.1.2 (7b)	Carriage permitted 3.2.1 (8)	Equipment required 8.1.5 (9)	Ventilation 7.1.6 (10)	Provisions concerning loading, unloading and carriage 7.1.6 (11)	Number of blue cones/lights 7.1.5 (12)	Remarks 3.2.1 (13)
2037	RECEPTACLES, SMALL, CONTAINING GAS (GAS CARTRIDGES) without a release device, non-refillable	2	5F		2.1	191 303 327 344	1 L	E0		PP, EX, A	VE01		1	
2037	RECEPTACLES, SMALL, CONTAINING GAS (GAS CARTRIDGES) without a release device, non-refillable	2	5O		2.2+5.1	191 303 327 344	1 L	E0		PP			0	
2037	RECEPTACLES, SMALL, CONTAINING GAS (GAS CARTRIDGES) without a release device, non-refillable	2	5T		2.3	303 327 344	120 ml	E0		PP, EP, TOX, A			2	
2037	RECEPTACLES, SMALL, CONTAINING GAS (GAS CARTRIDGES) without a release device, non-refillable	2	5TC		2.3+8	303 327 344	120 ml	E0		PP, EP, TOX, A	VE02		2	
2037	RECEPTACLES, SMALL, CONTAINING GAS (GAS CARTRIDGES) without a release device, non-refillable	2	5TF		2.3+2.1	303 327 344	120 ml	E0		PP, EP, EX, TOX, A	VE01, VE02		2	
2037	RECEPTACLES, SMALL, CONTAINING GAS (GAS CARTRIDGES) without a release device, non-refillable	2	5TFC		2.3+2.1+8	303 327 344	120 ml	E0		PP, EP, EX, TOX, A	VE01, VE02		2	
2037	RECEPTACLES, SMALL, CONTAINING GAS (GAS CARTRIDGES) without a release device, non-refillable	2	5TO		2.3+5.1	303 327 344	120 ml	E0		PP, EP, TOX, A	VE02		2	
2037	RECEPTACLES, SMALL, CONTAINING GAS (GAS CARTRIDGES) without a release device, non-refillable	2	5TOC		2.3+5.1+8	303 327 344	120 ml	E0		PP, EP, TOX, A	VE02		2	
2038	DINITROTOLUENES, LIQUID	6.1	T1	II	6.1	802	100 ml	E4		PP, EP, TOX, A	VE02		2	
2044	2,2-DIMETHYLPROPANE	2	2F		2.1	662	0	E0		PP, EX, A	VE01		1	
2045	ISOBUTYRALDEHYDE (ISOBUTYL ALDEHYDE)	3	F1	II	3		1 L	E2	T	PP, EX, A	VE01		1	
2046	CYMENES	3	F1	III	3		5 L	E1	T	PP, EX, A	VE01		0	
2047	DICHLOROPROPENES	3	F1	II	3		1 L	E2	T	PP, EX, A	VE01		1	
2047	DICHLOROPROPENES	3	F1	III	3		5 L	E1	T	PP, EX, A	VE01		0	
2048	DICYCLOPENTADIENE	3	F1	III	3		5 L	E1	T	PP, EX, A	VE01		0	
2049	DIETHYLBENZENE	3	F1	III	3		5 L	E1	T	PP, EX, A	VE01		0	
2050	DIISOBUTYLENE, ISOMERIC COMPOUNDS	3	F1	II	3		1 L	E2	T	PP, EX, A	VE01		1	
2051	2-DIMETHYLAMINOETHANOL	8	CF1	II	8+3		1 L	E2	T	PP, EP, EX, A	VE01		1	
2052	DIPENTENE	3	F1	III	3		5 L	E1	T	PP, EX, A	VE01		0	
2053	METHYL ISOBUTYL CARBINOL	3	F1	III	3		5 L	E1	T	PP, EX, A	VE01		0	
2054	MORPHOLINE	8	CF1	I	8+3		0	E0	T	PP, EP, EX, A	VE01		1	
2055	STYRENE MONOMER, STABILIZED	3	F1	III	3	386 676	5 L	E1	T	PP, EX, A	VE01		0	
2056	TETRAHYDROFURAN	3	F1	II	3		1 L	E2	T	PP, EX, A	VE01		1	
2057	TRIPROPYLENE	3	F1	II	3		1 L	E2	T	PP, EX, A	VE01		1	
2057	TRIPROPYLENE	3	F1	III	3		5 L	E1	T	PP, EX, A	VE01		0	
2058	VALERALDEHYDE	3	F1	II	3		1 L	E2	T	PP, EX, A	VE01		1	
2059	NITROCELLULOSE SOLUTION, FLAMMABLE with not more than 12.6% nitrogen, by dry mass, and not more than 55% nitrocellulose	3	D	I	3	198 531	0	E0		PP, EX, A	VE01		1	

UN No. or ID No. (1)	Name and description (2)	Class (3a)	Classi-fication Code (3b)	Packing group (4)	Labels (5)	Special provisions (6)	Limited and excepted quantities (7a)	Limited and excepted quantities (7b)	Carriage permitted (8)	Equipment required (9)	Venti-lation (10)	Provisions concerning loading, unloading and carriage (11)	Number of blue cones/ lights (12)	Remarks (13)
		2.2	2.2	2.1.1.3	5.2.2	3.3	3.4	3.5.1.2	3.2.1	8.1.5	7.1.6	7.1.6	7.1.5	3.2.1
(1)	(2)	(3a)	(3b)	(4)	(5)	(6)	(7a)	(7b)	(8)	(9)	(10)	(11)	(12)	(13)
2059	NITROCELLULOSE SOLUTION, FLAMMABLE with not more than 12.6% nitrogen, by dry mass, and not more than 55% nitrocellulose (vapour pressure at 50 °C more than 110 kPa)	3	D	II	3	198 531 640C	1 L	E0		PP, EX, A	VE01		1	
2059	NITROCELLULOSE SOLUTION, FLAMMABLE with not more than 12.6% nitrogen, by dry mass, and not more than 55% nitrocellulose (vapour pressure at 50 °C not more than 110 kPa)	3	D	II	3	198 531 640D	1 L	E0		PP, EX, A	VE01		1	
2059	NITROCELLULOSE SOLUTION, FLAMMABLE with not more than 12.6% nitrogen, by dry mass, and not more than 55% nitrocellulose	3	D	III	3	198 531	5 L	E0		PP, EX, A	VE01		0	
2067	AMMONIUM NITRATE BASED FERTILIZER	5.1	O2	III	5.1	306 307	5 kg	E1	B	PP		CO02, ST01, LO04 HA09	0	CO02, LO04 and HA09 apply only when this substance is carried in bulk or without packaging
2071	AMMONIUM NITRATE BASED FERTILIZER	9	M11			193			B	PP		CO02, ST02 HA09	0	Dangerous only in bulk or without packaging. CO02, ST02 and HA09 apply only when this substance is carried in bulk or without packaging
2073	AMMONIA SOLUTION, relative density less than 0.880 at 15 °C in water, with more than 35% but not more than 50% ammonia	2	4A		2.2	532	120 ml	E0		PP			0	
2074	ACRYLAMIDE, SOLID	6.1	T2	III	6.1	802	5 kg	E1		PP, EP	VE02		0	
2075	CHLORAL, ANHYDROUS, STABILIZED	6.1	T1	II	6.1	802	100 ml	E4		PP, EP, TOX, A	VE02		2	
2076	CRESOLS, LIQUID	6.1	TC1	II	6.1+8	802	100 ml	E4		PP, EP, TOX, A	VE02		2	
2077	alpha-NAPHTHYLAMINE	6.1	T2	III	6.1	802	5 kg	E1		PP, EP			0	
2078	TOLUENE DIISOCYANATE	6.1	T1	II	6.1	279 802	100 ml	E4	T*	PP, EP, TOX, A	VE02		2	* only for 2,4 TOLUENE DIISOCYANATE
2079	DIETHYLENETRIAMINE	8	C7	II	8		1 L	E2	T	PP, EP			0	
2186	HYDROGEN CHLORIDE, REFRIGERATED LIQUID	2	3TC						CARRIAGE PROHIBITED					
2187	CARBON DIOXIDE, REFRIGERATED LIQUID	2	3A		2.2		120 ml	E1	T	PP			0	
2188	ARSINE	2	2TF		2.3+2.1		0	E0		PP, EP, EX, TOX, A	VE01, VE02		2	
2189	DICHLOROSILANE	2	2TFC		2.3+2.1+8		0	E0		PP, EP, EX, TOX, A	VE01, VE02		2	
2190	OXYGEN DIFLUORIDE, COMPRESSED	2	1TOC		2.3+5.1+8		0	E0		PP, EP, TOX, A	VE02		2	
2191	SULPHURYL FLUORIDE	2	2T		2.3		0	E0		PP, EP, TOX, A	VE02		2	
2192	GERMANE	2	2TF		2.3+2.1	632	0	E0		PP, EP, EX, A	VE01, VE02		2	
2193	HEXAFLUOROETHANE (REFRIGERANT GAS R 116)	2	2A		2.2	662	120 ml	E1		PP			0	
2194	SELENIUM HEXAFLUORIDE	2	2TC		2.3+8		0	E0		PP, EP, TOX, A	VE02		2	
2195	TELLURIUM HEXAFLUORIDE	2	2TC		2.3+8		0	E0		PP, EP, TOX, A	VE02		2	
2196	TUNGSTEN HEXAFLUORIDE	2	2TC		2.3+8		0	E0		PP, EP, TOX, A	VE02		2	
2197	HYDROGEN IODIDE, ANHYDROUS	2	2TC		2.3+8		0	E0		PP, EP, TOX, A	VE02		2	
2198	PHOSPHORUS PENTAFLUORIDE	2	2TC		2.3+8		0	E0		PP, EP, TOX, A	VE02		2	

UN No. or ID No. (1)	Name and description (2)	Class (3a)	Classification Code (3b)	Packing group (4)	Labels (5)	Special provisions (6)	Limited and excepted quantities 3.4 (7a)	3.5.1.2 (7b)	Carriage permitted (8)	Equipment required (9)	Ventilation (10)	Provisions concerning loading, unloading and carriage (11)	Number of blue cones/lights (12)	Remarks (13)
2199	PHOSPHINE	2	2TF		2.3+2.1	632	0	E0		PP, EP, EX, TOX, A	VE01, VE02		2	
2200	PROPADIENE, STABILIZED	2	2F		2.1	386 662 676	0	E0		PP, EX, A	VE01		1	
2201	NITROUS OXIDE, REFRIGERATED LIQUID	2	3O		2.2+5.1		0	E0		PP			0	
2202	HYDROGEN SELENIDE, ANHYDROUS	2	2TF		2.3+2.1		0	E0		PP, EP, EX, TOX, A	VE01, VE02		2	
2203	SILANE	2	2F		2.1	632 662	0	E0		PP, EX, A	VE01		1	
2204	CARBONYL SULPHIDE	2	2TF		2.3+2.1		0	E0		PP, EP, EX, TOX, A	VE01, VE02		2	
2205	ADIPONITRILE	6.1	T1	III	6.1	802	5 L	E1	T	PP, EP, TOX, A	VE02		0	
2206	ISOCYANATES, TOXIC, N.O.S. or ISOCYANATE SOLUTION, TOXIC, N.O.S.	6.1	T1	II	6.1	274 551 802	100 ml	E4	T	PP, EP, TOX, A	VE02		2	
2206	ISOCYANATES, TOXIC, N.O.S. or ISOCYANATE SOLUTION, TOXIC, N.O.S.	6.1	T1	III	6.1	274 551 802	5 L	E1		PP, EP, TOX, A	VE02		0	
2208	CALCIUM HYPOCHLORITE MIXTURE, DRY with more than 10% but not more than 39% available chlorine	5.1	O2	III	5.1	314	5 kg	E1		PP			0	
2209	FORMALDEHYDE SOLUTION with not less than 25% formaldehyde	8	C9	III	8	533	5 L	E1	T	PP, EP			0	
2210	MANEB or MANEB PREPARATION with not less than 60% maneb	4.2	SW	III	4.2+4.3	273	0	E1	B	PP, EX, A	VE01, VE03	IN01, IN03	0	VE03, IN01 and IN03 apply only when this substance is carried in bulk or without packaging
2211	POLYMERIC BEADS, EXPANDABLE, evolving flammable vapour	9	M3	III	none	382 633 675	5 kg	E1	B	PP, EP, EX, A	VE01, VE03	IN01	0	VE03 and IN01 apply only when this substance is carried in bulk or without packaging
2212	ASBESTOS, AMPHIBOLE (amosite, tremolite, actinolite, anthophyllite, crocidolite)	9	M1	II	9	168 274 542 802	1 kg	E0		PP			0	
2213	PARAFORMALDEHYDE	4.1	F1	III	4.1		5 kg	E1		PP			0	
2214	PHTHALIC ANHYDRIDE with more than 0.05% of maleic anhydride	8	C4	III	8	169	5 kg	E1		PP, EP			0	
2215	MALEIC ANHYDRIDE, MOLTEN	8	C3	III	8		0	E0	T	PP, EP			0	
2215	MALEIC ANHYDRIDE	8	C4	III	8		5 kg	E1		PP, EP			0	
2216	FISH MEAL, STABILISED or FISH SCRAP, STABILISED	9	M11						B	PP			0	
2217	SEED CAKE with not more than 1.5% oil and not more than 11% moisture	4.2	S2	III	4.2	142 800	0	E0	B	PP		IN01	0	IN01 applies only when this substance is carried in bulk or without packaging
2218	ACRYLIC ACID, STABILIZED	8	CF1	II	8+3	386 676	1 L	E2	T	PP, EP, EX, A	VE01		1	
2219	ALLYL GLYCIDYL ETHER	3	F1	III	3		5 L	E1		PP, EX, A	VE01		0	

UN No. or ID No.	Name and description	Class	Classification Code	Packing group	Labels	Special provisions	Limited and excepted quantities		Carriage permitted	Equipment required	Ventilation	Provisions concerning loading, unloading and carriage	Number of blue cones/lights	Remarks
	3.1.2	2.2	2.2	2.1.1.3	5.2.2	3.3	3.4	3.5.1.2	3.2.1	8.1.5	7.1.6	7.1.6	7.1.5	3.2.1
(1)	(2)	(3a)	(3b)	(4)	(5)	(6)	(7a)	(7b)	(8)	(9)	(10)	(11)	(12)	(13)
2222	ANISOLE	3	F1	III	3		5 L	E1		PP, EX, A	VE01		0	
2224	BENZONITRILE	6.1	T1	II	6.1	802	100 ml	E4		PP, EP, TOX, A	VE02		2	
2225	BENZENESULPHONYL CHLORIDE	8	C3	III	8		5 L	E1		PP, EP			0	
2226	BENZOTRICHLORIDE	8	C9	II	8		1 L	E2		PP, EP	VE01		0	
2227	n-BUTYL METHACRYLATE, STABILIZED	3	F1	III	3	386 676	5 L	E1	T	PP, EX, A			0	
2232	2-CHLOROETHANAL	6.1	T1	I	6.1	354 802	0	E0		PP, EP, TOX, A	VE02		2	
2233	CHLOROANISIDINES	6.1	T2	III	6.1	802	5 kg	E1		PP, EP			0	
2234	CHLOROBENZOTRIFLUORIDES	3	F1	III	3		5 L	E1		PP, EX, A	VE01		0	
2235	CHLOROBENZYL CHLORIDES, LIQUID	6.1	T1	III	6.1	802	5 L	E1		PP, EP, TOX, A	VE02		0	
2236	3-CHLORO-4-METHYLPHENYL ISOCYANATE, LIQUID	6.1	T1	II	6.1	802	100 ml	E4		PP, EP, TOX, A	VE02		2	
2237	CHLORONITROANILINES	6.1	T2	III	6.1	802	5 kg	E1		PP, EP			0	
2238	CHLOROTOLUENES	3	F1	III	3		5 L	E1	T	PP, EX, A	VE01		0	
2239	CHLOROTOLUIDINES, SOLID	6.1	T2	III	6.1	802	5 kg	E1		PP, EP			0	
2240	CHROMOSULPHURIC ACID	8	C1	I	8		0	E0		PP, EP			0	
2241	CYCLOHEPTANE	3	F1	II	3		1 L	E2	T	PP, EX, A	VE01		1	
2242	CYCLOHEPTENE	3	F1	II	3		1 L	E2		PP, EX, A	VE01		1	
2243	CYCLOHEXYL ACETATE	3	F1	III	3		5 L	E1		PP, EX, A	VE01		0	
2244	CYCLOPENTANOL	3	F1	III	3		5 L	E1		PP, EX, A	VE01		0	
2245	CYCLOPENTANONE	3	F1	III	3		5 L	E1		PP, EX, A	VE01		0	
2246	CYCLOPENTENE	3	F1	II	3		1 L	E2		PP, EX, A	VE01		1	
2247	n-DECANE	3	F1	III	3		5 L	E1	T	PP, EX, A	VE01		0	
2248	Di-n-BUTYLAMINE	8	CF1	II	8+3		1 L	E2	T	PP, EP, EX, A	VE01		1	
2249	DICHLORODIMETHYL ETHER, SYMMETRICAL	6.1	TF1						CARRIAGE PROHIBITED					
2250	DICHLOROPHENYL ISOCYANATES	6.1	T2	II	6.1	802	500 g	E4		PP, EP			2	
2251	BICYCLO[2.2.1]HEPTA-2,5-DIENE, STABILIZED (2,5-NORBORNADIENE, STABILIZED)	3	F1	II	3	386 676	1 L	E2		PP, EX, A	VE01		1	
2252	1,2-DIMETHOXYETHANE	3	F1	II	3		1 L	E2		PP, EX, A	VE01		1	
2253	N,N-DIMETHYLANILINE	6.1	T1	II	6.1	802	100 ml	E4		PP, EP, TOX, A	VE02		2	
2254	MATCHES, FUSEE	4.1	F1	III	4.1	293	5 kg	E0		PP			0	
2256	CYCLOHEXENE	3	F1	II	3		1 L	E2		PP, EX, A	VE01		1	
2257	POTASSIUM	4.3	W2	I	4.3		0	E0		PP, EX, A	VE01	HA08	0	
2258	1,2-PROPYLENEDIAMINE	8	CF1	II	8+3		1 L	E2		PP, EP, EX, A	VE01		1	
2259	TRIETHYLENETETRAMINE	8	C7	II	8		1 L	E2		PP, EP			0	
2260	TRIPROPYLAMINE	3	FC	III	3+8		5 L	E1	T	PP, EP, EX, A	VE01		0	
2261	XYLENOLS, SOLID	6.1	T2	II	6.1	802	500 g	E4		PP, EP			2	
2262	DIMETHYLCARBAMOYL CHLORIDE	8	C3	II	8		1 L	E2	T	PP, EP			0	
2263	DIMETHYLCYCLOHEXANES	3	F1	II	3		1 L	E2	T	PP, EX, A	VE01		1	
2264	N,N-DIMETHYLCYCLOHEXYLAMINE	8	CF1	II	8+3		1 L	E2	T	PP, EP, EX, A	VE01		1	
2265	N,N-DIMETHYLFORMAMIDE	3	F1	III	3		5 L	E1	T	PP, EX, A	VE01		0	
2266	DIMETHYL-N-PROPYLAMINE	3	FC	II	3+8		1 L	E2	T	PP, EP, EX, A	VE01		1	
2267	DIMETHYLTHIOPHOSPHORYL CHLORIDE	6.1	TC1	II	6.1+8	802	100 ml	E4		PP, EP, TOX, A	VE02		2	
2269	3,3'-IMINODIPROPYLAMINE	8	C7	III	8		5 L	E1		PP, EP			0	
2270	ETHYLAMINE, AQUEOUS SOLUTION with not less than 50% but not more than 70% ethylamine	3	FC	II	3+8		1 L	E2		PP, EP, EX, A	VE01		1	
2271	ETHYL AMYL KETONE	3	F1	III	3		5 L	E1		PP, EX, A	VE01		0	

UN No. or ID No.	Name and description	Class	Classi-fication Code	Packing group	Labels	Special provis-ions	Limited and excepted quantities		Carriage permitted	Equipment required	Venti-lation	Provisions concerning loading, unloading and carriage	Number of blue cones/ lights	Remarks
							3.4	3.5.1.2	3.2.1	8.1.5	7.1.6	7.1.6	7.1.5	3.2.1
(1)	(2)	(3a)	(3b)	(4)	(5)	(6)	(7a)	(7b)	(8)	(9)	(10)	(11)	(12)	(13)
2272	N-ETHYLANILINE	6.1	T1	III	6.1	802	5 L	E1		PP, EP, TOX, A	VE02		0	
2273	2-ETHYLANILINE	6.1	T1	III	6.1	802	5 L	E1		PP, EP, TOX, A	VE02		0	
2274	N-ETHYL-N-BENZYLANILINE	6.1	T1	III	6.1	802	5 L	E1		PP, EP, TOX, A	VE02		0	
2275	2-ETHYLBUTANOL	3	F1	III	3		5 L	E1		PP, EX, A	VE01		0	
2276	2-ETHYLHEXYLAMINE	3	FC	III	3+8		5 L	E1	T	PP, EP, EX, A	VE01		0	
2277	ETHYL METHACRYLATE, STABILIZED	3	F1	II	3	386 676	1 L	E2		PP, EX, A	VE01		1	
2278	n-HEPTENE	3	F1	II	3		1 L	E2	T	PP, EX, A	VE01		1	
2279	HEXACHLOROBUTADIENE	6.1	T1	III	6.1	802	5 L	E1		PP, EP, TOX, A	VE02		0	
2280	HEXAMETHYLENEDIAMINE, SOLID	8	C8	III	8		5 kg	E1	T	PP, EP			0	
2281	HEXAMETHYLENE DIISOCYANATE	6.1	T1	II	6.1	802	100 ml	E4		PP, EP, TOX, A	VE02		2	
2282	HEXANOLS	3	F1	III	3		5 L	E1		PP, EX, A	VE01		0	
2283	ISOBUTYL METHACRYLATE, STABILIZED	3	F1	III	3	386 676	5 L	E1	T	PP, EX, A	VE01		0	
2284	ISOBUTYRONITRILE	3	FT1	II	3+6.1	802	1 L	E2		PP, EP, EX, TOX, A	VE01, VE02		2	
2285	ISOCYANATOBENZO-TRIFLUORIDES	6.1	TF1	II	6.1+3	802	100 ml	E4		PP, EP, EX, TOX, A	VE01, VE02		2	
2286	PENTAMETHYLHEPTANE	3	F1	III	3		5 L	E1	T	PP, EX, A	VE01		0	
2287	ISOHEPTENES	3	F1	II	3		1 L	E2		PP, EX, A	VE01		1	
2288	ISOHEXENES	3	F1	II	3		1 L	E2	T	PP, EX, A	VE01		1	
2289	ISOPHORONEDIAMINE	8	C7	III	8		5 L	E1	T	PP, EP	VE01		0	
2290	ISOPHORONE DIISOCYANATE	6.1	T1	III	6.1	802	5 L	E1		PP, EP, TOX, A	VE02		0	
2291	LEAD COMPOUND, SOLUBLE, N.O.S.	6.1	T5	III	6.1	199 274 535 802	5 kg	E1	B	PP, EP, A			0	
2293	4-METHOXY-4-METHYLPENTAN-2-ONE	3	F1	III	3		5 L	E1		PP, EX, A	VE01		0	
2294	N-METHYLANILINE	6.1	T1	III	6.1	802	5 L	E1		PP, EP, TOX, A	VE02		0	
2295	METHYL CHLOROACETATE	6.1	TF1	I	6.1+3	802	0	E0		PP, EP, EX, TOX, A	VE01, VE02		2	
2296	METHYLCYCLOHEXANE	3	F1	II	3		1 L	E2	T	PP, EX, A	VE01		1	
2297	METHYLCYCLOHEXANONE	3	F1	III	3		5 L	E1		PP, EX, A	VE01		0	
2298	METHYLCYCLOPENTANE	3	F1	II	3		1 L	E2		PP, EX, A	VE01		1	
2299	METHYL DICHLOROACETATE	6.1	T1	III	6.1	802	5 L	E1		PP, EP, TOX, A	VE02		0	
2300	2-METHYL-5-ETHYLPYRIDINE	6.1	T1	III	6.1	802	5 L	E1		PP, EP, TOX, A	VE02		0	
2301	2-METHYLFURAN	3	F1	II	3		1 L	E2		PP, EX, A	VE01		1	
2302	5-METHYLHEXAN-2-ONE	3	F1	III	3		5 L	E1	T	PP, EX, A	VE01		0	
2303	ISOPROPENYLBENZENE	3	F1	III	3	536	5 L	E1	T	PP, EX, A	VE01		0	
2304	NAPHTHALENE, MOLTEN	4.1	F2	III	4.1		0	E0		PP			0	
2305	NITROBENZENESULPHONIC ACID	8	C4	II	8		1 kg	E2		PP, EP			0	
2306	NITROBENZOTRIFLUORIDES, LIQUID	6.1	T1	II	6.1	802	100 ml	E4		PP, EP, TOX, A	VE02		2	
2307	3-NITRO-4-CHLORO-BENZOTRIFLUORIDE	6.1	T1	II	6.1	802	100 ml	E4		PP, EP, TOX, A	VE02		2	
2308	NITROSYLSULPHURIC ACID, LIQUID	8	C1	II	8		1 L	E2		PP, EP			0	
2309	OCTADIENE	3	F1	II	3		1 L	E2	T	PP, EX, A	VE01		1	

UN No. or ID No.	Name and description	Class	Classification Code	Packing group	Labels	Special provisions	Limited and excepted quantities		Carriage permitted	Equipment required	Venti-lation	Provisions concerning loading, unloading and carriage	Number of blue cones/ lights	Remarks
		3.1.2	2.2	2.2	2.1.1.3	5.2.2	3.3	3.4	3.5.1.2	3.2.1	8.1.5	7.1.6	7.1.6	7.1.5	3.2.1
(1)	(2)	(3a)	(3b)	(4)	(5)	(6)	(7a)	(7b)	(8)	(9)	(10)	(11)	(12)	(13)
2310	PENTANE-2,4-DIONE	3	FT1	III	3+6.1	802	5 L	E1		PP, EP, EX, TOX, A	VE01, VE02		0	
2311	PHENETIDINES	6.1	T1	III	6.1	279 802	5 L	E1	T	PP, EP, TOX, A	VE02		0	
2312	PHENOL, MOLTEN	6.1	T1	II	6.1	802	0	E0	T	PP, EP, TOX, A	VE02		2	
2313	PICOLINES	3	F1	III	3	802	5 L	E1		PP, EX, A	VE01		0	
2315	POLYCHLORINATED BIPHENYLS, LIQUID	9	M2	II	9	305 802	1 L	E2		PP, EP			0	
2316	SODIUM CUPROCYANIDE, SOLID	6.1	T5	I	6.1	802	0	E5		PP, EP			2	
2317	SODIUM CUPROCYANIDE SOLUTION	6.1	T4	I	6.1	802	0	E5		PP, EP			2	
2318	SODIUM HYDROSULPHIDE with less than 25% water of crystallization	4.2	S4	II	4.2	504	0	E2		PP			0	
2319	TERPENE HYDROCARBONS, N.O.S.	3	F1	III	3		5 L	E1		PP, EX, A	VE01		0	
2320	TETRAETHYLENEPENTAMINE	8	C7	III	8		5 L	E1	T	PP, EP			0	
2321	TRICHLOROBENZENES, LIQUID	6.1	T1	III	6.1	802	5 L	E1	T	PP, EP, TOX, A	VE02		0	
2322	TRICHLOROBUTENE	6.1	T1	II	6.1	802	100 ml	E4		PP, EP, TOX, A	VE02		2	
2323	TRIETHYL PHOSPHITE	3	F1	III	3		5 L	E1	T	PP, EX, A	VE01		0	
2324	TRIISOBUTYLENE	3	F1	III	3		5 L	E1	T	PP, EX, A	VE01		0	
2325	1,3,5-TRIMETHYLBENZENE	3	F1	III	3		5 L	E1	T	PP, EX, A	VE01		0	
2326	TRIMETHYLCYCLOHEXYLAMINE	8	C7	III	8		5 L	E1		PP, EP			0	
2327	TRIMETHYLHEXAMETHYLENEDIAMINES	8	C7	III	8		5 L	E1		PP, EP			0	
2328	TRIMETHYLHEXAMETHYLENE DIISOCYANATE	6.1	T1	III	6.1	802	5 L	E1		PP, EP, TOX, A	VE02		0	
2329	TRIMETHYL PHOSPHITE	3	F1	III	3		5 L	E1		PP, EX, A	VE01		0	
2330	UNDECANE	3	F1	III	3		5 L	E1		PP, EX, A	VE01		0	
2331	ZINC CHLORIDE, ANHYDROUS	8	C2	III	8		5 kg	E1		PP, EP			0	
2332	ACETALDEHYDE OXIME	3	F1	III	3		5 L	E1		PP, EX, A	VE01		0	
2333	ALLYL ACETATE	3	FT1	II	3+6.1	802	1 L	E2	T	PP, EP, EX, TOX, A	VE01, VE02		2	
2334	ALLYLAMINE	6.1	TF1	I	6.1+3	354 802	0	E0		PP, EP, EX, TOX, A	VE01, VE02		2	
2335	ALLYL ETHYL ETHER	3	FT1	II	3+6.1	802	1 L	E2		PP, EP, EX, TOX, A	VE01, VE02		2	
2336	ALLYL FORMATE	3	FT1	I	3+6.1	802	0	E0		PP, EP, EX, TOX, A	VE01, VE02		2	
2337	PHENYL MERCAPTAN	6.1	TF1	I	6.1+3	354 802	0	E0		PP, EP, EX, TOX, A	VE01, VE02		2	
2338	BENZOTRIFLUORIDE	3	F1	II	3		1 L	E2		PP, EX, A	VE01		1	
2339	2-BROMOBUTANE	3	F1	II	3		1 L	E2		PP, EX, A	VE01		1	
2340	2-BROMOETHYL ETHYL ETHER	3	F1	II	3		1 L	E2		PP, EX, A	VE01		1	
2341	1-BROMO-3-METHYLBUTANE	3	F1	III	3		5 L	E1		PP, EX, A	VE01		0	
2342	BROMOMETHYLPROPANES	3	F1	II	3		1 L	E2		PP, EX, A	VE01		1	
2343	2-BROMOPENTANE	3	F1	II	3		1 L	E2		PP, EX, A	VE01		1	
2344	BROMOPROPANES	3	F1	II	3		1 L	E2		PP, EX, A	VE01		1	
2344	BROMOPROPANES	3	F1	III	3		5 L	E1		PP, EX, A	VE01		0	
2345	3-BROMOPROPYNE	3	F1	II	3		1 L	E2		PP, EX, A	VE01		1	
2346	BUTANEDIONE	3	F1	II	3		1 L	E2		PP, EX, A	VE01		1	
2347	BUTYL MERCAPTAN	3	F1	II	3		1 L	E2		PP, EX, A	VE01		1	

-273-

UN No. or ID No. (1)	Name and description 3.1.2 (2)	Class 2.2 (3a)	Classi-fication Code 2.2 (3b)	Packing group 2.1.1.3 (4)	Labels 5.2.2 (5)	Special provis-ions 3.3 (6)	Limited and excepted quantities 3.4 (7a)	3.5.1.2 (7b)	Carriage permitted 3.2.1 (8)	Equipment required 8.1.5 (9)	Venti-lation 7.1.6 (10)	Provisions concerning loading, unloading and carriage 7.1.6 (11)	Number of blue cones/ lights 7.1.5 (12)	Remarks 3.2.1 (13)
2348	BUTYL ACRYLATES, STABILIZED	3	F1	III	3	386 676	5 L	E1		PP, EX, A	VE01		0	
2350	BUTYL METHYL ETHER	3	F1	II	3		1 L	E2	T	PP, EX, A	VE01		1	
2351	BUTYL NITRITES	3	F1	II	3		1 L	E2		PP, EX, A	VE01		1	
2351	BUTYL NITRITES	3	F1	III	3		5 L	E1		PP, EX, A	VE01		0	
2352	BUTYL VINYL ETHER, STABILIZED	3	F1	II	3	386 676	1 L	E2		PP, EX, A	VE01		1	
2353	BUTYRYL CHLORIDE	3	FC	II	3+8		1 L	E2		PP, EP, EX, A	VE01		1	
2354	CHLOROMETHYL ETHYL ETHER	3	FT1	II	3+6.1	802	1 L	E2		PP, EP, EX, TOX, A	VE01, VE02		2	
2356	2-CHLOROPROPANE	3	F1	I	3		0	E3	T	PP, EX, A	VE01		1	
2357	CYCLOHEXYLAMINE	8	CF1	II	8+3		1 L	E2		PP, EP, EX, A	VE01		1	
2358	CYCLOOCTATETRAENE	3	F1	II	3		1 L	E2		PP, EX, A	VE01		1	
2359	DIALLYLAMINE	3	FTC	II	3+6.1+8	802	1 L	E2		PP, EP, EX, TOX, A	VE01, VE02		2	
2360	DIALLYL ETHER	3	FT1	II	3+6.1	802	1 L	E2		PP, EP, EX, TOX, A	VE01, VE02		2	
2361	DIISOBUTYLAMINE	3	FC	III	3+8		5 L	E1		PP, EP, EX, A	VE01		0	
2362	1,1-DICHLOROETHANE	3	F1	II	3		1 L	E2	T	PP, EX, A	VE01		1	
2363	ETHYL MERCAPTAN	3	F1	I	3		0	E0		PP, EX, A	VE01		1	
2364	n-PROPYLBENZENE	3	F1	III	3		5 L	E1		PP, EX, A	VE01		0	
2366	DIETHYL CARBONATE	3	F1	III	3		5 L	E1		PP, EX, A	VE01		0	
2367	alpha-METHYLVALERALDEHYDE	3	F1	II	3		1 L	E2		PP, EX, A	VE01		1	
2368	alpha-PINENE	3	F1	III	3		5 L	E1		PP, EX, A	VE01		0	
2370	1-HEXENE	3	F1	II	3		1 L	E2	T	PP, EX, A	VE01		1	
2371	ISOPENTENES	3	F1	I	3		0	E3		PP, EX, A	VE01		1	
2372	1,2-DI-(DIMETHYLAMINO) ETHANE	3	F1	II	3		1 L	E2		PP, EX, A	VE01		1	
2373	DIETHOXYMETHANE	3	F1	II	3		1 L	E2		PP, EX, A	VE01		1	
2374	3,3-DIETHOXYPROPENE	3	F1	II	3		1 L	E2		PP, EX, A	VE01		1	
2375	DIETHYL SULPHIDE	3	F1	II	3		1 L	E2		PP, EX, A	VE01		1	
2376	2,3-DIHYDROPYRAN	3	F1	II	3		1 L	E2		PP, EX, A	VE01		1	
2377	1,1-DIMETHOXYETHANE	3	F1	II	3		1 L	E2		PP, EX, A	VE01		1	
2378	2-DIMETHYLAMINOACETONITRILE	3	FT1	II	3+6.1	802	1 L	E2		PP, EP, EX, TOX, A	VE01, VE02		2	
2379	1,3-DIMETHYLBUTYLAMINE	3	FC	II	3+8		1 L	E2		PP, EP, EX, A	VE01		1	
2380	DIMETHYLDIETHOXYSILANE	3	F1	II	3		1 L	E2		PP, EX, A	VE01		1	
2381	DIMETHYL DISULPHIDE	3	FT1	II	3+6.1	802	1 L	E0	T	PP, EP, EX, TOX, A	VE01, VE02		2	
2382	DIMETHYLHYDRAZINE, SYMMETRICAL	6.1	TF1	I	6.1+3	354 802	0	E0	T	PP, EP, EX, TOX, A	VE01, VE02		2	
2383	DIPROPYLAMINE	3	FC	II	3+8		1 L	E2	T	PP, EP, EX, A	VE01		1	
2384	DI-n-PROPYL ETHER	3	F1	II	3		1 L	E2		PP, EX, A	VE01		1	
2385	ETHYL ISOBUTYRATE	3	F1	II	3		1 L	E2		PP, EX, A	VE01		1	
2386	1-ETHYLPIPERIDINE	3	FC	II	3+8		1 L	E2		PP, EP, EX, A	VE01		1	
2387	FLUOROBENZENE	3	F1	II	3		1 L	E2		PP, EX, A	VE01		1	
2388	FLUOROTOLUENES	3	F1	II	3		1 L	E2		PP, EX, A	VE01		1	
2389	FURAN	3	F1	I	3		0	E3		PP, EX, A	VE01		1	
2390	2-IODOBUTANE	3	F1	II	3		1 L	E2		PP, EX, A	VE01		1	

UN No. or ID No. (1)	Name and description (2)	Class (3a)	Classification Code (3b)	Packing group (4)	Labels (5)	Special provisions (6)	Limited and excepted quantities 3.4 (7a)	Limited and excepted quantities 3.5.1.2 (7b)	Carriage permitted (8)	Equipment required (9)	Ventilation (10)	Provisions concerning loading, unloading and carriage (11)	Number of blue cones/lights (12)	Remarks (13)
2391	IODOMETHYLPROPANES	3	F1	II	3		1 L	E2		PP, EX, A	VE01		1	
2392	IODOPROPANES	3	F1	III	3		5 L	E1		PP, EX, A	VE01		0	
2393	ISOBUTYL FORMATE	3	F1	II	3		1 L	E2		PP, EX, A	VE01		1	
2394	ISOBUTYL PROPIONATE	3	F1	III	3		5 L	E1		PP, EX, A	VE01		0	
2395	ISOBUTYRYL CHLORIDE	3	FC	II	3+8		1 L	E2		PP, EP, EX, A	VE01		1	
2396	METHACRYLALDEHYDE, STABILIZED	3	FT1	II	3+6.1	386 676 802	1 L	E2		PP, EP, EX, TOX, A	VE01, VE02		2	
2397	3-METHYLBUTAN-2-ONE	3	F1	II	3		1 L	E2	T	PP, EX, A	VE01		1	
2398	METHYL tert-BUTYL ETHER	3	F1	II	3		1 L	E2	T	PP, EX, A	VE01		1	
2399	1-METHYLPIPERIDINE	3	FC	II	3+8		1 L	E2		PP, EP, EX, A	VE01		1	
2400	METHYL ISOVALERATE	3	F1	II	3		1 L	E2		PP, EX, A	VE01		1	
2401	PIPERIDINE	8	CF1	I	8+3		0	E0		PP, EP, EX, A	VE01		1	
2402	PROPANETHIOLS	3	F1	II	3		1 L	E2		PP, EX, A	VE01		1	
2403	ISOPROPENYL ACETATE	3	F1	II	3		1 L	E2		PP, EX, A	VE01		1	
2404	PROPIONITRILE	3	FT1	II	3+6.1	802	1 L	E0	T	PP, EP, EX, TOX, A	VE01, VE02		2	
2405	ISOPROPYL BUTYRATE	3	F1	III	3		5 L	E1		PP, EX, A	VE01		0	
2406	ISOPROPYL ISOBUTYRATE	3	F1	II	3		1 L	E2		PP, EX, A	VE01		1	
2407	ISOPROPYL CHLOROFORMATE	6.1	TFC	I	6.1+3+8	354 802	0	E0		PP, EP, EX, TOX, A	VE01, VE02		2	
2409	ISOPROPYL PROPIONATE	3	F1	II	3		1 L	E2		PP, EX, A	VE01		1	
2410	1,2,3,6-TETRAHYDROPYRIDINE	3	F1	II	3		1 L	E2		PP, EX, A	VE01		1	
2411	BUTYRONITRILE	3	FT1	II	3+6.1	802	1 L	E2		PP, EP, EX, TOX, A	VE01, VE02		2	
2412	TETRAHYDROTHIOPHENE	3	F1	II	3		1 L	E2		PP, EX, A	VE01		1	
2413	TETRAPROPYL ORTHOTITANATE	3	F1	III	3		5 L	E1		PP, EX, A	VE01		0	
2414	THIOPHENE	3	F1	II	3		1 L	E2		PP, EX, A	VE01		1	
2416	TRIMETHYL BORATE	3	F1	II	3		1 L	E2		PP, EX, A	VE01		1	
2417	CARBONYL FLUORIDE	2	2TC		2.3+8		0	E0		PP, EP, TOX, A	VE02		2	
2418	SULPHUR TETRAFLUORIDE	2	2TC		2.3+8		0	E0		PP, EP, TOX, A	VE02		2	
2419	BROMOTRIFLUOROETHYLENE	2	2F		2.1	662	0	E0		PP, EX, A	VE01		1	
2420	HEXAFLUOROACETONE	2	2TOC		2.3+8		0	E0		PP, EP, TOX, A	VE02		2	
2421	NITROGEN TRIOXIDE	2	2TOC			CARRIAGE PROHIBITED									
2422	OCTAFLUOROBUT-2-ENE (REFRIGERANT GAS R 1318)	2	2A		2.2	662	120 ml	E1		PP			0	
2424	OCTAFLUOROPROPANE (REFRIGERANT GAS R 218)	2	2A		2.2	662	120 ml	E1		PP			0	
2426	AMMONIUM NITRATE, LIQUID (hot concentrated solution)	5.1	O1		5.1	252 644	0	E0		PP			0	
2427	POTASSIUM CHLORATE, AQUEOUS SOLUTION	5.1	O1	II	5.1		1 L	E2		PP			0	
2427	POTASSIUM CHLORATE, AQUEOUS SOLUTION	5.1	O1	III	5.1		5 L	E1		PP			0	
2428	SODIUM CHLORATE, AQUEOUS SOLUTION	5.1	O1	II	5.1		1 L	E2		PP			0	
2428	SODIUM CHLORATE, AQUEOUS SOLUTION	5.1	O1	III	5.1		5 L	E1		PP			0	
2429	CALCIUM CHLORATE, AQUEOUS SOLUTION	5.1	O1	II	5.1		1 L	E2		PP			0	
2429	CALCIUM CHLORATE, AQUEOUS SOLUTION	5.1	O1	III	5.1		5 L	E1		PP			0	

UN No. or ID No. (1)	Name and description 3.1.2 (2)	Class 2.2 (3a)	Classification Code 2.2 (3b)	Packing group 2.1.1.3 (4)	Labels 5.2.2 (5)	Special provisions 3.3 (6)	Limited quantities 3.4 (7a)	Excepted quantities 3.5.1.2 (7b)	Carriage permitted 3.2.1 (8)	Equipment required 8.1.5 (9)	Ventilation 7.1.6 (10)	Provisions concerning loading, unloading and carriage 7.1.6 (11)	Number of blue cones/lights 7.1.5 (12)	Remarks 3.2.1 (13)
2430	ALKYLPHENOLS, SOLID, N.O.S. (including C_2-C_{12} homologues)	8	C4	I	8		0	E0		PP, EP			0	
2430	ALKYLPHENOLS, SOLID, N.O.S. (including C_2-C_{12} homologues)	8	C4	II	8		1 kg	E2	T	PP, EP			0	
2430	ALKYLPHENOLS, SOLID, N.O.S. (including C_2-C_{12} homologues)	8	C4	III	8		5 kg	E1		PP, EP			0	
2431	ANISIDINES	6.1	T1	III	6.1	802	5 L	E1		PP, EP, TOX, A	VE02		0	
2432	N,N-DIETHYLANILINE	6.1	T1	III	6.1	279 802	5 L	E1	T	PP, EP, TOX, A	VE02		0	
2433	CHLORONITROTOLUENES, LIQUID	6.1	T1	III	6.1	802	5 L	E1		PP, EP, TOX, A	VE02		0	
2434	DIBENZYLDICHLOROSILANE	8	C3	II	8		0	E0		PP, EP			0	
2435	ETHYLPHENYLDICHLOROSILANE	8	C3	II	8		0	E0		PP, EP			0	
2436	THIOACETIC ACID	3	F1	II	3		1 L	E2		PP, EX, A	VE01		1	
2437	METHYLPHENYLDICHLOROSILANE	8	C3	II	8		0	E0		PP, EP			0	
2438	TRIMETHYLACETYL CHLORIDE	6.1	TFC	I	6.1+3+8	802	0	E0		PP, EP, EX, TOX, A	VE01, VE02		2	
2439	SODIUM HYDROGENDIFLUORIDE	8	C2	II	8		1 kg	E2		PP, EP			0	
2440	STANNIC CHLORIDE PENTAHYDRATE	8	C2	III	8		5 kg	E1		PP, EP			0	
2441	TITANIUM TRICHLORIDE, PYROPHORIC or TITANIUM TRICHLORIDE MIXTURE, PYROPHORIC	4.2	SC4	I	4.2+8	537	0	E0		PP, EP			0	
2442	TRICHLOROACETYL CHLORIDE	8	C3	II	8		0	E0		PP, EP			0	
2443	VANADIUM OXYTRICHLORIDE	8	C1	II	8		1 L	E0		PP, EP			0	
2444	VANADIUM TETRACHLORIDE	8	C1	I	8		0	E0		PP, EP			0	
2446	NITROCRESOLS, SOLID	6.1	T2	III	6.1	802	5 kg	E1		PP, EP			0	
2447	PHOSPHORUS, WHITE, MOLTEN	4.2	ST3	I	4.2+6.1	802	0	E0	T	PP, EP, TOX, A	VE02		2	
2448	SULPHUR, MOLTEN	4.1	F3	III	4.1	538	0	E0		PP			0	
2451	NITROGEN TRIFLUORIDE	2	2O		2.2+5.1	662	0	E0		PP			0	
2452	ETHYLACETYLENE, STABILIZED	2	2F		2.1	386 662 676	0	E0		PP, EX, A	VE01		1	
2453	ETHYL FLUORIDE (REFRIGERANT GAS R 161)	2	2F		2.1	662	0	E0		PP, EX, A	VE01		1	
2454	METHYL FLUORIDE (REFRIGERANT GAS R 41)	2	2F		2.1	662	0	E0		PP, EX, A	VE01		1	
2455	METHYL NITRITE	2	2A						CARRIAGE PROHIBITED					
2456	2-CHLOROPROPENE	3	F1	I	3		0	E3		PP, EX, A	VE01		1	
2457	2,3-DIMETHYLBUTANE	3	F1	II	3		1 L	E2		PP, EX, A	VE01		1	
2458	HEXADIENES	3	F1	II	3		1 L	E2	T	PP, EX, A	VE01		1	
2459	2-METHYL-1-BUTENE	3	F1	I	3		0	E3		PP, EX, A	VE01		1	
2460	2-METHYL-2-BUTENE	3	F1	II	3		1 L	E2		PP, EX, A	VE01		1	
2461	METHYLPENTADIENE	3	F1	II	3		1 L	E2		PP, EX, A	VE01		1	
2463	ALUMINIUM HYDRIDE	4.3	W2	I	4.3		0	E0		PP, EP		HA08	0	
2464	BERYLLIUM NITRATE	5.1	OT2	II	5.1+6.1	802	1 kg	E2		PP, EP			2	
2465	DICHLOROISOCYANURIC ACID, DRY or DICHLOROISOCYANURIC ACID SALTS	5.1	O2	II	5.1	135	1 kg	E2		PP			0	
2466	POTASSIUM SUPEROXIDE	5.1	O2	I	5.1		0	E0		PP			0	
2468	TRICHLOROISOCYANURIC ACID, DRY	5.1	O2	II	5.1		1 kg	E2		PP			0	
2469	ZINC BROMATE	5.1	O2	III	5.1		5 kg	E1		PP			0	
2470	PHENYLACETONITRILE, LIQUID	6.1	T1	III	6.1	802	5 L	E1		PP, EP, TOX, A	VE02		0	
2471	OSMIUM TETROXIDE	6.1	T5	I	6.1	802	0	E5		PP, EP			2	

UN No. or ID No. (1)	Name and description 3.1.2 (2)	Class 2.2 (3a)	Classification Code 2.2 (3b)	Packing group 2.1.1.3 (4)	Labels 5.2.2 (5)	Special provisions 3.3 (6)	Limited and excepted quantities 3.4 (7a)	3.5.1.2 (7b)	Carriage permitted 3.2.1 (8)	Equipment required 8.1.5 (9)	Ventilation 7.1.6 (10)	Provisions concerning loading, unloading and carriage 7.1.6 (11)	Number of blue cones/lights 7.1.5 (12)	Remarks 3.2.1 (13)
2473	SODIUM ARSANILATE	6.1	T3	III	6.1	802	5 kg	E1		PP, EP, TOX, A	VE02		0	
2474	THIOPHOSGENE	6.1	T1	I	6.1	279 354 802	0	E0		PP, EP, TOX, A	VE02		2	
2475	VANADIUM TRICHLORIDE	8	C2	III	8		5 kg	E1		PP, EP			0	
2477	METHYL ISOTHIOCYANATE	6.1	TF1	I	6.1+3	354 802	0	E0	T	PP, EP, EX, TOX, A	VE01, VE02		2	
2478	ISOCYANATES, FLAMMABLE, TOXIC, N.O.S. or ISOCYANATE SOLUTION, FLAMMABLE, TOXIC, N.O.S.	3	FT1	II	3+6.1	274 539 802	1 L	E2		PP, EP, EX, TOX, A	VE01, VE02		2	
2478	ISOCYANATES, FLAMMABLE, TOXIC, N.O.S. or ISOCYANATE SOLUTION, FLAMMABLE, TOXIC, N.O.S.	3	FT1	III	3+6.1	274 802	5 L	E1		PP, EP, EX, TOX, A	VE01, VE02		0	
2480	METHYL ISOCYANATE	6.1	TF1	I	6.1+3	354 802	0	E0		PP, EP, EX, TOX, A	VE01, VE02		2	
2481	ETHYL ISOCYANATE	6.1	TF1	I	6.1+3	354 802	0	E0		PP, EP, EX, TOX, A	VE01, VE02		2	
2482	n-PROPYL ISOCYANATE	6.1	TF1	I	6.1+3	354 802	0	E0		PP, EP, EX, TOX, A	VE01, VE02		2	
2483	ISOPROPYL ISOCYANATE	6.1	TF1	I	6.1+3	354 802	0	E0		PP, EP, EX, TOX, A	VE01, VE02		2	
2484	tert-BUTYL ISOCYANATE	6.1	TF1	I	6.1+3	354 802	0	E0		PP, EP, EX, TOX, A	VE01, VE02		2	
2485	n-BUTYL ISOCYANATE	6.1	TF1	I	6.1+3	354 802	0	E0	T	PP, EP, EX, TOX, A	VE01, VE02		2	
2486	ISOBUTYL ISOCYANATE	6.1	TF1	I	6.1+3	354 802	0	E0	T	PP, EP, EX, TOX, A	VE01, VE02		2	
2487	PHENYL ISOCYANATE	6.1	TF1	I	6.1+3	354 802	0	E0	T	PP, EP, EX, TOX, A	VE01, VE02		2	
2488	CYCLOHEXYL ISOCYANATE	6.1	TF1	I	6.1+3	354 802	0	E0		PP, EP, EX, TOX, A	VE01, VE02		2	
2490	DICHLOROISOPROPYL ETHER	6.1	T1	II	6.1	802	100 ml	E4	T	PP, EP, TOX, A	VE02		2	
2491	ETHANOLAMINE or ETHANOLAMINE SOLUTION	8	C7	III	8		5 L	E1	T	PP, EP			0	
2493	HEXAMETHYLENEIMINE	3	FC	II	3+8		1 L	E2	T	PP, EP, EX, A	VE01		1	
2495	IODINE PENTAFLUORIDE	5.1	OTC	I	5.1+6.1+8	802	0	E0		PP, EP, TOX, A	VE02		2	
2496	PROPIONIC ANHYDRIDE	8	C3	III	8		5 L	E1	T	PP, EP.			0	
2498	1,2,3,6-TETRAHYDROBENZALDEHYDE	3	F1	III	3		5 L	E1		PP, EX, A	VE01		0	
2501	TRIS-(1-AZIRIDINYL) PHOSPHINE OXIDE SOLUTION	6.1	T1	II	6.1	802	100 ml	E4		PP, EP, TOX, A	VE02		2	
2501	TRIS-(1-AZIRIDINYL) PHOSPHINE OXIDE SOLUTION	6.1	T1	III	6.1	802	5 L	E1		PP, EP, TOX, A	VE02		0	
2502	VALERYL CHLORIDE	8	CF1	II	8+3		1 L	E2		PP, EP, EX, A	VE01		1	
2503	ZIRCONIUM TETRACHLORIDE	8	C2	III	8		5 kg	E1		PP, EP			0	
2504	TETRABROMOETHANE	6.1	T1	III	6.1	802	5 L	E1		PP, EP, TOX, A	VE02		0	
2505	AMMONIUM FLUORIDE	6.1	T5	III	6.1	802	5 kg	E1	B	PP, EP			0	

UN No. or ID No.	Name and description	Class	Classification Code	Packing group	Labels	Special provisions	Limited quantities	excepted quantities	Carriage permitted	Equipment required	Ventilation	Provisions concerning loading, unloading and carriage	Number of blue cones/lights	Remarks
		2.2	2.2	2.1.1.3	5.2.2	3.3	3.4	3.5.1.2	3.2.1	8.1.5	7.1.6	7.1.6	7.1.5	3.2.1
(1)	(2)	(3a)	(3b)	(4)	(5)	(6)	(7a)	(7b)	(8)	(9)	(10)	(11)	(12)	(13)
2506	AMMONIUM HYDROGEN SULPHATE	8	C2	II	8		1 kg	E2	B	PP, EP		CO03	0	CO03 applies only when this substance is carried in bulk or without packaging
2507	CHLOROPLATINIC ACID, SOLID	8	C2	III	8		5 kg	E1		PP, EP			0	
2508	MOLYBDENUM PENTACHLORIDE	8	C2	III	8		5 kg	E1		PP, EP			0	
2509	POTASSIUM HYDROGEN SULPHATE	8	C2	II	8		1 kg	E2	B	PP, EP		CO03	0	CO03 applies only when this substance is carried in bulk or without packaging
2511	2-CHLOROPROPIONIC ACID	8	C3	III	8		5 L	E1		PP, EP			0	
2512	AMINOPHENOLS (o-, m-, p-)	6.1	T2	III	6.1	279 802	5 kg	E1		PP, EP			0	
2513	BROMOACETYL BROMIDE	8	C3	II	8		1 L	E2		PP, EP			0	
2514	BROMOBENZENE	3	F1	III	3		5 L	E1		PP, EX, A	VE01		0	
2515	BROMOFORM	6.1	T1	III	6.1	802	5 L	E1		PP, EP, TOX, A	VE02		0	
2516	CARBON TETRABROMIDE	6.1	T2	III	6.1	802	5 kg	E1		PP, EP			0	
2517	1-CHLORO-1,1-DIFLUOROETHANE (REFRIGERANT GAS R 142b)	2	2F		2.1	662	0	E0		PP, EX, A	VE01		1	
2518	1,5,9-CYCLODODECATRIENE	6.1	T1	III	6.1	802	5 L	E1	T	PP, EP, TOX, A	VE02		0	
2520	CYCLOOCTADIENES	3	F1	III	3	802	5 L	E1		PP, EX, A	VE01		0	
2521	DIKETENE, STABILIZED	6.1	TF1	I	6.1+3	354 386 676 802	0	E0		PP, EP, EX, TOX, A	VE01, VE02		2	
2522	2-DIMETHYLAMINOETHYL METHACRYLATE, STABILIZED	6.1	T1	II	6.1	386 676 802	100 ml	E4		PP, EP, TOX, A	VE02		2	
2524	ETHYL ORTHOFORMATE	3	F1	III	3		5 L	E1		PP, EX, A	VE01		0	
2525	ETHYL OXALATE	6.1	T1	III	6.1	802	5 L	E1		PP, EP, TOX, A	VE02		0	
2526	FURFURYLAMINE	3	FC	III	3+8		5 L	E1		PP, EP, EX, A	VE01		0	
2527	ISOBUTYL ACRYLATE, STABILIZED	3	F1	III	3	386 676	5 L	E1	T	PP, EX, A	VE01		0	
2528	ISOBUTYL ISOBUTYRATE	3	F1	III	3		5 L	E1	T	PP, EX, A	VE01		0	
2529	ISOBUTYRIC ACID	3	FC	III	3+8		5 L	E1		PP, EP, EX, A	VE01		0	
2531	METHACRYLIC ACID, STABILIZED	8	C3	II	8	386 676	1 L	E2	T	PP, EP			0	
2533	METHYL TRICHLOROACETATE	6.1	T1	III	6.1	802	5 L	E1		PP, EP, TOX, A	VE02		0	
2534	METHYLCHLOROSILANE	2	2TFC		2.3+2.1+8		0	E0		PP, EP, EX, TOX, A	VE01, VE02		2	
2535	4-METHYLMORPHOLINE (N-METHYLMORPHOLINE)	3	FC	II	3+8		1 L	E2		PP, EP, EX, A	VE01		1	
2536	METHYLTETRAHYDROFURAN	3	F1	II	3		1 L	E2		PP, EX, A	VE01		1	
2538	NITRONAPHTHALENE	4.1	F1	III	4.1		5 kg	E1		PP			0	
2541	TERPINOLENE	3	F1	III	3		5 L	E1		PP, EX, A	VE01		0	
2542	TRIBUTYLAMINE	6.1	T1	II	6.1	802	100 ml	E4		PP, EP, TOX, A	VE02		2	
2545	HAFNIUM POWDER, DRY	4.2	S4	I	4.2	540	0	E0		PP			0	
2545	HAFNIUM POWDER, DRY	4.2	S4	II	4.2	540	0	E2		PP			0	
2545	HAFNIUM POWDER, DRY	4.2	S4	III	4.2	540	0	E1		PP			0	
2546	TITANIUM POWDER, DRY	4.2	S4	I	4.2	540	0	E0		PP			0	

UN No. or ID No.	Name and description	Class	Classification Code	Packing group	Labels	Special provisions	Limited and excepted quantities		Carriage permitted	Equipment required	Ventilation	Provisions concerning loading, unloading and carriage	Number of blue cones/lights	Remarks
3.1.2	3.1.2	2.2	2.2	2.1.1.3	5.2.2	3.3	3.4	3.5.1.2	3.2.1	8.1.5	7.1.6	7.1.6	7.1.5	3.2.1
(1)	(2)	(3a)	(3b)	(4)	(5)	(6)	(7a)	(7b)	(8)	(9)	(10)	(11)	(12)	(13)
2546	TITANIUM POWDER, DRY	4.2	S4	II	4.2	540	0	E2		PP			0	
2546	TITANIUM POWDER, DRY	4.2	S4	III	4.2	540	0	E1		PP			0	
2547	SODIUM SUPEROXIDE	5.1	O2	I	5.1		0	E0		PP			0	
2548	CHLORINE PENTAFLUORIDE	2	2TOC		2.3+5.1+8		0	E0		PP, EP, TOX, A	VE02		2	
2552	HEXAFLUOROACETONE HYDRATE, LIQUID	6.1	T1	II	6.1	802	100 ml	E4		PP, EP, TOX, A	VE02		2	
2554	METHYLALLYL CHLORIDE	3	F1	II	3		1 L	E2		PP, EX, A	VE01		1	
2555	NITROCELLULOSE WITH WATER (not less than 25% water, by mass)	4.1	D	II	4.1	394 541	0	E0		PP			0	
2556	NITROCELLULOSE WITH ALCOHOL (not less than 25% alcohol, by mass, and not more than 12.6% nitrogen, by dry mass)	4.1	D	II	4.1	394 541	0	E0		PP			0	
2557	NITROCELLULOSE, with not more than 12.6% nitrogen, by dry mass, MIXTURE WITH or WITHOUT PLASTICIZER, WITH or WITHOUT PIGMENT	4.1	D	II	4.1	241 394 541	0	E0		PP			0	
2558	EPIBROMOHYDRIN	6.1	TF1	I	6.1+3	802	0	E0		PP, EP, EX, TOX, A	VE01, VE02		2	
2560	2-METHYLPENTAN-2-OL	3	F1	III	3		5 L	E1		PP, EX, A	VE01		0	
2561	3-METHYL-1-BUTENE	3	F1	I	3		0	E3		PP, EX, A	VE01		1	
2564	TRICHLOROACETIC ACID SOLUTION	8	C3	II	8		1 L	E2	T	PP, EP			0	
2564	TRICHLOROACETIC ACID SOLUTION	8	C3	III	8		5 L	E1	T	PP, EP			0	
2565	DICYCLOHEXYLAMINE	8	C7	III	8		5 L	E1		PP, EP			0	
2567	SODIUM PENTACHLOROPHENATE	6.1	T2	II	6.1	802	500 g	E4		PP, EP			2	
2570	CADMIUM COMPOUND	6.1	T5	I	6.1	274 596 802	0	E5		PP, EP			2	
2570	CADMIUM COMPOUND	6.1	T5	II	6.1	274 596 802	500 g	E4		PP, EP			2	
2570	CADMIUM COMPOUND	6.1	T5	III	6.1	274 596 802	5 kg	E1		PP, EP			0	
2571	ALKYLSULPHURIC ACIDS	8	C3	II	8		1 L	E2		PP, EP			0	
2572	PHENYLHYDRAZINE	6.1	T1	II	6.1	802	100 ml	E4		PP, EP, TOX, A	VE02		2	
2573	THALLIUM CHLORATE	5.1	OT2	II	5.1+6.1	802	1 kg	E2		PP, EP			2	
2574	TRICRESYL PHOSPHATE with more than 3% ortho isomer	6.1	T1	II	6.1	802	100 ml	E4	T	PP, EP, TOX, A	VE02		2	
2576	PHOSPHORUS OXYBROMIDE, MOLTEN	8	C1	II	8		0	E0		PP, EP			0	
2577	PHENYLACETYL CHLORIDE	8	C3	II	8		1 L	E2		PP, EP			0	
2578	PHOSPHORUS TRIOXIDE	8	C2	III	8		5 kg	E1		PP, EP			0	
2579	PIPERAZINE	8	C8	III	8		5 kg	E1	T	PP, EP			0	
2580	ALUMINIUM BROMIDE SOLUTION	8	C1	III	8		5 L	E1		PP, EP			0	
2581	ALUMINIUM CHLORIDE SOLUTION	8	C1	III	8		5 L	E1		PP, EP			0	
2582	FERRIC CHLORIDE SOLUTION	8	C1	III	8		5 L	E1	T	PP, EP			0	
2583	ALKYLSULPHONIC ACIDS, SOLID or ARYLSULPHONIC ACIDS, SOLID with more than 5% free sulphuric acid	8	C2	II	8		1 kg	E2		PP, EP			0	

UN No. or ID No. (1)	Name and description (2) 3.1.2	Class (3a) 2.2	Classi-fication Code (3b) 2.2	Packing group (4) 2.1.1.3	Labels (5) 5.2.2	Special provis-ions (6) 3.3	Limited and excepted quantities 3.4 (7a)	3.5.1.2 (7b)	Carriage permitted (8) 3.2.1	Equipment required (9) 8.1.5	Venti-lation (10) 7.1.6	Provisions concerning loading, unloading and carriage (11) 7.1.6	Number of blue cones/ lights (12) 7.1.5	Remarks (13) 3.2.1
2584	ALKYLSULPHONIC ACIDS, LIQUID or ARYLSULPHONIC ACIDS, LIQUID with more than 5% free sulphuric acid	8	C1	II	8		1 L	E2		PP, EP			0	
2585	ALKYLSULPHONIC ACIDS, SOLID or ARYLSULPHONIC ACIDS, SOLID with not more than 5% free sulphuric acid	8	C4	III	8		5 kg	E1		PP, EP			0	
2586	ALKYLSULPHONIC ACIDS, LIQUID or ARYLSULPHONIC ACIDS, LIQUID with not more than 5% free sulphuric acid	8	C3	III	8		5 L	E1	T	PP, EP			0	
2587	BENZOQUINONE	6.1	T2	II	6.1	802	500 g	E4		PP, EP			2	
2588	PESTICIDE, SOLID, TOXIC, N.O.S.	6.1	T7	I	6.1	61 274 648 802	0	E5		PP, EP			2	
2588	PESTICIDE, SOLID, TOXIC, N.O.S.	6.1	T7	II	6.1	61 274 648 802	500 g	E4		PP, EP			2	
2588	PESTICIDE, SOLID, TOXIC, N.O.S.	6.1	T7	III	6.1	61 274 648 802	5 kg	E1		PP, EP			0	
2589	VINYL CHLOROACETATE	6.1	TF1	II	6.1+3	802	100 ml	E4		PP, EP, EX, TOX, A	VE01, VE02		2	
2590	ASBESTOS, CHRYSOTILE	9	M1	III	9	168 802	5 kg	E1		PP			0	
2591	XENON, REFRIGERATED LIQUID	2	3A		2.2	593	120 ml	E1		PP			0	
2599	CHLOROTRIFLUOROMETHANE AND TRIFLUOROMETHANE AZEOTROPIC MIXTURE with approximately 60% chlorotrifluoromethane (REFRIGERANT GAS R 503)	2	2A		2.2	662	120 ml	E1		PP			0	
2601	CYCLOBUTANE	2	2F		2.1	662	0	E0		PP, EX, A	VE01		1	
2602	DICHLORODIFLUOROMETHANE AND 1,1-DIFLUOROETHANE AZEOTROPIC MIXTURE with approximately 74% dichlorodifluoromethane (REFRIGERANT GAS R 500)	2	2A		2.2	662	120 ml	E1		PP			0	
2603	CYCLOHEPTATRIENE	3	FT1	II	3+6.1	802	1 L	E2		PP, EP, EX, TOX, A	VE01, VE02		2	
2604	BORON TRIFLUORIDE DIETHYL ETHERATE	8	CF1	I	8+3		0	E0		PP, EP, EX, A	VE01		1	
2605	METHOXYMETHYL ISOCYANATE	6.1	TF1	I	6.1+3	354 802	0	E0		PP, EP, EX, TOX, A	VE01, VE02		2	
2606	METHYL ORTHOSILICATE	6.1	TF1	I	6.1+3	354 802	0	E0		PP, EP, EX, TOX, A	VE01, VE02		2	
2607	ACROLEIN DIMER, STABILIZED	3	F1	III	3	386 676	5 L	E1	T	PP, EX, A	VE01		1	
2608	NITROPROPANES	3	F1	III	3		5 L	E1		PP, EX, A	VE01		0	
2609	TRIALLYL BORATE	6.1	T1	III	6.1	802	5 L	E1		PP, EP, TOX, A	VE02		0	
2610	TRIALLYLAMINE	3	FC	III	3+8		5 L	E1		PP, EP, EX, A	VE01		0	

UN No. or ID No.	Name and description	Class	Classi-fication Code	Packing group	Labels	Special provis-ions	Limited and excepted quantities		Carriage permitted	Equipment required	Venti-lation	Provisions concerning loading, unloading and carriage	Number of blue cones/ lights	Remarks
							3.4	3.5.1.2	3.2.1	8.1.5	7.1.6	7.1.6	7.1.5	3.2.1
(1)	(2)	(3a)	(3b)	(4)	(5)	(6)	(7a)	(7b)	(8)	(9)	(10)	(11)	(12)	(13)
2611	PROPYLENE CHLOROHYDRIN	6.1	TF1	II	6.1+3	802	100 ml	E4		PP, EP, EX, TOX, A	VE01, VE02		2	
2612	METHYL PROPYL ETHER	3	F1	II	3		1 L	E2		PP, EX, A	VE01		1	
2614	METHALLYL ALCOHOL	3	F1	III	3		5 L	E1		PP, EX, A	VE01		0	
2615	ETHYL PROPYL ETHER	3	F1	II	3		1 L	E2	T	PP, EX, A	VE01		1	
2616	TRIISOPROPYL BORATE	3	F1	II	3		1 L	E2		PP, EX, A	VE01		1	
2616	TRIISOPROPYL BORATE	3	F1	III	3		5 L	E1		PP, EX, A	VE01		0	
2617	METHYLCYCLOHEXANOLS, flammable	3	F1	III	3		5 L	E1		PP, EX, A	VE01		0	
2618	VINYLTOLUENES, STABILIZED	3	F1	III	3	386 676	5 L	E1	T	PP, EX, A	VE01		0	
2619	BENZYLDIMETHYLAMINE	8	CF1	II	8+3		1 L	E2		PP, EP, EX, A	VE01		1	
2620	AMYL BUTYRATES	3	F1	III	3		5 L	E1		PP, EX, A	VE01		0	
2621	ACETYL METHYL CARBINOL	3	F1	III	3		5 L	E1		PP, EX, A	VE01		0	
2622	GLYCIDALDEHYDE	3	FT1	II	3+6.1	802	1 L	E2		PP, EP, EX, TOX, A	VE01, VE02		2	
2623	FIRELIGHTERS, SOLID with flammable liquid	4.1	F1	III	4.1		5 kg	E1		PP			0	
2624	MAGNESIUM SILICIDE	4.3	W2	II	4.3		500 g	E2		PP, EX, A	VE01		0	
2626	CHLORIC ACID, AQUEOUS SOLUTION with not more than 10% chloric acid	5.1	O1	II	5.1	613	1 L	E0		PP		HA08	0	
2627	NITRITES, INORGANIC, N.O.S.	5.1	O2	II	5.1	103 274	1 kg	E2		PP			0	
2628	POTASSIUM FLUOROACETATE	6.1	T2	I	6.1	802	0	E5		PP, EP			2	
2629	SODIUM FLUOROACETATE	6.1	T2	I	6.1	802	0	E5		PP, EP			2	
2630	SELENATES or SELENITES	6.1	T5	I	6.1	274 802	0	E5		PP, EP			2	
2642	FLUOROACETIC ACID	6.1	T2	I	6.1	802	0	E5		PP, EP			2	
2643	METHYL BROMOACETATE	6.1	T1	II	6.1	802	100 ml	E4		PP, EP, TOX, A	VE02		2	
2644	METHYL IODIDE	6.1	T1	I	6.1	354 802	0	E0		PP, EP, TOX, A	VE02		2	
2645	PHENACYL BROMIDE	6.1	T2	II	6.1	802	500 g	E4		PP, EP			2	
2646	HEXACHLOROCYCLOPENTADIENE	6.1	T1	I	6.1	354 802	0	E0		PP, EP, TOX, A	VE02		2	
2647	MALONONITRILE	6.1	T2	II	6.1	802	500 g	E4		PP, EP			2	
2648	1,2-DIBROMOBUTAN-3-ONE	6.1	T1	II	6.1	802	100 ml	E4		PP, EP, TOX, A	VE02		2	
2649	1,3-DICHLOROACETONE	6.1	T2	II	6.1	802	500 g	E4		PP, EP			2	
2650	1,1-DICHLORO-1-NITROETHANE	6.1	T1	II	6.1	802	100 ml	E4		PP, EP, TOX, A	VE02		2	
2651	4,4'-DIAMINODIPHENYL-METHANE	6.1	T2	III	6.1	802	5 kg	E1	T	PP, EP			0	
2653	BENZYL IODIDE	6.1	T1	II	6.1	802	100 ml	E4		PP, EP, TOX, A	VE02		2	
2655	POTASSIUM FLUOROSILICATE	6.1	T5	III	6.1	802	5 kg	E1		PP, EP			0	
2656	QUINOLINE	6.1	T1	III	6.1	802	5 L	E1		PP, EP, TOX, A	VE02		0	
2657	SELENIUM DISULPHIDE	6.1	T5	II	6.1	802	500 g	E4		PP, EP			2	
2659	SODIUM CHLOROACETATE	6.1	T2	III	6.1	802	5 kg	E1		PP, EP			0	
2660	NITROTOLUIDINES (MONO)	6.1	T2	III	6.1	802	5 kg	E1		PP, EP			0	
2661	HEXACHLOROACETONE	6.1	T1	III	6.1	802	5 L	E1		PP, EP, TOX, A	VE02		0	
2664	DIBROMOMETHANE	6.1	T1	III	6.1	802	5 L	E1		PP, EP, TOX, A	VE02		0	
2667	BUTYLTOLUENES	6.1	T1	III	6.1	802	5 L	E1		PP, EP, TOX, A	VE01, VE02		0	
2668	CHLOROACETONITRILE	6.1	TF1	I	6.1+3	354 802	0	E0		PP, EP, TOX, A	VE01, VE02		2	

UN No. or ID No.	Name and description	Class	Classification Code	Packing group	Labels	Special provisions	Limited and excepted quantities		Carriage permitted	Equipment required	Venti-lation	Provisions concerning loading, unloading and carriage	Number of blue cones/ lights	Remarks
	3.1.2	2.2	2.2	2.1.1.3	5.2.2	3.3	3.4	3.5.1.2	3.2.1	8.1.5	7.1.6	7.1.6	7.1.5	3.2.1
(1)	(2)	(3a)	(3b)	(4)	(5)	(6)	(7a)	(7b)	(8)	(9)	(10)	(11)	(12)	(13)
2669	CHLOROCRESOLS, SOLUTION	6.1	T1	II	6.1	802	100 ml	E4		PP, EP, TOX, A	VE02		2	
2669	CHLOROCRESOLS, SOLUTION	6.1	T1	III	6.1	802	5 L	E1		PP, EP, TOX, A	VE02		0	
2670	CYANURIC CHLORIDE	8	C4	II	8		1 kg	E2		PP, EP			0	
2671	AMINOPYRIDINES (o-, m-, p-)	6.1	T2	II	6.1	802	500 g	E4		PP, EP			2	
2672	AMMONIA SOLUTION, relative density between 0.880 and 0.957 at 15 °C in water, with more than 10% but not more than 35% ammonia	8	C5	III	8	543	5 L	E1	T	PP, EP			0	
2673	2-AMINO-4-CHLOROPHENOL	6.1	T2	II	6.1	802	500 g	E4		PP, EP			2	
2674	SODIUM FLUOROSILICATE	6.1	T5	III	6.1	802	5 kg	E1		PP, EP			0	
2676	STIBINE	2	2TF		2.3+2.1		0	E0		PP, EP, EX, TOX, A	VE01, VE02		2	
2677	RUBIDIUM HYDROXIDE SOLUTION	8	C5	II	8		1 L	E2		PP, EP			0	
2677	RUBIDIUM HYDROXIDE SOLUTION	8	C5	III	8		5 L	E1		PP, EP			0	
2678	RUBIDIUM HYDROXIDE	8	C6	II	8		1 kg	E2		PP, EP			0	
2679	LITHIUM HYDROXIDE SOLUTION	8	C5	II	8		1 L	E2		PP, EP			0	
2679	LITHIUM HYDROXIDE SOLUTION	8	C5	III	8		5 L	E1		PP, EP			0	
2680	LITHIUM HYDROXIDE	8	C6	II	8		1 kg	E2		PP, EP			0	
2681	CAESIUM HYDROXIDE SOLUTION	8	C5	II	8		1 L	E2		PP, EP			0	
2681	CAESIUM HYDROXIDE SOLUTION	8	C5	III	8		5 L	E1		PP, EP			0	
2682	CAESIUM HYDROXIDE	8	C6	II	8		1 kg	E2		PP, EP			0	
2683	AMMONIUM SULPHIDE SOLUTION	8	CFT	II	8+3+6.1	802	1 L	E2	T	PP, EP, EX, TOX, A	VE01, VE02		2	
2684	3-DIETHYLAMINOPROPYLAMINE	3	FC	III	3+8		5 L	E1		PP, EP, EX, A	VE01		0	
2685	N,N-DIETHYLETHYLENEDIAMINE	8	CF1	II	8+3		1 L	E2		PP, EP, EX, A	VE01		1	
2686	2-DIETHYLAMINOETHANOL	8	CF1	II	8+3		1 L	E2		PP, EP, EX, A	VE01		1	
2687	DICYCLOHEXYLAMMONIUM NITRITE	4.1	F3	III	4.1		5 kg	E1		PP			0	
2688	1-BROMO-3-CHLOROPROPANE	6.1	T1	III	6.1	802	5 L	E1		PP, EP, TOX, A	VE02		0	
2689	GLYCEROL alpha-MONOCHLOROHYDRIN	6.1	T1	III	6.1	802	5 L	E1		PP, EP, TOX, A	VE02		0	
2690	N,n-BUTYLIMIDAZOLE	6.1	T1	II	6.1	802	100 ml	E4	T	PP, EP, TOX, A	VE02		2	
2691	PHOSPHORUS PENTABROMIDE	8	C2	II	8		1 kg	E0		PP, EP			0	
2692	BORON TRIBROMIDE	8	C1	I	8		0	E0		PP, EP			0	
2693	BISULPHITES, AQUEOUS SOLUTION, N.O.S.	8	C1	III	8	274	5 L	E1	T	PP, EP			0	
2698	TETRAHYDROPHTHALIC ANHYDRIDES with more than 0.05% of maleic anhydride	8	C4	III	8	169	5 kg	E1		PP, EP			0	
2699	TRIFLUOROACETIC ACID	8	C3	I	8		0	E0		PP, EP			0	
2705	1-PENTOL	8	C9	II	8		1 L	E2		PP, EP			0	
2707	DIMETHYLDIOXANES	3	F1	II	3		1 L	E2		PP, EX, A	VE01		1	
2707	DIMETHYLDIOXANES	3	F1	III	3		5 L	E1		PP, EX, A	VE01		0	
2709	BUTYLBENZENES	3	F1	III	3		5 L	E1	T	PP, EX, A	VE01		0	
2710	DIPROPYL KETONE	3	F1	III	3		5 L	E1		PP, EX, A	VE01		0	
2713	ACRIDINE	6.1	T2	III	6.1	802	5 kg	E1		PP, EP			0	
2714	ZINC RESINATE	4.1	F3	III	4.1		5 kg	E1		PP			0	
2715	ALUMINIUM RESINATE	4.1	F3	III	4.1		5 kg	E1		PP			0	
2716	1,4-BUTYNEDIOL	6.1	T2	III	6.1	802	5 kg	E1		PP, EP			0	
2717	CAMPHOR, synthetic	4.1	F1	III	4.1		5 kg	E1		PP			0	
2719	BARIUM BROMATE	5.1	OT2	II	5.1+6.1	802	1 kg	E2		PP, EP			2	

(1)	(2)	(3a)	(3b)	(4)	(5)	(6)	(7a)	(7b)	(8)	(9)	(10)	(11)	(12)	(13)
UN No. or ID No.	Name and description	Class	Classification Code	Packing group	Labels	Special provisions	Limited and excepted quantities		Carriage permitted	Equipment required	Ventilation	Provisions concerning loading, unloading and carriage	Number of blue cones/lights	Remarks
3.1.2	3.1.2	2.2	2.2	2.1.1.3	5.2.2	3.3	3.4	3.5.1.2	3.2.1	8.1.5	7.1.6	7.1.6	7.1.5	3.2.1
2720	CHROMIUM NITRATE	5.1	O2	III	5.1		5 kg	E1	B	PP		CO02, LO04	0	CO02 and LO04 apply only when this substance is carried in bulk or without packaging
2721	COPPER CHLORATE	5.1	O2	II	5.1		1 kg	E2		PP			0	
2722	LITHIUM NITRATE	5.1	O2	III	5.1		5 kg	E1	B	PP		CO02, LO04	0	CO02 and LO04 apply only when this substance is carried in bulk or without packaging
2723	MAGNESIUM CHLORATE	5.1	O2	II	5.1		1 kg	E2		PP			0	
2724	MANGANESE NITRATE	5.1	O2	III	5.1		5 kg	E1	B	PP		CO02, LO04	0	CO02 and LO04 apply only when this substance is carried in bulk or without packaging
2725	NICKEL NITRATE	5.1	O2	III	5.1		5 kg	E1	B	PP		CO02, LO04	0	CO02 and LO04 apply only when this substance is carried in bulk or without packaging
2726	NICKEL NITRITE	5.1	O2	III	5.1		5 kg	E1		PP			0	
2727	THALLIUM NITRATE	6.1	TO2	II	6.1+5.1	802	500 g	E4		PP, EP			2	
2728	ZIRCONIUM NITRATE	5.1	O2	III	5.1		5 kg	E1	B	PP		CO02, LO04	0	CO02 and LO04 apply only when this substance is carried in bulk or without packaging
2729	HEXACHLOROBENZENE	6.1	T2	III	6.1	802	5 kg	E1		PP, EP			0	
2730	NITROANISOLES, LIQUID	6.1	T1	III	6.1	279 802	5 L	E1		PP, EP, TOX, A	VE02		0	
2732	NITROBROMOBENZENES, LIQUID	6.1	T1	III	6.1	802	5 L	E1		PP, EP, TOX, A	VE02		0	
2733	AMINES, FLAMMABLE, CORROSIVE, N.O.S. or POLYAMINES, FLAMMABLE, CORROSIVE, N.O.S.	3	FC	I	3+8	274 544	0	E0		PP, EP, EX, A	VE01		1	
2733	AMINES, FLAMMABLE, CORROSIVE, N.O.S. or POLYAMINES, FLAMMABLE, CORROSIVE, N.O.S.	3	FC	II	3+8	274 544	1 L	E2	T	PP, EP, EX, A	VE01		1	
2733	AMINES, FLAMMABLE, CORROSIVE, N.O.S. or POLYAMINES, FLAMMABLE, CORROSIVE, N.O.S.	3	FC	III	3+8	274 544	5 L	E1		PP, EP, EX, A	VE01		0	
2734	AMINES, LIQUID, CORROSIVE, FLAMMABLE, N.O.S. or POLYAMINES, LIQUID, CORROSIVE, FLAMMABLE, N.O.S.	8	CF1	I	8+3	274	0	E0		PP, EP, EX, A	VE01		1	
2734	AMINES, LIQUID, CORROSIVE, FLAMMABLE, N.O.S. or POLYAMINES, LIQUID, CORROSIVE, FLAMMABLE, N.O.S.	8	CF1	II	8+3	274	1 L	E2		PP, EP, EX, A	VE01		1	
2735	AMINES, LIQUID, CORROSIVE, N.O.S. or POLYAMINES, LIQUID, CORROSIVE, N.O.S.	8	C7	I	8	274	0	E0	T	PP, EP			0	
2735	AMINES, LIQUID, CORROSIVE, N.O.S. or POLYAMINES, LIQUID, CORROSIVE, N.O.S.	8	C7	II	8	274	1 L	E2	T	PP, EP			0	
2735	AMINES, LIQUID, CORROSIVE, N.O.S. or POLYAMINES, LIQUID, CORROSIVE, N.O.S.	8	C7	III	8	274	5 L	E1	T	PP, EP			0	
2738	N-BUTYLANILINE	6.1	T1	II	6.1	802	100 ml	E4		PP, EP, TOX, A	VE02		2	
2739	BUTYRIC ANHYDRIDE	8	C3	III	8		5 L	E1		PP, EP			0	

(1)	(2)	(3a)	(3b)	(4)	(5)	(6)	(7a)	(7b)	(8)	(9)	(10)	(11)	(12)	(13)
UN No. or ID No.	Name and description 3.1.2	Class 2.2	Classification Code 2.2	Packing group 2.1.1.3	Labels 5.2.2	Special provisions 3.3	Limited and excepted quantities 3.4	3.5.1.2	Carriage permitted 3.2.1	Equipment required 8.1.5	Ventilation 7.1.6	Provisions concerning loading, unloading and carriage 7.1.6	Number of blue cones/lights 7.1.5	Remarks 3.2.1
2740	n-PROPYL CHLOROFORMATE	6.1	TFC	I	6.1+3+8	802	0	E0		PP, EP, EX, TOX, A	VE01, VE02		2	
2741	BARIUM HYPOCHLORITE with more than 22% available chlorine	5.1	OT2	II	5.1+6.1	802	1 kg	E2		PP, EP			2	
2742	CHLOROFORMATES, TOXIC, CORROSIVE, FLAMMABLE, N.O.S.	6.1	TFC	II	6.1+3+8	274 561 802	100 ml	E4		PP, EP, EX, TOX, A	VE01, VE02		2	
2743	n-BUTYL CHLOROFORMATE	6.1	TFC	II	6.1+3+8	802	100 ml	E0		PP, EP, EX, TOX, A	VE01, VE02		2	
2744	CYCLOBUTYL CHLOROFORMATE	6.1	TFC	II	6.1+3+8	802	100 ml	E4		PP, EP, EX, TOX, A	VE01, VE02		2	
2745	CHLOROMETHYL CHLOROFORMATE	6.1	TC1	II	6.1+8	802	100 ml	E4		PP, EP, TOX, A	VE02		2	
2746	PHENYL CHLOROFORMATE	6.1	TC1	II	6.1+8	802	100 ml	E4		PP, EP, TOX, A	VE02		2	
2747	tert-BUTYLCYCLOHEXYL CHLOROFORMATE	6.1	T1	III	6.1	802	5 L	E1		PP, EP, TOX, A	VE02		0	
2748	2-ETHYLHEXYL CHLOROFORMATE	6.1	TC1	II	6.1+8	802	100 ml	E4		PP, EP, TOX, A	VE02		2	
2749	TETRAMETHYLSILANE	3	F1	I	3		0	E0		PP, EX, A	VE01		1	
2750	1,3-DICHLOROPROPANOL-2	6.1	T1	II	6.1	802	100 ml	E4		PP, EP, TOX, A	VE02		2	
2751	DIETHYLTHIOPHOSPHORYL CHLORIDE	8	C3	II	8		1 L	E2		PP, EP			0	
2752	1,2-EPOXY-3-ETHOXYPROPANE	3	F1	III	3		5 L	E1		PP, EX, A	VE01		0	
2753	N-ETHYLBENZYLTOLUIDINES, LIQUID	6.1	T1	III	6.1	802	5 L	E1		PP, EP, TOX, A	VE02		0	
2754	N-ETHYLTOLUIDINES	6.1	T1	II	6.1	802	100 ml	E4	T	PP, EP, TOX, A	VE02		2	
2757	CARBAMATE PESTICIDE, SOLID, TOXIC	6.1	T7	I	6.1	61 274 648 802	0	E5		PP, EP			2	
2757	CARBAMATE PESTICIDE, SOLID, TOXIC	6.1	T7	II	6.1	61 274 648 802	500 g	E4		PP, EP			2	
2757	CARBAMATE PESTICIDE, SOLID, TOXIC	6.1	T7	III	6.1	61 274 648 802	5 kg	E1		PP, EP			0	
2758	CARBAMATE PESTICIDE, LIQUID, FLAMMABLE, TOXIC, flash-point less than 23 °C	3	FT2	I	3+6.1	61 274 802	0	E0		PP, EP, EX, TOX, A	VE01, VE02		2	
2758	CARBAMATE PESTICIDE, LIQUID, FLAMMABLE, TOXIC, flash-point less than 23 °C	3	FT2	II	3+6.1	61 274 802	1 L	E2		PP, EP, EX, TOX, A	VE01, VE02		2	
2759	ARSENICAL PESTICIDE, SOLID, TOXIC	6.1	T7	I	6.1	61 274 648 802	0	E5		PP, EP			2	
2759	ARSENICAL PESTICIDE, SOLID, TOXIC	6.1	T7	II	6.1	61 274 648 802	500 g	E4		PP, EP			2	

UN No. or ID No. (1)	Name and description 3.1.2 (2)	Class 2.2 (3a)	Classification Code 2.2 (3b)	Packing group 2.1.1.3 (4)	Labels 5.2.2 (5)	Special provisions 3.3 (6)	Limited quantities 3.4 (7a)	Excepted quantities 3.5.1.2 (7b)	Carriage permitted 3.2.1 (8)	Equipment required 8.1.5 (9)	Ventilation 7.1.6 (10)	Provisions concerning loading, unloading and carriage 7.1.6 (11)	Number of blue cones/lights 7.1.5 (12)	Remarks 3.2.1 (13)
2759	ARSENICAL PESTICIDE, SOLID, TOXIC	6.1	T7	III	6.1	61 274 648 802	5 kg	E1		PP, EP			0	
2760	ARSENICAL PESTICIDE, LIQUID, FLAMMABLE, TOXIC, flash-point less than 23 °C	3	FT2	I	3+6.1	61 274 802	0	E0		PP, EP, EX, TOX, A	VE01, VE02		2	
2760	ARSENICAL PESTICIDE, LIQUID, FLAMMABLE, TOXIC, flash-point less than 23 °C	3	FT2	II	3+6.1	61 274 802	1 L	E2		PP, EP, EX, TOX, A	VE01, VE02		2	
2761	ORGANOCHLORINE PESTICIDE, SOLID, TOXIC	6.1	T7	I	6.1	61 274 648 802	0	E5		PP, EP			2	
2761	ORGANOCHLORINE PESTICIDE, SOLID, TOXIC	6.1	T7	II	6.1	61 274 648 802	500 g	E4		PP, EP			2	
2761	ORGANOCHLORINE PESTICIDE, SOLID, TOXIC	6.1	T7	III	6.1	61 274 648 802	5 kg	E1		PP, EP			0	
2762	ORGANOCHLORINE PESTICIDE, LIQUID, FLAMMABLE, TOXIC, flash-point less than 23 °C	3	FT2	I	3+6.1	61 274 802	0	E0		PP, EP, EX, TOX, A	VE01, VE02		2	
2762	ORGANOCHLORINE PESTICIDE, LIQUID, FLAMMABLE, TOXIC, flash-point less than 23 °C	3	FT2	II	3+6.1	61 274 802	1 L	E2		PP, EP, EX, TOX, A	VE01, VE02		2	
2763	TRIAZINE PESTICIDE, SOLID, TOXIC	6.1	T7	I	6.1	61 274 648 802	0	E5		PP, EP			2	
2763	TRIAZINE PESTICIDE, SOLID, TOXIC	6.1	T7	II	6.1	61 274 648 802	500 g	E4		PP, EP			2	
2763	TRIAZINE PESTICIDE, SOLID, TOXIC	6.1	T7	III	6.1	61 274 648 802	5 kg	E1		PP, EP			0	
2764	TRIAZINE PESTICIDE, LIQUID, FLAMMABLE, TOXIC, flash-point less than 23 °C	3	FT2	I	3+6.1	61 274 802	0	E0		PP, EP, EX, TOX, A	VE01, VE02		2	
2764	TRIAZINE PESTICIDE, LIQUID, FLAMMABLE, TOXIC, flash-point less than 23 °C	3	FT2	II	3+6.1	61 274 802	1 L	E2		PP, EP, EX, TOX, A	VE01, VE02		2	

UN No. or ID No.	Name and description	Class	Classification Code	Packing group	Labels	Special provisions	Limited and excepted quantities		Carriage permitted	Equipment required	Ventilation	Provisions concerning loading, unloading and carriage	Number of blue cones/lights	Remarks
3.1.2	3.1.2	2.2	2.2	2.1.1.3	5.2.2	3.3	3.4	3.5.1.2	3.2.1	8.1.5	7.1.6	7.1.6	7.1.5	3.2.1
(1)	(2)	(3a)	(3b)	(4)	(5)	(6)	(7a)	(7b)	(8)	(9)	(10)	(11)	(12)	(13)
2771	THIOCARBAMATE PESTICIDE, SOLID, TOXIC	6.1	T7	I	6.1	61 274 648 802	0	E5		PP, EP			2	
2771	THIOCARBAMATE PESTICIDE, SOLID, TOXIC	6.1	T7	II	6.1	61 274 648 802	500 g	E4		PP, EP			2	
2771	THIOCARBAMATE PESTICIDE, SOLID, TOXIC	6.1	T7	III	6.1	61 274 648 802	5 kg	E1		PP, EP			0	
2772	THIOCARBAMATE PESTICIDE, LIQUID, FLAMMABLE, TOXIC, flash-point less than 23 °C	3	FT2	I	3+6.1	61 274 648 802	0	E0		PP, EP, EX, TOX, A	VE01, VE02		2	
2772	THIOCARBAMATE PESTICIDE, LIQUID, FLAMMABLE, TOXIC, flash-point less than 23 °C	3	FT2	II	3+6.1	61 274 648 802	1 L	E2		PP, EP, EX, TOX, A	VE01, VE02		2	
2775	COPPER BASED PESTICIDE, SOLID, TOXIC	6.1	T7	I	6.1	61 274 648 802	0	E5		PP, EP			2	
2775	COPPER BASED PESTICIDE, SOLID, TOXIC	6.1	T7	II	6.1	61 274 648 802	500 g	E4		PP, EP			2	
2775	COPPER BASED PESTICIDE, SOLID, TOXIC	6.1	T7	III	6.1	61 274 648 802	5 kg	E1		PP, EP			0	
2776	COPPER BASED PESTICIDE, LIQUID, FLAMMABLE, TOXIC, flash-point less than 23 °C	3	FT2	I	3+6.1	61 274 648 802	0	E0		PP, EP, EX, TOX, A	VE01, VE02		2	
2776	COPPER BASED PESTICIDE, LIQUID, FLAMMABLE, TOXIC, flash-point less than 23 °C	3	FT2	II	3+6.1	61 274 648 802	1 L	E2		PP, EP, EX, TOX, A	VE01, VE02		2	
2777	MERCURY BASED PESTICIDE, SOLID, TOXIC	6.1	T7	I	6.1	61 274 648 802	0	E5		PP, EP			2	
2777	MERCURY BASED PESTICIDE, SOLID, TOXIC	6.1	T7	II	6.1	61 274 648 802	500 g	E4		PP, EP			2	
2777	MERCURY BASED PESTICIDE, SOLID, TOXIC	6.1	T7	III	6.1	61 274 648 802	5 kg	E1		PP, EP			0	

UN No. or ID No. (1) 3.1.2	Name and description (2) 3.1.2	Class (3a) 2.2	Classification Code (3b) 2.2	Packing group (4) 2.1.1.3	Labels (5) 5.2.2	Special provisions (6) 3.3	Limited quantities (7a) 3.4	Excepted quantities (7b) 3.5.1.2	Carriage permitted (8) 3.2.1	Equipment required (9) 8.1.5	Ventilation (10) 7.1.6	Provisions concerning loading, unloading and carriage (11) 7.1.6	Number of blue cones/lights (12) 7.1.5	Remarks (13) 3.2.1
2778	MERCURY BASED PESTICIDE, LIQUID, FLAMMABLE, TOXIC, flash-point less than 23 °C	3	FT2	I	3+6.1	61 274 802	0	E0		PP, EP, EX, TOX, A	VE01, VE02		2	
2778	MERCURY BASED PESTICIDE, LIQUID, FLAMMABLE, TOXIC, flash-point less than 23 °C	3	FT2	II	3+6.1	61 274 802	1 L	E2		PP, EP, EX, TOX, A	VE01, VE02		2	
2779	SUBSTITUTED NITROPHENOL PESTICIDE, SOLID, TOXIC	6.1	T7	I	6.1	61 274 648 802	0	E5		PP, EP			2	
2779	SUBSTITUTED NITROPHENOL PESTICIDE, SOLID, TOXIC	6.1	T7	II	6.1	61 274 648 802	500 g	E4		PP, EP			2	
2779	SUBSTITUTED NITROPHENOL PESTICIDE, SOLID, TOXIC	6.1	T7	III	6.1	61 274 648 802	5 kg	E1		PP, EP			0	
2780	SUBSTITUTED NITROPHENOL PESTICIDE, LIQUID, FLAMMABLE, TOXIC, flash-point less than 23 °C	3	FT2	I	3+6.1	61 274 802	0	E0		PP, EP, EX, TOX, A	VE01, VE02		2	
2780	SUBSTITUTED NITROPHENOL PESTICIDE, LIQUID, FLAMMABLE, TOXIC, flash-point less than 23 °C	3	FT2	II	3+6.1	61 274 802	1 L	E2		PP, EP, EX, TOX, A	VE01, VE02		2	
2781	BIPYRIDILIUM PESTICIDE, SOLID, TOXIC	6.1	T7	I	6.1	61 274 648 802	0	E5		PP, EP			2	
2781	BIPYRIDILIUM PESTICIDE, SOLID, TOXIC	6.1	T7	II	6.1	61 274 648 802	500 g	E4		PP, EP			2	
2781	BIPYRIDILIUM PESTICIDE, SOLID, TOXIC	6.1	T7	III	6.1	61 274 648 802	5 kg	E1		PP, EP			0	
2782	BIPYRIDILIUM PESTICIDE, LIQUID, FLAMMABLE, TOXIC, flash-point less than 23 °C	3	FT2	I	3+6.1	61 274 802	0	E0		PP, EP, EX, TOX, A	VE01, VE02		2	
2782	BIPYRIDILIUM PESTICIDE, LIQUID, FLAMMABLE, TOXIC, flash-point less than 23 °C	3	FT2	II	3+6.1	61 274 802	1 L	E2		PP, EP, EX, TOX, A	VE01, VE02		2	
2783	ORGANOPHOSPHORUS PESTICIDE, SOLID, TOXIC	6.1	T7	I	6.1	61 274 648 802	0	E5		PP, EP			2	

UN No. or ID No.	Name and description	Class	Classification Code	Packing group	Labels	Special provisions	Limited and excepted quantities		Carriage permitted	Equipment required	Ventilation	Provisions concerning loading, unloading and carriage	Number of blue cones/lights	Remarks
	3.1.2	2.2	2.2	2.1.1.3	5.2.2	3.3	3.4	3.5.1.2	3.2.1	8.1.5	7.1.6	7.1.6	7.1.5	3.2.1
(1)	(2)	(3a)	(3b)	(4)	(5)	(6)	(7a)	(7b)	(8)	(9)	(10)	(11)	(12)	(13)
2783	ORGANOPHOSPHORUS PESTICIDE, SOLID, TOXIC	6.1	T7	II	6.1	61 274 648 802	500 g	E4		PP, EP			2	
2783	ORGANOPHOSPHORUS PESTICIDE, SOLID, TOXIC	6.1	T7	III	6.1	61 274 648 802	5 kg	E1		PP, EP			0	
2784	ORGANOPHOSPHORUS PESTICIDE, LIQUID, FLAMMABLE, TOXIC, flash-point less than 23 °C	3	FT2	I	3+6.1	61 274 802	0	E0		PP, EP, EX, TOX, A	VE01, VE02		2	
2784	ORGANOPHOSPHORUS PESTICIDE, LIQUID, FLAMMABLE, TOXIC, flash-point less than 23 °C	3	FT2	II	3+6.1	61 274 802	1 L	E2		PP, EP, EX, TOX, A	VE01, VE02		2	
2785	4-THIAPENTANAL	6.1	T1	III	6.1	802	5 L	E1	T	PP, EP, TOX, A	VE02		0	
2786	ORGANOTIN PESTICIDE, SOLID, TOXIC	6.1	T7	I	6.1	61 274 802	0	E5		PP, EP			2	
2786	ORGANOTIN PESTICIDE, SOLID, TOXIC	6.1	T7	II	6.1	61 274 648 802	500 g	E4		PP, EP			2	
2786	ORGANOTIN PESTICIDE, SOLID, TOXIC	6.1	T7	III	6.1	61 274 648 802	5 kg	E1		PP, EP			0	
2787	ORGANOTIN PESTICIDE, LIQUID, FLAMMABLE, TOXIC, flash-point less than 23 °C	3	FT2	I	3+6.1	61 274 802	0	E0		PP, EP, EX, TOX, A	VE01, VE02		2	
2787	ORGANOTIN PESTICIDE, LIQUID, FLAMMABLE, TOXIC, flash-point less than 23 °C	3	FT2	II	3+6.1	61 274 802	1 L	E2		PP, EP, EX, TOX, A	VE01, VE02		2	
2788	ORGANOTIN COMPOUND, LIQUID, N.O.S.	6.1	T3	I	6.1	43 274 802	0	E5		PP, EP, TOX, A	VE02		2	
2788	ORGANOTIN COMPOUND, LIQUID, N.O.S.	6.1	T3	II	6.1	43 274 802	100 ml	E4		PP, EP, TOX, A	VE02		2	
2788	ORGANOTIN COMPOUND, LIQUID, N.O.S.	6.1	T3	III	6.1	43 274 802	5 L	E1		PP, EP, TOX, A	VE02		0	
2789	ACETIC ACID, GLACIAL or ACETIC ACID SOLUTION, more than 80% acid, by mass	8	CF1	II	8+3		1 L	E2	T	PP, EP, EX, A	VE01		1	
2790	ACETIC ACID SOLUTION, not less than 50% but not more than 80% acid, by mass	8	C3	II	8		1 L	E2	T	PP, EP			0	
2790	ACETIC ACID SOLUTION, more than 10% and less than 50% acid, by mass	8	C3	III	8	597 647	5 L	E1	T	PP, EP			0	

(1)	(2)	(3a)	(3b)	(4)	(5)	(6)	(7a)	(7b)	(8)	(9)	(10)	(11)	(12)	(13)
UN No. or ID No.	Name and description	Class	Classi-fication Code	Packing group	Labels	Special provis-ions	Limited and excepted quantities		Carriage permitted	Equipment required	Venti-lation	Provisions concerning loading, unloading and carriage	Number of blue cones/ lights	Remarks
3.1.2	3.1.2	2.2	2.2	2.1.1.3	5.2.2	3.3	3.4	3.5.1.2	3.2.1	8.1.5	7.1.6	7.1.6	7.1.5	3.2.1
2793	FERROUS METAL BORINGS, SHAVINGS, TURNINGS or CUTTINGS in a form liable to self-heating	4.2	S4	III	4.2	592	0	E1	B	PP		LO02	0	LO02 applies only when this substance is carried in bulk or without packaging
2794	BATTERIES, WET, FILLED WITH ACID, electric storage	8	C11		8	295 598	1 L	E0		PP, EP			0	
2795	BATTERIES, WET, FILLED WITH ALKALI, electric storage	8	C11		8	295 598	1 L	E0		PP, EP			0	
2796	SULPHURIC ACID with not more than 51% acid or BATTERY FLUID, ACID	8	C1	II	8		1 L	E2	T	PP, EP			0	
2797	BATTERY FLUID, ALKALI	8	C5	II	8		1 L	E2	T	PP, EP			0	
2798	PHENYLPHOSPHORUS DICHLORIDE	8	C3	II	8		1 L	E0		PP, EP			0	
2799	PHENYLPHOSPHORUS THIODICHLORIDE	8	C3	II	8		1 L	E0		PP, EP			0	
2800	BATTERIES, WET, NON-SPILLABLE, electric storage	8	C11		8	238 295 598	1 L	E0		PP, EP			0	
2801	DYE, LIQUID, CORROSIVE, N.O.S. or DYE INTERMEDIATE, LIQUID, CORROSIVE, N.O.S.	8	C9	I	8	274	0	E0		PP, EP			0	
2801	DYE, LIQUID, CORROSIVE, N.O.S. or DYE INTERMEDIATE, LIQUID, CORROSIVE, N.O.S.	8	C9	II	8	274	1 L	E2		PP, EP			0	
2801	DYE, LIQUID, CORROSIVE, N.O.S. or DYE INTERMEDIATE, LIQUID, CORROSIVE, N.O.S.	8	C9	III	8	274	5 L	E1		PP, EP			0	
2802	COPPER CHLORIDE	8	C2	III	8		5 kg	E1		PP, EP			0	
2803	GALLIUM	8	C10	III	8		5 kg	E0		PP, EP			0	
2805	LITHIUM HYDRIDE, FUSED SOLID	4.3	W2	II	4.3		500 g	E2		PP, EX, A	VE01	HA08	0	
2806	LITHIUM NITRIDE	4.3	W2	I	4.3		0	E0		PP, EX, A	VE01	HA08	0	
2807	Magnetized material	9	M11						NOT SUBJECT TO ADN					
2809	MERCURY	8	CT1	III	8+6.1	365	5 kg	E0		PP, EP, EX, TOX, A	VE02		0	
2810	TOXIC LIQUID, ORGANIC, N.O.S.	6.1	T1	I	6.1	274 315 614 802	0	E5	T	PP, EP, TOX, A	VE02		2	
2810	TOXIC LIQUID, ORGANIC, N.O.S.	6.1	T1	II	6.1	274 614 802	100 ml	E4	T	PP, EP, TOX, A	VE02		2	
2810	TOXIC LIQUID, ORGANIC, N.O.S.	6.1	T1	III	6.1	274 614 802	5 L	E1	T	PP, EP, TOX, A	VE02		0	
2811	TOXIC SOLID, ORGANIC, N.O.S.	6.1	T2	I	6.1	274 614 802	0	E5	T	PP, EP			2	
2811	TOXIC SOLID, ORGANIC, N.O.S.	6.1	T2	II	6.1	274 614 802	500 g	E4		PP, EP			2	
2811	TOXIC SOLID, ORGANIC, N.O.S.	6.1	T2	III	6.1	274 614 802	5 kg	E1	T	PP, EP			0	
2812	Sodium aluminate, solid	8	C6						NOT SUBJECT TO ADN					

UN No. or ID No. (1)	Name and description (2)	Class (3a)	Classification Code (3b)	Packing group (4)	Labels (5)	Special provisions (6)	Limited quantities (7a)	Excepted quantities (7b)	Carriage permitted (8)	Equipment required (9)	Ventilation (10)	Provisions concerning loading, unloading and carriage (11)	Number of blue cones/lights (12)	Remarks (13)
2813	WATER-REACTIVE SOLID, N.O.S.	4.3	W2	I	4.3	274	0	E0		PP, EX, A	VE01	HA08	0	
2813	WATER-REACTIVE SOLID, N.O.S.	4.3	W2	II	4.3	274	500 g	E2		PP, EX, A	VE01	HA08	0	
2813	WATER-REACTIVE SOLID, N.O.S.	4.3	W2	III	4.3	274	1 kg	E1		PP, EX, A	VE01	HA08	0	
2814	INFECTIOUS SUBSTANCE, AFFECTING HUMANS	6.2	I1		6.2	318 802	0	E0		PP			0	
2814	INFECTIOUS SUBSTANCE, AFFECTING HUMANS, in refrigerated liquid nitrogen	6.2	I1		6.2 +2.2	318 802	0	E0		PP			0	
2814	INFECTIOUS SUBSTANCE, AFFECTING HUMANS (animal material only)	6.2	I1		6.2	318 802	0	E0		PP			0	
2815	N-AMINOETHYLPIPERAZINE	8	CT1	III	8+6.1		5 L	E1	T	PP, EP			0	
2817	AMMONIUM HYDROGENDIFLUORIDE SOLUTION	8	CT1	II	8+6.1	802	1 L	E2		PP, EP			2	
2817	AMMONIUM HYDROGENDIFLUORIDE SOLUTION	8	CT1	III	8+6.1	802	5 L	E1		PP, EP			0	
2818	AMMONIUM POLYSULPHIDE SOLUTION	8	CT1	II	8+6.1	802	1 L	E2		PP, EP			2	
2818	AMMONIUM POLYSULPHIDE SOLUTION	8	CT1	III	8+6.1	802	5 L	E1		PP, EP			0	
2819	AMYL ACID PHOSPHATE	8	C3	III	8		5 L	E1		PP, EP			0	
2820	BUTYRIC ACID	8	C3	III	8		5 L	E1	T	PP, EP			0	
2821	PHENOL SOLUTION	6.1	T1	II	6.1	802	100 ml	E4		PP, EP, TOX, A	VE02		2	
2821	PHENOL SOLUTION	6.1	T1	III	6.1	802	5 L	E1		PP, EP, TOX, A	VE02		0	
2822	2-CHLOROPYRIDINE	6.1	T1	II	6.1	802	100 ml	E4		PP, EP, TOX, A	VE02		2	
2823	CROTONIC ACID, SOLID	8	C4	III	8		5 kg	E1		PP, EP			0	
2826	ETHYL CHLOROTHIOFORMATE	8	CF1	II	8+3		0	E0	T	PP, EP	VE01		1	
2829	CAPROIC ACID	8	C3	III	8		5 L	E1		PP, EP			0	
2830	LITHIUM FERROSILICON	4.3	W2	II	4.3	802	500 g	E2		PP, EX, A	VE01	HA08	0	
2831	1,1,1-TRICHLOROETHANE	6.1	T1	III	6.1	802	5 L	E1	T	PP, EP, TOX, A	VE02		0	
2834	PHOSPHOROUS ACID	8	C2	III	8		5 kg	E0		PP, EP			0	
2835	SODIUM ALUMINIUM HYDRIDE	4.3	W2	II	4.3		500 g	E2		PP, EX, A	VE01	HA08	0	
2837	BISULPHATES, AQUEOUS SOLUTION	8	C1	II	8		1 L	E2		PP, EP			0	
2837	BISULPHATES, AQUEOUS SOLUTION	8	C1	III	8		5 L	E1		PP, EP			0	
2838	VINYL BUTYRATE, STABILIZED	3	F1	II	3	386 676	1 L	E2		PP, EX, A	VE01		1	
2839	ALDOL	6.1	T1	II	6.1	802	100 ml	E4		PP, EP, TOX, A	VE02		2	
2840	BUTYRALDOXIME	3	F1	III	3		5 L	E1		PP, EX, A	VE01		0	
2841	DI-n-AMYLAMINE	3	FT1	III	3+6.1	802	5 L	E1		PP, EP, EX, TOX, A	VE01, VE02		2	
2842	NITROETHANE	3	F1	III	3		5 L	E1		PP, EX, A	VE01		0	
2844	CALCIUM MANGANESE SILICON	4.3	W2	III	4.3	274	1 kg	E1		PP, EX, A	VE01	HA08	0	
2845	PYROPHORIC LIQUID, ORGANIC, N.O.S.	4.2	S1	I	4.2	274	0	E0		PP			0	
2846	PYROPHORIC SOLID, ORGANIC, N.O.S.	4.2	S2	I	4.2	274	0	E0		PP			0	
2849	3-CHLOROPROPANOL-1	6.1	T1	III	6.1	802	5 L	E1	T	PP, EP, TOX, A	VE02		2	
2850	PROPYLENE TETRAMER	3	F1	III	3		1 L	E2		PP, EX, A	VE01		0	
2851	BORON TRIFLUORIDE DIHYDRATE	8	C1	II	8		0	E0		PP, EP			0	
2852	DIPICRYL SULPHIDE, WETTED with not less than 10% water, by mass	4.1	D	I	4.1	545	0	E0		PP			1	
2853	MAGNESIUM FLUOROSILICATE	6.1	T5	III	6.1	802	5 kg	E1		PP, EP			0	
2854	AMMONIUM FLUOROSILICATE	6.1	T5	III	6.1	802	5 kg	E1		PP, EP			0	
2855	ZINC FLUOROSILICATE	6.1	T5	III	6.1	802	5 kg	E1		PP, EP			0	
2856	FLUOROSILICATES, N.O.S.	6.1	T5	III	6.1	274 802	5 kg	E1		PP, EP			0	

UN No. or ID No.	Name and description	Class	Classification Code	Packing group	Labels	Special provisions	Limited and excepted quantities		Carriage permitted	Equipment required	Venti-lation	Provisions concerning loading, unloading and carriage	Number of blue cones/lights	Remarks
							3.4	3.5.1.2	3.2.1	8.1.5	7.1.6	7.1.6	7.1.5	3.2.1
(1)	(2)	(3a)	(3b)	(4)	(5)	(6)	(7a)	(7b)	(8)	(9)	(10)	(11)	(12)	(13)
2857	REFRIGERATING MACHINES containing non-flammable, non-toxic gases or ammonia solutions (UN 2672)	2	6A		2.2	119	0	E0		PP			0	
2858	ZIRCONIUM, DRY, coiled wire, finished metal sheets, strip (thinner than 254 microns but not thinner than 18 microns)	4.1	F3	III	4.1	546	5 kg	E1		PP			0	
2859	AMMONIUM METAVANADATE	6.1	T5	II	6.1	802	500 g	E4		PP, EP			2	
2861	AMMONIUM POLYVANADATE	6.1	T5	II	6.1	802	500 g	E4		PP, EP			2	
2862	VANADIUM PENTOXIDE, non-fused form	6.1	T5	III	6.1	600 802	5 kg	E1		PP, EP			0	
2863	SODIUM AMMONIUM VANADATE	6.1	T5	II	6.1	802	500 g	E4		PP, EP			2	
2864	POTASSIUM METAVANADATE	6.1	T5	II	6.1	802	500 g	E4		PP, EP			2	
2865	HYDROXYLAMINE SULPHATE	8	C2	III	8		5 kg	E1		PP, EP			0	
2869	TITANIUM TRICHLORIDE MIXTURE	8	C2	II	8		1 kg	E2		PP, EP			0	
2869	TITANIUM TRICHLORIDE MIXTURE	8	C2	III	8		5 kg	E1		PP, EP			0	
2870	ALUMINIUM BOROHYDRIDE	4.2	SW	I	4.2+4.3		0	E0		PP, EX, A	VE01		0	
2870	ALUMINIUM BOROHYDRIDE IN DEVICES	4.2	SW	I	4.2+4.3		0	E0		PP, EX, A	VE01		0	
2871	ANTIMONY POWDER	6.1	T5	III	6.1	802	5 kg	E1		PP, EP			0	
2872	DIBROMOCHLOROPROPANES	6.1	T1	II	6.1	802	100 ml	E4		PP, EP, TOX, A	VE02		2	
2872	DIBROMOCHLOROPROPANES	6.1	T1	III	6.1	802	5 L	E1		PP, EP, TOX, A	VE02		0	
2873	DIBUTYLAMINOETHANOL	6.1	T1	III	6.1	802	5 L	E1		PP, EP, TOX, A	VE02		0	
2874	FURFURYL ALCOHOL	6.1	T1	III	6.1	802	5 L	E1	T	PP, EP, TOX, A	VE02		0	
2875	HEXACHLOROPHENE	6.1	T2	III	6.1	802	5 kg	E1		PP, EP			0	
2876	RESORCINOL	6.1	T2	III	6.1	802	5 kg	E1		PP, EP			0	
2878	TITANIUM SPONGE GRANULES or TITANIUM SPONGE POWDERS	4.1	F3	III	4.1	802	5 kg	E1		PP			0	
2879	SELENIUM OXYCHLORIDE	8	CT1	I	8+6.1	802	0	E0		PP, EP, TOX, A	VE02		2	
2880	CALCIUM HYPOCHLORITE, HYDRATED, or CALCIUM HYPOCHLORITE, HYDRATED MIXTURE, with not less than 5.5% but not more than 16% water	5.1	O2	II	5.1	314 322	1 kg	E2		PP			0	
2880	CALCIUM HYPOCHLORITE, HYDRATED or CALCIUM HYPOCHLORITE HYDRATED MIXTURE, with not less than 5.5% but not more than 16% water	5.1	O2	III	5.1	314	5 kg	E1		PP			0	
2881	METAL CATALYST, DRY	4.2	S4	I	4.2	274	0	E0		PP			0	
2881	METAL CATALYST, DRY	4.2	S4	II	4.2	274	0	E0		PP			0	
2881	METAL CATALYST, DRY	4.2	S4	III	4.2	274	0	E1		PP			0	
2900	INFECTIOUS SUBSTANCE, AFFECTING ANIMALS only	6.2	I2		6.2	318 802	0	E0		PP			0	
2900	INFECTIOUS SUBSTANCE, AFFECTING ANIMALS only, in refrigerated liquid nitrogen	6.2	I2		6.2 +2.2	318 802	0	E0		PP			0	
2900	INFECTIOUS SUBSTANCE, AFFECTING ANIMALS only (animal material only)	6.2	I2		6.2	318 802	0	E0		PP			0	
2901	BROMINE CHLORIDE	2	2TOC		2.3+5.1+8		0	E0		PP, EP, TOX, A	VE02		2	
2902	PESTICIDE, LIQUID, TOXIC, N.O.S.	6.1	T6	I	6.1	61 274 648 802	0	E5		PP, EP, TOX, A	VE02		2	

UN No. or ID No. (1)	Name and description 3.1.2 (2)	Class 2.2 (3a)	Classification Code 2.2 (3b)	Packing group 2.1.1.3 (4)	Labels 5.2.2 (5)	Special provisions 3.3 (6)	Limited and excepted quantities 3.4 (7a)	Limited and excepted quantities 3.5.1.2 (7b)	Carriage permitted 3.2.1 (8)	Equipment required 8.1.5 (9)	Ventilation 7.1.6 (10)	Provisions concerning loading, unloading and carriage 7.1.6 (11)	Number of blue cones/lights 7.1.5 (12)	Remarks 3.2.1 (13)
2902	PESTICIDE, LIQUID, TOXIC, N.O.S.	6.1	T6	II	6.1	61 274 648 802	100 ml	E4		PP, EP, TOX, A	VE02		2	
2902	PESTICIDE, LIQUID, TOXIC, N.O.S.	6.1	T6	III	6.1	61 274 648 802	5 L	E1		PP, EP, TOX, A	VE02		0	
2903	PESTICIDE, LIQUID, TOXIC, FLAMMABLE, N.O.S., flash-point not less than 23 °C	6.1	TF2	I	6.1+3	61 274 802	0	E5		PP, EP, EX, TOX, A	VE01, VE02		2	
2903	PESTICIDE, LIQUID, TOXIC, FLAMMABLE, N.O.S., flash-point not less than 23 °C	6.1	TF2	II	6.1+3	61 274 802	100 ml	E4		PP, EP, EX, TOX, A	VE01, VE02		2	
2903	PESTICIDE, LIQUID, TOXIC, FLAMMABLE, N.O.S., flash-point not less than 23 °C	6.1	TF2	III	6.1+3	61 274 802	5 L	E1		PP, EP, EX, TOX, A	VE01, VE02		0	
2904	CHLOROPHENOLATES, LIQUID or PHENOLATES, LIQUID	8	C9	III	8		5 L	E1	T *	PP, EP			0	* applies only to phenolates but not to chlorophenolates
2905	CHLOROPHENOLATES, SOLID or PHENOLATES, SOLID	8	C10	III	8		5 kg	E1		PP, EP			0	
2907	ISOSORBIDE DINITRATE MIXTURE with not less than 60% lactose, mannose, starch or calcium hydrogen phosphate	4.1	D	II	4.1	127	0	E0		PP			0	
2908	RADIOACTIVE MATERIAL, EXCEPTED PACKAGE - EMPTY PACKAGING	7				290 368	0	E0		PP			0	
2909	RADIOACTIVE MATERIAL, EXCEPTED PACKAGE - ARTICLES MANUFACTURED FROM NATURAL URANIUM or DEPLETED URANIUM or NATURAL THORIUM	7				290	0	E0		PP			0	
2910	RADIOACTIVE MATERIAL, EXCEPTED PACKAGE - LIMITED QUANTITY OF MATERIAL	7				290 368	0	E0		PP			0	
2911	RADIOACTIVE MATERIAL, EXCEPTED PACKAGE - INSTRUMENTS or ARTICLES	7				290	0	E0		PP			0	
2912	RADIOACTIVE MATERIAL, LOW SPECIFIC ACTIVITY (LSA-I), non fissile or fissile-excepted	7			7X	172 317 325	0	E0	B	PP		RA01	2	
2913	RADIOACTIVE MATERIAL, SURFACE CONTAMINATED OBJECTS (SCO-I, SCO-II or SCO-III), non fissile or fissile-excepted	7			7X	172 317 325	0	E0	B	PP		RA02	2	
2915	RADIOACTIVE MATERIAL, TYPE A PACKAGE, non-special form, non fissile or fissile-excepted	7			7X	172 317 325	0	E0		PP			2	
2916	RADIOACTIVE MATERIAL, TYPE B(U) PACKAGE, non fissile or fissile-excepted	7			7X	172 317 325 337	0	E0		PP			2	

(1) UN No. or ID No.	(2) Name and description 3.1.2	(3a) Class 2.2	(3b) Classification Code 2.2	(4) Packing group 2.1.1.3	(5) Labels 5.2.2	(6) Special provisions 3.3	(7a) Limited and excepted quantities 3.4	(7b) 3.5.1.2	(8) Carriage permitted 3.2.1	(9) Equipment required 8.1.5	(10) Venti-lation 7.1.6	(11) Provisions concerning loading, unloading and carriage 7.1.6	(12) Number of blue cones/lights 7.1.5	(13) Remarks 3.2.1
2917	RADIOACTIVE MATERIAL, TYPE B(M) PACKAGE, non fissile or fissile-excepted	7			7X	172 317 325 337	0	E0		PP			2	
2919	RADIOACTIVE MATERIAL, TRANSPORTED UNDER SPECIAL ARRANGEMENT, non fissile or fissile-excepted	7			7X	172 325 317	0	E0		PP			2	
2920	CORROSIVE LIQUID, FLAMMABLE, N.O.S.	8	CF1	I	8+3	274	0	E0		PP, EP, EX, A	VE01		1	
2920	CORROSIVE LIQUID, FLAMMABLE, N.O.S.	8	CF1	II	8+3	274	1 L	E2	T	PP, EP, EX, A	VE01		1	
2921	CORROSIVE SOLID, FLAMMABLE, N.O.S.	8	CF2	I	8+4.1	274	0	E0		PP, EP			1	
2921	CORROSIVE SOLID, FLAMMABLE, N.O.S.	8	CF2	II	8+4.1	274	1 kg	E2		PP, EP			1	
2922	CORROSIVE LIQUID, TOXIC, N.O.S.	8	CT1	I	8+6.1	274 802	0	E0	T	PP, EP, TOX, A	VE02		2	
2922	CORROSIVE LIQUID, TOXIC, N.O.S.	8	CT1	II	8+6.1	274 802	1 L	E2	T	PP, EP, TOX, A	VE02		2	
2922	CORROSIVE LIQUID, TOXIC, N.O.S.	8	CT1	III	8+6.1	274 802	5 L	E1	T	PP, EP, TOX, A	VE02		0	
2923	CORROSIVE SOLID, TOXIC, N.O.S.	8	CT2	I	8+6.1	274 802	0	E0		PP, EP			2	
2923	CORROSIVE SOLID, TOXIC, N.O.S.	8	CT2	II	8+6.1	274 802	1 kg	E2		PP, EP			2	
2923	CORROSIVE SOLID, TOXIC, N.O.S.	8	CT2	III	8+6.1	274 802	5 kg	E1		PP, EP			0	
2924	FLAMMABLE LIQUID, CORROSIVE, N.O.S.	3	FC	I	3+8	274	0	E0	T	PP, EP, EX, A	VE01		1	
2924	FLAMMABLE LIQUID, CORROSIVE, N.O.S.	3	FC	II	3+8	274	1 L	E2	T	PP, EP, EX, A	VE01		1	
2924	FLAMMABLE LIQUID, CORROSIVE, N.O.S.	3	FC	III	3+8	274	5 L	E1	T	PP, EP, EX, A	VE01		0	
2925	FLAMMABLE SOLID, CORROSIVE, ORGANIC, N.O.S.	4.1	FC1	II	4.1+8	274	1 kg	E2		PP, EP			1	
2925	FLAMMABLE SOLID, CORROSIVE, ORGANIC, N.O.S.	4.1	FC1	III	4.1+8	274	5 kg	E1		PP, EP			0	
2926	FLAMMABLE SOLID, TOXIC, ORGANIC, N.O.S.	4.1	FT1	II	4.1+6.1	274	1 kg	E2		PP, EP			2	
2926	FLAMMABLE SOLID, TOXIC, ORGANIC, N.O.S.	4.1	FT1	III	4.1+6.1	274	5 kg	E1		PP, EP			0	
2927	TOXIC LIQUID, CORROSIVE, ORGANIC, N.O.S.	6.1	TC1	I	6.1+8	274 315 802	0	E5	T	PP, EP, TOX, A	VE02		2	
2927	TOXIC LIQUID, CORROSIVE, ORGANIC, N.O.S.	6.1	TC1	II	6.1+8	274 802	100 ml	E4	T	PP, EP, TOX, A	VE02		2	
2928	TOXIC SOLID, CORROSIVE, ORGANIC, N.O.S.	6.1	TC2	I	6.1+8	274 802	0	E5		PP, EP			2	
2928	TOXIC SOLID, CORROSIVE, ORGANIC, N.O.S.	6.1	TC2	II	6.1+8	274 802	500 g	E4		PP, EP			2	
2929	TOXIC LIQUID, FLAMMABLE, ORGANIC, N.O.S.	6.1	TF1	I	6.1+3	274 315 802	0	E5	T	PP, EP, EX, TOX, A	VE01, VE02		2	
2929	TOXIC LIQUID, FLAMMABLE, ORGANIC, N.O.S.	6.1	TF1	II	6.1+3	274 802	100 ml	E4	T	PP, EP, EX, TOX, A	VE01, VE02		2	

UN No. or ID No.	Name and description	Class	Classification Code	Packing group	Labels	Special provisions	Limited and excepted quantities		Carriage permitted	Equipment required	Ventilation	Provisions concerning loading, unloading and carriage	Number of blue cones/ lights	Remarks
	3.1.2	2.2	2.2	2.1.1.3	5.2.2	3.3	3.4	3.5.1.2	3.2.1	8.1.5	7.1.6	7.1.6	7.1.5	3.2.1
(1)	(2)	(3a)	(3b)	(4)	(5)	(6)	(7a)	(7b)	(8)	(9)	(10)	(11)	(12)	(13)
2930	TOXIC SOLID, FLAMMABLE, ORGANIC, N.O.S.	6.1	TF3	I	6.1+4.1	274 802	0	E5		PP, EP			2	
2930	TOXIC SOLID, FLAMMABLE, ORGANIC, N.O.S.	6.1	TF3	II	6.1+4.1	274 802	500 g	E4		PP, EP			2	
2931	VANADYL SULPHATE	6.1	T5	II	6.1	802	500 g	E4		PP, EP			2	
2933	METHYL 2-CHLOROPROPIONATE	3	F1	III	3		5 L	E1		PP, EX, A	VE01		0	
2934	ISOPROPYL 2-CHLOROPROPIONATE	3	F1	III	3		5 L	E1		PP, EX, A	VE01		0	
2935	ETHYL 2-CHLOROPROPIONATE	3	F1	III	3		5 L	E1	T	PP, EX, A	VE01		0	
2936	THIOLACTIC ACID	6.1	T1	II	6.1	802	100 ml	E4		PP, EP, TOX, A	VE02		2	
2937	alpha-METHYLBENZYL ALCOHOL, LIQUID	6.1	T1	III	6.1	802	5 L	E1		PP, EP, TOX, A	VE02		0	
2940	9-PHOSPHABICYCLONONANES (CYCLOOCTADIENE PHOSPHINES)	4.2	S2	II	4.2		0	E2		PP			0	
2941	FLUOROANILINES	6.1	T1	III	6.1	802	5 L	E1		PP, EP, TOX, A	VE02		0	
2942	2-TRIFLUOROMETHYLANILINE	6.1	T1	III	6.1	802	5 L	E1		PP, EP, TOX, A	VE02		0	
2943	TETRAHYDROFURFURYLAMINE	3	F1	III	3		5 L	E1		PP, EX, A	VE01		1	
2945	N-METHYLBUTYLAMINE	3	FC	II	3+8		1 L	E2		PP, EP, EX, A	VE01		1	
2946	2-AMINO-5-DIETHYLAMINOPENTANE	6.1	T1	III	6.1	802	5 L	E1		PP, EP, TOX, A	VE02		0	
2947	ISOPROPYL CHLOROACETATE	3	F1	III	3		5 L	E1	T	PP, EX, A	VE01		0	
2948	3-TRIFLUOROMETHYLANILINE	6.1	T1	II	6.1	802	100 ml	E4		PP, EP, TOX, A	VE02		2	
2949	SODIUM HYDROSULPHIDE, HYDRATED with not less than 25% water of crystallization	8	C6	II	8	523	1 kg	E2		PP, EP			0	
2950	MAGNESIUM GRANULES, COATED, particle size not less than 149 microns	4.3	W2	III	4.3		1 kg	E1		PP, EX, TOX, A	VE01	HA08	0	
2956	5-tert-BUTYL-2,4,6-TRINITRO-m-XYLENE (MUSK XYLENE)	4.1	SR1	III	4.1	638	5 kg	E0		PP			0	
2965	BORON TRIFLUORIDE DIMETHYL ETHERATE	4.3	WFC	I	4.3+3+8		0	E0	T	PP, EP, EX, A	VE01	HA08	1	
2966	THIOGLYCOL	6.1	T1	II	6.1	802	100 ml	E4		PP, EP, TOX, A	VE02		2	
2967	SULPHAMIC ACID	8	C2	III	8		5 kg	E1		PP, EP			0	
2968	MANEB, STABILIZED or MANEB PREPARATION, STABILIZED against self-heating	4.3	W2	III	4.3	547	1 kg	E1		PP, EX, A	VE01	HA08	0	
2969	CASTOR BEANS or CASTOR MEAL or CASTOR POMACE or CASTOR FLAKE	9	M11	II	9	141	5 kg	E2	B	PP			0	
2977	RADIOACTIVE MATERIAL, URANIUM HEXAFLUORIDE, FISSILE	7			7X+7E +6.1+8		0	E0		PP, EP			2	
2978	RADIOACTIVE MATERIAL, URANIUM HEXAFLUORIDE, non fissile or fissile-excepted	7			7X+6.1+8	317	0	E0		PP, EP			2	
2983	ETHYLENE OXIDE AND PROPYLENE OXIDE MIXTURE, not more than 30% ethylene oxide	3	FT1	I	3+6.1	802	0	E0	T	PP, EP, EX, TOX, A	VE01, VE02		2	
2984	HYDROGEN PEROXIDE, AQUEOUS SOLUTION with not less than 8% but less than 20% hydrogen peroxide (stabilized as necessary)	5.1	O1	III	5.1	65	5 L	E1	T	PP			0	
2985	CHLOROSILANES, FLAMMABLE, CORROSIVE, N.O.S.	3	FC	II	3+8	548	0	E0		PP, EP, EX, A	VE01		1	
2986	CHLOROSILANES, CORROSIVE, FLAMMABLE, N.O.S.	8	CF1	II	8+3	548	0	E0		PP, EP, EX, A	VE01		1	
2987	CHLOROSILANES, CORROSIVE, N.O.S.	8	C3	II	8	548	0	E0		PP, EP			0	
2988	CHLOROSILANES, WATER-REACTIVE, FLAMMABLE, CORROSIVE, N.O.S.	4.3	WFC	I	4.3+3+8	549	0	E0		PP, EP, EX, A	VE01	HA08	1	

UN No. or ID No.	Name and description	Class	Classification Code	Packing group	Labels	Special provisions	Limited and excepted quantities		Carriage permitted	Equipment required	Ventilation	Provisions concerning loading, unloading and carriage	Number of blue cones/lights	Remarks
3.1.2	3.1.2	2.2	2.2	2.1.1.3	5.2.2	3.3	3.4	3.5.1.2	3.2.1	8.1.5	7.1.6	7.1.6	7.1.5	3.2.1
(1)	(2)	(3a)	(3b)	(4)	(5)	(6)	(7a)	(7b)	(8)	(9)	(10)	(11)	(12)	(13)
2989	LEAD PHOSPHITE, DIBASIC	4.1	F3	II	4.1		1 kg	E2		PP			1	
2989	LEAD PHOSPHITE, DIBASIC	4.1	F3	III	4.1		5 kg	E1		PP			0	
2990	LIFE-SAVING APPLIANCES, SELF-INFLATING	9	M5		9	296 635	0	E0		PP			0	
2991	CARBAMATE PESTICIDE, LIQUID, TOXIC, FLAMMABLE, flash-point not less than 23 °C	6.1	TF2	I	6.1+3	61 274 802	0	E5		PP, EP, EX, TOX, A	VE01, VE02		2	
2991	CARBAMATE PESTICIDE, LIQUID, TOXIC, FLAMMABLE, flash-point not less than 23 °C	6.1	TF2	II	6.1+3	61 274 802	100 ml	E4		PP, EP, EX, TOX, A	VE01, VE02		2	
2991	CARBAMATE PESTICIDE, LIQUID, TOXIC, FLAMMABLE, flash-point not less than 23 °C	6.1	TF2	III	6.1+3	61 274 802	5 L	E1		PP, EP, EX, TOX, A	VE01, VE02		0	
2992	CARBAMATE PESTICIDE, LIQUID, TOXIC	6.1	T6	I	6.1	61 274 648 802	0	E5		PP, EP, TOX, A	VE02		2	
2992	CARBAMATE PESTICIDE, LIQUID, TOXIC	6.1	T6	II	6.1	61 274 648 802	100 ml	E4		PP, EP, TOX, A	VE02		2	
2992	CARBAMATE PESTICIDE, LIQUID, TOXIC	6.1	T6	III	6.1	61 274 648 802	5 L	E1		PP, EP, TOX, A	VE02		0	
2993	ARSENICAL PESTICIDE, LIQUID, TOXIC, FLAMMABLE, flash-point not less than 23 °C	6.1	TF2	I	6.1+3	61 274 802	0	E5		PP, EP, EX, TOX, A	VE01, VE02		2	
2993	ARSENICAL PESTICIDE, LIQUID, TOXIC, FLAMMABLE, flash-point not less than 23 °C	6.1	TF2	II	6.1+3	61 274 802	100 ml	E4		PP, EP, EX, TOX, A	VE01, VE02		2	
2993	ARSENICAL PESTICIDE, LIQUID, TOXIC, FLAMMABLE, flash-point not less than 23 °C	6.1	TF2	III	6.1+3	61 274 802	5 L	E1		PP, EP, EX, TOX, A	VE01, VE02		0	
2994	ARSENICAL PESTICIDE, LIQUID, TOXIC	6.1	T6	I	6.1	61 274 648 802	0	E5		PP, EP, TOX, A	VE02		2	
2994	ARSENICAL PESTICIDE, LIQUID, TOXIC	6.1	T6	II	6.1	61 274 648 802	100 ml	E4		PP, EP, TOX, A	VE02		2	
2994	ARSENICAL PESTICIDE, LIQUID, TOXIC	6.1	T6	III	6.1	61 274 648 802	5 L	E1		PP, EP, TOX, A	VE02		0	

UN No. or ID No.	Name and description	Class	Classification Code	Packing group	Labels	Special provisions	Limited and excepted quantities		Carriage permitted	Equipment required	Ventilation	Provisions concerning loading, unloading and carriage	Number of blue cones/ lights	Remarks
							3.4	3.5.1.2	3.2.1	8.1.5	7.1.6	7.1.6	7.1.5	3.2.1
(1)	(2)	(3a)	(3b)	(4)	(5)	(6)	(7a)	(7b)	(8)	(9)	(10)	(11)	(12)	(13)
2995	ORGANOCHLORINE PESTICIDE, LIQUID, TOXIC, FLAMMABLE, flash-point not less than 23 °C	6.1	TF2	I	6.1+3	61 274 802	0	E5		PP, EP, EX, TOX, A	VE01, VE02		2	
2995	ORGANOCHLORINE PESTICIDE, LIQUID, TOXIC, FLAMMABLE, flash-point not less than 23 °C	6.1	TF2	II	6.1+3	61 274 802	100 ml	E4		PP, EP, EX, TOX, A	VE01, VE02		2	
2995	ORGANOCHLORINE PESTICIDE, LIQUID, TOXIC, FLAMMABLE, flash-point not less than 23 °C	6.1	TF2	III	6.1+3	61 274 802	5 L	E1		PP, EP, EX, TOX, A	VE01, VE02		0	
2996	ORGANOCHLORINE PESTICIDE, LIQUID, TOXIC	6.1	T6	I	6.1	61 274 648 802	0	E5		PP, EP, TOX, A	VE02		2	
2996	ORGANOCHLORINE PESTICIDE, LIQUID, TOXIC	6.1	T6	II	6.1	61 274 648 802	100 ml	E4		PP, EP, TOX, A	VE02		2	
2996	ORGANOCHLORINE PESTICIDE, LIQUID, TOXIC	6.1	T6	III	6.1	61 274 648 802	5 L	E1		PP, EP, TOX, A	VE02		0	
2997	TRIAZINE PESTICIDE, LIQUID, TOXIC, FLAMMABLE, flash-point not less than 23 °C	6.1	TF2	I	6.1+3	61 274 802	0	E5		PP, EP, EX, TOX, A	VE01, VE02		2	
2997	TRIAZINE PESTICIDE, LIQUID, TOXIC, FLAMMABLE, flash-point not less than 23 °C	6.1	TF2	II	6.1+3	61 274 802	100 ml	E4		PP, EP, EX, TOX, A	VE01, VE02		2	
2997	TRIAZINE PESTICIDE, LIQUID, TOXIC, FLAMMABLE, flash-point not less than 23 °C	6.1	TF2	III	6.1+3	61 274 802	5 L	E1		PP, EP, EX, TOX, A	VE01, VE02		0	
2998	TRIAZINE PESTICIDE, LIQUID, TOXIC	6.1	T6	I	6.1	61 274 648 802	0	E5		PP, EP, TOX, A	VE02		2	
2998	TRIAZINE PESTICIDE, LIQUID, TOXIC	6.1	T6	II	6.1	61 274 648 802	100 ml	E4		PP, EP, TOX, A	VE02		2	
2998	TRIAZINE PESTICIDE, LIQUID, TOXIC	6.1	T6	III	6.1	61 274 648 802	5 L	E1		PP, EP, TOX, A	VE02		0	
3005	THIOCARBAMATE PESTICIDE, LIQUID, TOXIC, FLAMMABLE, flash-point not less than 23 °C	6.1	TF2	I	6.1+3	61 274 802	0	E5		PP, EP, EX, TOX, A	VE01, VE02		2	

UN No. or ID No.	Name and description	Class	Classification Code	Packing group	Labels	Special provisions	Limited and excepted quantities		Carriage permitted	Equipment required	Venti- lation	Provisions concerning loading, unloading and carriage	Number of blue cones/ lights	Remarks
							3.4	3.5.1.2						
3.1.2	3.1.2	2.2	2.2	2.1.1.3	5.2.2	3.3			3.2.1	8.1.5	7.1.6	7.1.6	7.1.5	3.2.1
(1)	(2)	(3a)	(3b)	(4)	(5)	(6)	(7a)	(7b)	(8)	(9)	(10)	(11)	(12)	(13)
3005	THIOCARBAMATE PESTICIDE, LIQUID, TOXIC, FLAMMABLE, flash-point not less than 23 °C	6.1	TF2	II	6.1+3	61 274 802	100 ml	E4		PP, EP, EX, TOX, A	VE01, VE02		2	
3005	THIOCARBAMATE PESTICIDE, LIQUID, TOXIC, FLAMMABLE, flash-point not less than 23 °C	6.1	TF2	III	6.1+3	61 274 802	5 L	E1		PP, EP, EX, TOX, A	VE01, VE02		0	
3006	THIOCARBAMATE PESTICIDE, LIQUID, TOXIC	6.1	T6	I	6.1	61 274 648 802	0	E5		PP, EP, TOX, A	VE02		2	
3006	THIOCARBAMATE PESTICIDE, LIQUID, TOXIC	6.1	T6	II	6.1	61 274 648 802	100 ml	E4		PP, EP, TOX, A	VE02		2	
3006	THIOCARBAMATE PESTICIDE, LIQUID, TOXIC	6.1	T6	III	6.1	61 274 648 802	5 L	E1		PP, EP, TOX, A	VE02		0	
3009	COPPER BASED PESTICIDE, LIQUID, TOXIC, FLAMMABLE, flash-point not less than 23 °C	6.1	TF2	I	6.1+3	61 274 802	0	E5		PP, EP, EX, TOX, A	VE01, VE02		2	
3009	COPPER BASED PESTICIDE, LIQUID, TOXIC, FLAMMABLE, flash-point not less than 23 °C	6.1	TF2	II	6.1+3	61 274 802	100 ml	E4		PP, EP, EX, TOX, A	VE01, VE02		2	
3009	COPPER BASED PESTICIDE, LIQUID, TOXIC, FLAMMABLE, flash-point not less than 23 °C	6.1	TF2	III	6.1+3	61 274 648 802	5 L	E1		PP, EP, EX, TOX, A	VE01, VE02		0	
3010	COPPER BASED PESTICIDE, LIQUID, TOXIC	6.1	T6	I	6.1	61 274 648 802	0	E5		PP, EP, TOX, A	VE02		2	
3010	COPPER BASED PESTICIDE, LIQUID, TOXIC	6.1	T6	II	6.1	61 274 648 802	100 ml	E4		PP, EP, TOX, A	VE02		2	
3010	COPPER BASED PESTICIDE, LIQUID, TOXIC	6.1	T6	III	6.1	61 274 648 802	5 L	E1		PP, EP, TOX, A	VE02		0	
3011	MERCURY BASED PESTICIDE, LIQUID, TOXIC, FLAMMABLE, flash-point not less than 23 °C	6.1	TF2	I	6.1+3	61 274 802	0	E5		PP, EP, EX, TOX, A	VE01, VE02		2	
3011	MERCURY BASED PESTICIDE, LIQUID, TOXIC, FLAMMABLE, flash-point not less than 23 °C	6.1	TF2	II	6.1+3	61 274 802	100 ml	E4		PP, EP, EX, TOX, A	VE01, VE02		2	
3011	MERCURY BASED PESTICIDE, LIQUID, TOXIC, FLAMMABLE, flash-point not less than 23 °C	6.1	TF2	III	6.1+3	61 274 802	5 L	E1		PP, EP, EX, TOX, A	VE01, VE02		0	

UN No. or ID No.	Name and description	Class	Classification Code	Packing group	Labels	Special provisions	Limited and excepted quantities		Carriage permitted	Equipment required	Ventilation	Provisions concerning loading, unloading and carriage	Number of blue cones/lights	Remarks
	3.1.2	2.2	2.2	2.1.1.3	5.2.2	3.3	3.4	3.5.1.2	3.2.1	8.1.5	7.1.6	7.1.6	7.1.5	3.2.1
(1)	(2)	(3a)	(3b)	(4)	(5)	(6)	(7a)	(7b)	(8)	(9)	(10)	(11)	(12)	(13)
3012	MERCURY BASED PESTICIDE, LIQUID, TOXIC	6.1	T6	I	6.1	61 274 648 802	0	E5		PP, EP, TOX, A	VE02		2	
3012	MERCURY BASED PESTICIDE, LIQUID, TOXIC	6.1	T6	II	6.1	61 274 648 802	100 ml	E4		PP, EP, TOX, A	VE02		2	
3012	MERCURY BASED PESTICIDE, LIQUID, TOXIC	6.1	T6	III	6.1	61 274 648 802	5 L	E1		PP, EP, TOX, A	VE02		0	
3013	SUBSTITUTED NITROPHENOL PESTICIDE, LIQUID, TOXIC, FLAMMABLE, flash-point not less than 23 °C	6.1	TF2	I	6.1+3	61 274 802	0	E5		PP, EP, EX, TOX, A	VE01, VE02		2	
3013	SUBSTITUTED NITROPHENOL PESTICIDE, LIQUID, TOXIC, FLAMMABLE, flash-point not less than 23 °C	6.1	TF2	II	6.1+3	61 274 802	100 ml	E4		PP, EP, EX, TOX, A	VE01, VE02		2	
3013	SUBSTITUTED NITROPHENOL PESTICIDE, LIQUID, TOXIC, FLAMMABLE, flash-point not less than 23 °C	6.1	TF2	III	6.1+3	61 274 802	5 L	E1		PP, EP, EX, TOX, A	VE01, VE02		0	
3014	SUBSTITUTED NITROPHENOL PESTICIDE, LIQUID, TOXIC	6.1	T6	I	6.1	61 274 648 802	0	E5		PP, EP, TOX, A	VE02		2	
3014	SUBSTITUTED NITROPHENOL PESTICIDE, LIQUID, TOXIC	6.1	T6	II	6.1	61 274 648 802	100 ml	E4		PP, EP, TOX, A	VE02		2	
3014	SUBSTITUTED NITROPHENOL PESTICIDE, LIQUID, TOXIC	6.1	T6	III	6.1	61 274 648 802	5 L	E1		PP, EP, TOX, A	VE02		0	
3015	BIPYRIDILIUM PESTICIDE, LIQUID, TOXIC, FLAMMABLE, flash-point not less than 23 °C	6.1	TF2	I	6.1+3	61 274 802	0	E5		PP, EP, EX, TOX, A	VE01, VE02		2	
3015	BIPYRIDILIUM PESTICIDE, LIQUID, TOXIC, FLAMMABLE, flash-point not less than 23 °C	6.1	TF2	II	6.1+3	61 274 802	100 ml	E4		PP, EP, EX, TOX, A	VE01, VE02		2	
3015	BIPYRIDILIUM PESTICIDE, LIQUID, TOXIC, FLAMMABLE, flash-point not less than 23 °C	6.1	TF2	III	6.1+3	61 274 802	5 L	E1		PP, EP, EX, TOX, A	VE01, VE02		0	
3016	BIPYRIDILIUM PESTICIDE, LIQUID, TOXIC	6.1	T6	I	6.1	61 274 648 802	0	E5		PP, EP, TOX, A	VE02		2	

(1)	(2)	(3a)	(3b)	(4)	(5)	(6)	(7a)	(7b)	(8)	(9)	(10)	(11)	(12)	(13)
UN No. or ID No.	Name and description	Class	Classification Code	Packing group	Labels	Special provisions	Limited and excepted quantities		Carriage permitted	Equipment required	Ventilation	Provisions concerning loading, unloading and carriage	Number of blue cones/ lights	Remarks
	3.1.2	2.2	2.2	2.1.1.3	5.2.2	3.3	3.4	3.5.1.2	3.2.1	8.1.5	7.1.6	7.1.6	7.1.5	3.2.1
(1)	(2)	(3a)	(3b)	(4)	(5)	(6)	(7a)	(7b)	(8)	(9)	(10)	(11)	(12)	(13)
3016	BIPYRIDILIUM PESTICIDE, LIQUID, TOXIC	6.1	T6	II	6.1	61 274 648 802	100 ml	E4		PP, EP, TOX, A	VE02		2	
3016	BIPYRIDILIUM PESTICIDE, LIQUID, TOXIC	6.1	T6	III	6.1	61 274 648 802	5 L	E1		PP, EP, TOX, A	VE02		0	
3017	ORGANOPHOSPHORUS PESTICIDE, LIQUID, TOXIC, FLAMMABLE, flash-point not less than 23 °C	6.1	TF2	I	6.1+3	61 274 802	0	E5		PP, EP, EX, TOX, A	VE01, VE02		2	
3017	ORGANOPHOSPHORUS PESTICIDE, LIQUID, TOXIC, FLAMMABLE, flash-point not less than 23 °C	6.1	TF2	II	6.1+3	61 274 802	100 ml	E4		PP, EP, EX, TOX, A	VE01, VE02		2	
3017	ORGANOPHOSPHORUS PESTICIDE, LIQUID, TOXIC, FLAMMABLE, flash-point not less than 23 °C	6.1	TF2	III	6.1+3	61 274 802	5 L	E1		PP, EP, EX, TOX, A	VE01, VE02		0	
3018	ORGANOPHOSPHORUS PESTICIDE, LIQUID, TOXIC	6.1	T6	I	6.1	61 274 648 802	0	E5		PP, EP, TOX, A	VE02		2	
3018	ORGANOPHOSPHORUS PESTICIDE, LIQUID, TOXIC	6.1	T6	II	6.1	61 274 648 802	100 ml	E4		PP, EP, TOX, A	VE02		2	
3018	ORGANOPHOSPHORUS PESTICIDE, LIQUID, TOXIC	6.1	T6	III	6.1	61 274 648 802	5 L	E1		PP, EP, TOX, A	VE02		0	
3019	ORGANOTIN PESTICIDE, LIQUID, TOXIC, FLAMMABLE, flash-point not less than 23 °C	6.1	TF2	I	6.1+3	61 274 802	0	E5		PP, EP, EX, TOX, A	VE01, VE02		2	
3019	ORGANOTIN PESTICIDE, LIQUID, TOXIC, FLAMMABLE, flash-point not less than 23 °C	6.1	TF2	II	6.1+3	61 274 802	100 ml	E4		PP, EP, EX, TOX, A	VE01, VE02		2	
3019	ORGANOTIN PESTICIDE, LIQUID, TOXIC, FLAMMABLE, flash-point not less than 23 °C	6.1	TF2	III	6.1+3	61 274 802	5 L	E1		PP, EP, EX, TOX, A	VE01, VE02		0	
3020	ORGANOTIN PESTICIDE, LIQUID, TOXIC	6.1	T6	I	6.1	61 274 648 802	0	E5		PP, EP, TOX, A	VE02		2	
3020	ORGANOTIN PESTICIDE, LIQUID, TOXIC	6.1	T6	II	6.1	61 274 648 802	100 ml	E4		PP, EP, TOX, A	VE02		2	

UN No. or ID No. (1)	Name and description (2)	Class (3a)	Classification Code (3b)	Packing group (4)	Labels (5)	Special provisions (6)	Limited quantities 3.4 (7a)	Excepted quantities 3.5.1.2 (7b)	Carriage permitted (8)	Equipment required (9)	Ventilation (10)	Provisions concerning loading, unloading and carriage (11)	Number of blue cones/lights (12)	Remarks (13)
3020	ORGANOTIN PESTICIDE, LIQUID, TOXIC	6.1	T6	III	6.1	61 274 648 802	5 L	E1		PP, EP, TOX, A	VE02		0	
3021	PESTICIDE, LIQUID, FLAMMABLE, TOXIC, N.O.S., flash-point less than 23 °C	3	FT2	I	3+6.1	61 274 802	0	E0		PP, EP, EX, TOX, A	VE01, VE02		2	
3021	PESTICIDE, LIQUID, FLAMMABLE, TOXIC, N.O.S., flash-point less than 23 °C	3	FT2	II	3+6.1	61 274 802	1 L	E2		PP, EP, EX, TOX, A	VE01, VE02		2	
3022	1,2-BUTYLENE OXIDE, STABILIZED	3	F1	II	3	386 676	1 L	E2		PP, EX, A	VE01		1	
3023	2-METHYL-2-HEPTANETHIOL	6.1	TF1	I	6.1+3	354 802	0	E0		PP, EP, EX, TOX, A	VE01, VE02		2	
3024	COUMARIN DERIVATIVE PESTICIDE, LIQUID, FLAMMABLE, TOXIC, flash-point less than 23 °C	3	FT2	I	3+6.1	61 274 802	0	E0		PP, EP, EX, TOX, A	VE01, VE02		2	
3024	COUMARIN DERIVATIVE PESTICIDE, LIQUID, FLAMMABLE, TOXIC, flash-point less than 23 °C	3	FT2	II	3+6.1	61 274 802	1 L	E2		PP, EP, EX, TOX, A	VE01, VE02		2	
3025	COUMARIN DERIVATIVE PESTICIDE, LIQUID, TOXIC, FLAMMABLE, flash-point not less than 23 °C	6.1	TF2	I	6.1+3	61 274 802	0	E5		PP, EP, EX, TOX, A	VE01, VE02		2	
3025	COUMARIN DERIVATIVE PESTICIDE, LIQUID, TOXIC, FLAMMABLE, flash-point not less than 23 °C	6.1	TF2	II	6.1+3	61 274 802	100 ml	E4		PP, EP, EX, TOX, A	VE01, VE02		2	
3025	COUMARIN DERIVATIVE PESTICIDE, LIQUID, TOXIC, FLAMMABLE, flash-point not less than 23 °C	6.1	TF2	III	6.1+3	61 274 802	5 L	E1		PP, EP, EX, TOX, A	VE01, VE02		0	
3026	COUMARIN DERIVATIVE PESTICIDE, LIQUID, TOXIC	6.1	T6	I	6.1	61 274 648 802	0	E5		PP, EP, TOX, A	VE02		2	
3026	COUMARIN DERIVATIVE PESTICIDE, LIQUID, TOXIC	6.1	T6	II	6.1	61 274 648 802	100 ml	E4		PP, EP, TOX, A	VE02		2	
3026	COUMARIN DERIVATIVE PESTICIDE, LIQUID, TOXIC	6.1	T6	III	6.1	61 274 648 802	5 L	E1		PP, EP, TOX, A	VE02		0	
3027	COUMARIN DERIVATIVE PESTICIDE, SOLID, TOXIC	6.1	T7	I	6.1	61 274 648 802	0	E5		PP, EP			2	

UN No. or ID No. (1)	Name and description 3.1.2 (2)	Class 2.2 (3a)	Classification Code 2.2 (3b)	Packing group 2.1.1.3 (4)	Labels 5.2.2 (5)	Special provisions 3.3 (6)	Limited and excepted quantities 3.4 (7a)	3.5.1.2 (7b)	Carriage permitted 3.2.1 (8)	Equipment required 8.1.5 (9)	Ventilation 7.1.6 (10)	Provisions concerning loading, unloading and carriage 7.1.6 (11)	Number of blue cones/lights 7.1.5 (12)	Remarks 3.2.1 (13)
3027	COUMARIN DERIVATIVE PESTICIDE, SOLID, TOXIC	6.1	T7	II	6.1	61 274 648 802	500 g	E4		PP, EP			2	
3027	COUMARIN DERIVATIVE PESTICIDE, SOLID, TOXIC	6.1	T7	III	6.1	61 274 648 802	5 kg	E1		PP, EP			0	
3028	BATTERIES, DRY, CONTAINING POTASSIUM HYDROXIDE SOLID, electric storage	8	C11		8	295 304 598	2 kg	E0		PP, EP			0	
3048	ALUMINIUM PHOSPHIDE PESTICIDE	6.1	T7	I	6.1	153 648 802	0	E0		PP, EP			2	
3054	CYCLOHEXYL MERCAPTAN	3	F1	III	3		5 L	E1		PP, EX, A	VE01		0	
3055	2-(2-AMINOETHOXY)ETHANOL	8	C7	III	8		5 L	E1		PP, EP			0	
3056	n-HEPTALDEHYDE	3	F1	III	3		5 L	E1		PP, EX, A	VE01		0	
3057	TRIFLUOROACETYL CHLORIDE	2	2TC		2.3+8		0	E0		PP, EP, TOX, A	VE02		2	
3064	NITROGLYCERIN, SOLUTION IN ALCOHOL with more than 1% but not more than 5% nitroglycerin	3	D	II	3	359	0	E0		PP, EX, A	VE01		1	
3065	ALCOHOLIC BEVERAGES, with more than 70% alcohol by volume	3	F1	II	3		5 L	E2		PP, EX, A	VE01		1	
3065	ALCOHOLIC BEVERAGES, with more than 24% but not more than 70% alcohol by volume	3	F1	III	3	144 145 247	5 L	E1		PP, EX, A	VE01		0	
3066	PAINT (including paint, lacquer, enamel, stain, shellac, varnish, polish, liquid filler and liquid lacquer base) or PAINT RELATED MATERIAL (including paint thinning and reducing compound)	8	C9	II	8	163 367	1 L	E2		PP, EP			0	
3066	PAINT (including paint, lacquer, enamel, stain, shellac, varnish, polish, liquid filler and liquid lacquer base) or PAINT RELATED MATERIAL (including paint thinning and reducing compound)	8	C9	III	8	163 367	5 L	E1		PP, EP			0	
3070	ETHYLENE OXIDE AND DICHLORODIFLUORO-METHANE MIXTURE with not more than 12.5% ethylene oxide	2	2A		2.2	392 662	120 ml	E1		PP			0	
3071	MERCAPTANS, LIQUID, TOXIC, FLAMMABLE, N.O.S. or MERCAPTAN MIXTURE, LIQUID, TOXIC, FLAMMABLE, N.O.S.	6.1	TF1	II	6.1+3	274 802	100 ml	E4		PP, EP, EX, TOX, A	VE01, VE02		2	
3072	LIFE-SAVING APPLIANCES NOT SELF-INFLATING containing dangerous goods as equipment	9	M5		9	296 635	0	E0		PP			0	
3073	VINYLPYRIDINES, STABILIZED	6.1	TFC	II	6.1+3+8	386 676 802	100 ml	E4		PP, EP, EX, TOX, A	VE01, VE02		2	

UN No. or ID No.	Name and description	Class	Classification Code	Packing group	Labels	Special provisions	Limited quantities	Excepted quantities	Carriage permitted	Equipment required	Ventilation	Provisions concerning loading, unloading and carriage	Number of blue cones/lights	Remarks
(1)	(2)	(3a)	(3b)	(4)	(5)	(6)	(7a)	(7b)	(8)	(9)	(10)	(11)	(12)	(13)
	3.1.2	2.2	2.2	2.1.1.3	5.2.2	3.3	3.4	3.5.1.2	3.2.1	8.1.5	7.1.6	7.1.6	7.1.5	3.2.1
3077	ENVIRONMENTALLY HAZARDOUS SUBSTANCE, SOLID, N.O.S.	9	M7	III	9	274 335 375 601	5 kg	E1	T* B**	PP, A***			0	* Only in the molten state. ** For carriage in bulk see also 7.1.4.1. *** Only in the case of transport in bulk.
3078	CERIUM, turnings or gritty powder	4.3	W2	II	4.3	550	500 g	E2		PP, EX, A	VE01	HA08	0	
3079	METHACRYLONITRILE, STABILIZED	6.1	TF1	I	6.1+3	354 386 676 802	0	E0	T	PP, EP, EX, TOX, A	VE01, VE02		2	
3080	ISOCYANATES, TOXIC, FLAMMABLE, N.O.S. or ISOCYANATE SOLUTION, TOXIC, FLAMMABLE, N.O.S.	6.1	TF1	II	6.1+3	274 551 802	100 ml	E4		PP, EP, EX, TOX, A	VE01, VE02		2	
3082	ENVIRONMENTALLY HAZARDOUS SUBSTANCE, LIQUID, N.O.S.	9	M6	III	9	274 335 375 601	5 L	E1	T	PP			0	
3083	PERCHLORYL FLUORIDE	2	2TO		2.3+5.1		0	E0		PP, EP, TOX, A	VE02		2	
3084	CORROSIVE SOLID, OXIDIZING, N.O.S.	8	CO2	I	8+5.1	274	0	E0		PP, EP			0	
3084	CORROSIVE SOLID, OXIDIZING, N.O.S.	8	CO2	II	8+5.1	274	1 kg	E2		PP, EP			0	
3085	OXIDIZING SOLID, CORROSIVE, N.O.S.	5.1	OC2	I	5.1+8	274	0	E0		PP, EP			0	
3085	OXIDIZING SOLID, CORROSIVE, N.O.S.	5.1	OC2	II	5.1+8	274	1 kg	E2		PP, EP			0	
3085	OXIDIZING SOLID, CORROSIVE, N.O.S.	5.1	OC2	III	5.1+8	274	5 kg	E1		PP, EP			0	
3086	TOXIC SOLID, OXIDIZING, N.O.S.	6.1	TO2	I	6.1+5.1	274 802	0	E5		PP, EP			2	
3086	TOXIC SOLID, OXIDIZING, N.O.S.	6.1	TO2	II	6.1+5.1	274 802	500 g	E4		PP, EP			2	
3087	OXIDIZING SOLID, TOXIC, N.O.S.	5.1	OT2	I	5.1+6.1	274 802	0	E0		PP, EP			2	
3087	OXIDIZING SOLID, TOXIC, N.O.S.	5.1	OT2	II	5.1+6.1	274 802	1 kg	E2		PP, EP			2	
3087	OXIDIZING SOLID, TOXIC, N.O.S.	5.1	OT2	III	5.1+6.1	274 802	5 kg	E1		PP, EP			0	
3088	SELF-HEATING SOLID, ORGANIC, N.O.S.	4.2	S2	II	4.2	274	0	E2		PP			0	
3088	SELF-HEATING SOLID, ORGANIC, N.O.S.	4.2	S2	III	4.2	274 665	0	E1		PP			0	
3089	METAL POWDER, FLAMMABLE, N.O.S.	4.1	F3	II	4.1	552	1 kg	E2		PP			1	
3089	METAL POWDER, FLAMMABLE, N.O.S.	4.1	F3	III	4.1	552	5 kg	E1		PP			0	
3090	LITHIUM METAL BATTERIES (including lithium alloy batteries)	9	M4		9A	188 230 310 376 377 387 636	0	E0		PP			0	

UN No. or ID No.	Name and description	Class	Classi-fication Code	Packing group	Labels	Special provis-ions	Limited and excepted quantities		Carriage permitted	Equipment required	Venti-lation	Provisions concerning loading, unloading and carriage	Number of blue cones/ lights	Remarks
							3.4	3.5.1.2						
3.1.2	3.1.2	2.2	2.2	2.1.1.3	5.2.2	3.3			3.2.1	8.1.5	7.1.6	7.1.6	7.1.5	3.2.1
(1)	(2)	(3a)	(3b)	(4)	(5)	(6)	(7a)	(7b)	(8)	(9)	(10)	(11)	(12)	(13)
3091	LITHIUM METAL BATTERIES CONTAINED IN EQUIPMENT or LITHIUM METAL BATTERIES PACKED WITH EQUIPMENT (including lithium alloy batteries)	9	M4		9A	188 230 310 360 376 377 387 390 670	0	E0		PP			0	
3092	1-METHOXY-2-PROPANOL	3	F1	III	3	274	5 L	E1	T	PP, EX, A	VE01		0	
3093	CORROSIVE LIQUID, OXIDIZING, N.O.S.	8	CO1	I	8+5.1	274	0	E0		PP, EP			0	
3093	CORROSIVE LIQUID, OXIDIZING, N.O.S.	8	CO1	II	8+5.1	274	1 L	E2		PP, EP			0	
3094	CORROSIVE LIQUID, WATER-REACTIVE, N.O.S.	8	CW1	I	8+4.3	274	0	E0		PP, EP			0	
3094	CORROSIVE LIQUID, WATER-REACTIVE, N.O.S.	8	CW1	II	8+4.3	274	1 L	E2		PP, EP			0	
3095	CORROSIVE SOLID, SELF-HEATING, N.O.S.	8	CS2	I	8+4.2	274	0	E0		PP, EP			0	
3095	CORROSIVE SOLID, SELF-HEATING, N.O.S.	8	CS2	II	8+4.2	274	1 kg	E2		PP, EP			0	
3096	CORROSIVE SOLID, WATER-REACTIVE, N.O.S.	8	CW2	I	8+4.3	274	0	E0		PP, EP			0	
3096	CORROSIVE SOLID, WATER-REACTIVE, N.O.S.	8	CW2	II	8+4.3	274	1 kg	E2		PP, EP			0	
3097	FLAMMABLE SOLID, OXIDIZING, N.O.S.	4.1	FO						CARRIAGE PROHIBITED					
3098	OXIDIZING LIQUID, CORROSIVE, N.O.S.	5.1	OC1	I	5.1+8	274	0	E0		PP, EP			0	
3098	OXIDIZING LIQUID, CORROSIVE, N.O.S.	5.1	OC1	II	5.1+8	274	1 L	E2		PP, EP			0	
3098	OXIDIZING LIQUID, CORROSIVE, N.O.S.	5.1	OC1	III	5.1+8	274	5 L	E1		PP, EP			0	
3099	OXIDIZING LIQUID, TOXIC, N.O.S.	5.1	OT1	I	5.1+6.1	274 802	0	E0		PP, EP, TOX, A	VE02		2	
3099	OXIDIZING LIQUID, TOXIC, N.O.S.	5.1	OT1	II	5.1+6.1	274 802	1 L	E2		PP, EP, TOX, A	VE02		2	
3099	OXIDIZING LIQUID, TOXIC, N.O.S.	5.1	OT1	III	5.1+6.1	274 802	5 L	E1		PP, EP, TOX, A	VE02		0	
3100	OXIDIZING SOLID, SELF-HEATING, N.O.S.	5.1	OS						CARRIAGE PROHIBITED					
3101	ORGANIC PEROXIDE TYPE B, LIQUID	5.2	P1		5.2+1	122 181 274	25 ml	E0		PP, EX, A	VE01	HA01, HA10	3	
3102	ORGANIC PEROXIDE TYPE B, SOLID	5.2	P1		5.2+1	122 181 274	100 g	E0		PP, EX, A	VE01	HA01, HA10	3	
3103	ORGANIC PEROXIDE TYPE C, LIQUID	5.2	P1		5.2	122 274	25 ml	E0		PP, EX, A	VE01		0	
3104	ORGANIC PEROXIDE TYPE C, SOLID	5.2	P1		5.2	122 274	100 g	E0		PP, EX, A	VE01		0	
3105	ORGANIC PEROXIDE TYPE D, LIQUID	5.2	P1		5.2	122 274	125 ml	E0		PP, EX, A	VE01		0	
3106	ORGANIC PEROXIDE TYPE D, SOLID	5.2	P1		5.2	122 274	500 g	E0		PP, EX, A	VE01		0	
3107	ORGANIC PEROXIDE TYPE E, LIQUID	5.2	P1		5.2	122 274	125 ml	E0		PP, EX, A	VE01		0	
3108	ORGANIC PEROXIDE TYPE E, SOLID	5.2	P1		5.2	122 274	500 g	E0		PP, EX, A	VE01		0	

UN No. or ID No.	Name and description	Class	Classi-fication Code	Packing group	Labels	Special provis-ions	Limited and excepted quantities		Carriage permitted	Equipment required	Venti-lation	Provisions concerning loading, unloading and carriage	Number of blue cones/ lights	Remarks
							3.4	3.5.1.2						
3.1.2	3.1.2	2.2	2.2	2.1.1.3	5.2.2	3.3	(7a)	(7b)	3.2.1	8.1.5	7.1.6	7.1.6	7.1.5	3.2.1
(1)	(2)	(3a)	(3b)	(4)	(5)	(6)			(8)	(9)	(10)	(11)	(12)	(13)
3109	ORGANIC PEROXIDE TYPE F, LIQUID	5.2	P1		5.2	122 274	125 ml	E0		PP, EX, A	VE01		0	
3110	ORGANIC PEROXIDE TYPE F, SOLID	5.2	P1		5.2	122 274	500 g	E0		PP, EX, A	VE01		0	
3111	ORGANIC PEROXIDE TYPE B, LIQUID, TEMPERATURE CONTROLLED	5.2	P2		5.2+1	122 181 274	0	E0		PP, EX, A	VE01	HA01, HA10	3	
3112	ORGANIC PEROXIDE TYPE B, SOLID, TEMPERATURE CONTROLLED	5.2	P2		5.2+1	122 181 274	0	E0		PP, EX, A	VE01	HA01, HA10	3	
3113	ORGANIC PEROXIDE TYPE C, LIQUID, TEMPERATURE CONTROLLED	5.2	P2		5.2	122 274	0	E0		PP, EX, A	VE01		0	
3114	ORGANIC PEROXIDE TYPE C, SOLID, TEMPERATURE CONTROLLED	5.2	P2		5.2	122 274	0	E0		PP, EX, A	VE01		0	
3115	ORGANIC PEROXIDE TYPE D, LIQUID, TEMPERATURE CONTROLLED	5.2	P2		5.2	122 274	0	E0		PP, EX, A	VE01		0	
3116	ORGANIC PEROXIDE TYPE D, SOLID, TEMPERATURE CONTROLLED	5.2	P2		5.2	122 274	0	E0		PP, EX, A	VE01		0	
3117	ORGANIC PEROXIDE TYPE E, LIQUID, TEMPERATURE CONTROLLED	5.2	P2		5.2	122 274	0	E0		PP, EX, A	VE01		0	
3118	ORGANIC PEROXIDE TYPE E, SOLID, TEMPERATURE CONTROLLED	5.2	P2		5.2	122 274	0	E0		PP, EX, A	VE01		0	
3119	ORGANIC PEROXIDE TYPE F, LIQUID, TEMPERATURE CONTROLLED	5.2	P2		5.2	122 274	0	E0		PP, EX, A	VE01		0	
3120	ORGANIC PEROXIDE TYPE F, SOLID, TEMPERATURE CONTROLLED	5.2	P2		5.2	122 274	0	E0		PP, EX, A	VE01		0	
3121	OXIDIZING SOLID, WATER-REACTIVE, N.O.S.	5.1	OW						CARRIAGE PROHIBITED					
3122	TOXIC LIQUID, OXIDIZING, N.O.S.	6.1	TO1	I	6.1+5.1	274 315 802	0	E0		PP, EP, TOX, A	VE02		2	
		6.1	TO1	II	6.1+5.1	274 802	100 ml	E4		PP, EP, TOX, A	VE02		2	
3123	TOXIC LIQUID, WATER-REACTIVE, N.O.S.	6.1	TW1	I	6.1+4.3	274 315 802	0	E0		PP, EP, TOX, A	VE02		2	
		6.1	TW1	II	6.1+4.3	274 802	100 ml	E4		PP, EP, TOX, A	VE02		2	
3124	TOXIC SOLID, SELF-HEATING, N.O.S.	6.1	TS	I	6.1+4.2	274 802	0	E5		PP, EP			2	
3124	TOXIC SOLID, SELF-HEATING, N.O.S.	6.1	TS	II	6.1+4.2	274 802	0	E4		PP, EP			2	
3125	TOXIC SOLID, WATER-REACTIVE, N.O.S.	6.1	TW2	I	6.1+4.3	274 802	0	E5		PP, EP			2	
3125	TOXIC SOLID, WATER-REACTIVE, N.O.S.	6.1	TW2	II	6.1+4.3	274 802	500 g	E4		PP, EP			2	
3126	SELF-HEATING SOLID, CORROSIVE, ORGANIC, N.O.S.	4.2	SC2	II	4.2+8	274	0	E2		PP, EP			0	

UN No. or ID No.	Name and description	Class	Classification Code	Packing group	Labels	Special provisions	Limited and excepted quantities		Carriage permitted	Equipment required	Ventilation	Provisions concerning loading, unloading and carriage	Number of blue cones/lights	Remarks
		2.2	2.2	2.1.1.3	5.2.2	3.3	3.4	3.5.1.2	3.2.1	8.1.5	7.1.6	7.1.6	7.1.5	3.2.1
(1)	(2)	(3a)	(3b)	(4)	(5)	(6)	(7a)	(7b)	(8)	(9)	(10)	(11)	(12)	(13)
3126	SELF-HEATING SOLID, CORROSIVE, ORGANIC, N.O.S.	4.2	SC2	III	4.2+8	274	0	E1		PP, EP			0	
3127	SELF-HEATING SOLID, OXIDIZING, N.O.S.	4.2	SO						CARRIAGE PROHIBITED					
3128	SELF-HEATING SOLID, TOXIC, ORGANIC, N.O.S.	4.2	ST2	II	4.2+6.1	274 802	0	E2		PP, EP			2	
3128	SELF-HEATING SOLID, TOXIC, ORGANIC, N.O.S.	4.2	ST2	III	4.2+6.1	274 802	0	E1		PP, EP			0	
3129	WATER-REACTIVE LIQUID, CORROSIVE, N.O.S.	4.3	WC1	I	4.3+8	274	0	E0		PP, EP, EX, A	VE01	HA08	0	
3129	WATER-REACTIVE LIQUID, CORROSIVE, N.O.S.	4.3	WC1	II	4.3+8	274	500 ml	E0		PP, EP, EX, A	VE01	HA08	0	
3129	WATER-REACTIVE LIQUID, CORROSIVE, N.O.S.	4.3	WC1	III	4.3+8	274	1 L	E1		PP, EP, EX, A	VE01	HA08	0	
3130	WATER-REACTIVE LIQUID, TOXIC, N.O.S.	4.3	WT1	I	4.3+6.1	274	0	E0		PP, EP, EX, TOX, A	VE01, VE02	HA08	2	
3130	WATER-REACTIVE LIQUID, TOXIC, N.O.S.	4.3	WT1	II	4.3+6.1	274 802	500 ml	E0		PP, EP, EX, TOX, A	VE01, VE02	HA08	2	
3130	WATER-REACTIVE LIQUID, TOXIC, N.O.S.	4.3	WT1	III	4.3+6.1	274 802	1 L	E1		PP, EP, EX, TOX, A	VE01, VE02	HA08	0	
3131	WATER-REACTIVE SOLID, CORROSIVE, N.O.S.	4.3	WC2	I	4.3+8	274	0	E0		PP, EP, EX, A	VE01	HA08	0	
3131	WATER-REACTIVE SOLID, CORROSIVE, N.O.S.	4.3	WC2	II	4.3+8	274	500 g	E2		PP, EP, EX, A	VE01	HA08	0	
3131	WATER-REACTIVE SOLID, CORROSIVE, N.O.S.	4.3	WC2	III	4.3+8	274	1 kg	E1		PP, EP, EX, A	VE01	HA08	0	
3132	WATER-REACTIVE SOLID, FLAMMABLE, N.O.S.	4.3	WF2	I	4.3+4.1	274	0	E0		PP,EX,A	VE01	HA08	1	
3132	WATER-REACTIVE SOLID, FLAMMABLE, N.O.S.	4.3	WF2	II	4.3+4.1	274	500 g	E2		PP,EX,A	VE01	HA08	1	
3133	WATER-REACTIVE SOLID, OXIDIZING, N.O.S.	4.3	WO	III	4.3+4.1	274	1 kg	E1		PP,EX,A	VE01	HA08	0	
3134	WATER-REACTIVE SOLID, TOXIC, N.O.S.	4.3	WT2	I	4.3+6.1	274 802	0	E0		PP, EP, EX, TOX, A	VE01	HA08	2	
3134	WATER-REACTIVE SOLID, TOXIC, N.O.S.	4.3	WT2	II	4.3+6.1	274 802	500 g	E2		PP, EP, EX, TOX, A	VE01	HA08	2	
3134	WATER-REACTIVE SOLID, TOXIC, N.O.S.	4.3	WT2	III	4.3+6.1	274 802	1 kg	E1		PP, EP, EX, TOX, A	VE01	HA08	0	
3135	WATER-REACTIVE SOLID, SELF-HEATING, N.O.S.	4.3	WS	I	4.3+4.2	274	0	E0		PP,EX,A	VE01	HA08	0	
3135	WATER-REACTIVE SOLID, SELF-HEATING, N.O.S.	4.3	WS	II	4.3+4.2	274	0	E2		PP,EX,A	VE01	HA08	0	
3135	WATER-REACTIVE SOLID, SELF-HEATING, N.O.S.	4.3	WS	III	4.3+4.2	274	0	E1		PP,EX,A	VE01	HA08	0	
3136	TRIFLUOROMETHANE, REFRIGERATED LIQUID	2	3A		2.2	593	120 ml	E1		PP	VE01		0	
3137	OXIDIZING SOLID, FLAMMABLE, N.O.S.	5.1	OF						CARRIAGE PROHIBITED					
3138	ETHYLENE, ACETYLENE AND PROPYLENE MIXTURE, REFRIGERATED LIQUID containing at least 71.5% ethylene with not more than 22.5% acetylene and not more than 6% propylene	2	3F		2.1		0	E0		PP, EX, A	VE01		1	
3139	OXIDIZING LIQUID, N.O.S.	5.1	O1	I	5.1	274	0	E0		PP			0	
3139	OXIDIZING LIQUID, N.O.S.	5.1	O1	II	5.1	274	1 L	E2		PP			0	
3139	OXIDIZING LIQUID, N.O.S.	5.1	O1	III	5.1	274	5 L	E1		PP			0	
3140	ALKALOIDS, LIQUID, N.O.S. or ALKALOID SALTS, LIQUID, N.O.S.	6.1	T1	I	6.1	43 274 802	0	E5		PP, EP, TOX, A	VE02		2	
3140	ALKALOIDS, LIQUID, N.O.S. or ALKALOID SALTS, LIQUID, N.O.S.	6.1	T1	II	6.1	43 274 802	100 ml	E4		PP, EP, TOX, A	VE02		2	

UN No. or ID No. (1)	Name and description 3.1.2 (2)	Class 2.2 (3a)	Classi-fication Code 2.2 (3b)	Packing group 2.1.1.3 (4)	Labels 5.2.2 (5)	Special provisions 3.3 (6)	Limited and excepted quantities 3.4 (7a)	3.5.1.2 (7b)	Carriage permitted 3.2.1 (8)	Equipment required 8.1.5 (9)	Venti-lation 7.1.6 (10)	Provisions concerning loading, unloading and carriage 7.1.6 (11)	Number of blue cones/lights 7.1.5 (12)	Remarks 3.2.1 (13)
3140	ALKALOIDS, LIQUID, N.O.S. or ALKALOID SALTS, LIQUID, N.O.S.	6.1	T1	III	6.1	43 274 802	5 L	E1		PP, EP, TOX, A	VE02		0	
3141	ANTIMONY COMPOUND, INORGANIC, LIQUID, N.O.S.	6.1	T4	III	6.1	45 274 512 802	5 L	E1		PP, EP, TOX, A	VE02		0	
3142	DISINFECTANT, LIQUID, TOXIC, N.O.S.	6.1	T1	I	6.1	274 802	0	E5		PP, EP, TOX, A	VE02		2	
3142	DISINFECTANT, LIQUID, TOXIC, N.O.S.	6.1	T1	II	6.1	274 802	100 ml	E4		PP, EP, TOX, A	VE02		2	
3142	DISINFECTANT, LIQUID, TOXIC, N.O.S.	6.1	T1	III	6.1	274 802	5 L	E1		PP, EP, TOX, A	VE02		0	
3143	DYE, SOLID, TOXIC, N.O.S. or DYE INTERMEDIATE, SOLID, TOXIC, N.O.S.	6.1	T2	I	6.1	274 802	0	E5		PP, EP			2	
3143	DYE, SOLID, TOXIC, N.O.S. or DYE INTERMEDIATE, SOLID, TOXIC, N.O.S.	6.1	T2	II	6.1	274 802	500 g	E4		PP, EP			2	
3143	DYE, SOLID, TOXIC, N.O.S. or DYE INTERMEDIATE, SOLID, TOXIC, N.O.S.	6.1	T2	III	6.1	274 802	5 kg	E1		PP, EP			0	
3144	NICOTINE COMPOUND, LIQUID, N.O.S. or NICOTINE PREPARATION, LIQUID, N.O.S.	6.1	T1	I	6.1	43 274 802	0	E5		PP, EP, TOX, A	VE02		2	
3144	NICOTINE COMPOUND, LIQUID, N.O.S. or NICOTINE PREPARATION, LIQUID, N.O.S.	6.1	T1	II	6.1	43 274 802	100 ml	E4		PP, EP, TOX, A	VE02		2	
3144	NICOTINE COMPOUND, LIQUID, N.O.S. or NICOTINE PREPARATION, LIQUID, N.O.S.	6.1	T1	III	6.1	43 274 802	5 L	E1		PP, EP, TOX, A	VE02		0	
3145	ALKYLPHENOLS, LIQUID, N.O.S. (including C_2-C_{12} homologues)	8	C3	I	8		0	E0		PP, EP			0	
3145	ALKYLPHENOLS, LIQUID, N.O.S. (including C_2-C_{12} homologues)	8	C3	II	8		1 L	E2	T	PP, EP			0	
3145	ALKYLPHENOLS, LIQUID, N.O.S. (including C_2-C_{12} homologues)	8	C3	III	8		5 L	E1	T	PP, EP			0	
3146	ORGANOTIN COMPOUND, SOLID, N.O.S.	6.1	T3	I	6.1	43 274 802	0	E5		PP, EP			2	
3146	ORGANOTIN COMPOUND, SOLID, N.O.S.	6.1	T3	II	6.1	43 274 802	500 g	E4		PP, EP			2	
3146	ORGANOTIN COMPOUND, SOLID, N.O.S.	6.1	T3	III	6.1	43 274 802	5 kg	E1		PP, EP			0	
3147	DYE, SOLID, CORROSIVE, N.O.S. or DYE INTERMEDIATE, SOLID, CORROSIVE, N.O.S.	8	C10	I	8	274	0	E0		PP, EP			0	
3147	DYE, SOLID, CORROSIVE, N.O.S. or DYE INTERMEDIATE, SOLID, CORROSIVE, N.O.S.	8	C10	II	8	274	1 kg	E2		PP, EP			0	

UN No. or ID No.	Name and description	Class	Classification Code	Packing group	Labels	Special provisions	Limited and excepted quantities		Carriage permitted	Equipment required	Ventilation	Provisions concerning loading, unloading and carriage	Number of blue cones/lights	Remarks
	3.1.2	2.2	2.2	2.1.1.3	5.2.2	3.3	3.4	3.5.1.2	3.2.1	8.1.5	7.1.6	7.1.6	7.1.5	3.2.1
(1)	(2)	(3a)	(3b)	(4)	(5)	(6)	(7a)	(7b)	(8)	(9)	(10)	(11)	(12)	(13)
3147	DYE, SOLID, CORROSIVE, N.O.S. or DYE INTERMEDIATE, SOLID, CORROSIVE, N.O.S.	8	C10	III	8	274	5 kg	E1		PP, EP			0	
3148	WATER-REACTIVE LIQUID, N.O.S.	4.3	W1	I	4.3	274	0	E0		PP, EX, A	VE01	HA08	0	
3148	WATER-REACTIVE LIQUID, N.O.S.	4.3	W1	II	4.3	274	500 ml	E2		PP, EX, A	VE01	HA08	0	
3148	WATER-REACTIVE LIQUID, N.O.S.	4.3	W1	III	4.3	274	1 L	E1		PP, EX, A	VE01	HA08	0	
3149	HYDROGEN PEROXIDE AND PEROXYACETIC ACID MIXTURE with acid(s), water and not more than 5% peroxyacetic acid, STABILIZED	5.1	OC1	II	5.1+8	196 553	1 L	E2		PP, EP	VE01		0	
3150	DEVICES, SMALL, HYDROCARBON GAS POWERED or HYDROCARBON GAS REFILLS FOR SMALL DEVICES with release device	2	6F		2.1		0	E0		PP, EX, A	VE01		1	
3151	POLYHALOGENATED BIPHENYLS, LIQUID or HALOGENATED MONOMETHYLDIPHENYLMETHANES, LIQUID or POLYHALOGENATED TERPHENYLS, LIQUID	9	M2	II	9	203 305 802	1 L	E2		PP, EP			0	
3152	POLYHALOGENATED BIPHENYLS, SOLID or HALOGENATED MONOMETHYLDIPHENYLMETHANES, SOLID or POLYHALOGENATED TERPHENYLS, SOLID	9	M2	II	9	203 305 802	1 kg	E2		PP, EP			0	
3153	PERFLUORO(METHYL VINYL ETHER)	2	2F		2.1	662	0	E0		PP, EX, A	VE01		1	
3154	PERFLUORO(ETHYL VINYL ETHER)	2	2F		2.1	662	0	E0		PP, EX, A	VE01		1	
3155	PENTACHLOROPHENOL	6.1	T2	II	6.1	43 802	500 g	E4		PP, EP			2	
3156	COMPRESSED GAS, OXIDIZING, N.O.S.	2	1O		2.2+5.1	274 655 662	0	E0		PP			0	
3157	LIQUEFIED GAS, OXIDIZING, N.O.S.	2	2O		2.2+5.1	274 662	0	E0		PP			0	
3158	GAS, REFRIGERATED LIQUID, N.O.S.	2	3A		2.2	274 593	120 ml	E1		PP			0	
3159	1,1,1,2-TETRAFLUOROETHANE (REFRIGERANT GAS R 134a)	2	2A		2.2	662	120 ml	E1		PP			0	
3160	LIQUEFIED GAS, TOXIC, FLAMMABLE, N.O.S.	2	2TF		2.3+2.1	274	0	E0		PP, EP, EX, TOX, A	VE01, VE02		2	
3161	LIQUEFIED GAS, FLAMMABLE, N.O.S.	2	2F		2.1	274 662	0	E0		PP, EX, A	VE01		1	
3162	LIQUEFIED GAS, TOXIC, N.O.S.	2	2T		2.3	274	0	E0		PP, EP, TOX, A	VE02		2	
3163	LIQUEFIED GAS, N.O.S.	2	2A		2.2	274 392 662	120 ml	E1		PP			0	
3164	ARTICLES, PRESSURIZED, PNEUMATIC or HYDRAULIC (containing non-flammable gas)	2	6A		2.2	283 371 594	120 ml	E0		PP			0	
3165	AIRCRAFT HYDRAULIC POWER UNIT FUEL TANK (containing a mixture of anhydrous hydrazine and methylhydrazine) (M86 fuel)	3	FTC	I	3+6.1+8	802	0	E0		PP, EP, EX, TOX, A	VE01, VE02		2	

UN No. or ID No. (1) 3.1.2	Name and description (2) 3.1.2	Class (3a) 2.2	Classi-fication Code (3b) 2.2	Packing group (4) 2.1.1.3	Labels (5) 5.2.2	Special provisions (6) 3.3	Limited quantities (7a) 3.4	excepted quantities (7b) 3.5.1.2	Carriage permitted (8) 3.2.1	Equipment required (9) 8.1.5	Ventilation (10) 7.1.6	Provisions concerning loading, unloading and carriage (11) 7.1.6		Number of blue cones/lights (12) 7.1.5	Remarks (13) 3.2.1
3166	VEHICLE, FLAMMABLE GAS POWERED or VEHICLE, FLAMMABLE LIQUID POWERED or VEHICLE, FUEL CELL, FLAMMABLE GAS POWERED or VEHICLE, FUEL CELL, FLAMMABLE LIQUID POWERED	9	M11			388 666 667 669				PP				0	
3167	GAS SAMPLE, NON-PRESSURIZED, FLAMMABLE, N.O.S., not refrigerated liquid	2	7F		2.1		0	E0		PP, EX, A	VE01			1	
3168	GAS SAMPLE, NON-PRESSURIZED, TOXIC, FLAMMABLE, N.O.S., not refrigerated liquid	2	7TF		2.3+2.1		0	E0		PP, EP, EX, TOX, A	VE01, VE02			2	
3169	GAS SAMPLE, NON-PRESSURIZED, TOXIC, N.O.S., not refrigerated liquid	2	7T		2.3		0	E0		PP, EP, TOX, A	VE02			2	
3170	ALUMINIUM SMELTING BY-PRODUCTS or ALUMINIUM REMELTING BY-PRODUCTS	4.3	W2	II	4.3	244	500 g	E2		PP, EX, A	VE01	HA08		0	
3170	ALUMINIUM SMELTING BY-PRODUCTS or ALUMINIUM REMELTING BY-PRODUCTS	4.3	W2	III	4.3	244	1 kg	E1	B	PP, EX, A	VE01, VE03	LO03 HA07, HA08	IN01, IN02, IN03	0	VE03, LO03, HA07, IN01, IN02 and IN03 apply only when this substance is carried in bulk or without packaging
3171	BATTERY POWERED VEHICLE or BATTERY POWERED EQUIPMENT	9	M11			388 666 667 669				PP				0	
3172	TOXINS, EXTRACTED FROM LIVING SOURCES, LIQUID, N.O.S.	6.1	T1	I	6.1	210 274 802	0	E5		PP, EP, TOX, A	VE02			2	
3172	TOXINS, EXTRACTED FROM LIVING SOURCES, LIQUID, N.O.S.	6.1	T1	II	6.1	210 274 802	100 ml	E4		PP, EP, TOX, A	VE02			2	
3172	TOXINS, EXTRACTED FROM LIVING SOURCES, LIQUID, N.O.S.	6.1	T1	III	6.1	210 274 802	5 L	E1		PP, EP, TOX, A	VE02			0	
3174	TITANIUM DISULPHIDE	4.2	S4	III	4.2		0	E1		PP				0	
3175	SOLIDS or mixtures of solids (such as preparations and wastes) CONTAINING FLAMMABLE LIQUID, N.O.S. having a flash-point up to 60°C	4.1	F1	II	4.1	216 274 601 800	1 kg	E2	B	PP, EX, A	VE01, VE03	IN01, IN02		1	VE03, IN01 and IN02 apply only when this substance is carried in bulk or without packaging
3175	SOLIDS CONTAINING FLAMMABLE LIQUID, MOLTEN, having a flash-point up to 60°C	4.1	F1	II	4.1	216 274 601 800	1 kg	E2	T	PP, EX, A	VE01, VE03	IN01, IN02		1	VE03, IN01 and IN02 apply only when this substance is carried in bulk or without packaging
3176	FLAMMABLE SOLID, ORGANIC, MOLTEN, N.O.S.	4.1	F2	II	4.1	274	0	E0		PP				1	
3176	FLAMMABLE SOLID, ORGANIC, MOLTEN, N.O.S.	4.1	F2	III	4.1	274	0	E0		PP				0	
3178	FLAMMABLE SOLID, INORGANIC, N.O.S.	4.1	F3	II	4.1	274	1 kg	E2		PP				1	
3178	FLAMMABLE SOLID, INORGANIC, N.O.S.	4.1	F3	III	4.1	274	5 kg	E1		PP				0	
3179	FLAMMABLE SOLID, TOXIC, INORGANIC, N.O.S.	4.1	FT2	II	4.1+6.1	274 802	1 kg	E2		PP, EP				2	
3179	FLAMMABLE SOLID, TOXIC, INORGANIC, N.O.S.	4.1	FT2	III	4.1+6.1	274 802	5 kg	E1		PP, EP				0	

UN No. or ID No.	Name and description	Class	Classification Code	Packing group	Labels	Special provisions	Limited and excepted quantities		Carriage permitted	Equipment required	Ventilation	Provisions concerning loading, unloading and carriage	Number of blue cones/lights	Remarks
							3.4	3.5.1.2	3.2.1	8.1.5	7.1.6	7.1.6	7.1.5	3.2.1
(1)	(2)	(3a)	(3b)	(4)	(5)	(6)	(7a)	(7b)	(8)	(9)	(10)	(11)	(12)	(13)
3180	FLAMMABLE SOLID, CORROSIVE, INORGANIC, N.O.S.	4.1	FC2	II	4.1+8	274	1 kg	E2		PP, EP				1	
3180	FLAMMABLE SOLID, CORROSIVE, INORGANIC, N.O.S.	4.1	FC2	III	4.1+8	274	5 kg	E1		PP, EP				0	
3181	METAL SALTS OF ORGANIC COMPOUNDS, FLAMMABLE, N.O.S.	4.1	F3	II	4.1	274	1 kg	E2		PP				1	
3181	METAL SALTS OF ORGANIC COMPOUNDS, FLAMMABLE, N.O.S.	4.1	F3	III	4.1	274	5 kg	E1		PP				0	
3182	METAL HYDRIDES, FLAMMABLE, N.O.S.	4.1	F3	II	4.1	274 554	1 kg	E2		PP				1	
3182	METAL HYDRIDES, FLAMMABLE, N.O.S.	4.1	F3	III	4.1	274 554	5 kg	E1		PP				0	
3183	SELF-HEATING LIQUID, ORGANIC, N.O.S.	4.2	S1	II	4.2	274	0	E2		PP				0	
3183	SELF-HEATING LIQUID, ORGANIC, N.O.S.	4.2	S1	III	4.2	274	0	E1		PP				0	
3184	SELF-HEATING LIQUID, TOXIC, ORGANIC, N.O.S.	4.2	ST1	II	4.2+6.1	274 802	0	E2		PP, EP, TOX, A	VE02			2	
3184	SELF-HEATING LIQUID, TOXIC, ORGANIC, N.O.S.	4.2	ST1	III	4.2+6.1	274 802	0	E1		PP, EP, TOX, A	VE02			0	
3185	SELF-HEATING LIQUID, CORROSIVE, ORGANIC, N.O.S.	4.2	SC1	II	4.2+8	274	0	E2		PP, EP				0	
3185	SELF-HEATING LIQUID, CORROSIVE, ORGANIC, N.O.S.	4.2	SC1	III	4.2+8	274	0	E1		PP, EP				0	
3186	SELF-HEATING LIQUID, INORGANIC, N.O.S.	4.2	S3	II	4.2	274	0	E2		PP				0	
3186	SELF-HEATING LIQUID, INORGANIC, N.O.S.	4.2	S3	III	4.2	274	0	E1		PP				0	
3187	SELF-HEATING LIQUID, TOXIC, INORGANIC, N.O.S.	4.2	ST3	II	4.2+6.1	274 802	0	E2		PP, EP, TOX, A	VE02			2	
3187	SELF-HEATING LIQUID, TOXIC, INORGANIC, N.O.S.	4.2	ST3	III	4.2+6.1	274 802	0	E1		PP, EP, TOX, A	VE02			0	
3188	SELF-HEATING LIQUID, CORROSIVE, INORGANIC, N.O.S.	4.2	SC3	II	4.2+8	274	0	E2		PP, EP				0	
3188	SELF-HEATING LIQUID, CORROSIVE, INORGANIC, N.O.S.	4.2	SC3	III	4.2+8	274	0	E1		PP, EP				0	
3189	METAL POWDER, SELF-HEATING, N.O.S.	4.2	S4	II	4.2	274 555	0	E2		PP				0	
3189	METAL POWDER, SELF-HEATING, N.O.S.	4.2	S4	III	4.2	274 555	0	E1		PP				0	
3190	SELF-HEATING SOLID, INORGANIC, N.O.S.	4.2	S4	II	4.2	274	0	E2		PP				0	
3190	SELF-HEATING SOLID, INORGANIC, N.O.S.	4.2	S4	III	4.2	274	0	E1	B	PP				0	
3191	SELF-HEATING SOLID, TOXIC, INORGANIC, N.O.S.	4.2	ST4	II	4.2+6.1	274 802	0	E2		PP, EP				2	
3191	SELF-HEATING SOLID, TOXIC, INORGANIC, N.O.S.	4.2	ST4	III	4.2+6.1	274 802	0	E1		PP, EP				0	
3192	SELF-HEATING SOLID, CORROSIVE, INORGANIC, N.O.S.	4.2	SC4	II	4.2+8	274	0	E2		PP, EP				0	
3192	SELF-HEATING SOLID, CORROSIVE, INORGANIC, N.O.S.	4.2	SC4	III	4.2+8	274	0	E1		PP, EP				0	
3194	PYROPHORIC LIQUID, INORGANIC, N.O.S.	4.2	S3	I	4.2	274	0	E0		PP				0	
3200	PYROPHORIC SOLID, INORGANIC, N.O.S.	4.2	S4	I	4.2	274	0	E0		PP				0	

UN No. or ID No. (1) 3.1.2	Name and description (2) 3.1.2	Class (3a) 2.2	Classification Code (3b) 2.2	Packing group (4) 2.1.1.3	Labels (5) 5.2.2	Special provisions (6) 3.3	Limited and excepted quantities 3.4 (7a)	3.5.1.2 (7b)	Carriage permitted (8) 3.2.1	Equipment required (9) 8.1.5	Ventilation (10) 7.1.6	Provisions concerning loading, unloading and carriage (11) 7.1.6	Number of blue cones/lights (12) 7.1.5	Remarks (13) 3.2.1
3205	ALKALINE EARTH METAL ALCOHOLATES, N.O.S.	4.2	S4	II	4.2	183 274	0	E2		PP			0	
3205	ALKALINE EARTH METAL ALCOHOLATES, N.O.S.	4.2	S4	III	4.2	183 274	0	E1		PP			0	
3206	ALKALI METAL ALCOHOLATES, SELF-HEATING, CORROSIVE, N.O.S.	4.2	SC4	II	4.2+8	182 274	0	E2		PP, EP			0	
3206	ALKALI METAL ALCOHOLATES, SELF-HEATING, CORROSIVE, N.O.S.	4.2	SC4	III	4.2+8	182 274	0	E1		PP, EP			0	
3208	METALLIC SUBSTANCE, WATER-REACTIVE, N.O.S.	4.3	W2	I	4.3	274 557	0	E0		PP, EX, A	VE01	HA08	0	
3208	METALLIC SUBSTANCE, WATER-REACTIVE, N.O.S.	4.3	W2	II	4.3	274 557	500 g	E2		PP, EX, A	VE01	HA08	0	
3208	METALLIC SUBSTANCE, WATER-REACTIVE, N.O.S.	4.3	W2	III	4.3	274 557	1 kg	E1		PP, EX, A	VE01	HA08	0	
3209	METALLIC SUBSTANCE, WATER-REACTIVE, SELF-HEATING, N.O.S.	4.3	WS	I	4.3+4.2	274 558	0	E0		PP, EX, A	VE01	HA08	0	
3209	METALLIC SUBSTANCE, WATER-REACTIVE, SELF-HEATING, N.O.S.	4.3	WS	II	4.3+4.2	274 558	0	E0		PP, EX, A	VE01	HA08	0	
3209	METALLIC SUBSTANCE, WATER-REACTIVE, SELF-HEATING, N.O.S.	4.3	WS	III	4.3+4.2	274 558	0	E1		PP, EX, A	VE01	HA08	0	
3210	CHLORATES, INORGANIC, AQUEOUS SOLUTION, N.O.S.	5.1	O1	II	5.1	274 351	1 L	E2		PP			0	
3210	CHLORATES, INORGANIC, AQUEOUS SOLUTION, N.O.S.	5.1	O1	III	5.1	274 351	5 L	E1		PP			0	
3211	PERCHLORATES, INORGANIC, AQUEOUS SOLUTION, N.O.S.	5.1	O1	II	5.1	274 351	1 L	E2		PP			0	
3211	PERCHLORATES, INORGANIC, AQUEOUS SOLUTION, N.O.S.	5.1	O1	III	5.1		5 L	E1		PP			0	
3212	HYPOCHLORITES, INORGANIC, N.O.S.	5.1	O2	II	5.1	274 349	1 kg	E2		PP			0	
3213	BROMATES, INORGANIC, AQUEOUS SOLUTION, N.O.S.	5.1	O1	II	5.1	274 350	1 L	E2		PP			0	
3213	BROMATES, INORGANIC, AQUEOUS SOLUTION, N.O.S.	5.1	O1	III	5.1	274 350	5 L	E1		PP			0	
3214	PERMANGANATES, INORGANIC, AQUEOUS SOLUTION, N.O.S.	5.1	O1	II	5.1	274 353	1 L	E2		PP			0	
3215	PERSULPHATES, INORGANIC, N.O.S.	5.1	O2	III	5.1		5 kg	E1		PP			0	
3216	PERSULPHATES, INORGANIC, AQUEOUS SOLUTION, N.O.S.	5.1	O1	III	5.1	274 511	5 L	E1		PP			0	
3218	NITRATES, INORGANIC, AQUEOUS SOLUTION, N.O.S.	5.1	O1	II	5.1	270 511	1 L	E2		PP			0	
3218	NITRATES, INORGANIC, AQUEOUS SOLUTION, N.O.S.	5.1	O1	III	5.1	270 511	5 L	E1		PP			0	
3219	NITRITES, INORGANIC, AQUEOUS SOLUTION, N.O.S.	5.1	O1	II	5.1	103 274	1 L	E2		PP			0	
3219	NITRITES, INORGANIC, AQUEOUS SOLUTION, N.O.S.	5.1	O1	III	5.1	103 274	5 L	E1		PP			0	

UN No. or ID No.	Name and description	Class	Classification Code	Packing group	Labels	Special provisions	Limited and excepted quantities		Carriage permitted	Equipment required	Ventilation	Provisions concerning loading, unloading and carriage	Number of blue cones/lights	Remarks
							3.4	3.5.1.2	3.2.1	8.1.5	7.1.6	7.1.6	7.1.5	3.2.1
3.1.2	3.1.2	2.2	2.2	2.1.1.3	5.2.2	3.3							7.1.5	
(1)	(2)	(3a)	(3b)	(4)	(5)	(6)	(7a)	(7b)	(8)	(9)	(10)	(11)	(12)	(13)
3220	PENTAFLUOROETHANE (REFRIGERANT GAS R 125)	2	2A		2.2	662	120 ml	E1		PP			0	
3221	SELF-REACTIVE LIQUID TYPE B	4.1	SR1		4.1+1	181 194 274	25 ml	E0		PP		HA01, HA10	3	
3222	SELF-REACTIVE SOLID TYPE B	4.1	SR1		4.1+1	181 194 274	100g	E0		PP		HA01, HA10	3	
3223	SELF-REACTIVE LIQUID TYPE C	4.1	SR1		4.1	194 274	25 ml	E0		PP			0	
3224	SELF-REACTIVE SOLID TYPE C	4.1	SR1		4.1	194 274	100g	E0		PP			0	
3225	SELF-REACTIVE LIQUID TYPE D	4.1	SR1		4.1	194 274	125 ml	E0		PP			0	
3226	SELF-REACTIVE SOLID TYPE D	4.1	SR1		4.1	194 274	500 g	E0		PP			0	
3227	SELF-REACTIVE LIQUID TYPE E	4.1	SR1		4.1	194 274	125 ml	E0		PP			0	
3228	SELF-REACTIVE SOLID TYPE E	4.1	SR1		4.1	194 274	500 g	E0		PP			0	
3229	SELF-REACTIVE LIQUID TYPE F	4.1	SR1		4.1	194 274	125 ml	E0		PP			0	
3230	SELF-REACTIVE SOLID TYPE F	4.1	SR1		4.1	194 274	500 g	E0		PP			0	
3231	SELF-REACTIVE LIQUID TYPE B, TEMPERATURE CONTROLLED	4.1	SR2		4.1+1	181 194 274	0	E0		PP		HA01, HA10	3	
3232	SELF-REACTIVE SOLID TYPE B, TEMPERATURE CONTROLLED	4.1	SR2		4.1+1	181 194 274	0	E0		PP		HA01, HA10	3	
3233	SELF-REACTIVE LIQUID TYPE C, TEMPERATURE CONTROLLED	4.1	SR2		4.1	194 274	0	E0		PP			0	
3234	SELF-REACTIVE SOLID TYPE C, TEMPERATURE CONTROLLED	4.1	SR2		4.1	194 274	0	E0		PP			0	
3235	SELF-REACTIVE LIQUID TYPE D, TEMPERATURE CONTROLLED	4.1	SR2		4.1	194 274	0	E0		PP			0	
3236	SELF-REACTIVE SOLID TYPE D, TEMPERATURE CONTROLLED	4.1	SR2		4.1	194 274	0	E0		PP			0	
3237	SELF-REACTIVE LIQUID TYPE E, TEMPERATURE CONTROLLED	4.1	SR2		4.1	194 274	0	E0		PP			0	
3238	SELF-REACTIVE SOLID TYPE E, TEMPERATURE CONTROLLED	4.1	SR2		4.1	194 274	0	E0		PP			0	
3239	SELF-REACTIVE LIQUID TYPE F, TEMPERATURE CONTROLLED	4.1	SR2		4.1	194 274	0	E0		PP			0	
3240	SELF-REACTIVE SOLID TYPE F, TEMPERATURE CONTROLLED	4.1	SR2		4.1	194 274	0	E0		PP			0	
3241	2-BROMO-2-NITROPROPANE-1,3-DIOL	4.1	SR1	III	4.1	638	5 kg	E1		PP			0	

UN No. or ID No. (1)	Name and description 3.1.2 (2)	Class 2.2 (3a)	Classi-fication Code 2.2 (3b)	Packing group 2.1.1.3 (4)	Labels 5.2.2 (5)	Special provisions 3.3 (6)	Limited and excepted quantities 3.4 (7a)	3.5.1.2 (7b)	Carriage permitted 3.2.1 (8)	Equipment required 8.1.5 (9)	Venti-lation 7.1.6 (10)	Provisions concerning loading, unloading and carriage 7.1.6 (11)	Number of blue cones/lights 7.1.5 (12)	Remarks 3.2.1 (13)
3242	AZODICARBONAMIDE	4.1	SR1	II	4.1	215 638	1 kg	E0		PP			0	
3243	SOLIDS CONTAINING TOXIC LIQUID, N.O.S.	6.1	T9	II	6.1	217 274 601 802	500 g	E4		PP, EP, TOX, A	VE02		2	
3244	SOLIDS CONTAINING CORROSIVE LIQUID, N.O.S.	8	C10	II	8	218 274	1 kg	E2		PP, EP			0	
3245	GENETICALLY MODIFIED MICROORGANISMS or GENETICALLY MODIFIED ORGANISMS	9	M8		9	219 637 802	0	E0		PP			0	
3245	GENETICALLY MODIFIED MICRO-ORGANISMS or GENETICALLY MODIFIED ORGANISMS, in refrigerated liquid nitrogen	9	M8		9 +2.2	219 637 802	0	E0		PP			0	
3246	METHANESULPHONYL CHLORIDE	6.1	TC1	I	6.1+8	354 802	0	E0		PP, EP, TOX, A	VE02		2	
3247	SODIUM PEROXOBORATE, ANHYDROUS	5.1	O2	II	5.1		1 kg	E2		PP			0	
3248	MEDICINE, LIQUID, FLAMMABLE, TOXIC, N.O.S.	3	FT1	II	3+6.1	220 221 601 802	1 L	E2		PP, EP, EX, TOX, A	VE01, VE02		2	
3248	MEDICINE, LIQUID, FLAMMABLE, TOXIC, N.O.S.	3	FT1	III	3+6.1	220 221 601 802	5 L	E1		PP, EP, EX, TOX, A	VE01, VE02		0	
3249	MEDICINE, SOLID, TOXIC, N.O.S.	6.1	T2	II	6.1	221 601 802	500 g	E4		PP, EP			2	
3249	MEDICINE, SOLID, TOXIC, N.O.S.	6.1	T2	III	6.1	221 601 802	5 kg	E1		PP, EP			0	
3250	CHLOROACETIC ACID, MOLTEN	6.1	TC1	II	6.1+8	802	0	E0		PP, EP, TOX, A	VE02		2	
3251	ISOSORBIDE-5-MONONITRATE	4.1	SR1	III	4.1	226 638	5 kg	E0		PP			0	
3252	DIFLUOROMETHANE (REFRIGERANT GAS R 32)	2	2F		2.1	662	0	E0		PP, EX, A	VE01		1	
3253	DISODIUM TRIOXOSILICATE	8	C6	III	8		5 kg	E1		PP, EP			0	
3254	TRIBUTYLPHOSPHANE	4.2	S1	I	4.2		0	E0		PP			0	
3255	tert-BUTYL HYPOCHLORITE	4.2	SC1						CARRIAGE PROHIBITED					
3256	ELEVATED TEMPERATURE LIQUID, FLAMMABLE, N.O.S., at or above its flash-point above 60°C, at or above its flash-point and below 100°C	3	F2	III	3	274 560	0	E0	T	PP, EX, A	VE01		0	
3256	ELEVATED TEMPERATURE LIQUID, FLAMMABLE, N.O.S. with flash-point above 60°C, at or above its flash-point and at or above 100°C	3	F2	III	3	274 560	0	E0	T	PP, EX, A	VE01		0	
3257	ELEVATED TEMPERATURE LIQUID, N.O.S., at or above 100°C and below its flash-point (including molten metals, molten salts, etc.)	9	M9	III	9	274 643 668	0	E0	T	PP			0	

UN No. or ID No. (1)	Name and description (2)	Class (3a)	Classification Code (3b)	Packing group (4)	Labels (5)	Special provisions (6)	Limited quantities 3.4 (7a)	Excepted quantities 3.5.1.2 (7b)	Carriage permitted (8)	Equipment required (9)	Ventilation (10)	Provisions concerning loading, unloading and carriage (11)	Number of blue cones/lights (12)	Remarks (13)
3258	ELEVATED TEMPERATURE SOLID, N.O.S., at or above 240 °C	9	M10	III	9	274 643	0	E0		PP			0	
3259	AMINES, SOLID, CORROSIVE, N.O.S. or POLYAMINES, SOLID, CORROSIVE, N.O.S.	8	C8	I	8	274	0	E0		PP, EP			0	
3259	AMINES, SOLID, CORROSIVE, N.O.S. or POLYAMINES, SOLID, CORROSIVE, N.O.S.	8	C8	II	8	274	1 kg	E2		PP, EP			0	
3259	AMINES, SOLID, CORROSIVE, N.O.S. or POLYAMINES, SOLID, CORROSIVE, N.O.S.	8	C8	III	8	274	5 kg	E1	T	PP, EP			0	
3260	CORROSIVE SOLID, ACIDIC, INORGANIC, N.O.S.	8	C2	I	8	274	0	E0		PP, EP			0	
3260	CORROSIVE SOLID, ACIDIC, INORGANIC, N.O.S.	8	C2	II	8	274	1 kg	E2		PP, EP			0	
3260	CORROSIVE SOLID, ACIDIC, INORGANIC, N.O.S.	8	C2	III	8	274	5 kg	E1		PP, EP			0	
3261	CORROSIVE SOLID, ACIDIC, ORGANIC, N.O.S.	8	C4	I	8	274	0	E0		PP, EP			0	
3261	CORROSIVE SOLID, ACIDIC, ORGANIC, N.O.S.	8	C4	II	8	274	1 kg	E2		PP, EP			0	
3261	CORROSIVE SOLID, ACIDIC, ORGANIC, N.O.S.	8	C4	III	8	274	5 kg	E1		PP, EP			0	
3262	CORROSIVE SOLID, BASIC, INORGANIC, N.O.S.	8	C6	I	8	274	0	E0		PP, EP			0	
3262	CORROSIVE SOLID, BASIC, INORGANIC, N.O.S.	8	C6	II	8	274	1 kg	E2		PP, EP			0	
3262	CORROSIVE SOLID, BASIC, INORGANIC, N.O.S.	8	C6	III	8	274	5 kg	E1		PP, EP			0	
3263	CORROSIVE SOLID, BASIC, ORGANIC, N.O.S.	8	C8	I	8	274	0	E0		PP, EP			0	
3263	CORROSIVE SOLID, BASIC, ORGANIC, N.O.S.	8	C8	II	8	274	1 kg	E2		PP, EP			0	
3263	CORROSIVE SOLID, BASIC, ORGANIC, N.O.S.	8	C8	III	8	274	5 kg	E1		PP, EP			0	
3264	CORROSIVE LIQUID, ACIDIC, INORGANIC, N.O.S.	8	C1	I	8	274	0	E0	T	PP, EP			0	
3264	CORROSIVE LIQUID, ACIDIC, INORGANIC, N.O.S.	8	C1	II	8	274	1 L	E2	T	PP, EP			0	
3264	CORROSIVE LIQUID, ACIDIC, INORGANIC, N.O.S.	8	C1	III	8	274	5 L	E1	T	PP, EP			0	
3265	CORROSIVE LIQUID, ACIDIC, ORGANIC, N.O.S.	8	C3	I	8	274	0	E0	T	PP, EP			0	
3265	CORROSIVE LIQUID, ACIDIC, ORGANIC, N.O.S.	8	C3	II	8	274	1 L	E2	T	PP, EP			0	
3265	CORROSIVE LIQUID, ACIDIC, ORGANIC, N.O.S.	8	C3	III	8	274	5 L	E1	T	PP, EP			0	
3266	CORROSIVE LIQUID, BASIC, INORGANIC, N.O.S.	8	C5	I	8	274	0	E0	T	PP, EP			0	
3266	CORROSIVE LIQUID, BASIC, INORGANIC, N.O.S.	8	C5	II	8	274	1 L	E2	T	PP, EP			0	
3266	CORROSIVE LIQUID, BASIC, INORGANIC, N.O.S.	8	C5	III	8	274	5 L	E1	T	PP, EP			0	
3267	CORROSIVE LIQUID, BASIC, ORGANIC, N.O.S.	8	C7	I	8	274	0	E0	T	PP, EP			0	
3267	CORROSIVE LIQUID, BASIC, ORGANIC, N.O.S.	8	C7	II	8	274	1 L	E2	T	PP, EP			0	
3267	CORROSIVE LIQUID, BASIC, ORGANIC, N.O.S.	8	C7	III	8	274	5 L	E1	T	PP, EP			0	
3268	SAFETY DEVICES, electrically initiated	9	M5		9	280 289	0	E0		PP			0	
3269	POLYESTER RESIN KIT, liquid base material	3	F3	II	3	236 340	5 L	See SP 340		PP, EX, A	VE01		1	
3269	POLYESTER RESIN KIT, liquid base material	3	F3	III	3	236 340	5 L	See SP 340		PP, EX, A	VE01		0	
3270	NITROCELLULOSE MEMBRANE FILTERS, with not more than 12.6% nitrogen, by dry mass	4.1	F1	II	4.1	237 286	1 kg	E2		PP			1	
3271	ETHERS, N.O.S.	3	F1	II	3	274	1 L	E2	T	PP, EX, A	VE01		1	
3271	ETHERS, N.O.S.	3	F1	III	3	274	5 L	E1	T	PP, EX, A	VE01		0	
3272	ESTERS, N.O.S.	3	F1	II	3	274	1 L	E2	T	PP, EX, A	VE01		1	
3272	ESTERS, N.O.S.	3	F1	III	3	274 601	5 L	E1	T	PP, EX, A	VE01		0	
3273	NITRILES, FLAMMABLE, TOXIC, N.O.S.	3	FT1	I	3+6.1	274 802	0	E0	T	PP, EP, EX, TOX, A	VE01, VE02		2	

UN No. or ID No. (1)	Name and description 3.1.2 (2)	Class 2.2 (3a)	Classification Code 2.2 (3b)	Packing group 2.1.1.3 (4)	Labels 5.2.2 (5)	Special provisions 3.3 (6)	Limited quantities 3.4 (7a)	Excepted quantities 3.5.1.2 (7b)	Carriage permitted 3.2.1 (8)	Equipment required 8.1.5 (9)	Ventilation 7.1.6 (10)	Provisions concerning loading, unloading and carriage 7.1.6 (11)	Number of blue cones/lights 7.1.5 (12)	Remarks 3.2.1 (13)
3273	NITRILES, FLAMMABLE, TOXIC, N.O.S.	3	FT1	II	3+6.1	274 802	1 L	E2		PP, EP, EX, TOX, A	VE01, VE02		2	
3274	ALCOHOLATES SOLUTION, N.O.S. in alcohol	3	FC	II	3+8	274	1 L	E2		PP, EP, EX, A	VE01		1	
3275	NITRILES, TOXIC, FLAMMABLE, N.O.S.	6.1	TF1	I	6.1+3	274 315 802	0	E5		PP, EP, EX, TOX, A	VE01, VE02		2	
3275	NITRILES, TOXIC, FLAMMABLE, N.O.S.	6.1	TF1	II	6.1+3	274 802	100 ml	E4		PP, EP, EX, TOX, A	VE01, VE02		2	
3276	NITRILES, LIQUID, TOXIC, N.O.S.	6.1	T1	I	6.1	274 315 802	0	E5		PP, EP, TOX, A	VE02		2	
3276	NITRILES, LIQUID, TOXIC, N.O.S.	6.1	T1	II	6.1	274 802	100 ml	E4		PP, EP, TOX, A	VE02		2	
3276	NITRILES, LIQUID, TOXIC, N.O.S.	6.1	T1	III	6.1	274 802	5 L	E1	T	PP, EP, TOX, A	VE02		0	
3277	CHLOROFORMATES, TOXIC, CORROSIVE, N.O.S.	6.1	TC1	II	6.1+8	274 561 802	100 ml	E4		PP, EP, TOX, A	VE02		2	
3278	ORGANOPHOSPHORUS COMPOUND, LIQUID, TOXIC, N.O.S.	6.1	T1	I	6.1	43 274 315 802	0	E5		PP, EP, TOX, A	VE02		2	
3278	ORGANOPHOSPHORUS COMPOUND, LIQUID, TOXIC, N.O.S.	6.1	T1	II	6.1	43 274 802	100 ml	E4		PP, EP, TOX, A	VE02		2	
3278	ORGANOPHOSPHORUS COMPOUND, LIQUID, TOXIC, N.O.S.	6.1	T1	III	6.1	43 274 802	5 L	E1		PP, EP, TOX, A	VE02		0	
3279	ORGANOPHOSPHORUS COMPOUND, TOXIC, FLAMMABLE, N.O.S.	6.1	TF1	I	6.1+3	43 274 315 802	0	E5		PP, EP, EX, TOX, A	VE01, VE02		2	
3279	ORGANOPHOSPHORUS COMPOUND, TOXIC, FLAMMABLE, N.O.S.	6.1	TF1	II	6.1+3	43 274 802	100 ml	E4		PP, EP, EX, TOX, A	VE01, VE02		2	
3280	ORGANOARSENIC COMPOUND, LIQUID, N.O.S.	6.1	T3	I	6.1	274 315 802	0	E5		PP, EP, TOX, A	VE02		2	
3280	ORGANOARSENIC COMPOUND, LIQUID, N.O.S.	6.1	T3	II	6.1	274 802	100 ml	E4		PP, EP, TOX, A	VE02		2	
3280	ORGANOARSENIC COMPOUND, LIQUID, N.O.S.	6.1	T3	III	6.1	274 802	5 L	E1		PP, EP, TOX, A	VE02		0	
3281	METAL CARBONYLS, LIQUID, N.O.S.	6.1	T3	I	6.1	274 315 562 802	0	E5		PP, EP, TOX, A	VE02		2	

UN No. or ID No.	Name and description	Class	Classification Code	Packing group	Labels	Special provisions	Limited quantities	excepted quantities	Carriage permitted	Equipment required	Ventilation	Provisions concerning loading, unloading and carriage	Number of blue cones/lights	Remarks
(1)	(2)	(3a)	(3b)	(4)	(5)	(6)	(7a)	(7b)	(8)	(9)	(10)	(11)	(12)	(13)
3.1.2	3.1.2	2.2	2.2	2.1.1.3	5.2.2	3.3	3.4	3.5.1.2	3.2.1	8.1.5	7.1.6	7.1.6	7.1.5	3.2.1
3281	METAL CARBONYLS, LIQUID, N.O.S.	6.1	T3	II	6.1	274 562 802	100 ml	E4		PP, EP, TOX, A	VE02		2	
3281	METAL CARBONYLS, LIQUID, N.O.S.	6.1	T3	III	6.1	274 562 802	5 L	E1		PP, EP, TOX, A	VE02		0	
3282	ORGANOMETALLIC COMPOUND, LIQUID, TOXIC, N.O.S.	6.1	T3	I	6.1	274 562 802	0	E5		PP, EP, TOX, A	VE02		2	
3282	ORGANOMETALLIC COMPOUND, LIQUID, TOXIC, N.O.S.	6.1	T3	II	6.1	274 562 802	100 ml	E4		PP, EP, TOX, A	VE02		2	
3282	ORGANOMETALLIC COMPOUND, LIQUID, TOXIC, N.O.S.	6.1	T3	III	6.1	274 562 802	5 L	E1		PP, EP, TOX, A	VE02		0	
3283	SELENIUM COMPOUND, SOLID, N.O.S.	6.1	T5	I	6.1	274 563 802	0	E5		PP, EP			2	
3283	SELENIUM COMPOUND, SOLID, N.O.S.	6.1	T5	II	6.1	274 563 802	500 g	E4		PP, EP			2	
3283	SELENIUM COMPOUND, SOLID, N.O.S.	6.1	T5	III	6.1	274 563 802	5 kg	E1		PP, EP			0	
3284	TELLURIUM COMPOUND, N.O.S.	6.1	T5	I	6.1	274 802	0	E5		PP, EP			2	
3284	TELLURIUM COMPOUND, N.O.S.	6.1	T5	II	6.1	274 802	500 g	E4		PP, EP			2	
3284	TELLURIUM COMPOUND, N.O.S.	6.1	T5	III	6.1	274 802	5 kg	E1		PP, EP			0	
3285	VANADIUM COMPOUND, N.O.S.	6.1	T5	I	6.1	274 564 802	0	E5		PP, EP			2	
3285	VANADIUM COMPOUND, N.O.S.	6.1	T5	II	6.1	274 564 802	500 g	E4		PP, EP			2	
3285	VANADIUM COMPOUND, N.O.S.	6.1	T5	III	6.1	274 564 802	5 kg	E1		PP, EP			0	
3286	FLAMMABLE LIQUID, TOXIC, CORROSIVE, N.O.S.	3	FTC	I	3+6.1+8	274 802	0	E0	T	PP, EP, EX, TOX, A	VE01, VE02		2	
3286	FLAMMABLE LIQUID, TOXIC, CORROSIVE, N.O.S.	3	FTC	II	3+6.1+8	274 802	1 L	E2	T	PP, EP, EX, TOX, A	VE01, VE02		2	
3287	TOXIC LIQUID, INORGANIC, N.O.S.	6.1	T4	I	6.1	274 315 802	0	E5	T	PP, EP, TOX, A	VE02		2	
3287	TOXIC LIQUID, INORGANIC, N.O.S.	6.1	T4	II	6.1	274 802	100 ml	E4	T	PP, EP, TOX, A	VE02		2	

UN No. or ID No. (1)	Name and description (2)	Class (3a)	Classification Code (3b)	Packing group (4)	Labels (5)	Special provisions (6)	Limited quantities (7a)	Excepted quantities (7b)	Carriage permitted (8)	Equipment required (9)	Ventilation (10)	Provisions concerning loading, unloading and carriage (11)	Number of blue cones/lights (12)	Remarks (13)
3287	TOXIC LIQUID, INORGANIC, N.O.S.	6.1	T4	III	6.1	274 802	5 L	E1	T	PP, EP, TOX, A	VE02		0	
3288	TOXIC SOLID, INORGANIC, N.O.S.	6.1	T5	I	6.1	274 802	0	E5		PP, EP			2	
3288	TOXIC SOLID, INORGANIC, N.O.S.	6.1	T5	II	6.1	274 802	500 g	E4		PP, EP			2	
3288	TOXIC SOLID, INORGANIC, N.O.S.	6.1	T5	III	6.1	274 802	5 kg	E1		PP, EP			0	
3289	TOXIC LIQUID, CORROSIVE, INORGANIC, N.O.S.	6.1	TC3	I	6.1+8	274 315 802	0	E5	T	PP, EP, TOX, A			2	
3289	TOXIC LIQUID, CORROSIVE, INORGANIC, N.O.S.	6.1	TC3	II	6.1+8	274 802	100 ml	E4	T	PP, EP, TOX, A	VE02		2	
3290	TOXIC SOLID, CORROSIVE, INORGANIC, N.O.S.	6.1	TC4	I	6.1+8	274 802	0	E5		PP, EP			2	
3290	TOXIC SOLID, CORROSIVE, INORGANIC, N.O.S.	6.1	TC4	II	6.1+8	274 802	500 g	E4		PP, EP			2	
3291	CLINICAL WASTE, UNSPECIFIED, N.O.S. or (BIO) MEDICAL WASTE, N.O.S. or REGULATED MEDICAL WASTE, N.O.S.	6.2	I3		6.2	565 802	0	E0		PP			0	
3291	CLINICAL WASTE, UNSPECIFIED, N.O.S. or (BIO) MEDICAL WASTE, N.O.S. or REGULATED MEDICAL WASTE, N.O.S., in refrigerated liquid nitrogen	6.2	I3		6.2 +2.2	565 802	0	E0		PP			0	
3292	BATTERIES, CONTAINING SODIUM, or CELLS, CONTAINING SODIUM	4.3	W3		4.3	239 295	0	E0		PP, EX, A	VE01	HA08	0	
3293	HYDRAZINE, AQUEOUS SOLUTION with not more than 37% hydrazine, by mass	6.1	T4	III	6.1	566 802	5 L	E1		PP, EP, TOX, A	VE02		0	
3294	HYDROGEN CYANIDE, SOLUTION IN ALCOHOL with not more than 45% hydrogen cyanide	6.1	TF1	I	6.1+3	610 802	0	E0		PP, EP, EX, TOX, A	VE01, VE02		2	
3295	HYDROCARBONS, LIQUID, N.O.S.	3	F1	I	3		500 ml	E3	T	PP, EX, A	VE01		1	
3295	HYDROCARBONS, LIQUID, N.O.S. (vapour pressure at 50 °C more than 110 kPa)	3	F1	II	3	640C	1 L	E2	T	PP, EX, A	VE01		1	
3295	HYDROCARBONS, LIQUID, N.O.S. (vapour pressure at 50 °C not more than 110 kPa)	3	F1	II	3	640D	1 L	E2	T	PP, EX, A	VE01		1	
3295	HYDROCARBONS, LIQUID, N.O.S.	3	F1	III	3		5 L	E1	T	PP, EX, A	VE01		0	
3296	HEPTAFLUOROPROPANE (REFRIGERANT GAS R 227)	2	2A		2.2		120 ml	E1		PP			0	
3297	ETHYLENE OXIDE AND CHLOROTETRAFLUOROETHANE MIXTURE with not more than 8.8% ethylene oxide	2	2A		2.2	392 662	120 ml	E1		PP			0	
3298	ETHYLENE OXIDE AND PENTAFLUOROETHANE MIXTURE with not more than 7.9% ethylene oxide	2	2A		2.2	392 662	120 ml	E1		PP			0	
3299	ETHYLENE OXIDE AND TETRAFLUOROETHANE MIXTURE with not more than 5.6% ethylene oxide	2	2A		2.2	392 662	120 ml	E1		PP			0	
3300	ETHYLENE OXIDE AND CARBON DIOXIDE MIXTURE with more than 87% ethylene oxide	2	2TF		2.3+2.1		0	E0		PP, EP, EX, TOX, A	VE01, VE02		2	
3301	CORROSIVE LIQUID, SELF-HEATING, N.O.S.	8	CS1	I	8+4.2	274	0	E0		PP, EP			0	
3301	CORROSIVE LIQUID, SELF-HEATING, N.O.S.	8	CS1	II	8+4.2	274	0	E2		PP, EP			0	

UN No. or ID No.	Name and description	Class	Classification Code	Packing group	Labels	Special provisions	Limited and excepted quantities		Carriage permitted	Equipment required	Venti-lation	Provisions concerning loading, unloading and carriage	Number of blue cones/ lights	Remarks
		2.2	2.2	2.1.1.3	5.2.2	3.3	3.4	3.5.1.2	3.2.1	8.1.5	7.1.6	7.1.6	7.1.5	3.2.1
(1)	(2)	(3a)	(3b)	(4)	(5)	(6)	(7a)	(7b)	(8)	(9)	(10)	(11)	(12)	(13)
3302	2-DIMETHYLAMINOETHYL ACRYLATE, STABILIZED	6.1	T1	II	6.1	386 676 802	100 ml	E4		PP, EP, TOX, A	VE02		2	
3303	COMPRESSED GAS, TOXIC, OXIDIZING, N.O.S.	2	1TO		2.3+5.1	274	0	E0		PP, EP, TOX, A	VE02		2	
3304	COMPRESSED GAS, TOXIC, CORROSIVE, N.O.S.	2	1TC		2.3+8	274	0	E0		PP, EP, TOX, A	VE02		2	
3305	COMPRESSED GAS, TOXIC, FLAMMABLE, CORROSIVE, N.O.S.	2	1TFC		2.3+2.1+8	274	0	E0		PP, EP, EX, TOX, A	VE01, VE02		2	
3306	COMPRESSED GAS, TOXIC, OXIDIZING, CORROSIVE, N.O.S.	2	1TOC		2.3+5.1+8	274	0	E0		PP, EP, TOX, A	VE02		2	
3307	LIQUEFIED GAS, TOXIC, OXIDIZING, N.O.S.	2	2TO		2.3+5.1	274	0	E0		PP, EP, TOX, A	VE02		2	
3308	LIQUEFIED GAS, TOXIC, CORROSIVE, N.O.S.	2	2TC		2.3+8	274	0	E0		PP, EP, TOX, A	VE02		2	
3309	LIQUEFIED GAS, TOXIC, FLAMMABLE, CORROSIVE, N.O.S.	2	2TFC		2.3+2.1+8	274	0	E0		PP, EP, EX, TOX, A	VE01, VE02		2	
3310	LIQUEFIED GAS, TOXIC, OXIDIZING, CORROSIVE, N.O.S.	2	2TOC		2.3+5.1+8	274	0	E0		PP, EP, TOX, A	VE02		2	
3311	GAS, REFRIGERATED LIQUID, OXIDIZING, N.O.S.	2	3O		2.2+5.1	274	0	E0		PP			0	
3312	GAS, REFRIGERATED LIQUID, FLAMMABLE, N.O.S.	2	3F		2.1	274	0	E0		PP, EX, A	VE01		1	
3313	ORGANIC PIGMENTS, SELF-HEATING	4.2	S2	II	4.2		0	E2		PP			0	
3313	ORGANIC PIGMENTS, SELF-HEATING	4.2	S2	III	4.2		0	E1		PP			0	
3314	PLASTICS MOULDING COMPOUND in dough, sheet or extruded rope form evolving flammable vapour	9	M3	III	none	207 633 675	5 kg	E1		PP, EX, A	VE01		0	
3315	CHEMICAL SAMPLE, TOXIC	6.1	T8	I	6.1	250 802	0	E0		PP, EP, TOX, A	VE02		2	
3316	CHEMICAL KIT or FIRST AID KIT	9	M11		9	251 340 671	See SP 251	See SP 340		PP			0	
3317	2-AMINO-4,6-DINITROPHENOL, WETTED with not less than 20% water, by mass	4.1	D	I	4.1		0	E0		PP			1	
3318	AMMONIA SOLUTION, relative density less than 0.880 at 15°C in water, with more than 50% ammonia	2	4TC		2.3+8	23	0	E0		PP, EP, TOX, A	VE02		2	
3319	NITROGLYCERIN MIXTURE, DESENSITIZED, SOLID, N.O.S. with more than 2% but not more than 10% nitroglycerin. by mass	4.1	D	II	4.1	272 274	0	E0		PP			0	
3320	SODIUM BOROHYDRIDE AND SODIUM HYDROXIDE SOLUTION, with not more than 12% sodium borohydride and not more than 40% sodium hydroxide by mass	8	C5	II	8		1 L	E2		PP, EP			0	
3320	SODIUM BOROHYDRIDE AND SODIUM HYDROXIDE SOLUTION, with not more than 12% sodium borohydride and not more than 40% sodium hydroxide by mass	8	C5	III	8		5 L	E1		PP, EP			0	
3321	RADIOACTIVE MATERIAL, LOW SPECIFIC ACTIVITY (LSA-II), non fissile or fissile-excepted	7			7X	172 317 325 336	0	E0		PP			2	

UN No. or ID No.	Name and description	Class	Classi-fication Code	Packing group	Labels	Special provis-ions	Limited and excepted quantities		Carriage permitted	Equipment required	Venti-lation	Provisions concerning loading, unloading and carriage	Number of blue cones/ lights	Remarks
	3.1.2	2.2	2.2	2.1.1.3	5.2.2	3.3	3.4	3.5.1.2	3.2.1	8.1.5	7.1.6	7.1.6	7.1.5	3.2.1
(1)	(2)	(3a)	(3b)	(4)	(5)	(6)	(7a)	(7b)	(8)	(9)	(10)	(11)	(12)	(13)
3322	RADIOACTIVE MATERIAL, LOW SPECIFIC ACTIVITY (LSA-III), non fissile or fissile-excepted	7			7X	172 317 325 336	0	E0		PP			2	
3323	RADIOACTIVE MATERIAL, TYPE C PACKAGE, non fissile or fissile-excepted	7			7X	172 317 325	0	E0		PP			2	
3324	RADIOACTIVE MATERIAL, LOW SPECIFIC ACTIVITY (LSA-II), FISSILE	7			7X+7E	172 326 336	0	E0		PP			2	
3325	RADIOACTIVE MATERIAL, LOW SPECIFIC ACTIVITY (LSA-III), FISSILE	7			7X+7E	172 326 336	0	E0		PP			2	
3326	RADIOACTIVE MATERIAL, SURFACE CONTAMINATED OBJECTS (SCO-I or SCO-II), FISSILE	7			7X+7E	172 326	0	E0		PP			2	
3327	RADIOACTIVE MATERIAL, TYPE A PACKAGE, FISSILE, non-special form	7			7X+7E	172 326	0	E0		PP			2	
3328	RADIOACTIVE MATERIAL, TYPE B(U) PACKAGE, FISSILE	7			7X+7E	172 326 337	0	E0		PP			2	
3329	RADIOACTIVE MATERIAL, TYPE B(M) PACKAGE, FISSILE	7			7X+7E	172 326 337	0	E0		PP			2	
3330	RADIOACTIVE MATERIAL, TYPE C PACKAGE, FISSILE	7			7X+7E	172 326	0	E0		PP			2	
3331	RADIOACTIVE MATERIAL, TRANSPORTED UNDER SPECIAL ARRANGEMENT, FISSILE	7			7X+7E	172 326	0	E0		PP			2	
3332	RADIOACTIVE MATERIAL, TYPE A PACKAGE, SPECIAL FORM, non fissile or fissile-excepted	7			7X	172 317	0	E0		PP			2	
3333	RADIOACTIVE MATERIAL, TYPE A PACKAGE, SPECIAL FORM, FISSILE	7			7X+7E	172	0	E0		PP			2	
3334	Aviation regulated liquid, n.o.s.	9	M11						NOT SUBJECT TO ADN					
3335	Aviation regulated solid, n.o.s.	9	M11						NOT SUBJECT TO ADN					
3336	MERCAPTANS, LIQUID, FLAMMABLE, N.O.S. or MERCAPTAN MIXTURE, LIQUID, FLAMMABLE, N.O.S.	3	F1	I	3	274	0	E0		PP, EX, A	VE01		1	
3336	MERCAPTANS, LIQUID, FLAMMABLE, N.O.S. or MERCAPTAN MIXTURE, LIQUID, FLAMMABLE, N.O.S. (vapour pressure at 50 °C more than 110 kPa)	3	F1	II	3	274 640C	1 L	E2		PP, EX, A	VE01		1	
3336	MERCAPTANS, LIQUID, FLAMMABLE, N.O.S. or MERCAPTAN MIXTURE, LIQUID, FLAMMABLE, N.O.S. (vapour pressure at 50 °C not more than 110 kPa)	3	F1	II	3	274 640D	1 L	E2		PP, EX, A	VE01		1	
3336	MERCAPTANS, LIQUID, FLAMMABLE, N.O.S. or MERCAPTAN MIXTURE, LIQUID, FLAMMABLE, N.O.S.	3	F1	III	3	274	5 L	E1		PP, EX, A	VE01		0	

(1)	(2)	(3a)	(3b)	(4)	(5)	(6)	(7a)	(7b)	(8)	(9)	(10)	(11)	(12)	(13)
UN No. or ID No.	Name and description	Class	Classification Code	Packing group	Labels	Special provisions	Limited and excepted quantities		Carriage permitted	Equipment required	Ventilation	Provisions concerning loading, unloading and carriage	Number of blue cones/lights	Remarks
	3.1.2	2.2	2.2	2.1.1.3	5.2.2	3.3	3.4	3.5.1.2	3.2.1	8.1.5	7.1.6	7.1.6	7.1.5	3.2.1
3337	REFRIGERANT GAS R 404A (Pentafluoroethane, 1,1,1-trifluoroethane, and 1,1,1,2-tetrafluoroethane zeotropic mixture with approximately 44% pentafluoroethane and 52% 1,1,1-trifluoroethane)	2	2A		2.2	662	120 ml	E1		PP			0	
3338	REFRIGERANT GAS R 407A (Difluoromethane, pentafluoroethane, and 1,1,1,2-tetrafluoroethane zeotropic mixture with approximately 20% difluoromethane and 40% pentafluoroethane)	2	2A		2.2	662	120 ml	E1		PP			0	
3339	REFRIGERANT GAS R 407B (Difluoromethane, pentafluoroethane, and 1,1,1,2-tetrafluoroethane zeotropic mixture with approximately 10% difluoromethane and 70% pentafluoroethane)	2	2A		2.2	662	120 ml	E1		PP			0	
3340	REFRIGERANT GAS R 407C (Difluoromethane, pentafluoroethane, and 1,1,1,2-tetrafluoroethane zeotropic mixture with approximately 23% difluoromethane and 25% pentafluoroethane)	2	2A		2.2	662	120 ml	E1		PP			0	
3341	THIOUREA DIOXIDE	4.2	S2	II	4.2		0	E2		PP			0	
3341	THIOUREA DIOXIDE	4.2	S2	III	4.2		0	E1		PP			0	
3342	XANTHATES	4.2	S2	II	4.2		0	E2		PP			0	
3342	XANTHATES	4.2	S2	III	4.2		0	E1		PP			0	
3343	NITROGLYCERIN MIXTURE, DESENSITIZED, LIQUID, FLAMMABLE, N.O.S. with not more than 30% nitroglycerin, by mass	3	D		3	274 278	0	E0		PP, EX, A	VE01		0	
3344	PENTAERYTHRITE TETRANITRATE (PENTAERYTHRITOL TETRANITRATE; PETN) MIXTURE, DESENSITIZED, SOLID, N.O.S. with more than 10% but not more than 20% PETN, by mass	4.1	D	II	4.1	272 274	0	E0		PP			1	
3345	PHENOXYACETIC ACID DERIVATIVE PESTICIDE, SOLID, TOXIC	6.1	T7	I	6.1	61 274 648 802	0	E5		PP, EP			2	
3345	PHENOXYACETIC ACID DERIVATIVE PESTICIDE, SOLID, TOXIC	6.1	T7	II	6.1	61 274 648 802	500 g	E4		PP, EP			2	
3345	PHENOXYACETIC ACID DERIVATIVE PESTICIDE, SOLID, TOXIC	6.1	T7	III	6.1	61 274 648 802	5 kg	E1		PP, EP			0	
3346	PHENOXYACETIC ACID DERIVATIVE PESTICIDE, LIQUID, FLAMMABLE, TOXIC, flash-point less than 23 °C	3	FT2	I	3+6.1	61 274 802	0	E0		PP, EP, EX, TOX, A	VE01, VE02		2	
3346	PHENOXYACETIC ACID DERIVATIVE PESTICIDE, LIQUID, FLAMMABLE, TOXIC, flash-point less than 23 °C	3	FT2	II	3+6.1	61 274 802	1 L	E2		PP, EP, EX, TOX, A	VE01, VE02		2	
3347	PHENOXYACETIC ACID DERIVATIVE PESTICIDE, LIQUID, TOXIC, FLAMMABLE, flash-point not less than 23 °C	6.1	TF2	I	6.1+3	61 274 802	0	E5		PP, EP, EX, TOX, A	VE01, VE02		2	

UN No. or ID No.	Name and description	Class	Classi-fication Code	Packing group	Labels	Special provis-ions	Limited and excepted quantities		Carriage permitted	Equipment required	Venti-lation	Provisions concerning loading, unloading and carriage	Number of blue cones/ lights	Remarks
	3.1.2	2.2	2.2	2.1.1.3	5.2.2	3.3	3.4	3.5.1.2	3.2.1	8.1.5	7.1.6	7.1.6	7.1.5	3.2.1
(1)	(2)	(3a)	(3b)	(4)	(5)	(6)	(7a)	(7b)	(8)	(9)	(10)	(11)	(12)	(13)
3347	PHENOXYACETIC ACID DERIVATIVE PESTICIDE, LIQUID, TOXIC, FLAMMABLE, flash-point not less than 23 °C	6.1	TF2	II	6.1+3	61 274 802	100 ml	E4		PP, EP, EX, TOX, A	VE01, VE02		2	
3347	PHENOXYACETIC ACID DERIVATIVE PESTICIDE, LIQUID, TOXIC, FLAMMABLE, flash-point not less than 23 °C	6.1	TF2	III	6.1+3	61 274 802	5 L	E1		PP, EP, EX, TOX, A	VE01, VE02		0	
3348	PHENOXYACETIC ACID DERIVATIVE PESTICIDE, LIQUID, TOXIC	6.1	T6	I	6.1	61 274 648 802	0	E5		PP, EP, TOX, A	VE02		2	
3348	PHENOXYACETIC ACID DERIVATIVE PESTICIDE, LIQUID, TOXIC	6.1	T6	II	6.1	61 274 648 802	100 ml	E4		PP, EP, TOX, A	VE02		2	
3348	PHENOXYACETIC ACID DERIVATIVE PESTICIDE, LIQUID, TOXIC	6.1	T6	III	6.1	61 274 648 802	5 L	E1		PP, EP, TOX, A	VE02		0	
3349	PYRETHROID PESTICIDE, SOLID, TOXIC	6.1	T7	I	6.1	61 274 648 802	0	E5		PP, EP			2	
3349	PYRETHROID PESTICIDE, SOLID, TOXIC	6.1	T7	II	6.1	61 274 648 802	500 g	E4		PP, EP			2	
3349	PYRETHROID PESTICIDE, SOLID, TOXIC	6.1	T7	III	6.1	61 274 648 802	5 kg	E1		PP, EP			0	
3350	PYRETHROID PESTICIDE, LIQUID, FLAMMABLE, TOXIC, flash-point less than 23 °C	3	FT2	I	3+6.1	61 274 802	0	E0		PP, EP, EX, TOX, A	VE01, VE02		2	
3350	PYRETHROID PESTICIDE, LIQUID, FLAMMABLE, TOXIC, flash-point less than 23 °C	3	FT2	II	3+6.1	61 274 802	1 L	E2		PP, EP, EX, TOX, A	VE01, VE02		2	
3351	PYRETHROID PESTICIDE, LIQUID, TOXIC, FLAMMABLE, flash-point not less than 23 °C	6.1	TF2	I	6.1+3	61 274 802	0	E5		PP, EP, EX, TOX, A	VE01, VE02		2	
3351	PYRETHROID PESTICIDE, LIQUID, TOXIC, FLAMMABLE, flash-point not less than 23 °C	6.1	TF2	II	6.1+3	61 274 802	100 ml	E4		PP, EP, EX, TOX, A	VE01, VE02		2	
3351	PYRETHROID PESTICIDE, LIQUID, TOXIC, FLAMMABLE, flash-point not less than 23 °C	6.1	TF2	III	6.1+3	61 274 802	5 L	E1		PP, EP, EX, TOX, A	VE01, VE02		0	

UN No. or ID No. (1)	Name and description 3.1.2 (2)	Class 2.2 (3a)	Classification Code 2.2 (3b)	Packing group 2.1.1.3 (4)	Labels 5.2.2 (5)	Special provisions 3.3 (6)	Limited and excepted quantities 3.4 (7a)	3.5.1.2 (7b)	Carriage permitted 3.2.1 (8)	Equipment required 8.1.5 (9)	Ventilation 7.1.6 (10)	Provisions concerning loading, unloading and carriage 7.1.6 (11)	Number of blue cones/ lights 7.1.5 (12)	Remarks 3.2.1 (13)
3352	PYRETHROID PESTICIDE, LIQUID, TOXIC	6.1	T6	I	6.1	61 274 648 802	0	E5		PP, EP, TOX, A	VE02		2	
3352	PYRETHROID PESTICIDE, LIQUID, TOXIC	6.1	T6	II	6.1	61 274 648 802	100 ml	E4		PP, EP, TOX, A	VE02		2	
3352	PYRETHROID PESTICIDE, LIQUID, TOXIC	6.1	T6	III	6.1	61 274 648 802	5 L	E1		PP, EP, TOX, A	VE02		0	
3354	INSECTICIDE GAS, FLAMMABLE, N.O.S.	2	2F		2.1	274 662	0	E0		PP, EX, A	VE01		1	
3355	INSECTICIDE GAS, TOXIC, FLAMMABLE, N.O.S.	2	2TF		2.3+2.1	274	0	E0		PP, EP, EX, TOX, A	VE01, VE02		2	
3356	OXYGEN GENERATOR, CHEMICAL	5.1	O3		5.1	284	0	E0		PP			0	
3357	NITROGLYCERIN MIXTURE, DESENSITIZED, LIQUID, N.O.S. with not more than 30% nitroglycerin, by mass	3	D	II	3	274 288	0	E0		PP, EX, A	VE01		1	
3358	REFRIGERATING MACHINES containing flammable, non-toxic, liquefied gas	2	6F		2.1	291	0	E0		PP, EX, A	VE01		1	
3359	FUMIGATED CARGO TRANSPORT UNIT	9	M11			302				PP				
3360	Fibres, vegetable, dry	4.1	F1						NOT SUBJECT TO ADN					
3361	CHLOROSILANES, TOXIC, CORROSIVE, N.O.S.	6.1	TC1	II	6.1+8	274 802	0	E0		PP, EP, TOX, A	VE02		2	
3362	CHLOROSILANES, TOXIC, CORROSIVE, FLAMMABLE, N.O.S.	6.1	TFC	II	6.1+3+8	274	0	E0		PP, EP, EX, TOX, A	VE01, VE02		2	
3363	DANGEROUS GOODS IN ARTICLES or DANGEROUS GOODS IN MACHINERY or DANGEROUS GOODS IN APPARATUS	9	M11		9	301 672	0	E0						
3364	TRINITROPHENOL (PICRIC ACID) WETTED with not less than 10% water, by mass	4.1	D	I	4.1		0	E0		PP			1	
3365	TRINITROCHLOROBENZENE (PICRYL CHLORIDE) WETTED with not less than 10% water, by mass	4.1	D	I	4.1		0	E0		PP			1	
3366	TRINITROTOLUENE (TNT), WETTED with not less than 10% water, by mass	4.1	D	I	4.1		0	E0		PP			1	
3367	TRINITROBENZENE, WETTED with not less than 10% water, by mass	4.1	D	I	4.1		0	E0		PP			1	
3368	TRINITROBENZOIC ACID, WETTED with not less than 10% water, by mass	4.1	D	I	4.1		0	E0		PP			1	
3369	SODIUM DINITRO-o-CRESOLATE, WETTED with not less than 10% water, by mass	4.1	DT	I	4.1+6.1	802	0	E0		PP, EP			2	
3370	UREA NITRATE, WETTED with not less than 10% water, by mass	4.1	D	I	4.1		0	E0		PP			1	
3371	2-METHYLBUTANAL	3	F1	II	3		1 L	E2		PP, EX, A	VE01		1	
3373	BIOLOGICAL SUBSTANCE, CATEGORY B	6.2	I4		6.2	319	0	E0		PP			0	

UN No. or ID No.	Name and description	Class	Classi-fication Code	Packing group	Labels	Special provis-ions	Limited and excepted quantities		Carriage permitted	Equipment required	Venti-lation	Provisions concerning loading, unloading and carriage	Number of blue cones/lights	Remarks
		2.2	2.2	2.1.1.3	5.2.2	3.3	3.4	3.5.1.2	3.2.1	8.1.5	7.1.6	7.1.6	7.1.5	3.2.1
(1)	(2)	(3a)	(3b)	(4)	(5)	(6)	(7a)	(7b)	(8)	(9)	(10)	(11)	(12)	(13)
3373	BIOLOGICAL SUBSTANCE, CATEGORY B (animal material only)	6.2	I4		6.2	319	0	E0		PP			0	
3374	ACETYLENE, SOLVENT FREE	2	2F		2.1	662	0	E0		PP, EX, A	VE01		1	
3375	AMMONIUM NITRATE EMULSION, or SUSPENSION or GEL, intermediate for blasting explosives, liquid	5.1	O1	II	5.1	309	0	E2		PP			0	
3375	AMMONIUM NITRATE EMULSION, or SUSPENSION or GEL, intermediate for blasting explosives, solid	5.1	O2	II	5.1	309	0	E2		PP			0	
3376	4-NITROPHENYLHYDRAZINE, with not less than 30% water, by mass	4.1	D	I	4.1		0	E0		PP			1	
3377	SODIUM PERBORATE MONOHYDRATE	5.1	O2	III	5.1		5 kg	E1		PP			0	
3378	SODIUM CARBONATE PEROXYHYDRATE	5.1	O2	II	5.1		1 kg	E2		PP			0	
3378	SODIUM CARBONATE PEROXYHYDRATE	5.1	O2	III	5.1		5 kg	E1		PP			0	
3379	DESENSITIZED EXPLOSIVE, LIQUID, N.O.S.	3	D	I	3	274 311	0	E0		PP, EX, A	VE01		1	
3380	DESENSITIZED EXPLOSIVE, SOLID, N.O.S.	4.1	D	I	4.1	274 311 394	0	E0		PP			1	
3381	TOXIC BY INHALATION LIQUID, N.O.S. with an LC_{50} lower than or equal to 200 ml/m^3 and saturated vapour concentration greater than or equal to 500 LC_{50}	6.1	T1 or T4	I	6.1	274 802	0	E0		PP, EP, TOX, A	VE02		2	
3382	TOXIC BY INHALATION LIQUID, N.O.S. with an LC_{50} lower than or equal to 1000 ml/m^3 and saturated vapour concentration greater than or equal to 10 LC_{50}	6.1	T1 or T4	I	6.1	274 802	0	E0		PP, EP, TOX, A	VE02		2	
3383	TOXIC BY INHALATION LIQUID, FLAMMABLE, N.O.S. with an LC_{50} lower than or equal to 200 ml/m^3 and saturated vapour concentration greater than or equal to 500 LC_{50}	6.1	TF1	I	6.1 +3	274 802	0	E0		PP, EP, EX, TOX, A	VE01, VE02		2	
3384	TOXIC BY INHALATION LIQUID, FLAMMABLE, N.O.S. with an LC_{50} lower than or equal to 1000 ml/m^3 and saturated vapour concentration greater than or equal to 10 LC_{50}	6.1	TF1	I	6.1 +3	274 802	0	E0		PP, EP, EX, TOX, A	VE01, VE02		2	
3385	TOXIC BY INHALATION LIQUID, WATER-REACTIVE, N.O.S. with an LC_{50} lower than or equal to 200 ml/m^3 and saturated vapour concentration greater than or equal to 500 LC_{50}	6.1	TW1	I	6.1 +4.3	274 802	0	E0		PP, EP, TOX, A	VE02		2	
3386	TOXIC BY INHALATION LIQUID, WATER-REACTIVE, N.O.S. with an LC_{50} lower than or equal to 1000 ml/m^3 and saturated vapour concentration greater than or equal to 10 LC_{50}	6.1	TW1	I	6.1 +4.3	274 802	0	E0		PP, EP, TOX, A	VE02		2	
3387	TOXIC BY INHALATION LIQUID, OXIDIZING, N.O.S. with an LC_{50} lower than or equal to 200 ml/m^3 and saturated vapour concentration greater than or equal to 500 LC_{50}	6.1	TO1	I	6.1 +5.1	274 802	0	E0		PP, EP, TOX, A	VE02		2	

UN No. or ID No. (1)	Name and description (2)	Class 2.2 (3a)	Classification Code 2.2 (3b)	Packing group 2.1.1.3 (4)	Labels 5.2.2 (5)	Special provisions 3.3 (6)	Limited quantities 3.4 (7a)	Limited and excepted quantities 3.5.1.2 (7b)	Carriage permitted 3.2.1 (8)	Equipment required 8.1.5 (9)	Ventilation 7.1.6 (10)	Provisions concerning loading, unloading and carriage 7.1.6 (11)	Number of blue cones/lights 7.1.5 (12)	Remarks 3.2.1 (13)
3388	TOXIC BY INHALATION LIQUID, OXIDIZING, N.O.S. with an LC_{50} lower than or equal to 1000 ml/m³ and saturated vapour concentration greater than or equal to 10 LC_{50}	6.1	TO1	I	6.1 +5.1	274 802	0	E0		PP, EP, TOX, A	VE02		2	
3389	TOXIC BY INHALATION LIQUID, CORROSIVE, N.O.S. with an LC_{50} lower than or equal to 200 ml/m³ and saturated vapour concentration greater than or equal to 500 LC_{50}	6.1	TC1 or TC3	I	6.1 +8	274 802	0	E0		PP, EP, TOX, A	VE02		2	
3390	TOXIC BY INHALATION LIQUID, CORROSIVE, N.O.S. with an LC_{50} lower than or equal to 1000 ml/m³ and saturated vapour concentration greater than or equal to 10 LC_{50}	6.1	TC1 or TC3	I	6.1 +8	274 802	0	E0		PP, EP, TOX, A	VE02		2	
3391	ORGANOMETALLIC SUBSTANCE, SOLID, PYROPHORIC	4.2	S5	I	4.2	274	0	E0		PP			0	
3392	ORGANOMETALLIC SUBSTANCE, LIQUID, PYROPHORIC	4.2	S5	I	4.2	274	0	E0		PP			0	
3393	ORGANOMETALLIC SUBSTANCE, SOLID, PYROPHORIC, WATER REACTIVE	4.2	SW	I	4.2 +4.3	274	0	E0		PP, EX, A	VE01		0	
3394	ORGANOMETALLIC SUBSTANCE, LIQUID, PYROPHORIC, WATER REACTIVE	4.2	SW	I	4.2 +4.3	274	0	E0		PP, EX, A	VE01		0	
3395	ORGANOMETALLIC SUBSTANCE, SOLID, WATER REACTIVE	4.3	W2	I	4.3	274	0	E0		PP, EX, A	VE01	HA08	0	
3395	ORGANOMETALLIC SUBSTANCE, SOLID, WATER REACTIVE	4.3	W2	II	4.3	274	500 g	E2		PP, EX, A	VE01	HA08	0	
3395	ORGANOMETALLIC SUBSTANCE, SOLID, WATER REACTIVE	4.3	W2	III	4.3	274	1 kg	E1		PP, EX, A	VE01	HA08	0	
3396	ORGANOMETALLIC SUBSTANCE, SOLID, WATER REACTIVE, FLAMMABLE	4.3	WF2	I	4.3 +4.1	274	0	E0		PP, EX, A	VE01	HA08	1	
3396	ORGANOMETALLIC SUBSTANCE, SOLID, WATER REACTIVE, FLAMMABLE	4.3	WF2	II	4.3 +4.1	274	500 g	E2		PP, EX, A	VE01	HA08	1	
3396	ORGANOMETALLIC SUBSTANCE, SOLID, WATER REACTIVE, FLAMMABLE	4.3	WF2	III	4.3 +4.1	274	1 kg	E1		PP, EX, A	VE01	HA08	0	
3397	ORGANOMETALLIC SUBSTANCE, SOLID, WATER REACTIVE, SELF-HEATING	4.3	WS	I	4.3 +4.2	274	0	E0		PP, EX, A	VE01	HA08	0	
3397	ORGANOMETALLIC SUBSTANCE, SOLID, WATER REACTIVE, SELF-HEATING	4.3	WS	II	4.3 +4.2	274	500 g	E2		PP, EX, A	VE01	HA08	0	
3397	ORGANOMETALLIC SUBSTANCE, SOLID, WATER REACTIVE, SELF-HEATING	4.3	WS	III	4.3 +4.2	274	1 kg	E1		PP, EX, A	VE01	HA08	0	
3398	ORGANOMETALLIC SUBSTANCE, LIQUID, WATER REACTIVE	4.3	W1	I	4.3	274	0	E0		PP, EX, A	VE01	HA08	0	
3398	ORGANOMETALLIC SUBSTANCE, LIQUID, WATER REACTIVE	4.3	W1	II	4.3	274	500 ml	E2		PP, EX, A	VE01	HA08	0	
3398	ORGANOMETALLIC SUBSTANCE, LIQUID, WATER REACTIVE	4.3	W1	III	4.3	274	1 L	E1		PP, EX, A	VE01	HA08	0	
3399	ORGANOMETALLIC SUBSTANCE, LIQUID, WATER REACTIVE, FLAMMABLE	4.3	WF1	I	4.3 +3	274	0	E0		PP, EX, A	VE01	HA08	1	

UN No. or ID No. (1)	Name and description (2)	Class (3a)	Classification Code (3b)	Packing group (4)	Labels (5)	Special provisions (6)	Limited and excepted quantities (7a)	(7b)	Carriage permitted (8)	Equipment required (9)	Ventilation (10)	Provisions concerning loading, unloading and carriage (11)	Number of blue cones/lights (12)	Remarks (13)
3399	ORGANOMETALLIC SUBSTANCE, LIQUID, WATER REACTIVE, FLAMMABLE	4.3	WF1	II	4.3+3	274	500 ml	E2		PP, EX, A	VE01	HA08	1	
3399	ORGANOMETALLIC SUBSTANCE, LIQUID, WATER REACTIVE, FLAMMABLE	4.3	WF1	III	4.3+3	274	1 L	E1		PP, EX, A	VE01	HA08	0	
3400	ORGANOMETALLIC SUBSTANCE, SOLID, SELF-HEATING	4.2	S5	II	4.2	274	500 g	E2		PP			0	
3400	ORGANOMETALLIC SUBSTANCE, SOLID, SELF-HEATING	4.2	S5	III	4.2	274	1 kg	E1		PP			0	
3401	ALKALI METAL AMALGAM, SOLID	4.3	W2	I	4.3	182	0	E0		PP, EX, A	VE01	HA08	0	
3402	ALKALINE EARTH METAL AMALGAM, SOLID	4.3	W2	I	4.3	183 506	0	E0		PP, EX, A	VE01	HA08	0	
3403	POTASSIUM METAL ALLOYS, SOLID	4.3	W2	I	4.3		0	E0		PP, EX, A	VE01	HA08	0	
3404	POTASSIUM SODIUM ALLOYS, SOLID	4.3	W2	I	4.3		0	E0		PP, EX, A	VE01	HA08	0	
3405	BARIUM CHLORATE SOLUTION	5.1	OT1	II	5.1+6.1	802	1 L	E2		PP, EP, TOX, A	VE02		2	
3405	BARIUM CHLORATE SOLUTION	5.1	OT1	III	5.1+6.1	802	5 L	E1		PP, EP, TOX, A	VE02		2	
3406	BARIUM PERCHLORATE SOLUTION	5.1	OT1	II	5.1+6.1	802	1 L	E2		PP, EP, TOX, A	VE02		2	
3406	BARIUM PERCHLORATE SOLUTION	5.1	OT1	III	5.1+6.1	802	5 L	E1		PP, EP, TOX, A	VE02		0	
3407	CHLORATE AND MAGNESIUM CHLORIDE MIXTURE SOLUTION	5.1	O1	II	5.1		1 L	E2		PP			0	
3407	CHLORATE AND MAGNESIUM CHLORIDE MIXTURE SOLUTION	5.1	O1	III	5.1		5 L	E1		PP			0	
3408	LEAD PERCHLORATE SOLUTION	5.1	OT1	II	5.1+6.1	802	1 L	E2		PP, EP			2	
3408	LEAD PERCHLORATE SOLUTION	5.1	OT1	III	5.1+6.1	802	5 L	E1		PP, EP			0	
3409	CHLORONITROBENZENES, LIQUID	6.1	T1	II	6.1	279 802	100 ml	E4		PP, EP, TOX, A	VE02		2	
3410	4-CHLORO-o-TOLUIDINE HYDROCHLORIDE SOLUTION	6.1	T1	III	6.1	802	5 L	E1		PP, EP, TOX, A	VE02		0	
3411	beta-NAPHTHYLAMINE SOLUTION	6.1	T1	II	6.1	802	100 ml	E4		PP, EP, TOX, A	VE02		2	
3411	beta-NAPHTHYLAMINE SOLUTION	6.1	T1	III	6.1	802	5 L	E1		PP, EP, TOX, A	VE02		0	
3412	FORMIC ACID with not less than 10% but not more than 85% acid by mass	8	C3	II	8		1 L	E2	T	PP, EP			0	
3412	FORMIC ACID with not less than 5% but less than 10% acid by mass	8	C3	III	8		5 L	E1	T	PP, EP			0	
3413	POTASSIUM CYANIDE SOLUTION	6.1	T4	I	6.1	802	0	E5		PP, EP, TOX, A	VE02		2	
3413	POTASSIUM CYANIDE SOLUTION	6.1	T4	II	6.1	802	100 ml	E4		PP, EP, TOX, A	VE02		2	
3413	POTASSIUM CYANIDE SOLUTION	6.1	T4	III	6.1	802	5 L	E1		PP, EP, TOX, A	VE02		0	
3414	SODIUM CYANIDE SOLUTION	6.1	T4	I	6.1	802	0	E5		PP, EP, TOX, A	VE02		2	
3414	SODIUM CYANIDE SOLUTION	6.1	T4	II	6.1	802	100 ml	E4		PP, EP, TOX, A	VE02		2	
3414	SODIUM CYANIDE SOLUTION	6.1	T4	III	6.1	802	5 L	E1		PP, EP, TOX, A	VE02		0	
3415	SODIUM FLUORIDE SOLUTION	6.1	T4	III	6.1	802	5 L	E1		PP, EP, TOX, A	VE02		0	
3416	CHLOROACETOPHENONE, LIQUID	6.1	T1	II	6.1	802	0	E0		PP, EP, TOX, A	VE02		2	
3417	XYLYL BROMIDE, SOLID	6.1	T2	II	6.1	802	0	E4		PP, EP	VE02		2	
3418	2,4-TOLUYLENEDIAMINE SOLUTION	6.1	T1	III	6.1	802	5 L	E1		PP, EP, TOX, A	VE02		0	
3419	BORON TRIFLUORIDE ACETIC ACID COMPLEX, SOLID	8	C4	II	8		1 kg	E2		PP, EP			0	
3420	BORON TRIFLUORIDE PROPIONIC ACID COMPLEX, SOLID	8	C4	II	8		1 kg	E2		PP, EP			0	
3421	POTASSIUM HYDROGENDIFLUORIDE SOLUTION	8	CT1	II	8+6.1	802	1 L	E2		PP, EP, TOX, A	VE02		2	

UN No. or ID No.	Name and description	Class	Classification Code	Packing group	Labels	Special provisions	Limited and excepted quantities		Carriage permitted	Equipment required	Ventilation	Provisions concerning loading, unloading and carriage	Number of blue cones/lights	Remarks
3.1.2	3.1.2	2.2	2.2	2.1.1.3	5.2.2	3.3	3.4	3.5.1.2	3.2.1	8.1.5	7.1.6	7.1.6	7.1.5	3.2.1
(1)	(2)	(3a)	(3b)	(4)	(5)	(6)	(7a)	(7b)	(8)	(9)	(10)	(11)	(12)	(13)
3421	POTASSIUM HYDROGENDIFLUORIDE SOLUTION	8	CT1	III	8+6.1	802	5 L	E1		PP, EP, TOX, A	VE02		0	
3422	POTASSIUM FLUORIDE SOLUTION	6.1	T4	III	6.1	802	5 L	E1		PP, EP, TOX, A	VE02		0	
3423	TETRAMETHYLAMMONIUM HYDROXIDE, SOLID	8	C8	II	8		1 kg	E2		PP, EP			0	
3424	AMMONIUM DINITRO -o-CRESOLATE SOLUTION	6.1	T1	II	6.1	802	100 ml	E4		PP, EP, TOX, A	VE02		2	
3424	AMMONIUM DINITRO -o-CRESOLATE SOLUTION	6.1	T1	III	6.1	802	5 L	E1		PP, EP, TOX, A	VE02		0	
3425	BROMOACETIC ACID, SOLID	8	C4	II	8		1 kg	E2		PP, EP			0	
3426	ACRYLAMIDE SOLUTION	6.1	T1	III	6.1	802	5 L	E1	T	PP, EP, TOX, A	VE02		0	
3427	CHLOROBENZYL CHLORIDES, SOLID	6.1	T2	III	6.1	802	5 kg	E1		PP, EP			0	
3428	3-CHLORO-4-METHYLPHENYL ISOCYANATE, SOLID	6.1	T2	II	6.1	802	500 g	E4		PP, EP			2	
3429	CHLOROTOLUIDINES, LIQUID	6.1	T1	III	6.1	802	5 L	E1	T	PP, EP, TOX, A	VE02		0	
3430	XYLENOLS, LIQUID	6.1	T1	II	6.1	802	100 ml	E4		PP, EP, TOX, A	VE02		2	
3431	NITROBENZOTRIFLUORIDES, SOLID	6.1	T2	II	6.1	802	500 g	E4		PP, EP			2	
3432	POLYCHLORINATED BIPHENYLS, SOLID	9	M2	II	9	305 802	1 kg	E2		PP, EP			0	
3434	NITROCRESOLS, LIQUID	6.1	T1	III	6.1	802	5 L	E1		PP, EP, TOX, A	VE02		0	
3436	HEXAFLUOROACETONE HYDRATE, SOLID	6.1	T2	II	6.1	802	500 g	E4		PP, EP			2	
3437	CHLOROCRESOLS, SOLID	6.1	T2	II	6.1	802	500 g	E4		PP, EP			2	
3438	alpha-METHYLBENZYL ALCOHOL, SOLID	6.1	T2	III	6.1	802	5 kg	E1		PP, EP			0	
3439	NITRILES, SOLID, TOXIC, N.O.S.	6.1	T2	I	6.1	274 802	0	E5		PP, EP			2	
3439	NITRILES, SOLID, TOXIC, N.O.S.	6.1	T2	II	6.1	274 802	500 g	E4		PP, EP			2	
3439	NITRILES, SOLID, TOXIC, N.O.S.	6.1	T2	III	6.1	274 802	5 kg	E1		PP, EP			0	
3440	SELENIUM COMPOUND, LIQUID, N.O.S.	6.1	T4	I	6.1	274 563 802	0	E5		PP, EP, TOX, A	VE02		2	
3440	SELENIUM COMPOUND, LIQUID, N.O.S.	6.1	T4	II	6.1	274 563 802	100 ml	E4		PP, EP, TOX, A	VE02		2	
3440	SELENIUM COMPOUND, LIQUID, N.O.S.	6.1	T4	III	6.1	274 563 802	5 L	E1		PP, EP, TOX, A	VE02		0	
3441	CHLORODINITROBENZENES, SOLID	6.1	T2	II	6.1	279 802	500 g	E4		PP, EP			2	
3442	DICHLOROANILINES, SOLID	6.1	T2	II	6.1	279 802	500 g	E4		PP, EP			2	
3443	DINITROBENZENES, SOLID	6.1	T2	II	6.1	802	500 g	E4		PP, EP			2	
3444	NICOTINE HYDROCHLORIDE, SOLID	6.1	T2	II	6.1	43 802	500 g	E4		PP, EP			2	
3445	NICOTINE SULPHATE, SOLID	6.1	T2	II	6.1	802	500 g	E4		PP, EP			2	
3446	NITROTOLUENES, SOLID	6.1	T2	II	6.1	802	500 g	E4		PP, EP			2	
3447	NITROXYLENES, SOLID	6.1	T2	I	6.1	802	500 g	E4	T	PP, EP			2	
3448	TEAR GAS SUBSTANCE, SOLID, N.O.S.	6.1	T2	I	6.1	274 802	0	E0		PP, EP			2	
3448	TEAR GAS SUBSTANCE, SOLID, N.O.S.	6.1	T2	II	6.1	274 802	0	E0		PP, EP			2	

UN No. or ID No. (1)	Name and description (2)	Class (3a)	Classification Code (3b)	Packing group (4)	Labels (5)	Special provisions (6)	Limited and excepted quantities 3.4 (7a)	3.5.1.2 (7b)	Carriage permitted (8)	Equipment required (9)	Venti- lation (10)	Provisions concerning loading, unloading and carriage (11)	Number of blue cones/ lights (12)	Remarks (13)
3449	BROMOBENZYL CYANIDES, SOLID	6.1	T2	I	6.1	138 802	0	E5		PP, EP			2	
3450	DIPHENYLCHLOROARSINE, SOLID	6.1	T3	I	6.1	802	0	E0		PP, EP			2	
3451	TOLUIDINES, SOLID	6.1	T2	II	6.1	279 802	500 g	E4	T	PP, EP			2	
3452	XYLIDINES, SOLID	6.1	T2	II	6.1	802	500 g	E4		PP, EP			2	
3453	PHOSPHORIC ACID, SOLID	8	C2	III	8		5 kg	E1		PP, EP			0	
3454	DINITROTOLUENES, SOLID	6.1	T2	II	6.1	802	500 g	E4		PP, EP			2	
3455	CRESOLS, SOLID	6.1	TC2	II	6.1+8	802	500 g	E4	T	PP, EP			2	
3456	NITROSYLSULPHURIC ACID, SOLID	8	C2	II	8		1 kg	E2		PP, EP			0	
3457	CHLORONITROTOLUENES, SOLID	6.1	T2	III	6.1	802	5 kg	E1		PP, EP			0	
3458	NITROANISOLES, SOLID	6.1	T2	III	6.1	279 802	5 kg	E1		PP, EP			0	
3459	NITROBROMOBENZENES, SOLID	6.1	T2	III	6.1	802	5 kg	E1		PP, EP			0	
3460	N-ETHYLBENZYLTOLUIDINES, SOLID	6.1	T2	III	6.1	802	5 kg	E1		PP, EP			0	
3462	TOXINS, EXTRACTED FROM LIVING SOURCES, SOLID, N.O.S.	6.1	T2	I	6.1	210 274 802	0	E5		PP, EP			2	
3462	TOXINS, EXTRACTED FROM LIVING SOURCES, SOLID, N.O.S.	6.1	T2	II	6.1	210 274 802	500 g	E4		PP, EP			2	
3462	TOXINS, EXTRACTED FROM LIVING SOURCES, SOLID, N.O.S.	6.1	T2	III	6.1	210 274 802	5 kg	E1		PP, EP			0	
3463	PROPIONIC ACID with not less than 90% acid by mass	8	CF1	II	8+3	43 274 802	1 L	E2	T	PP, EP, EX, A	VE01		1	
3464	ORGANOPHOSPHORUS COMPOUND, SOLID, TOXIC, N.O.S.	6.1	T2	I	6.1	43 274 802	0	E5		PP, EP			2	
3464	ORGANOPHOSPHORUS COMPOUND, SOLID, TOXIC, N.O.S.	6.1	T2	II	6.1	43 274 802	500 g	E4		PP, EP			2	
3464	ORGANOPHOSPHORUS COMPOUND, SOLID, TOXIC, N.O.S.	6.1	T2	III	6.1	43 274 802	5 kg	E1		PP, EP			0	
3465	ORGANOARSENIC COMPOUND, SOLID, N.O.S.	6.1	T3	I	6.1	274 802	0	E5		PP, EP			2	
3465	ORGANOARSENIC COMPOUND, SOLID, N.O.S.	6.1	T3	II	6.1	274 802	500 g	E4		PP, EP			2	
3465	ORGANOARSENIC COMPOUND, SOLID, N.O.S.	6.1	T3	III	6.1	274 802	5 kg	E1		PP, EP			0	
3466	METAL CARBONYLS, SOLID, N.O.S	6.1	T3	I	6.1	274 562 802	0	E5		PP, EP			2	
3466	METAL CARBONYLS, SOLID, N.O.S	6.1	T3	II	6.1	274 562 802	500 g	E4		PP, EP			2	

UN No. or ID No. (1)	Name and description (2)	Class (3a)	Classification Code (3b)	Packing group (4)	Labels (5)	Special provisions (6)	Limited and excepted quantities (7a) 3.4	(7b) 3.5.1.2	Carriage permitted (8)	Equipment required (9)	Ventilation (10)	Provisions concerning loading, unloading and carriage (11)	Number of blue cones/lights (12)	Remarks (13)
		2.2	2.2	2.1.1.3	5.2.2	3.3	3.4	3.5.1.2	3.2.1	8.1.5	7.1.6	7.1.6	7.1.5	3.2.1
3466	METAL CARBONYLS, SOLID, N.O.S	6.1	T3	III	6.1	274 562 802	5 kg	E1		PP, EP			0	
3467	ORGANOMETALLIC COMPOUND, SOLID, TOXIC, N.O.S.	6.1	T3	I	6.1	274 562 802	0	E5		PP, EP			2	
3467	ORGANOMETALLIC COMPOUND, SOLID, TOXIC, N.O.S.	6.1	T3	II	6.1	274 562 802	500 g	E4		PP, EP			2	
3467	ORGANOMETALLIC COMPOUND, SOLID, TOXIC, N.O.S	6.1	T3	III	6.1	274 562 802	5 kg	E1		PP, EP			0	
3468	HYDROGEN IN A METAL HYDRIDE STORAGE SYSTEM or HYDROGEN IN A METAL HYDRIDE STORAGE SYSTEM CONTAINED IN EQUIPMENT or HYDROGEN IN A METAL HYDRIDE STORAGE SYSTEM PACKED WITH EQUIPMENT	2	1F		2.1	321 356	0	E0		PP, EX, A	VE01		1	
3469	PAINT, FLAMMABLE, CORROSIVE (including paint, lacquer, enamel, stain, shellac, varnish, polish, liquid filler and liquid lacquer base) or PAINT RELATED MATERIAL, FLAMMABLE, CORROSIVE (including paint thinning or reducing compound)	3	FC	I	3+8	163 367	0	E0		PP, EX, A	VE01		1	
3469	PAINT, FLAMMABLE, CORROSIVE (including paint, lacquer, enamel, stain, shellac, varnish, polish, liquid filler and liquid lacquer base) or PAINT RELATED MATERIAL, FLAMMABLE, CORROSIVE (including paint thinning or reducing compound)	3	FC	II	3+8	163 367	1 L	E2		PP, EX, A	VE01		1	
3469	PAINT, FLAMMABLE, CORROSIVE (including paint, lacquer, enamel, stain, shellac, varnish, polish, liquid filler and liquid lacquer base) or PAINT RELATED MATERIAL, FLAMMABLE, CORROSIVE (including paint thinning or reducing compound)	3	FC	III	3+8	163 367	5 L	E1		PP, EX, A	VE01		0	
3470	PAINT, CORROSIVE, FLAMMABLE (including paint, lacquer, enamel, stain, shellac, varnish, polish, liquid filler and liquid lacquer base) or PAINT RELATED MATERIAL CORROSIVE, FLAMMABLE (including paint thinning or reducing compound)	8	CF1	II	8+3	163 367	1 L	E2		PP, EP, EX, A	VE01		1	
3471	HYDROGENDIFLUORIDES SOLUTION, N.O.S.	8	CT1	II	8+6.1	802	1 L	E2		PP, EP			2	
3471	HYDROGENDIFLUORIDES SOLUTION, N.O.S.	8	CT1	III	8+6.1	802	5 L	E1		PP, EP			0	
3472	CROTONIC ACID, LIQUID	8	C3	III	8		5 L	E1		PP, EP			0	
3473	FUEL CELL CARTRIDGES or FUEL CELL CARTRIDGES CONTAINED IN EQUIPMENT or FUEL CELL CARTRIDGES PACKED WITH EQUIPMENT containing flammable liquids	3	F3		3	328	1 L	E0		PP, EX, A	VE01		1	
3474	1-HYDROXYBENZOTRIAZOLE MONOHYDRATE	4.1	D	I	4.1		0	E0		PP			1	
3475	ETHANOL AND GASOLINE MIXTURE or ETHANOL AND MOTOR SPIRIT MIXTURE or ETHANOL AND PETROL MIXTURE, with more than 10% ethanol	3	F1	II	3	333	1 L	E2	T	PP, EX, A	VE01		1	

UN No. or ID No. (1)	Name and description (2)	Class (3a)	Classification Code (3b)	Packing group (4)	Labels (5)	Special provisions (6)	Limited quantities (7a)	Excepted quantities (7b)	Carriage permitted (8)	Equipment required (9)	Ventilation (10)	Provisions concerning loading, unloading and carriage (11)	Number of blue cones/lights (12)	Remarks (13)
3476	FUEL CELL CARTRIDGES or FUEL CELL CARTRIDGES CONTAINED IN EQUIPMENT or FUEL CELL CARTRIDGES PACKED WITH EQUIPMENT, containing water-reactive substances	4.3	W3		4.3	328 334	500 ml or 500 g	E0		PP, EX, A	VE01	HA08	0	
3477	FUEL CELL CARTRIDGES or FUEL CELL CARTRIDGES CONTAINED IN EQUIPMENT or FUEL CELL CARTRIDGES PACKED WITH EQUIPMENT, containing corrosive substances	8	C11		8	328 334	1 L or 1 kg	E0		PP, EP, A			0	
3478	FUEL CELL CARTRIDGES or FUEL CELL CARTRIDGES CONTAINED IN EQUIPMENT or FUEL CELL CARTRIDGES PACKED WITH EQUIPMENT, containing liquefied flammable gas	2	6F		2.1	328 338	120 ml	E0		PP, EX, A	VE01		1	
3479	FUEL CELL CARTRIDGES or FUEL CELL CARTRIDGES CONTAINED IN EQUIPMENT or FUEL CELL CARTRIDGES PACKED WITH EQUIPMENT, containing hydrogen in metal hydride	2	6F		2.1	328 339	120 ml	E0		PP, EX, A	VE01		1	
3480	LITHIUM ION BATTERIES (including lithium ion polymer batteries)	9	M4		9A	188 230 310 348 376 377 387 636	0	E0		PP			0	
3481	LITHIUM ION BATTERIES CONTAINED IN EQUIPMENT or LITHIUM ION BATTERIES PACKED WITH EQUIPMENT (including lithium ion polymer batteries)	9	M4		9A	188 230 310 348 360 376 377 387 390 670	0	E0		PP			0	
3482	ALKALI METAL DISPERSION, FLAMMABLE or ALKALINE EARTH METAL DISPERSION, FLAMMABLE	4.3	WF1	I	4.3+3	182 183 506	0	E0		PP, EX, A	VE01	HA08	1	
3483	MOTOR FUEL ANTI-KNOCK MIXTURE, FLAMMABLE	6.1	TF1	I	6.1+3	802	0	E0		PP, EP, EX, TOX, A	VE01, VE02		2	
3484	HYDRAZINE AQUEOUS SOLUTION, FLAMMABLE with more than 37% hydrazine, by mass	8	CFT	I	8+3+6.1	530	0	E0		PP, EP, EX, TOX, A	VE01, VE02		2	
3485	CALCIUM HYPOCHLORITE, DRY, CORROSIVE or CALCIUM HYPOCHLORITE MIXTURE, DRY, CORROSIVE with more than 39% available chlorine (8.8% available oxygen)	5.1	OC2	II	5.1+8	314	1 kg	E2		PP			0	
3486	CALCIUM HYPOCHLORITE MIXTURE, DRY, CORROSIVE with more than 10% but not more than 39% available chlorine	5.1	OC2	III	5.1+8	314	5 kg	E1		PP			0	

UN No. or ID No.	Name and description	Class	Classification Code	Packing group	Labels	Special provisions	Limited and excepted quantities		Carriage permitted	Equipment required	Ventilation	Provisions concerning loading, unloading and carriage	Number of blue cones/lights	Remarks
3.1.2	3.1.2	2.2	2.2	2.1.1.3	5.2.2	3.3	3.4	3.5.1.2	3.2.1	8.1.5	7.1.6	7.1.6	7.1.5	3.2.1
(1)	(2)	(3a)	(3b)	(4)	(5)	(6)	(7a)	(7b)	(8)	(9)	(10)	(11)	(12)	(13)
3487	CALCIUM HYPOCHLORITE, HYDRATED, CORROSIVE or CALCIUM HYPOCHLORITE, HYDRATED MIXTURE, CORROSIVE with not less than 5.5% but not more than 16% water	5.1	OC2	II	5.1+8	314 322	1 kg	E2		PP			0	
3487	CALCIUM HYPOCHLORITE, HYDRATED, CORROSIVE or CALCIUM HYPOCHLORITE, HYDRATED MIXTURE, CORROSIVE with not less than 5.5% but not more than 16% water	5.1	OC2	III	5.1+8	314	5 kg	E1		PP			0	
3488	TOXIC BY INHALATION LIQUID, FLAMMABLE, CORROSIVE, N.O.S. with an LC_{50} lower than or equal to 200 ml/m³ and saturated vapour concentration greater than or equal to 500 LC_{50}	6.1	TFC	I	6.1+3+8	274 802	0	E0		PP, EP, EX, TOX, A	VE01, VE02		2	
3489	TOXIC BY INHALATION LIQUID, FLAMMABLE, CORROSIVE, N.O.S. with an LC_{50} lower than or equal to 1000 ml/m³ and saturated vapour concentration greater than or equal to 10 LC_{50}	6.1	TFC	I	6.1+3+8	274	0	E0		PP, EP, EX, TOX, A	VE01, VE02		2	
3490	TOXIC BY INHALATION LIQUID, WATER-REACTIVE, FLAMMABLE, N.O.S. with an LC_{50} lower than or equal to 200 ml/m³ and saturated vapour concentration greater than or equal to 500 LC_{50}	6.1	TFW	I	6.1+4.3+3	274 802	0	E0		PP, EP, EX, TOX, A	VE01, VE02		2	
3491	TOXIC BY INHALATION LIQUID, WATER-REACTIVE, FLAMMABLE, N.O.S. with an LC_{50} lower than or equal to 1000 ml/m³ and saturated vapour concentration greater than or equal to 10 LC_{50}	6.1	TFW	I	6.1+4.3+3	274 802	0	E0		PP, EP, EX, TOX, A	VE01, VE02		2	
3494	PETROLEUM SOUR CRUDE OIL, FLAMMABLE, TOXIC	3	FT1	I	3+6.1	343 802	0	E0	T	PP, EP, EX, TOX, A	VE01, VE02		2	
3494	PETROLEUM SOUR CRUDE OIL, FLAMMABLE, TOXIC	3	FT1	II	3+6.1	343 802	1 L	E2	T	PP, EP, EX, TOX, A	VE01, VE02		2	
3494	PETROLEUM SOUR CRUDE OIL, FLAMMABLE, TOXIC	3	FT1	III	3+6.1	343 802	5 L	E1	T	PP, EP, EX, TOX, A	VE01, VE02		0	
3495	IODINE	8	CT2	III	8+6.1	279 802	5 kg	E1		PP, EP, TOX, A	VE02		0	
3496	Batteries, nickel-metal hydride	9	M11						NOT SUBJECT TO ADN					
3497	KRILL MEAL	4.2	S2	II	4.2	300	0	E2		PP			0	
3497	KRILL MEAL	4.2	S2	III	4.2	300	0	E1		PP			0	
3498	IODINE MONOCHLORIDE, LIQUID	8	C1	II	8		1L	E0		PP, EP			0	
3499	CAPACITOR, ELECTRIC DOUBLE LAYER (with an energy storage capacity greater than 0.3 Wh)	9	M11		9	361	0	E0		PP			0	
3500	CHEMICAL UNDER PRESSURE, N.O.S	2	8A		2.2	274 659	0	E0		PP			0	
3501	CHEMICAL UNDER PRESSURE, FLAMMABLE, N.O.S.	2	8F		2.1	274 659	0	E0		PP, EX, A	VE01		1	
3502	CHEMICAL UNDER PRESSURE, TOXIC, N.O.S.	2	8T		2.2+6.1	274 659	0	E0		PP, EP, TOX, A	VE02		2	

UN No. or ID No.	Name and description	Class	Classification Code	Packing group	Labels	Special provisions	Limited and excepted quantities		Carriage permitted	Equipment required	Venti-lation	Provisions concerning loading, unloading and carriage	Number of blue cones/ lights	Remarks
		2.2	2.2	- 2.1.1.3	5.2.2	3.3	3.4	3.5.1.2	3.2.1	8.1.5	7.1.6	7.1.6	7.1.5	3.2.1
(1)	(2)	(3a)	(3b)	(4)	(5)	(6)	(7a)	(7b)	(8)	(9)	(10)	(11)	(12)	(13)
3503	CHEMICAL UNDER PRESSURE, CORROSIVE, N.O.S.	2	8C		2.2+8	274 659	0	E0		PP, EP	VE02		0	
3504	CHEMICAL UNDER PRESSURE, FLAMMABLE, TOXIC, N.O.S.	2	8TF		2.1+6.1	274 659	0	E0		PP, EP, EX, TOX, A	VE01, VE02		2	
3505	CHEMICAL UNDER PRESSURE, FLAMMABLE, CORROSIVE, N.O.S.	2	8FC		2.1+8	274 659	0	E0		PP, EP, EX, A	VE01		1	
3506	MERCURY CONTAINED IN MANUFACTURED ARTICLES	8	CT3		8+6.1	366	5kg	E0		PP, EP, TOX, A	VE02		0	
3507	URANIUM HEXAFLUORIDE, RADIOACTIVE MATERIAL, EXCEPTED PACKAGE, less than 0.1 kg per package, non-fissile or fissile-excepted	6.1		I	6.1+8	317 369	0	E0		PP, EP			0	
3508	CAPACITOR, ASYMMETRIC (with an energy storage capacity greater than 0.3Wh)	9	M11		9	372	0			PP			0	
3509	PACKAGING DISCARDED, EMPTY, UNCLEANED	9	M11		9	663	0	E0		PP			0	
3510	ADSORBED GAS, FLAMMABLE, N.O.S.	2	9F		2.1	274	0	E0		PP, EX, A	VE01		1	
3511	ADSORBED GAS, N.O.S.	2	9A		2.2	274	0	E0		PP			0	
3512	ADSORBED GAS, TOXIC, N.O.S.	2	9T		2.3	274	0	E0		PP, EP, TOX, A	VE02		2	
3513	ADSORBED GAS, OXIDIZING, N.O.S.	2	9O		2.2+5.1	274	0	E0		PP			0	
3514	ADSORBED GAS, TOXIC, FLAMMABLE, N.O.S.	2	9TF		2.3+2.1	274	0	E0		PP, EP, EX, TOX, A	VE01, VE02		2	
3515	ADSORBED GAS, TOXIC, OXIDIZING, N.O.S.	2	9TO		2.3+5.1	274	0	E0		PP, EP, TOX, A	VE02		2	
3516	ADSORBED GAS, TOXIC, CORROSIVE, N.O.S.	2	9TC		2.3+8	274 379	0	E0		PP, EP, TOX, A	VE02		2	
3517	ADSORBED GAS, TOXIC, FLAMMABLE, CORROSIVE, N.O.S.	2	9TFC		2.3+2.1+8	274	0	E0		PP, EP, EX, TOX, A	VE01, VE02		2	
3518	ADSORBED GAS, TOXIC, OXIDIZING, CORROSIVE, N.O.S.	2	9TOC		2.3+5.1+8	274	0	E0		PP, EP, TOX, A	VE02		2	
3519	BORON TRIFLUORIDE, ADSORBED	2	9TC		2.3+8		0	E0		PP, EP, TOX, A	VE02		2	
3520	CHLORINE, ADSORBED	2	9TOC		2.3+5.1+8		0	E0		PP, EP, TOX, A	VE02		2	
3521	SILICON TETRAFLUORIDE, ADSORBED	2	9TC		2.3+8		0	E0		PP, EP, TOX, A	VE02		2	
3522	ARSINE, ADSORBED	2	9TF		2.3+2.1		0	E0		PP, EP, EX, TOX, A	VE01, VE02		2	
3523	GERMANE, ADSORBED	2	9TF		2.3+2.1		0	E0		PP, EP, EX, TOX, A	VE01, VE02		2	
3524	PHOSPHORUS PENTAFLUORIDE, ADSORBED	2	9TC		2.3+8		0	E0		PP, EP, TOX, A	VE02		2	
3525	PHOSPHINE, ADSORBED	2	9TF		2.3+2.1		0	E0		PP, EP, EX, TOX, A	VE01, VE02		2	
3526	HYDROGEN SELENIDE, ADSORBED	2	9TF		2.3+2.1		0	E0		PP, EP, EX, TOX, A	VE01, VE02		2	
3527	POLYESTER RESIN KIT, solid base material	4.1	F4	II	4.1	236 340	5Kg	See SP 340		PP			1	
3527	POLYESTER RESIN KIT, solid base material	4.1	F4	III	4.1	236 340	5Kg	See SP 340		PP			0	

UN No. or ID No.	Name and description	Class	Classification Code	Packing group	Labels	Special provisions	Limited and excepted quantities		Carriage permitted	Equipment required	Ventilation	Provisions concerning loading, unloading and carriage	Number of blue cones/ lights	Remarks
	3.1.2	2.2	2.2	2.1.1.3	5.2.2	3.3	3.4	3.5.1.2	3.2.1	8.1.5	7.1.6	7.1.6	7.1.5	3.2.1
(1)	(2)	(3a)	(3b)	(4)	(5)	(6)	(7a)	(7b)	(8)	(9)	(10)	(11)	(12)	(13)
3528	ENGINE, INTERNAL COMBUSTION, FLAMMABLE LIQUID POWERED or ENGINE, FUEL CELL, FLAMMABLE LIQUID POWERED or MACHINERY, INTERNAL COMBUSTION, FLAMMABLE LIQUID POWERED or MACHINERY, FUEL CELL, FLAMMABLE LIQUID POWERED	3	F3		3	363 667 669	0	E0		PP, EX, A	VE01		0	
3529	ENGINE, INTERNAL COMBUSTION, FLAMMABLE GAS POWERED or ENGINE, FUEL CELL, FLAMMABLE GAS POWERED or MACHINERY, INTERNAL COMBUSTION, FLAMMABLE GAS POWERED or MACHINERY, FUEL CELL, FLAMMABLE GAS POWERED	2	6F		2.1	363 667 669	0	E0		PP, EX, A	VE01		0	
3530	ENGINE, INTERNAL COMBUSTION or MACHINERY, INTERNAL COMBUSTION	9	M11		9	363 667 669	0	E0		PP			0	
3531	POLYMERIZING SUBSTANCE, SOLID, STABILIZED, N.O.S.	4.1	PM1	III	4.1	274 386 676	0	E0		PP			0	
3532	POLYMERIZING SUBSTANCE, LIQUID, STABILIZED, N.O.S.	4.1	PM1	III	4.1	274 386 676	0	E0		PP			0	
3533	POLYMERIZING SUBSTANCE, SOLID, TEMPERATURE CONTROLLED, N.O.S.	4.1	PM2	III	4.1	274 386 676	0	E0		PP			0	
3534	POLYMERIZING SUBSTANCE, LIQUID, TEMPERATURE CONTROLLED, N.O.S.	4.1	PM2	III	4.1	274 386 676	0	E0		PP			0	
3535	TOXIC SOLID, FLAMMABLE, INORGANIC, N.O.S.	6.1	TF3	I	6.1 +4.1	274	0	E5		PP, EP, EX, A	VE01		2	
3535	TOXIC SOLID, FLAMMABLE, INORGANIC, N.O.S.	6.1	TF3	II	6.1 +4.1	274	500 g	E4		PP, EP, EX, A	VE01		2	
3536	LITHIUM BATTERIES INSTALLED IN CARGO TRANSPORT UNIT lithium ion batteries or lithium metal batteries	9	M4		9	389	0	E0		PP			0	
3537	ARTICLES CONTAINING FLAMMABLE GAS, N.O.S.	2	6F		See 5.2.2.1.12	274 802	0	E0		PP, EX, A	VE01		1	
3538	ARTICLES CONTAINING NON-FLAMMABLE, NON TOXIC GAS, N.O.S.	2	6A		See 5.2.2.1.12	274 396	0	E0		PP			0	
3539	ARTICLES CONTAINING TOXIC GAS, N.O.S.	2	6T		See 5.2.2.1.12	274 802	0	E0		PP, EP, TOX, A	VE02		2	
3540	ARTICLES CONTAINING FLAMMABLE LIQUID, N.O.S.	3	F3		See 5.2.2.1.12	274 802	0	E0		PP, EX, A	VE01		1	
3541	ARTICLES CONTAINING FLAMMABLE SOLID, N.O.S.	4.1	F4		See 5.2.2.1.12	274 802	0	E0		PP			0	
3542	ARTICLES CONTAINING A SUBSTANCE LIABLE TO SPONTANEOUS COMBUSTION, N.O.S.	4.2	S6		See 5.2.2.1.12	274 802	0	E0		PP			0	

UN No. or ID No.	Name and description	Class	Classi-fication Code	Packing group	Labels	Special provis-ions	Limited and excepted quantities		Carriage permitted	Equipment required	Venti-lation	Provisions concerning loading, unloading and carriage	Number of blue cones/ lights	Remarks
	3.1.2	2.2	2.2	2.1.1.3	5.2.2	3.3	3.4	3.5.1.2	3.2.1	8.1.5	7.1.6	7.1.6	7.1.5	3.2.1
(1)	(2)	(3a)	(3b)	(4)	(5)	(6)	(7a)	(7b)	(8)	(9)	(10)	(11)	(12)	(13)
3543	ARTICLES CONTAINING A SUBSTANCE WHICH IN CONTACT WITH WATER EMITS FLAMMABLE GASES, N.O.S.	4.3	W3		See 5.2.2.1.12	274 802	0	E0		PP, EX, A	VE01	HA08	0	
3544	ARTICLES CONTAINING OXIDIZING SUBSTANCE, N.O.S.	5.1	O3		See 5.2.2.1.12	274 802	0	E0		PP			0	
3545	ARTICLES CONTAINING ORGANIC PEROXIDE, N.O.S.	5.2	P1 or P2		See 5.2.2.1.12	274 802	0	E0		PP, EX, A	VE01		0	
3546	ARTICLES CONTAINING TOXIC SUBSTANCE, N.O.S.	6.1	T10		See 5.2.2.1.12	274 802	0	E0		PP, EP, TOX, A	VE02		0	
3547	ARTICLES CONTAINING CORROSIVE SUBSTANCE, N.O.S.	8	C11		See 5.2.2.1.12	274 802	0	E0		PP, EP			0	
3548	ARTICLES CONTAINING MISCELLANEOUS DANGEROUS GOODS, N.O.S.	9	M11		See 5.2.2.1.12	274 802	0	E0		PP			0	
3549	MEDICAL WASTE, CATEGORY A, AFFECTING HUMANS, solid or MEDICAL WASTE, CATEGORY A, AFFECTING ANIMALS only, solid	6.2	I3		6.2	395 802	0	E0		PP			0	
3550	COBALT DIHYDROXIDE POWDER, containing not less than 10 % respirable particles	6.1	T5	I	6.1	802	0	E5		PP, EP			2	
9000	AMMONIA, DEEPLY REFRIGERATED	2	3TC		2.3+8				T	PP, EP, TOX, A	VE02		2	Only admitted for carriage in tank vessels
9001	SUBSTANCE WITH A FLASHPOINT ABOVE 60 °C, HEATED within a range of 15 K below the flashpoint	3	F4		none				T	PP			0	Dangerous only when carried in tank vessels
9002	SUBSTANCES WITH A SELF-IGNITION TEMPERATURE OF 200 °C AND BELOW, N.O.S.	3	F5		none				T	PP			0	Dangerous only when carried in tank vessels
9003	SUBSTANCES WITH A FLASH-POINT ABOVE 60 °C AND NOT MORE THAN 100 °C, which do not belong to another Class	9	M12		none				T	PP			0	Dangerous only when carried in tank vessels
9004	DIPHENYLMETHANE-4, 4'-DIISOCYANATE	9	M12		none				T	PP			0	Dangerous only when carried in tank vessels
9005	ENVIRONMENTALLY HAZARDOUS SUBSTANCE, SOLID, N.O.S. MOLTEN	9	M12		none				T	PP			0	Dangerous only when carried in tank vessels
9006	ENVIRONMENTALLY HAZARDOUS SUBSTANCE, LIQUID, N.O.S.	9	M12		none				T	PP			0	Dangerous only when carried in tank vessels

3.2.2   **Table B: List of dangerous goods in alphabetical order**

The following Table B is an alphabetical list of the substances and articles which are listed in the UN numerical order in Table A of 3.2.1. It does not form an integral part of ADN. It has been prepared, with all necessary care by the Secretariat of the United Nations Economic Commission for Europe, in order to facilitate the consultation of the annexed Regulations, but it cannot be relied upon as a substitute for the careful study and observance of the actual provisions of those annexed Regulations which, in case of conflict, are deemed to be authoritative.

NOTE 1: For the purpose of determining the alphabetical order the following information has been ignored, even when it forms part of the proper shipping name: numbers; Greek letters; the abbreviations "sec" and "tert"; the prefixes "cis" and "trans"; and the letters "N" (nitrogen), "n" (normal), "o" (ortho) "m" (meta), "p" (para) and "N.O.S." (not otherwise specified).

NOTE 2: The name of a substance or article in block capital letters indicates a proper shipping name (see 3.1.2).

NOTE 3: The name of a substance or article in block capital letters followed by the word "see" indicates an alternative proper shipping name or part of a proper shipping name (except for PCBs) (see 3.1.2.1).

NOTE 4: An entry in lower case letters followed by the word "see" indicates that the entry is not a proper shipping name; it is a synonym.

NOTE 5: Where an entry is partly in block capital letters and partly in lower case letters, the latter part is considered not to be part of the proper shipping name (see 3.1.2.1).

NOTE 6: A proper shipping name may be used in the singular or plural, as appropriate, for the purposes of documentation and package marking (see 3.1.2.3).

NOTE 7: For the exact determination of a proper shipping name, see 3.1.2.

Name and description	UN No.	Class	Remarks	Name and description	UN No.	Class	Remarks
Accumulators, electric, see	2794	8		ACROLEIN, STABILIZED	1092	6.1	
	2795	8		ACRYLAMIDE, SOLID	2074	6.1	
	2800	8					
	3028	8		ACRYLAMIDE, SOLUTION	3426	6.1	
	3292	4.3					
ACETAL	1088	3		ACRYLIC ACID, STABILIZED	2218	8	
ACETALDEHYDE	1089	3		ACRYLONITRILE, STABILIZED	1093	3	
ACETALDEHYDE AMMONIA	1841	9		Actinolite, see	2212	9	
ACETALDEHYDE OXIME	2332	3		Activated carbon, see	1362	4.2	
ACETIC ACID, GLACIAL	2789	8		Activated charcoal, see	1362	4.2	
ACETIC ACID SOLUTION, more than 10% but not more than 80% acid, by mass	2790	8		ADHESIVES containing flammable liquid	1133	3	
ACETIC ACID SOLUTION, more than 80% acid, by mass	2789	8		ADIPONITRILE	2205	6.1	
ACETIC ANHYDRIDE	1715	8		ADSORBED GAS, FLAMMABLE, N.O.S.	3510	2	
Acetoin, see	2621	3		ADSORBED GAS, N.O.S.	3511	2	
ACETONE	1090	3		ADSORBED GAS, OXIDIZING, N.O.S.	3513	2	
ACETONE CYANOHYDRIN, STABILIZED	1541	6.1		ADSORBED GAS, TOXIC, CORROSIVE, N.O.S.	3516	2	
ACETONE OILS	1091	3		ADSORBED GAS, TOXIC, FLAMMABLE, CORROSIVE, N.O.S.	3517	2	
ACETONITRILE	1648	3					
ACETYL BROMIDE	1716	8		ADSORBED GAS, TOXIC, FLAMMABLE, N.O.S.	3514	2	
ACETYL CHLORIDE	1717	3		ADSORBED GAS, TOXIC, N.O.S.	3512	2	
ACETYLENE, DISSOLVED	1001	2		ADSORBED GAS, TOXIC, OXIDIZING, CORROSIVE, N.O.S.	3518	2	
ACETYLENE, SOLVENT FREE	3374	2					
Acetylene tetrabromide, see	2504	6.1		ADSORBED GAS, TOXIC, OXIDIZING, N.O.S.	3515	2	
Acetylene tetrachloride, see	1702	6.1					
ACETYL IODIDE	1898	8		Aeroplane flares, see	0093	1	
					0403	1	
ACETYL METHYL CARBINOL	2621	3			0404	1	
Acid butyl phosphate, see	1718	8			0420	1	
					0421	1	
Acid mixture, hydrofluoric and sulphuric, see	1786	8		AEROSOLS	1950	2	
Acid mixture, nitrating acid, see	1796	8		AGENT, BLASTING, TYPE B	0331	1	
Acid mixture, spent, nitrating acid, see	1826	8		AGENT, BLASTING, TYPE E	0332	1	
Acraldehyde, inhibited, see	1092	6.1		Air bag inflators, see	0503	1	
					3268	9	
ACRIDINE	2713	6.1		Air bag modules, see	0503	1	
ACROLEIN DIMER, STABILIZED	2607	3			3268	9	

Name and description	UN No.	Class	Remarks	Name and description	UN No.	Class	Remarks
AIR, COMPRESSED	1002	2		ALKALINE EARTH METAL ALLOY, N.O.S.	1393	4.3	
Aircraft evacuation slides, see	2990	9		ALKALINE EARTH METAL AMALGAM, LIQUID	1392	4.3	
AIRCRAFT HYDRAULIC POWER UNIT FUEL TANK (containing a mixture of anhydrous hydrazine and methylhydrazine) (M86 fuel)	3165	3		ALKALINE EARTH METAL AMALGAM, SOLID	3402	4.3	
Aircraft survival kits, see	2990	9		ALKALINE EARTH METAL DISPERSION	1391	4.3	
AIR, REFRIGERATED LIQUID	1003	2		ALKALINE EARTH METAL DISPERSION, FLAMMABLE	1391	4.3	
ALCOHOLATES SOLUTION, N.O.S., in alcohol	3274	3		ALKALOIDS, LIQUID, N.O.S.	3140	6.1	
Alcohol, denaturated, see	1986	3		ALKALOIDS, SOLID, N.O.S.	1544	6.1	
	1987	3		ALKALOID SALTS, LIQUID, N.O.S.	3140	6.1	
Alcohol, industrial, see	1986	3					
	1987	3		ALKALOID SALTS, SOLID, N.O.S.	1544	6.1	
ALCOHOLS, N.O.S.	1987	3					
ALCOHOLS, FLAMMABLE, TOXIC, N.O.S.	1986	3		Alkyl aluminium halides, see	3394	4.2	
				ALKYLPHENOLS, LIQUID, N.O.S. (including C2-C12 homologues)	3145	8	
ALCOHOLIC BEVERAGES, with more than 24% but not more than 70% alcohol by volume	3065	3		ALKYLPHENOLS, SOLID, N.O.S. (including C2-C12 homologues)	2430	8	
ALCOHOLIC BEVERAGES, with more than 70% alcohol by volume	3065	3		ALKYLSULPHONIC ACIDS, LIQUID with more than 5% free sulphuric acid	2584	8	
Aldehyde, see	1989	3		ALKYLSULPHONIC ACIDS, LIQUID with not more than 5% free sulphuric acid	2586	8	
ALDEHYDES, N.O.S.	1989	3					
ALDEHYDES, FLAMMABLE, TOXIC, N.O.S.	1988	3		ALKYLSULPHONIC ACIDS, SOLID with more than 5% free sulphuric acid	2583	8	
ALDOL	2839	6.1		ALKYLSULPHONIC ACIDS, SOLID with not more than 5% free sulphuric acid	2585	8	
ALKALI METAL ALCOHOLATES, SELF-HEATING, CORROSIVE, N.O.S.	3206	4.2					
ALKALI METAL ALLOY, LIQUID, N.O.S.	1421	4.3		ALKYLSULPHURIC ACIDS	2571	8	
				Allene, see	2200	2	
ALKALI METAL AMALGAM, LIQUID	1389	4.3		ALLYL ACETATE	2333	3	
ALKALI METAL AMALGAM, SOLID	3401	4.3		ALLYL ALCOHOL	1098	6.1	
ALKALI METAL AMIDES	1390	4.3		ALLYLAMINE	2334	6.1	
ALKALI METAL DISPERSION	1391	4.3		ALLYL BROMIDE	1099	3	
ALKALI METAL DISPERSION, FLAMMABLE	3482	4.3		ALLYL CHLORIDE	1100	3	
Alkaline corrosive battery fluid, see	2797	8		Allyl chlorocarbonate, see	1722	6.1	
ALKALINE EARTH METAL ALCOHOLATES, N.O.S.	3205	4.2		ALLYL CHLOROFORMATE	1722	6.1	

Name and description	UN No.	Class	Remarks	Name and description	UN No.	Class	Remarks
ALLYL ETHYL ETHER	2335	3		ALUMINIUM SMELTING BY-PRODUCTS	3170	4.3	
ALLYL FORMATE	2336	3		Amatols, see	0082	1	
ALLYL GLYCIDYL ETHER	2219	3		AMINES, FLAMMABLE, CORROSIVE, N.O.S.	2733	3	
ALLYL IODIDE	1723	3		AMINES, LIQUID, CORROSIVE, N.O.S.	2735	8	
ALLYL ISOTHIOCYANATE, STABILIZED	1545	6.1		AMINES, LIQUID, CORROSIVE, FLAMMABLE, N.O.S.	2734	8	
ALLYLTRICHLOROSILANE, STABILIZED	1724	8		AMINES, SOLID, CORROSIVE, N.O.S.	3259	8	
Aluminium alkyls, see	3394	4.2		Aminobenzene, see	1547	6.1	
Aluminium alkyl halides, liquid, see	3394	4.2		2-Aminobenzotrifluoruride, see	2942	6.1	
Aluminium alkyl halides, solid, see	3393	4.2		3-Aminobenzotrifluoruride, see	2948	6.1	
Aluminium alkyl hydrides, see	3394	4.2		Aminobutane, see	1125	3	
ALUMINIUM BOROHYDRIDE	2870	4.2		2-AMINO-4-CHLOROPHENOL	2673	6.1	
ALUMINIUM BOROHYDRIDE IN DEVICES	2870	4.2		2-AMINO-5-DIETHYLAMINOPENTANE	2946	6.1	
ALUMINIUM BROMIDE, ANHYDROUS	1725	8		2-AMINO-4,6-DINITROPHENOL, WETTED with not less than 20% water, by mass	3317	4.1	
ALUMINIUM BROMIDE SOLUTION	2580	8		2-(2-AMINOETHOXY) ETHANOL	3055	8	
ALUMINIUM CARBIDE	1394	4.3		N-AMINOETHYLPIPERAZINE	2815	8	
ALUMINIUM CHLORIDE, ANHYDROUS	1726	8		1-Amino-2-nitrobenzene, see	1661	6.1	
ALUMINIUM CHLORIDE SOLUTION	2581	8		1-Amino-3-nitrobenzene, see	1661	6.1	
Aluminium dross, see	3170	4.3		1-Amino-4-nitrobenzene, see	1661	6.1	
ALUMINIUM FERROSILICON POWDER	1395	4.3		AMINOPHENOLS (o-, m-, p-)	2512	6.1	
ALUMINIUM HYDRIDE	2463	4.3		AMINOPYRIDINES (o-, m-, p-)	2671	6.1	
ALUMINIUM NITRATE	1438	5.1		AMMONIA, ANHYDROUS	1005	2	
ALUMINIUM PHOSPHIDE	1397	4.3		AMMONIA, DEEPLY REFRIGERATED	9000	2	Admitted only for carriage in tank vessels
ALUMINIUM PHOSPHIDE PESTICIDE	3048	6.1					
ALUMINIUM POWDER, COATED	1309	4.1					
ALUMINIUM POWDER, UNCOATED	1396	4.3		AMMONIA SOLUTION, relative density between 0.880 and 0.957 at 15 °C in water, with more than 10% but not more than 35% ammonia	2672	8	
ALUMINIUM REMELTING BY-PRODUCTS	3170	4.3					
ALUMINIUM RESINATE	2715	4.1		AMMONIA SOLUTION, relative density less than 0.880 at 15 °C in water, with more than 35% but not more than 50% ammonia	2073	2	
ALUMINIUM SILICON POWDER, UNCOATED	1398	4.3					

Name and description	UN No.	Class	Remarks	Name and description	UN No.	Class	Remarks
AMMONIA SOLUTION, relative density less than 0.880 at 15 °C in water, with more than 50% ammonia	3318	2		AMMONIUM NITRATE BASED FERTILIZER	2071	9	
AMMONIUM ARSENATE	1546	6.1		AMMONIUM NITRATE GEL, intermediate for blasting explosives, liquid	3375	5.1	
Ammonium bichromate, see	1439	5.1		AMMONIUM NITRATE GEL, intermediate for blasting explosives, solid	3375	5.1	
Ammonium bifluoride solid, see	1727	8		AMMONIUM NITRATE, LIQUID (hot concentrated solution)	2426	5.1	
Ammonium bifluoride solution, see	2817	8					
Ammonium bisulphate, see	2506	8		AMMONIUM NITRATE SUSPENSION, intermediate for blasting explosives, liquid	3375	5.1	
Ammonium bisulphite solution, see	2693	8					
AMMONIUM DICHROMATE	1439	5.1		AMMONIUM NITRATE SUSPENSION, intermediate for blasting explosives, solid	3375	5.1	
AMMONIUM DINITRO-o-CRESOLATE, SOLID	1843	6.1					
AMMONIUM DINITRO-o-CRESOLATE, SOLUTION	3424	6.1		AMMONIUM PERCHLORATE	0402	1	
AMMONIUM FLUORIDE	2505	6.1			1442	5.1	
AMMONIUM FLUOROSILICATE	2854	6.1		Ammonium permanganate, see	1482	5.1	
Ammonium hexafluorosilicate, see	2854	6.1		AMMONIUM PERSULPHATE	1444	5.1	
AMMONIUM HYDROGENDIFLUORIDE, SOLID	1727	8		AMMONIUM PICRATE dry or wetted with less than 10% water, by mass	0004	1	
AMMONIUM HYDROGENDIFLUORIDE SOLUTION	2817	8		AMMONIUM PICRATE, WETTED with not less than 10% water, by mass	1310	4.1	
AMMONIUM HYDROGEN SULPHATE	2506	8		AMMONIUM POLYSULPHIDE SOLUTION	2818	8	
Ammonium hydrosulphide solution (treat as ammonium sulphide solution), see	2683	8		AMMONIUM POLYVANADATE	2861	6.1	
				Ammonium silicofluoride, see	2854	6.1	
AMMONIUM METAVANADATE	2859	6.1		AMMONIUM SULPHIDE SOLUTION	2683	8	
AMMONIUM NITRATE	0222	1					
AMMONIUM NITRATE with not more than 0.2% combustible substances, including any organic substance calculated as carbon, to the exclusion of any other added substance	1942	5.1		Ammunition, blank, see	0014	1	
					0326	1	
					0327	1	
					0338	1	
					0413	1	
				Ammunition, fixed	0005	1	
AMMONIUM NITRATE EMULSION, intermediate for blasting explosives, liquid	3375	5.1		Ammunition, semi-fixed	0006	1	
				Ammunition, separate loading, see	0007	1	
					0321	1	
					0348	1	
AMMONIUM NITRATE EMULSION, intermediate for blasting explosives, solid	3375	5.1			0412	1	
Ammonium nitrate explosive, see	0082	1		AMMUNITION, ILLUMINATING with or without burster, expelling charge or propelling charge	0171	1	
	0331	1			0254	1	
					0297	1	
AMMONIUM NITRATE BASED FERTILIZER	2067	5.1		AMMUNITION, INCENDIARY, liquid or gel, with burster, expelling charge or propelling charge	0247	1	

Name and description	UN No.	Class	Remarks	Name and description	UN No.	Class	Remarks
AMMUNITION, INCENDIARY with or without burster, expelling charge or propelling charge	0009 0010 0300	1 1 1		AMMUNITION, TOXIC with burster, expelling charge or propelling charge	0021	1	Carriage prohi- bited
Ammunition, incendiary (water- activated contrivances) with burster, expelling charge or propelling charge, see	0248 0249	1 1		Ammunition, toxic (water-activated contrivances) with burster, expelling charge or propelling charge, see	0248 0249	1 1	
AMMUNITION, INCENDIARY, WHITE PHOSPHORUS with burster, expelling charge or propelling charge	0243 0244	1 1		AMMUNITION, TOXIC, NON- EXPLOSIVE without burster or expelling charge, non-fuzed	2016	6.1	
				Amosite, see	2212	9	
Ammunition, industrial, see	0275 0276 0277 0278 0323 0381	1 1 1 1 1 1		Amphibole asbestos, see	2212	9	
				AMYL ACETATES	1104	3	
				AMYL ACID PHOSPHATE	2819	8	
				Amyl aldehyde, see	2058	3	
Ammunition, lachrymatory, see	0018 0019 0301 2017	1 1 1 1		AMYLAMINE	1106	3	
				n-Amylamine, see	1106	3	
AMMUNITION, PRACTICE	0362 0488	1 1		AMYL BUTYRATES	2620	3	
				AMYL CHLORIDE	1107	3	
AMMUNITION, PROOF	0363	1		n-AMYLENE, see	1108	3	
AMMUNITION, SMOKE with or without burster, expelling charge or propelling charge	0015 0016 0303	1 1 1		AMYL FORMATES	1109	3	
				AMYL MERCAPTAN	1111	3	
Ammunition, smoke (water-activated contrivances), white phosphorus with burster, expelling charge or propelling charge, see	0248	1		n-AMYL METHYL KETONE	1110	3	
				AMYL NITRATE	1112	3	
Ammunition, smoke (water-activated contrivances), without white phosphorus or phosphides with burster, expelling charge or propelling charge, see	0249	1		AMYL NITRITE	1113	3	
				AMYLTRICHLOROSILANE	1728	8	
				Anaesthetic ether, see	1155	3	
AMMUNITION, SMOKE, WHITE PHOSPHORUS with burster, expelling charge or propelling charge	0245 0246	1 1		ANILINE	1547	6.1	
				Aniline chloride, see	1548	6.1	
Ammunition, sporting, see	0012 0328 0339 0417	1 1 1 1		ANILINE HYDROCHLORIDE	1548	6.1	
				Aniline oil, see	1547	6.1	
				Aniline salt, see	1548	6.1	
AMMUNITION, TEAR- PRODUCING, NON-EXPLOSIVE without burster or expelling charge, non-fuzed	2017	6.1		ANISIDINES	2431	6.1	
				ANISOLE	2222	3	
AMMUNITION, TEAR- PRODUCING with burster, expelling charge or propelling charge	0018 0019 0301	1 1 1		ANISOYL CHLORIDE	1729	8	
				Anthophyllite, see	2212	9	
AMMUNITION, TOXIC with burster, expelling charge or propelling charge	0020	1	Carriage prohi- bited	Antimonous chloride, see	1733	8	

Name and description	UN No.	Class	Remarks	Name and description	UN No.	Class	Remarks
ANTIMONY COMPOUND, INORGANIC, LIQUID, N.O.S.	3141	6.1		Arsenic chloride, see	1560	6.1	
ANTIMONY COMPOUND, INORGANIC, SOLID, N.O.S.	1549	6.1		ARSENIC COMPOUND, LIQUID, N.O.S., inorganic, including: Arsenates, n.o.s., Arsenites, n.o.s.; and Arsenic sulphides, n.o.s.	1556	6.1	
Antimony hydride, see	2676	2		ARSENIC COMPOUND, SOLID, N.O.S., inorganic, including: Arsenates, n.o.s.; Arsenites, n.o.s.; and Arsenic sulphides, n.o.s.	1557	6.1	
ANTIMONY LACTATE	1550	6.1					
Antimony (III) lactate, see	1550	6.1					
ANTIMONY PENTACHLORIDE, LIQUID	1730	8		Arsenic (III) oxide, see	1561	6.1	
				Arsenic (V) oxide, see	1559	6.1	
ANTIMONY PENTACHLORIDE SOLUTION	1731	8		ARSENIC PENTOXIDE	1559	6.1	
ANTIMONY PENTAFLUORIDE	1732	8		Arsenic sulphides, see	1556 1557	6.1 6.1	
Antimony perchloride, liquid, see	1730	8		ARSENIC TRICHLORIDE	1560	6.1	
ANTIMONY POTASSIUM TARTRATE	1551	6.1		ARSENIC TRIOXIDE	1561	6.1	
ANTIMONY POWDER	2871	6.1		Arsenious chloride, see	1560	6.1	
ANTIMONY TRICHLORIDE	1733	8		Arsenites, n.o.s., see	1556 1557	6.1 6.1	
A.n.t.u., see	1651	6.1		Arsenous chloride, see	1560	6.1	
ARGON, COMPRESSED	1006	2		ARSINE	2188	2	
ARGON, REFRIGERATED LIQUID	1951	2		ARSINE, ADSORBED	3522	2	
Arsenates, n.o.s., see	1556 1557	6.1 6.1		ARTICLES CONTAINING A SUBSTANCE LIABLE TO SPONTANEOUS COMBUSTION, N.O.S.	3542	4.2	
ARSENIC	1558	6.1					
ARSENIC ACID, LIQUID	1553	6.1		ARTICLES CONTAINING A SUBSTANCE WHICH EMITS FLAMMABLE GAS IN CONTACT WITH WATER, N.O.S.	3543	4.3	
ARSENIC ACID, SOLID	1554	6.1					
ARSENICAL DUST	1562	6.1					
Arsenical flue dust, see	1562	6.1		ARTICLES CONTAINING CORROSIVE SUBSTANCE, N.O.S.	3547	8	
ARSENICAL PESTICIDE, LIQUID, FLAMMABLE, TOXIC, flash-point less than 23 °C	2760	3		ARTICLES CONTAINING FLAMMABLE GAS, N.O.S	3537	2	
ARSENICAL PESTICIDE, LIQUID, TOXIC	2994	6.1		ARTICLES CONTAINING FLAMMABLE LIQUID, N.O.S.	3540	3	
ARSENICAL PESTICIDE, LIQUID, TOXIC, FLAMMABLE, flash-point not less than 23 °C	2993	6.1		ARTICLES CONTAINING FLAMMABLE SOLID, N.O.S.	3541	4.1	
				ARTICLES CONTAINING MISCELLANEOUS DANGEROUS GOODS, N.O.S.	3548	9	
ARSENICAL PESTICIDE, SOLID, TOXIC	2759	6.1					
ARSENIC BROMIDE	1555	6.1		ARTICLES CONTAINING NON-FLAMMABLE, NON TOXIC GAS, N.O.S.	3538	2	
Arsenic (III) bromide, see	1555	6.1					
				ARTICLES CONTAINING ORGANIC PEROXIDE, N.O.S.	3545	5.2	

Name and description	UN No.	Class	Remarks	Name and description	UN No.	Class	Remarks
ARTICLES CONTAINING OXIDIZING SUBSTANCE, N.O.S.	3544	5.1		ASBESTOS, AMPHIBOLE	2212	2	
				ASBESTOS, CHRYSOTILE	2590	2	
ARTICLES CONTAINING TOXIC GAS, N.O.S.	3539	2		Asphalt, with a flash-point above 60°C, at or above its flash-point, see	3256	3	
ARTICLES CONTAINING TOXIC SUBSTANCE, N.O.S.	3546	6.1		Asphalt, at or above 100 °C and below its flash-point, see	3257	9	
ARTICLES, EEI, see	0486	1		Aviation regulated liquid, n.o.s.	3334	9	Not subject to ADN
ARTICLES, EXPLOSIVE, EXTREMELY INSENSITIVE	0486	1					
				Aviation regulated solid, n.o.s.	3335	9	Not subject to ADN
ARTICLES, EXPLOSIVE, N.O.S.	0349	1					
	0350	1					
	0351	1		AZODICARBONAMIDE	3242	4.1	
	0352	1					
	0353	1		Bag charges, see	0242	1	
	0354	1			0279	1	
	0355	1			0414	1	
	0356	1					
	0462	1		Ballistite, see	0160	1	
	0463	1			0161	1	
	0464	1					
	0465	1		Bangalore torpedoes, see	0136	1	
	0466	1			0137	1	
	0467	1			0138	1	
	0468	1			0294	1	
	0469	1					
	0470	1					
	0471	1		BARIUM	1400	4.3	
	0472	1					
				BARIUM ALLOYS, PYROPHORIC	1854	4.2	
ARTICLES, PRESSURIZED, HYDRAULIC (containing non-flammable gas)	3164	2		BARIUM AZIDE, dry or wetted with less than 50% water, by mass	0224	1	
ARTICLES, PRESSURIZED, PNEUMATIC (containing non-flammable gas)	3164	2		BARIUM AZIDE, WETTED with not less than 50% water, by mass	1571	4.1	
				Barium binoxide, see	1449	5.1	
ARTICLES, PYROPHORIC	0380	1		BARIUM BROMATE	2719	5.1	
ARTICLES, PYROTECHNIC for technical purposes	0428	1		BARIUM CHLORATE, SOLID	1445	5.1	
	0429	1					
	0430	1		BARIUM CHLORATE, SOLUTION	3405	5.1	
	0431	1					
	0432	1		BARIUM COMPOUND, N.O.S.	1564	6.1	
ARYLSULPHONIC ACIDS, LIQUID with more than 5% free sulphuric acid	2584	8		BARIUM CYANIDE	1565	6.1	
				Barium dioxide, see	1449	5.1	
ARYLSULPHONIC ACIDS, LIQUID with not more than 5% free sulphuric acid	2586	8		BARIUM HYPOCHLORITE with more than 22% available chlorine	2741	5.1	
ARYLSULPHONIC ACIDS, SOLID with more than 5% free sulphuric acid	2583	8		BARIUM NITRATE	1446	5.1	
				BARIUM OXIDE	1884	6.1	
ARYLSULPHONIC ACIDS, SOLID with not more than 5% free sulphuric acid	2585	8		BARIUM PERCHLORATE, SOLID	1447	5.1	
				BARIUM PERCHLORATE, SOLUTION	3406	5.1	

Name and description	UN No.	Class	Remarks	Name and description	UN No.	Class	Remarks
BARIUM PERMANGANATE	1448	5.1		BENZYL BROMIDE	1737	6.1	
BARIUM PEROXIDE	1449	5.1		BENZYL CHLORIDE	1738	6.1	
Barium selenate, see	2630	6.1		Benzyl chlorocarbonate, see	1739	8	
Barium selenite, see	2630	6.1		BENZYL CHLOROFORMATE	1739	8	
Barium superoxide, see	1449	5.1		Benzyl cyanide, see	2470	6.1	
BATTERIES, CONTAINING SODIUM	3292	4.3		BENZYLDIMETHYLAMINE	2619	8	
BATTERIES, DRY, CONTAINING POTASSIUM HYDROXIDE SOLID, electric storage	3028	8		BENZYLIDENE CHLORIDE	1886	6.1	
				BENZYL IODIDE	2653	6.1	
Batteries, nickel-metal hydride	3496	9	Not subject to ADN	BERYLLIUM COMPOUND, N.O.S.	1566	6.1	
				BERYLLIUM NITRATE	2464	5.1	
				BERYLLIUM POWDER	1567	6.1	
BATTERY POWERED EQUIPMENT	3171	9		Bhusa	1327	4.1	Not subject to ADN
BATTERY POWERED VEHICLE	3171	9					
BATTERIES, WET, FILLED WITH ACID, electric storage	2794	8		BICYCLO[2.2.1]HEPTA-2,5-DIENE, STABILIZED	2251	3	
BATTERIES, WET, FILLED WITH ALKALI, electric storage	2795	8		Bifluorides, n.o.s., see	1740	8	
BATTERIES, WET, NON-SPILLABLE, electric storage	2800	8		BIOLOGICAL SUBSTANCE, CATEGORY B	3373	6.2	
BATTERY FLUID, ACID	2796	8		BIOLOGICAL SUBSTANCE, CATEGORY B (animal material only)	3373	6.2	
BATTERY FLUID, ALKALI	2797	8					
				(BIO) MEDICAL WASTE, N.O.S.	3291	6.2	
BENZALDEHYDE	1990	9		BIPYRIDILIUM PESTICIDE, LIQUID, FLAMMABLE, TOXIC, flash-point less than 23 °C	2782	3	
BENZENE	1114	3					
BENZENESULPHONYL CHLORIDE	2225	8		BIPYRIDILIUM PESTICIDE, LIQUID, TOXIC	3016	6.1	
Benzenethiol, see	2337	6.1		BIPYRIDILIUM PESTICIDE, LIQUID, TOXIC, FLAMMABLE, flash-point not less than 23 °C	3015	6.1	
BENZIDINE	1885	6.1					
Benzol, see	1114	3					
Benzolene, see	1268	3		BIPYRIDILIUM PESTICIDE, SOLID, TOXIC	2781	6.1	
BENZONITRILE	2224	6.1		BISULPHATES, AQUEOUS SOLUTION	2837	8	
BENZOQUINONE	2587	6.1		BISULPHITES, AQUEOUS SOLUTION, N.O.S.	2693	8	
Benzosulphochloride, see	2225	8					
BENZOTRICHLORIDE	2226	8		Bitumen, with a flash-point above 60 °C, at or above its flash-point, see	3256	3	
BENZOTRIFLUORIDE	2338	3		Bitumen, at or above 100 °C and below its flash-point, see	3257	9	
BENZOYL CHLORIDE	1736	8					
				BLACK POWDER, COMPRESSED	0028	1	

Name and description	UN No.	Class	Remarks	Name and description	UN No.	Class	Remarks
BLACK POWDER, granular or as a meal	0027	1		BORON TRIFLUORIDE DIMETHYL ETHERATE	2965	4.3	
BLACK POWDER, IN PELLETS	0028	1		BORON TRIFLUORIDE PROPIONIC ACID COMPLEX, LIQUID	1743	8	
Blasting cap assemblies, see	0360	1					
	0361	1		BORON TRIFLUORIDE PROPIONIC ACID COMPLEX, SOLID	3420	8	
Blasting caps, electric, see	0030	1					
	0255	1		BROMATES, INORGANIC, N.O.S.	1450	5.1	
	0456	1					
Bleaching powder, see	2208	5.1		BROMATES, INORGANIC, AQUEOUS SOLUTION, N.O.S	3213	5.1	
BOMBS with bursting charge	0033	1					
	0034	1		BROMINE	1744	8	
	0035	1					
	0291	1		BROMINE CHLORIDE	2901	2	
Bombs, illuminating, see	0254	1		BROMINE PENTAFLUORIDE	1745	5.1	
BOMBS, PHOTO-FLASH	0037	1		BROMINE SOLUTION	1744	8	
	0038	1					
	0039	1		BROMINE TRIFLUORIDE	1746	5.1	
	0299	1					
BOMBS, SMOKE, NON-EXPLOSIVE with corrosive liquid, without initiating device	2028	8		BROMOACETIC ACID, SOLID	3425	8	
				BROMOACETIC ACID, SOLUTION	1938	8	
Bombs, target identification, see	0171	1		BROMOACETONE	1569	6.1	
	0254	1					
	0297	1		omega-Bromoacetone, see	2645	6.4	
BOMBS WITH FLAMMABLE LIQUID with bursting charge	0399	1		BROMOACETYL BROMIDE	2513	8	
	0400	1					
BOOSTERS WITH DETONATOR	0225	1		BROMOBENZENE	2514	3	
	0268	1		BROMOBENZYL CYANIDES, LIQUID	1694	6.1	
BOOSTERS without detonator	0042	1					
	0283	1		BROMOBENZYL CYANIDES, SOLID	3449	6.1	
Borate and chlorate mixture, see	1458	5.1					
				1-BROMOBUTANE	1126	3	
BORNEOL	1312	4.1		2-BROMOBUTANE	2339	3	
BORON TRIBROMIDE	2692	8		BROMOCHLOROMETHANE	1887	6.1	
BORON TRICHLORIDE	1741	2		1-BROMO-3-CHLOROPROPANE	2688	6.1	
BORON TRIFLUORIDE ACETIC ACID COMPLEX, LIQUID	1742	8		1-Bromo-2,3-epoxypropane, see	2558	6.1	
BORON TRIFLUORIDE ACETIC ACID COMPLEX, SOLID	3419	8		Bromoethane, see	1891	6.1	
				2-BROMOETHYL ETHYL ETHER	2340	3	
BORON TRIFLUORIDE, ADSORBED	3519	2		BROMOFORM	2515	6.1	
BORON TRIFLUORIDE	1008	2		Bromomethane, see	1062	2	
BORON TRIFLUORIDE DIETHYL ETHERATE	2604	8		1-BROMO-3-METHYLBUTANE	2341	3	
BORON TRIFLUORIDE DIHYDRATE	2851	8		BROMOMETHYLPROPANES	2342	3	

Name and description	UN No.	Class	Remarks	Name and description	UN No.	Class	Remarks
2-BROMO-2-NITROPROPANE-1,3-DIOL	3241	4.1		Butyl alcohols, see	1120	3	
2-BROMOPENTANE	2343	3		n-BUTYLAMINE	1125	3	
BROMOPROPANES	2344	3		N-BUTYLANILINE	2738	6.1	
3-BROMOPROPYNE	2345	3		sec-Butyl benzene, see	2709	3	
BROMOTRIFLUOROETHYLENE	2419	2		BUTYLBENZENES	2709	3	
BROMOTRIFLUOROMETHANE	1009	2		n-Butyl bromide, see	1126	3	
BRUCINE	1570	6.1		n-Butyl chloride, see	1127	3	
BURSTERS, explosive	0043	1		n-BUTYL CHLOROFORMATE	2743	6.1	
BUTADIENES, STABILIZED or BUTADIENES AND HYDROCARBON MIXTURE, STABILIZED, containing more than 40% butadienes	1010	2		tert-BUTYLCYCLOHEXYL CHLOROFORMATE	2747	6.1	
				BUTYLENE	1012	2	
BUTADIENE, STABILIZED, (1,2-butadiene)	1010	2		1-butylene, see	1012	2	
				cis-2-butylene, see	1012	2	
BUTADIENE, STABILIZED, (1,3-butadiene)	1010	2		trans-2-butylene, see	1012	2	
				Butylenes, mixture, see	1012	2	
BUTANE	1011	2		1,2-BUTYLENE OXIDE, STABILIZED	3022	3	
BUTANEDIONE	2346	3					
Butane-1-thiol, see	2347	3		Butyl ethers, see	1149	3	
BUTANOLS	1120	3		Butyl ethyl ether, see	1179	3	
1-Butanol, see	1120	3		n-BUTYL FORMATE	1128	3	
Butan-2-ol, see	1120	3		tert-BUTYL HYPOCHLORITE	3255	4.2	Carriage prohibited
Butanol, secondary, see	1120	3					
Butanol, tertiary, see	1120	3		N,n-BUTYLIMIDAZOLE	2690	6.1	
Butanone, see	1193	3		N,n-Butyliminazole, see	2690	6.1	
2-Butenal, see	1143	6.1		n-BUTYL ISOCYANATE	2485	6.1	
Butene, see	1012	2		tert-BUTYL ISOCYANATE	2484	6.1	
Bute-1-ene-3-one, see	1251	3		Butyl lithium, see	3394	4.2	
1,2-Buteneoxide, see	3022	3		BUTYL MERCAPTAN	2347	3	
2-Buten-1-ol, see	2614	3		n-BUTYL METHACRYLATE, STABILIZED	2227	3	
BUTYL ACETATES	1123	3		BUTYL METHYL ETHER	2350	3	
Butyl acetate, secondary, see	1123	3		BUTYL NITRITES	2351	3	
BUTYL ACID PHOSPHATE	1718	8		Butylphenols, liquid, see	3145	8	
BUTYL ACRYLATES, STABILIZED	2348	3		Butylphenols, solid, see	2430	8	
				BUTYL PROPIONATES	1914	3	
n-Butyl alcohol, see	1120	3					

Name and description	UN No.	Class	Remarks	Name and description	UN No.	Class	Remarks
p-tert-Butyltoluene, see	2667	6.1		CALCIUM CARBIDE	1402	4.3	
BUTYLTOLUENES	2667	6.1		CALCIUM CHLORATE	1452	5.1	
BUTYLTRICHLOROSILANE	1747	8		CALCIUM CHLORATE, AQUEOUS SOLUTION	2429	5.1	
5-tert-BUTYL-2,4,6-TRINITRO-m-XYLENE	2956	4.1		CALCIUM CHLORITE	1453	5.1	
BUTYL VINYL ETHER, STABILIZED	2352	3		CALCIUM CYANAMIDE with more than 0.1% calcium carbide	1403	4.3	
But-1-yne, see	2452	2		CALCIUM CYANIDE	1575	6.1	
1,4-BUTYNEDIOL	2716	6.1		CALCIUM DITHIONITE	1923	4.2	
2-Butyne-1,4-diol, see	2716	6.1		CALCIUM HYDRIDE	1404	4.3	
BUTYRALDEHYDE	1129	3		CALCIUM HYDROSULPHITE, see	1923	4.2	
n-Butyraldehyde, see	1129	3		CALCIUM HYPOCHLORITE, DRY	1748	5.1	
BUTYRALDOXIME	2840	3		CALCIUM HYPOCHLORITE, DRY with more than 39% available chlorine (8.8% available oxygen)	1748	5.1	
BUTYRIC ACID	2820	8					
BUTYRIC ANHYDRIDE	2739	8		CALCIUM HYPOCHLORITE, DRY, CORROSIVE with more than 39% available chlorine (8.8% available oxygen)	3485	5.1	
Butyrone, see	2710	3					
BUTYRONITRILE	2411	3		CALCIUM HYPOCHLORITE, HYDRATED with not less than 5.5% but not more than 16% water	2880	5.1	
Butyroyl chloride, see	2353	3					
BUTYRYL CHLORIDE	2353	3		CALCIUM HYPOCHLORITE, HYDRATED MIXTURE with not less than 5.5% but not more than 16% water	2880	5.1	
Cable cutters, explosive, see	0070	1					
CACODYLIC ACID	1572	6.1					
CADMIUM COMPOUND	2570	6.1		CALCIUM HYPOCHLORITE, HYDRATED, CORROSIVE with not less than 5.5% but not more than 16% water	3487	5.1	
CAESIUM	1407	4.3					
CAESIUM HYDROXIDE	2682	8		CALCIUM HYPOCHLORITE, HYDRATED MIXTURE, CORROSIVE with not less than 5.5% but not more than 16% water	3487	5.1	
CAESIUM HYDROXIDE SOLUTION	2681	8					
CAESIUM NITRATE	1451	5.1		CALCIUM HYPOCHLORITE MIXTURE, DRY with more than 10% but not more than 39% available chlorine	2208	5.1	
Caffeine, see	1544	6.1					
Cajeputene, see	2052	3					
CALCIUM	1401	4.3		CALCIUM HYPOCHLORITE MIXTURE, DRY with more than 39% available chlorine (8.8% available oxygen)	1748	5.1	
CALCIUM ALLOYS, PYROPHORIC	1855	4.2					
CALCIUM ARSENATE	1573	6.1		CALCIUM HYPOCHLORITE MIXTURE, DRY, CORROSIVE with more than 10% but not more than 39% available chlorine	3486	5.1	
CALCIUM ARSENATE AND CALCIUM ARSENITE MIXTURE, SOLID	1574	6.1					
Calcium bisulphite solution, see	2693	8					

Name and description	UN No.	Class	Remarks	Name and description	UN No.	Class	Remarks
CALCIUM HYPOCHLORITE MIXTURE, DRY, CORROSIVE with more than 39% available chlorine (8.8% available oxygen)	3485	5.1		Carbolic acid, see	1671 2312 2821	6.1 6.1 6.1	
CALCIUM MANGANESE SILICON	2844	4.3		CARBON, animal or vegetable origin	1361	4.2	
CALCIUM NITRATE	1454	5.1		CARBON, ACTIVATED	1362	4.2	
Calcium oxide	1910	8	Not subject to ADN	Carbon bisulphide, see	1131	3	
				Carbon black (animal or vegetable origin), see	1361	4.2	
CALCIUM PERCHLORATE	1455	5.1		CARBON DIOXIDE	1013	2	
CALCIUM PERMANGANATE	1456	5.1		Carbon dioxide and ethylene oxide mixture, see	1041 1952 3300	2 2 2	
CALCIUM PEROXIDE	1457	5.1					
CALCIUM PHOSPHIDE	1360	4.3		CARBON DIOXIDE, REFRIGERATED LIQUID	2187	2	
CALCIUM, PYROPHORIC	1855	4.2					
CALCIUM RESINATE	1313	4.1		Carbon dioxide, solid	1845	9	Not subject to ADN
CALCIUM RESINATE, FUSED	1314	4.1					
Calcium selenate, see	2630	6.1		CARBON DISULPHIDE	1131	3	
CALCIUM SILICIDE	1405	4.3		Carbonic anhydride, see	1013 1845 2187	2 9 2	
Calcium silicon, see	1405	4.3					
Calcium superoxide, see	1457	5.1		CARBON MONOXIDE, COMPRESSED	1016	2	
Camphanone, see	2717	4.1		Carbon oxysulphide, see	2204	2.3	
CAMPHOR OIL	1130	3		Carbon sulphide, see	1131	3	
CAMPHOR, synthetic	2717	4.1		CARBON TETRABROMIDE	2516	6.1	
CAPACITOR, ASYMMETRIC (with an energy storage capacity greater than 0.3Wh)	3508	9		CARBON TETRACHLORIDE	1846	6.1	
				Carbonyl chloride, see	1076	2	
CAPACITOR, ELECTRIC DOUBLE LAYER (with an energy storage capacity greater than 0.3 Wh)	3499	9		CARBONYL FLUORIDE	2417	2	
				CARBONYL SULPHIDE	2204	2	
CAPROIC ACID	2829	8		Cartridge cases, empty, primed, see	0055 0379	1 1	
CARBAMATE PESTICIDE, LIQUID, FLAMMABLE, TOXIC, flash-point less than 23 °C	2758	3		Cartridges, actuating, for fire extinguisher or apparatus valve, see	0275 0276 0323 0381	1 1 1 1	
CARBAMATE PESTICIDE, LIQUID, TOXIC	2992	6.1					
				Cartridges, explosive, see	0048	1	
CARBAMATE PESTICIDE, LIQUID, TOXIC, FLAMMABLE, flash-point not less than 23 °C	2991	6.1		CARTRIDGES, FLASH	0049 0050	1 1	
CARBAMATE PESTICIDE, SOLID, TOXIC	2757	6.1					

Name and description	UN No.	Class	Remarks	Name and description	UN No.	Class	Remarks
CARTRIDGES FOR WEAPONS with bursting charge	0005	1		Caustic soda, see	1824	8	
	0006	1		Caustic soda liquor, see	1824	8	
	0007	1					
	0321	1		CELLS, CONTAINING SODIUM	3292	4.3	
	0348	1					
	0412	1		CELLULOID in block, rods, rolls, sheets, tubes, etc., except scrap	2000	4.1	
CARTRIDGES FOR WEAPONS, BLANK	0014	1					
	0326	1		CELLULOID, SCRAP	2002	4.2	
	0327	1					
	0338	1		Cement, see	1133	3	
	0413	1					
				CERIUM, slabs, ingots or rods	1333	4.1	
CARTRIDGES FOR WEAPONS, INERT PROJECTILE	0012	1					
	0328	1		CERIUM, turnings or gritty powder	3078	4.3	
	0339	1					
	0417	1		Cer mishmetall, see	1323	4.1	
Cartridges, illuminating, see	0171	1		Charcoal, activated, see	1362	4.1	
	0254	1					
	0297	1		Charcoal, non-activated, see	1361	4.2	
CARTRIDGES, OIL WELL	0277	1		CHARGES, BURSTING, PLASTICS BONDED	0457	1	
	0278	1			0458	1	
					0459	1	
CARTRIDGES, POWER DEVICE	0275	1			0460	1	
	0276	1					
	0323	1		CHARGES, DEMOLITION	0048	1	
	0381	1					
				CHARGES, DEPTH	0056	1	
CARTRIDGES, SIGNAL	0054	1					
	0312	1		Charges, expelling, explosive, for fire extinguishers, see	0275	1	
	0405	1			0276	1	
					0323	1	
CARTRIDGES, SMALL ARMS	0012	1			0381	1	
	0339	1					
	0417	1		CHARGES, EXPLOSIVE, COMMERCIAL without detonator	0442	1	
					0443	1	
CARTRIDGES, SMALL ARMS, BLANK or CARTRIDGES FOR TOOLS, BLANK	0014	1			0444	1	
	0327	1			0445	1	
	0338	1					
				CHARGES, PROPELLING	0271	1	
Cartridges, starter, jet engine, see	0275	1			0272	1	
	0276	1			0415	1	
	0323	1			0491	1	
	0381	1					
				CHARGES, PROPELLING, FOR CANNON	0242	1	
CASES, CARTRIDGE, EMPTY, WITH PRIMER	0055	1			0279	1	
	0379	1			0414	1	
CASES, COMBUSTIBLE, EMPTY, WITHOUT PRIMER	0446	1		CHARGES, SHAPED, FLEXIBLE, LINEAR	0237	1	
	0447	1			0288	1	
Casinghead gasoline, see	1203	3		CHARGES, SHAPED, without detonator	0059	1	
					0439	1	
CASTOR BEANS	2969	9			0440	1	
					0441	1	
CASTOR FLAKE	2969	9					
				CHARGES, SUPPLEMENTARY, EXPLOSIVE	0060	1	
CASTOR MEAL	2969	9					
CASTOR POMACE	2969	9		CHEMICAL KIT	3316	9	
CAUSTIC ALKALI LIQUID, N.O.S.	1719	8		CHEMICAL SAMPLE, TOXIC	3315	6.1	
Caustic potash, see	1814	8					

Name and description	UN No.	Class	Remarks	Name and description	UN No.	Class	Remarks
CHEMICAL UNDER PRESSURE, N.O.S.	3500	2		CHLOROACETONITRILE	2668	6.1	
CHEMICAL UNDER PRESSURE, FLAMMABLE, N.O.S.	3501	2		CHLOROACETOPHENONE, LIQUID	3416	6.1	
CHEMICAL UNDER PRESSURE, TOXIC, N.O.S.	3502	2		CHLOROACETOPHENONE, SOLID	1697	6.1	
CHEMICAL UNDER PRESSURE, CORROSIVE, N.O.S.	3503	2		CHLOROACETYL CHLORIDE	1752	6.1	
CHEMICAL UNDER PRESSURE, FLAMMABLE, TOXIC, N.O.S.	3504	2		CHLOROANILINES, LIQUID	2019	6.1	
				CHLOROANILINES, SOLID	2018	6.1	
CHEMICAL UNDER PRESSURE, FLAMMABLE, CORROSIVE, N.O.S.	3505	2		CHLOROANISIDINES	2233	6.1	
				CHLOROBENZENE	1134	3	
Chile saltpetre, see	1498	5.1		CHLOROBENZOTRIFLUORIDES	2234	3	
CHLORAL, ANHYDROUS, STABILIZED	2075	6.1		CHLOROBENZYL CHLORIDES, LIQUID	2235	6.1	
CHLORATE AND BORATE MIXTURE	1458	5.1		CHLOROBENZYL CHLORIDES, SOLID	3427	6.1	
CHLORATE AND MAGNESIUM CHLORIDE MIXTURE, SOLID	1459	5.1		1-Chloro-3-bromopropane, see	2688	6.1	
				1-Chlorobutane, see	1127	3	
CHLORATE AND MAGNESIUM CHLORIDE MIXTURE, SOLUTION	3407	5.1		2-Chlorobutane, see	1127	3	
				CHLOROBUTANES	1127	3	
CHLORATES, INORGANIC, N.O.S.	1461	5.1		CHLOROCRESOLS, SOLUTION	2669	6.1	
				CHLOROCRESOLS, SOLID	3437	6.1	
CHLORATES, INORGANIC, AQUEOUS SOLUTION, N.O.S.	3210	5.1		CHLORODIFLUORO-BROMOMETHANE	1974	2	
CHLORIC ACID, AQUEOUS SOLUTION with not more than 10% chloric acid	2626	5.1		1-CHLORO-1,1-DIFLUORO-ETHANE	2517	2	
CHLORINE	1017	2		CHLORODIFLUOROMETHANE	1018	2	
CHLORINE, ADSORBED	3520	2		CHLORODIFLUORO-METHANE AND CHLORO-PENTAFLUOROETHANE MIXTURE with fixed boiling point, with approximately 49% chlorodifluoromethane	1973	2	
CHLORINE PENTAFLUORIDE	2548	2					
CHLORINE TRIFLUORIDE	1749	2					
CHLORITES, INORGANIC, N.O.S.	1462	5.1					
CHLORITE SOLUTION	1908	8		3-Chloro-1,2-dihydroxypropane, see	2689	6.1	
Chloroacetaldehyde, see	2232	6.1		Chlorodimethyl ether, see	1239	6.1	
CHLOROACETIC ACID, MOLTEN	3250	6.1		1-Chloro-2,2-dimethylpropane, see	1107	3	
CHLOROACETIC ACID, SOLID	1751	6.1		CHLORODINITROBENZENES, LIQUID	1577	6.1	
CHLOROACETIC ACID SOLUTION	1750	6.1		CHLORODINITROBENZENES, SOLID	3441	6.1	
CHLOROACETONE, STABILIZED	1695	6.1					

Name and description	UN No.	Class	Remarks	Name and description	UN No.	Class	Remarks
2-CHLOROETHANAL	2232	6.1		CHLOROPHENOLATES, LIQUID	2904	8	
Chloroethane, see	1037	2		CHLOROPHENOLATES, SOLID	2905	8	
Chloroethane nitrile, see	2668	6.1		CHLOROPHENOLS, LIQUID	2021	6.1	
2-Chloroethanol, see	1135	6.1		CHLOROPHENOLS, SOLID	2020	6.1	
CHLOROFORM	1888	6.1		CHLOROPHENYL-TRICHLOROSILANE	1753	8	
CHLOROFORMATES, TOXIC, CORROSIVE, N.O.S.	3277	6.1		CHLOROPICRIN	1580	6.1	
CHLOROFORMATES, TOXIC, CORROSIVE, FLAMMABLE, N.O.S.	2742	6.1		CHLOROPICRIN AND METHYL BROMIDE MIXTURE, with more than 2% chloropicrin	1581	2	
Chloromethane, see	1063	2		CHLOROPICRIN AND METHYL CHLORIDE MIXTURE	1582	2	
1-Chloro-3-methylbutane, see	1107	3		CHLOROPICRIN MIXTURE, N.O.S.	1583	6.1	
2-Chloro-2-methylbutane, see	1107	3					
CHLOROMETHYL CHLOROFORMATE	2745	6.1		CHLOROPLATINIC ACID, SOLID	2507	8	
Chloromethyl cyanide, see	2668	6.1		CHLOROPRENE, STABILIZED	1991	3	
CHLOROMETHYL ETHYL ETHER	2354	3		1-CHLOROPROPANE	1278	3	
				2-CHLOROPROPANE	2356	3	
1-Chloro-3-methylbutane, see	1107	3		3-Chloro-propanediol-1,2, see	2689	6.1	
1-Chloro-3-methylbutane, see	1107	3		3-CHLOROPROPANOL-1	2849	6.1	
Chloromethyl methyl ether, see	1239	6.1		2-CHLOROPROPENE	2456	3	
3-CHLORO-4-METHYLPHENYL ISOCYANATE, LIQUID	2236	6.1		3-Chloropropene, see	1100	3	
3-CHLORO-4-METHYLPHENYL ISOCYANATE, SOLID	3428	6.1		3-Chloroprop-1-ene, see	1100	3	
1-Chloro-2-methylpropane, see	1127	3		2-CHLOROPROPIONIC ACID	2511	8	
2-Chloro-2-methylpropane, see	1127	3		2-CHLOROPYRIDINE	2822	6.1	
3-Chloro-2-methylprop-1-ene, see	2554	3		CHLOROSILANES, CORROSIVE, N.O.S.	2987	8	
CHLORONITROANILINES	2237	6.1		CHLOROSILANES, CORROSIVE, FLAMMABLE, N.O.S.	2986	8	
CHLORONITROBENZENES LIQUID	3409	6.1		CHLOROSILANES, FLAMMABLE, CORROSIVE, N.O.S.	2985	3	
CHLORONITROBENZENES SOLID	1578	6.1		CHLOROSILANES, TOXIC, CORROSIVE, N.O.S.	3361	6.1	
CHLORONITROTOLUENES, LIQUID	2433	6.1		CHLOROSILANES, TOXIC, CORROSIVE, FLAMMABLE, N.O.S.	3362	6.1	
CHLORONITROTOLUENES, SOLID	3457	6.1					
CHLOROPENTAFLUORO-ETHANE	1020	2		CHLOROSILANES, WATER-REACTIVE, FLAMMABLE, CORROSIVE, N.O.S.	2988	4.3	
1-Chloropentane	1107	3					

Name and description	UN No.	Class	Remarks	Name and description	UN No.	Class	Remarks
CHLOROSULPHONIC ACID (with or without sulphur trioxide)	1754	8		CLINICAL WASTE, UNSPECIFIED, N.O.S.	3291	6.2	
1-CHLORO-1,2,2,2-TETRAFLUOROETHANE	1021	2		COAL GAS, COMPRESSED	1023	2	
CHLOROTOLUENES	2238	3		COAL TAR DISTILLATES, FLAMMABLE	1136	3	
4-CHLORO-o-TOLUIDINE HYDROCHLORIDE, SOLID	1579	6.1		Coal tar naphtha, see	1268	3	
				Coal tar oil, see	1136	3	
4-CHLORO-o-TOLUIDINE HYDROCHLORIDE, SOLUTION	3410	6.1		COATING SOLUTION (includes surface treatments or coatings used for industrial or other purposes such as vehicle under coating, drum or barrel lining)	1139	3	
CHLOROTOLUIDINES LIQUID	3429	6.1					
CHLOROTOLUIDINES SOLID	2239	6.1					
1-CHLORO-2,2,2-TRIFLUOROETHANE	1983	2		COBALT DIHYDROXIDE POWDER, containing not less than 10 % respirable particles	3550	6.1	
Chlorotrifluoroethylene, see	1082	2					
CHLOROTRIFLUOROMETHANE	1022	2		COBALT NAPHTHENATES, POWDER	2001	4.1	
CHLOROTRIFLUOROMETHANE AND TRIFLUOROMETHANE AZEOTROPIC MIXTURE with approximately 60% chlorotrifluoromethane	2599	2		COBALT RESINATE, PRECIPITATED	1318	4.1	
				Cocculus, see	3172	6.1	
					3462	6.1	
Chromic acid, solid, see	1463	5.1		Collodion cottons, see	0340	1	
					0341	1	
CHROMIC ACID SOLUTION	1755	8			0342	1	
					2059	3	
Chromic anhydride, solid, see	1463	5.1			2555	4.1	
					2556	4.1	
CHROMIC FLUORIDE, SOLID	1756	8			2557	4.1	
CHROMIC FLUORIDE SOLUTION	1757	8		COMPONENTS, EXPLOSIVE TRAIN, N.O.S.	0382	1	
					0383	1	
Chromic nitrate, see	2720	5.1			0384	1	
					0461	1	
Chromium (VI) dichloride dioxide, see	1758	8		Composition B, see	0118	1	
Chromium (III) fluoride, solid, see	1756	8		COMPRESSED GAS, N.O.S.	1956	2	
CHROMIUM NITRATE	2720	5.1		COMPRESSED GAS, FLAMMABLE, N.O.S.	1954	2	
Chromium (III) nitrate, see	2720	5.1					
CHROMIUM OXYCHLORIDE	1758	8		COMPRESSED GAS, OXIDIZING, N.O.S.	3156	2	
CHROMIUM TRIOXIDE, ANHYDROUS	1463	5.1		COMPRESSED GAS, TOXIC, N.O.S.	1955	2	
CHROMOSULPHURIC ACID	2240	8		COMPRESSED GAS, TOXIC, CORROSIVE, N.O.S.	3304	2	
Chrysotile, see	2590	9		COMPRESSED GAS, TOXIC, FLAMMABLE, N.O.S.	1953	2	
Cinene, see	2052	3					
Cinnamene, see	2055	3		COMPRESSED GAS, TOXIC, FLAMMABLE, CORROSIVE, N.O.S.	3305	2	
Cinnamol, see	2055	3					

Name and description	UN No.	Class	Remarks	Name and description	UN No.	Class	Remarks
COMPRESSED GAS, TOXIC, OXIDIZING, N.O.S.	3303	2		CORROSIVE LIQUID, BASIC, ORGANIC, N.O.S.	3267	8	
COMPRESSED GAS, TOXIC, OXIDIZING, CORROSIVE, N.O.S.	3306	2		CORROSIVE LIQUID, FLAMMABLE, N.O.S.	2920	8	
CONTRIVANCES, WATER-ACTIVATED with burster, expelling charge or propelling charge	0248 0249	1 1		CORROSIVE LIQUID, OXIDIZING, N.O.S.	3093	8	
COPPER ACETOARSENITE	1585	6.1		CORROSIVE LIQUID, SELF-HEATING, N.O.S.	3301	8	
COPPER ARSENITE	1586	6.1		CORROSIVE LIQUID, TOXIC, N.O.S.	2922	8	
Copper (II) arsenite, see	1586	6.1		CORROSIVE LIQUID, WATER-REACTIVE, N.O.S.	3094	8	
COPPER BASED PESTICIDE, LIQUID, FLAMMABLE, TOXIC, flash-point less than 23 °C	2776	3		CORROSIVE SOLID, N.O.S.	1759	8	
COPPER BASED PESTICIDE, LIQUID, TOXIC	3010	6.1		CORROSIVE SOLID, ACIDIC, INORGANIC, N.O.S.	3260	8	
COPPER BASED PESTICIDE, LIQUID, TOXIC, FLAMMABLE, flash-point not less than 23 °C	3009	6.1		CORROSIVE SOLID, ACIDIC, ORGANIC, N.O.S.	3261	8	
COPPER BASED PESTICIDE, SOLID, TOXIC	2775	6.1		CORROSIVE SOLID, BASIC, INORGANIC, N.O.S.	3262	8	
COPPER CHLORATE	2721	5.1		CORROSIVE SOLID, BASIC, ORGANIC, N.O.S.	3263	8	
Copper (II) chlorate, see	2721	5.1		CORROSIVE SOLID, FLAMMABLE, N.O.S.	2921	8	
COPPER CHLORIDE	2802	8		CORROSIVE SOLID, OXIDIZING, N.O.S.	3084	8	
COPPER CYANIDE	1587	6.1					
Copper selenate, see	2630	6.1		CORROSIVE SOLID, SELF-HEATING, N.O.S.	3095	8	
Copper selenite, see	2630	6.1		CORROSIVE SOLID, TOXIC, N.O.S.	2923	8	
COPRA	1363	4.2					
CORD, DETONATING, flexible	0065 0289	1 1		CORROSIVE SOLID, WATER-REACTIVE, N.O.S.	3096	8	
CORD, DETONATING, metal clad	0102 0290	1 1		COTTON WASTE, OILY	1364	4.2	
CORD, DETONATING, MILD EFFECT, metal clad	0104	1		COTTON, WET	1365	4.2	
CORD, IGNITER	0066	1		COUMARIN DERIVATIVE PESTICIDE, LIQUID, FLAMMABLE, TOXIC, flash-point less than 23 °C	3024	3	
Cordite, see	0160 0161	1 1		COUMARIN DERIVATIVE PESTICIDE, LIQUID, TOXIC	3026	6.1	
CORROSIVE LIQUID, N.O.S.	1760	8					
CORROSIVE LIQUID, ACIDIC, INORGANIC, N.O.S.	3264	8		COUMARIN DERIVATIVE PESTICIDE, LIQUID, TOXIC, FLAMMABLE, flash-point not less than 23 °C	3025	6.1	
CORROSIVE LIQUID, ACIDIC, ORGANIC, N.O.S.	3265	8					
CORROSIVE LIQUID, BASIC, INORGANIC, N.O.S.	3266	8		COUMARIN DERIVATIVE PESTICIDE, SOLID, TOXIC	3027	6.1	

Name and description	UN No.	Class	Remarks	Name and description	UN No.	Class	Remarks
Creosote, see	2810	6.1		CYANOGEN CHLORIDE, STABILIZED	1589	2	
Creosote salts, see	1334	4.1		CYANURIC CHLORIDE	2670	8	
CRESOLS, LIQUID	2076	6.1		CYCLOBUTANE	2601	2	
CRESOLS, SOLID	3455	6.1		CYCLOBUTYL CHLOROFORMATE	2744	6.1	
CRESYLIC ACID	2022	6.1		1,5,9-CYCLODODECATRIENE	2518	6.1	
Crocidolite, see	2212	9		CYCLOHEPTANE	2241	3	
CROTONALDEHYDE	1143	6.1		CYCLOHEPTATRIENE	2603	3	
CROTONALDEHYDE, STABILIZED	1143	6.1		1,3,5-Cycloheptatriene, see	2603	3	
CROTONIC ACID, LIQUID	3472	8		CYCLOHEPTENE	2242	3	
CROTONIC ACID, SOLID	2823	8		1,4-Cyclohexadienedione, see	2587	6.1	
Crotonic aldehyde / Crotonic aldehyde, stabilized, see	1143	6.1		CYCLOHEXANE	1145	3	
CROTONYLENE	1144	3		Cyclohexanthiol, see	3054	3	
Crude naphtha, see	1268	3		CYCLOHEXANONE	1915	3	
Cumene, see	1918	3		CYCLOHEXENE	2256	3	
Cupric chlorate, see	2721	5.1		CYCLOHEXENYLTRI-CHLOROSILANE	1762	8	
CUPRIETHYLENEDIAMINE SOLUTION	1761	8		CYCLOHEXYL ACETATE	2243	3	
Cutback bitumen, with a flash-point not greater than 60 °C, see	1999	3		CYCLOHEXYLAMINE	2357	8	
				CYCLOHEXYL ISOCYANATE	2488	6.1	
Cutback bitumen, with a flash-point above 60 °C, at or above its flash-point, see	3256	3		CYCLOHEXYL MERCAPTAN	3054	3	
Cutback bitumen, at or above 100 °C and below its flash-point, see	3257	9		CYCLOHEXYLTRI-CHLOROSILANE	1763	8	
CUTTERS, CABLE, EXPLOSIVE	0070	1		CYCLONITE AND CYCLOTETRAMETHYLENE-TETRANITRAMINE MIXTURE, WETTED with not less than 15% water, by mass or DESENSITIZED with not less than 10% phlegmatiser by mass, see	0391	1	
CYANIDE SOLUTION, N.O.S.	1935	6.1					
CYANIDES, INORGANIC, SOLID, N.O.S.	1588	6.1					
Cyanides, organic, flammable, toxic, n.o.s., see	3273	3		CYCLONITE, DESENSITIZED, see	0483	1	
Cyanides, organic, toxic, n.o.s., see	3276	6.1		CYCLONITE, WETTED with not less than 15% water, by mass, see	0072	1	
	3439	6.1		CYCLOOCTADIENES	2520	3	
Cyanides, organic, toxic, flammable, n.o.s., see	3275	6.1		CYCLOOCTADIENE PHOSPHINES, see	2940	4.2	
Cyanoacetonitrile, see	2647	6.1		CYCLOOCTATETRAENE	2358	3	
CYANOGEN	1026	2		CYCLOPENTANE	1146	3	
CYANOGEN BROMIDE	1889	6.1		CYCLOPENTANOL	2244	3	

Name and description	UN No.	Class	Remarks	Name and description	UN No.	Class	Remarks
CYCLOPENTANONE	2245	3		DESENSITIZED EXPLOSIVE, SOLID, N.O.S.	3380	4.1	
CYCLOPENTENE	2246	3		Detonating relays, see	0029	1	
CYCLOPROPANE	1027	2			0267	1	
CYCLOTETRAMETHYLENE-TETRANITRAMINE, DESENSITIZED	0484	1			0360	1	
					0361	1	
					0455	1	
					0500	1	
CYCLOTETRAMETHYLENE-TETRANITRAMINE, WETTED with not less than 15% water, by mass	0226	1		DETONATOR ASSEMBLIES, NON-ELECTRIC for blasting	0360	1	
					0361	1	
					0500	1	
CYCLOTRIMETHYLENE-TRINITRAMINE AND CYCLOTETRAMETHYLENE-TETRANITRAMINE MIXTURE, DESENSITIZED with not less than 10% phlegmatiser by mass	0391	1		DETONATORS FOR AMMUNITION	0073	1	
					0364	1	
					0365	1	
					0366	1	
CYCLOTRIMETHYLENE-TRINITRAMINE AND CYCLOTETRAMETHYLENE-TETRANITRAMINE MIXTURE, WETTED with not less than 15% water, by mass	0391	1		DETONATORS, ELECTRIC for blasting	0030	1	
					0255	1	
					0456	1	
				DETONATORS, ELECTRONIC programmable for blasting	0511	1	
					0512	1	
					0513	1	
CYCLOTRIMETHYLENE-TRINITRAMINE, DESENSITIZED	0483	1		DETONATORS, NON-ELECTRIC for blasting	0029	1	
					0267	1	
					0455	1	
CYCLOTRIMETHYLENE-TRINITRAMINE, WETTED with not less than 15% water, by mass	0072	1		DEUTERIUM, COMPRESSED	1957	2	
				DEVICES, SMALL, HYDROCARBON GAS POWERED with release device	3150	2	
CYMENES	2046	3		DIACETONE ALCOHOL	1148	3	
Cymol, see	2046	3		DIALKYL-(C_{12}-C_{18})-DIMETHYL-AMMONIUM and 2-PROPANOL	3175	4.1	
Deanol, see	2051	8					
DANGEROUS GOODS IN ARTICLES	3363	9		DIALLYLAMINE	2359	3	
				DIALLYL ETHER	2360	3	
DANGEROUS GOODS IN MACHINERY OR DANGEROUS GOODS IN APPARATUS	3363	9		4,4'-DIAMINODIPHENYL-METHANE	2651	6.1	
DECABORANE	1868	4.1		1,2-Diaminoethane, see	1604	8	
DECAHYDRONAPHTHALENE	1147	3		Diaminopropylamine, see	2269	8	
Decalin, see	1147	3		DI-n-AMYLAMINE	2841	3	
n-DECANE	2247	3		DIAZODINITROPHENOL, WETTED with not less than 40% water, or mixture of alcohol and water, by mass	0074	1	
DEFLAGRATING METAL SALTS OF AROMATIC NITRODERIVATIVES, N.O.S.	0132	1					
Depth charge, see	0056	1		Dibenzopyridine, see	2713	6.1	
				DIBENZYLDICHLOROSILANE	2434	8	
DESENSITIZED EXPLOSIVE, LIQUID, N.O.S.	3379	3		DIBORANE	1911	2	
				1,2-DIBROMOBUTAN-3-ONE	2648	6.1	

Name and description	UN No.	Class	Remarks	Name and description	UN No.	Class	Remarks
DIBROMOCHLOROPROPANES	2872	6.1		DICHLOROMETHANE	1593	6.1	
1,2-Dibromo-3-chloropropane, see	2872	6.1		1,1-DICHLORO-1-NITROETHANE	2650	6.1	
DIBROMODIFLUOROMETHANE	1941	9		DICHLOROPENTANES	1152	3	
DIBROMOMETHANE	2664	6.1		Dichlorophenol, see	2020	6.1	
					2021	6.1	
DI-n-BUTYLAMINE	2248	8		DICHLOROPHENYL ISOCYANATES	2250	6.1	
DIBUTYLAMINOETHANOL	2873	6.1					
2-Dibutylaminoethanol, see	2873	6.1		N,N-Di-n-butylaminoethanol, see	2873	6.1	
N,N-Di-n-butylaminoethanol, see	2873	6.1		DICHLOROPHENYLTRI-CHLOROSILANE	1766	8	
DIBUTYL ETHERS	1149	3		1,2-DICHLOROPROPANE	1279	3	
DICHLOROACETIC ACID	1764	8		1,3-DICHLORO-PROPANOL-2	2750	6.1	
1,3-DICHLOROACETONE	2649	6.1		1,3-Dichloro-2-propanone, see	2649	6.1	
DICHLOROACETYL CHLORIDE	1765	8		DICHLOROPROPENES	2047	3	
DICHLOROANILINES, LIQUID	1590	6.1		DICHLOROSILANE	2189	2	
DICHLOROANILINES, SOLID	3442	6.1		1,2-DICHLORO-1,1,2,2-TETRAFLUOROETHANE	1958	2	
o-DICHLOROBENZENE	1591	6.1		Dichloro-s-triazine-2,4,6-trione, see	2465	5.1	
2,2'-DICHLORODIETHYL ETHER	1916	6.1		1,4-Dicyanobutane, see	2205	6.1	
DICHLORODIFLUORO-METHANE	1028	2		Dicycloheptadiene, see	2251	3	
				DICYCLOHEXYLAMINE	2565	8	
DICHLORODIFLUORO-METHANE AND 1,1-DIFLUOROETHANE AZEOTROPIC MIXTURE with approximately 74% dichlorodifluoromethane	2602	2		Dicyclohexylamine nitrite, see	2687	4.1	
				DICYCLOHEXYLAMMONIUM NITRITE	2687	4.1	
				DICYCLOPENTADIENE	2048	3	
Dichlorodifluoromethane and ethylene oxide mixture, see	3070	2		1,2-DI-(DIMETHYLAMINO) ETHANE	2372	3	
DICHLORODIMETHYL ETHER, SYMMETRICAL	2249	6.1	Carriage prohibited	DIDYMIUM NITRATE	1465	5.1	
1,1-DICHLOROETHANE	2362	3		DIESEL FUEL	1202	3	
1,2-Dichloroethane, see	1184	3		1,1-Diethoxyethane, see	1088	3	
1,2-DICHLOROETHYLENE	1150	3		1,2-Diethoxyethane, see	1153	3	
Di(2-chloroethyl) ether, see	1916	6.1		DIETHOXYMETHANE	2373	3	
DICHLOROFLUOROMETHANE	1029	2		3,3-DIETHOXYPROPENE	2374	3	
alpha-Dichlorohydrin, see	2750	6.1		DIETHYLAMINE	1154	3	
DICHLOROISOCYANURIC ACID, DRY	2465	5.1		2-DIETHYLAMINOETHANOL	2686	8	
DICHLOROISOCYANURIC ACID SALTS	2465	5.1		3-DIETHYL-AMINOPROPYLAMINE	2684	3	
DICHLOROISOPROPYL ETHER	2490	6.1		N,N-DIETHYLANILINE	2432	6.1	

Name and description	UN No.	Class	Remarks	Name and description	UN No.	Class	Remarks
DIETHYLBENZENE	2049	3		DIFLUOROPHOSPHORIC ACID, ANHYDROUS	1768	8	
Diethylcarbinol, see	1105	3		2,3-DIHYDROPYRAN	2376	3	
DIETHYL CARBONATE	2366	3					
DIETHYLDICHLOROSILANE	1767	8		DIISOBUTYLAMINE	2361	3	
Diethylenediamine, see	2579	8		DIISOBUTYLENE, ISOMERIC COMPOUNDS	2050	3	
DIETHYLENEGLYCOL DINITRATE, DESENSITIZED with not less than 25% non-volatile, water-insoluble phlegmatizer, by mass	0075	1		alpha-Diisobutylene, see	2050	3	
				beta-Diisobutylene, see	2050	3	
				DIISOBUTYL KETONE	1157	3	
DIETHYLENETRIAMINE	2079	8		DIISOOCTYL ACID PHOSPHATE	1902	8	
N,N-Diethylethanolamine, see	2686	3		DIISOPROPYLAMINE	1158	3	
DIETHYL ETHER	1155	3		DIISOPROPYL ETHER	1159	3	
N,N-DIETHYLETHYLENE-DIAMINE	2685	8		DIKETENE, STABILIZED	2521	6.1	
Di-(2-ethylhexyl) phosphoric acid, see	1902	8		1,1-DIMETHOXYETHANE	2377	3	
				1,2-DIMETHOXYETHANE	2252	3	
DIETHYL KETONE	1156	3		Dimethoxystrychnine, see	1570	6.1	
DIETHYL SULPHATE	1594	6.1		DIMETHYLAMINE, ANHYDROUS	1032	2	
DIETHYL SULPHIDE	2375	3					
DIETHYLTHIOPHOSPHORYL CHLORIDE	2751	8		DIMETHYLAMINE AQUEOUS SOLUTION	1160	3	
Diethylzinc, see	3394	4.2		2-DIMETHYLAMINO-ACETONITRILE	2378	3	
2,4-Difluoroaniline, see	2941	6.1		2-DIMETHYLAMINOETHANOL	2051	8	
Difluorochloroethane, see	2517	2		2-DIMETHYLAMINOETHYL ACRYLATE, STABILIZED	3302	6.1	
1,1-DIFLUOROETHANE	1030	2					
1,1-DIFLUOROETHYLENE	1959	2		2-DIMETHYLAMINOETHYL-METHACRYLATE, STABILIZED	2522	6.1	
DIFLUOROMETHANE	3252	2		N,N-DIMETHYLANILINE	2253	6.1	
Difluoromethane, pentafluoroethane, and 1,1,1,2-tetrafluoroethane zeotropic mixture with approximately 10% difluoromethane and 70% pentafluoroethane, see	3339	2		Dimethylarsenic acid, see	1572	6.1	
				N,N-Dimethylbenzylamine, see	2619	8	
				2,3-DIMETHYLBUTANE	2457	3	
Difluoromethane, pentafluoroethane, and 1,1,1,2-tetrafluoroethane zeotropic mixture with approximately 20% difluoromethane and 40% pentafluoroethane, see	3338	2		1,3-DIMETHYLBUTYLAMINE	2379	3	
				DIMETHYLCARBAMOYL CHLORIDE	2262	8	
Difluoromethane, pentafluoroethane, and 1,1,1,2-tetrafluoroethane zeotropic mixture with approximately 23% difluoromethane and 25% pentafluoroethane, see	3340	2		DIMETHYL CARBONATE	1161	3	
				DIMETHYLCYCLOHEXANES	2263	3	
				N,N-DIMETHYLCYCLO-HEXYLAMINE	2264	8	

Name and description	UN No.	Class	Remarks	Name and description	UN No.	Class	Remarks
DIMETHYLDICHLOROSILANE	1162	3		DINITROPHENOLATES, WETTED with not less than 15% water, by mass	1321	4.1	
DIMETHYLDIETHOXYSILANE	2380	3					
DIMETHYLDIOXANES	2707	3		DINITRORESORCINOL, dry or wetted with less than 15% water, by mass	0078	1	
DIMETHYL DISULPHIDE	2381	3					
Dimethylethanolamine, see	2051	8		DINITRORESORCINOL, WETTED with not less than 15% water, by mass	1322	4.1	
DIMETHYL ETHER	1033	2					
N,N-DIMETHYLFORMAMIDE	2265	3		DINITROSOBENZENE	0406	1	
DIMETHYLHYDRAZINE, SYMMETRICAL	2382	6.1		Dinitrotoluene mixed with sodium chlorate, see	0083	1	
DIMETHYLHYDRAZINE, UNSYMMETRICAL	1163	6.1		DINITROTOLUENES, LIQUID	2038	6.1	
1,1-Dimethylhydrazine, see	1163	6.1		DINITROTOLUENES, MOLTEN	1600	6.1	
N,N-Dimethyl-4-nitrosoaniline, see	1369	4.2		DINITROTOLUENES, SOLID	3454	6.1	
2,2-DIMETHYLPROPANE	2044	2		DIOXANE	1165	3	
DIMETHYL-N-PROPYLAMINE	2266	3		DIOXOLANE	1166	3	
DIMETHYL SULPHATE	1595	6.1		DIPENTENE	2052	3	
DIMETHYL SULPHIDE	1164	3		DIPHENYLAMINE CHLOROARSINE	1698	6.1	
DIMETHYL THIOPHOSPHORYL CHLORIDE	2267	6.1		DIPHENYLCHLOROARSINE, LIQUID	1699	6.1	
Dimethylzinc, see	3394	4.2		DIPHENYLCHLOROARSINE, SOLID	3450	6.1	
DINGU, see	0489	1		DIPHENYLDICHLOROSILANE	1769	8	
DINITROANILINES	1596	6.1		DIPHENYLMETHANE-4, 4'-DIISOCYANATE	9004	9	Danger-ous in tank vessels only
DINITROBENZENES, LIQUID	1597	6.1					
DINITROBENZENES, SOLID	3443	6.1					
Dinitrochlorobenzene, see	1577 3441	6.1 6.1		DIPHENYLMETHYL BROMIDE	1770	8	
DINITRO-o-CRESOL	1598	6.1		DIPICRYLAMINE, see	0079	1	
DINITROGEN TETROXIDE	1067	2		DIPICRYL SULPHIDE, dry or wetted with less than 10% water, by mass	0401	1	
DINITROGLYCOLURIL	0489	1					
DINITROPHENOL, dry or wetted with less than 15% water, by mass	0076	1		DIPICRYL SULPHIDE, WETTED with not less than 10% water, by mass	2852	4.1	
DINITROPHENOL SOLUTION	1599	6.1		DIPROPYLAMINE	2383	3	
DINITROPHENOL, WETTED with not less than 15% water, by mass	1320	4.1		Dipropylene triamine, see	2269	8	
DINITROPHENOLATES, alkali metals, dry or wetted with less than 15% water, by mass	0077	1		DI-n-PROPYL ETHER	2384	3	
				DIPROPYL KETONE	2710	3	
				DISINFECTANT, LIQUID, CORROSIVE, N.O.S.	1903	8	

Name and description	UN No.	Class	Remarks	Name and description	UN No.	Class	Remarks
DISINFECTANT, LIQUID, TOXIC, N.O.S.	3142	6.1		Empty battery-vehicle, uncleaned			See 4.3.2.4 of ADR, 5.1.3 and 5.4.1.1.6
DISINFECTANT, SOLID, TOXIC, N.O.S.	1601	6.1					
DISODIUM TRIOXOSILICATE	3253	8		Empty IBC, uncleaned			See 4.1.1.11 of ADR, 5.1.3 and 5.4.1.1.6
DIVINYL ETHER, STABILIZED	1167	3					
DODECYLTRICHLOROSILANE	1771	8					
Dry ice, see	1845	9	Not subject to ADN	Empty large packaging, uncleaned			See 4.1.1.11 of ADR, 5.1.3 and 5.4.1.1.6
DYE INTERMEDIATE, LIQUID, CORROSIVE, N.O.S.	2801	8					
DYE INTERMEDIATE, LIQUID, TOXIC, N.O.S.	1602	6.1		Empty MEGC, uncleaned			See 4.3.2.4 of ADR, 5.1.3 and 5.4.1.1.6
DYE INTERMEDIATE, SOLID, CORROSIVE, N.O.S.	3147	8					
DYE INTERMEDIATE, SOLID, TOXIC, N.O.S.	3143	6.1		Empty packaging, uncleaned			See 4.1.1.11 of ADR, 5.1.3 and 5.4.1.1.6
DYE, LIQUID, CORROSIVE, N.O.S.	2801	8					
DYE, LIQUID, TOXIC, N.O.S.	1602	6.1		Empty receptacle, uncleaned			See 5.1.3 and 5.4.1.1.6
DYE, SOLID, CORROSIVE, N.O.S.	3147	8					
DYE, SOLID, TOXIC, N.O.S.	3143	6.1		Empty tank, uncleaned			See 4.3.2.4 of ADR, 5.1.3 and 5.4.1.1.6
Dynamite, see	0081	1					
Electric storage batteries, see	2794	8					
	2795	8		Empty vehicle, uncleaned			See 5.1.3 and 5.4.1.1.6
	2800	8					
	3028	8					
Electrolyte (acid or alkaline) for batteries, see	2796	8		Enamel, see	1263	3	
	2797	8			3066	8	
					3469	3	
ELEVATED TEMPERATURE LIQUID, N.O.S., at or above 100 °C and below its flash-point (including molten metals, molten salts, etc.)	3257	9			3470	8	
				ENGINE, FUEL CELL, FLAMMABLE GAS POWERED	3529	2.1	
ELEVATED TEMPERATURE LIQUID, FLAMMABLE, N.O.S. with flash-point above 60 °C, at or above its flash-point and below 100°C	3256	3		ENGINE, FUEL CELL, FLAMMABLE LIQUID POWERED	3528	3	
				ENGINE, INTERNAL COMBUSTION	3530	9	
ELEVATED TEMPERATURE LIQUID, FLAMMABLE, N.O.S. with flash-point above 60 °C, at or above its flash-point and at or above 100°C	3256	3		ENGINE, INTERNAL COMBUSTION, FLAMMABLE GAS POWERED	3529	2.1	
				ENGINE, INTERNAL COMBUSTION, FLAMMABLE LIQUID POWERED	3528	3	
ELEVATED TEMPERATURE SOLID, N.O.S., at or above 240 °C	3258	9					

Name and description	UN No.	Class	Remarks	Name and description	UN No.	Class	Remarks
Engines, rocket, see	0250	1		ETHYL ACRYLATE, STABILIZED	1917	3	
	0322	1		ETHYL ALCOHOL, see	1170	3	
ENVIRONMENTALLY HAZARDOUS SUBSTANCE, LIQUID, N.O.S.	3082	9		ETHYL ALCOHOL SOLUTION, see	1170	3	
ENVIRONMENTALLY HAZARDOUS SUBSTANCE, SOLID, N.O.S.	3077	9		ETHYLAMINE	1036	2	
EPIBROMOHYDRIN	2558	6.1		ETHYLAMINE, AQUEOUS SOLUTION with not less than 50% but not more than 70% ethylamine	2270	3	
EPICHLOROHYDRIN	2023	6.1		ETHYL AMYL KETONE	2271	3	
1,2-Epoxybutane, stabilized, see	3022	3		N-ETHYLANILINE	2272	6.1	
Epoxyethane, see	1040	2		2-ETHYLANILINE	2273	6.1	
1,2-EPOXY-3-ETHOXYPROPANE	2752	3		ETHYLBENZENE	1175	3	
2,3-Epoxy-1-propanal, see	2622	3		N-ETHYL-N-BENZYLANILINE	2274	6.1	
2,3-Epoxypropyl ethyl ether, see	2752	3		N-ETHYLBENZYLTOLUIDINES, LIQUID	2753	6.1	
ESTERS, N.O.S.	3272	3		N-ETHYLBENZYLTOLUIDINES, SOLID	3460	6.1	
Ethanal, see	1089	3		ETHYL BORATE	1176	3	
ETHANE	1035	2		ETHYL BROMIDE	1891	6.1	
ETHANE, REFRIGERATED LIQUID	1961	2		ETHYL BROMOACETATE	1603	6.1	
Ethanethiol, see	2363	3		2-ETHYLBUTANOL	2275	3	
ETHANOL	1170	3		2-ETHYLBUTYL ACETATE	1177	3	
ETHANOL AND GASOLINE MIXTURE or ETHANOL AND MOTOR SPIRIT MIXTURE or ETHANOL AND PETROL MIXTURE, with more than 10% ethanol	3475	3		ETHYL BUTYL ETHER	1179	3	
				2-ETHYLBUTYRALDEHYDE	1178	3	
				ETHYL BUTYRATE	1180	3	
ETHANOL SOLUTION	1170	3		ETHYL CHLORIDE	1037	2	
ETHANOLAMINE	2491	8		ETHYL CHLOROACETATE	1181	6.1	
ETHANOLAMINE SOLUTION	2491	8		Ethyl chlorocarbonate, see	1182	6.1	
Ether, see	1155	3		ETHYL CHLOROFORMATE	1182	6.1	
ETHERS, N.O.S.	3271	3		ETHYL 2-CHLOROPROPIONATE	2935	3	
2-Ethoxyethanol, see	1171	3		Ethyl-alpha-chloropropionate, see	2935	3	
2-Ethoxyethyl acetate, see	1172	3		ETHYL CHLOROTHIOFORMATE	2826	8	
Ethoxy propane-1, see	2615	3		ETHYL CROTONATE	1862	3	
ETHYL ACETATE	1173	3		ETHYLDICHLOROARSINE	1892	6.1	
ETHYLACETYLENE, STABILIZED	2452	2		ETHYLDICHLOROSILANE	1183	4.3	

Name and description	UN No.	Class	Remarks	Name and description	UN No.	Class	Remarks
ETHYLENE, ACETYLENE AND PROPYLENE MIXTURE, REFRIGERATED LIQUID containing at least 71.5% ethylene with not more than 22.5% acetylene and not more than 6% propylene	3138	2		ETHYLENE OXIDE AND PENTAFLUOROETHANE MIXTURE with not more than 7.9% ethylene oxide	3298	2	
ETHYLENE CHLOROHYDRIN	1135	6.1		ETHYLENE OXIDE AND PROPYLENE OXIDE MIXTURE, not more than 30% ethylene oxide	2983	3	
ETHYLENE	1962	2		ETHYLENE OXIDE AND TETRAFLUOROETHANE MIXTURE with not more than 5.6% ethylene oxide	3299	2	
ETHYLENEDIAMINE	1604	8					
ETHYLENE DIBROMIDE	1605	6.1					
Ethylene dibromide and methyl bromide, liquid mixture, see	1647	6.1		ETHYLENE OXIDE WITH NITROGEN up to a total pressure of 1 MPa (10 bar) at 50 °C	1040	2	
ETHYLENE DICHLORIDE	1184	3		ETHYLENE, REFRIGERATED LIQUID	1038	2	
ETHYLENE GLYCOL DIETHYL ETHER	1153	3		ETHYL ETHER, see	1155	3	
ETHYLENE GLYCOL MONOETHYL ETHER	1171	3		ETHYL FLUORIDE	2453	2	
				ETHYL FORMATE	1190	3	
ETHYLENE GLYCOL MONOETHYL ETHER ACETATE	1172	3		2-ETHYLHEXYLAMINE	2276	3	
ETHYLENE GLYCOL MONOMETHYL ETHER	1188	3		2-ETHYLHEXYL CHLOROFORMATE	2748	6.1	
ETHYLENE GLYCOL MONOMETHYL ETHER ACETATE	1189	3		Ethylidene chloride, see	2362	3	
				ETHYL ISOBUTYRATE	2385	3	
ETHYLENEIMINE, STABILIZED	1185	6.1		ETHYL ISOCYANATE	2481	6.1	
ETHYLENE OXIDE	1040	2		ETHYL LACTATE	1192	3	
ETHYLENE OXIDE AND CARBON DIOXIDE MIXTURE with more than 87% ethylene oxide	3300	2		ETHYL MERCAPTAN	2363	3	
				ETHYL METHACRYLATE, STABILIZED	2277	3	
ETHYLENE OXIDE AND CARBON DIOXIDE MIXTURE with more than 9% but not more than 87% ethylene oxide	1041	2		ETHYL METHYL ETHER	1039	2	
				ETHYL METHYL KETONE	1193	3	
ETHYLENE OXIDE AND CARBON DIOXIDE MIXTURE with not more than 9% ethylene oxide	1952	2		ETHYL NITRITE SOLUTION	1194	3	
				ETHYL ORTHOFORMATE	2524	3	
				ETHYL OXALATE	2525	6.1	
ETHYLENE OXIDE AND CHLOROTETRAFLUORO-ETHANE MIXTURE with not more than 8.8% ethylene oxide	3297	2		ETHYLPHENYL-DICHLOROSILANE	2435	8	
				1-ETHYLPIPERIDINE	2386	3	
ETHYLENE OXIDE AND DICHLORODIFLUORO-METHANE MIXTURE with not more than 12.5% ethylene oxide	3070	2		ETHYL PROPIONATE	1195	3	
				ETHYL PROPYL ETHER	2615	3	
				Ethyl silicate, see	1292	3	
				Ethyl sulphate, see	1594	6.1	

Name and description	UN No.	Class	Remarks	Name and description	UN No.	Class	Remarks
N-ETHYLTOLUIDINES	2754	6.1		FERROSILICON with 30% or more but less than 90% silicon	1408	4.3	
ETHYLTRICHLOROSILANE	1196	3		FERROUS ARSENATE	1608	6.1	
EXPLOSIVE, BLASTING, TYPE A	0081	1		FERROUS METAL BORINGS in a form liable to self-heating	2793	4.2	
EXPLOSIVE, BLASTING, TYPE B	0082 0331	1 1		FERROUS METAL CUTTINGS in a form liable to self-heating	2793	4.2	
EXPLOSIVE, BLASTING, TYPE C	0083	1		FERROUS METAL SHAVINGS in a form liable to self-heating	2793	4.2	
EXPLOSIVE, BLASTING, TYPE D	0084	1		FERROUS METAL TURNINGS in a form liable to self-heating	2793	4.2	
EXPLOSIVE, BLASTING, TYPE E	0241 0332	1 1		FERTILIZER AMMONIATING SOLUTION with free ammonia	1043	2	
Explosives, emulsion, see	0241 0332	1 1		Fertilizer with ammonium nitrate, n.o.s., see	2067	5.1	
Explosive, seismic, see	0081 0082 0083 0331	1 1 1 1		Fibres, animal, burnt, wet or damp	1372	4.2	Not subject to ADN
Explosive, slurry, see	0241 0332	1 1		FIBRES, ANIMAL, N.O.S. with oil	1373	4.2	
Explosive, water gel, see	0241 0332	1 1		FIBRES IMPREGNATED WITH WEAKLY NITRATED NITROCELLULOSE, N.O.S.	1353	4.1	
Extracts, aromatic, liquid, see	1197	3		FIBRES, SYNTHETIC, N.O.S. with oil	1373	4.2	
Extracts, flavouring, liquid, see	1197	3		Fibres, vegetable, burnt, wet or damp	1372	4.2	Not subject to ADN
EXTRACTS, LIQUID, for flavour or aroma	1197	3		Fibres, vegetable, dry	3360	4.1	Not subject to ADN
FABRICS, ANIMAL, N.O.S. with oil	1373	4.2		FIBRES, VEGETABLE, N.O.S. with oil	1373	4.2	
FABRICS IMPREGNATED WITH WEAKLY NITRATED NITROCELLULOSE, N.O.S.	1353	4.1		Filler, liquid, see	1263 3066 3469 3470	3 8 3 8	
FABRICS, SYNTHETIC, N.O.S. with oil	1373	4.2		Films, nitrocellulose base, from which gelatin has been removed; film scrap, see	2002	4.2	
FABRICS, VEGETABLE, N.O.S. with oil	1373	4.2		FILMS, NITROCELLULOSE BASE, gelatin coated, except scrap	1324	4.1	
FERRIC ARSENATE	1606	6.1					
FERRIC ARSENITE	1607	6.1		FIRE EXTINGUISHER CHARGES, corrosive liquid	1774	8	
FERRIC CHLORIDE, ANHYDROUS	1773	8		Fire extinguisher charges, expelling, explosive, see	0275 0276 0323 0381	1 1 1 1	
FERRIC CHLORIDE SOLUTION	2582	8					
FERRIC NITRATE	1466	5.1					
FERROCERIUM	1323	4.1		FIRE EXTINGUISHERS with compressed or liquefied gas	1044	2	

Name and description	UN No.	Class	Remarks
FIRELIGHTERS, SOLID with flammable liquid	2623	4.1	
FIREWORKS	0333	1	See 2.2.1.1.7
	0334	1	
	0335	1	
	0336	1	
	0337	1	
FIRST AID KIT	3316	9	
FISH MEAL, STABILIZED	2216	9	
FISH MEAL, UNSTABILIZED	1374	4.2	
FISH SCRAP, STABILIZED, see	2216	9	
FISH SCRAP, UNSTABILIZED, see	1374	4.2	
Flammable gas in lighters, see	1057	2	
FLAMMABLE LIQUID, N.O.S	1993	3	
FLAMMABLE LIQUID, CORROSIVE, N.O.S.	2924	3	
FLAMMABLE LIQUID, TOXIC, N.O.S.	1992	3	
FLAMMABLE LIQUID, TOXIC, CORROSIVE, N.O.S.	3286	3	
FLAMMABLE SOLID, CORROSIVE, INORGANIC, N.O.S.	3180	4.1	
FLAMMABLE SOLID, CORROSIVE, ORGANIC, N.O.S.	2925	4.1	
FLAMMABLE SOLID, INORGANIC, N.O.S.	3178	4.1	
FLAMMABLE SOLID, ORGANIC, N.O.S.	1325	4.1	
FLAMMABLE SOLID, ORGANIC, MOLTEN, N.O.S.	3176	4.1	
FLAMMABLE SOLID, OXIDIZING, N.O.S.	3097	4.1	Carriage prohibited
FLAMMABLE SOLID, TOXIC, INORGANIC, N.O.S.	3179	4.1	
FLAMMABLE SOLID, TOXIC, ORGANIC, N.O.S.	2926	4.1	
FLARES, AERIAL	0093	1	
	0403	1	
	0404	1	
	0420	1	
	0421	1	
Flares, aeroplane, see	0093	1	
	0403	1	
	0404	1	
	0420	1	
	0421	1	
Flares, highway, Flares, distress, small, Flares, railway or highway, see	0191	1	
	0373	1	
FLARES, SURFACE	0092	1	
	0418	1	
	0419	1	
Flares, water-activated, see	0248	1	
	0249	1	
FLASH POWDER	0094	1	
	0305	1	
Flue dusts, toxic, see	1562	6.1	
Fluoric acid, see	1790	8	
FLUORINE, COMPRESSED	1045	2	
FLUOROACETIC ACID	2642	6.1	
FLUOROANILINES	2941	6.1	
2-Fluoroaniline, see	2941	6.1	
4-Fluoroaniline, see	2941	6.1	
o-Fluoroaniline, see	2941	6.1	
p-Fluoroaniline, see	2941	6.1	
FLUOROBENZENE	2387	3	
FLUOROBORIC ACID	1775	8	
Fluoroethane, see	2453	2	
Fluoroform, see	1984	2	
Fluoromethane, see	2454	2	
FLUOROPHOSPHORIC ACID, ANHYDROUS	1776	8	
FLUOROSILICATES, N.O.S.	2856	6.1	
FLUOROSILICIC ACID	1778	8	
FLUOROSULPHONIC ACID	1777	8	
FLUOROTOLUENES	2388	3	
FORMALDEHYDE SOLUTION with not less than 25% formaldehyde	2209	8	
FORMALDEHYDE SOLUTION, FLAMMABLE	1198	3	
Formalin, see	1198	3	
	2209	8	

Name and description	UN No.	Class	Remarks	Name and description	UN No.	Class	Remarks
Formamidine sulphinic acid, see	3341	4.2		Fuze, combination, percussion or time, see	0106	1	
					0107	1	
FORMIC ACID with more than 85% acid by mass	1779	8			0257	1	
					0316	1	
					0317	1	
FORMIC ACID with not more than 85% acid by mass	3412	8			0367	1	
					0368	1	
Formic aldehyde, see	1198	3		FUZES, DETONATING	0106	1	
	2209	8			0107	1	
					0257	1	
2-Formyl-3,4-dihydro-2H-pyran, see	2607	3			0367	1	
FRACTURING DEVICES, EXPLOSIVE without detonator, for oil wells	0099	1		FUZES, DETONATING with protective features	0408	1	
					0409	1	
					0410	1	
FUEL, AVIATION, TURBINE ENGINE	1863	3		FUZES, IGNITING	0316	1	
					0317	1	
					0368	1	
FUEL CELL CARTRIDGES	3478	2					
	3479	2		GALLIUM	2803	8	
	3473	3					
	3476	4.3		GAS CARTRIDGES without a release device, non-refillable, see	2037	2	
	3477	8					
FUEL CELL CARTRIDGES CONTAINED IN EQUIPMENT	3478	2		Gas drips, hydrocarbon, see	3295	3	
	3479	2					
	3473	3		GAS OIL	1202	3	
	3476	4.3					
	3477	8		GASOLINE	1203	3	
FUEL CELL CARTRIDGES PACKED WITH EQUIPMENT	3478	2		Gasoline and ethanol mixture, with more than 10% ethanol, see	3475	3	
	3479	2					
	3473	3		Gasoline, casinghead, see	1203	3	
	3476	4.3					
	3477	8		GAS, REFRIGERATED LIQUID, N.O.S.	3158	2	
Fumaroyl dichloride, see	1780	3					
FUMARYL CHLORIDE	1780	8		GAS, REFRIGERATED LIQUID, FLAMMABLE, N.O.S.	3312	2	
FUMIGATED CARGO TRANSPORT UNIT	3359	9		GAS, REFRIGERATED LIQUID, OXIDIZING, N.O.S.	3311	2	
FURALDEHYDES	1199	6.1		GAS SAMPLE, NON-PRESSURIZED, FLAMMABLE, N.O.S., not refrigerated liquid	3167	2	
FURAN	2389	3					
FURFURYL ALCOHOL	2874	6.1		GAS SAMPLE, NON-PRESSURIZED, TOXIC, N.O.S., not refrigerated liquid	3169	2	
FURFURYLAMINE	2526	3					
Furyl carbinol, see	2874	6.1		GAS SAMPLE, NON-PRESSURIZED, TOXIC, FLAMMABLE, N.O.S., not refrigerated liquid	3168	2	
FUSE, DETONATING, metal clad	0102	1					
	0290	1					
FUSE, DETONATING, MILD EFFECT, metal clad	0104	1					
				Gelatin, blasting, see	0081	1	
FUSE, IGNITER, tubular, metal clad	0103	1		Gelatin, dynamites, see	0081	1	
FUSE, NON-DETONATING	0101	1		GENETICALLY MODIFIED MICROORGANISMS	3245	9	
FUSEL OIL	1201	3					
FUSE, SAFETY	0105	1					

Name and description	UN No.	Class	Remarks	Name and description	UN No.	Class	Remarks
GENETICALLY MODIFIED ORGANISMS	3245	9		HAFNIUM POWDER, WETTED with not less than 25% water	1326	4.1	
GERMANE	2192	2		HALOGENATED MONOMETHYLDIPHENYL-METHANES, LIQUID	3151	9	
GERMANE, ADSORBED	3523	2		HALOGENATED MONOMETHYLDIPHENYL-METHANES, SOLID	3152	9	
Germanium hydride, see	2192	2					
Glycer-1,3-dichlorohydrin, see	2750	6.1					
GLYCEROL alpha-MONOCHLOROHYDRIN	2689	6.1		Hay	1327	4.1	Not subject to ADN
Glyceryl trinitrate, see	0143	1					
	0144	1		HEATING OIL, LIGHT	1202	3	
	1204	3					
	3064	3		Heavy hydrogen, see	1957	2	
GLYCIDALDEHYDE	2622	3		HELIUM, COMPRESSED	1046	2	
GRENADES, hand or rifle, with bursting charge	0284	1		HELIUM, REFRIGERATED LIQUID	1963	2	
	0285	1					
	0292	1		HEPTAFLUOROPROPANE	3296	2	
	0293	1					
Grenades, illuminating, see	0171	1		n-HEPTALDEHYDE	3056	3	
	0254	1					
	0297	1		n-Heptanal, see	3056	3	
GRENADES, PRACTICE, hand or rifle	0110	1		HEPTANES	1206	3	
	0318	1					
	0372	1		4-Heptanone, see	2710	3	
	0452	1		n-HEPTENE	2278	3	
Grenades, smoke, see	0015	1		HEXACHLOROACETONE	2661	6.1	
	0016	1		HEXACHLOROBENZENE	2729	6.1	
	0245	1					
	0246	1		HEXACHLOROBUTADIENE	2279	6.1	
	0303	1		Hexachloro-1,3-butadiene, see	2279	6.1	
GUANIDINE NITRATE	1467	5.1					
GUANYLNITROSAMINO-GUANYLIDENE HYDRAZINE, WETTED with not less than 30% water, by mass	0113	1		HEXACHLOROCYCLO-PENTADIENE	2646	6.1	
				HEXACHLOROPHENE	2875	6.1	
				Hexachloro-2-propanone, see	2661	6.1	
GUANYLNITROSAMINO-GUANYLTETRAZENE, WETTED with not less than 30% water, or mixture of alcohol and water, by mass	0114	1		HEXADECYLTRICHLORO-SILANE	1781	8	
				HEXADIENES	2458	3	
GUNPOWDER, COMPRESSED, see	0028	1		HEXAETHYL TETRAPHOSPHATE	1611	6.1	
GUNPOWDER, granular or as a meal, see	0027	1		HEXAETHYL TETRAPHOSPHATE AND COMPRESSED GAS MIXTURE	1612	2	
GUNPOWDER, IN PELLETS, see	0028	1		HEXAFLUOROACETONE	2420	2	
Gutta percha solution, see	1287	3					
HAFNIUM POWDER, DRY	2545	4.2		HEXAFLUOROACETONE HYDRATE, LIQUID	2552	6.1	

Name and description	UN No.	Class	Remarks	Name and description	UN No.	Class	Remarks
HEXAFLUOROACETONE HYDRATE, SOLID	3436	6.1		HEXYLTRICHLOROSILANE	1784	8	
HEXAFLUOROETHANE	2193	2		HMX, see	0391	1	
HEXAFLUOROPHOSPHORIC ACID	1782	8		HMX, DESENSITIZED, see	0484	1	
				HMX, WETTED with not less than 15% water, by mass, see	0226	1	
HEXAFLUOROPROPYLENE	1858	2		HYDRAZINE, ANHYDROUS	2029	8	
Hexahydrocresol, see	2617	3		HYDRAZINE AQUEOUS SOLUTION, with more than 37% hydrazine by mass	2030	8	
Hexahydromethyl phenol, see	2617	3					
HEXALDEHYDE	1207	3		HYDRAZINE, AQUEOUS SOLUTION with not more than 37% hydrazine, by mass	3293	6.1	
HEXAMETHYLENEDIAMINE, SOLID	2280	8					
HEXAMETHYLENEDIAMINE SOLUTION	1783	8		HYDRAZINE AQUEOUS SOLUTION, FLAMMABLE with more than 37% hydrazine, by mass	3484	8	
HEXAMETHYLENE DIISOCYANATE	2281	6.1		Hydrides, metal, water-reactive, n.o.s., see	1409	4.3	
HEXAMETHYLENEIMINE	2493	3		Hydriodic acid, anhydrous, see	2197	2	
HEXAMETHYLENETETRAMINE	1328	4.1		HYDRIODIC ACID	1787	8	
Hexamine, see	1328	4.1		HYDROBROMIC ACID	1788	8	
HEXANES	1208	3		HYDROCARBON GAS MIXTURE, COMPRESSED, N.O.S.	1964	2	
HEXANITRODIPHENYLAMINE	0079	1					
HEXANITROSTILBENE	0392	1		HYDROCARBON GAS MIXTURE, LIQUEFIED, N.O.S. such as mixtures A, A01, A02, A0, A1, B1, B2, B or C	1965	2	
Hexanoic acid, see	2829	8					
HEXANOLS	2282	3					
1-HEXENE	2370	3		HYDROCARBON GAS REFILLS FOR SMALL DEVICES with release device	3150	2	
HEXOGEN AND CYCLOTETRA-METHYLENE-TETRANITRAMINE MIXTURE, WETTED with not less than 15% water, by mass or DESENSITIZED with not less than 10% phlegmatiser by mass, see	0391	1					
				HYDROCARBONS, LIQUID, N.O.S.	3295	3	
				HYDROCHLORIC ACID	1789	8	
HEXOGEN, DESENSITIZED, see	0483	1		HYDROCYANIC ACID, AQUEOUS SOLUTION with not more than 20% hydrogen cyanide	1613	6.1	
HEXOGEN, WETTED with not less than 15% water, by mass, see	0072	1					
HEXOLITE, dry or wetted with less than 15% water, by mass	0118	1		HYDROFLUORIC ACID with more than 60% but not more than 85% hydrogen fluoride	1790	8	
HEXOTOL, dry or wetted with less than 15% water, by mass, see	0118	1		HYDROFLUORIC ACID with more than 85% hydrogen fluoride	1790	8	
HEXOTONAL	0393	1		HYDROFLUORIC ACID with not more than 60% hydrogen fluoride	1790	8	
HEXOTONAL, cast, see	0393	1		HYDROFLUORIC ACID AND SULPHURIC ACID MIXTURE	1786	8	
HEXYL, see	0079	1		Hydrofluoroboric acid, see	1775	8	

Name and description	UN No.	Class	Remarks	Name and description	UN No.	Class	Remarks
Hydrofluorosilicic acid, see	1778	8		HYDROGEN PEROXIDE AND PEROXYACETIC ACID MIXTURE with acid(s), water and not more than 5% peroxyacetic acid, STABILIZED	3149	5.1	
HYDROGEN AND METHANE MIXTURE, COMPRESSED	2034	2					
Hydrogen arsenide, see	2188	2		HYDROGEN PEROXIDE, AQUEOUS SOLUTION with not less than 8% but less than 20% hydrogen peroxide (stabilized as necessary)	2984	5.1	
HYDROGEN BROMIDE, ANHYDROUS	1048	2					
Hydrogen bromide solution, see	1788	8		HYDROGEN PEROXIDE, AQUEOUS SOLUTION with not less than 20% but not more than 60% hydrogen peroxide (stabilized as necessary)	2014	5.1	
HYDROGEN CHLORIDE, ANHYDROUS	1050	2					
HYDROGEN CHLORIDE, REFRIGERATED LIQUID	2186	2	Carriage prohibited	HYDROGEN PEROXIDE, AQUEOUS SOLUTION, STABILIZED with more than 60% hydrogen peroxide and not more than 70% hydrogen peroxide	2015	5.1	
HYDROGEN, COMPRESSED	1049	2					
HYDROGEN CYANIDE, AQUEOUS SOLUTION with not more than 20% hydrogen cyanide, see	1613	6.1		HYDROGEN PEROXIDE, AQUEOUS SOLUTION, STABILIZED with more than 70% hydrogen peroxide	2015	5.1	
HYDROGEN CYANIDE, SOLUTION IN ALCOHOL with not more than 45% hydrogen cyanide	3294	6.1		HYDROGEN PEROXIDE, STABILIZED	2015	5.1	
HYDROGEN CYANIDE, STABILIZED containing less than 3% water	1051	6.1		HYDROGEN, REFRIGERATED LIQUID	1966	2	
HYDROGEN CYANIDE, STABILIZED, containing less than 3% water and absorbed in a porous inert material	1614	6.1		HYDROGEN SELENIDE, ADSORBED	3526	2	
HYDROGENDIFLUORIDES, SOLID, N.O.S.	1740	8		HYDROGEN SELENIDE, ANHYDROUS	2202	2	
				Hydrogen silicide, see	2203	2	
HYDROGENDIFLUORIDES SOLUTION, N.O.S.	3471	8		HYDROGEN SULPHIDE	1053	2	
HYDROGEN FLUORIDE, ANHYDROUS	1052	8		Hydroselenic acid, see	2202	2	
				Hydrosilicofluoric acid, see	1778	8	
Hydrogen fluoride solution, see	1790	8		1-HYDROXYBENZOTRIAZOLE, ANHYDROUS, dry or wetted with less than 20% water, by mass	0508	1	
HYDROGEN IN A METAL HYDRIDE STORAGE SYSTEM	3468	2					
HYDROGEN IN A METAL HYDRIDE STORAGE SYSTEM CONTAINED IN EQUIPMENT	3468	2		1-HYDROXYBENZOTRIAZOLE MONOHYDRATE	3474	4.1	
				3-Hydroxybutan-2-one, see	2621	3	
HYDROGEN IN A METAL HYDRIDE STORAGE SYSTEM PACKED WITH EQUIPMENT	3468	2		HYDROXYLAMINE SULPHATE	2865	8	
				1-Hydroxy-3-methyl-2-penten-4-yne, see	2705	8	
HYDROGEN IODIDE, ANHYDROUS	2197	2		3-Hydroxyphenol, see	2876	6.1	
Hydrogen iodide solution, see	1787	8		HYPOCHLORITES, INORGANIC, N.O.S.	3212	5.1	

Name and description	UN No.	Class	Remarks	Name and description	UN No.	Class	Remarks
HYPOCHLORITE SOLUTION	1791	8		Iron sesquichloride, anhydrous, see	1773	8	
IGNITERS	0121	1		IRON SPONGE, SPENT obtained from coal gas purification	1376	4.2	
	0314	1					
	0315	1		Iron swarf, see	2793	4.2	
	0325	1					
	0454	1		ISOBUTANE	1969	2	
3,3'-IMINODIPROPYLAMINE	2269	8		ISOBUTANOL	1212	3	
India rubber, see	1287	3		Isobutene, see	1055	2	
INFECTIOUS SUBSTANCE, AFFECTING ANIMALS only	2900	6.2		ISOBUTYL ACETATE	1213	3	
				ISOBUTYL ACRYLATE, STABILIZED	2527	3	
INFECTIOUS SUBSTANCE, AFFECTING HUMANS	2814	6.2		ISOBUTYL ALCOHOL, see	1212	3	
Ink, printer's, flammable, see	1210	3		ISOBUTYL ALDEHYDE, see	2045	3	
INSECTICIDE GAS, N.O.S.	1968	2		ISOBUTYLAMINE	1214	3	
INSECTICIDE GAS, FLAMMABLE, N.O.S.	3354	2		ISOBUTYLENE	1055	2	
				ISOBUTYL FORMATE	2393	3	
INSECTICIDE GAS, TOXIC, N.O.S.	1967	2		ISOBUTYL ISOBUTYRATE	2528	3	
INSECTICIDE GAS, TOXIC, FLAMMABLE, N.O.S.	3355	2		ISOBUTYL ISOCYANATE	2486	6.1	
				ISOBUTYL METHACRYLATE, STABILIZED	2283	3	
IODINE MONOCHLORIDE SOLIDE	1792	8		ISOBUTYL PROPIONATE	2394	3	
IODINE MONOCHLORIDE, LIQUID	3498	8		ISOBUTYRALDEHYDE	2045	3	
IODINE PENTAFLUORIDE	2495	5.1		ISOBUTYRIC ACID	2529	3	
2-IODOBUTANE	2390	3		ISOBUTYRONITRILE	2284	3	
Iodomethane, see	2644	6.1		ISOBUTYRYL CHLORIDE	2395	3	
IODOMETHYLPROPANES	2391	3		ISOCYANATES, FLAMMABLE, TOXIC, N.O.S.	2478	3	
IODOPROPANES	2392	3		ISOCYANATES, TOXIC, N.O.S.	2206	6.1	
alpha-Iodotoluene, see	2653	6.1		ISOCYANATES, TOXIC, FLAMMABLE, N.O.S.	3080	6.1	
I.p.d.i., see	2290	6.1					
Iron chloride, anhydrous, see	1773	8		ISOCYANATE SOLUTION, FLAMMABLE, TOXIC, N.O.S.	2478	3	
Iron (III) chloride, anhydrous, see	1773	8		ISOCYANATE SOLUTION, TOXIC, N.O.S.	2206	6.1	
Iron chloride solution, see	2582	8					
IRON OXIDE, SPENT obtained from coal gas purification	1376	4.2		ISOCYANATE SOLUTION, TOXIC, FLAMMABLE, N.O.S.	3080	6.1	
IRON PENTACARBONYL	1994	6.1		ISOCYANATO-BENZOTRIFLUORIDES	2285	6.1	
Iron perchloride, anhydrous, see	1773	8					
Iron powder, pyrophoric, see	1383	4.2		3-Isocyanatomethyl-3,5,5-tri-methylcyclohexyl isocyanate, see	2290	6.1	

Name and description	UN No.	Class	Remarks	Name and description	UN No.	Class	Remarks
Isododecane, see	2286	3		ISOPROPYL PROPIONATE	2409	3	
ISOHEPTENE	2287	3		Isolpropyltoluene, see	2046	3	
ISOHEXENE	2288	3		Isopropyltoluol, see	2046	3	
Isooctane, see	1262	3		ISOSORBIDE DINITRATE MIXTURE with not less than 60% lactose, mannose, starch or calcium hydrogen phosphate	2907	4.1	
ISOOCTENE	1216	3					
Isopentane, see	1265	3		ISOSORBIDE-5-MONONITRATE	3251	4.1	
ISOPENTENES	2371	3		Isovaleraldehyde, see	2058	3	
Isopentylamine, see	1106	3		JET PERFORATING GUNS, CHARGED, oil well, without detonator	0124	1	
Isopentyl nitrite, see	1113	3			0494	1	
ISOPHORONEDIAMINE	2289	8		Jet tappers, without detonator, see	0059	1	
ISOPHORONE DIISOCYANATE	2290	6.1		KEROSENE	1223	3	
ISOPRENE, STABILIZED	1218	3		KETONES, LIQUID, N.O.S.	1224	3	
ISOPROPANOL	1219	3		KRILL MEAL	3497	4.2	
ISOPROPENYL ACETATE	2403	3		KRYPTON, COMPRESSED	1056	2	
ISOPROPENYLBENZENE	2303	3		KRYPTON, REFRIGERATED LIQUID	1970	2	
ISOPROPYL ACETATE	1220	3					
ISOPROPYL ACID PHOSPHATE	1793	8		Lacquer, see	1263	3	
					3066	8	
ISOPROPYL ALCOHOL, see	1219	3			3469	3	
					3470	8	
ISOPROPYLAMINE	1221	3		Lacquer base, liquid, see	1263	3	
					3066	8	
ISOPROPYLBENZENE	1918	3			3469	3	
					3470	8	
ISOPROPYL BUTYRATE	2405	3		Lacquer base or lacquer chips, nitrocellulose, dry, see	2557	4.1	
Isopropyl chloride, see	2356	3					
ISOPROPYL CHLOROACETATE	2947	3		Lacquer base or lacquer chips, plastic, wet with alcohol or solvent, see	1263	3	
					2059	3	
ISOPROPYL CHLOROFORMATE	2407	6.1			2555	4.1	
					2556	4.1	
ISOPROPYL 2-CHLORO-PROPIONATE	2934	3		LEAD ACETATE	1616	6.1	
Isopropyl-alpha-chloropropionate, see	2934	3		Lead (II) acetate, see	1616	6.1	
				LEAD ARSENATES	1617	6.1	
Isopropyl ether, see	1159	3		LEAD ARSENITES	1618	6.1	
Isopropylethylene, see	2561	3		LEAD AZIDE, WETTED with not less than 20% water, or mixture of alcohol and water, by mass	0129	1	
Isopropyl formate, see	1281	3					
ISOPROPYL ISOBUTYRATE	2406	3		Lead chloride, solid, see	2291	6.1	
ISOPROPYL ISOCYANATE	2483	6.1		LEAD COMPOUND, SOLUBLE, N.O.S.	2291	6.1	
Isopropyl mercaptan, see	2402	3					
ISOPROPYL NITRATE	1222	3		LEAD CYANIDE	1620	6.1	

Name and description	UN No.	Class	Remarks	Name and description	UN No.	Class	Remarks
Lead (II) cyanide	1620	6.1		LIQUEFIED GAS, TOXIC, CORROSIVE, N.O.S.	3308	2	
LEAD DIOXIDE	1872	5.1		LIQUEFIED GAS, TOXIC, FLAMMABLE, N.O.S.	3160	2	
LEAD NITRATE	1469	5.1		LIQUEFIED GAS, TOXIC, FLAMMABLE, CORROSIVE, N.O.S.	3309	2	
Lead (II) nitrate	1469	5.1					
LEAD PERCHLORATE, SOLID	1470	5.1		LIQUEFIED GAS, TOXIC, OXIDIZING, N.O.S.	3307	2	
LEAD PERCHLORATE, SOLUTION	3408	5.1		LIQUEFIED GAS, TOXIC, OXIDIZING, CORROSIVE, N.O.S.	3310	2	
Lead (II) perchlorate	1470	5.1					
	3408	5.1		Liquefied petroleum gas, see	1075	2	
Lead peroxide, see	1872	5.1		Liquid filler, see	1263	3	
LEAD PHOSPHITE, DIBASIC	2989	4.1			3066	8	
					3469	3	
LEAD STYPHNATE, WETTED with not less than 20% water, or mixture of alcohol and water, by mass	0130	1			3470	8	
				Liquid lacquer base, see	1263	3	
					3066	8	
LEAD SULPHATE with more than 3% free acid	1794	8			3469	3	
					3470	8	
Lead tetraethyl, see	1649	6.1		LITHIUM	1415	4.3	
Lead tetramethyl, see	1649	6.1		Lithium alkyls, liquid, see	3394	4.2	
				Lithium alkyls, solid, see	3393	4.2	
LEAD TRINITRORESORCINATE, WETTED with not less than 20% water, or mixture of alcohol and water, by mass, see	0130	1		LITHIUM ALUMINIUM HYDRIDE	1410	4.3	
				LITHIUM ALUMINIUM HYDRIDE, ETHEREAL	1411	4.3	
LIFE-SAVING APPLIANCES NOT SELF-INFLATING containing dangerous goods as equipment	3072	9		LITHIUM BATTERIES INSTALLED IN CARGO TRANSPORT UNIT lithium ion batteries or lithium metal batteries	3536	9	
LIFE-SAVING APPLIANCES, SELF-INFLATING	2990	9					
LIGHTER REFILLS containing flammable gas	1057	2		LITHIUM ION BATTERIES (including lithium ion polymer batteries)	3480	9	
LIGHTERS containing flammable gas	1057	2		LITHIUM ION BATTERIES CONTAINED IN EQUIPMENT (including lithium ion polymer batteries)	3481	9	
LIGHTERS, FUSE	0131	1					
Limonene, inactive, see	2052	3		LITHIUM ION BATTERIES PACKED WITH EQUIPMENT (including lithium ion polymer batteries)	3481	9	
LIQUEFIED GAS, N.O.S.	3163	2					
LIQUEFIED GAS, FLAMMABLE, N.O.S.	3161	2					
LIQUEFIED GASES, non-flammable, charged with nitrogen, carbon dioxide or air	1058	2		LITHIUM METAL BATTERIES (including lithium alloy batteries)	3090	9	
LIQUEFIED GAS, OXIDIZING, N.O.S.	3157	2		LITHIUM METAL BATTERIES CONTAINED IN EQUIPMENT (including lithium alloy batteries)	3091	9	
LIQUEFIED GAS, TOXIC, N.O.S.	3162	2					

Name and description	UN No.	Class	Remarks	Name and description	UN No.	Class	Remarks
LITHIUM METAL BATTERIES PACKED WITH EQUIPMENT (including lithium alloy batteries)	3091	9		MAGNESIUM ALLOYS with more than 50% magnesium in pellets, turnings or ribbons	1869	4.1	
LITHIUM BOROHYDRIDE	1413	4.3		MAGNESIUM ALLOYS POWDER	1418	4.3	
LITHIUM FERROSILICON	2830	4.3		MAGNESIUM ALUMINIUM PHOSPHIDE	1419	4.3	
LITHIUM HYDRIDE	1414	4.3		MAGNESIUM ARSENATE	1622	6.1	
LITHIUM HYDRIDE, FUSED SOLID	2805	4.3		Magnesium bisulphite solution, see	2693	8	
LITHIUM HYDROXIDE	2680	8		MAGNESIUM BROMATE	1473	5.1	
LITHIUM HYDROXIDE SOLUTION	2679	8		MAGNESIUM CHLORATE	2723	5.1	
LITHIUM HYPOCHLORITE, DRY	1471	5.1		Magnesium chloride and chlorate mixture, see	1459 3407	5.1 5.1	
LITHIUM HYPOCHLORITE MIXTURE	1471	5.1		MAGNESIUM DIAMIDE	2004	4.2	
Lithium in cartouches, see	1415	4.3		Magnesium diphenyl, see	3393	4.2	
LITHIUM NITRATE	2722	5.1		MAGNESIUM FLUOROSILICATE	2853	6.1	
LITHIUM NITRIDE	2806	4.3		MAGNESIUM GRANULES, COATED, particle size not less than 149 microns	2950	4.3	
LITHIUM PEROXIDE	1472	5.1		MAGNESIUM HYDRIDE	2010	4.3	
Lithium silicide, see	1417	4.3		MAGNESIUM NITRATE	1474	5.1	
LITHIUM SILICON	1417	4.3		MAGNESIUM PERCHLORATE	1475	5.1	
L.n.g., see	1972	2		MAGNESIUM PEROXIDE	1476	5.1	
LONDON PURPLE	1621	6.1		MAGNESIUM PHOSPHIDE	2011	4.3	
L.p.g., see	1075	2		MAGNESIUM POWDER	1418	4.3	
Lye, see	1823	8		Magnesium scrap, see	1869	4.1	
Lythene, see	1268	3		MAGNESIUM SILICIDE	2624	4.3	
MACHINERY, FUEL CELL, FLAMMABLE GAS POWERED	3529	2.1		Magnesium silicofluoride, see	2853	6.1	
MACHINERY, FUEL CELL, FLAMMABLE LIQUID POWERED	3528	3		Magnetized material	2807	9	Not subject to ADN
MACHINERY, INTERNAL COMBUSTION	3530	9		MALEIC ANHYDRIDE	2215	8	
MACHINERY, INTERNAL COMBUSTION, FLAMMABLE GAS POWERED	3529	2.1		MALEIC ANHYDRIDE, MOLTEN	2215	8	
				Malonic dinitrile, see	2647	6.1	
MACHINERY, INTERNAL COMBUSTION, FLAMMABLE LIQUID POWERED	3528	3		Malonodinitrile, see	2647	6.1	
				MALONONITRILE	2647	6.1	
MAGNESIUM in pellets, turnings or ribbons	1869	4.1		MANEB	2210	4.2	
Magnesium alkyls, see	3394	4.2		MANEB PREPARATION with not less than 60% maneb	2210	4.2	

Name and description	UN No.	Class	Remarks	Name and description	UN No.	Class	Remarks
MANEB PREPARATION, STABILIZED against self-heating	2968	4.3		MERCAPTAN MIXTURE, LIQUID, FLAMMABLE, TOXIC, N.O.S.	1228	3	
MANEB, STABILIZED against self-heating	2968	4.3		MERCAPTAN MIXTURE, LIQUID, TOXIC, FLAMMABLE, N.O.S.	3071	6.1	
Manganese ethylene-di-dithiocarbamate, see	2210	4.2		2-Mercaptoethanol, see	2966	6.1	
Manganese ethylene-1,2-dithiocarbamate, see	2210	4.2		2-Mercaptopropionic acid, see	2936	6.1	
MANGANESE NITRATE	2724	5.1		5-MERCAPTOTETRAZOL-1-ACETIC ACID	0448	1	
Manganese (II) nitrate, see	2724	5.1		MERCURIC ARSENATE	1623	6.1	
MANGANESE RESINATE	1330	4.1		MERCURIC CHLORIDE	1624	6.1	
Manganous nitrate, see	2724	5.1		MERCURIC NITRATE	1625	6.1	
MANNITOL HEXANITRATE, WETTED with not less than 40% water, or mixture of alcohol and water, by mass	0133	1		MERCURIC POTASSIUM CYANIDE	1626	6.1	
				Mercuric sulphate, see	1645	6.1	
MATCHES, FUSEE	2254	4.1		Mercurol, see	1639	6.1	
MATCHES, SAFETY (book, card or strike on box)	1944	4.1		Mercurous bisulphate, see	1645	6.1	
MATCHES, "STRIKE ANYWHERE"	1331	4.1		Mercurous chloride, see	2025	6.1	
MATCHES, WAX "VESTA"	1945	4.1		MERCUROUS NITRATE	1627	6.1	
MEDICAL WASTE, CATEGORY A, AFFECTING ANIMALS only, solid	3549	6.2		Mercurous sulphate, see	1645	6.1	
				MERCURY	2809	8	
MEDICAL WASTE, CATEGORY A, AFFECTING HUMANS, solid	3549	6.2		MERCURY ACETATE	1629	6.1	
MEDICAL WASTE, N.O.S.	3291	6.2		MERCURY AMMONIUM CHLORIDE	1630	6.1	
MEDICINE, LIQUID, FLAMMABLE, TOXIC, N.O.S.	3248	3		MERCURY BASED PESTICIDE, LIQUID, FLAMMABLE, TOXIC, flash-point less than 23 °C	2778	3	
MEDICINE, LIQUID, TOXIC, N.O.S.	1851	6.1		MERCURY BASED PESTICIDE, LIQUID, TOXIC	3012	6.1	
MEDICINE, SOLID, TOXIC, N.O.S.	3249	6.1		MERCURY BASED PESTICIDE, LIQUID, TOXIC, FLAMMABLE, flash-point not less than 23 °C	3011	6.1	
p-Mentha-1,8-diene, see	2052	8					
MERCAPTANS, LIQUID, FLAMMABLE, N.O.S.	3336	3		MERCURY BASED PESTICIDE, SOLID, TOXIC	2777	6.1	
MERCAPTANS, LIQUID, FLAMMABLE, TOXIC, N.O.S.	1228	3		MERCURY BENZOATE	1631	6.1	
				Mercury bichloride, see	1624	6.1	
MERCAPTANS, LIQUID, TOXIC, FLAMMABLE, N.O.S.	3071	6.1		MERCURY BROMIDES	1634	6.1	
MERCAPTAN MIXTURE, LIQUID, FLAMMABLE, N.O.S.	3336	3		MERCURY COMPOUND, LIQUID, N.O.S.	2024	6.1	

Name and description	UN No.	Class	Remarks	Name and description	UN No.	Class	Remarks
MERCURY COMPOUND, SOLID, N.O.S.	2025	6.1		METAL HYDRIDES, WATER-REACTIVE, N.O.S.	1409	4.3	
MERCURY CONTAINED IN MANUFACTURED ARTICLES	3506	8		METALLIC SUBSTANCE, WATER-REACTIVE, N.O.S.	3208	4.3	
MERCURY CYANIDE	1636	6.1		METALLIC SUBSTANCE, WATER-REACTIVE, SELF-HEATING, N.O.S.	3209	4.3	
MERCURY FULMINATE, WETTED with not less than 20% water, or mixture of alcohol and water, by mass	0135	1		METAL POWDER, FLAMMABLE, N.O.S.	3089	4.1	
MERCURY GLUCONATE	1637	6.1		METAL POWDER, SELF-HEATING, N.O.S.	3189	4.2	
MERCURY IODIDE	1638	6.1		METAL SALTS OF ORGANIC COMPOUNDS, FLAMMABLE, N.O.S.	3181	4.1	
MERCURY NUCLEATE	1639	6.1					
MERCURY OLEATE	1640	6.1		METHACRYLALDEHYDE, STABILIZED	2396	3	
MERCURY OXIDE	1641	6.1		METHACRYLIC ACID, STABILIZED	2531	8	
MERCURY OXYCYANIDE, DESENSITIZED	1642	6.1		METHACRYLONITRILE, STABILIZED	3079	6.1	
MERCURY POTASSIUM IODIDE	1643	6.1		METHALLYL ALCOHOL	2614	3	
MERCURY SALICYLATE	1644	6.1		Methanal, see	1198 2209	3 8	
MERCURY SULPHATE	1645	6.1					
MERCURY THIOCYANATE	1646	6.1		Methane and hydrogen mixture, see	2034	2	
Metal alkyl halides, water-reactive, n.o.s. / Metal aryl halides, water-reactive, n.o.s., see	3394	4.2		METHANE, COMPRESSED	1971	2	
Metal alkyl hydrides, water-reactive, n.o.s. / Metal aryl hydrides, water-reactive, n.o.s., see	3394	4.2		METHANE, REFRIGERATED LIQUID	1972	2	
Metal alkyls, water-reactive, n.o.s. / Metal aryls, water-reactive, n.o.s., see	3393	4.2		METHANESULPHONYL CHLORIDE	3246	6.1	
Mesitylene, see	2325	3		METHANOL	1230	3	
MESITYL OXIDE	1229	3		2-Methoxyethyl acetate, see	1189	3	
METAL CARBONYLS, LIQUID, N.O.S.	3281	6.1		METHOXYMETHYL ISOCYANATE	2605	6.1	
METAL CARBONYLS, SOLID, N.O.S.	3466	6.1		4-METHOXY-4-METHYLPENTAN-2-ONE	2293	3	
METAL CATALYST, DRY	2881	4.2		1-Methoxy-2-nitrobenzene, see	2730 3458	6.1 6.1	
METAL CATALYST, WETTED with a visible excess of liquid	1378	4.2		1-Methoxy-3-nitrobenzene, see	2730 3458	6.1 6.1	
METALDEHYDE	1332	4.1		1-Methoxy-4-nitrobenzene, see	2730 3458	6.1 6.1	
METAL HYDRIDES, FLAMMABLE, N.O.S.	3182	4.1		1-METHOXY-2-PROPANOL	3092	3	
				METHYL ACETATE	1231	3	

Name and description	UN No.	Class	Remarks	Name and description	UN No.	Class	Remarks
METHYLACETYLENE AND PROPADIENE MIXTURE, STABILIZED such as mixture P1 or mixture P2	1060	2		METHYL BUTYRATE	1237	3	
beta-Methyl acrolein, see	1143	6.1		METHYL CHLORIDE	1063	2	
				Methyl chloride and chloropicrin mixture, see	1582	2	
METHYL ACRYLATE, STABILIZED	1919	3		METHYL CHLORIDE AND METHYLENE CHLORIDE MIXTURE	1912	2	
METHYLAL	1234	3					
Methyl alcohol, see	1230	3		METHYL CHLOROACETATE	2295	6.1	
Methyl allyl alcohol, see	2614	3		Methyl chlorocarbonate, see	1238	6.1	
				Methyl chloroform, see	2831	6.1	
METHYLALLYL CHLORIDE	2554	3		METHYL CHLOROFORMATE	1238	6.1	
METHYLAMINE, ANHYDROUS	1061	2		METHYL CHLOROMETHYL ETHER	1239	6.1	
METHYLAMINE, AQUEOUS SOLUTION	1235	3					
METHYLAMYL ACETATE	1233	3		METHYL 2-CHLORO-PROPIONATE	2933	3	
Methyl amyl alcohol, see	2053	3		Methyl alpha-chloropropionate, see	2933	3	
Methyl amyl ketone, see	1110	3		METHYLCHLOROSILANE	2534	2	
N-METHYLANILINE	2294	6.1		Methyl cyanide, see	1648	3	
Methylated spirit, see	1986	3		METHYLCYCLOHEXANE	2296	3	
	1987	3		METHYLCYCLOHEXANOLS, flammable	2617	3	
alpha-METHYLBENZYL ALCOHOL, LIQUID	2937	6.1		METHYLCYCLOHEXANONE	2297	3	
alpha-METHYLBENZYL ALCOHOL, SOLID	3438	6.1		METHYLCYCLOPENTANE	2298	3	
METHYL BROMIDE with not more than 2% chloropicrin	1062	2		METHYL DICHLOROACETATE	2299	6.1	
				METHYLDICHLOROSILANE	1242	4.3	
Methyl bromide and chloropicrin mixture, with more than 2% chloropicrin, see	1581	2		Methylene bromide, see	2664	6.1	
				Methylene chloride, see	1593	6.1	
METHYL BROMIDE AND ETHYLENE DIBROMIDE MIXTURE, LIQUID	1647	6.1		Methylene chloride and methyl chloride mixture, see	1912	2	
METHYL BROMOACETATE	2643	6.1		Methylene cyanide, see	2647	6.1	
2-METHYLBUTANAL	3371	3		p,p'-Methylene dianiline, see	2651	6.1	
3-METHYLBUTAN-2-ONE	2397	3		Methylene dibromide, see	2664	6.1	
2-METHYL-1-BUTENE	2459	3		2,2'-Methylene-di-(3,4,6-trichlorophenol), see	2875	6.1	
2-METHYL-2-BUTENE	2460	3					
3-METHYL-1-BUTENE	2561	3		Methyl ethyl ether, see	1039	2	
N-METHYLBUTYLAMINE	2945	3		METHYL ETHYL KETONE, see	1193	3	
				2-METHYL-5-ETHYLPYRIDINE	2300	6.1	
METHYL tert-BUTYL ETHER	2398	3		METHYL FLUORIDE	2454	2	

Name and description	UN No.	Class	Remarks	Name and description	UN No.	Class	Remarks
METHYL FORMATE	1243	3		METHYL PROPIONATE	1248	3	
2-METHYLFURAN	2301	3		Methylpropylbenzene, see	2046	3	
Methyl glycol, see	1188	3		METHYL PROPYL ETHER	2612	3	
Methyl glycol acetate, see	1189	3		METHYL PROPYL KETONE	1249	3	
2-METHYL-2-HEPTANETHIOL	3023	6.1		Methyl pyridines, see	2313	3	
5-METHYLHEXAN-2-ONE	2302	3		Methylstyrene, inhibited, see	2618	3	
METHYLHYDRAZINE	1244	6.1		alpha-Methylstyrene, see	2303	3	
METHYL IODIDE	2644	6.1		Methyl sulphate, see	1595	6.1	
METHYL ISOBUTYL CARBINOL	2053	3		Methyl sulphide, see	1164	3	
METHYL ISOBUTYL KETONE	1245	3		METHYLTETRAHYDROFURAN	2536	3	
METHYL ISOCYANATE	2480	6.1		METHYL TRICHLOROACETATE	2533	6.1	
METHYL ISOPROPENYL KETONE, STABILIZED	1246	3		METHYLTRICHLOROSILANE	1250	3	
METHYL ISOTHIOCYANATE	2477	6.1		alpha-METHYLVALERAL-DEHYDE	2367	3	
METHYL ISOVALERATE	2400	3		Methyl vinyl benzene, inhibited, see	2618	3	
METHYL MAGNESIUM BROMIDE IN ETHYL ETHER	1928	4.3		METHYL VINYL KETONE, STABILIZED	1251	6.1	
METHYL MERCAPTAN	1064	2		M.i.b.c., see	2053	3	
Methyl mercaptopropionaldehyde, see	2785	6.1		MINES with bursting charge	0136	1	
					0137	1	
					0138	1	
METHYL METHACRYLATE MONOMER, STABILIZED	1247	3			0294	1	
				Mirbane oil, see	1662	6.1	
4-METHYLMORPHOLINE	2535	3		Missiles, guided, see	0180	1	
N-METHYLMORPHOLINE, see	2535	3			0181	1	
					0182	1	
METHYL NITRITE	2455	2	Carriage prohibited		0183	1	
					0295	1	
					0397	1	
					0398	1	
METHYL ORTHOSILICATE	2606	6.1			0436	1	
					0437	1	
METHYLPENTADIENE	2461	3			0438	1	
Methylpentanes, see	1208	3		Mixtures A, A01, A02, A0, A1, B1, B2, B or C, see	1965	2	
2-METHYLPENTAN-2-OL	2560	3		Mixture F1, mixture F2 or mixture F3, see	1078	2	
4-Methylpentan-2-ol, see	2053	3					
3-Methyl-2-penten-4ynol, see	2705	8		MIXTURES OF 1,3-BUTADIENE AND HYDROCARBONS, STABILIZED, having a vapour pressure at 70 °C not exceeding 1.1 MPa (11 bar) and a density at 50 °C not lower than 0.525 kg/l	1010	2	
METHYLPHENYL-DICHLOROSILANE	2437	8					
2-Methyl-2-phenylpropane, see	2709	3					
1-METHYLPIPERIDINE	2399	3		Mixture P1 or mixture P2, see	1060	2	

Name and description	UN No.	Class	Remarks	Name and description	UN No.	Class	Remarks
MOLYBDENUM PENTACHLORIDE	2508	8		1-Naphthylthiourea, see	1651	6.1	
Monochloroacetic acid, see	1750	6.1		NAPHTHYLUREA	1652	6.1	
	1751	6.1		NATURAL GAS, COMPRESSED with high methane content	1971	2	
Monochlorobenzene, see	1134	3		NATURAL GAS, REFRIGERATED LIQUID with high methane content	1972	2	
Monochlorodifluoromethane, see	1018	2					
Monochlorodifluoromethane and monochloropentafluoroethane mixture, see	1973	2		Natural gasoline, see	1203	3	
				Neohexane, see	1208	3	
Monochlorodifluoromono-bromomethane, see	1974	2		NEON, COMPRESSED	1065	2	
				NEON, REFRIGERATED LIQUID	1913	2	
Monochloropentafluoroethane and monochlorodifluoromethane mixture, see	1973	2		Neothyl, see	2612	3	
				NICKEL CARBONYL	1259	6.1	
Monoethylamine, see	1036	2		NICKEL CYANIDE	1653	6.1	
MONONITROTOLUIDINES, see	2660	6.1		Nickel (II) cyanide, see	1653	6.1	
Monopropylamine, see	1277	3		NICKEL NITRATE	2725	5.1	
MORPHOLINE	2054	8		Nickel (II) nitrate, see	2725	5.1	
MOTOR FUEL ANTI-KNOCK MIXTURE	1649	6.1		NICKEL NITRITE	2726	5.1	
MOTOR FUEL ANTI-KNOCK MIXTURE, FLAMMABLE	3483	6.1		Nickel (II) nitrite, see	2726	5.1	
				Nickelous nitrate, see	2725	5.1	
MOTOR SPIRIT	1203	3		Nickelous nitrite, see	2726	5.1	
Motor spirit and ethanol mixture, with more than 10% ethanol, see	3475	3		Nickel tetracarbonyl, see	1259	6.1	
Muriatic acid, see	1789	8		NICOTINE	1654	6.1	
MUSK XYLENE, see	2956	4.1		NICOTINE COMPOUND, LIQUID, N.O.S	3144	6.1	
Mysorite, see	2212	9		NICOTINE COMPOUND, SOLID, N.O.S	1655	6.1	
Naphta, see	1268	3					
Naphta, petroleum, see	1268	3		NICOTINE HYDROCHLORIDE, LIQUID	1656	6.1	
Naphta, solvent, see	1268	3		NICOTINE HYDROCHLORIDE, SOLID	3444	6.1	
NAPHTHALENE, CRUDE	1334	4.1					
NAPHTHALENE, MOLTEN	2304	4.1		NICOTINE HYDROCHLORIDE SOLUTION	1656	6.1	
NAPHTHALENE, REFINED	1334	4.1		NICOTINE PREPARATION, LIQUID, N.O.S.	3144	6.1	
alpha-NAPHTHYLAMINE	2077	6.1					
beta-NAPHTHYLAMINE, SOLID	1650	6.1		NICOTINE PREPARATION, SOLID, N.O.S.	1655	6.1	
beta-NAPHTHYLAMINE, SOLUTION	3411	6.1		NICOTINE SALICYLATE	1657	6.1	
NAPHTHYLTHIOUREA	1651	6.1		NICOTINE SULPHATE, SOLID	3445	6.1	

Name and description	UN No.	Class	Remarks	Name and description	UN No.	Class	Remarks
NICOTINE SULPHATE, SOLUTION	1658	6.1		NITROANISOLES, SOLID	3458	6.1	
NICOTINE TARTRATE	1659	6.1		NITROBENZENE	1662	6.1	
NITRATES, INORGANIC, N.O.S.	1477	5.1		Nitrobenzene bromide, see	2732	6.1	
NITRATES, INORGANIC, AQUEOUS SOLUTION, N.O.S.	3218	5.1		NITROBENZENESULPHONIC ACID	2305	8	
NITRATING ACID MIXTURE with more than 50% nitric acid	1796	8		Nitrobenzol, see	1662	6.1	
NITRATING ACID MIXTURE with not more than 50% nitric acid	1796	8		5-NITROBENZOTRIAZOL	0385	1	
NITRATING ACID MIXTURE, SPENT, with more than 50% nitric acid	1826	8		NITROBENZOTRIFLUORIDES, LIQUID	2306	6.1	
NITRATING ACID MIXTURE, SPENT, with not more than 50% nitric acid	1826	8		NITROBENZOTRIFLUORIDES, SOLID	3431	6.1	
NITRIC ACID, other than red fuming, with at least 65% but not more than 70% nitric acid	2031	8		NITROBROMOBENZENES, LIQUID	2732	6.1	
NITRIC ACID, other than red fuming, with less than 65% nitric acid	2031	8		NITROBROMOBENZENES, SOLID	3459	6.1	
NITRIC ACID, other than red fuming, with more than 70% nitric acid	2031	8		NITROCELLULOSE, dry or wetted with less than 25% water (or alcohol), by mass	0340	1	
NITRIC ACID, RED FUMING	2032	8		NITROCELLULOSE, unmodified or plasticized with less than 18% plasticizing substance, by mass	0341	1	
NITRIC OXIDE, COMPRESSED	1660	2		NITROCELLULOSE MEMBRANE FILTERS, with not more than 12.6% nitrogen, by dry mass	3270	4.1	
NITRIC OXIDE AND DINITROGEN TETROXIDE MIXTURE	1975	2		NITROCELLULOSE, with not more than 12.6% nitrogen, by dry mass, MIXTURE WITH PLASTICIZER, WITH PIGMENT	2557	4.1	
NITRIC OXIDE AND NITROGEN DIOXIDE MIXTURE, see	1975	2		NITROCELLULOSE, with not more than 12.6% nitrogen, by dry mass, MIXTURE WITH PLASTICIZER, WITHOUT PIGMENT	2557	4.1	
NITRILES, FLAMMABLE, TOXIC, N.O.S.	3273	3		NITROCELLULOSE, with not more than 12.6% nitrogen, by dry mass, MIXTURE WITHOUT PLASTICIZER, WITH PIGMENT	2557	4.1	
NITRILES, LIQUID, TOXIC, N.O.S.	3276	6.1		NITROCELLULOSE, with not more than 12.6% nitrogen, by dry mass, MIXTURE WITHOUT PLASTICIZER, WITHOUT PIGMENT	2557	4.1	
NITRILES, SOLID, TOXIC, N.O.S.	3439	6.1					
NITRILES, TOXIC, FLAMMABLE, N.O.S.	3275	6.1					
NITRITES, INORGANIC, N.O.S.	2627	5.1		NITROCELLULOSE, PLASTICIZED with not less than 18% plasticizing substance, by mass	0343	1	
NITRITES, INORGANIC, AQUEOUS SOLUTION, N.O.S.	3219	5.1					
NITROANILINES (o-, m-, p-)	1661	6.1		NITROCELLULOSE SOLUTION, FLAMMABLE with not more than 12.6% nitrogen, by dry mass, and not more than 55% nitrocellulose	2059	3	
NITROANISOLES, LIQUID	2730	6.1					

Name and description	UN No.	Class	Remarks	Name and description	UN No.	Class	Remarks
NITROCELLULOSE, WETTED with not less than 25% alcohol, by mass	0342	1		NITROGLYCERIN SOLUTION IN ALCOHOL with not more than 1% nitroglycerin	1204	3	
NITROCELLULOSE WITH ALCOHOL (not less than 25% alcohol, by mass, and not more than 12.6% nitrogen, by dry mass)	2556	4.1		NITROGUANIDINE, dry or wetted with less than 20% water, by mass	0282	1	
NITROCELLULOSE WITH WATER (not less than 25% water, by mass)	2555	4.1		NITROGUANIDINE, WETTED with not less than 20% water, by mass	1336	4.1	
Nitrochlorobenzenes, see	1578 3409	6.1 6.1		NITROHYDROCHLORIC ACID	1798	8	Carriage prohibited
3-NITRO-4-CHLOROBENZO-TRIFLUORIDE	2307	6.1		NITROMANNITE, WETTED, see	0133	1	
NITROCRESOLS, LIQUID	3434	6.1		NITROMETHANE	1261	3	
NITROCRESOLS, SOLID	2446	6.1		Nitromuriatic acid, see	1798	8	
NITROETHANE	2842	3		NITRONAPHTHALENE	2538	4.1	
NITROGEN, COMPRESSED	1066	2		NITROPHENOLS (o-, m-, p-)	1663	6.1	
NITROGEN DIOXIDE, see	1067	2		4-NITROPHENYLHYDRAZINE, with not less than 30% water, by mass	3376	4.1	
NITROGEN, REFRIGERATED LIQUID	1977	2		NITROPROPANES	2608	3	
NITROGEN TRIFLUORIDE	2451	2		p-NITROSODIMETHYLANILINE	1369	4.2	
NITROGEN TRIOXIDE	2421	2	Carriage prohibited	NITROSTARCH, dry or wetted with less than 20% water, by mass	0146	1	
NITROGLYCERIN, DESENSITIZED with not less than 40% non-volatile water-insoluble phlegmatizer, by mass	0143	1		NITROSTARCH, WETTED with not less than 20% water, by mass	1337	4.1	
				NITROSYL CHLORIDE	1069	2	
NITROGLYCERIN MIXTURE, DESENSITIZED, LIQUID, N.O.S. with not more than 30% nitroglycerin, by mass	3357	3		NITROSYLSULPHURIC ACID, LIQUID	2308	8	
NITROGLYCERIN MIXTURE, DESENSITIZED, LIQUID, FLAMMABLE, N.O.S. with not more than 30% nitroglycerin, by mass	3343	3		NITROSYLSULPHURIC ACID, SOLID	3456	8	
				NITROTOLUENES, LIQUID	1664	6.1	
				NITROTOLUENES, SOLID	3446	6.1	
				NITROTOLUIDINES	2660	6.1	
NITROGLYCERIN MIXTURE, DESENSITIZED, SOLID, N.O.S. with more than 2% but not more than 10% nitroglycerin, by mass	3319	4.1		NITROTRIAZOLONE	0490	1	
				NITRO UREA	0147	1	
				NITROUS OXIDE	1070	2	
NITROGLYCERIN, SOLUTION IN ALCOHOL with more than 1% but not more than 5% nitroglycerin	3064	3		NITROUS OXIDE, REFRIGERATED LIQUID	2201	2	
NITROGLYCERIN SOLUTION IN ALCOHOL with more than 1% but not more than 10% nitroglycerin	0144	1		NITROXYLENES, LIQUID	1665	6.1	
				NITROXYLENES, SOLID	3447	6.1	

Name and description	UN No.	Class	Remarks	Name and description	UN No.	Class	Remarks
Non-activated carbon, see	1361	4.2		ORGANIC PEROXIDE TYPE B, SOLID, TEMPERATURE CONTROLLED	3112	5.2	
Non-activated charcoal, see	1361	4.2					
NONANES	1920	3		ORGANIC PEROXIDE TYPE C, LIQUID	3103	5.2	
NONYLTRICHLOROSILANE	1799	8					
2,5-NORBORNADIENE, STABILIZED, see	2251	3		ORGANIC PEROXIDE TYPE C, LIQUID, TEMPERATURE CONTROLLED	3113	5.2	
Normal propyl alcohol, see	1274	3		ORGANIC PEROXIDE TYPE C, SOLID	3104	5.2	
NTO, see	0490	1					
OCTADECYLTRICHLORO-SILANE	1800	8		ORGANIC PEROXIDE TYPE C, SOLID, TEMPERATURE CONTROLLED	3114	5.2	
OCTADIENE	2309	3		ORGANIC PEROXIDE TYPE D, LIQUID	3105	5.2	
OCTAFLUOROBUT-2-ENE	2422	2					
OCTAFLUOROCYCLOBUTANE	1976	2		ORGANIC PEROXIDE TYPE D, LIQUID, TEMPERATURE CONTROLLED	3115	5.2	
OCTAFLUOROPROPANE	2424	2					
OCTANES	1262	3		ORGANIC PEROXIDE TYPE D, SOLID	3106	5.2	
OCTOGEN, see	0226	1		ORGANIC PEROXIDE TYPE D, SOLID, TEMPERATURE CONTROLLED	3116	5.2	
	0391	1					
	0484	1					
OCTOL, dry or wetted with less than 15% water, by mass, see	0266	1		ORGANIC PEROXIDE TYPE E, LIQUID	3107	5.2	
OCTOLITE, dry or wetted with less than 15% water, by mass	0266	1		ORGANIC PEROXIDE TYPE E, LIQUID, TEMPERATURE CONTROLLED	3117	5.2	
OCTONAL	0496	1		ORGANIC PEROXIDE TYPE E, SOLID	3108	5.2	
OCTYL ALDEHYDES	1191	3					
tert-Octyl mercaptan, see	3023	6.1		ORGANIC PEROXIDE TYPE E, SOLID, TEMPERATURE CONTROLLED	3118	5.2	
OCTYLTRICHLOROSILANE	1801	8					
Oenanthol, see	3056	3		ORGANIC PEROXIDE TYPE F, LIQUID	3109	5.2	
OIL GAS, COMPRESSED	1071	2					
Oil seeds, crushed seeds and seedcakes containing vegetable oil, treated with solvents, not subject to spontaneous combustion	3175	4.1		ORGANIC PEROXIDE TYPE F, LIQUID, TEMPERATURE CONTROLLED	3119	5.2	
				ORGANIC PEROXIDE TYPE F, SOLID	3110	5.2	
Oleum, see	1831	8		ORGANIC PEROXIDE TYPE F, SOLID, TEMPERATURE CONTROLLED	3120	5.2	
ORGANIC PEROXIDE TYPE B, LIQUID	3101	5.2					
ORGANIC PEROXIDE TYPE B, LIQUID, TEMPERATURE CONTROLLED	3111	5.2		Organic peroxides, see 2.2.52.4 for an alphabetic list of currently assigned organic peroxides and see	3101 to 3120	5.2	
ORGANIC PEROXIDE TYPE B, SOLID	3102	5.2		ORGANIC PIGMENTS, SELF-HEATING	3313	4.2	

Name and description	UN No.	Class	Remarks	Name and description	UN No.	Class	Remarks
ORGANOARSENIC COMPOUND, LIQUID, N.O.S.	3280	6.1		ORGANOMETALLIC SUBSTANCE, LIQUID, WATER-REACTIVE, FLAMMABLE	3399	4.3	
ORGANOARSENIC COMPOUND, SOLID, N.O.S.	3465	6.1		ORGANOMETALLIC SUBSTANCE, SOLID, WATER-REACTIVE, FLAMMABLE	3396	4.3	
ORGANOCHLORINE PESTICIDE, LIQUID, FLAMMABLE, TOXIC, flash-point less than 23 °C	2762	3		ORGANOMETALLIC SUBSTANCE, SOLID, WATER-REACTIVE, SELF-HEATING	3397	4.3	
ORGANOCHLORINE PESTICIDE, LIQUID, TOXIC	2996	6.1		ORGANOPHOSPHORUS COMPOUND, LIQUID; TOXIC, N.O.S.	3278	6.1	
ORGANOCHLORINE PESTICIDE, LIQUID, TOXIC, FLAMMABLE, flash-point not less than 23 °C	2995	6.1		ORGANOPHOSPHORUS COMPOUND, SOLID, TOXIC, N.O.S.	3464	6.1	
ORGANOCHLORINE PESTICIDE, SOLID, TOXIC	2761	6.1		ORGANOPHOSPHORUS COMPOUND, TOXIC, FLAMMABLE, N.O.S.	3279	6.1	
ORGANOMETALLIC COMPOUND, LIQUID, TOXIC, N.O.S.	3282	6.1		ORGANOPHOSPHORUS PESTICIDE, LIQUID, FLAMMABLE, TOXIC, flash-point less than 23 °C	2784	3	
ORGANOMETALLIC COMPOUND, SOLID, TOXIC, N.O.S.	3467	6.1		ORGANOPHOSPHORUS PESTICIDE, LIQUID, TOXIC	3018	6.1	
Organometallic compound, solid, water-reactive, flammable, n.o.s., see	3396	4.3		ORGANOPHOSPHORUS PESTICIDE, LIQUID, TOXIC, FLAMMABLE, flash-point not less than 23 °C	3017	6.1	
Organometallic compound or Organometallic compound solution or Organometallic compound dispersion, water-reactive, flammable, n.o.s., see	3399	4.3		ORGANOPHOSPHORUS PESTICIDE, SOLID, TOXIC	2783	6.1	
ORGANOMETALLIC SUBSTANCE, LIQUID, PYROPHORIC	3392	4.2		ORGANOTIN COMPOUND, LIQUID, N.O.S.	2788	6.1	
ORGANOMETALLIC SUBSTANCE, SOLID, PYROPHORIC	3391	4.2		ORGANOTIN COMPOUND, SOLID, N.O.S.	3146	6.1	
ORGANOMETALLIC SUBSTANCE, SOLID, SELF-HEATING	3400	4.2		ORGANOTIN PESTICIDE, LIQUID, FLAMMABLE, TOXIC, flash-point less than 23 °C	2787	3	
ORGANOMETALLIC SUBSTANCE, LIQUID, PYROPHORIC, WATER-REACTIVE	3394	4.2		ORGANOTIN PESTICIDE, LIQUID, TOXIC	3020	6.1	
ORGANOMETALLIC SUBSTANCE, SOLID, PYROPHORIC, WATER-REACTIVE	3393	4.2		ORGANOTIN PESTICIDE, LIQUID, TOXIC, FLAMMABLE, flash-point not less than 23 °C	3019	6.1	
ORGANOMETALLIC SUBSTANCE, LIQUID, WATER-REACTIVE	3398	4.3		ORGANOTIN PESTICIDE, SOLID, TOXIC	2786	6.1	
				Orthophospohoric acid, see	1805	8	
ORGANOMETALLIC SUBSTANCE, SOLID, WATER-REACTIVE	3395	4.3		OSMIUM TETROXIDE	2471	6.1	
				OXIDIZING LIQUID, N.O.S.	3139	5.1	

Name and description	UN No.	Class	Remarks	Name and description	UN No.	Class	Remarks
OXIDIZING LIQUID, CORROSIVE, N.O.S.	3098	5.1		PARALDEHYDE	1264	3	
OXIDIZING LIQUID, TOXIC, N.O.S.	3099	5.1		PCBs, see	2315	9	
					3432	9	
				PENTABORANE	1380	4.2	
OXIDIZING SOLID, N.O.S.	1479	5.1		PENTACHLOROETHANE	1669	6.1	
OXIDIZING SOLID, CORROSIVE, N.O.S.	3085	5.1		PENTACHLOROPHENOL	3155	6.1	
OXIDIZING SOLID, FLAMMABLE, N.O.S.	3137	5.1	Carriage prohibited	PENTAERYTHRITE TETRANITRATE with not less than 7% wax, by mass	0411	1	
OXIDIZING SOLID, SELF-HEATING, N.O.S.	3100	5.1	Carriage prohibited	PENTAERYTHRITE TETRANITRATE, DESENSITIZED with not less than 15% phlegmatizer, by mass	0150	1	
OXIDIZING SOLID, TOXIC, N.O.S.	3087	5.1		PENTAERYTHRITE TETRANITRATE MIXTURE, DESENSITIZED, SOLID, N.O.S. with more than 10% but not more than 20% PETN, by mass	3344	4.1	
OXIDIZING SOLID, WATER-REACTIVE, N.O.S.	3121	5.1	Carriage prohibited				
Oxirane, see	1040	2		PENTAERYTHRITE TETRANITRATE, WETTED with not less than 25% water, by mass	0150	1	
OXYGEN, COMPRESSED	1072	2					
OXYGEN DIFLUORIDE, COMPRESSED	2190	2		PENTAERYTHRITOL TETRANITRATE, see	0150	1	
					0411	1	
					3344	4.1	
OXYGEN GENERATOR, CHEMICAL	3356	5.1		PENTAFLUOROETHANE	3220	2	
OXYGEN, REFRIGERATED LIQUID	1073	2		Pentafluoroethane, 1,1,1-trifluoroethane, and 1,1,1,2-tetrafluoroethane zeotropic mixture with approximately 44% pentafluoroethane and 52% 1,1,1-trifluoroethane, see	3337	2	
1-Oxy-4-nitrobenzene, see	1663	6.1					
PACKAGINGS, DISCARDED, EMPTY, UNCLEANED	3509	9		PENTAMETHYLHEPTANE	2286	3	
PAINT (including paint, lacquer, enamel, stain, shellac, varnish, polish, liquid filler and liquid lacquer base)	1263	3		Pentanal, see	2058	3	
	3066	8					
	3469	3		PENTANE-2,4-DIONE	2310	3	
	3470	8		PENTANES, liquid	1265	3	
PAINT RELATED MATERIAL (including paint thinning and reducing compound)	1263	3		n-Pentane, see	1265	3	
	3066	8					
	3469	3		PENTANOLS	1105	3	
	3470	8					
Paint thinning and reducing compound, see	1263	3		n-Pentanol, see	1105	3	
	3066	8		3-Pentanol, see	1105	3	
	3469	3					
	3470	8		1-PENTENE	1108	3	
PAPER, UNSATURATED OIL TREATED, incompletely dried (including carbon paper)	1379	4.2		1-PENTOL	2705	8	
Paraffin, see	1223	3		PENTOLITE, dry or wetted with less than 15% water, by mass	0151	1	
PARAFORMALDEHYDE	2213	4.1		Pentyl nitrite, see	1113	3	

Name and description	UN No.	Class	Remarks	Name and description	UN No.	Class	Remarks
PERCHLORATES, INORGANIC, N.O.S.	1481	5.1		Pesticide, toxic, under compressed gas, n.o.s, see	1950	2	
PERCHLORATES, INORGANIC, AQUEOUS SOLUTION, N.O.S.	3211	5.1		PETN, see	0150	1	
					0411	1	
PERCHLORIC ACID with more than 50% but not more than 72% acid, by mass	1873	5.1			3344	4.1	
				PETN/TNT, see	0151	1	
				PETROL	1203	3	
PERCHLORIC ACID with not more than 50% acid, by mass	1802	8		Petrol and ethanol mixture, with more than 10% ethanol, see	3475	3	
Perchlorobenzene, see	2729	6.1		PETROLEUM CRUDE OIL	1267	3	
Perchlorocyclopentadiene, see	2646	6.1		PETROLEUM DISTILLATES, N.O.S.	1268	3	
Perchloroethylene, see	1897	6.1		Petroleum ether, see	1268	3	
PERCHLOROMETHYL MERCAPTAN	1670	6.1		PETROLEUM GASES, LIQUEFIED	1075	2	
PERCHLORYL FLUORIDE	3083	2		Petroleum naphtha, see	1268	3	
Perfluoroacetylchloride, see	3057	2		Petroleum oil, see	1268	3	
PERFLUORO(ETHYL VINYL ETHER)	3154	2		PETROLEUM PRODUCTS, N.O.S.	1268	3	
PERFLUORO(METHYL VINYL ETHER)	3153	2		Petroleum raffinate, see	1268	3	
Perfluoropropane, see	2424	2		PETROLEUM SOUR CRUDE OIL, FLAMMABLE, TOXIC	3494	3	
PERFUMERY PRODUCTS with flammable solvents	1266	3		Petroleum spirit, see	1268	3	
PERMANGANATES, INORGANIC, N.O.S.	1482	5.1		PHENACYL BROMIDE	2645	6.1	
				PHENETIDINES	2311	6.1	
PERMANGANATES, INORGANIC, AQUEOUS SOLUTION, N.O.S.	3214	5.1		PHENOLATES, LIQUID	2904	8	
				PHENOLATES, SOLID	2905	8	
PEROXIDES, INORGANIC, N.O.S.	1483	5.1		PHENOL, MOLTEN	2312	6.1	
PERSULPHATES, INORGANIC, N.O.S.	3215	5.1		PHENOL, SOLID	1671	6.1	
PERSULPHATES, INORGANIC, AQUEOUS SOLUTION, N.O.S.	3216	5.1		PHENOL SOLUTION	2821	6.1	
				PHENOLSULPHONIC ACID, LIQUID	1803	8	
PESTICIDE, LIQUID, FLAMMABLE, TOXIC, N.O.S., flash-point less than 23 °C	3021	3		PHENOXYACETIC ACID DERIVATIVE PESTICIDE, LIQUID, FLAMMABLE, TOXIC, flash-point less than 23 °C	3346	3	
PESTICIDE, LIQUID, TOXIC, N.O.S.	2902	6.1		PHENOXYACETIC ACID DERIVATIVE PESTICIDE, LIQUID, TOXIC	3348	6.1	
PESTICIDE, LIQUID, TOXIC, FLAMMABLE, N.O.S., flash-point not less than 23 °C	2903	6.1		PHENOXYACETIC ACID DERIVATIVE PESTICIDE, LIQUID, TOXIC, FLAMMABLE, flash-point not less than 23 °C	3347	6.1	
PESTICIDE, SOLID, TOXIC, N.O.S.	2588	6.1					

Name and description	UN No.	Class	Remarks	Name and description	UN No.	Class	Remarks
PHENOXYACETIC ACID DERIVATIVE PESTICIDE, SOLID, TOXIC	3345	6.1		Phosphoric acid, anhydrous, see	1807	8	
PHENYLACETONITRILE, LIQUID	2470	6.1		PHOSPHOROUS ACID	2834	8	
PHENYLACETYL CHLORIDE	2577	8		PHOSPHORUS, AMORPHOUS	1338	4.1	
Phenylamine, see	1547	6.1		Phosphorus bromide, see	1808	8	
1-Phenylbutane, see	2709	3		Phosphorus chloride, see	1809	6.1	
2-Phenylbutane, see	2709	3		PHOSPHORUS HEPTASULPHIDE, free from yellow and white phosphorus	1339	4.1	
PHENYLCARBYLAMINE CHLORIDE	1672	6.1		PHOSPHORUS OXYBROMIDE	1939	8	
PHENYL CHLOROFORMATE	2746	6.1		PHOSPHORUS OXYBROMIDE, MOLTEN	2576	8	
Phenyl cyanide, see	2224	6.1		PHOSPHORUS OXYCHLORIDE	1810	6.1	
PHENYLENEDIAMINES (o-, m-, p-)	1673	6.1		PHOSPHORUS PENTABROMIDE	2691	8	
Phenylethylene, see	2055	3		PHOSPHORUS PENTACHLORIDE	1806	8	
PHENYLHYDRAZINE	2572	6.1		PHOSPHORUS PENTAFLUORIDE	2198	2	
PHENYL ISOCYANATE	2487	6.1		PHOSPHORUS PENTAFLUORIDE, ADSORBED	3524	2	
Phenylisocyanodichloride, see	1672	6.1		PHOSPHORUS PENTASULPHIDE, free from yellow and white phosphorus	1340	4.3	
PHENYL MERCAPTAN	2337	6.1		PHOSPHORUS PENTOXIDE	1807	8	
PHENYLMERCURIC ACETATE	1674	6.1		PHOSPHORUS SESQUISULPHIDE, free from yellow and white phosphorus	1341	4.1	
PHENYLMERCURIC COMPOUND, N.O.S.	2026	6.1		Phosphorus (V) sulphide, free from yellow and white phosphorus, see	1340	4.3	
PHENYLMERCURIC HYDROXIDE	1894	6.1		Phosphorus sulphochloride, see	1837	8	
PHENYLMERCURIC NITRATE	1895	6.1		PHOSPHORUS TRIBROMIDE	1808	8	
PHENYLPHOSPHORUS DICHLORIDE	2798	8		PHOSPHORUS TRICHLORIDE	1809	6.1	
PHENYLPHOSPHORUS THIODICHLORIDE	2799	8		PHOSPHORUS TRIOXIDE	2578	8	
2-Phenylpropene, see	2303	3		PHOSPHORUS TRISULPHIDE, free from yellow and white phosphorus	1343	4.1	
PHENYLTRICHLOROSILANE	1804	8		PHOSPHORUS, WHITE, DRY	1381	4.2	
PHOSGENE	1076	2		PHOSPHORUS, WHITE IN SOLUTION	1381	4.2	
9-PHOSPHABICYCLONONANES	2940	4.2		PHOSPHORUS, WHITE, MOLTEN	2447	4.2	
PHOSPHINE	2199	2		PHOSPHORUS, WHITE, UNDER WATER	1381	4.2	
PHOSPHINE, ADSORBED	3525	2		PHOSPHORUS, YELLOW, DRY	1381	4.2	
Phosphoretted hydrogen, see	2199	2					
PHOSPHORIC ACID, SOLUTION	1805	8					
PHOSPHORIC ACID, SOLID	3453	8					

Name and description	UN No.	Class	Remarks	Name and description	UN No.	Class	Remarks
PHOSPHORUS, YELLOW, IN SOLUTION	1381	4.2		POLYCHLORINATED BIPHENYLS, SOLID	3432	9	
PHOSPHORUS, YELLOW, UNDER WATER	1381	4.2		POLYESTER RESIN KIT, liquid base material	3269	3	
Phosphoryl chloride, see	1810	6.1		POLYESTER RESIN KIT, solid base material	3527	4.1	
PHTHALIC ANHYDRIDE with more than 0.05% of maleic anhydride	2214	8		POLYHALOGENATED BIPHENYLS, LIQUID	3151	9	
PICOLINES	2313	3		POLYHALOGENATED BIPHENYLS, SOLID	3152	9	
PICRAMIDE, see	0153	1					
PICRIC ACID WETTED, see	1344	4.1		POLYHALOGENATED TERPHENYLS, LIQUID	3151	9	
	3364	4.1					
PICRITE, see	0282	1		POLYHALOGENATED TERPHENYLS, SOLID	3152	9	
PICRITE, WETTED, see	1336	4.1					
Picrotoxin, see	3172	6.1		POLYMERIC BEADS, EXPANDABLE, evolving flammable vapour	2211	9	
	3462	6.1					
PICRYL CHLORIDE, see	0155	1					
PICRYL CHLORIDE, WETTED, see	3365	4.1		POLYMERIZING SUBSTANCE, LIQUID, STABILIZED, N.O.S.	3532	4.1	
alpha-PINENE	2368	3		POLYMERIZING SUBSTANCE, LIQUID, TEMPERATURE CONTROLLED, N.O.S.	3534	4.1	
PINE OIL	1272	3					
PIPERAZINE	2579	8		POLYMERIZING SUBSTANCE, SOLID, STABILIZED, N.O.S.	3531	4.1	
PIPERIDINE	2401	8		POLYMERIZING SUBSTANCE, SOLID, TEMPERATURE CONTROLLED, N.O.S.	3533	4.1	
Pivaloyl chloride, see	2438	6.1					
Plastic explosives , see	0084	1		Polystyrene beads, expandable, see	2211	9	
PLASTICS MOULDING COMPOUND in dough, sheet or extruded rope form evolving flammable vapour	3314	9		POTASSIUM	2257	4.3	
				POTASSIUM ARSENATE	1677	6.1	
PLASTICS, NITROCELLULOSE-BASED, SELF-HEATING, N.O.S.	2006	4.2		POTASSIUM ARSENITE	1678	6.1	
				Potassium bifluoride, see	1811	8	
Polish, see	1263	3		Potassium bisulphate, see	2509	8	
	3066	8					
	3469	3		Potassium bisulphite solution, see	2693	8	
	3470	8					
POLYAMINES, FLAMMABLE, CORROSIVE, N.O.S.	2733	3		POTASSIUM BOROHYDRIDE	1870	4.3	
POLYAMINES, LIQUID, CORROSIVE, N.O.S.	2735	8		POTASSIUM BROMATE	1484	5.1	
				POTASSIUM CHLORATE	1485	5.1	
POLYAMINES, LIQUID, CORROSIVE, FLAMMABLE, N.O.S.	2734	8		POTASSIUM CHLORATE, AQUEOUS SOLUTION	2427	5.1	
POLYAMINES, SOLID, CORROSIVE, N.O.S.	3259	8		Potassium chlorate mixed with mineral oil, see	0083	1	
POLYCHLORINATED BIPHENYLS, LIQUID	2315	9		POTASSIUM CUPROCYANIDE	1679	6.1	

Name and description	UN No.	Class	Remarks	Name and description	UN No.	Class	Remarks
POTASSIUM CYANIDE, SOLID	1680	6.1		POTASSIUM PEROXIDE	1491	5.1	
POTASSIUM CYANIDE, SOLUTION	3413	6.1		POTASSIUM PERSULPHATE	1492	5.1	
Potassium dicyanocuprate (I), see	1679	6.1		POTASSIUM PHOSPHIDE	2012	4.3	
POTASSIUM DITHIONITE	1929	4.2		Potassium selenate, see	2630	6.1	
POTASSIUM FLUORIDE, SOLID	1812	6.1		Potassium selenite, see	2630	6.1	
POTASSIUM FLUORIDE, SOLUTION	3422	6.1		Potassium silicofluoride, see	2655	6.1	
POTASSIUM FLUOROACETATE	2628	6.1		POTASSIUM SODIUM ALLOYS, LIQUID	1422	4.3	
POTASSIUM FLUOROSILICATE	2655	6.1		POTASSIUM SODIUM ALLOYS, SOLID	3404	4.3	
Potassium hexafluorosilicate, see	2655	6.1		POTASSIUM SULPHIDE with less than 30% water of crystallization	1382	4.2	
Potassium hydrate, see	1814	8		POTASSIUM SULPHIDE, ANHYDROUS	1382	4.2	
POTASSIUM HYDROGENDIFLUORIDE, SOLID	1811	8		POTASSIUM SULPHIDE, HYDRATED with not less than 30% water of crystallization	1847	8	
POTASSIUM HYDROGENDIFLUORIDE, SOLUTION	3421	8		POTASSIUM SUPEROXIDE	2466	5.1	
POTASSIUM HYDROGEN SULPHATE	2509	8		Potassium tetracyano-mercurate (II), see	1626	6.1	
POTASSIUM HYDROSULPHITE, see	1929	4.2		POWDER CAKE, WETTED with not less than 17% alcohol, by mass	0433	1	
Potassium hydroxide, liquid, see	1814	8		POWDER CAKE, WETTED with not less than 25% water, by mass	0159	1	
POTASSIUM HYDROXIDE, SOLID	1813	8		POWDER PASTE, see	0159 0433	1 1	
POTASSIUM HYDROXIDE SOLUTION	1814	8		POWDER, SMOKELESS	0160 0161 0509	1 1 1	
POTASSIUM METAL ALLOYS, LIQUID	1420	4.3		Power devices, explosive, see	0275 0276 0323 0381	1 1 1 1	
POTASSIUM METAL ALLOYS, SOLID	3403	4.3		PRIMERS, CAP TYPE	0044 0377 0378	1 1 1	
POTASSIUM METAVANADATE	2864	6.1		Primers, small arms, see	0044	1	
POTASSIUM MONOXIDE	2033	8		PRIMERS, TUBULAR	0319 0320 0376	1 1 1	
POTASSIUM NITRATE	1486	5.1					
Potassium nitrate and sodium nitrate mixture, see	1499	5.1		PRINTING INK, flammable or PRINTING INK RELATED MATERIAL (including printing ink thinning or reducing compound), flammable	1210	3	
POTASSIUM NITRATE AND SODIUM NITRITE MIXTURE	1487	5.1					
POTASSIUM NITRITE	1488	5.1					
POTASSIUM PERCHLORATE	1489	5.1					
POTASSIUM PERMANGANATE	1490	5.1					

Name and description	UN No.	Class	Remarks	Name and description	UN No.	Class	Remarks
Projectiles, illuminating, see	0171	1		n-PROPYLBENZENE	2364	3	
	0254	1		Propyl chloride, see	1278	3	
	0297	1					
PROJECTILES, inert with tracer	0345	1		n-PROPYL CHLOROFORMATE	2740	6.1	
	0424	1					
	0425	1		PROPYLENE	1077	2	
PROJECTILES with burster or expelling charge	0346	1		PROPYLENE CHLOROHYDRIN	2611	6.1	
	0347	1					
	0426	1		1,2-PROPYLENEDIAMINE	2258	8	
	0427	1					
	0434	1		Propylene dichloride, see	1279	3	
	0435	1					
				PROPYLENEIMINE, STABILIZED	1921	3	
PROJECTILES with bursting charge	0167	1					
	0168	1		PROPYLENE OXIDE	1280	3	
	0169	1					
	0324	1		PROPYLENE TETRAMER	2850	3	
	0344	1					
				Propylene trimer, see	2057	3	
PROPADIENE, STABILIZED	2200	2					
				PROPYL FORMATES	1281	3	
Propadiene and methyl acetylene mixture, stabilized, see	1060	2		n-PROPYL ISOCYANATE	2482	6.1	
PROPANE	1978	2		Propyl mercaptan, see	2402	3	
PROPANETHIOLS	2402	3		n-PROPYL NITRATE	1865	3	
n-PROPANOL	1274	3		PROPYLTRICHLOROSILANE	1816	8	
PROPELLANT, LIQUID	0495	1		Pyrazine hexahydride, see	2579	8	
	0497	1		PYRETHROID PESTICIDE, LIQUID, FLAMMABLE, TOXIC, flash-point less than 23 °C	3350	3	
PROPELLANT, SOLID	0498	1					
	0499	1					
	0501	1		PYRETHROID PESTICIDE, LIQUID, TOXIC	3352	6.1	
Propellant with a single base, Propellant with a double base, Propellant with a triple base, see	0160	1					
	0161	1		PYRETHROID PESTICIDE, LIQUID, TOXIC, FLAMMABLE, flash-point not less than 23 °C	3351	6.1	
Propene, see	1077	2		PYRETHROID PESTICIDE, SOLID, TOXIC	3349	6.1	
PROPIONALDEHYDE	1275	3					
PROPIONIC ACID with not less than 10% and less than 90% acid by mass	1848	8		PYRIDINE	1282	3	
				Pyrophoric organometallic compound, water-reactive, n.o.s., liquid, see	3394	4.2	
PROPIONIC ACID with not less than 90% acid by mass	3463	8					
				Pyrophoric organometallic compound, water-reactive, n.o.s., solid, see	3393	4.2	
PROPIONIC ANHYDRIDE	2496	8					
PROPIONITRILE	2404	3		PYROPHORIC ALLOY, N.O.S.	1383	4.2	
PROPIONYL CHLORIDE	1815	3		PYROPHORIC LIQUID, INORGANIC, N.O.S.	3194	4.2	
n-PROPYL ACETATE	1276	3					
PROPYL ALCOHOL, NORMAL, see	1274	3		PYROPHORIC LIQUID, ORGANIC, N.O.S.	2845	4.2	
PROPYLAMINE	1277	3		PYROPHORIC METAL, N.O.S.	1383	4.2	

Name and description	UN No.	Class	Remarks	Name and description	UN No.	Class	Remarks
PYROPHORIC SOLID, INORGANIC, N.O.S.	3200	4.2		RADIOACTIVE MATERIAL, SURFACE CONTAMINATED OBJECTS (SCO-I, SCO-II or SCO-III), non fissile or fissile-excepted	2913	7	
PYROPHORIC SOLID, ORGANIC, N.O.S.	2846	4.2					
PYROSULPHURYL CHLORIDE	1817	8		RADIOACTIVE MATERIAL, TRANSPORTED UNDER SPECIAL ARRANGEMENT, FISSILE	3331	7	
Pyroxylin solution, see	2059	3					
PYRROLIDINE	1922	3		RADIOACTIVE MATERIAL, TRANSPORTED UNDER SPECIAL ARRANGEMENT, non fissile or fissile-excepted	2919	7	
QUINOLINE	2656	6.1					
Quinone, see	2587	6.1		RADIOACTIVE MATERIAL, TYPE A PACKAGE, FISSILE, non-special form	3327	7	
RADIOACTIVE MATERIAL, EXCEPTED PACKAGE - ARTICLES MANUFACTURED FROM NATURAL URANIUM or DEPLETED URANIUM or NATURAL THORIUM	2909	7		RADIOACTIVE MATERIAL, TYPE A PACKAGE, non-special form, non fissile or fissile-excepted	2915	7	
RADIOACTIVE MATERIAL, EXCEPTED PACKAGE - EMPTY PACKAGING	2908	7		RADIOACTIVE MATERIAL, TYPE A PACKAGE, SPECIAL FORM, FISSILE	3333	7	
RADIOACTIVE MATERIAL, EXCEPTED PACKAGE - INSTRUMENTS or ARTICLES	2911	7		RADIOACTIVE MATERIAL, TYPE A PACKAGE, SPECIAL FORM, non fissile or fissile-excepted	3332	7	
RADIOACTIVE MATERIAL, EXCEPTED PACKAGE - LIMITED QUANTITY OF MATERIAL	2910	7		RADIOACTIVE MATERIAL, TYPE B(M) PACKAGE, FISSILE	3329	7	
RADIOACTIVE MATERIAL, LOW SPECIFIC ACTIVITY (LSA-I), non fissile or fissile-excepted	2912	7		RADIOACTIVE MATERIAL, TYPE B(M) PACKAGE, non fissile or fissile-excepted	2917	7	
RADIOACTIVE MATERIAL, LOW SPECIFIC ACTIVITY (LSA-II), FISSILE	3324	7		RADIOACTIVE MATERIAL, TYPE B(U) PACKAGE, FISSILE	3328	7	
RADIOACTIVE MATERIAL, LOW SPECIFIC ACTIVITY (LSA-II), non fissile or fissile-excepted	3321	7		RADIOACTIVE MATERIAL, TYPE B(U) PACKAGE, non fissile or fissile-excepted	2916	7	
RADIOACTIVE MATERIAL, LOW SPECIFIC ACTIVITY (LSA-III), FISSILE	3325	7		RADIOACTIVE MATERIAL, TYPE C PACKAGE, FISSILE	3330	7	
RADIOACTIVE MATERIAL, LOW SPECIFIC ACTIVITY (LSA-III), non fissile or fissile-excepted	3322	7		RADIOACTIVE MATERIAL, TYPE C PACKAGE, non fissile or fissile-excepted	3323	7	
				RADIOACTIVE MATERIAL, URANIUM HEXAFLUORIDE, FISSILE	2977	7	
RADIOACTIVE MATERIAL, SURFACE CONTAMINATED OBJECTS (SCO-I or SCO-II), FISSILE	3326	7		RADIOACTIVE MATERIAL, URANIUM HEXAFLUORIDE, non fissile or fissile-excepted	2978	7	
				Rags, oily	1856	4.2	Not subject to ADN

Name and description	UN No.	Class	Remarks	Name and description	UN No.	Class	Remarks
RDX, see	0072	1		REFRIGERANT GAS R 407C	3340	2	
	0391	1		REFRIGERANT GAS R 500, see	2602	2	
	0483	1		REFRIGERANT GAS R 502, see	1973	2	
RECEPTACLES, SMALL, CONTAINING GAS without a release device, non-refillable	2037	2		REFRIGERANT GAS R 503, see	2599	2	
Red phosphorus, see	1338	4.1		REFRIGERANT GAS R 1132a, see	1959	2	
REFRIGERANT GAS, N.O.S., such as mixture F1, mixture F2 or mixture P2	1078	2		REFRIGERANT GAS R 1216, see	1858	2	
				REFRIGERANT GAS R 1318, see	2422	2	
REFRIGERANT GAS R 12, see	1028	2		REFRIGERANT GAS RC 318, see	1976	2	
REFRIGERANT GAS R 12B1, see	1974	2		REFRIGERATING MACHINES containing flammable, non-toxic, liquefied gas	3358	2	
REFRIGERANT GAS R 13, see	1022	2					
REFRIGERANT GAS R 13B1, see	1009	2		REFRIGERATING MACHINES containing non-flammable, non-toxic, gases or ammonia solutions (UN 2672)	2857	2	
REFRIGERANT GAS R 14, see	1982	2					
REFRIGERANT GAS R 21, see	1029	2					
REFRIGERANT GAS R 22, see	1018	2		REGULATED MEDICAL WASTE, N O S	3291	6.2	
REFRIGERANT GAS R 23, see	1984	2		RELEASE DEVICES, EXPLOSIVE	0173	1	
REFRIGERANT GAS R 32, see	3252	2		RESIN SOLUTION, flammable	1866	3	
REFRIGERANT GAS R 40, see	1063	2		Resorcin, see	2876	6.1	
REFRIGERANT GAS R 41, see	2454	2		RESORCINOL	2876	6.1	
REFRIGERANT GAS R 114, see	1958	2		RIVETS, EXPLOSIVE	0174	1	
REFRIGERANT GAS R 115, see	1020	2		Road oil, with a flash-point not greater than 60 °C, see	1999	3	
REFRIGERANT GAS R 116, see	2193	2		Road oil, with a flash-point above 60 °C, at or above its flash-point, see	3256	3	
REFRIGERANT GAS R 124, see	1021	2					
REFRIGERANT GAS R 125, see	3220	2		Road oil, at or above 100 °C and below its flash-point, see	3257	9	
REFRIGERANT GAS R 133a, see	1983	2					
REFRIGERANT GAS R 134a, see	3159	2		ROCKET MOTORS	0186	1	
					0280	1	
					0281	1	
REFRIGERANT GAS R 142b, see	2517	2			0510	1	
REFRIGERANT GAS R 143a, see	2035	2		ROCKET MOTORS, LIQUID FUELLED	0395	1	
					0396	1	
REFRIGERANT GASR 152a, see	1030	2		ROCKET MOTORS WITH HYPERGOLIC LIQUIDS with or without expelling charge	0250	1	
REFRIGERANT GAS R 161, see	2453	2			0322	1	
REFRIGERANT GAS R 218, see	2424	2		ROCKETS with bursting charge	0180	1	
REFRIGERANT GAS R 227, see	3296	2			0181	1	
					0182	1	
REFRIGERANT GAS R 404A	3337	2			0295	1	
REFRIGERANT GAS R 407A	3338	2		ROCKETS with expelling charge	0436	1	
					0437	1	
REFRIGERANT GAS R 407B	3339	2			0438	1	

Name and description	UN No.	Class	Remarks	Name and description	UN No.	Class	Remarks
ROCKETS with inert head	0183	1		SELENIUM COMPOUND, SOLID, N.O.S.	3283	6.1	
	0502	1					
ROCKETS, LINE-THROWING	0238	1		SELENIUM DISULPHIDE	2657	6.1	
	0240	1		SELENIUM HEXAFLUORIDE	2194	2	
	0453	1		SELENIUM OXYCHLORIDE	2879	8	
ROCKETS, LIQUID FUELLED with bursting charge	0397	1		SELF-HEATING LIQUID, CORROSIVE, INORGANIC, N.O.S.	3188	4.2	
	0398	1					
ROSIN OIL	1286	3		SELF-HEATING LIQUID, CORROSIVE, ORGANIC, N.O.S.	3185	4.2	
RUBBER SCRAP, powdered or granulated, not exceeding 840 microns and rubber content exceeding 45 %	1345	4.1		SELF-HEATING LIQUID, INORGANIC, N.O.S.	3186	4.2	
				SELF-HEATING LIQUID, ORGANIC, N.O.S.	3183	4.2	
RUBBER SHODDY, powdered or granulated, not exceeding 840 microns and rubber content exceeding 45 %	1345	4.1		SELF-HEATING LIQUID, TOXIC, INORGANIC, N.O.S.	3187	4.2	
				SELF-HEATING LIQUID, TOXIC, ORGANIC, N.O.S.	3184	4.2	
RUBBER SOLUTION	1287	3					
RUBIDIUM	1423	4.3		SELF-HEATING SOLID, CORROSIVE, INORGANIC, N.O.S.	3192	4.2	
RUBIDIUM HYDROXIDE	2678	8		SELF-HEATING SOLID, CORROSIVE, ORGANIC, N.O.S.	3126	4.2	
RUBIDIUM HYDROXIDE SOLUTION	2677	8		SELF-HEATING SOLID, INORGANIC, N.O.S.	3190	4.2	
Rubidium nitrate, see	1477	5.1		SELF-HEATING SOLID, ORGANIC, N.O.S.	3088	4.2	
SAFETY DEVICES, electrically initiated	3268	9		SELF-HEATING SOLID, OXIDIZING, N.O.S	3127	4.2	Carriage prohibited
SAFETY DEVICES, PYROTECHNIC	0503	1		SELF-HEATING SOLID, TOXIC, INORGANIC, N.O.S.	3191	4.2	
Saltpetre, see	1486	5.1		SELF-HEATING SOLID, TOXIC, ORGANIC, N.O.S.	3128	4.2	
SAMPLES, EXPLOSIVE, other than initiating explosive	0190	1					
Sand acid, see	1778	8		SELF-REACTIVE LIQUID TYPE B	3221	4.1	
Seat-belt pretensioners, see	0503	1		SELF-REACTIVE LIQUID TYPE B, TEMPERATURE CONTROLLED	3231	4.1	
	3268	9					
SEED CAKE with more than 1.5% oil and not more than 11% moisture	1386	4.2		SELF-REACTIVE LIQUID TYPE C	3223	4.1	
SEED CAKE with not more than 1.5% oil and not more than 11% moisture	2217	4.2		SELF-REACTIVE LIQUID TYPE C, TEMPERATURE CONTROLLED	3233	4.1	
Seed expellers, see	1386	4.2		SELF-REACTIVE LIQUID TYPE D	3225	4.1	
	2217	4.2					
SELENATES	2630	6.1		SELF-REACTIVE LIQUID TYPE D, TEMPERATURE CONTROLLED	3235	4.1	
SELENIC ACID	1905	8					
SELENITES	2630	6.1					
SELENIUM COMPOUND, LIQUID, N.O.S.	3440	6.1					

Name and description	UN No.	Class	Remarks	Name and description	UN No.	Class	Remarks
SELF-REACTIVE LIQUID TYPE E	3227	4.1		Signals, distress, ship, water-activated, see	0249	1	
SELF-REACTIVE LIQUID TYPE E, TEMPERATURE CONTROLLED	3237	4.1		SIGNALS, RAILWAY TRACK, EXPLOSIVE	0192	1	
					0193	1	
					0492	1	
SELF-REACTIVE LIQUID TYPE F	3229	4.1			0493	1	
				SIGNALS, SMOKE	0196	1	
					0197	1	
SELF-REACTIVE LIQUID TYPE F, TEMPERATURE CONTROLLED	3239	4.1			0313	1	
					0487	1	
					0507	1	
SELF-REACTIVE SOLID TYPE B	3222	4.1		SILANE	2203	2	
				Silicofluoric acid, see	1778	8	
SELF-REACTIVE SOLID TYPE B, TEMPERATURE CONTROLLED	3232	4.1		Silicofluorides, n.o.s., see	2856	6.1	
				Silicon chloride, see	1818	8	
SELF-REACTIVE SOLID TYPE C	3224	4.1		SILICON POWDER, AMORPHOUS	1346	4.1	
SELF-REACTIVE SOLID TYPE C, TEMPERATURE CONTROLLED	3234	4.1		SILICON TETRACHLORIDE	1818	8	
				SILICON TETRAFLUORIDE	1859	2	
SELF-REACTIVE SOLID TYPE D	3226	4.1		SILICON TETRAFLUORIDE, ADSORBED	3521	2	
SELF-REACTIVE SOLID TYPE D, TEMPERATURE CONTROLLED	3236	4.1		SILVER ARSENITE	1683	6.1	
				SILVER CYANIDE	1684	6.1	
SELF-REACTIVE SOLID TYPE E	3228	4.1		SILVER NITRATE	1493	5.1	
SELF-REACTIVE SOLID TYPE E, TEMPERATURE CONTROLLED	3238	4.1		SILVER PICRATE, WETTED with not less than 30% water, by mass	1347	4.1	
				SLUDGE ACID	1906	8	
SELF-REACTIVE SOLID TYPE F	3230	4.1		SODA LIME with more than 4% sodium hydroxide	1907	8	
SELF-REACTIVE SOLID TYPE F, TEMPERATURE CONTROLLED	3240	4.1		SODIUM	1428	4.3	
				Sodium aluminate, solid	2812	8	Not subject to ADN
SHALE OIL	1288	3					
Shaped charges, see	0059	1					
	0439	1		SODIUM ALUMINATE SOLUTION	1819	8	
	0440	1					
	0441	1		SODIUM ALUMINIUM HYDRIDE	2835	4.3	
Shellac, see	1263	3					
	3066	8		SODIUM AMMONIUM VANADATE	2863	6.1	
	3469	3					
	3470	8		SODIUM ARSANILATE	2473	6.1	
SIGNAL DEVICES, HAND	0191	1					
	0373	1		SODIUM ARSENATE	1685	6.1	
SIGNALS, DISTRESS, ship	0194	1		SODIUM ARSENITE, AQUEOUS SOLUTION	1686	6.1	
	0195	1					
	0505	1					
	0506	1					

Name and description	UN No.	Class	Remarks	Name and description	UN No.	Class	Remarks
SODIUM ARSENITE, SOLID	2027	6.1		Sodium dioxide, see	1504	5.1	
SODIUM AZIDE	1687	6.1		SODIUM DITHIONITE	1384	4.2	
Sodium bifluoride, see	2439	8		SODIUM FLUORIDE, SOLID	1690	6.1	
Sodium binoxide, see	1504	5.1		SODIUM FLUORIDE, SOLUTION	3415	6.1	
Sodium bisulphite solution, see	2693	8		SODIUM FLUOROACETATE	2629	6.1	
SODIUM BOROHYDRIDE	1426	4.3		SODIUM FLUOROSILICATE	2674	6.1	
SODIUM BOROHYDRIDE AND SODIUM HYDROXIDE SOLUTION, with not more than 12% sodium borohydride and not more than 40% sodium hydroxide by mass	3320	8		Sodium hexafluorosilicate, see	2674	6.1	
				Sodium hydrate, see	1824	8	
				SODIUM HYDRIDE	1427	4.3	
SODIUM BROMATE	1494	5.1		Sodium hydrogen 4-amino-phenylarsenate, see	2473	6.1	
SODIUM CACODYLATE	1688	6.1		SODIUM HYDROGENDIFLUORIDE	2439	8	
SODIUM CARBONATE PEROXYHYDRATE	3378	5.1		SODIUM HYDROSULPHIDE with less than 25% water of crystallization	2318	4.2	
SODIUM CHLORATE	1495	5.1		SODIUM HYDROSULPHIDE, HYDRATED with not less than 25% water of crystallization	2949	8	
SODIUM CHLORATE, AQUEOUS SOLUTION	2428	5.1					
Sodium chlorate mixed with dinitrotoluene, see	0083	1		SODIUM HYDROSULPHITE, see	1384	4.2	
				SODIUM HYDROXIDE, SOLID	1823	8	
SODIUM CHLORITE	1496	5.1		SODIUM HYDROXIDE SOLUTION	1824	8	
SODIUM CHLOROACETATE	2659	6.1					
SODIUM CUPROCYANIDE, SOLID	2316	6.1		Sodium metasilicate pentahydrate, see	3253	8	
SODIUM CUPROCYANIDE SOLUTION	2317	6.1		SODIUM METHYLATE	1431	4.2	
SODIUM CYANIDE, SOLID	1689	6.1		SODIUM METHYLATE SOLUTION in alcohol	1289	3	
SODIUM CYANIDE, SOLUTION	3414	6.1		SODIUM MONOXIDE	1825	8	
Sodium dicyanocuprate (I), solid, see	2316	6.1		SODIUM NITRATE	1498	5.1	
Sodium dicyanocuprate (I) solution, see	2317	6.1		SODIUM NITRATE AND POTASSIUM NITRATE MIXTURE	1499	5.1	
Sodium dimethylarsenate, see	1688	6.1		SODIUM NITRITE	1500	5.1	
SODIUM DINITRO-o-CRESOLATE, dry or wetted with less than 15% water, by mass	0234	1		Sodium nitrite and potassium nitrate mixture, see	1487	5.1	
				SODIUM PENTACHLOROPHENATE	2567	6.1	
SODIUM DINITRO-o-CRESOLATE, WETTED with not less than 10% water, by mass	3369	4.1		SODIUM PERBORATE MONOHYDRATE	3377	5.1	
SODIUM DINITRO-o-CRESOLATE, WETTED with not less than 15% water, by mass	1348	4.1		SODIUM PERCHLORATE	1502	5.1	
				SODIUM PERMANGANATE	1503	5.1	

Name and description	UN No.	Class	Remarks	Name and description	UN No.	Class	Remarks
SODIUM PEROXIDE	1504	5.1		STANNIC CHLORIDE PENTAHYDRATE	2440	8	
SODIUM PEROXOBORATE, ANHYDROUS	3247	5.1		STANNIC PHOSPHIDES	1433	4.3	
SODIUM PERSULPHATE	1505	5.1		Steel swarf, see	2793	4.2	
SODIUM PHOSPHIDE	1432	4.3		STIBINE	2676	2	
SODIUM PICRAMATE, dry or wetted with less than 20% water, by mass	0235	1		Straw	1327	4.1	Not subject to ADN
SODIUM PICRAMATE, WETTED with not less than 20% water, by mass	1349	4.1		Strontium alloys, pyrophoric, see	1383	4.2	
				STRONTIUM ARSENITE	1691	6.1	
Sodium potassium alloys, liquid, see	1422	4.3		STRONTIUM CHLORATE	1506	5.1	
Sodium selenate, see	2630	6.1		Strontium dioxide, see	1509	5.1	
Sodium selenite, see	2630	6.1		STRONTIUM NITRATE	1507	5.1	
Sodium silicofluoride, see	2674	6.1		STRONTIUM PERCHLORATE	1508	5.1	
SODIUM SULPHIDE, ANHYDROUS	1385	4.2		STRONTIUM PEROXIDE	1509	5.1	
				STRONTIUM PHOSPHIDE	2013	4.3	
SODIUM SULPHIDE with less than 30% water of crystallization	1385	4.2		STRYCHNINE	1692	6.1	
SODIUM SULPHIDE, HYDRATED with not less than 30% water	1849	8		STRYCHNINE SALTS	1692	6.1	
				STYPHNIC ACID, see	0219	1	
					0394	1	
SODIUM SUPEROXIDE	2547	5.1					
SOLIDS CONTAINING CORROSIVE LIQUID, N.O.S.	3244	8		STYRENE MONOMER, STABILIZED	2055	3	
SOLIDS or mixtures of solids (such as preparations and wastes) CONTAINING FLAMMABLE LIQUID, N.O.S. having a flash-point up to 60°C	3175	4.1		SUBSTANCES, EVI, N.O.S., see	0482	1	
				SUBSTANCES, EXPLOSIVE, N.O.S.	0357	1	
					0358	1	
					0359	1	
					0473	1	
SOLIDS CONTAINING TOXIC LIQUID, N.O.S.	3243	6.1			0474	1	
					0475	1	
					0476	1	
Solvents, flammable, n.o.s., see	1993	3			0477	1	
					0478	1	
Solvents, flammable, toxic, n.o.s., see	1992	3			0479	1	
					0480	1	
SOUNDING DEVICES, EXPLOSIVE	0204	1			0481	1	
	0296	1			0485	1	
	0374	1					
	0375	1		SUBSTANCES, EXPLOSIVE, VERY INSENSITIVE, N.O.S.	0482	1	
Squibs, see	0325	1					
	0454	1		Substances liable to spontaneous combustion, n.o.s., see	2845	4.2	
					2846	4.2	
Stain, see	1263	3			3194	4.2	
	3066	8			3200	4.2	
	3469	3					
	3470	8					
STANNIC CHLORIDE, ANHYDROUS	1827	8					

Name and description	UN No.	Class	Remarks	Name and description	UN No.	Class	Remarks
SUBSTANCES WITH A FLASH-POINT ABOVE 60 °C which are carried heated within a limiting range of 15K below their flash-point	9001	3	Dangerous in tank vessels only	SULPHUR TETRAFLUORIDE	2418	2	
				SULPHUR TRIOXIDE, STABILIZED	1829	8	
				SULPHURYL CHLORIDE	1834	6.1	
SUBSTANCES WITH A FLASH-POINT ABOVE 60 °C AND NOT MORE THAN 100 °C, which do not belong to another Class	9003	9	Dangerous in tank vessels only	SULPHURYL FLUORIDE	2191	2	
				Table Tennis Balls, see	2000	4.1	
SUBSTANCES WITH AN AUTO-IGNITION TEMPERATURE OF 200 °C AND BELOW, n.o.s.	9002	3	Dangerous in tank vessels only	Talcum with tremolite and/or actinolite, see	2212	9	
				TARS, LIQUID, including road oils and cutback bitumens, with a flash-point not greater than 60 °C	1999	3	
SUBSTITUTED NITROPHENOL PESTICIDE, LIQUID, FLAMMABLE, TOXIC, flash-point less than 23 °C	2780	3		Tars, liquid, with a flash-point above 60 °C, at or above its flash-point, see	3256	3	
SUBSTITUTED NITROPHENOL PESTICIDE, LIQUID, TOXIC	3014	6.1		Tars, liquid, at or above 100 °C and below its flash-point, see	3257	9	
SUBSTITUTED NITROPHENOL PESTICIDE, LIQUID, TOXIC, FLAMMABLE, flash-point not less than 23 °C	3013	6.1		Tartar emetic, see	1551	6.1	
				TEAR GAS CANDLES	1700	6.1	
SUBSTITUTED NITROPHENOL PESTICIDE, SOLID, TOXIC	2779	6.1		TEAR GAS SUBSTANCE, LIQUID, N.O.S.	1693	6.1	
SULPHAMIC ACID	2967	8		TEAR GAS SUBSTANCE, SOLID, N.O.S.	3448	6.1	
SULPHUR	1350	4.1		TELLURIUM COMPOUND, N.O.S.	3284	6.1	
SULPHUR CHLORIDES	1828	8		TELLURIUM HEXAFLUORIDE	2195	2	
Sulphur dichloride, see	1828	8		TERPENE HYDROCARBONS, N.O.S.	2319	3	
SULPHUR DIOXIDE	1079	2		TERPINOLENE	2541	3	
Sulphuretted hydrogen, see	1053	2		TETRABROMOETHANE	2504	6.1	
SULPHUR HEXAFLUORIDE	1080	2		1,1,2,2-TETRACHLOROETHANE	1702	6.1	
SULPHURIC ACID with more than 51% acid	1830	8		TETRACHLOROETHYLENE	1897	6.1	
SULPHURIC ACID with not more than 51% acid	2796	8		TETRAETHYL DITHIO-PYROPHOSPHATE	1704	6.1	
				TETRAETHYLENEPENTAMINE	2320	8	
SULPHURIC ACID, FUMING	1831	8		Tetraethyl lead, see	1649	6.1	
SULPHURIC ACID, SPENT	1832	8		TETRAETHYL SILICATE	1292	3	
Sulphuric and hydrofluoric acid mixture, see	1786	8		Tetraethyoxysilane, see	1292	3	
SULPHUR, MOLTEN	2448	4.1		Tetrafluorodichloroethane, see	1958	2	
Sulphur monochloride, see	1828	8		1,1,1,2-TETRAFLUOROETHANE	3159	2	
SULPHUROUS ACID	1833	8		TETRAFLUOROETHYLENE, STABILIZED	1081	2	

Name and description	UN No.	Class	Remarks	Name and description	UN No.	Class	Remarks
TETRAFLUOROMETHANE	1982	2		Thallous chlorate, see	2573	5.1	
1,2,3,6-TETRAHYDRO-BENZALDEHYDE	2498	3		4-THIAPENTANAL	2785	6.1	
TETRAHYDROFURAN	2056	3		Thia-4-pentanal, see	2785	6.1	
TETRAHYDRO-FURFURYLAMINE	2943	3		THIOACETIC ACID	2436	3	
Tetrahydro-1,4-oxazine, see	2054	3		THIOCARBAMATE PESTICIDE, LIQUID, FLAMMABLE, TOXIC, flash-point less than 23 °C	2772	3	
TETRAHYDROPHTHALIC ANHYDRIDES with more than 0.05% of maleic anhydride	2698	8		THIOCARBAMATE PESTICIDE, LIQUID, TOXIC	3006	6.1	
1,2,3,6-TETRAHYDROPYRIDINE	2410	3		THIOCARBAMATE PESTICIDE, LIQUID, TOXIC, FLAMMABLE, flash-point not less than 23 °C	3005	6.1	
TETRAHYDROTHIOPHENE	2412	3		THIOCARBAMATE PESTICIDE, SOLID, TOXIC	2771	6.1	
Tetramethoxysilane, see	2606	6.1					
TETRAMETHYLAMMONIUM HYDROXIDE, SOLID	3423	8		THIOGLYCOL	2966	6.1	
				THIOGLYCOLIC ACID	1940	8	
TETRAMETHYLAMMONIUM HYDROXIDE, SOLUTION	1835	8		THIOLACTIC ACID	2936	6.1	
Tetramethylene, see	2601	2		THIONYL CHLORIDE	1836	8	
Tetramethylene cyanide, see	2205	6.1		THIOPHENE	2414	3	
Tetramethyl lead, see	1649	6.1		Thiophenol, see	2337	6.1	
TETRAMETHYLSILANE	2749	3		THIOPHOSGENE	2474	6.1	
TETRANITROANILINE	0207	1		THIOPHOSPHORYL CHLORIDE	1837	8	
TETRANITROMETHANE	1510	6.1		THIOUREA DIOXIDE	3341	4.2	
TETRAPROPYL ORTHOTITANATE	2413	3		Tin (IV) chloride, anhydrous, see	1827	8	
				Tin (IV) chloride pentahydrate, see	2440	8	
TETRAZENE, WETTED with not less than 30% water, or mixture of alcohol and water, by mass, see	0114	1		TINCTURES, MEDICINAL	1293	3	
				Tin tetrachloride, see	1827	8	
TETRAZOL-1-ACETIC ACID	0407	1		TITANIUM DISULPHIDE	3174	4.2	
1H-TETRAZOLE	0504	1		TITANIUM HYDRIDE	1871	4.1	
TETRYL, see	0208	1		TITANIUM POWDER, DRY	2546	4.2	
Textile waste, wet	1857	4.2	Not subject to ADN	TITANIUM POWDER, WETTED with not less than 25% water	1352	4.1	
THALLIUM CHLORATE	2573	5.1		TITANIUM SPONGE GRANULES	2878	4.1	
Thallium (I) chlorate, see	2573	5.1		TITANIUM SPONGE POWDERS	2878	4.1	
THALLIUM COMPOUND, N.O.S.	1707	6.1		TITANIUM TETRACHLORIDE	1838	6.1	
THALLIUM NITRATE	2727	6.1		TITANIUM TRICHLORIDE MIXTURE	2869	8	
Thallium (I) nitrate, see	2727	6.1					

Name and description	UN No.	Class	Remarks	Name and description	UN No.	Class	Remarks
TITANIUM TRICHLORIDE MIXTURE, PYROPHORIC	2441	4.2		TOXIC BY INHALATION LIQUID, CORROSIVE, N.O.S. with an LC_{50} lower than or equal to 200 ml/m^3 and saturated vapour concentration greater than or equal to 500 LC_{50}	3389	6.1	
TITANIUM TRICHLORIDE, PYROPHORIC	2441	4.2					
TNT, see	0209	1		TOXIC BY INHALATION LIQUID, CORROSIVE, N.O.S. with an LC_{50} lower than or equal to 1000 ml/m^3 and saturated vapour concentration greater than or equal to 10 LC_{50}	3390	6.1	
	0388	1					
	0389	1					
TNT mixed with aluminium, see	0390	1					
TNT, WETTED with not less than 30% water, by mass, see	1356	4.1		TOXIC BY INHALATION LIQUID, FLAMMABLE, N.O.S. with an LC_{50} lower than or equal to 200 ml/m^3 and saturated vapour concentration greater than or equal to 500 LC_{50}	3383	6.1	
TNT, WETTED with not less than 10% water, by mass, see	3366	4.1					
Toe puffs, nitrocellulose base, see	1353	4.1		TOXIC BY INHALATION LIQUID, FLAMMABLE, N.O.S. with an LC_{50} lower than or equal to 1000 ml/m^3 and saturated vapour concentration greater than or equal to 10 LC_{50}	3384	6.1	
TOLUENE	1294	3					
TOLUENE DIISOCYANATE	2078	6.1					
TOLUIDINES, LIQUID	1708	6.1		TOXIC BY INHALATION LIQUID, FLAMMABLE, CORROSIVE, N.O.S. with an LC_{50} lower than or equal to 200 ml/m^3 and saturated vapour concentration greater than or equal to 500 LC_{50}	3488	6.1	
TOLUIDINES, SOLID	3451	6.1					
Toluol, see	1294	3					
2,4-TOLUYLENEDIAMINE, SOLID	1709	6.1		TOXIC BY INHALATION LIQUID, FLAMMABLE, CORROSIVE, N.O.S. with an LC_{50} lower than or equal to 1000 ml/m^3 and saturated vapour concentration greater than or equal to 10 LC_{50}	3489	6.1	
2,4-TOLUYLENEDIAMINE, SOLUTION	3418	6.1					
Toluylene diisocyanate, see	2078	6.1					
Tolylene diisocyanate, see	2078	6.1		TOXIC BY INHALATION LIQUID, OXIDIZING, N.O.S. with an LC_{50} lower than or equal to 200 ml/m^3 and saturated vapour concentration greater than or equal to 500 LC_{50}	3387	6.1	
Tolylethylene, inhibited, see	2618	3					
TORPEDOES with bursting charge	0329	1					
	0330	1		TOXIC BY INHALATION LIQUID, OXIDIZING, N.O.S. with an LC_{50} lower than or equal to 1000 ml/m^3 and saturated vapour concentration greater than or equal to 10 LC_{50}	3387	6.1	
	0451	1					
TORPEDOES, LIQUID FUELLED with inert head	0450	1					
TORPEDOES, LIQUID FUELLED with or without bursting charge	0449	1		TOXIC BY INHALATION LIQUID, OXIDIZING, N.O.S. with an LC_{50} lower than or equal to 1000 ml/m^3 and saturated vapour concentration greater than or equal to 10 LC_{50}	3388	6.1	
TOXIC BY INHALATION LIQUID, N.O.S. with an LC_{50} lower than or equal to 200 ml/m^3 and saturated vapour concentration greater than or equal to 500 LC_{50}	3381	6.1					
TOXIC BY INHALATION LIQUID, N.O.S. with an LC_{50} lower than or equal to 1000 ml/m^3 and saturated vapour concentration greater than or equal to 10 LC_{50}	3382	6.1		TOXIC BY INHALATION LIQUID, WATER-REACTIVE, N.O.S. with an LC_{50} lower than or equal to 200 ml/m^3 and saturated vapour concentration greater than or equal to 500 LC_{50}	3385	6.1	

Name and description	UN No.	Class	Remarks	Name and description	UN No.	Class	Remarks
TOXIC BY INHALATION LIQUID, WATER-REACTIVE, N.O.S. with an LC_{50} lower than or equal to 1000 ml/m^3 and saturated vapour concentration greater than or equal to 10 LC_{50}	3386	6.1		TOXINS, EXTRACTED FROM LIVING SOURCES, LIQUID, N.O.S.	3172	6.1	
				TOXINS, EXTRACTED FROM LIVING SOURCES, SOLID, N.O.S.	3462	6.1	
TOXIC BY INHALATION LIQUID, WATER-REACTIVE, FLAMMABLE, N.O.S. with an LC_{50} lower than or equal to 200 ml/m^3 and saturated vapour concentration greater than or equal to 500 LC_{50}	3490	6.1		TRACERS FOR AMMUNITION	0212 / 0306	1 / 1	
				Tremolite, see	2212	9	
				TRIALLYLAMINE	2610	3	
				TRIALLYL BORATE	2609	6.1	
TOXIC BY INHALATION LIQUID, WATER-REACTIVE, FLAMMABLE, N.O.S. with an LC_{50} lower than or equal to 1000 ml/m^3 and saturated vapour concentration greater than or equal to 10 LC_{50}	3491	6.1		TRIAZINE PESTICIDE, LIQUID, FLAMMABLE, TOXIC, flash-point less than 23 °C	2764	3	
				TRIAZINE PESTICIDE, LIQUID, TOXIC	2998	6.1	
TOXIC LIQUID, CORROSIVE, INORGANIC, N.O.S.	3289	6.1		TRIAZINE PESTICIDE, LIQUID, TOXIC, FLAMMABLE, flash-point not less than 23 °C	2997	6.1	
TOXIC LIQUID, CORROSIVE, ORGANIC, N.O.S.	2927	6.1		TRIAZINE PESTICIDE, SOLID, TOXIC	2763	6.1	
TOXIC LIQUID, FLAMMABLE, ORGANIC, N.O.S.	2929	6.1		Tribromoborane, see	2692	8	
TOXIC LIQUID, INORGANIC, N.O.S.	3287	6.1		TRIBUTYLAMINE	2542	6.1	
TOXIC LIQUID, ORGANIC, N.O.S.	2810	6.1		TRIBUTYLPHOSPHANE	3254	4.2	
TOXIC LIQUID, OXIDIZING, N.O.S.	3122	6.1		Trichloroacetaldehyde, see	2075	6.1	
				TRICHLOROACETIC ACID	1839	8	
TOXIC LIQUID, WATER-REACTIVE, N.O.S.	3123	6.1		TRICHLOROACETIC ACID SOLUTION	2564	8	
TOXIC SOLID, CORROSIVE, INORGANIC, N.O.S.	3290	6.1		Trichlororaceticaldehyde, see	2075	6.1	
TOXIC SOLID, CORROSIVE, ORGANIC, N.O.S.	2928	6.1		TRICHLOROACETYL CHLORIDE	2442	8	
TOXIC SOLID, FLAMMABLE, INORGANIC, N.O.S.	3535	6.1		TRICHLOROBENZENES, LIQUID	2321	6.1	
				TRICHLOROBUTENE	2322	6.1	
TOXIC SOLID, FLAMMABLE, ORGANIC, N.O.S.	2930	6.1		1,1,1-TRICHLOROETHANE	2831	6.1	
				TRICHLOROETHYLENE	1710	6.1	
TOXIC SOLID, INORGANIC, N.O.S.	3288	6.1		TRICHLOROISOCYANURIC ACID, DRY	2468	5.1	
TOXIC SOLID, ORGANIC, N.O.S.	2811	6.1		Trichloronitromethane, see	1580	6.1	
TOXIC SOLID, OXIDIZING, N.O.S.	3086	6.1		TRICHLOROSILANE	1295	4.3	
TOXIC SOLID, SELF-HEATING, N.O.S.	3124	6.1		1,3,5-Trichloro-s-triazine-2,4,6-trione, see	2468	5.1	
TOXIC SOLID, WATER-REACTIVE, N.O.S.	3125	6.1		2,4,6-Trichloro-1,3,5- triazine, see	2670	8	

Name and description	UN No.	Class	Remarks	Name and description	UN No.	Class	Remarks
TRICRESYL PHOSPHATE with more than 3% ortho isomer	2574	6.1		TRIMETHYLHEXAMETHYLENE DIISOCYANATE	2328	6.1	
TRIETHYLAMINE	1296	3		2,4,4-Trimethylpentene-1, see	2050	3	
Triethyl borate, see	1176	3		2,4,4-Trimethylpentene-2, see	2050	3	
TRIETHYLENETETRAMINE	2259	8		TRIMETHYL PHOSPHITE	2329	3	
Triethyl orthoformate, see	2524	3		TRINITROANILINE	0153	1	
TRIETHYL PHOSPHITE	2323	3		TRINITROANISOLE	0213	1	
TRIFLUOROACETIC ACID	2699	8		TRINITROBENZENE, dry or wetted with less than 30% water, by mass	0214	1	
TRIFLUOROACETYL CHLORIDE	3057	2		TRINITROBENZENE, WETTED with not less than 10% water, by mass	3367	4.1	
Trifluorobromomethane, see	1009	2		TRINITROBENZENE, WETTED with not less than 30% water, by mass	1354	4.1	
Trifluorochloroethane, see	1983	2					
TRIFLUOROCHLOROETHYLENE, STABILIZED, REFRIGERANT GAS R 1113	1082	2		TRINITROBENZENE-SULPHONIC ACID	0386	1	
Trifluorochloromethane, see	1022	2		TRINITROBENZOIC ACID, dry or wetted with less than 30% water, by mass	0215	1	
1,1,1-TRIFLUOROETHANE	2035	2					
TRIFLUOROMETHANE	1984	2		TRINITROBENZOIC ACID, WETTED with not less than 10% water, by mass	3368	4.1	
TRIFLUOROMETHANE, REFRIGERATED LIQUID	3136	2		TRINITROBENZOIC ACID, WETTED with not less than 30% water, by mass	1355	4.1	
2-TRIFLUOROMETHYLANILINE	2942	6.1					
3-TRIFLUOROMETHYLANILINE	2948	6.1		TRINITROCHLOROBENZENE	0155	1	
TRIISOBUTYLENE	2324	3		TRINITROCHLOROBENZENE, WETTED with not less than 10% water, by mass	3365	4.1	
TRIISOPROPYL BORATE	2616	3					
TRIMETHYLACETYL CHLORIDE	2438	6.1		TRINITRO-m-CRESOL	0216	1	
TRIMETHYLAMINE, ANHYDROUS	1083	2		TRINITROFLUORENONE	0387	1	
TRIMETHYLAMINE, AQUEOUS SOLUTION, not more than 50% trimethylamine, by mass	1297	3		TRINITRONAPHTHALENE	0217	1	
				TRINITROPHENETOLE	0218	1	
1,3,5-TRIMETHYLBENZENE	2325	3		TRINITROPHENOL, dry or wetted with less than 30% water, by mass	0154	1	
TRIMETHYL BORATE	2416	3					
TRIMETHYLCHLOROSILANE	1298	3		TRINITROPHENOL (PICRIC ACID), WETTED with not less than 30% water, by mass	1344	4.1	
TRIMETHYLCYCLO-HEXYLAMINE	2326	8					
Trimethylene chlorobromide, see	2688	6.1		TRINITROPHENOL, WETTED with not less than 10% water, by mass	3364	4.1	
TRIMETHYLHEXA-METHYLENEDIAMINES	2327	8					
				TRINITROPHENYL-METHYLNITRAMINE	0208	1	

Name and description	UN No.	Class	Remarks	Name and description	UN No.	Class	Remarks
TRINITRORESORCINOL, dry or wetted with less than 20% water, or mixture of alcohol and water, by mass	0219	1		UREA NITRATE, WETTED with not less than 20% water, by mass	1357	4.1	
				Valeral, see	2058	3	
TRINITRORESORCINOL, WETTED with not less than 20% water, or mixture of alcohol and water, by mass	0394	1		VALERALDEHYDE	2058	3	
				n-Valeraldehyde, see	2058	3	
				Valeric aldehyde, see	2058	3	
TRINITROTOLUENE (TNT), dry or wetted with less than 30% water, by mass	0209	1		VALERYL CHLORIDE	2502	8	
				VANADIUM COMPOUND, N.O.S.	3285	6.1	
TRINITROTOLUENE AND HEXANITROSTILBENE MIXTURE	0388	1		Vanadium (IV) oxide sulphate, see	2931	6.1	
				Vanadium oxysulphate, see	2931	6.1	
TRINITROTOLUENE MIXTURE CONTAINING TRINITROBENZENE AND HEXANITROSTILBENE	0389	1		VANADIUM OXYTRICHLORIDE	2443	8	
				VANADIUM PENTOXIDE, non-fused form	2862	6.1	
TRINITROTOLUENE AND TRINITROBENZENE MIXTURE	0388	1		VANADIUM TETRACHLORIDE	2444	8	
				VANADIUM TRICHLORIDE	2475	8	
TRINITROTOLUENE, WETTED with not less than 10% water, by mass	3366	4.1		VANADYL SULPHATE	2931	6.1	
TRINITROTOLUENE, WETTED with not less than 30% water, by mass	1356	4.1		Varnish, see	1263 3066 3469 3470	3 8 3 8	
TRIPROPYLAMINE	2260	3		VEHICLE, FLAMMABLE GAS POWERED	3166	9	
TRIPROPYLENE	2057	3					
TRIS-(1-AZIRIDINYL) PHOSPHINE OXIDE SOLUTION	2501	6.1		VEHICLE, FLAMMABLE LIQUID POWERED	3166	9	
TRITONAL	0390	1					
Tropilidene, see	2603	3		VEHICLE, FUEL CELL, FLAMMABLE GAS POWERED	3166	9	
TUNGSTEN HEXAFLUORIDE	2196	2					
TURPENTINE	1299	3		VEHICLE, FUEL CELL, FLAMMABLE LIQUID POWERED	3166	9	
TURPENTINE SUBSTITUTE	1300	3					
UNDECANE	2330	3		Villiaumite, see	1690	6.1	
URANIUM HEXAFLUORIDE, RADIOACTIVE MATERIAL, EXCEPTED PACKAGE, less than 0.1 kg per package, non-fissile or fissile-excepted	3507	6.1		VINYL ACETATE, STABILIZED	1301	3	
				Vinylbenzene, see	2055	3	
				VINYL BROMIDE, STABILIZED	1085	2	
UREA HYDROGEN PEROXIDE	1511	5.1		VINYL BUTYRATE, STABILIZED	2838	3	
UREA NITRATE, dry or wetted with less than 20% water, by mass	0220	1		VINYL CHLORIDE, STABILIZED	1086	2	
				VINYL CHLOROACETATE	2589	6.1	
UREA NITRATE, WETTED with not less than 10% water, by mass	3370	4.1		VINYL ETHYL ETHER, STABILIZED	1302	3	

Name and description	UN No.	Class	Remarks	Name and description	UN No.	Class	Remarks
VINYL FLUORIDE, STABILIZED	1860	2		WOOD PRESERVATIVES, LIQUID	1306	3	
VINYLIDENE CHLORIDE, STABILIZED	1303	3		Wool waste, wet	1387	4.2	Not subject to ADN
VINYL ISOBUTYL ETHER, STABILIZED	1304	3					
VINYL METHYL ETHER, STABILIZED	1087	2		XANTHATES	3342	4.2	
				XENON	2036	2	
VINYLPYRIDINES, STABILIZED	3073	6.1		XENON, REFRIGERATED LIQUID	2591	2	
VINYLTOLUENES, STABILIZED	2618	3		XYLENES	1307	3	
VINYLTRICHLOROSILANE	1305	3		XYLENOLS, LIQUID	3430	6.1	
Warheads for guided missiles, see	0286	1		XYLENOLS, SOLID	2261	6.1	
	0287	1		XYLIDINES, LIQUID	1711	6.1	
	0369	1					
	0370	1		XYLIDINES, SOLID	3452	6.1	
	0371	1					
WARHEADS, ROCKET with burster or expelling charge	0370	1		Xylols, see	1307	3	
	0371	1		XYLYL BROMIDE, LIQUID	1701	6.1	
WARHEADS, ROCKET with bursting charge	0286	1		XYLYL BROMIDE, SOLID	3417	6.1	
	0287	1					
	0369	1		ZINC AMMONIUM NITRITE	1512	5.1	
WARHEADS, TORPEDO with bursting charge	0221	1		ZINC ARSENATE	1712	6.1	
				ZINC ARSENATE AND ZINC ARSENITE MIXTURE	1712	6.1	
WATER-REACTIVE LIQUID, N.O.S.	3148	4.3		ZINC ARSENITE	1712	6.1	
WATER-REACTIVE LIQUID, CORROSIVE, N.O.S.	3129	4.3		ZINC ASHES	1435	4.3	
WATER-REACTIVE LIQUID, TOXIC, N.O.S.	3130	4.3		Zinc bisulphite solution, see	2693	8	
WATER-REACTIVE SOLID, N.O.S.	2813	4.3		ZINC BROMATE	2469	5.1	
				ZINC CHLORATE	1513	5.1	
WATER-REACTIVE SOLID, CORROSIVE, N.O.S.	3131	4.3		ZINC CHLORIDE, ANHYDROUS	2331	8	
WATER-REACTIVE SOLID, FLAMMABLE, N.O.S.	3132	4.3		ZINC CHLORIDE SOLUTION	1840	8	
				ZINC CYANIDE	1713	6.1	
WATER-REACTIVE SOLID, OXIDIZING, N.O.S.	3133	4.3	Carriage prohibited	ZINC DITHIONITE	1931	9	
				ZINC DUST	1436	4.3	
WATER-REACTIVE SOLID, SELF-HEATING, N.O.S.	3135	4.3		ZINC FLUOROSILICATE	2855	6.1	
WATER-REACTIVE SOLID, TOXIC, N.O.S.	3134	4.3		Zinc hexafluorosilicate, see	2855	6.1	
				ZINC HYDROSULPHITE, see	1931	9	
White arsenic, see	1561	6.1		ZINC NITRATE	1514	5.1	
White spirit, see	1300	3		ZINC PERMANGANATE	1515	5.1	

Name and description	UN No.	Class	Remarks	Name and description	UN No.	Class	Remarks
ZINC PEROXIDE	1516	5.1		ZIRCONIUM NITRATE	2728	5.1	
ZINC PHOSPHIDE	1714	4.3		ZIRCONIUM PICRAMATE, dry or wetted with less than 20% water, by mass	0236	1	
ZINC POWDER	1436	4.3					
ZINC RESINATE	2714	4.1		ZIRCONIUM PICRAMATE, WETTED with not less than 20% water, by mass	1517	4.1	
Zinc selenate, see	2630	4.1					
Zinc selenite, see	2630	4.1					
Zinc silicofluoride, see	2855	6.1		ZIRCONIUM POWDER, DRY	2008	4.2	
ZIRCONIUM, DRY, coiled wire, finished metal sheets, strip (thinner than 254 microns but not thinner than 18 microns)	2858	4.1		ZIRCONIUM POWDER, WETTED with not less than 25% water	1358	4.1	
				ZIRCONIUM SCRAP	1932	4.2	
ZIRCONIUM, DRY, finished sheets, strip or coiled wire	2009	4.2		ZIRCONIUM SUSPENDED IN A FLAMMABLE LIQUID	1308	3	
ZIRCONIUM HYDRIDE	1437	4.1		ZIRCONIUM TETRACHLORIDE	2503	8	

3.2.3   (See Volume I)

3.2.4   (See Volume I)

CHAPTER 3.3

SPECIAL PROVISIONS APPLICABLE TO CERTAIN ARTICLES OR SUBSTANCES

3.3.1   When Column (6) of Table A of Chapter 3.2 indicates that a special provision is relevant to a substance or article, the meaning and requirements of that special provision are as set forth below. Where a special provision includes a requirement for package marking, the provisions of 5.2.1.2 (a) and (b) shall be met. If the required mark is in the form of specific wording indicated in quotation marks, such as "LITHIUM BATTERIES FOR DISPOSAL", the size of the mark shall be at least 12 mm, unless otherwise indicated in the special provision or elsewhere in ADN.

16   Samples of new or existing explosive substances or articles may be carried as directed by the competent authorities (see 2.2.1.1.3) for purposes including: testing, classification, research and development, quality control, or as a commercial sample. Explosive samples which are not wetted or desensitised shall be limited to 10 kg in small packages as specified by the competent authorities. Explosive samples which are wetted or desensitised shall be limited to 25 kg.

23   Even though this substance has a flammability hazard, it only exhibits such hazard under extreme fire conditions in confined areas.

32   This substance is not subject to the requirements of ADN when in any other form.

37   This substance is not subject to the requirements of ADN when coated.

38   This substance is not subject to the requirements of ADN when it contains not more than 0.1% calcium carbide.

39   This substance is not subject to the requirements of ADN when it contains less than 30% or not less than 90% silicon.

43   When offered for carriage as pesticides, these substances shall be carried under the relevant pesticide entry and in accordance with the relevant pesticide provisions (see 2.2.61.1.10 to 2.2.61.1.11.2).

45   Antimony sulphides and oxides which contain not more than 0.5% of arsenic calculated on the total mass are not subject to the requirements of ADN.

47   Ferricyanides and ferrocyanides are not subject to the requirements of ADN.

48   The carriage of this substance, when it contains more than 20% hydrocyanic acid, is prohibited.

59   These substances are not subject to the requirements of ADN when they contain not more than 50% magnesium.

60   If the concentration is more than 72%, the carriage of this substance is prohibited.

61   The technical name which shall supplement the proper shipping name shall be the ISO common name (see also ISO 1750:1981 "*Pesticides and other agrochemicals - common names*", as amended), other names listed in the WHO "*Recommended Classification of Pesticides by Hazard and Guidelines to Classification*" or the name of the active substance (see also 3.1.2.8.1 and 3.1.2.8.1.1).

62   This substance is not subject to the requirements of ADN when it contains not more than 4% sodium hydroxide.

65   Hydrogen peroxide aqueous solutions with less than 8% hydrogen peroxide are not subject to the requirements of ADN.

66   Cinnabar is not subject to the requirements of ADN.

103   The carriage of ammonium nitrites and mixtures of an inorganic nitrite with an ammonium salt is prohibited.

105   Nitrocellulose meeting the descriptions of UN No. 2556 or UN No. 2557 may be classified in Class 4.1.

113   The carriage of chemically unstable mixtures is prohibited.

119   Refrigerating machines include machines or other appliances which have been designed for the specific purpose of keeping food or other items at a low temperature in an internal compartment, and air conditioning units. Refrigerating machines and refrigerating machine components are not subject to the provisions of ADN if they contain less than 12 kg of gas in Class 2, group A or O according to 2.2.2.1.3, or if they contain less than 12 litres ammonia solution (UN No. 2672).

      NOTE: For the purposes of carriage, heat pumps may be considered as refrigerating machines.

122   The subsidiary hazards, control and emergency temperatures if any, and the UN number (generic entry) for each of the currently assigned organic peroxide formulations are given in 2.2.52.4, 4.1.4.2 packing instruction IBC520 and 4.2.5.2.6 portable tank instruction T23 of ADR.

123   *(Reserved)*

127   Other inert material or inert material mixture may be used, provided this inert material has identical phlegmatizing properties.

131   The phlegmatized substance shall be significantly less sensitive than dry PETN.

135   The dihydrated sodium salt of dichloroisocyanuric acid does not meet the criteria for inclusion in Class 5.1 and is not subject to ADN unless meeting the criteria for inclusion in another Class.

138   p-Bromobenzyl cyanide is not subject to the requirements of ADN.

141   Products which have undergone sufficient heat treatment so that they present no hazard during carriage are not subject to the requirements of ADN.

142   Solvent extracted soya bean meal containing not more than 1.5% oil and 11% moisture, which is substantially free of flammable solvent, is not subject to the requirements of ADN.

144   An aqueous solution containing not more than 24% alcohol by volume is not subject to the requirements of ADN.

145   Alcoholic beverages of packing group III, when carried in receptacles of 250 litres or less, are not subject to the requirements of ADN.

152   The classification of this substance will vary with particle size and packaging, but borderlines have not been experimentally determined. Appropriate classifications shall be made in accordance with 2.2.1.

153   This entry applies only if it is demonstrated, on the basis of tests, that the substances when in contact with water are not combustible nor show a tendency to auto-ignition and that the mixture of gases evolved is not flammable.

163   A substance mentioned by name in Table A of Chapter 3.2 shall not be carried under this entry. Substances carried under this entry may contain 20% or less nitrocellulose provided the nitrocellulose contains not more than 12.6% nitrogen (by dry mass).

168   Asbestos which is immersed or fixed in a natural or artificial binder (such as cement, plastics, asphalt, resins or mineral ore) in such a way that no escape of hazardous quantities of respirable asbestos fibres can occur during carriage is not subject to the requirements of ADN. Manufactured articles containing asbestos and not meeting this provision are nevertheless not subject to the requirements of ADN when packed so that no escape of hazardous quantities of respirable asbestos fibres can occur during carriage.

169   Phthalic anhydride in the solid state and tetrahydrophthalic anhydrides, with not more than 0.05% maleic anhydride, are not subject to the requirements of ADN. Phthalic anhydride molten at a temperature above its flash-point, with not more than 0.05% maleic anhydride, shall be classified under UN No. 3256.

172   Where a radioactive material has (a) subsidiary hazard(s):

(a)   The substance shall be allocated to packing group I, II or III, if appropriate, by application of the packing group criteria provided in Part 2 corresponding to the nature of the predominant subsidiary hazard;

(b)   Packages shall be labelled with subsidiary risk labels corresponding to each subsidiary hazard exhibited by the material; corresponding placards shall be affixed to cargo transport units in accordance with the relevant provisions of 5.3.1;

(c)   For the purposes of documentation and package marking, the proper shipping name shall be supplemented with the name of the constituents which most predominantly contribute to this (these) subsidiary hazard(s) and which shall be enclosed in parenthesis;

(d)   The dangerous goods transport document shall indicate the label model number(s) corresponding to each subsidiary hazard in parenthesis after the Class number "7" and, where assigned the packing group as required by 5.4.1.1.1 (d).

For packing, see also 4.1.9.1.5 of ADR.

177   Barium sulphate is not subject to the requirements of ADN.

178   This designation shall be used only when no other appropriate designation exists in Table A of Chapter 3.2, and only with the approval of the competent authority of the country of origin (see 2.2.1.1.3).

181   Packages containing this type of substance shall bear a label conforming to model No. 1 (see 5.2.2.2.2) unless the competent authority of the country of origin has permitted this label to be dispensed with for the specific packaging employed because test data have proved that the substance in this packaging does not exhibit explosive behaviour (see 5.2.2.1.9).

182   The group of alkali metals includes lithium, sodium, potassium, rubidium and caesium.

183   The group of alkaline earth metals includes magnesium, calcium, strontium and barium.

186   *(Deleted)*

188   Cells and batteries offered for carriage are not subject to other provisions of ADN if they meet the following:

(a)   For a lithium metal or lithium alloy cell, the lithium content is not more than 1 g, and for a lithium-ion cell, the Watt-hour rating is not more than 20 Wh;

NOTE: When lithium batteries in conformity with 2.2.9.1.7 (f) are carried in accordance with this special provision, the total lithium content of all lithium metal cells contained in the battery shall not exceed 1.5 g and the total capacity of all lithium ion cells contained in the battery shall not exceed 10 Wh (see special provision 387).

(b)   For a lithium metal or lithium alloy battery the aggregate lithium content is not more than 2 g, and for a lithium-ion battery, the Watt-hour rating is not more than 100 Wh. Lithium ion batteries subject to this provision shall be marked with the Watt-hour rating on the outside case except those manufactured before 1 January 2009;

NOTE: When lithium batteries in conformity with 2.2.9.1.7 (f) are carried in accordance with this special provision, the total lithium content of all lithium metal cells contained in the battery shall not exceed 1.5 g and the total capacity of all lithium ion cells contained in the battery shall not exceed 10 Wh (see special provision 387).

(c)   Each cell or battery meets the provisions of 2.2.9.1.7 (a), (e), (f) if applicable, and (g);

(d)   Cells and batteries, except when installed in equipment, shall be packed in inner packagings that completely enclose the cell or battery. Cells and batteries shall be protected so as to prevent short circuits. This includes protection against contact with electrically conductive material within the same packaging that could lead to a short circuit. The inner packagings shall be packed in strong outer packagings which conform to the provisions of 4.1.1.1, 4.1.1.2 and 4.1.1.5 of ADR;

(e)   Cells and batteries when installed in equipment shall be protected from damage and short circuit, and the equipment shall be equipped with an effective means of preventing accidental activation. This requirement does not apply to devices which are intentionally active in carriage (radio frequency identification (RFID) transmitters, watches, sensors, etc.) and which are not capable of generating a dangerous evolution of heat. When batteries are installed in equipment, the equipment shall be packed in strong outer packagings constructed of suitable material of adequate strength and design in relation to the packaging's capacity and its intended use unless the battery is afforded equivalent protection by the equipment in which it is contained;

(f) Each package shall be marked with the appropriate lithium battery mark, as illustrated in 5.2.1.9;

This requirement does not apply to:

(i) packages containing only button cell batteries installed in equipment (including circuit boards); and

(ii) packages containing no more than four cells or two batteries installed in equipment, where there are not more than two packages in the consignment.

When packages are placed in an overpack, the lithium battery mark shall either be clearly visible or be reproduced on the outside of the overpack and the overpack shall be marked with the word "OVERPACK". The lettering of the "OVERPACK" mark shall be at least 12 mm high.

NOTE: *Packages containing lithium batteries packed in conformity with the provisions of Part 4, Chapter 11, packing instructions 965 or 968 Section IB of the ICAO Technical Instructions that bear the mark as shown in 5.2.1.9 (lithium battery mark) and the label shown in 5.2.2.2.2, model No. 9A shall be deemed to meet the provisions of this special provision.*

(g) Except when cells or batteries are installed in equipment, each package shall be capable of withstanding a 1.2 m drop test in any orientation without damage to cells or batteries contained therein, without shifting of the contents so as to allow battery to battery (or cell to cell) contact and without release of contents; and

(h) Except when cells or batteries are installed in or packed with equipment, packages shall not exceed 30 kg gross mass.

As used above and elsewhere in ADN, "lithium content" means the mass of lithium in the anode of a lithium metal or lithium alloy cell. As used in this special provision "equipment" means apparatus for which the lithium cells or batteries will provide electrical power for its operation.

Separate entries exist for lithium metal batteries and lithium ion batteries to facilitate the carriage of these batteries for specific modes of carriage and to enable the application of different emergency response actions.

A single cell battery as defined in Part III, sub-section 38.3.2.3 of the *Manual of Tests and Criteria* is considered a "cell" and shall be carried according to the requirements for "cells" for the purpose of this special provision.

190 Aerosol dispensers shall be provided with protection against inadvertent discharge. Aerosols with a capacity not exceeding 50 ml containing only non-toxic constituents are not subject to the requirements of ADN.

191 Receptacles, small, with a capacity not exceeding 50 ml, containing only non-toxic constituents are not subject to the requirements of ADN.

193 This entry may only be used for ammonium nitrate based compound fertilizers. They shall be classified in accordance with the procedure as set out in the Manual of Tests and Criteria, Part III, Section 39. Fertilizers meeting the criteria for this UN number are subject to the requirements of ADN only when carried in bulk.

194 The control and emergency temperatures, if any, and the UN number (generic entry) for each of the currently assigned self-reactive substances are given in 2.2.41.4.

196 Formulations which in laboratory testing neither detonate in the cavitated state nor deflagrate, which show no effect when heated under confinement and which exhibit no explosive power may be carried under this entry. The formulation must also be thermally stable (i.e. the SADT is 60 °C or higher for a 50 kg package). Formulations not meeting these criteria shall be carried under the provisions of Class 5.2, (see 2.2.52.4).

198 Nitrocellulose solutions containing not more than 20% nitrocellulose may be carried as paint, perfumery products or printing ink, as applicable (see UN Nos. 1210, 1263, 1266, 3066, 3469 and 3470).

199 Lead compounds which, when mixed in a ratio of 1:1000 with 0.07M hydrochloric acid and stirred for one hour at a temperature of 23 °C ± 2 °C, exhibit a solubility of 5% or less (see ISO 3711:1990 *Lead chromate pigments and lead chromate-molybdate pigments – Specifications and methods of test"*) are considered insoluble and are not subject to the requirements of ADN unless they meet the criteria for inclusion in another class.

201 Lighters and lighter refills shall comply with the provisions of the country in which they were filled. They shall be provided with protection against inadvertent discharge. The liquid portion of the gas shall not exceed 85% of the capacity of the receptacle at 15 °C. The receptacles, including the closures, shall be capable of withstanding an internal pressure of twice the pressure of the liquefied petroleum gas at 55 °C. The valve mechanisms and ignition devices shall be securely sealed, taped or otherwise fastened or designed to prevent operation or leakage of the contents during carriage. Lighters shall not contain more than 10 g of liquefied petroleum gas. Lighter refills shall not contain more than 65 g of liquefied petroleum gas.

NOTE: *For waste lighters collected separately see Chapter 3.3, special provision 654.*

203 This entry shall not be used for polychlorinated biphenyls, liquid, UN No. 2315 and polychlorinated biphenyls, solid, UN No. 3432.

204 *(Deleted)*

205 This entry shall not be used for UN No. 3155 PENTACHLOROPHENOL.

207 Plastics moulding compounds may be made from polystyrene, poly(methyl methacrylate) or other polymeric material.

208 The commercial grade of calcium nitrate fertilizer, when consisting mainly of a double salt (calcium nitrate and ammonium nitrate) containing not more than 10% ammonium nitrate and at least 12% water of crystallization, is not subject to the requirements of ADN.

210 Toxins from plant, animal or bacterial sources which contain infectious substances, or toxins that are contained in infectious substances, shall be classified in Class 6.2.

215 This entry only applies to the technically pure substance or to formulations derived from it having an SADT higher than 75 °C and therefore does not apply to formulations which are self-reactive substances (for self-reactive substances, see 2.2.41.4). Homogeneous mixtures containing not more than 35% by mass of azodicarbonamide and at least 65% of inert substance are not subject to the requirements of ADN unless criteria of other classes are met.

216   Mixtures of solids which are not subject to the requirements of ADN and flammable liquids may be carried under this entry without first applying the classification criteria of Class 4.1, provided there is no free liquid visible at the time the substance is loaded or at the time the packaging or cargo transport unit is closed. Sealed packets and articles containing less than 10 ml of a packing group II or III flammable liquid absorbed into a solid material are not subject to ADN provided there is no free liquid in the packet or article.

217   Mixtures of solids which are not subject to the requirements of ADN and toxic liquids may be carried under this entry without first applying the classification criteria of Class 6.1, provided there is no free liquid visible at the time the substance is loaded or at the time the packaging or cargo transport unit is closed. This entry shall not be used for solids containing a packing group I liquid.

218   Mixtures of solids which are not subject to the requirements of ADN and corrosive liquids may be carried under this entry without first applying the classification criteria of Class 8, provided there is no free liquid visible at the time the substance is loaded or at the time the packaging or cargo transport unit is closed.

219   Genetically modified microorganisms (GMMOs) and genetically modified organisms (GMOs) packed and marked in accordance with packing instruction P904 of 4.1.4.1 of ADR are not subject to any other requirements of ADN.

        If GMMOs or GMOs meet the criteria for inclusion in Class 6.1 or 6.2 (see 2.2.61.1 and 2.2.62.1) the requirements in ADN for the carriage of toxic substances or infectious substances apply.

220   Only the technical name of the flammable liquid component of this solution or mixture shall be shown in parentheses immediately following the proper shipping name.

221   Substances included under this entry shall not be of packing group I.

224   Unless it can be demonstrated by testing that the sensitivity of the substance in its frozen state is no greater than in its liquid state, the substance shall remain liquid during normal transport conditions. It shall not freeze at temperatures above -15 °C.

225   Fire extinguishers under this entry may include installed actuating cartridges (cartridges, power device of classification code 1.4C or 1.4S), without changing the classification of Class 2, group A or O according to 2.2.2.1.3 provided the total quantity of deflagrating (propellant) explosives does not exceed 3.2 g per extinguishing unit.

        Fire extinguishers shall be manufactured, tested, approved and labelled according to the provisions applied in the country of manufacture.

        NOTE: *Provisions applied in the country of manufacture" means the provisions applicable in the country of manufacture or those applicable in the country of use.*

        Fire extinguishers under this entry include:

        (a)   portable fire extinguishers for manual handling and operation;

                NOTE: This entry applies to portable fire extinguishers, even if some components that are necessary for their proper functioning (e.g. hoses and nozzles) are temporarily detached, as long as the safety of the pressurized extinguishing agent containers is not compromised and the fire extinguishers continue to be identified as a portable fire extinguisher.

        (b)   fire extinguishers for installation in aircraft;

(c)   fire extinguishers mounted on wheels for manual handling;

(d)   fire extinguishing equipment or machinery mounted on wheels or wheeled platforms or units carried similar to (small) trailers, and

(e)   fire extinguishers composed of a non-rollable pressure drum and equipment, and handled e.g. by fork lift or crane when loaded or unloaded.

NOTE: Pressure receptacles which contain gases for use in the above-mentioned fire extinguishers or for use in stationary fire-fighting installations shall meet the requirements of Chapter 6.2 of ADR and all requirements applicable to the relevant dangerous goods when these pressure receptacles are carried separately.

226   Formulations of this substance containing not less than 30% non-volatile, non-flammable phlegmatizer are not subject to the requirements of ADN.

227   When phlegmatized with water and inorganic inert material the content of urea nitrate may not exceed 75% by mass and the mixture shall not be capable of being detonated by the Series 1, type (a), test in the *Manual of Tests and Criteria*, Part 1.

228   Mixtures not meeting the criteria for flammable gases (see 2.2.2.1.5) shall be carried under UN No. 3163.

230   Lithium cells and batteries may be carried under this entry if they meet the provisions of 2.2.9.1.7.

235   This entry applies to articles which contain Class 1 explosive substances and which may also contain dangerous goods of other classes. These articles are used to enhance safety in vehicles, vessels or aircraft – e.g. air bag inflators, air bag modules, seat-belt pretensioners, and pyromechanical devices.

236   Polyester resin kits consist of two components: a base material (either Class 3 or Class 4.1, packing group II or III) and an activator (organic peroxide). The organic peroxide shall be type D, E, or F, not requiring temperature control. The packing group shall be II or III, according to the criteria of either Class 3 or Class 4.1, as appropriate, applied to the base material. The quantity limit shown in column (7a) of Table A of Chapter 3.2 applies to the base material.

237   The membrane filters, including paper separators, coating or backing materials, etc., that are present in carriage, shall not be liable to propagate a detonation as tested by one of the tests described in the *Manual of Tests and Criteria*, Part I, Test series 1 (a).

In addition, the competent authority may determine, on the basis of the results of suitable burning rate tests taking account of the standard tests in the *Manual of Tests and Criteria*, Part III, sub-section 33.2, that nitrocellulose membrane filters in the form in which they are to be carried are not subject to the requirements applicable to flammable solids in Class 4.1.

238   (a)   Batteries can be considered as non-spillable provided that they are capable of withstanding the vibration and pressure differential tests given below, without leakage of battery fluid.

Vibration test: The battery is rigidly clamped to the platform of a vibration machine and a simple harmonic motion having an amplitude of 0.8 mm (1.6 mm maximum total excursion) is applied. The frequency is varied at the rate of 1 Hz/min between the limits of 10 Hz and 55 Hz. The entire range of frequencies and return is traversed in 95 ± 5 minutes for each mounting position (direction of vibration) of the battery. The battery is tested in three mutually perpendicular positions (to include testing with fill openings and vents, if any, in an inverted position) for equal time periods.

Pressure differential test: Following the vibration test, the battery is stored for six hours at $24\,°C \pm 4\,°C$ while subjected to a pressure differential of at least 88 kPa. The battery is tested in three mutually perpendicular positions (to include testing with fill openings and vents, if any, in an inverted position) for at least six hours in each position.

(b)   Non-spillable batteries are not subject to the requirements of ADN if, at a temperature of 55 °C, the electrolyte will not flow from a ruptured or cracked case and there is no free liquid to flow and if, as packaged for carriage, the terminals are protected from short circuit.

239   Batteries or cells shall not contain dangerous substances other than sodium, sulphur or sodium compounds (e.g. sodium polysulphides and sodium tetrachloroaluminate). Batteries or cells shall not be offered for carriage at a temperature such that liquid elemental sodium is present in the battery or cell unless approved and under the conditions established by the competent authority of the country of origin. If the country of origin is not a Contracting Party to ADN, the approval and conditions of carriage shall be recognized by the competent authority of the first country Contracting Party to ADN reached by the consignment.

Cells shall consist of hermetically sealed metal casings which fully enclose the dangerous substances and which are so constructed and closed as to prevent the release of the dangerous substances under normal conditions of carriage.

Batteries shall consist of cells secured within and fully enclosed by a metal casing so constructed and closed as to prevent the release of the dangerous substances under normal conditions of carriage.

240   *(Deleted)*

241   The formulation shall be prepared so that it remains homogeneous and does not separate during carriage. Formulations with low nitrocellulose contents and not showing dangerous properties when tested for their liability to detonate, deflagrate or explode when heated under defined confinement by tests of Test series 1 (a), 2 (b) and 2 (c) respectively in the *Manual of Tests and Criteria*, Part I and not being a flammable solid when tested in accordance with Test N.1 in the *Manual of Tests and Criteria*, Part III, sub-section 33.2.4 (chips, if necessary, crushed and sieved to a particle size of less than 1.25 mm) are not subject to the requirements of ADN.

242   Sulphur is not subject to the requirements of ADN when it has been formed to a specific shape (e.g. prills, granules, pellets, pastilles or flakes).

243   Gasoline, motor spirit and petrol for use in spark-ignition engines (e.g. in automobiles, stationary engines and other engines) shall be assigned to this entry regardless of variations in volatility.

244   This entry includes e.g. aluminium dross, aluminium skimmings, spent cathodes, spent potliner, and aluminium salt slags.

247   Alcoholic beverages containing more than 24% alcohol but not more than 70% by volume, when carried as part of the manufacturing process, may be carried in wooden barrels with a capacity of more than 250 litres and not more than 500 litres meeting the general requirements of 4.1.1 of ADR, as appropriate, on the following conditions:

(a)   The wooden barrels shall be checked and tightened before filling;

(b)   Sufficient ullage (not less than 3%) shall be left to allow for the expansion of the liquid;

(c)   The wooden barrels shall be carried with the bungholes pointing upwards;

(d)   The wooden barrels shall be carried in containers meeting the requirements of the CSC. Each wooden barrel shall be secured in custom-made cradles and be wedged by appropriate means to prevent it from being displaced in any way during carriage.

249   Ferrocerium, stabilized against corrosion, with a minimum iron content of 10% is not subject to the requirements of ADN.

250   This entry may only be used for samples of chemicals taken for analysis in connection with the implementation of the Convention on the Prohibition of the Development, Production, Stockpiling and Use of Chemical Weapons and on their Destruction. The carriage of substances under this entry shall be in accordance with the chain of custody and security procedures specified by the Organisation for the Prohibition of Chemical Weapons.

The chemical sample may only be carried providing prior approval has been granted by the competent authority or the Director General of the Organisation for the Prohibition of Chemical Weapons and providing the sample complies with the following provisions:

(a)   It shall be packed according to packing instruction 623 in the ICAO Technical Instructions; and

(b)   During carriage, a copy of the document of approval for transport, showing the quantity limitations and the packing provisions shall be attached to the transport document.

251   The entry CHEMICAL KIT or FIRST AID KIT is intended to apply to boxes, cases etc. containing small quantities of various dangerous goods which are used for example for medical, analytical or testing or repair purposes.

Such kits shall only contain dangerous goods that are permitted as:

(a)   Excepted quantities not exceeding the quantity indicated by the code in column (7b) of Table A of Chapter 3.2, provided that the net quantity per inner packaging and net quantity per package are as prescribed in 3.5.1.2 and 3.5.1.3; or;

(b)   Limited quantities as indicated in column (7a) of Table A of Chapter 3.2, provided that the net quantity per inner packaging does not exceed 250 ml or 250 g.

Components shall not react dangerously (see "dangerous reaction" in 1.2.1). The total quantity of dangerous goods in any one kit shall not exceed either 1 *l* or 1 kg.

For the purposes of completion of the transport document as set out in 5.4.1.1.1, the packing group shown on the document shall be the most stringent packing group assigned to any individual substance in the kit. Where the kit contains only dangerous goods to which no packing group is assigned, no packing group need be indicated on the dangerous goods transport document.

Kits which are carried on board vessels for first-aid or operating purposes are not subject to the requirements of ADN.

Chemical kits and first aid kits containing dangerous goods in inner packagings which do not exceed the quantity limits for limited quantities applicable to individual substances as specified in Column (7a) of Table A of Chapter 3.2 may be carried in accordance with Chapter 3.4.

252   Provided the ammonium nitrate remains in solution under all conditions of carriage, aqueous solutions of ammonium nitrate, with not more than 0.2% combustible material, in a concentration not exceeding 80%, are not subject to the requirements of ADN.

266   This substance, when containing less alcohol, water or phlegmatizer than specified, shall not be carried unless specifically authorized by the competent authority (see 2.2.1.1).

267   Any explosives, blasting, type C containing chlorates shall be segregated from explosives containing ammonium nitrate or other ammonium salts.

270   Aqueous solutions of Class 5.1 inorganic solid nitrate substances are considered as not meeting the criteria of Class 5.1 if the concentration of the substances in solution at the minimum temperature encountered during carriage is not greater than 80% of the saturation limit.

271   Lactose or glucose or similar materials may be used as a phlegmatizer provided that the substance contains not less than 90%, by mass, of phlegmatizer. The competent authority may authorize these mixtures to be classified in Class 4.1 on the basis of a test Series 6 (c) of Section 16 of Part I of the *Manual of Tests and Criteria* on at least three packages as prepared for carriage. Mixtures containing at least 98%, by mass, of phlegmatizer are not subject to the requirements of ADN. Packages containing mixtures with not less than 90%, by mass, of phlegmatizer need not bear a label conforming to model No. 6.1.

272   This substance shall not be carried under the provisions of Class 4.1 unless specifically authorized by the competent authority (see UN No. 0143 or UN No. 0150 as appropriate).

273   Maneb and maneb preparations stabilized against self-heating need not be classified in Class 4.2 when it can be demonstrated by testing that a cubic volume of 1 m^3 of substance does not self-ignite and that the temperature at the centre of the sample does not exceed 200 °C, when the sample is maintained at a temperature of not less than 75 °C ± 2 °C for a period of 24 hours.

274   The provisions of 3.1.2.8 apply.

278   These substances shall not be classified and carried unless authorized by the competent authority on the basis of results from Series 2 tests and a Series 6(c) test of Part I of the *Manual of Tests and Criteria* on packages as prepared for carriage (see 2.2.1.1). The competent authority shall assign the packing group on the basis of 2.2.3 criteria and the package type used for the Series 6(c) test.

279   The substance is assigned to this classification or packing group based on human experience rather than the strict application of classification criteria set out in ADN.

280   This entry applies to safety devices for vehicles, vessels or aircraft, e.g. air bag inflators, air bag modules, seat-belt pretensioners, and pyromechanical devices, which contain dangerous goods of Class 1 or of other classes, when carried as component parts and if these articles as presented for carriage have been tested in accordance with Test Series 6(c) of Part 1 of the Manual of Tests and Criteria, with no explosion of the device, no fragmentation of device casing or pressure receptacle, and no projection hazard nor thermal effect which would significantly hinder fire-fighting or emergency response efforts in the immediate vicinity. This entry does not apply to life saving appliances described in special provision 296 (UN Nos. 2990 and 3072).

283   Articles containing gas, intended to function as shock absorbers, including impact energy-absorbing devices, or pneumatic springs are not subject to the requirements of ADN provided:

(a)   Each article has a gas space capacity not exceeding 1.6 litres and a charge pressure not exceeding 280 bar where the product of the capacity (litres) and charge pressure (bars) does not exceed 80 (i.e. 0.5 litres gas space and 160 bar charge pressure, 1 litre gas space and 80 bar charge pressure, 1.6 litres gas space and 50 bar charge pressure, 0.28 litres gas space and 280 bar charge pressure);

(b)   Each article has a minimum burst pressure of 4 times the charge pressure at 20 °C for products not exceeding 0.5 litres gas space capacity and 5 times charge pressure for products greater than 0.5 litres gas space capacity;

(c)   Each article is manufactured from material which will not fragment upon rupture;

(d)   Each article is manufactured in accordance with a quality assurance standard acceptable to the competent authority; and

(e)   The design type has been subjected to a fire test demonstrating that the article relieves its pressure by means of a fire degradable seal or other pressure relief device, such that the article will not fragment and that the article does not rocket.

See also 1.1.3.2 (d) of ADR for equipment used for the operation of the vehicle.

284   An oxygen generator, chemical, containing oxidizing substances shall meet the following conditions:

(a)   The generator when containing an explosive actuating device shall only be carried under this entry when excluded from Class 1 in accordance with the NOTE under paragraph 2.2.1.1.1 (b);

(b)   The generator, without its packaging, shall be capable of withstanding a 1.8 m drop test onto a rigid, non-resilient, flat and horizontal surface, in the position most likely to cause damage, without loss of its contents and without actuation;

(c)   When a generator is equipped with an actuating device, it shall have at least two positive means of preventing unintentional actuation.

286   Nitrocellulose membrane filters covered by this entry, each with a mass not exceeding 0.5 g, are not subject to the requirements of ADN when contained individually in an article or a sealed packet.

288   These substances shall not be classified and carried unless authorized by the competent authority on the basis of results from Series 2 tests and a Series 6 (c) test of Part I of the *Manual of Tests and Criteria* on packages as prepared for carriage (see 2.2.1.1).

289   Safety devices, electrically initiated and safety devices, pyrotechnic installed in vehicles, wagons, vessels or aircraft or in completed components such as steering columns, door panels, seats, etc. are not subject to ADN.

290   When this radioactive material meets the definitions and criteria of other classes as defined in Part 2, it shall be classified in accordance with the following:

(a)   Where the substance meets the criteria for dangerous goods in excepted quantities as set out in Chapter 3.5, the packagings shall be in accordance with 3.5.2 and meet the testing requirements of 3.5.3. All other requirements applicable to radioactive material, excepted packages as set out in 1.7.1.5 shall apply without reference to the other class;

(b)   Where the quantity exceeds the limits specified in 3.5.1.2 the substance shall be classified in accordance with the predominant subsidiary hazard. The transport document shall describe the substance with the UN number and proper shipping name applicable to the other class supplemented with the name applicable to the radioactive excepted package according to Column (2) of Table A of Chapter 3.2, and the substance shall be carried in accordance with the provisions applicable to that UN number. An example of the information shown on the transport document is:

"UN 1993, Flammable liquid, N.O.S. (ethanol and toluene mixture), Radioactive material, excepted package – limited quantity of material, 3, PG II".

In addition, the requirements of 2.2.7.2.4.1 shall apply;

(c)   The provisions of Chapter 3.4 for the carriage of dangerous goods packed in limited quantities shall not apply to substances classified in accordance with sub-paragraph (b);

(d)   When the substance meets a special provision that exempts this substance from all dangerous goods provisions of the other classes it shall be classified in accordance with the applicable UN number of Class 7 and all requirements specified in 1.7.1.5 shall apply.

291   Flammable liquefied gases shall be contained within refrigerating machine components. These components shall be designed and tested to at least three times the working pressure of the machinery. The refrigerating machines shall be designed and constructed to contain the liquefied gas and preclude the risk of bursting or cracking of the pressure retaining components during normal conditions of carriage. Refrigerating machines and refrigerating-machine components are not subject to the requirements of ADN if they contain less than 12 kg of gas.

NOTE: *For the purposes of carriage, heat pumps may be considered as refrigerating machines.*

292   *(Deleted)*

293   The following definitions apply to matches:

(a)   Fusee matches are matches the heads of which are prepared with a friction-sensitive igniter composition and a pyrotechnic composition which burns with little or no flame, but with intense heat;

(b)   Safety matches are matches that are combined with or attached to the box, book or card that can be ignited by friction only on a prepared surface;

(c)   Strike anywhere matches are matches that can be ignited by friction on a solid surface;

(d)   Wax Vesta matches are matches that can be ignited by friction either on a prepared surface or on a solid surface.

295   Batteries need not be individually marked and labelled if the pallet bears the appropriate mark and label.

296   These entries apply for life-saving appliances such as life rafts, personal flotation devices and self-inflating slides. UN No. 2990 applies to self-inflating appliances and UN No. 3072 applies to life-saving appliances that are not self-inflating. Life-saving appliances may contain:

(a)   Signal devices (Class 1) which may include smoke and illumination signal flares packed in packagings that prevent them from being inadvertently activated;

(b)   For UN No. 2990 only, cartridges, power devices of Division 1.4, compatibility group S, may be contained for purposes of the self-inflating mechanism and provided that the quantity of explosives per appliance does not exceed 3.2 g;

(c)   Class 2 compressed or liquefied gases, group A or O, according to 2.2.2.1.3;

(d)   Electric storage batteries (Class 8) and lithium batteries (Class 9);

(e)   First aid kits or repair kits containing small quantities of dangerous goods (e.g.: substances of Class 3, 4.1, 5.2, 8 or 9); or

(f)   "Strike anywhere" matches packed in packagings that prevent them from being inadvertently activated.

Life-saving appliances packed in strong rigid outer packagings with a total maximum gross mass of 40 kg, containing no dangerous goods other than compressed or liquefied gases of Class 2, group A or group O, in receptacles with a capacity not exceeding 120 ml, installed solely for the purpose of the activation of the appliance, are not subject to the requirements of ADN.

300   Fish meal, fish scrap and krill meal shall not be loaded if the temperature at the time of loading exceeds 35 °C or 5 °C above the ambient temperature whichever is higher.

301   This entry only applies to articles such as machinery, apparatus or devices containing dangerous goods as a residue or an integral element of the articles. It shall not be used for articles for which a proper shipping name already exists in Table A of Chapter 3.2. Articles carried under this entry shall only contain dangerous goods which are authorized to be carried in accordance with the provisions of Chapter 3.4 (Limited quantities). The quantity of dangerous goods in articles shall not exceed the quantity specified in Column (7a) of Table A of Chapter 3.2 for each item of dangerous goods contained. If the articles contain more than one item of dangerous goods, the individual dangerous goods shall be enclosed to prevent them reacting dangerously with one another during carriage (see 4.1.1.6 of ADR). When it is required to ensure liquid dangerous goods remain in their intended orientation, orientation arrows shall be displayed on at least two opposite vertical sides with the arrows pointing in the correct direction in accordance with 5.2.1.10.

302   Fumigated cargo transport units containing no other dangerous goods are only subject to the provisions of 5.5.2.

303   Receptacles shall be assigned to the classification code of the gas or mixture of gases contained therein determined in accordance with the provisions of section 2.2.2.

304   This entry may only be used for the transport of non-activated batteries which contain dry potassium hydroxide and which are intended to be activated prior to use by addition of an appropriate amount of water to the individual cells.

305   These substances are not subject to the requirements of ADN when in concentrations of not more than 50 mg/kg.

306   This entry may only be used for substances that are too insensitive for acceptance into Class 1 when tested in accordance with Test Series 2 (see *Manual of Tests and Criteria*, Part I).

307   This entry may only be used for ammonium nitrate based fertilizers. They shall be classified in accordance with the procedure as set out in the Manual of Tests and Criteria, Part III, Section 39 subject to the restrictions of 2.2.51.2.2, thirteenth and fourteenth indents. When used in the said Section 39, the term "competent authority" means the competent authority of the country of origin. If the country of origin is not a Contracting Party to ADN, the classification and conditions of carriage shall be recognized by the competent authority of the first country Contracting Party to ADN reached by the consignment.

309   This entry applies to non-sensitized emulsions, suspensions and gels consisting primarily of a mixture of ammonium nitrate and fuel, intended to produce a Type E blasting explosive only after further processing prior to use.

    The mixture for emulsions typically has the following composition: 60-85% ammonium nitrate, 5-30% water, 2-8% fuel, 0.5-4% emulsifier agent, 0-10% soluble flame suppressants, and trace additives. Other inorganic nitrate salts may replace part of the ammonium nitrate.

    The mixture for suspensions and gels typically has the following composition: 60-85% ammonium nitrate, 0-5% sodium or potassium perchlorate, 0-17% hexamine nitrate or monomethylamine nitrate, 5-30% water, 2-15% fuel, 0.5-4% thickening agent, 0-10% soluble flame suppressants, and trace additives. Other inorganic nitrate salts may replace part of the ammonium nitrate.

    Substances shall satisfy the criteria for classification as an ammonium nitrate emulsion, suspension or gel, intermediate for blasting explosives (ANE) of Test Series 8 of the *Manual of Tests and Criteria*, Part I, Section 18 and be approved by the competent authority.

310   The testing requirements in the Manual of Tests and Criteria, part III, sub-section 38.3 do not apply to production runs, consisting of not more than 100 cells or batteries, or to pre-production prototypes of cells or batteries when these prototypes are carried for testing when packaged in accordance with packing instruction P910 of 4.1.4.1 of ADR or LP905 of 4.1.4.3 of ADR, as applicable.

    The transport document shall include the following statement: "Carriage in accordance with special provision 310".

    Damaged or defective cells, batteries, or cells and batteries contained in equipment shall be carried in accordance with special provision 376.

Cells, batteries or cells and batteries contained in equipment carried for disposal or recycling may be packaged in accordance with special provision 377 and packing instruction P909 of 4.1.4.1 of ADR.

311   Substances shall not be carried under this entry unless approved by the competent authority on the basis of the results of appropriate tests according to Part I of the *Manual of Tests and Criteria*. Packaging shall ensure that the percentage of diluent does not fall below that stated in the competent authority approval, at any time during carriage.

312   *(Deleted)*

313   *(Deleted)*

314   (a)   These substances are liable to exothermic decomposition at elevated temperatures. Decomposition can be initiated by heat or by impurities (e.g. powdered metals (iron, manganese, cobalt, magnesium) and their compounds);

       (b)   During the course of carriage, these substances shall be shaded from direct sunlight and all sources of heat and be placed in adequately ventilated areas.

315   This entry shall not be used for Class 6.1 substances which meet the inhalation toxicity criteria for packing group I described in 2.2.61.1.8.

316   This entry applies only to calcium hypochlorite, dry, when carried in non-friable tablet form.

317   "Fissile-excepted" applies only to those fissile material and packages containing fissile material which are excepted in accordance with 2.2.7.2.3.5.

318   For the purposes of documentation, the proper shipping name shall be supplemented with the technical name (see 3.1.2.8). When the infectious substances to be carried are unknown, but suspected of meeting the criteria for inclusion in category A and assignment to UN No. 2814 or 2900, the words "suspected category A infectious substance" shall be shown, in parentheses, following the proper shipping name on the transport document.

319   Substances packed and packages marked in accordance with packing instruction P650 of ADR are not subject to any other requirements of ADN.

321   These storage systems shall always be considered as containing hydrogen.

322   When carried in non-friable tablet form, these goods are assigned to packing group III.

323   *(Reserved)*

324   This substance needs to be stabilized when in concentrations of not more than 99%.

325   In the case of non-fissile or fissile excepted uranium hexafluoride, the material shall be classified under UN No. 2978.

326   In the case of fissile uranium hexafluoride, the material shall be classified under UN No. 2977.

327   Waste aerosols and waste gas cartridges consigned in accordance with 5.4.1.1.3.1 may be carried under UN Nos. 1950 or 2037, as appropriate, for the purposes of reprocessing or disposal. They need not be protected against movement and inadvertent discharge provided that measures to prevent dangerous build up of pressure and dangerous atmospheres are addressed. Waste aerosols, other than those leaking or severely deformed, shall be packed in accordance with packing instruction P207 of ADR and special provision PP87 of ADR, or packing instruction LP200 of ADR and special packing provision L2 of ADR. Waste gas cartridges, other than those leaking or severely deformed, shall be packed in accordance with packing instruction P003 and special packing provisions PP17 and PP96 of ADR, or packing instruction LP200 and special packing provision L2 of ADR. Leaking or severely deformed aerosols and gas cartridges shall be carried in salvage pressure receptacles or salvage packagings provided appropriate measures are taken to ensure there is no dangerous build up of pressure.

NOTE: For maritime carriage, waste aerosols and waste gas cartridges shall not be carried in closed containers.

Waste gas cartridges that were filled with non-flammable, non-toxic gases of Class 2, group A or O and have been pierced are not subject to ADN.

328   This entry applies to fuel cell cartridges including when contained in equipment or packed with equipment. Fuel cell cartridges installed in or integral to a fuel cell system are regarded as contained in equipment. Fuel cell cartridge means an article that stores fuel for discharge into the fuel cell through (a) valve(s) that control(s) the discharge of fuel into the fuel cell. Fuel cell cartridges, including when contained in equipment, shall be designed and constructed to prevent fuel leakage under normal conditions of carriage.

Fuel cell cartridge design types using liquids as fuels shall pass an internal pressure test at a pressure of 100 kPa (gauge) without leakage.

Except for fuel cell cartridges containing hydrogen in metal hydride which shall be in compliance with special provision 339, each fuel cell cartridge design type shall be shown to pass a 1.2 meter drop test onto an unyielding surface in the orientation most likely to result in failure of the containment system with no loss of contents.

When lithium metal or lithium ion batteries are contained in the fuel cell system, the consignment shall be consigned under this entry and under the appropriate entries for UN 3091 LITHIUM METAL BATTERIES CONTAINED IN EQUIPMENT or UN 3481 LITHIUM ION BATTERIES CONTAINED IN EQUIPMENT.

329   *(Reserved)*

331   *(Reserved)*

332   Magnesium nitrate hexahydrate is not subject to the requirements of ADN.

333   Ethanol and gasoline, motor spirit or petrol mixtures for use in spark-ignition engines (e.g. in automobiles, stationary engines and other engines) shall be assigned to this entry regardless of variations in volatility.

334   A fuel cell cartridge may contain an activator provided it is fitted with two independent means of preventing unintended mixing with the fuel during carriage.

335 Mixtures of solids which are not subject to the requirements of ADN and environmentally hazardous liquids or solids shall be classified as UN 3077 and may be carried under this entry provided there is no free liquid visible at the time the substance is loaded or at the time the packaging or cargo transport unit is closed. Each cargo transport unit shall be leakproof when used for carriage in bulk. If free liquid is visible at the time the mixture is loaded or at the time the packaging or cargo transport unit is closed, the mixture shall be classified as UN 3082. Sealed packets and articles containing less than 10 ml of an environmentally hazardous liquid, absorbed into a solid material but with no free liquid in the packet or article, or containing less than 10 g of an environmentally hazardous solid, are not subject to the requirements of ADN.

336 A single package of non-combustible solid LSA-II or LSA-III material, if carried by air, shall not contain an activity greater than 3 000 A_2.

337 Type B(U) and Type B(M) packages, if carried by air, shall not contain activities greater than the following:

(a) For low dispersible radioactive material: as authorized for the package design as specified in the certificate of approval;

(b) For special form radioactive material: 3 000 A_1 or 100 000 A_2, whichever is the lower; or

(c) For all other radioactive material: 3 000 A_2.

338 Each fuel cell cartridge carried under this entry and designed to contain a liquefied flammable gas shall:

(a) Be capable of withstanding, without leakage or bursting, a pressure of at least two times the equilibrium pressure of the contents at 55 °C;

(b) Not contain more than 200 ml liquefied flammable gas, the vapour pressure of which shall not exceed 1 000 kPa at 55 °C; and

(c) Pass the hot water bath test prescribed in 6.2.6.3.1 of ADR.

339 Fuel cell cartridges containing hydrogen in a metal hydride carried under this entry shall have a water capacity less than or equal to 120 ml.

The pressure in the fuel cell cartridge shall not exceed 5 MPa at 55 °C. The design type shall withstand, without leaking or bursting, a pressure of twice the design pressure of the cartridge at 55 °C or 200 kPa more than the design pressure of the cartridge at 55 °C, whichever is greater. The pressure at which this test is conducted is referred to in the drop test and the hydrogen cycling test as the "minimum shell burst pressure".

Fuel cell cartridges shall be filled in accordance with procedures provided by the manufacturer. The manufacturer shall provide the following information with each fuel cell cartridge:

(a) Inspection procedures to be carried out before initial filling and before refilling of the fuel cell cartridge;

(b) Safety precautions and potential hazards to be aware of;

(c) Method for determining when the rated capacity has been achieved;

(d) Minimum and maximum pressure range;

(e)   Minimum and maximum temperature range; and

(f)   Any other requirements to be met for initial filling and refilling including the type of equipment to be used for initial filling and refilling.

The fuel cell cartridges shall be designed and constructed to prevent fuel leakage under normal conditions of carriage. Each cartridge design type, including cartridges integral to a fuel cell, shall be subjected to and shall pass the following tests:

Drop test

A 1.8 metre drop test onto an unyielding surface in four different orientations:

(a)   Vertically, on the end containing the shut-off valve assembly;

(b)   Vertically, on the end opposite to the shut-off valve assembly;

(c)   Horizontally, onto a steel apex with a diameter of 38 mm, with the steel apex in the upward position; and

(d)   At a 45° angle on the end containing the shut-off valve assembly.

There shall be no leakage, determined by using a soap bubble solution or other equivalent means on all possible leak locations, when the cartridge is charged to its rated charging pressure. The fuel cell cartridge shall then be hydrostatically pressurized to destruction. The recorded burst pressure shall exceed 85% of the minimum shell burst pressure.

Fire test

A fuel cell cartridge filled to rated capacity with hydrogen shall be subjected to a fire engulfment test. The cartridge design, which may include a vent feature integral to it, is deemed to have passed the fire test if:

(a)   The internal pressure vents to zero gauge pressure without rupture of the cartridge; or

(b)   The cartridge withstands the fire for a minimum of 20 minutes without rupture.

Hydrogen cycling test

This test is intended to ensure that a fuel cell cartridge design stress limits are not exceeded during use.

The fuel cell cartridge shall be cycled from not more than 5% rated hydrogen capacity to not less than 95% rated hydrogen capacity and back to not more than 5% rated hydrogen capacity. The rated charging pressure shall be used for charging and temperatures shall be held within the operating temperature range. The cycling shall be continued for at least 100 cycles.

Following the cycling test, the fuel cell cartridge shall be charged and the water volume displaced by the cartridge shall be measured. The cartridge design is deemed to have passed the hydrogen cycling test if the water volume displaced by the cycled cartridge does not exceed the water volume displaced by an uncycled cartridge charged to 95% rated capacity and pressurized to 75% of its minimum shell burst pressure.

Production leak test

Each fuel cell cartridge shall be tested for leaks at 15 °C ± 5 °C, while pressurized to its rated charging pressure. There shall be no leakage, determined by using a soap bubble solution or other equivalent means on all possible leak locations.

Each fuel cell cartridge shall be permanently marked with the following information:

(a) The rated charging pressure in MPa;

(b) The manufacturer's serial number of the fuel cell cartridges or unique identification number; and

(c) The date of expiry based on the maximum service life (year in four digits; month in two digits).

340 Chemical kits, first aid kits and polyester resin kits containing dangerous substances in inner packagings which do not exceed the quantity limits for excepted quantities applicable to individual substances as specified in column (7b) of Table A of Chapter 3.2, may be carried in accordance with Chapter 3.5. Class 5.2 substances, although not individually authorized as excepted quantities in column (7b) of Table A of Chapter 3.2, are authorized in such kits and are assigned Code E2 (see 3.5.1.2).

341 *(Reserved)*

342 Glass inner receptacles (such as ampoules or capsules) intended only for use in sterilization devices, when containing less than 30 ml of ethylene oxide per inner packaging with not more than 300 ml per outer packaging, may be carried in accordance with the provisions in Chapter 3.5, irrespective of the indication of "E0" in column (7b) of Table A of Chapter 3.2 provided that:

(a) After filling, each glass inner receptacle has been determined to be leak-tight by placing the glass inner receptacle in a hot water bath at a temperature, and for a period of time, sufficient to ensure that an internal pressure equal to the vapour pressure of ethylene oxide at 55 °C is achieved. Any glass inner receptacle showing evidence of leakage, distortion or other defect under this test shall not be carried under the terms of this special provision;

(b) In addition to the packaging required by 3.5.2, each glass inner receptacle is placed in a sealed plastics bag compatible with ethylene oxide and capable of containing the contents in the event of breakage or leakage of the glass inner receptacle; and

(c) Each glass inner receptacle is protected by a means of preventing puncture of the plastics bag (e.g. sleeves or cushioning) in the event of damage to the packaging (e.g. by crushing).

343 This entry applies to crude oil containing hydrogen sulphide in sufficient concentration that vapours evolved from the crude oil can present an inhalation hazard. The packing group assigned shall be determined by the flammability hazard and inhalation hazard, in accordance with the degree of danger presented.

344 The provisions of 6.2.6 of ADR shall be met.

345 This gas contained in open cryogenic receptacles with a maximum capacity of 1 litre constructed with glass double walls having the space between the inner and outer wall evacuated (vacuum insulated) is not subject to ADN provided each receptacle is carried in an outer packaging with suitable cushioning or absorbent materials to protect it from impact damage.

346 Open cryogenic receptacles conforming to the requirements of packing instruction P203 of 4.1.4.1 of ADR and containing no dangerous goods except for UN No. 1977 nitrogen, refrigerated liquid, which is fully absorbed in a porous material, are not subject to any other requirements of ADN.

347 This entry shall only be used if the results of Test series 6 (d) of Part I of the *Manual of Tests and Criteria* have demonstrated that any hazardous effects arising from functioning are confined within the package.

348 Batteries manufactured after 31 December 2011 shall be marked with the Watt-hour rating on the outside case.

349 Mixtures of a hypochlorite with an ammonium salt are not to be accepted for carriage. UN No. 1791 hypochlorite solution is a substance of Class 8.

350 Ammonium bromate and its aqueous solutions and mixtures of a bromate with an ammonium salt are not to be accepted for carriage.

351 Ammonium chlorate and its aqueous solutions and mixtures of a chlorate with an ammonium salt are not to be accepted for carriage.

352 Ammonium chlorite and its aqueous solutions and mixtures of a chlorite with an ammonium salt are not to be accepted for carriage.

353 Ammonium permanganate and its aqueous solutions and mixtures of a permanganate with an ammonium salt are not to be accepted for carriage.

354 This substance is toxic by inhalation.

355 Oxygen cylinders for emergency use carried under this entry may include installed actuating cartridges (cartridges, power device of Division 1.4, Compatibility Group C or S), without changing the classification in Class 2 provided the total quantity of deflagrating (propellant) explosives does not exceed 3.2 g per oxygen cylinder. The cylinders with the installed actuating cartridges as prepared for carriage shall have an effective means of preventing inadvertent activation.

356 Metal hydride storage systems intended to be installed in vehicles, wagons, vessels, machinery, engines or aircraft shall be approved by the competent authority of the country of manufacture[1] before acceptance for carriage. The transport document shall include an indication that the package was approved by the competent authority of the country of manufacture[1] or a copy of the competent authority of the country of manufacture[1] approval shall accompany each consignment.

357 Petroleum crude oil containing hydrogen sulphide in sufficient concentration that vapours evolved from the crude oil can present an inhalation hazard shall be consigned under the entry UN 3494 PETROLEUM SOUR CRUDE OIL, FLAMMABLE, TOXIC.

---

[1] *If the country of manufacture is not a Contracting Party to ADN, the approval shall be recognized by the competent authority of a Contracting Party to ADN.*

358   Nitroglycerin solution in alcohol with more than 1% but not more than 5% nitroglycerin may be classified in Class 3 and assigned to UN No. 3064 provided all the requirements of packing instruction P300 of 4.1.4.1 of ADR are complied with.

359   Nitroglycerin solution in alcohol with more than 1% but not more than 5% nitroglycerin shall be classified in Class 1 and assigned to UN No. 0144 if not all the requirements of packing instruction P300 of 4.1.4.1 of ADR are complied with.

360   Vehicles only powered by lithium metal batteries or lithium ion batteries shall be assigned to the entry UN 3171 battery-powered vehicle. Lithium batteries installed in cargo transport units, designed only to provide power external to the transport unit shall be assigned to entry UN 3536 LITHIUM BATTERIES INSTALLED IN CARGO TRANSPORT UNIT lithium ion batteries or lithium metal batteries.

361   This entry applies to electric double layer capacitors with an energy storage capacity greater than 0.3 Wh. Capacitors with an energy storage capacity of 0.3 Wh or less are not subject to ADN. Energy storage capacity means the energy held by a capacitor, as calculated using the nominal voltage and capacitance. All capacitors to which this entry applies, including capacitors containing an electrolyte that does not meet the classification criteria of any class of dangerous goods, shall meet the following conditions:

   (a)   Capacitors not installed in equipment shall be carried in an uncharged state. Capacitors installed in equipment shall be carried either in an uncharged state or protected against short circuit;

   (b)   Each capacitor shall be protected against a potential short circuit hazard in carriage as follows:

      (i)   When a capacitor's energy storage capacity is less than or equal to 10Wh or when the energy storage capacity of each capacitor in a module is less than or equal to 10 Wh, the capacitor or module shall be protected against short circuit or be fitted with a metal strap connecting the terminals; and

      (ii)   When the energy storage capacity of a capacitor or a capacitor in a module is more than 10 Wh, the capacitor or module shall be fitted with a metal strap connecting the terminals;

   (c)   Capacitors containing dangerous goods shall be designed to withstand a 95 kPa pressure differential;

   (d)   Capacitors shall be designed and constructed to safely relieve pressure that may build up in use, through a vent or a weak point in the capacitor casing. Any liquid which is released upon venting shall be contained by the packaging or by the equipment in which a capacitor is installed; and

   (e)   Capacitors shall be marked with the energy storage capacity in Wh.

Capacitors containing an electrolyte not meeting the classification criteria of any class of dangerous goods, including when installed in equipment, are not subject to other provisions of ADN.

Capacitors containing an electrolyte meeting the classification criteria of any class of dangerous goods, with an energy storage capacity of 10 Wh or less are not subject to other provisions of ADN when they are capable of withstanding a 1.2 metre drop test unpackaged on an unyielding surface without loss of contents.

Capacitors containing an electrolyte meeting the classification criteria of any class of dangerous goods that are not installed in equipment and with an energy storage capacity of more than 10 Wh are subject to ADN.

Capacitors installed in equipment and containing an electrolyte meeting the classification criteria of any class of dangerous goods are not subject to other provisions of ADN provided the equipment is packaged in a strong outer packaging constructed of suitable material and of adequate strength and design, in relation to the packaging's intended use and in such a manner as to prevent accidental functioning of capacitors during carriage. Large robust equipment containing capacitors may be offered for carriage unpackaged or on pallets when capacitors are afforded equivalent protection by the equipment in which they are contained.

NOTE: Capacitors which by design maintain a terminal voltage (e.g. asymmetrical capacitors) do not belong to this entry.

362   *(Reserved).*

363   This entry may only be used when the conditions of this special provision are met. No other requirements of ADN apply.

(a)   This entry applies to engines or machinery, powered by fuels classified as dangerous goods via internal combustion systems or fuel cells (e.g. combustion engines, generators, compressors, turbines, heating units, etc.), except vehicle equipment assigned to UN No. 3166 referred to in special provision 666;

NOTE: This entry does not apply to equipment referred to in 1.1.3.2 (a), (d) and (e), 1.1.3.3 and 1.1.3.7.

(b)   Engines or machinery which are empty of liquid or gaseous fuels and which do not contain other dangerous goods, are not subject to ADN.

NOTE 1: An engine or machinery is considered to be empty of liquid fuel when the liquid fuel tank has been drained and the engine or machinery cannot be operated due to a lack of fuel. Engine or machinery components such as fuel lines, fuel filters and injectors do not need to be cleaned, drained or purged to be considered empty of liquid fuels. In addition, the liquid fuel tank does not need to be cleaned or purged.

NOTE 2: An engine or machinery is considered to be empty of gaseous fuels when the gaseous fuel tanks are empty of liquid (for liquefied gases), the pressure in the tanks does not exceed 2 bar and the fuel shut-off or isolation valve is closed and secured.

(c)   Engines and machinery containing fuels meeting the classification criteria of Class 3, shall be assigned to the entries UN No. 3528 ENGINE, INTERNAL COMBUSTION, FLAMMABLE LIQUID POWERED or UN No. 3528 ENGINE, FUEL CELL, FLAMMABLE LIQUID POWERED or UN No. 3528 MACHINERY, INTERNAL COMBUSTION, FLAMMABLE LIQUID POWERED or UN No. 3528 MACHINERY, FUEL CELL, FLAMMABLE LIQUID POWERED, as appropriate.

(d)   Engines and machinery containing fuels meeting the classification criteria of flammable gases of Class 2, shall be assigned to the entries UN No. 3529 ENGINE, INTERNAL COMBUSTION, FLAMMABLE GAS POWERED or UN No. 3529 ENGINE, FUEL CELL, FLAMMABLE GAS POWERED or UN No. 3529 MACHINERY, INTERNAL COMBUSTION, FLAMMABLE GAS POWERED or UN No. 3529 MACHINERY, FUEL CELL, FLAMMABLE GAS POWERED, as appropriate.

Engines and machinery powered by both a flammable gas and a flammable liquid shall be assigned to the appropriate UN No. 3529 entry.

(e)   Engines and machinery containing liquid fuels meeting the classification criteria of 2.2.9.1.10 for environmentally hazardous substances and not meeting the classification criteria of any other class shall be assigned to the entries UN No. 3530 ENGINE, INTERNAL COMBUSTION or UN No. 3530 MACHINERY, INTERNAL COMBUSTION, as appropriate.

(f)   Engines or machinery may contain other dangerous goods than fuels (e.g. batteries, fire extinguishers, compressed gas accumulators or safety devices) required for their functioning or safe operation without being subject to any additional requirements for these other dangerous goods, unless otherwise specified in ADN. However, lithium batteries shall meet the provisions of 2.2.9.1.7, except as provided for in special provision 667.

(g)   The engine or machinery, including the means of containment containing dangerous goods, shall be in compliance with the construction requirements specified by the competent authority of the country of manufacture[2];

(h)   Any valves or openings (e.g. venting devices) shall be closed during carriage;

(i)   The engines or machinery shall be oriented to prevent inadvertent leakage of dangerous goods and secured by means capable of restraining the engines or machinery to prevent any movement during carriage which would change the orientation or cause them to be damaged;

(j)   For UN No. 3528 and UN No. 3530:

Where the engine or machinery contains more than 60 l of liquid fuel and has a capacity of more than 450 l but not more than 3 000 l, it shall be labelled on two opposite sides in accordance with 5.2.2.

Where the engine or machinery contains more than 60 l of liquid fuel and has a capacity of more than 3 000 l, it shall be placarded on two opposite sides. Placards shall correspond to the labels required in Column (5) of Table A of Chapter 3.2 and shall conform to the specifications given in 5.3.1.7. Placards shall be displayed on a background of contrasting colour, or shall have either a dotted or solid outer boundary line.

NOTE: On engines and machinery with a capacity of more than 450 l but containing 60 l of liquid fuel or less, labelling and placarding compliant with the above requirements are permitted.

---

[2]   *For example, compliance with the relevant provisions of Directive 2006/42/EC of the European Parliament and of the Council of 17 May 2006 on machinery, and amending Directive 95/16/EC (Official Journal of the European Union No. L 157 of 9 June 2006, pp. 0024-0086).*

(k)   For UN No. 3529:

Where the fuel tank of the engine or machinery has a water capacity of more than 450 l but not more than 1 000 l, it shall be labelled on two opposite sides in accordance with 5.2.2.

Where the fuel tank of the engine or machinery has a water capacity of more than 1 000 l, it shall be placarded on two opposite sides. Placards shall correspond to the labels required in Column (5) of Table A of Chapter 3.2 and shall conform to the specifications given in 5.3.1.7. Placards shall be displayed on a background of contrasting colour, or shall have either a dotted or solid outer boundary line.

(l)   When the engine or machinery contains more than 1 000 *l* of liquid fuels, for UN No. 3528 and UN No. 3530, or the fuel tank has a water capacity of more than 1 000 *l*, for UN No. 3529:

–   A transport document in accordance with 5.4.1 is required. This transport document shall contain the following additional statement "Transport in accordance with special provision 363".

(m)   The requirements specified in packing instruction P005 of 4.1.4.1 of ADR shall be met.

364   This article may only be carried under the provisions of Chapter 3.4 if, as presented for carriage, the package is capable of passing the test in accordance with Test Series 6(d) of Part I of the *Manual of Tests and Criteria* as determined by the competent authority.

365   For manufactured instruments and articles containing mercury, see UN No. 3506.

366   Manufactured instruments and articles containing not more than 1 kg of mercury are not subject to ADN.

367   For the purposes of documentation:

The proper shipping name "Paint related material" may be used for consignments of packages containing "Paint" and "Paint related material" in the same package;

The proper shipping name "Paint related material, corrosive, flammable" may be used for consignments of packages containing "Paint, corrosive, flammable" and "Paint related material, corrosive, flammable" in the same package;

The proper shipping name "Paint related material, flammable, corrosive" may be used for consignments of packages containing "Paint, flammable, corrosive" and "Paint related material, flammable, corrosive" in the same package; and

The proper shipping name "Printing ink related material" may be used for consignments of packages containing "Printing ink" and "Printing ink related material" in the same package.

368   In the case of non-fissile or fissile-excepted uranium hexafluoride, the material shall be classified under UN No. 3507 or UN No. 2978.

369   In accordance with 2.1.3.5.3 (a), this radioactive material in an excepted package possessing toxic and corrosive properties is classified in Class 6.1 with radioactivity and corrosivity subsidiary hazards.

Uranium hexafluoride may be classified under this entry only if the conditions of 2.2.7.2.4.1.2, 2.2.7.2.4.1.5, 2.2.7.2.4.5.2 and, for fissile-excepted material, of 2.2.7.2.3.5 are met.

In addition to the provisions applicable to the carriage of Class 6.1 substances with a corrosivity subsidiary hazard, the provisions of 5.1.3.2, 5.1.5.2.2, 5.1.5.4.1 (b), 7.5.11 CV33 (3.1), (5.1) to (5.4) and (6) of ADR shall apply.

No Class 7 label is required to be displayed.

370   This entry only applies to ammonium nitrate that meets one of the following criteria:

(a)   ammonium nitrate with more than 0.2% combustible substances, including any organic substance calculated as carbon, to the exclusion of any added substance; or

(b)   ammonium nitrate with not more than 0.2% combustible substances, including any organic substance calculated as carbon, to the exclusion of any added substance, that gives a positive result when tested in accordance with Test Series 2 (see Manual of Tests and Criteria, Part I). See also UN No. 1942.

This entry shall not be used for ammonium nitrate for which a proper shipping name already exists in Table A of Chapter 3.2 including ammonium nitrate mixed with fuel oil (ANFO) or any of the commercial grades of ammonium nitrate.

371   (1)   This entry also applies to articles, containing a small pressure receptacle with a release device. Such articles shall comply with the following requirements:

(i)   The water capacity of the pressure receptacle shall not exceed 0.5 litres and the working pressure shall not exceed 25 bar at 15 °C;

(ii)   The minimum burst pressure of the pressure receptacle shall be at least four times the pressure of the gas at 15 °C;

(iii)   Each article shall be manufactured in such a way that unintentional firing or release is avoided under normal conditions of handling, packing, carriage and use. This may be fulfilled by an additional locking device linked to the activator;

(iv)   Each article shall be manufactured in such a way as to prevent hazardous projections of the pressure receptacle or parts of the pressure receptacle;

(v)   Each pressure receptacle shall be manufactured from material which will not fragment upon rupture;

(vi)   The design type of the article shall be subjected to a fire test. For this test, the provisions of paragraphs 16.6.1.2 except letter g, 16.6.1.3.1 to 16.6.1.3.6, 16.6.1.3.7 (b) and 16.6.1.3.8 of the *Manual of Tests and Criteria* shall be applied. It shall be demonstrated that the article relieves its pressure by means of a fire degradable seal or other pressure relief device, in such a way that the pressure receptacle will not fragment and that the article or fragments of the article do not rocket more than 10 metres;

(vii) The design type of the article shall be subjected to the following test. A stimulating mechanism shall be used to initiate one article in the middle of the packaging. There shall be no hazardous effects outside the package such as disruption of the package, metal fragments or a receptacle which passes through the packaging.

(2) The manufacturer shall produce technical documentation of the design type, manufacture as well as the tests and their results. The manufacturer shall apply procedures to ensure that articles produced in series are made of good quality, conform to the design type and are able to meet the requirements in (1). The manufacturer shall provide such information to the competent authority on request.

372 This entry applies to asymmetric capacitors with an energy storage capacity greater than 0.3 Wh. Capacitors with an energy storage capacity of 0.3 Wh or less are not subject to ADN.

Energy storage capacity means the energy stored in a capacitor, as calculated according to the following equation,

$$Wh = 1/2C_N(U_R^2-U_L^2) \times (1/3600),$$

using the nominal capacitance (C_N), rated voltage (U_R) and rated lower limit voltage (U_L).

All asymmetric capacitors to which this entry applies shall meet the following conditions:

(a) Capacitors or modules shall be protected against short circuit;

(b) Capacitors shall be designed and constructed to safely relieve pressure that may build up in use, through a vent or a weak point in the capacitor casing. Any liquid which is released upon venting shall be contained by packaging or by equipment in which a capacitor is installed;

(c) Capacitors shall be marked with the energy storage capacity in Wh; and

(d) Capacitors containing an electrolyte meeting the classification criteria of any class of dangerous goods shall be designed to withstand a 95 kPa pressure differential;

Capacitors containing an electrolyte not meeting the classification criteria of any class of dangerous goods, including when configured in a module or when installed in equipment are not subject to other provisions of ADN.

Capacitors containing an electrolyte meeting the classification criteria of any class of dangerous goods, with an energy storage capacity of 20 Wh or less, including when configured in a module, are not subject to other provisions of ADN when the capacitors are capable of withstanding a 1.2 metre drop test unpackaged on an unyielding surface without loss of contents.

Capacitors containing an electrolyte meeting the classification criteria of any class of dangerous goods that are not installed in equipment and with an energy storage capacity of more than 20 Wh are subject to ADN.

Capacitors installed in equipment and containing an electrolyte meeting the classification criteria of any class of dangerous goods, are not subject to other provisions of ADN provided that the equipment is packaged in a strong outer packaging constructed of suitable material, and of adequate strength and design, in relation to the packaging's intended use and in such a manner as to prevent accidental functioning of capacitors during carriage. Large robust equipment containing capacitors may be offered for carriage unpackaged or on pallets when capacitors are afforded equivalent protection by the equipment in which they are contained.

NOTE: Notwithstanding the provisions of this special provision, nickel-carbon asymmetric capacitors containing Class 8 alkaline electrolytes shall be carried as UN 2795 BATTERIES, WET, FILLED WITH ALKALI, electric storage.

373   Neutron radiation detectors containing non-pressurized boron trifluoride gas may be carried under this entry provided that the following conditions are met:

(a)   Each radiation detector shall meet the following conditions.

   (i)   The pressure in each detector shall not exceed 105 kPa absolute at 20 °C;

   (ii)   The amount of gas shall not exceed 13 g per detector;

   (iii)   Each detector shall be manufactured under a registered quality assurance programme;

   NOTE: ISO 9001 may be used for this purpose.

   (iv)   Each neutron radiation detector shall be of welded metal construction with brazed metal to ceramic feed through assemblies. These detectors shall have a minimum burst pressure of 1800 kPa as demonstrated by design type qualification testing; and

   (v)   Each detector shall be tested to a 1×10^{-10} cm^3/s leaktightness standard before filling.

(b)   Radiation detectors carried as individual components shall be carried as follows:

   (i)   Detectors shall be packed in a sealed intermediate plastics liner with sufficient absorbent or adsorbent material to absorb or adsorb the entire gas contents;

   (ii)   They shall be packed in strong outer packaging. The completed package shall be capable of withstanding a 1.8 m drop test without leakage of gas contents from detectors;

   (iii)   The total amount of gas from all detectors per outer packaging shall not exceed 52 g.

(c) Completed neutron radiation detection systems containing detectors meeting the conditions of paragraph (a) shall be carried as follows:

   (i) The detectors shall be contained in a strong sealed outer casing;

   (ii) The casing shall contain sufficient absorbent or adsorbent material to absorb or adsorb the entire gas contents;

   (iii) The completed systems shall be packed in strong outer packagings capable of withstanding a 1.8 m drop test without leakage unless a system's outer casing affords equivalent protection.

Packing instruction P200 of 4.1.4.1 of ADR is not applicable.

The transport document shall include the following statement "Transport in accordance with special provision 373".

Neutron radiation detectors containing not more than 1 g of boron trifluoride, including those with solder glass joints, are not subject to ADN provided they meet the requirements in paragraph (a) and are packed in accordance with paragraph (b). Radiation detection systems containing such detectors are not subject to ADN provided they are packed in accordance with paragraph (c).

374 *(Reserved)*

375 These substances when carried in single or combination packagings containing a net quantity per single or inner packaging of 5 l or less for liquids or having a net mass per single or inner packaging of 5 kg or less for solids, are not subject to any other provisions of ADN provided the packagings meet the general provisions of 4.1.1.1, 4.1.1.2 and 4.1.1.4 to 4.1.1.8 of ADR.

376 Lithium ion cells or batteries and lithium metal cells or batteries identified as being damaged or defective such that they do not conform to the type tested according to the applicable provisions of the Manual of Tests and Criteria shall comply with the requirements of this special provision.

For the purposes of this special provision, these may include, but are not limited to:

– Cells or batteries identified as being defective for safety reasons;

– Cells or batteries that have leaked or vented;

– Cells or batteries that cannot be diagnosed prior to carriage; or

– Cells or batteries that have sustained physical or mechanical damage.

NOTE: In assessing a cell or battery as damaged or defective, an assessment or evaluation shall be performed based on safety criteria from the cell, battery or product manufacturer or by a technical expert with knowledge of the cell's or battery's safety features. An assessment or evaluation may include, but is not limited to, the following criteria:

(a) Acute hazard, such as gas, fire, or electrolyte leaking;

(b) The use or misuse of the cell or battery;

(c) Signs of physical damage, such as deformation to cell or battery casing, or colours on the casing;

(d)   *External and internal short circuit protection, such as voltage or isolation measures;*

(e)   *The condition of the cell or battery safety features; or*

(f)   *Damage to any internal safety components, such as the battery management system.*

Cells and batteries shall be carried according to the provisions applicable to UN No. 3090, UN No. 3091, UN No. 3480 and No. UN 3481, except special provision 230 and as otherwise stated in this special provision.

Cells and batteries shall be packed in accordance with packing instructions P908 of 4.1.4.1 of ADR or LP904 of 4.1.4.3 of ADR, as applicable.

Cells and batteries identified as damaged or defective and liable to rapidly disassemble, dangerously react, produce a flame or a dangerous evolution of heat or a dangerous emission of toxic, corrosive or flammable gases or vapours under normal conditions of carriage shall be packed and carried in accordance with packing instruction P911 of 4.1.4.1 of ADR or LP906 of 4.1.4.3 of ADR, as applicable. Alternative packing and/or carriage conditions may be authorized by the competent authority of any ADN Contracting Party who may also recognize an approval granted by the competent authority of a country which is not an ADN Contracting Party provided that this approval has been granted in accordance with the procedures applicable according to RID, ADR, ADN, the IMDG Code or the ICAO Technical Instructions. In both cases the cells and batteries are assigned to transport category 0.

Packages shall be marked "DAMAGED/DEFECTIVE LITHIUM ION BATTERIES" or "DAMAGED/DEFECTIVE LITHIUM METAL BATTERIES", as applicable.

The transport document shall include the following statement "Transport in accordance with special provision 376".

If applicable, a copy of the competent authority approval shall accompany the carriage.

377   Lithium ion and lithium metal cells and batteries and equipment containing such cells and batteries carried for disposal or recycling, either packed together with or packed without non-lithium batteries, may be packaged in accordance with packing instruction P909 of 4.1.4.1 of ADR.

These cells and batteries are not subject to the provisions of 2.2.9.1.7 (a) to (g).

Packages shall be marked "LITHIUM BATTERIES FOR DISPOSAL" or "LITHIUM BATTERIES FOR RECYCLING".

Identified damaged or defective batteries shall be carried in accordance with special provision 376.

378   Radiation detectors containing this gas in non-refillable pressure receptacles not meeting the requirements of Chapter 6.2 and packing instruction P200 of 4.1.4.1 of ADR may be carried under this entry provided:

(a)   The working pressure in each receptacle does not exceed 50 bar;

(b)   The receptacle capacity does not exceed 12 litres;

(c)   Each receptacle has a minimum burst pressure of at least 3 times the working pressure when a relief device is fitted and at least 4 times the working pressure when no relief device is fitted;

(d)   Each receptacle is manufactured from material which will not fragment upon rupture;

(e)   Each detector is manufactured under a registered quality assurance programme;

NOTE: ISO 9001 may be used for this purpose.

(f)   Detectors are carried in strong outer packagings. The complete package shall be capable of withstanding a 1.2 metre drop test without breakage of the detector or rupture of the outer packaging. Equipment that includes a detector shall be packed in a strong outer packaging unless the detector is afforded equivalent protection by the equipment in which it is contained; and

(g)   The transport document includes the following statement "Transport in accordance with special provision 378".

Radiation detectors, including detectors in radiation detection systems, are not subject to any other requirements of ADN if the detectors meet the requirements in (a) to (f) above and the capacity of detector receptacles does not exceed 50 ml.

379   Anhydrous ammonia adsorbed or absorbed on a solid contained in ammonia dispensing systems or receptacles intended to form part of such systems are not subject to the other provisions of ADN if the following conditions are observed:

(a)   The adsorption or absorption presents the following properties:

(i)   The pressure at a temperature of 20 °C in the receptacle is less than 0.6 bar;

(ii)   The pressure at a temperature of 35 °C in the receptacle is less than 1 bar;

(iii)   The pressure at a temperature of 85 °C in the receptacle is less than 12 bar.

(b)   The adsorbent or absorbent material shall not have dangerous properties listed in classes 1 to 8;

(c)   The maximum contents of a receptacle shall be 10 kg; and

(d)   Receptacles containing adsorbed or absorbed ammonia shall meet the following conditions:

(i)   Receptacles shall be made of a material compatible with ammonia as specified in ISO 11114-1:2012 + A1:2017;

(ii)   Receptacles and their means of closure shall be hermetically sealed and able to contain the generated ammonia;

(iii)   Each receptacle shall be able to withstand the pressure generated at 85 °C with a volumetric expansion no greater than 0.1%;

(iv)   Each receptacle shall be fitted with a device that allows for gas evacuation once pressure exceeds 15 bar without violent rupture, explosion or projection; and

(v)   Each receptacle shall be able to withstand a pressure of 20 bar without leakage when the pressure relief device is deactivated.

When carried in an ammonia dispenser, the receptacles shall be connected to the dispenser in such a way that the assembly is guaranteed to have the same strength as a single receptacle.

The properties of mechanical strength mentioned in this special provision shall be tested using a prototype of a receptacle and/or dispenser filled to nominal capacity, by increasing the temperature until the specified pressures are reached.

The test results shall be documented, shall be traceable and shall be communicated to the relevant authorities upon request.

380   *(Reserved)*

381   *(Reserved)*

382   Polymeric beads may be made from polystyrene, poly (methyl methacrylate) or other polymeric material. When it can be demonstrated that no flammable vapour, resulting in a flammable atmosphere, is evolved according to test U1 (Test method for substances liable to evolve flammable vapours) of Part III, sub-section 38.4.4 of the Manual of Tests and Criteria, polymeric beads, expandable need not be classified under this UN number. This test should only be performed when de-classification of a substance is considered.

383   Table tennis balls manufactured from celluloid are not subject to ADN where the net mass of each table tennis ball does not exceed 3.0 g and the total net mass of table tennis balls does not exceed 500 g per package.

384   *(Reserved)*

385   *(Deleted)*

386   When substances are stabilized by temperature control, the provisions of 2.2.41.1.21, 7.1.7, special provision V8 of Chapter 7.2 of ADR, special provision S4 of Chapter 8.5 of ADR and the requirements of Chapter 9.6 of ADR apply. When chemical stabilization is employed, the person offering the packaging, IBC or tank for carriage shall ensure that the level of stabilization is sufficient to prevent the substance in the packaging, IBC or tank from dangerous polymerization at a bulk mean loading temperature of 50 °C, or, in the case of a portable tank, 45 °C. Where chemical stabilization becomes ineffective at lower temperatures within the anticipated duration of carriage, temperature control is required. In making this determination factors to be taken into consideration include, but are not limited to, the capacity and geometry of the packaging, IBC or tank and the effect of any insulation present, the temperature of the substance when offered for carriage, the duration of the journey and the ambient temperature conditions typically encountered in the journey (considering also the season of year), the effectiveness and other properties of the stabilizer employed, applicable operational controls imposed by regulation (e.g. requirements to protect from sources of heat, including other cargo carried at a temperature above ambient) and any other relevant factors.

387 Lithium batteries in conformity with 2.2.9.1.7 (f) containing both primary lithium metal cells and rechargeable lithium ion cells shall be assigned to UN Nos. 3090 or 3091 as appropriate. When such batteries are carried in accordance with special provision 188, the total lithium content of all lithium metal cells contained in the battery shall not exceed 1.5 g and the total capacity of all lithium ion cells contained in the battery shall not exceed 10 Wh.

388 UN No. 3166 entries apply to vehicles powered by flammable liquid or gas internal combustion engines or fuel cells.

Vehicles powered by a fuel cell engine shall be assigned to the entries UN No. 3166 VEHICLE, FUEL CELL, FLAMMABLE GAS POWERED or UN No. 3166 VEHICLE, FUEL CELL, FLAMMABLE LIQUID POWERED, as appropriate. These entries include hybrid electric vehicles powered by both a fuel cell and an internal combustion engine with wet batteries, sodium batteries, lithium metal batteries or lithium ion batteries, carried with the battery(ies) installed.

Other vehicles which contain an internal combustion engine shall be assigned to the entries UN No. 3166 VEHICLE, FLAMMABLE GAS POWERED or UN No. 3166 VEHICLE, FLAMMABLE LIQUID POWERED, as appropriate. These entries include hybrid electric vehicles powered by both an internal combustion engine and wet batteries, sodium batteries, lithium metal batteries or lithium ion batteries, carried with the battery(ies) installed.

If a vehicle is powered by a flammable liquid and a flammable gas internal combustion engine, it shall be assigned to UN No. 3166 VEHICLE, FLAMMABLE GAS POWERED.

Entry UN No. 3171 only applies to vehicles powered by wet batteries, sodium batteries, lithium metal batteries or lithium ion batteries and equipment powered by wet batteries or sodium batteries carried with these batteries installed.

For the purpose of this special provision, vehicles are self-propelled apparatus designed to carry one or more persons or goods. Examples of such vehicles are cars, motorcycles, scooters, three- and four-wheeled vehicles or motorcycles, trucks, locomotives, bicycles (pedal cycles with a motor) and other vehicles of this type (e.g. self-balancing vehicles or vehicles not equipped with at least one seating position), wheelchairs, lawn tractors, self-propelled farming and construction equipment, boats and aircraft. This includes vehicles carried in a packaging. In this case some parts of the vehicle may be detached from its frame to fit into the packaging.

Examples of equipment are lawnmowers, cleaning machines or model boats and model aircraft. Equipment powered by lithium metal batteries or lithium ion batteries shall be assigned to the entries UN No. 3091 LITHIUM METAL BATTERIES CONTAINED IN EQUIPMENT or UN No. 3091 LITHIUM METAL BATTERIES PACKED WITH EQUIPMENT or UN No. 3481 LITHIUM ION BATTERIES CONTAINED IN EQUIPMENT or UN No. 3481 LITHIUM ION BATTERIES PACKED WITH EQUIPMENT, as appropriate. Lithium ion batteries or lithium metal batteries installed in a cargo transport unit and designed only to provide power external to the cargo transport unit shall be assigned to the entry UN 3536 LITHIUM BATTERIES INSTALLED IN CARGO TRANSPORT UNIT lithium ion batteries or lithium metal batteries.

Dangerous goods, such as batteries, airbags, fire extinguishers, compressed gas accumulators, safety devices and other integral components of the vehicle that are necessary for the operation of the vehicle or for the safety of its operator or passengers, shall be securely installed in the vehicle and are not otherwise subject to ADN.

However, lithium batteries shall meet the provisions of 2.2.9.1.7, except as otherwise provided for in special provision 667.

Where a lithium battery installed in a vehicle or equipment is damaged or defective, the vehicle or equipment shall be carried in accordance with the conditions defined in special provision 667 (c).

389   This entry only applies to lithium ion batteries or lithium metal batteries installed in a cargo transport unit and designed only to provide power external to the cargo transport unit. The lithium batteries shall meet the provisions of 2.2.9.1.7 (a) to (g) and contain the necessary systems to prevent overcharge and over discharge between the batteries.

The batteries shall be securely attached to the interior structure of the cargo transport unit (e.g., by means of placement in racks, cabinets, etc.) in such a manner as to prevent short circuits, accidental operation, and significant movement relative to the cargo transport unit under the shocks, loadings and vibrations normally incident to carriage. Dangerous goods necessary for the safe and proper operation of the cargo transport unit (e.g., fire extinguishing systems and air conditioning systems), shall be properly secured to or installed in the cargo transport unit and are not otherwise subject to ADN. Dangerous goods not necessary for the safe and proper operation of the cargo transport unit shall not be carried within the cargo transport unit.

The batteries inside the cargo transport unit are not subject to marking or labelling requirements. Except as provided in 1.1.3.6 of RID or ADR, the cargo transport unit shall bear orange-coloured plates in accordance with 5.3.2.2 and placards in accordance with 5.3.1.1 on two opposing sides.

390   When a package contains a combination of lithium batteries contained in equipment and lithium batteries packed with equipment, the following requirements apply for the purposes of package marking and documentation:

(a)   the package shall be marked "UN 3091" or "UN 3481", as appropriate. If a package contains both lithium ion batteries and lithium metal batteries packed with and contained in equipment, the package shall be marked as required for both battery types. However, button cell batteries installed in equipment (including circuit boards) need not be considered;

(b)   the transport document shall indicate "UN 3091 LITHIUM METAL BATTERIES PACKED WITH EQUIPMENT" or "UN 3481 LITHIUM ION BATTERIES PACKED WITH EQUIPMENT", as appropriate. If a package contains both lithium metal batteries and lithium ion batteries packed with and contained in equipment, then the transport document shall indicate both "UN 3091 LITHIUM METAL BATTERIES PACKED WITH EQUIPMENT" and "UN 3481 LITHIUM ION BATTERIES PACKED WITH EQUIPMENT".

391   *(Reserved)*

392   For the carriage of fuel gas containment systems designed and approved to be fitted in motor vehicles containing this gas the provisions of 4.1.4.1 and Chapter 6.2 of ADR need not be applied when carried for disposal, recycling, repair, inspection, maintenance or from where they are manufactured to a vehicle assembly plant, provided the following conditions are met:

(a)   The fuel gas containment systems shall meet the requirements of the standards or regulations for fuel tanks for vehicles, as applicable. Examples of applicable standards and regulations are:

LPG tanks	
UN Regulation No. 67 Revision 2	Uniform provisions concerning: I. Approval of specific equipment of vehicles of category M and N using liquefied petroleum gases in their propulsion system; II. Approval of vehicles of category M and N fitted with specific equipment for the use of liquefied petroleum gases in their propulsion system with regard to the installation of such equipment
UN Regulation No. 115	Uniform provisions concerning the approval of: I. Specific LPG (liquefied petroleum gases) retrofit systems to be installed in motor vehicles for the use of LPG in their propulsion systems; II Specific CNG (compressed natural gas) retrofit systems to be installed in motor vehicles for the use of CNG in their propulsion system
CNG and LNG tanks	
UN Regulation No. 110	Uniform provisions concerning the approval of: I. Specific components of motor vehicles using compressed natural gas (CNG) and/or liquefied natural gas (LNG) in their propulsion system II. Vehicles with regard to the installation of specific components of an approved type for the use of compressed natural gas (CNG) and/or liquefied natural gas (LNG) in their propulsion system
UN Regulation No. 115	Uniform provisions concerning the approval of: I. Specific LPG (liquefied petroleum gases) retrofit systems to be installed in motor vehicles for the use of LPG in their propulsion systems; II Specific CNG (compressed natural gas) retrofit systems to be installed in motor vehicles for the use of CNG in their propulsion system
ISO 11439:2013	Gas cylinders — High pressure cylinders for the on-board storage of natural gas as a fuel for automotive vehicles
ISO 15500-Series	Road vehicles -- Compressed natural gas (CNG) fuel system components – several parts as applicable
ANSI NGV 2	Compressed natural gas vehicle fuel containers
CSA B51 Part 2:2014	Boiler, pressure vessel, and pressure piping code Part 2 Requirements for high-pressure cylinders for on-board storage of fuels for automotive vehicles

Hydrogen pressure tanks	
Global Technical Regulation (GTR) No. 13	Global technical regulation on hydrogen and fuel cell vehicles (ECE/TRANS/180/Add.13).
ISO/TS 15869:2009	Gaseous hydrogen and hydrogen blends - Land vehicle fuel tanks
Regulation (EC) No.79/2009	Regulation (EC) No. 79/2009 of the European Parliament and of the Council of 14 January 2009 on type approval of hydrogen-powered motor vehicles, and amending Directive 2007/46/EC
Regulation (EU) No. 406/2010	Commission Regulation (EU) No 406/2010 of 26 April 2010 implementing Regulation (EC) No 79/2009 of the European Parliament and of the Council on type-approval of hydrogen-powered motor vehicles
UN Regulation No. 134	Uniform provisions concerning the approval of motor vehicles and their components with regard to the safety-related performance of hydrogen-fuelled vehicles (HFCV)
CSA B51 Part 2: 2014	Boiler, pressure vessel, and pressure piping code – Part 2: Requirements for high-pressure cylinders for on-board storage of fuels for automotive vehicles

Gas tanks designed and constructed in accordance with previous versions of relevant standards or regulations for gas tanks for motor vehicles, which were applicable at the time of the certification of the vehicles for which the gas tanks were designed and constructed may continue to be carried;

(b)   The fuel gas containment systems shall be leakproof and shall not exhibit any signs of external damage which may affect their safety;

NOTE 1: *Criteria may be found in standard ISO 11623:2015 Gas cylinders – Composite construction – Periodic inspection and testing (or ISO 19078:2013 Gas cylinders – Inspection of the cylinder installation, and requalification of high pressure cylinders for the on-board storage of natural gas as a fuel for automotive vehicles).*

NOTE 2: *If the fuel gas containment systems are not leakproof or are overfilled or if they exhibit damage that could affect their safety (e.g. in case of a safety related recall), they shall only be carried in salvage pressure receptacles in conformity with ADN.*

(c)   If a fuel gas containment system is equipped with two valves or more integrated in line, the two valves shall be closed as to be gastight under normal conditions of carriage. If only one valve exists or only one valve works, all openings with the exception of the opening of the pressure relief device shall be closed as to be gastight under normal conditions of carriage;

(d)   Fuel gas containment systems shall be carried in such a way as to prevent obstruction of the pressure relief device or any damage to the valves and any other pressurised part of the fuel gas containment systems and unintentional release of the gas under normal conditions of carriage. The fuel gas containment system shall be secured in order to prevent slipping, rolling or vertical movement;

(e)   Valves shall be protected by one of the methods described in 4.1.6.8 (a) to (e) of ADR;

(f)   Except for the case of fuel gas containment systems removed for disposal, recycling, repair, inspection or maintenance, they shall be filled with not more than 20% of their nominal filling ratio or nominal working pressure, as applicable;

(g)   Notwithstanding the provisions of Chapter 5.2, when fuel gas containment systems are consigned in a handling device, marks and labels may be affixed to the handling device; and

(h)   Notwithstanding the provisions of 5.4.1.1.1 (f) the information on the total quantity of dangerous goods may be replaced by the following information:

(i)   The number of fuel gas containment systems; and

(ii)   In the case of liquefied gases the total net mass (kg) of gas of each fuel gas containment system and, in the case of compressed gases, the total water capacity (l) of each fuel gas containment system followed by the nominal working pressure.

Examples for information in the transport document:

Example 1: "UN 1971 natural gas, compressed, 2.1, 1 fuel gas containment system of 50 *l* in total, 200 bar".

Example 2: "UN 1965 hydrocarbon gas mixture, liquefied, n.o.s., 2.1, 3 fuel gas containment systems, each of 15 kg net mass of gas"

393   The nitrocellulose shall meet the criteria of the Bergmann-Junk test or methyl violet paper test in the Manual of Tests and Criteria Appendix 10. Tests of type 3 (c) need not be applied.

394   The nitrocellulose shall meet the criteria of the Bergmann-Junk test or methyl violet paper test in the Manual of Tests and Criteria Appendix 10.

395   This entry shall only be used for solid medical waste of Category A carried for disposal.

396   Large and robust articles may be carried with connected gas cylinders with the valves open regardless of 4.1.6.5 of ADR provided:

(a)   The gas cylinders contain nitrogen of UN No. 1066 or compressed gas of UN No. 1956 or compressed air of UN No. 1002;

(b)   The gas cylinders are connected with the article through pressure regulators and fixed piping in such a way that the pressure of the gas (gauge pressure) in the article does not exceed 35 kPa (0.35 bar);

(c)   The gas cylinders are properly secured so that they cannot move in relation to the article and are fitted with strong and pressure resistant hoses and pipes;

(d)   The gas cylinders, pressure regulators, piping and other components are protected from damage and impacts during carriage by wooden crates or other suitable means;

(e) The transport document includes the following statement "TRANSPORT IN ACCORDANCE WITH SPECIAL PROVISION 396";

(f) Cargo transport units containing articles carried with cylinders with open valves containing a gas presenting a risk of asphyxiation are well ventilated and marked in accordance with 5.5.3.6.

397 Mixtures of nitrogen and oxygen containing not less than 19.5% and not more than 23.5% oxygen by volume may be carried under this entry when no other oxidizing gases are present. A Class 5.1 subsidiary hazard label (model No. 5.1, see 5.2.2.2.2) is not required for any concentrations within this limit.

398 This entry applies to mixtures of butylenes, 1-butylene, cis-2-butylene and trans-2-butylene. For isobutylene, see UN No. 1055.

NOTE: For additional information to be added in the transport document, see 5.4.1.2.2 (e).

399-499 *(Reserved)*

500 *(Deleted)*

501 For naphthalene, molten, see UN No. 2304.

502 UN No. 2006 plastics, nitrocellulose-based, self-heating, n.o.s., and UN No. 2002 celluloid scrap are substances of Class 4.2.

503 For phosphorus, white, molten, see UN No. 2447.

504 UN No. 1847 potassium sulphide, hydrated with not less than 30% water of crystallization, UN No. 1849 sodium sulphide, hydrated with not less than 30% water of crystallization and UN No. 2949 sodium hydrosulphide, hydrated with not less than 25% water of crystallization are substances of Class 8.

505 UN No. 2004 magnesium diamide is a substance of Class 4.2.

506 Alkaline earth metals and alkaline earth metal alloys in pyrophoric form are substances of Class 4.2.

UN No. 1869 magnesium or magnesium alloys containing more than 50% magnesium as pellets, turnings or ribbons, are substances of Class 4.1.

507 UN No. 3048 aluminium phosphide pesticides, with additives inhibiting the emission of toxic flammable gases are substances of Class 6.1.

508 UN No. 1871 titanium hydride and UN No. 1437 zirconium hydride are substances of Class 4.1. UN No. 2870 aluminium borohydride is a substance of Class 4.2.

509 UN No. 1908 chlorite solution is a substance of Class 8.

510 UN No. 1755 chromic acid solution is a substance of Class 8.

511 UN No. 1625 mercuric nitrate, UN No. 1627 mercurous nitrate and UN No. 2727 thallium nitrate are substances of Class 6.1. Thorium nitrate, solid, uranyl nitrate hexahydrate solution and uranyl nitrate, solid are substances of Class 7.

512   UN No. 1730 antimony pentachloride, liquid, UN No. 1731 antimony pentachloride solution, UN No. 1732 antimony pentafluoride and UN No. 1733 antimony trichloride are substances of Class 8.

513   UN No. 0224 barium azide, dry or wetted with less than 50% water, by mass, is a substance of Class 1. UN No. 1571 barium azide, wetted with not less than 50% water, by mass, is a substance of Class 4.1. UN No. 1854 barium alloys, pyrophoric, are substances of Class 4.2. UN No. 1445 barium chlorate, solid, UN No. 1446 barium nitrate, UN No. 1447 barium perchlorate, solid, UN No. 1448 barium permanganate, UN No. 1449 barium peroxide, UN No. 2719 barium bromate, UN No. 2741 barium hypochlorite with more than 22% available chlorine, UN No. 3405 barium chlorate, solution and UN No. 3406 barium perchlorate, solution, are substances of Class 5.1. UN No. 1565 barium cyanide and UN No. 1884 barium oxide are substances of Class 6.1.

514   UN No. 2464 beryllium nitrate is a substance of Class 5.1.

515   UN No. 1581 chloropicrin and methyl bromide mixture and UN No. 1582 chloropicrin and methyl chloride mixture are substances of Class 2.

516   UN No. 1912 methyl chloride and methylene chloride mixture is a substance of Class 2.

517   UN No. 1690 sodium fluoride, solid, UN No. 1812 potassium fluoride, solid, UN No. 2505 ammonium fluoride, UN No. 2674 sodium fluorosilicate, UN No. 2856 fluorosilicates, n.o.s., UN No. 3415 sodium fluoride, solution and UN No. 3422 potassium fluoride, solution, are substances of Class 6.1.

518   UN No. 1463 chromium trioxide, anhydrous (chromic acid, solid) is a substance of Class 5.1.

519   UN No. 1048 hydrogen bromide, anhydrous, is a substance of Class 2.

520   UN No. 1050 hydrogen chloride, anhydrous, is a substance of Class 2.

521   Solid chlorites and hypochlorites are substances of Class 5.1.

522   UN No. 1873 perchloric acid aqueous solution with more than 50% but not more than 72% pure acid, by mass are substances of Class 5.1. Perchloric acid solutions containing more than 72% pure acid, by mass, or mixtures of perchloric acid with any liquid other than water, are not to be accepted for carriage.

523   UN No. 1382 anhydrous potassium sulphide and UN No. 1385 anhydrous sodium sulphide and their hydrates with less than 30% water of crystallization, and UN No. 2318 sodium hydrosulphide with less than 25% water of crystallization are substances of Class 4.2.

524   UN No. 2858 finished zirconium products of a thickness of 18 μm or more are substances of Class 4.1.

525   Solutions of inorganic cyanides with a total cyanide ion content of more than 30% shall be classified in packing group I, solutions with a total cyanide ion content of more than 3% and not more than 30% in packing group II and solutions with a cyanide ion content of more than 0.3% and not more than 3% in packing group III.

526   UN No. 2000 celluloid is assigned to Class 4.1.

527   (Reserved)

528　UN No. 1353 fibres or fabrics impregnated with weakly nitrated cellulose, non-self heating are substances of Class 4.1.

529　UN No. 0135 mercury fulminate, wetted with not less than 20% water, or mixture of alcohol and water, by mass, is a substance of Class 1. Mercurous chloride (calomel) is a substance of Class 6.1 (UN No. 2025).

530　UN No. 3293 hydrazine, aqueous solution with not more than 37% hydrazine, by mass, is a substance of Class 6.1.

531　Mixtures having a flash-point below 23 °C and containing more than 55% nitrocellulose, whatever its nitrogen content or containing not more than 55% nitrocellulose with a nitrogen content above 12.6% (by dry mass), are substances of Class 1 (see UN Nos. 0340 or 0342) or of Class 4.1 (UN Nos. 2555, 2556 or 2557).

532　UN No. 2672 ammonia solution containing not less than 10% but not more than 35% ammonia is a substance of Class 8.

533　UN No. 1198 formaldehyde solutions, flammable are substances of Class 3. Formaldehyde solutions, non-flammable, with less than 25% formaldehyde are not subject to the requirements of ADN.

534　While in some climatic conditions, petrol (gasoline) may have a vapour pressure at 50 °C of more than 110 kPa (1.10 bar) but not more than 150 kPa (1.50 bar) it is to continue to be considered as a substance having a vapour pressure at 50 °C of not more than 110 kPa (1.10 bar).

535　UN No. 1469 lead nitrate, UN No. 1470 lead perchlorate, solid and UN No. 3408 lead perchlorate, solution are substances of Class 5.1.

536　For naphthalene, solid, see UN No. 1334.

537　UN No. 2869 titanium trichloride mixture, not pyrophoric, is a substance of Class 8.

538　For sulphur (in the solid state), see UN No. 1350.

539　Solutions of isocyanates having a flash-point of not less than 23 °C are substances of Class 6.1.

540　UN No. 1326 hafnium powder, wetted, UN No. 1352 titanium powder, wetted or UN No. 1358 zirconium powder, wetted, with not less than 25% water, are substances of Class 4.1.

541　Nitrocellulose mixtures with a water content, alcohol content or plasticizer content lower than the stated limits are substances of Class 1.

542　Talc containing tremolite and/or actinolite is covered by this entry.

543　UN No. 1005 ammonia, anhydrous, UN No. 3318 ammonia solution with more than 50% ammonia and UN No. 2073 ammonia solution, with more than 35% but not more than 50% ammonia, are substances of Class 2. Ammonia solutions with not more than 10% ammonia are not subject to the requirements of ADN.

544　UN No. 1032 dimethylamine, anhydrous, UN No. 1036 ethylamine, UN No. 1061 methylamine, anhydrous and UN No. 1083 trimethylamine, anhydrous, are substances of Class 2.

545   UN No. 0401 dipicryl sulphide, wetted with less than 10% water by mass is a substance of Class 1.

546   UN No. 2009 zirconium, dry, finished sheets, strip or coiled wire, in thicknesses of less than 18 μm, is a substance of Class 4.2. Zirconium, dry, finished sheets, strip or coiled wire, in thicknesses of 254 μm or more, is not subject to the requirements of ADN.

547   UN No. 2210 maneb or UN No. 2210 maneb preparations in self-heating form are substances of Class 4.2.

548   Chlorosilanes which, in contact with water, emit flammable gases, are substances of Class 4.3.

549   Chlorosilanes having a flash-point of less than 23 °C and which, in contact with water, do not emit flammable gases are substances of Class 3. Chlorosilanes having a flash-point equal to or greater than 23 °C and which, in contact with water, do not emit flammable gases are substances of Class 8.

550   UN No. 1333 cerium in slabs, rods or ingots is a substance of Class 4.1.

551   Solutions of these isocyanates having a flash-point below 23 °C are substances of Class 3.

552   Metals and metal alloys in powdered or other flammable form, liable to spontaneous combustion, are substances of Class 4.2. Metals and metal alloys in powdered or other flammable form which, in contact with water, emit flammable gases are substances of Class 4.3.

553   This mixture of hydrogen peroxide and peroxyacetic acid shall, in laboratory testing (see *Manual of Tests and Criteria*, Part II, section 20), neither detonate in the cavitated state nor deflagrate at all and shall show no effect when heated under confinement nor any explosive power. The formulation shall be thermally stable (self-accelerating decomposition temperature 60 °C or higher for a 50 kg package), and a liquid compatible with peroxyacetic acid shall be used for desensitization. Formulations not meeting these criteria are to be regarded as substances of Class 5.2 (see *Manual of Tests and Criteria*, Part II, paragraph 20.4.3 (g)).

554   Metal hydrides which, in contact with water, emit flammable gases are substances of Class 4.3. UN No. 2870 aluminium borohydride or UN No. 2870 aluminium borohydride in devices is a substance of Class 4.2.

555   Dust and powder of metals in non-spontaneously combustible form, non-toxic which nevertheless, in contact with water, emit flammable gases, are substances of Class 4.3.

556   *(Deleted)*

557   Dust and powder of metals in pyrophoric form are substances of Class 4.2.

558   Metals and metal alloys in pyrophoric form are substances of Class 4.2. Metals and metal alloys which, in contact with water, do not emit flammable gases and are not pyrophoric or self-heating, but which are easily ignited, are substances of Class 4.1.

559   *(Deleted)*

560   An elevated temperature liquid, n.o.s. at or above 100 °C (including molten metals and molten salts) or, for a substance having a flash-point, at a temperature below its flash-point, is a substance of Class 9 (UN No. 3257).

561   Chloroformates having predominantly corrosive properties are substances of Class 8.

562   Spontaneously combustible organometallic compounds are substances of Class 4.2. Water-reactive organometallic compounds, flammable, are substances of Class 4.3.

563   UN No. 1905 selenic acid is a substance of Class 8.

564   UN No. 2443 vanadium oxytrichloride, UN No. 2444 vanadium tetrachloride and UN No. 2475 vanadium trichloride are substances of Class 8.

565   Unspecified wastes resulting from medical/veterinary treatment of humans/animals or from biological research, and which are unlikely to contain substances of Class 6.2 shall be assigned to this entry. Decontaminated clinical wastes or wastes resulting from biological research which previously contained infectious substances are not subject to the requirements of Class 6.2.

566   UN No. 2030 hydrazine aqueous solution, with more than 37% hydrazine, by mass, is a substance of Class 8.

567   (*Deleted*)

568   Barium azide with a water content lower than the stated limit is a substance of Class 1, UN No. 0224.

569-579   (*Reserved*)

580   (*Deleted*)

581   This entry covers mixtures of propadiene with 1 to 4% methylacetylene as well as the following mixtures:

Mixture	Content, % by volume			Permitted technical name for purposes of 5.4.1.1
	Methylacetylene and propadiene, not more than	Propane and propylene, not more than	C$_4$-saturated hydrocarbons, not less than	
P1	63	24	14	"Mixture P1"
P2	48	50	5	"Mixture P2"

582   This entry covers, *inter alia*, mixtures of gases indicated by the letter R ..., with the following properties:

Mixture	Maximum vapour pressure at 70 °C (MPa)	Minimum density at 50 °C (kg/l)	Permitted technical name for purposes of 5.4.1.1
F1	1.3	1.30	"Mixture F1"
F2	1.9	1.21	"Mixture F2"
F3	3.0	1.09	"Mixture F3"

NOTE 1: *Trichlorofluoromethane (refrigerant R 11), 1,1,2-trichloro-1,2,2-trifluoroethane (refrigerant R 113), 1,1,1-trichloro-2,2,2-trifluoroethane (refrigerant R 113a), 1-chloro-1,2,2-trifluoroethane (refrigerant R 133) and 1-chloro-1,1,2-trifluoroethane (refrigerant R 133 b) are not substances of Class 2. They may, however, enter into the composition of mixtures F 1 to F 3.*

NOTE 2: *The reference densities correspond to the densities of dichlorofluoromethane (1.30 kg/l), dichloridifluoromethane (1.21 kg/l) and chlorodifluoromethane (1.09 kg/l).*

583   This entry covers, *inter alia*, mixtures of gases, with the following properties:

Mixture	Maximun vapour pressure at 70 °C (MPa)	Minimun density at 50 °C (kg/l)	Permitted technical name[a] for purposes of 5.4.1.1
A	1.1	0.525	"Mixture A" or "Butane"
A01	1.6	0.516	"Mixture A01" or "Butane"
A02	1.6	0.505	"Mixture A02" or "Butane"
A0	1.6	0.495	"Mixture A0" or "Butane"
A1	2.1	0.485	"Mixture A1"
B1	2.6	0.474	"Mixture B1"
B2	2.6	0.463	"Mixture B2"
B	2.6	0.450	"Mixture B"
C	3.1	0.440	"Mixture C" or "Propane"

[a] *For carriage in tanks, the trade names "Butane" or "Propane" may be used only as a complement.*

584   This gas is not subject to the requirements of ADN when:

– it contains not more than 0.5% air in the gaseous state;

– it is contained in metal capsules (sodors, sparklets) free from defects which may impair their strength;

– the leakproofness of the closure of the capsule is ensured;

– a capsule contains not more than 25 g of this gas;

– a capsule contains not more than 0.75 g of this gas per cm^3 of capacity.

585   (*Deleted*).

586   Hafnium, titanium and zirconium powders shall contain a visible excess of water. Hafnium, titanium and zirconium powders, wetted, mechanically produced, of a particle size of 53 μm and over, or chemically produced, of a particle size of 840 μm and over, are not subject to the requirements of ADN.

587   Barium stearate and barium titanate are not subject to the requirements of ADN.

588   Solid hydrated forms of aluminium bromide and aluminium chloride are not subject to the requirements of ADN.

589   (*Deleted*)

590   Ferric chloride hexahydrate is not subject to the requirements of ADN.

591   Lead sulphate with not more than 3% free acid is not subject to the requirements of Class 8 of ADN.

592   Uncleaned empty packagings (including empty IBCs and large packagings), empty tank-vehicles, empty tank wagons, empty demountable tanks, empty portable tanks, empty tank-containers and empty small containers which have contained this substance are not subject to the requirements of ADN.

593   This gas, when used for cooling goods not fulfilling the criteria of any class, e.g. medical or biological specimens, if contained in double wall receptacles which comply with the provisions of packing instruction P203, paragraph (6) for open cryogenic receptacles of 4.1.4.1 of ADR, is not subject to the requirements of ADN except as specified in 5.5.3.

594 The following articles, manufactured and filled according to the provisions applied in the country of manufacture, are not subject to the requirements of ADN:

(a) UN No. 1044 fire extinguishers provided with protection against inadvertent discharge, when:

– they are packaged in a strong outer packaging; or

– they are large fire extinguishers which meet the requirements of special packing provision PP91 of packing instruction P003 in 4.1.4.1 of ADR;

(b) UN No. 3164 articles, pressurized pneumatic or hydraulic, designed to withstand stresses greater than the internal gas pressure by virtue of transmission of force, intrinsic strength or construction, when they are packaged in a strong outer packaging.

NOTE: "Provisions applied in the country of manufacture" means the provisions applicable in the country of manufacture or those applicable in the country of use.

596 Cadmium pigments, such as cadmium sulphides, cadmium sulphoselenides and cadmium salts of higher fatty acids (e.g. cadmium stearate), are not subject to the requirements of ADN.

597 Acetic acid solutions with not more than 10% pure acid by mass are not subject to the requirements of ADN.

598 The following are not subject to the requirements of ADN:

(a) New storage batteries when:

– they are secured in such a way that they cannot slip, fall or be damaged;

– they are provided with carrying devices, unless they are suitably stacked, e.g. on pallets;

– there are no dangerous traces of alkalis or acids on the outside;

– they are protected against short circuits;

(b) Used storage batteries when:

– their cases are undamaged;

– they are secured in such a way that they cannot leak, slip, fall or be damaged, e.g. by stacking on pallets;

– there are no dangerous traces of alkalis or acids on the outside of the articles;

– they are protected against short circuits.

"Used storage batteries" means storage batteries carried for recycling at the end of their normal service life.

599 (*Deleted*)

600 Vanadium pentoxide, fused and solidified, is not subject to the requirements of ADN.

601   Pharmaceutical products (medicines) ready for use, which are substances manufactured and packaged for retail sale or distribution for personal or household consumption are not subject to the requirements of ADN.

602   Phosphorus sulphides which are not free from yellow and white phosphorus are not to be accepted for carriage.

603   Anhydrous hydrogen cyanide not meeting the description for UN No. 1051 or UN No. 1614 is not to be accepted for carriage. Hydrogen cyanide (hydrocyanic acid) containing less than 3% water is stable, if the pH-value is 2.5 ± 0.5 and the liquid is clear and colourless.

604 to 606   (Deleted)

607   Mixtures of potassium nitrate and sodium nitrite with an ammonium salt are not to be accepted for carriage.

608   (Deleted)

609   Tetranitromethane not free from combustible impurities is not to be accepted for carriage.

610   The carriage of this substance, when it contains more than 45% hydrogen cyanide is prohibited.

611   Ammonium nitrate containing more than 0.2% combustible substances (including any organic substance calculated as carbon) is not to be accepted for carriage unless it is a constituent of a substance or article of Class 1.

612   (Reserved)

613   Chloric acid solution containing more than 10% chloric acid and mixtures of chloric acid with any liquid other than water is not to be accepted for carriage.

614   2,3,7,8-tetrachlorodibenzo-p-dioxin (TCDD) in concentrations considered highly toxic according to the criteria in 2.2.61.1 is not to be accepted for carriage.

615   (Reserved)

616   Substances containing more than 40% liquid nitric esters shall satisfy the exudation test specified in 2.3.1.

617   In addition to the type of explosive, the commercial name of the particular explosive shall be marked on the package.

618   In receptacles containing 1,2-butadiene, the oxygen concentration in the gaseous phase shall not exceed 50 ml/m^3.

619 to 622 (Reserved)

623   UN No. 1829 sulphur trioxide shall be inhibited. Sulphur trioxide, 99.95% pure or above, may be carried without inhibitor in tanks provided that its temperature is maintained at or above 32.5 °C. For the carriage of this substance without inhibitor in tanks at a minimum temperature of 32.5 °C, the specification **"Transport under minimum temperature of the product of 32.5 °C"** shall appear in the transport document.

625   Packages containing these articles shall be clearly marked as follows:

"UN 1950 AEROSOLS"

626-631   *(Reserved)*

632   Considered to be spontaneously flammable (pyrophoric).

633   Packages and small containers containing this substance shall bear the following mark: **"Keep away from any source of ignition"**. This mark shall be in an official language of the forwarding country, and also, if that language is not English, French or German, in English, French or German, unless any agreements concluded between the countries concerned in the transport operation provide otherwise.

635   Packages containing these articles need not bear a label conforming to model No. 9 unless the article is fully enclosed by packaging, crates or other means that prevent the ready identification of the article.

636   Up to the intermediate processing facility, lithium cells and batteries with a gross mass of not more than 500 g each, lithium ion cells with a Watt-hour rating of not more than 20 Wh, lithium ion batteries with a Watt-hour rating of not more than 100 Wh, lithium metal cells with a lithium content of not more than 1 g and lithium metal batteries with an aggregate lithium content of not more than 2 g, not contained in equipment, collected and handed over for carriage for sorting, disposal or recycling, together with or without other non-lithium cells or batteries, are not subject to the other provisions of ADN including special provision 376 and 2.2.9.1.7, if the following conditions are met:

   (a)   The cells and batteries are packed according to packing instruction P909 of 4.1.4.1 of ADR except for the additional requirements 1 and 2;

   (b)   A quality assurance system is in place to ensure that the total amount of lithium cells and batteries per transport unit does not exceed 333 kg;

           NOTE: The total quantity of lithium cells and batteries in the mix may be assessed by means of a statistical method included in the quality assurance system. A copy of the quality assurance records shall be made available to the competent authority upon request.

   (c)   Packages are marked "LITHIUM BATTERIES FOR DISPOSAL" or "LITHIUM BATTERIES FOR RECYCLING" as appropriate.

637   Genetically modified microorganisms and genetically modified organisms are those which are not dangerous for humans and animals, but which could alter animals, plants, microbiological substances and ecosystems in such a way as cannot occur naturally. Genetically modified microorganisms and genetically modified organisms are not subject to the requirements of ADN when authorized for use by the competent authorities of the countries of origin, transit and destination[3].

---

[3]   *See in particular Part C of Directive 2001/18/EC of the European Parliament and of the Council on the deliberate release into the environment of genetically modified organisms and repealing Council Directive 90/220/EEC (Official Journal of the European Communities, No. L 106, of 17 April 2001, pp. 8-14), which sets out the authorization procedures for the European Community.*

Live vertebrate or invertebrate animals shall not be used to carry these substances classified under this UN number unless the substance can be carried in no other way.

For the carriage of easily perishable substances under this UN number appropriate information shall be given, e.g.: **"Cool at +2 °/+4 °C"** or **"Carry in frozen state"** or **"Do not freeze"**.

638 Substances related to self-reactive substances (see 2.2.41.1.19).

639 See 2.2.2.3, classification code 2F, UN No. 1965, Note 2.

640 The physical and technical characteristics mentioned in column (2) of Table A of Chapter 3.2 determine different tank codes for the carriage of substances of the same packing group in tanks conforming to Chapter 6.8 of RID or ADR.

In order to identify these physical and technical characteristics of the product carried in the tank, the following shall be added to the particulars required in the transport document only in case of carriage in tanks conforming to Chapter 6.8 of ADR or RID:

"Special provision 640X" where "X" is the applicable capital letter appearing after the reference to special provision 640 in column (6) of Table A of Chapter 3.2.

These particulars may, however, be dispensed with in the case of carriage in the type of tank which, for substances of a specific packing group of a specific UN number, meets at least the most stringent requirements.

641 *(Reserved)*

642 Except as authorized under 1.1.4.2, this entry of the UN Model Regulations shall not be used for the carriage of fertilizer ammoniating solutions with free ammonia. Otherwise, for carriage of ammonia solution, see UN Nos. 2073, 2672 and 3318.

643 Stone or aggregate asphalt mixture is not subject to the requirements for Class 9.

644 This substance is admitted for carriage provided that:

–   The pH is between 5 and 7 measured in an aqueous solution of 10% of the substance carried;

–   The solution does not contain more than 93% ammonium nitrate;

–   The solution does not contain more than 0.2% combustible material or chlorine compounds in quantities such that the chlorine level exceeds 0.02%.

645 The classification code as mentioned in Column (3b) of Table A of Chapter 3.2 shall be used only with the approval of the competent authority of a Contracting Party to ADN prior to carriage. The approval shall be given in writing as a classification approval certificate (see 5.4.1.2.1 (g)) and shall be provided with a unique reference. When assignment to a division is made in accordance with the procedure in 2.2.1.1.7.2, the competent authority may require the default classification to be verified on the basis of test data derived from Test Series 6 of the *Manual of Tests and Criteria*, Part I, Section 16.

646 Carbon made by steam activation process is not subject to the requirements of ADN.

647 Except for carriage in tank vessels, the carriage of vinegar and acetic acid with not more than 25% pure acid by mass is subject only to the following requirements:

(a) Packagings, including IBCs and large packagings, and tanks shall be manufactured from stainless steel or plastic material which is permanently resistant to corrosion of vinegar/acetic acid food grade;

(b) Packagings, including IBCs and large packagings, and tanks shall be subjected to a visual inspection by the owner at least once a year. The results of the inspections shall be recorded and the records kept for at least one year. Damaged packagings, including IBCs and large packagings, and tanks shall not be filled;

(c) Packagings, including IBCs and large packagings, and tanks shall be filled in a way that no product is spilled or adheres to the outer surface;

(d) Seals and closures shall be resistant to vinegar/acetic acid food grade. Packagings, including IBCs and large packagings, and tanks shall be hermetically sealed by the person in charge of packaging and/or filling so that under normal conditions of carriage there will be no leakage;

(e) Combination packagings with inner packaging made of glass or plastic (see packing instruction P001 in 4.1.4.1 of ADR) which fulfil the general packing requirements of 4.1.1.1, 4.1.1.2, 4.1.1.4, 4.1.1.5, 4.1.1.6, 4.1.1.7 and 4.1.1.8 of ADR may be used;

The other provisions of ADN do not apply except those relating to carriage in tank vessels.

648 Articles impregnated with this pesticide, such as fibreboard plates, paper strips, cotton-wool balls, sheets of plastics material, in hermetically closed wrappings, are not subject to the provisions of ADN.

649 *(Deleted)*

650 Waste consisting of packaging residues, solidified residues and liquid residues of paint may be carried under the conditions of packing group II. In addition to the provisions of UN No. 1263, packing group II, the waste may also be packed and carried as follows:

(a) The waste may be packed in accordance with packing instruction P002 of 4.1.4.1 of ADR or to packing instruction IBC006 of 4.1.4.2 of ADR;

(b) The waste may be packed in flexible IBCs of types 13H3, 13H4 and 13H5 in overpacks with complete walls;

(c) Testing of packagings and IBCs indicated under (a) or (b) may be carried out in accordance with the requirements of Chapters 6.1 or 6.5 of ADR, as appropriate, in relation to solids, at the packing group II performance level.

The tests shall be carried out on packagings and IBCs, filled with a representative sample of the waste, as prepared for carriage;

(d)   Carriage in bulk in sheeted wagons, movable roof wagons/sheeted vehicles, closed containers or sheeted large containers, all with complete walls is allowed. The wagons, containers or body of vehicles shall be leakproof or rendered leakproof, for example by means of a suitable and sufficiently stout inner lining;

(e)   If the waste is carried under the conditions of this special provision, the goods shall be declared in accordance with 5.4.1.1.3.1 in the transport document, as follows: "UN 1263 WASTE PAINT, 3, II", or "UN 1263 WASTE PAINT, 3, PG II".

651   Special provision V2 (1) of ADR does not apply if the net explosive mass per transport unit does not exceed 4 000 kg, provided that the net explosive mass per vehicle does not exceed 3 000 kg.

652   *(Reserved)*

653   The carriage of this gas in cylinders having a test pressure capacity product of maximum 15.2 MPa.litre (152 bar.litre) is not subject to the other provisions of ADN if the following conditions are met:

–   The provisions for construction, testing and filling of cylinders are observed;

–   The cylinders are contained in outer packagings which at least meet the requirements of Part 4 for combination packagings. The general provisions of packing of 4.1.1.1, 4.1.1.2 and 4.1.1.5 to 4.1.1.7 of ADR shall be observed;

–   The cylinders are not packed together with other dangerous goods;

–   The total gross mass of a package does not exceed 30 kg; and

–   Each package is clearly and durably marked with "UN 1006" for argon compressed, "UN 1013" for carbon dioxide, "UN 1046" for helium compressed or "UN 1066" for nitrogen compressed. This mark is displayed within a diamond-shaped area surrounded by a line that measures at least 100 mm by 100 mm.

654   Waste lighters collected separately and consigned in accordance with 5.4.1.1.3.1 may be carried under this entry for the purposes of disposal. They need not be protected against inadvertent discharge provided that measures are taken to prevent the dangerous build up of pressure and dangerous atmospheres.

Waste lighters, other than those leaking or severely deformed, shall be packed in accordance with packing instruction P003 of ADR. In addition the following provisions shall apply:

–   only rigid packagings of a maximum capacity of 60 litres shall be used;

–   the packagings shall be filled with water or any other appropriate protection material to avoid any ignition;

–   under normal conditions of carriage all ignition devices of the lighters shall fully be covered by the protection material;

–   the packagings shall be adequately vented to prevent the creation of flammable atmosphere and the build up of pressure;

–   the packages shall only be carried in ventilated or open wagons/vehicles or containers.

Leaking or severely deformed lighters shall be carried in salvage packagings, provided appropriate measures are taken to ensure there is no dangerous build up of pressure.

NOTE: *Special provision 201 and special packing provisions PP84 and RR5 of packing instruction P002 in 4.1.4.1 of ADR do not apply to waste lighters.*

655 Cylinders designed, constructed, approved and marked in accordance with Directive 97/23/EC[4] or Directive 2014/68/EU[5] and used for breathing apparatus may be carried without conforming to Chapter 6.2 of ADR, provided that they are subject to inspections and tests specified in 6.2.1.6.1 of ADR and the interval between tests specified in packing instruction P200 in 4.1.4.1 of ADR is not exceeded. The pressure used for the hydraulic pressure test is the pressure marked on the cylinder in accordance with Directive 97/23/EC[4] or Directive 2014/68/EU[5].

656 *(Deleted)*

657 This entry shall be used for the technically pure substance only; for mixtures of LPG components, see UN 1965 or see UN 1075 in conjunction with NOTE 2 in 2.2.2.3.

658 UN No. 1057 LIGHTERS complying with standard EN ISO 9994:2019 "Lighters – Safety Specification" and UN No. 1057 LIGHTER REFILLS, may be carried subject only to the provisions of 3.4.1 (a) to (f), 3.4.2 (except for the total gross mass of 30 kg), 3.4.3 (except for the total gross mass of 20 kg), 3.4.11 and 3.4.12, provided the following conditions are met:

(a) The total gross mass of each package is not more than 10 kg;

(b) Not more than 100 kg gross mass of such packages is carried in a wagon or vehicle or large container; and

(c) Each outer packaging is clearly and durably marked with "UN 1057 LIGHTERS" or "UN 1057 LIGHTER REFILLS", as appropriate.

659 Substances to which PP86 or TP7 are assigned in Column (9a) and Column (11) of Table A in Chapter 3.2 of ADR and therefore require air to be eliminated from the vapour space, shall not be used for carriage under this UN number but shall be carried under their respective UN numbers as listed in Table A of Chapter 3.2.

NOTE: *See also 2.2.2.1.7.*

660 *(Deleted)*

661 *(Deleted).*

---

[4] *Directive 97/23/EC of the European Parliament and of the Council of 29 May 1997 on the approximation of the laws of the Member States concerning pressure equipment (PED) (Official Journal of the European Communities No. L 181 of 9 July 1997, p. 1 - 55).*

[5] *Directive 2014/68/EU of the European Parliament and of the Council of 15 May 2014 on the harmonisation of the laws of the Member States relating to the making available on the market of pressure equipment (PED) (Official Journal of the European Union No. L 189 of 27 June 2014, p. 164 - 259).*

662 Cylinders not conforming to the provisions of Chapter 6.2 which are used exclusively on board a ship or aircraft, may be carried for the purpose of filling or inspection and subsequent return, provided the cylinders are designed and constructed in accordance with a standard recognized by the competent authority of the country of approval and all the other relevant requirements of ADN and other conditions are met including:

(a)   The cylinders shall be carried with valve protection in conformity with 4.1.6.8;

(b)   The cylinders shall be marked and labelled in conformity with 5.2.1 and 5.2.2; and

(c)   All the relevant filling requirements of packing instruction P200 of 4.1.4.1 of ADR are complied with.

The transport document shall include the following statement: "Carriage in accordance with Special Provision 662".

663 This entry may only be used for packagings, large packagings or IBCs, or parts thereof, which have contained dangerous goods which are carried for disposal, recycling or recovery of their material, other than reconditioning, repair, routine maintenance, remanufacturing or reuse, and which have been emptied to the extent that only residues of dangerous goods adhering to the packaging parts are present when they are handed over for carriage.

Scope:

Residues present in the packagings, discarded, empty, uncleaned shall only be of dangerous goods of classes 3, 4.1, 5.1, 6.1, 8 or 9. In addition, they shall not be:

–   Substances assigned to packing group I or that have "0" assigned in Column (7a) of Table A of Chapter 3.2; nor

–   Substances classified as desensitized explosive substances of Class 3 or Class 4.1; nor

–   Substances classified as self-reactive substances of Class 4.1; nor

–   Radioactive material; nor

–   Asbestos (UN 2212 and UN 2590), polychlorinated biphenyls (UN 2315 and UN 3432) and polyhalogenated biphenyls, halogenated monomethyldiphenylmethanes or polyhalogenated terphenyls (UN 3151 and UN 3152).

General provisions:

Packagings, discarded, empty, uncleaned with residues presenting a primary or subsidiary hazard of Class 5.1 shall not be loaded in bulk together with packagings, discarded, empty, uncleaned with residues presenting a hazard of other classes. Packagings, discarded, empty, uncleaned with residues presenting a primary or subsidiary hazard of Class 5.1 shall not be packed with other packagings, discarded, empty, uncleaned with residues presenting hazards of other classes in the same outer packaging.

Documented sorting procedures shall be implemented on the loading site to ensure compliance with the provisions applicable to this entry.

NOTE: All the other provisions of ADN apply.

664   *(Reserved)*

665   Except in the case of carriage in bulk, unground hard coal, coke and anthracite, meeting the classification criteria of Class 4.2, packing group III, are not subject to the requirements of ADN.

666   Vehicles and battery powered equipment, referred to by special provision 388, when carried as a load, as well as any dangerous goods they contain that are necessary for their operation or the operation of their equipment, are not subject to any other provisions of ADN, provided the following conditions are met:

(a)   For liquid fuels, any valves between the engine or equipment and the fuel tank shall be closed during carriage unless it is essential for the equipment to remain operational. Where appropriate, the vehicles shall be loaded upright and secured against falling;

(b)   For gaseous fuels, the valves between the gas tank and engine shall be closed and the electric contact open unless it is essential for the equipment to remain operational;

(c)   Metal hydride storage systems shall be approved by the competent authority of the country of manufacture. If the country of manufacture is not a contracting party to ADN the approval shall be recognized by the competent authority of a contracting party to ADN;

(d)   The provisions of (a) and (b) do not apply to vehicles which are empty of liquid or gaseous fuels,

NOTE 1: A vehicle is considered to be empty of liquid fuel when the liquid fuel tank has been drained and the vehicle cannot be operated due to a lack of fuel. Vehicle components such as fuel lines, fuel filters and injectors do not need to be cleaned, drained or purged to be considered empty of liquid fuels. In addition, the liquid fuel tank does not need to be cleaned or purged.

NOTE 2: A vehicle is considered to be empty of gaseous fuels when the gaseous fuel tanks are empty of liquid (for liquefied gases), the pressure in the tanks does not exceed 2 bar and the fuel shut-off or isolation valve is closed and secured.

667   (a)   The provisions of 2.2.9.1.7 (a) do not apply when pre-production prototype lithium cells or batteries or lithium cells or batteries of a small production run, consisting of not more than 100 cells or batteries, are installed in the vehicle, engine or machinery;

(b)   The provisions of 2.2.9.1.7 do not apply to lithium cells or batteries installed in damaged or defective vehicles, engine or machinery. In such cases the following conditions shall be met:

(i)   If the damage or defect has no significant impact on the safety of the cell or battery, damaged and defective vehicles, engines or machinery, may be carried under the conditions defined in special provisions 363 or 666, as appropriate;

(ii) If the damage or defect has a significant impact on the safety of the cell or battery, the lithium cell or battery shall be removed and carried according to special provision 376.

However, if it is not possible to safely remove the cell or battery or it is not possible to verify the status of the cell or battery, the vehicle, engine or machinery may be towed or carried as specified in (i).

(c) The procedures described in (b) also apply to damaged lithium cells or batteries in vehicles, engines or machinery.

668 Elevated temperature substances for the purpose of applying road markings are not subject to the requirements of ADN, provided that the following conditions are met:

(a) They do not fulfil the criteria of any class other than Class 9;

(b) The temperature of the outer surface of the boiler does not exceed 70 °C;

(c) The boiler is closed in such a way that any loss of product is prevented during carriage;

(d) The maximum capacity of the boiler is limited to 3 000 l.

669 A trailer fitted with equipment powered by a liquid or gaseous fuel or an electric energy storage and production system, that is intended for use during carriage operated by this trailer as a part of a transport unit, shall be assigned to UN Nos. 3166 or 3171 and be subject to the same conditions as specified for these UN Nos., when carried as a load on a vessel, provided that the total capacity of the tanks containing liquid fuel does not exceed 500 litres.

670 (a) Lithium cells and batteries installed in equipment from private households collected and handed over for carriage for depollution, dismantling, recycling or disposal are not subject to the other provisions of ADN including special provision 376 and 2.2.9.1.7 when:

(i) They are not the main power source for the operation of the equipment in which they are contained;

(ii) The equipment in which they are contained does not contain any other lithium cell or battery used as the main power source; and

(iii) They are afforded protection by the equipment in which they are contained.

Examples for cells and batteries covered by this paragraph are button cells used for data integrity in household appliances (e.g. refrigerators, washing machines, dishwashers) or in other electrical or electronic equipment;

(b) Up to the intermediate processing facility lithium cells and batteries contained in equipment from private households not meeting the requirements of (a) collected and handed over for carriage for depollution, dismantling, recycling or disposal are not subject to the other provisions of ADN including special provision 376 and 2.2.9.1.7, if the following conditions are met:

(i)   The equipment is packed in accordance with packing instruction P909 of 4.1.4.1 of ADR except for the additional requirements 1 and 2; or it is packed in strong outer packagings, e.g. specially designed collection receptacles, which meet the following requirements:

–   The packagings shall be constructed of suitable material and be of adequate strength and design in relation to the packaging capacity and its intended use. The packagings need not meet the requirements of 4.1.1.3 of ADR;

–   Appropriate measures shall be taken to minimize the damage of the equipment when filling and handling the packaging, e.g. use of rubber mats; and

–   The packagings shall be constructed and closed so as to prevent any loss of contents during carriage, e.g. by lids, strong inner liners, covers for transport. Openings designed for filling are acceptable if they are constructed so as to prevent loss of content;

(ii)   A quality assurance system is in place to ensure that the total amount of lithium cells and batteries per transport unit does not exceed 333 kg;

NOTE: The total quantity of lithium cells and batteries in the equipment from private households may be assessed by means of a statistical method included in the quality assurance system. A copy of the quality assurance records shall be made available to the competent authority upon request.

(iii)   Packages are marked "LITHIUM BATTERIES FOR DISPOSAL" or "LITHIUM BATTERIES FOR RECYCLING" as appropriate.

If equipment containing lithium cells or batteries is carried unpackaged or on pallets in accordance with packing instruction P909 (3) of 4.1.4.1 of ADR, this mark may alternatively be affixed to the external surface of the vehicles, wagons or containers).

NOTE: "Equipment from private households" means equipment which comes from private households and equipment which comes from commercial, industrial, institutional and other sources which, because of its nature and quantity, is similar to that from private households. Equipment likely to be used by both private households and users other than private households shall in any event be considered to be equipment from private households.

671   For the purposes of the exemption related to quantities carried on board vessels (see 1.1.3.6), the transport category shall be determined in relation to the packing group (see paragraph 3 of special provision 251):

–   Transport category 3 for kits assigned to packing group III;

–   Transport category 2 for kits assigned to packing group II;

–   Transport category 1 for kits assigned to packing group I.

Kits containing only dangerous goods to which no packing group is assigned shall be allocated to transport category 2 for completion of transport documents and the exemption related to quantities carried per vessel (see 1.1.3.6).

672 Articles, such as machinery, apparatus or devices carried under this entry and in conformity with special provision 301 are not subject to any other provision of ADN provided they are either:

     –   packed in a strong outer packaging constructed of suitable material, and of adequate strength and design in relation to the packaging's capacity and its intended use, and meeting the applicable requirements of 4.1.1.1 of ADR; or

     –   carried without outer packaging if the article is constructed and designed so that the receptacles containing the dangerous goods are afforded adequate protection.

673 *(Reserved)*

674 This special provision applies to periodic inspection and test of over-moulded cylinders as defined in 1.2.1.

Over-moulded cylinders subject to 6.2.3.5.3.1 of ADR shall be subject to periodic inspection and test in accordance with 6.2.1.6.1 of ADR, adapted by the following alternative method:

     –   Substitute test required in 6.2.1.6.1 d) of ADR by alternative destructive tests;

     –   Perform specific additional destructive tests related to the characteristics of over-moulded cylinders.

The procedures and requirements of this alternative method are described below.

Alternative method:

(a) General

The following provisions apply to over-moulded cylinders produced serially and based on welded steel cylinder shells in accordance with EN 1442:2017, EN 14140:2014 + AC:2015 or annex I, parts 1 to 3 to Council Directive 84/527/EEC. The design of the over-moulding shall prevent water from penetrating on to the inner steel cylinder shell. The conversion of the steel cylinder shell to an over-moulded cylinder shall comply with the relevant requirements of EN 1442:2017 and EN 14140:2014 + AC:2015.

Over-moulded cylinders shall be equipped with self-closing valves.

(b) Basic population

A basic population of over-moulded cylinders is defined as the production of cylinders from only one over-moulding manufacturer using new inner steel cylinder shells manufactured by only one manufacturer within one calendar year, based on the same design type, the same materials and production processes.

(c) Sub-groups of a basic population

Within the above defined basic population, over-moulded cylinders belonging to different owners shall be separated into specific sub-groups, one per owner.

If the whole basic population is owned by one owner, the sub-group equals the basic population.

(d) Traceability

Inner steel cylinder shell marks in accordance with 6.2.3.9 of ADR shall be repeated on the over-moulding. In addition, each over-moulded cylinder shall be fitted with an individual resilient electronic identification device. The detailed characteristics of the over-moulded cylinders shall be recorded by the owner in a central database. The database shall be used to:

− Identify the specific sub-group;

− Make available to inspection bodies, filling centres and competent authorities the specific technical characteristics of the cylinders consisting of at least the following: serial number, steel cylinder shell production batch, over-moulding production batch, date of over-moulding;

− Identify the cylinder by linking the electronic device to the database with the serial number;

− Check individual cylinder history and determine measures (e.g. filling, sampling, retesting, withdrawal);

− Record performed measures including the date and the address of where it was done.

The recorded data shall be kept available by the owner of the over-moulded cylinders for the entire life of the sub-group.

(e) Sampling for statistical assessment

The sampling shall be random among a sub-group as defined in sub-paragraph (c). The size of each sample per sub-group shall be in accordance with the table in sub-paragraph (g).

(f) Test procedure for destructive testing

The inspection and test required by 6.2.1.6.1 of ADR shall be carried out except (d) which shall be substituted by the following test procedure:

− Burst test (according to EN 1442:2017 or EN 14140:2014 + AC:2015).

In addition, the following tests shall be performed:

− Adhesion test (according to EN 1442:2017 or EN 14140:2014 + AC:2015);

− Peeling and Corrosion tests (according to EN ISO 4628-3:2016).

Adhesion test, peeling and corrosion tests, and burst test shall be performed on each related sample according to the table in sub-paragraph (g) and shall be conducted after the first 3 years in service and every 5 years thereafter.

(g) Statistical evaluation of test results – Method and minimum requirements

The procedure for statistical evaluation according to the related rejection criteria is described in the following.

Test interval (years)	Type of test	Standard	Rejection criteria	Sampling out of a sub-group
After 3 years in service (see (f))	Burst test	EN 1442:2017	Burst pressure point of the representative sample must be above the lower limit of tolerance interval on the Sample Performance Chart $\Omega_m \geq 1 + \Omega_s \times k3(n;p;1-\alpha)$ [a] No individual test result shall be less than the test pressure	$3\sqrt[3]{Q}$ or Q/200 whichever is lower, and with a minimum of 20 per sub-group (Q)
	Peeling and corrosion	EN ISO 4628-3:2016	Max corrosion grade: Ri2	Q/1 000
	Adhesion of Polyurethane	ISO 2859-1:1999 + A1:2011 EN 1442:2017 EN 14140:2014 + AC:2015	Adhesion value > 0.5 N/mm²	See ISO 2859-1:1999 + A1:2011 applied to Q/1000
Every 5 years thereafter (see (f))	Burst test	EN 1442:2017	Burst pressure point of the representative sample must be above the lower limit of tolerance interval on the Sample Performance Chart $\Omega_m \geq 1 + \Omega_s \times k3(n;p;1-\alpha)$ [a] No individual test result shall be less than the test pressure	$6\sqrt[3]{Q}$ or Q/100 whichever is lower, and with a minimum of 40 per sub-group (Q)
	Peeling and corrosion	EN ISO 4628-3:2016	Max corrosion grade: Ri2	Q/1 000
	Adhesion of Polyurethane	ISO 2859-1:1999 + A1:2011 EN 1442:2017 EN 14140:2014 + AC:2015	Adhesion value > 0.5 N/mm²	See ISO 2859-1:1999 + A1:2011 applied to Q/1000

[a] *Burst pressure point (BPP) of the representative sample is used for the evaluation of test results by using a Sample Performance Chart:*

Step 1: Determination of the burst pressure point (BPP) of a representative sample

Each sample is represented by a point whose coordinates are the mean value of burst test results and the standard deviation of burst test results, each normalised to the relevant test pressure.

$$BPP: (\Omega_s = \frac{s}{PH} ; \Omega_m = \frac{x}{PH})$$

with

x: sample mean value;

s: sample standard deviation;

PH: test pressure

Step 2: Plotting on a Sample Performance Chart

Each BPP is plotted on a Sample Performance Chart with following axis:

- *Abscissa : Standard Deviation normalised to test pressure (Ω_s)*

- *Ordinate : Mean value normalised to test pressure (Ω_m)*

Step 3: Determination of the relevant lower limit of tolerance interval in the Sample Performance Chart

Results for burst pressure shall first be checked according to the Joint Test (multidirectional test) using a significance level of α=0.05 (see paragraph 7 of ISO 5479:1997) to determine whether the distribution of results for each sample is normal or non-normal.

- *For a normal distribution, the determination of the relevant lower limit of tolerance is given in step 3.1.*

- *For a non-normal distribution, the determination of the relevant lower limit of tolerance is given in step 3.2.*

Step 3.1: Lower limit of tolerance interval for results following a normal distribution

In accordance with the standard ISO 16269-6:2014, and considering that the variance is unknown, the unilateral statistical tolerance interval shall be considered for a confidence level of 95% and a fraction of population equal to 99.9999%.

By application in the Sample Performance Chart, the lower limit of tolerance interval is represented by a line of constant survival rate defined by the formula:

$$\Omega_m = 1 + \Omega_s \times k3\,(n; p; 1 - \alpha)$$

with

k3: factor function of n, p and 1-α;

p: proportion of the population selected for the tolerance interval (99.9999%);

1- α: confidence level (95%);

n: sample size.

The value for k3 dedicated to Normal Distributions shall be taken from the table at end of Step 3.

Step 3.2: Lower limit of tolerance interval for results following a non-normal distribution

The unilateral statistical tolerance interval shall be calculated for a confidence level of 95% and a fraction of population equal to 99.9999%.

The lower limit of tolerance is represented by a line of constant survival rate defined by the formula given in previous step 3.1, with factors k3 based and calculated on the properties of a Weibull Distribution.

The value for k3 dedicated to Weibull Distributions shall be taken from the table below at end of Step 3.

Table for k3		
p=99.9999% and (1- α)=0.95		
Sample size n	Normal distribution k3	Weibull distribution k3
20	6.901	16.021
22	6.765	15.722
24	6.651	15.472
26	6.553	15.258
28	6.468	15.072
30	6.393	14.909
35	6.241	14.578
40	6.123	14.321
45	6.028	14.116
50	5.949	13.947
60	5.827	13.683
70	5.735	13.485
80	5.662	13.329
90	5.603	13.203
100	5.554	13.098
150	5.393	12.754
200	5.300	12.557
250	5.238	12.426
300	5,193	12.330
400	5.131	12.199
500	5.089	12.111
1000	4.988	11.897
∞	4.753	11.408

NOTE: *If sample size is between two values, the closest lower sample size shall be selected.*

(h)   Measures if the acceptance criteria are not met

If a result of the burst test, peeling and corrosion test or adhesion test does not comply with the criteria detailed in the table in paragraph (g), the affected sub-group of over-moulded cylinders shall be segregated by the owner for further investigations and not be filled or made available for transport and use.

In agreement with the competent authority or the Xa-body which issued the design approval, additional tests shall be performed to determine the root cause of the failure.

If the root cause cannot be proved to be limited to the affected sub-group of the owner, the competent authority or the Xa-body shall take measures concerning the whole basic population and potentially other years of production.

If the root cause can be proved to be limited to a part of the affected sub-group, not affected parts may be authorized by the competent authority to return to service. It shall be proved that no individual over-moulded cylinder returning to service is affected.

(i) Filling centre requirements

The owner shall make available to the competent authority documentary evidence that the filling centres:

– Comply with the provisions of packing instruction P200 (7) of 4.1.4.1 of ADR and that the requirements of the standard on pre-fill inspections referenced in table P200 (11) of 4.1.4.1 of ADR are fulfilled and correctly applied;

– Have the appropriate means to identify over-moulded cylinders through the electronic identification device;

– Have access to the database as defined in (d);

– Have the capacity to update the database;

– Apply a quality system, according to the standard ISO 9000 (series) or equivalent, certified by an accredited independent body recognized by the competent authority.

675 For packages containing these dangerous goods, mixed loading with substances and articles of Class 1, with the exception of 1.4S, shall be prohibited.

676 For the carriage of packages containing polymerizing substances the provisions of special provision 386, in conjunction with 7.1.7.3, 7.1.7.4, 5.4.1.1.15 and 5.4.1.2.3.1, need not be applied, when carried for disposal or recycling provided the following conditions are met:

(a) Before loading an examination has shown that there is no significant deviation between the outside temperature of the package and the ambient temperature;

(b) The carriage is effected within a period of not more than 24 hours from that examination;

(c) The packages are protected from direct sunlight and from the impact of other sources of heat (e.g. additional loads that are being carried above ambient temperature) during carriage;

(d) The ambient temperatures during the carriage are below 45 °C;

(e) Vehicles and containers are adequately ventilated;

(f) The substances are packed in packages with a maximum capacity of 1 000 litres.

In assessing the substances for carriage under the conditions of this special provision, additional measures to prevent dangerous polymerization may be considered, for example the addition of inhibitors.

800 Oil seeds, crushed seeds and seedcake containing vegetable oil, treated with solvents, not subject to spontaneous combustion, are allocated to UN No. 3175. These substances are not subject to ADN when they have been prepared or treated to ensure that they cannot give off dangerous gases in dangerous quantities (no risk of explosion) during carriage and when this is mentioned in the transport document.

801 Ferrosilicon with between 25 and 30% or more than 90% silicon content by mass is a dangerous substance of Class 4.3 for carriage in bulk or without packaging by inland navigation vessel.

802 See 7.1.4.10.

803 Hard coal, coke and anthracite, when carried in bulk, are not subject to the provisions of ADN if:

(a) The temperature of the cargo has been determined using an appropriate procedure and is not higher than 60°C before, during or immediately after loading of the hold;

(b) Depending on the temperature of the cargo before, during and immediately after loading of the hold, the expected duration of carriage without temperature monitoring does not exceed the maximum number of days shown in the table below:

Maximum temperature on loading (°C)	Maximum duration of journey (days)
60	10
50	18
40	32
30	57

(c) Where the effective duration of carriage exceeds the maximum duration shown in sub-paragraph (b), temperature monitoring is carried out from the first day over the maximum duration. The necessary monitoring apparatus shall be on board as from the first day of the carriage following the maximum duration of the journey;

(d) The master is given, at the time of loading and in a traceable form, instructions on how to proceed if there is a significant heating of the cargo.

CHAPTER 3.4

DANGEROUS GOODS PACKED IN LIMITED QUANTITIES

3.4.1   This Chapter provides the provisions applicable to the carriage of dangerous goods of certain classes packed in limited quantities. The applicable quantity limit for the inner packaging or article is specified for each substance in Column (7a) of Table A of Chapter 3.2. In addition, the quantity "0" has been indicated in this column for each entry not permitted to be carried in accordance with this Chapter.

Limited quantities of dangerous goods packed in such limited quantities, meeting the provisions of this Chapter are not subject to any other provisions of ADN except the relevant provisions of:

(a)   Part 1, Chapters 1.1, 1.2, 1.3, 1.4, 1.5, 1.6, 1.8, 1.9;

(b)   Part 2;

(c)   Part 3, Chapters 3.1, 3.2, 3.3 (except special provisions 61, 178, 181, 220, 274, 625, 633 and 650 (e));

(d)   Part 4, paragraphs 4.1.1.1, 4.1.1.2, 4.1.1.4 to 4.1.1.8 of ADR;

(e)   Part 5, 5.1.2.1(a) (i) and (b), 5.1.2.2, 5.1.2.3, 5.2.1.10, 5.4.2;

(f)   Part 6, construction requirements of 6.1.4 and paragraphs 6.2.5.1 and 6.2.6.1 to 6.2.6.3 of ADR;

3.4.2   Dangerous goods shall be packed only in inner packagings placed in suitable outer packagings. Intermediate packagings may be used. In addition, for articles of Division 1.4, Compatibility Group S, the provisions of section 4.1.5 of ADR shall be fully complied with. The use of inner packagings is not necessary for the carriage of articles such as aerosols or "receptacles, small, containing gas". The total gross mass of the package shall not exceed 30 kg.

3.4.3   Except for articles of Division 1.4, Compatibility Group S, shrink-wrapped or stretch-wrapped trays meeting the conditions of 4.1.1.1, 4.1.1.2 and 4.1.1.4 to 4.1.1.8 of ADR are acceptable as outer packagings for articles or inner packagings containing dangerous goods carried in accordance with this Chapter. Inner packagings that are liable to break or be easily punctured, such as those made of glass, porcelain, stoneware or certain plastics, shall be placed in suitable intermediate packagings meeting the provisions of 4.1.1.1, 4.1.1.2 and 4.1.1.4 to 4.1.1.8 of ADR, and be so designed that they meet the construction requirements of 6.1.4 of ADR. The total gross mass of the package shall not exceed 20 kg.

3.4.4   Liquid goods of Class 8, packing group II in glass, porcelain or stoneware inner packagings shall be enclosed in a compatible and rigid intermediate packaging.

3.4.5 and 3.4.6 (*Reserved*)

3.4.7   **Marking of packages containing limited quantities**

3.4.7.1   Except for air transport, packages containing dangerous goods in limited quantities shall bear the mark shown in Figure 3.4.7.1:

Figure 3.4.7.1

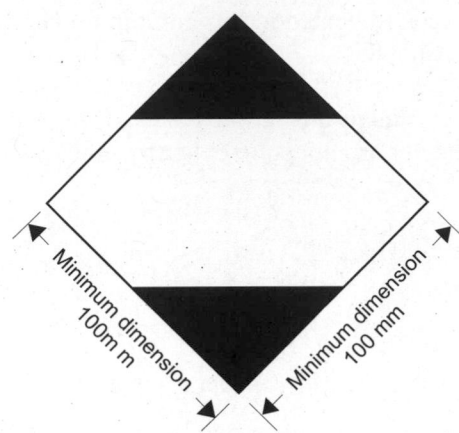

Mark for packages containing limited quantities

The mark shall be readily visible, legible and able to withstand open weather exposure without a substantial reduction in effectiveness.

The mark shall be in the form of a square set at an angle of 45° (diamond-shaped). The top and bottom portions and the surrounding line shall be black. The centre area shall be white or a suitable contrasting background. The minimum dimensions shall be 100 mm x 100 mm and the minimum width of the line forming the diamond shall be 2 mm. Where dimensions are not specified, all features shall be in approximate proportion to those shown.

3.4.7.2   If the size of the package so requires, the minimum outer dimensions shown in Figure 3.4.7.1 may be reduced to be not less than 50 mm x 50 mm provided the mark remains clearly visible. The minimum width of the line forming the diamond may be reduced to a minimum of 1 mm.

3.4.8   **Marking of packages containing limited quantities conforming to Part 3, Chapter 4 of the ICAO Technical Instructions**

3.4.8.1   Packages containing dangerous goods packed in conformity with the provisions of Part 3, Chapter 4 of the ICAO Technical Instructions may bear the mark shown in Figure 3.4.8.1 to certify conformity with these provisions:

Figure 3.4.8.1

Mark for packages containing limited quantities
conforming to Part 3, Chapter 4 of the ICAO Technical Instructions

The mark shall be readily visible, legible and able to withstand open weather exposure without a substantial reduction in effectiveness.

The mark shall be in the form of a square set at an angle of 45° (diamond-shaped). The top and bottom portions and the surrounding line shall be black. The centre area shall be white or a suitable contrasting background. The minimum dimensions shall be 100 mm x 100 mm and the minimum width of the line forming the diamond shall be 2 mm. The symbol "Y" shall be placed in the centre of the mark and shall be clearly visible. Where dimensions are not specified, all features shall be in approximate proportion to those shown.

3.4.8.2   If the size of the package so requires, the minimum outer dimensions shown in Figure 3.4.8.1 may be reduced to be not less than 50 mm x 50 mm provided the mark remains clearly visible. The minimum width of the line forming the diamond may be reduced to a minimum of 1 mm. The symbol "Y" shall remain in approximate proportion to that shown in Figure 3.4.8.1.

3.4.9   Packages containing dangerous goods bearing the mark shown in 3.4.8 with or without the additional labels and marks for air transport shall be deemed to meet the provisions of section 3.4.1 as appropriate and of sections 3.4.2 to 3.4.4 and need not bear the mark shown in 3.4.7.

3.4.10   Packages containing dangerous goods in limited quantities bearing the mark shown in 3.4.7 and conforming with the provisions of the ICAO Technical Instructions, including all necessary marks and labels specified in Parts 5 and 6, shall be deemed to meet the provisions of section 3.4.1 as appropriate and of sections 3.4.2 to 3.4.4.

3.4.11   **Use of overpacks**

For an overpack containing dangerous goods packed in limited quantities, the following applies:

Unless the marks representative of all dangerous goods in an overpack are visible, the overpack shall be:

(a)   marked with the word "OVERPACK". The lettering of the "OVERPACK" mark shall be at least 12 mm high. The mark shall be in an official language of the country of origin and also, if that language is not English, French or German, in English, French or German, unless agreements, if any, concluded between the countries concerned in the transport operation provide otherwise; and

(b)   marked with the marks required by this Chapter.

Except for air transport, the other provisions of 5.1.2.1 apply only if other dangerous goods which are not packed in limited quantities are contained in the overpack and only in relation to these other dangerous goods.

3.4.12   In advance of carriage, consignors of dangerous goods packed in limited quantities shall inform the carrier in a traceable form of the total gross mass of such goods to be consigned.

3.4.13   (a)   Transport units with a maximum mass exceeding 12 tonnes carrying dangerous goods packed in limited quantities shall be marked in accordance with 3.4.15 at the front and at the rear except when the transport unit contains other dangerous goods for which orange-coloured plate marking in accordance with 5.3.2 is required. In this latter case, the transport unit may display the required orange-coloured plate marking only, or both the orange-coloured plate marking in accordance with 5.3.2 and the marks in accordance with 3.4.15.

(b)   Wagons carrying packages with dangerous goods in limited quantities shall be marked in accordance with 3.4.15 on both sides except when placards in accordance with section 5.3.1 are already affixed.

(c)   Containers carrying dangerous goods packed in limited quantities, on transport units with a maximum mass exceeding 12 tonnes, shall be marked in accordance with 3.4.15 on all four sides except when the container contains other dangerous goods for which placarding in accordance with 5.3.1 is required. In this latter case, the container may display the required placards only, or both the placards in accordance with 5.3.1 and the marks in accordance with 3.4.15.

If the containers are loaded on a transport unit or wagon, the carrying transport unit or wagon need not be marked, except when the marks affixed to the containers are not visible from the outside of this carrying transport unit or wagon. In this latter case, the same marks shall also be affixed at the front and the rear of the carrying transport unit, or on both sides of the carrying wagon.

3.4.14   The marks specified in 3.4.13 may be dispensed with, if the total gross mass of the packages containing dangerous goods packed in limited quantities carried does not exceed 8 tonnes per transport unit or wagon.

3.4.15   The marks specified in 3.4.13 shall be the same as the one required in 3.4.7, except that their minimum dimensions shall be 250 mm x 250 mm. These marks shall be removed or covered if no dangerous goods in limited quantities are carried.

CHAPTER 3.5

DANGEROUS GOODS PACKED IN EXCEPTED QUANTITIES

3.5.1   **Excepted quantities**

3.5.1.1   Excepted quantities of dangerous goods of certain classes, other than articles, meeting the provisions of this Chapter are not subject to any other provisions of ADN except for:

(a)   The training requirements in Chapter 1.3;

(b)   The classification procedures and packing group criteria in Part 2;

(c)   The packaging requirements of 4.1.1.1, 4.1.1.2, 4.1.1.4 and 4.1.1.6 of ADR.

NOTE: In the case of radioactive material, the requirements for radioactive material in excepted packages in 1.7.1.5 apply.

3.5.1.2   Dangerous goods which may be carried as excepted quantities in accordance with the provisions of this Chapter are shown in column (7b) of Table A of Chapter 3.2 by means of an alphanumeric code as follows:

Code	Maximum net quantity per inner packaging (in grams for solids and ml for liquids and gases)	Maximum net quantity per outer packaging (in grams for solids and ml for liquids and gases, or sum of grams and ml in the case of mixed packing)
E0	Not permitted as Excepted Quantity	
E1	30	1000
E2	30	500
E3	30	300
E4	1	500
E5	1	300

For gases, the volume indicated for inner packagings refers to the water capacity of the inner receptacle and the volume indicated for outer packagings refers to the combined water capacity of all inner packagings within a single outer packaging.

3.5.1.3   Where dangerous goods in excepted quantities for which different codes are assigned are packaged together the total quantity per outer packaging shall be limited to that corresponding to the most restrictive code.

3.5.1.4   Excepted quantities of dangerous goods assigned to codes E1, E2, E4 and E5 with a maximum net quantity of dangerous goods per inner packaging limited to 1 ml for liquids and gases and 1 g for solids and a maximum net quantity of dangerous goods per outer packaging which does not exceed 100 g for solids or 100 ml for liquids and gases are only subject to:

(a)   The provisions of 3.5.2, except that an intermediate packaging is not required if the inner packagings are securely packed in an outer packaging with cushioning material in such a way that, under normal conditions of carriage, they cannot break, be punctured, or leak their contents; and for liquids, the outer packaging contains sufficient absorbent material to absorb the entire contents of the inner packagings; and

(b)   The provisions of 3.5.3.

3.5.2 **Packagings**

Packagings used for the carriage of dangerous goods in excepted quantities shall be in compliance with the following:

(a)   There shall be an inner packaging and each inner packaging shall be constructed of plastic (with a minimum thickness of 0.2 mm when used for liquids), or of glass, porcelain, stoneware, earthenware or metal (see also 4.1.1.2 of ADR) and the closure of each inner packaging shall be held securely in place with wire, tape or other positive means; any receptacle having a neck with moulded screw threads shall have a leakproof threaded type cap. The closure shall be resistant to the contents;

(b)   Each inner packaging shall be securely packed in an intermediate packaging with cushioning material in such a way that, under normal conditions of carriage, they cannot break, be punctured or leak their contents. For liquid dangerous goods, the intermediate or outer packaging shall contain sufficient absorbent material to absorb the entire contents of the inner packagings. When placed in the intermediate packaging, the absorbent material may be the cushioning material. Dangerous goods shall not react dangerously with cushioning, absorbent material and packaging material or reduce the integrity or function of the materials. Regardless of its orientation, the package shall completely contain the contents in case of breakage or leakage;

(c)   The intermediate packaging shall be securely packed in a strong, rigid outer packaging (wooden, fibreboard or other equally strong material);

(d)   Each package type shall be in compliance with the provisions in 3.5.3;

(e)   Each package shall be of such a size that there is adequate space to apply all necessary marks; and

(f)   Overpacks may be used and may also contain packages of dangerous goods or goods not subject to the requirements of ADN.

3.5.3 **Tests for packages**

3.5.3.1   The complete package as prepared for carriage, with inner packagings filled to not less than 95% of their capacity for solids or 98% for liquids, shall be capable of withstanding, as demonstrated by testing which is appropriately documented, without breakage or leakage of any inner packaging and without significant reduction in effectiveness:

(a)   Drops onto a rigid, non-resilient flat and horizontal surface from a height of 1.8 m:

(i)   Where the sample is in the shape of a box, it shall be dropped in each of the following orientations:

–   flat on the base;

–   flat on the top;

–   flat on the longest side;

–   flat on the shortest side;

–   on a corner.

      (ii)   Where the sample is in the shape of a drum, it shall be dropped in each of the following orientations:

- diagonally on the top chime, with the centre of gravity directly above the point of impact;

- diagonally on the base chime;

- flat on the side.

NOTE: Each of the above drops may be performed on different but identical packages.

(b)   A force applied to the top surface for a duration of 24 hours, equivalent to the total weight of identical packages if stacked to a height of 3 m (including the sample).

3.5.3.2   For the purposes of testing, the substances to be carried in the packaging may be replaced by other substances except where this would invalidate the results of the tests. For solids, when another substance is used, it must have the same physical characteristics (mass, grain size, etc.) as the substance to be carried. In the drop tests for liquids, when another substance is used, its relative density (specific gravity) and viscosity should be similar to those of the substance to be carried.

3.5.4   Marking of packages

3.5.4.1   Packages containing excepted quantities of dangerous goods prepared in accordance with this Chapter shall be durably and legibly marked with the mark shown in 3.5.4.2. The first or only label number indicated in column (5) of Table A of Chapter 3.2 for each of the dangerous goods contained in the package shall be shown in the mark. Where the name of the consignor or consignee is not shown elsewhere on the package this information shall be included within the mark.

3.5.4.2   *Excepted quantities mark*

Figure 3.5.4.2

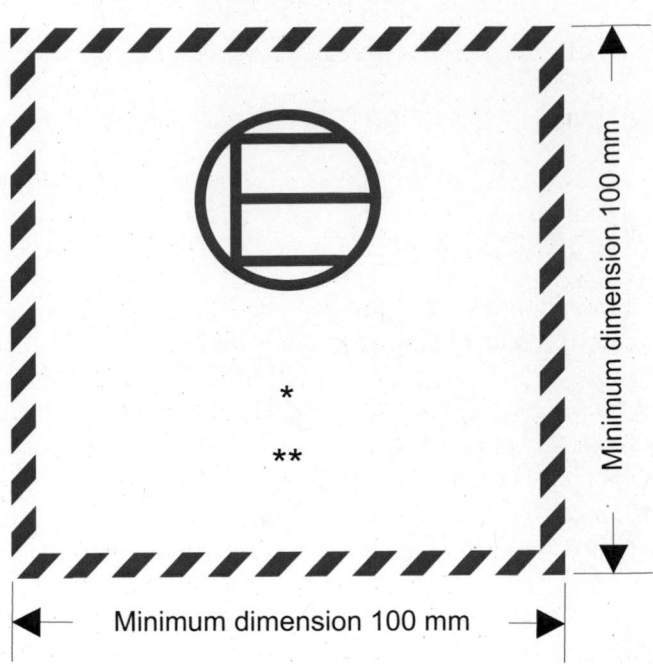

Excepted quantities mark

*   *The first or only label number indicated in column (5) of Table A of Chapter 3.2 shall be shown in this location.*

**   *The name of the consignor or of the consignee shall be shown in this location if not shown elsewhere on the package.*

The mark shall be in the form of a square. The hatching and symbol shall be of the same colour, black or red, on white or suitable contrasting background. The minimum dimensions shall be 100 mm x 100 mm. Where dimensions are not specified, all features shall be in approximate proportion to those shown.

3.5.4.3   *Use of overpacks*

For an overpack containing dangerous goods packed in excepted quantities, the following applies:

Unless the marks representative of all dangerous goods in an overpack are visible, the overpack shall be:

(a)   marked with the word "OVERPACK". The lettering of the "OVERPACK" mark shall be at least 12 mm high. The mark shall be in an official language of the country of origin and also, if that language is not English, French or German, in English, French or German, unless agreements, if any, concluded between the countries concerned in the transport operation provide otherwise; and

(b)   marked with the marks required by this Chapter.

The other provisions of 5.1.2.1 apply only if other dangerous goods which are not packed in excepted quantities are contained in the overpack and only in relation to these other dangerous goods.

3.5.5   **Maximum number of packages in any vehicle, wagon or container**

The number of packages in any vehicle, wagon or container shall not exceed 1 000.

3.5.6   **Documentation**

If a document or documents (such as a bill of lading, air waybill or CMR/CIM consignment note) accompanies(y) dangerous goods in excepted quantities, at least one of these documents shall include the statement "Dangerous Goods in Excepted Quantities" and indicate the number of packages.